W9-DIW-551

STUDIES IN ECONOMIC HISTORY AND POLICY
THE UNITED STATES IN THE TWENTIETH CENTURY

Energy policy in America since 1945

STUDIES IN ECONOMIC HISTORY AND POLICY
THE UNITED STATES IN THE TWENTIETH CENTURY

Edited by
Louis Galambos and Robert Gallman

Other books in the series:

Peter D. McClelland and Alan L. Magdovitz: *Crisis in the making: the political economy of New York State since 1945*
Hugh Rockoff: *Drastic measures: a history of wage and price controls in the United States*
William N. Parker: *Europe, America, and the wider world: essays on the economic history of Western capitalism*

Energy policy in America since 1945

A study of business–government relations

RICHARD H. K. VIETOR
Harvard Business School

The right of the
University of Cambridge
to print and sell
all manner of books
was granted by
Henry VIII in 1534.
The University has printed
and published continuously
since 1584.

Cambridge University Press

Cambridge
London   New York   New Rochelle
Melbourne   Sydney

Published by the Press Syndicate of the University of Cambridge
The Pitt Building, Trumpington Street, Cambridge CB2 1RP
32 East 57th Street, New York, NY 10022, USA
10 Stamford Road, Oakleigh, Melbourne 3166, Australia

First published 1984
First paperback edition 1987

Printed in the United States of America

Library of Congress Cataloging in Publication Data
Vietor, Richard H. K., 1945–
Energy policy in America since 1945.
(Studies in economic history and policy)
Includes index.
1. Energy policy – United States – History –
20th century.   I. Title.   II. Series.
HD9502.U52V53   1984   333.79'0973   84-5833
ISBN 0 521 26658 0 hard covers
ISBN 0 521 33572 8 paperback

TO NICHOLAS, CHRISTOPHER, AND MEREDITH

TO NICHOLAS, CHRISTOPHER, AND MEREDITH

Contents

Charts and figures

Charts

Figures

x

Tables

xi

Editors' preface

While the United States has had a series of public policies related to energy sources since the nineteenth century, the general public has only become aware of and concerned about these policies in the years since World War II. The reason for this neglect is that for most of our history we have been an unusually energy-rich nation. The major thrust of policy was to encourage private entrepreneurs to convert natural resources into commercial products as rapidly as possible. When, on occasion, surpluses pushed prices down too far, our twentieth-century government intervened to stabilize energy prices, but these programs were only of great interest to those groups directly involved in developing the resources.

When, however, conditions of surplus gave way to shortages of vital energy sources – as has been the case in recent years – most Americans became very concerned about federal policies in the energy field. Unfortunately, there were few reliable, scholarly accounts to which they could turn for an accurate description and balanced analysis of how those policies had evolved in the years since 1945. Now they can read Richard Vietor's penetrating study of *Energy Policy in America since 1945*. As editors of the series Studies in Economic History and Policy: The United States in the Twentieth Century, we are especially pleased to publish this survey of political developments in the field of energy. As Vietor demonstrates, public policy failed when it became unresponsive over the long term to market forces. The "politics of stasis" left our economy burdened with regulations and price controls that led inevitably to a series of major economic crises. Our attempts to balance the equities of the organized interests with stakes in the energy struggle magnified our difficulties.

While Vietor is critical of our public blunders, he also provides his readers with a carefully reasoned account of what the government has done and can do effectively. In this and other regards, his book is a model of sound scholarly analysis and comprehensive historical research.

Louis Galambos
Professor of History
The Johns Hopkins University

Robert Gallman
Kenan Professor of Economics
University of North Carolina

Acknowledgments

My work on this book was supported by several institutions, by colleagues and other professionals, and by my family.

The Graduate School of Arts & Sciences at the University of Missouri and the National Endowment for the Humanities each provided a fellowship for a summer of research. Since 1978, the Division of Research at the Harvard Graduate School of Business Administration has generously absorbed my expenses for travel, word-processing, editing, graphics, and research assistance. I am especially grateful to Richard Rosenbloom and Raymond Corey, Directors of the Division of Research, who helped secure time for the work, and then waited patiently for results. Dean John McArthur has been a consistent source of encouragement.

Robert Anderson, now retired from the Department of the Interior, is one of the many archivists and librarians whose help was indispensable. For six weeks, Mr. Anderson guided me through the Secretary's Central Files. And there were others like him at the National Archives, the Federal Records Center, four presidential libraries, the government-document division of Widener Library, and the Baker Library at Harvard.

Several companies cooperated in my field research: The Gulf Oil Corporation, The El Paso Company, Continental Oil, and the American Petroleum Institute. Warren Davis, now retired as Chief Economist, coordinated and facilitated my work at Gulf. He also contributed his own wisdom, accumulated over thirty years in the industry. J. L. Schweizer, Howard Boyd, Ed Najaiko, J. T. McDonnell, A. M. Derrick, Frank O'Hara, and John Bailey were among the thoughtful managers who patiently explained the complex regulatory relationships between their firms and government.

In Washington, I had help from a number of government officials. One of them was James Schlesinger, former Secretary of Energy, who candidly shared with me his insights and perspective on the Carter administration's energy policies. This was invaluable.

I have learned much about public policy and business-government relations from colleagues. Four in particular to whom I'm obliged – Douglas Anderson, Thomas McCraw, Bruce Scott, and Robert Stobaugh – helped make this a better book by sharing their own work and providing careful criticism of the entire manuscript. So did Max Hall, whose painstaking editorial criticism was an education in itself. Others, including Alfred Chandler, Louis Galambos, George Lodge, Michael Rukstad, Philip Scarpino, Richard Tedlow, and Louis Wells, made valuable comments on various parts of the manuscript. Christopher Gibbs was a sounding-board as well as a capable research assistant.

I appreciate the numerous ways in which Cynthia Carey, my secretary, has helped.

Over the course of seven years, much of the time I devoted to this book was taken from my family – my wife Cindy and our three young children. They should know that I understand, and am grateful for, their contribution; especially Cindy, whose patience and encouragement keep our lives on track.

Abbreviations

DDEPL	Dwight D. Eisenhower Presidential Library
DOE/EIA	Department of Energy, Energy Information Agency
GTAC/OCR/FRC	General Technical Advisory Committee, Office of Coal Research, Federal Records Center
HTPL	Harry Truman Presidential Library
JFKL	John F. Kennedy Library
LBJL	LBJ Library, Austin, Texas
LBJPL	Lyndon B. Johnson Presidential Library
NA/RG48	National Archives Record Group 48
NPC/DOI	National Petroleum Council, Department of the Interior
OCR/DOI	Office of Coal Research, Department of the Interior
OCR/FRC	Office of Coal Research, Federal Records Center
OOG/DOI	Office of Oil and Gas, Department of the Interior (Appears as O&G/DOI after name was changed to Oil & Gas Division)
OS/DOI	Oil Shale, Department of the Interior
OS/MFGP/DOI	Oil Shale, Minerals, Fuels, Commodities, Products, Department of the Interior
PG/OCR/FRC	Project Gasoline, Office of Coal Research, Federal Records Center

1. Introduction: The political economy of energy

This book has two objectives. One is to present the history of fossil-fuel energy policy in the United States since World War II. The other is to provide a useful framework for understanding how business and government interact.

The two objectives are not independent; they grow out of each other. The energy policies of the United States have been by-products of the nation's distinctive political economy. Policy-making was shaped in large part by government-business relations, American style, with non-business interest groups enlarging their political role during the 1970's. For better or worse, government intervention into the energy industries has been the norm not the exception. Through fragmentary initiatives that affected production, importation, and consumption of fossil fuels, the federal government fostered the energy conditions that prevail in the 1980's.

The course of relations between business and government has been governed by shifts in energy market conditions – changes in price or the parity of supply and demand. That fact is so strikingly pervasive that it is a major theme of the book, and I am making it the first of five general propositions about the American political economy at the end of this chapter. Changes in supply and price brought political pressures from producers, consumers, or government officials to restore the status quo or alter the effects of the market to serve distributive objectives not related to economic efficiency.

Relationships between business firms and the agencies of government fluctuated during the postwar era, at times dramatically, but narrowly within the bounds of two methods for allocating economic goods: the market mechanism at one extreme, and centralized administrative management at the other. Neither extreme has prevailed for any significant time during the past 35 years. The tension between the two methods – the balance of power and responsibility for determining output, consumption, and price – is my definition of business-government relations. The availability of institutional means for discussing issues and solving problems effectively contributes to their tenor.

Prior to the early 1970's, neither historians nor most other observers benefited from a generic perspective on "energy." Available literature generally

1

focused on a single fuel or a particular government agency.[1] Work by economists, rather than historians or political scientists, tended to dominate what
literature there was.[2] Scarcely any of this work concerned itself with the relationship between business and government in the area of domestic energy
policy. Since 1973, public and scholarly interest in energy problems has resulted in a surfeit of studies that vary widely in quality and purpose. Still,
historical studies have continued to lag, and the few available do not connect
politics to markets.[3]

In this study, I attempt to integrate the economics and public policy of three
basic fuel industries – coal, petroleum, and natural gas – as well as developments in synthetic fuels that firms in all three industries have pursued. To do
this, I have relied mostly on primary sources: the records of government agencies; briefs and decisions of regulatory commissions; congressional hearings;
presidential papers; corporate files; and interviews.

Although I aimed at comprehensiveness, some limitations on this study were
necessary. Its focus is on government policies affecting the production of fossil
fuels. It excludes the development of nuclear power, which, however important,
occurred as an isolated political phenomenon. It excludes the regulation of most
"downstream" activities – refining, transportation, and retail distribution – as
well as electric power generation, which is regulated principally by states. The
story is primarily domestic, although related to the foreign oil policies of the
United States and developments in international oil markets.

As to the book's temporal boundaries, World War II is more than a conven-
ient starting point. In the political economy of energy, that war proved to be a
significant watershed. It accelerated the transition from dependence on coal to
cleaner, more transportable petroleum and natural gas (see Chart 1–1). Mobilization also provided an unprecedented experience in the management of
energy markets by a forced partnership of business and government. The study
concludes with the Carter administration's final attempt in 1980 to fabricate a
comprehensive federal energy policy for demand as well as supply.

[1] See Gerald Nash, *U.S. Oil Policy, 1890–1964* (Pittsburgh: University of Pittsburgh Press,
1968); Robert Engler, *The Politics of Oil* (Chicago: University of Chicago Press, 1961); Christopher
Tugendhat, *Oil: The Biggest Business* (New York: Putnam Sons, 1968); E. W. Zimmermann, *Conser-
vation in the Production of Petroleum* (New Haven: Yale University Press, 1957); Clark Hawkins, *The
Field Price Regulation of Natural Gas* (Tallahassee: Florida State University Press, 1969); Richard
Hewlett and Oscar Anderson, *The New World, 1939–1946: A History of the USAEC*, vol. I, and
Atomic Shield, 1947–1952: A History of the USAEC, vol. II (University Park: Pennsylvania State
University Press, 1962 and 1969).
[2] For example, see Sam Schurr and Bruce Netschert, *Energy in the American Economy* (Baltimore:
Johns Hopkins University Press, 1960); Paul MacAvoy, *Price Formation in Natural Gas Fields: A
Study of Competition, Monopoly, and Regulation* (New Haven: Yale University Press, 1962); James
McKie, *The Regulation of Natural Gas* (Washington: American Enterprise Institute, 1957); Alfred
Kahn and M. DeChazeau, *Integration and Concentration in the Petroleum Industry* (New Haven: Yale
University Press, 1962): M. A. Adelman, *The World Petroleum Market* (Baltimore: Johns Hopkins
University Press, 1972).
[3] Craufurd D. Goodwin, ed., *Energy Policy in Perspective* (Washington: The Brookings Institution,
1981).

The story falls naturally into three periods, corresponding to conditions of energy supply and price that affected issues of public policy.

The first period runs from 1945 through 1958. During those years, the U.S. economy shifted from its primary dependence on solid fuels to fluid fuels. The coal industry stagnated. The price of coal, adjusted for inflation, fell 7.4 percent, while its share of the domestic energy market shrunk from 43 to 22 percent. Demand for natural gas boomed. Its contribution to energy consumption climbed from 14 to 30 percent, while its real price gained 56 percent (from a very low base). Domestic and foreign oil shared the rest of coal's loss. Although an oil shortage in the late 1940's drove oil prices up sharply, the real price declined throughout the 1950's as the growth of domestic reserves outstripped demand.

During this first period, the domestic energy market also shifted from wartime scarcity to super-excess capacity. Accordingly, conflict over energy policy likewise shifted from stimulating supply to protecting market share. Plans for a synthetic fuel industry based on coal staggered and collapsed, despite the coal industry's plight. In natural gas, the disparity between immense reserves and marketable supply posed a problem of allocating economic rent. And cheap foreign oil, the bane of domestic producers, became the balance wheel of policy and of the market.

The second period, from 1959 to 1968, was a decade of "stasis" in energy policy, and seemingly so in energy markets. Relative market shares and prices for all three fuels were stable, although natural gas drifted slightly higher. But public policy, not the price mechanism, was responsible for this pseudo-stability. Business and government were preoccupied with the tactical issues of administering it: import quotas and "prorationing" for crude oil, cost-based rate regulation for natural gas, and a feeble pilot-plant program for coal-derived, synthetic fuels. Meanwhile, economic growth and domestic depletion quietly eroded the surplus. Contented consumers never even noticed, until crisis struck after the end of the period.

The third period, 1969 through 1980, saw the painful process of national adjustment to a belated realization that cheap domestic reserves of petroleum and natural gas were depleted. Domestic shortages of petroleum allowed the Organization of Petroleum Exporting Countries (OPEC) to raise prices 1700 percent (in current dollars) over the period. In the United States, the price of "new" natural gas rose nearly as much. But because of price controls on "old" oil and gas, average prices rose far less. Since coal prices increased even less, the decline in that fuel's market share finally halted, then reversed. So dramatic was this shift in market equilibria that it had powerful effects on industry structure, public policy, and business-government relations. National policies were rebuilt to redistribute oil revenues, raise the price of natural gas, develop synfuels, utilize coal, and finally, curb demand.

The three parts of this book correspond to those three periods. Before beginning Part I, however, I will highlight some special aspects of energy-policy issues, and offer some preliminary generalizations about the political economy.

Chart 1-1
U.S. Consumption of Energy Fuels
1915-1980
(Percent on a BTU-equivalent Basis)

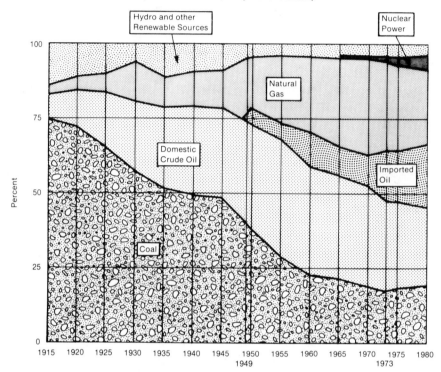

Sources: Sam Shurr et al., Energy in the American Economy, 1850–1975 (Baltimore: Johns Hopkins University Press, 1960); American Petroleum Institute, Basic Petroleum Data Book, November 1976; Exxon Background Series, World Energy Outlook (New York: Exxon Corporation, 1981).

Geophysical reality is fundamental to the whole subject. The essential physical characteristic of fossil fuels is that their supply is finite. Depletion is inherent in their use.[4] Technological innovation, higher prices, or luck may yield increased

[4]   The concept of "entropy," derived from the second law of thermodynamics, explains the depletion of stored solar energy that fossil fuels contain. Entropy is a measure of the unavailability of thermal energy for conversion into mechanical work. Thus, a ton of coal is low in entropy before it is burned to generate electricity. But the char that remains after combustion represents high entropy, as does the air pollution that is generated. By definition, rising entropy is inevitable in all human and physical activity. Only the rate is variable. Since fossil fuels have an immense potential for mechanical work, their production and consumption is a highly entropic activity. This unique characteristic of the energy industries certainly contributes to their distinctive economic and political salience. For discussion of the economic implications of entropy, see Nicholas Georgescu-Roegen, *The Entropy Law and the Economic Process* (Cambridge: Harvard University Press, 1971) and "Energy and Economic Myths," *Southern Economic Journal*, 41 (January, 1975), 347–381.

reserves, but inevitably a growing rate of extraction and consumption must result in the depletion of the earth's fixed stock. This fact has serious implications for the long-run economics of energy, and, with significant variations among fuels and regions, for the short-run economics as well.[5] It was depletion of easily accessible oil and gas reserves in the continental United States, in the absence of a working price mechanism, that precipitated the energy crisis of the early 1970's.

Because of depletion, production of fossil fuels is a rising-cost enterprise in the long run. As accessible reserves are extracted, they can only be replaced by deeper, less concentrated, and more remote reserves. This implies rising exploration costs under any given conditions of knowledge. Production costs likewise rise, as M. A. Adelman has shown, as any individual deposit is further developed. A rising cost curve is even applicable to the Persian Gulf region, although it is so gradual as to be scarcely significant with respect to prices and supply in the short run.[6]

In the United States, the rising costs inherent in depletion appear to have outstripped the rate of cost savings from technological progress, at least since the late 1940's.[7] Decreased yields from exploratory wells, together with increased costs of drilling, are simple indicators of this trend. During the period of surplus, the percentage of wells that resulted in significant finds – reserves greater than one million barrels of oil or 6 billion cubic feet of gas – declined by more than a third, from 2.7 to 1.5 percent. Drilling costs for all wells increased 77 percent (30 percent when adjusted for inflation).[8] Because of economies of scale and improvements in mining technology, the production costs of coal kept falling in that period, and only began rising in the 1970's.

The *economics* of energy markets has some interesting characteristics. One is the relation of price to demand. Since energy is so essential to industrial activity, the demand for fossil fuels has been highly inelastic in the short run. This means that an increase in price did not precipitate a proportionate decrease in the quantities demanded. Thus, when marketable supplies were tight, as in the late 1940's and early 1970's, price increases did little to restore equilibrium by effecting a quick reduction in demand. Similarly, when there were surpluses, as in the 1960's, soft prices did little to stimulate an immediate increase in demand.

Not only demand but also supply has been price inelastic, owing to political rather than market stimuli. Especially for petroleum, rising prices generally did

5 A thoughtful discussion of depletion and future prospects for expanding reserves in the United States can be found in Robert Stobaugh and Daniel Yergin, eds., *Energy Future: Report of the Energy Project at the Harvard Business School* (New York: Random House, 1979), pp. 3–55; on the relationship of technological change to costs, see note on pp. 264–265.

6 M. A. Adelman, *The World Petroleum Market*, p. 21.

7 John E. Hodges and Henry Steele, *An Investigation of the Problems of Cost Determination for the Discovery, Development, and Production of Liquid Hydrocarbons and Natural Gas Reserves* (Rice Institute Pamphlet, October, 1959); M. A. Adelman, "Trends in the Cost of Finding and Developing Crude Oil and Gas in the United States," in Stephen L. Gardner and Steve H. Hanke, eds., *Essays in Petroleum Economics* (Boulder: Colorado School of Mines Press, 1967).

8 American Petroleum Institute, *Basic Petroleum Databook*, 1976, Section III, tables 7 and 10.

not elicit an increase in available supply, and declining prices did not result in reduced supplies. The reason is that governments managed oil markets by controlling supply. In the United States, price was held above marginal costs by state commissions that regulated output, and by the federal government's import quotas. This caused a substantial excess capacity that lasted until the early 1970's. In the Middle East, the production decisions of governments appear to have been income-driven. Declining real price stimulated increased production until 1973, when sufficient income from higher prices resulted in production cutbacks.[9]

These frictions in energy markets, whether real or contrived, have amplified the effects of innovation, depletion, and disruption. They have contributed to imbalances that threatened producers, angered consumers, and perplexed politicians. The perception of energy's importance to the social order made these price-and-supply problems more politically salient. The experience of two world wars, in which adequate fuel was crucial to victory, left a lasting impression on government officials. More recent disruptions from turmoil in the Middle East reinforced that impression, and disbursed it among consumers.

Such frictions and imbalances in supply and price help explain the public's antipathy to the economic rents that accrue from the process of depletion. "Economic rent," by no means limited to energy fuels, is the profit that scarce resources command.[10] Discovered reserves gain value over time as depletion increases the cost of their replacement. Without regulation, for example, gas found in 1950 at a cost of 10 cents per thousand cubic feet could have sold for $1.00 in 1973, a price that reflected current marginal costs. The 90-cent difference is economic rent. Consumers and a majority of politicians were unwilling to let producers capture that rent, which finally resulted in shortages.

There are similar rents in the oil business, but they have been overshadowed by a much larger kind of rent – the unearned return from a price that exceeds long-run marginal costs. This is "monopoly profit," which can only be achieved by agreement among producers or by government fiat to restrict supply. Although international oil companies did this in the Middle East with decreasing effectiveness, the role of producing and consuming governments was more significant. The Texas Railroad Commission and other state agencies did just this from the 1930's until 1972. In 1973, the governments of OPEC picked up where the state governments left off.

The distinction between economic rent and monopoly profit is not merely semantic. Economic rent, though inherent in depletion, provides the incentive and cash flow necessary to stimulate new supplies at ever rising replacement costs. Monopoly profits are contrived and misallocate resources.

---

[9]   For discussion of the backward bending supply curve in the Middle East, see Bruce Scott, "OPEC, the American Scapegoat," *Harvard Business Review*, Vol. 59, No. 1 (January, 1981), p. 6.
[10]   Stephen Breyer, *Regulation and its Reform* (Cambridge: Harvard University Press, 1982), pp. 21–23; also, Alfred Kahn, *The Economics of Regulation: Principles and Institutions* (New York: John Wiley & Sons, 1970), vol. I, p. 68.

In addition to the special aspects of geology and economics, there is *ideology*. Conflict and confusion over ideology has been just beneath the surface in most issues of energy policy. The conflict stemmed from differences in the two models of resource allocation suggested earlier: (1) collectivist concern for the "public interest," as presumably served by administrative allocation, and (2) reliance on the self-interested actions of individuals, that is, the market mechanism. The confusion resulted from the fact that few participants in energy politics either understood these ideological archetypes or were consistent in their commitment to them.

The collectivist perspective has three facets relevant to energy issues: a notion of the "commons," a concern for distributive equity, and a distrust of big business. The perspective of the commons, by emphasizing bounds and limits, inspired a quantity-oriented approach to energy policy among some social activists, geologists, and politicians.[11] This view often rejected the sanctity of property rights and usually distrusted the price mechanism as a rational governor of resource depletion. Commitment to distributive equity manifested itself in the rationing of energy revenues among producers and the reallocation of rents to consumers. Aversion to big business, with its roots in American populism, was closely related to these. Bigness implied abuse of the commons, abuse of equity, and excessive political power. This aversion motivated some of the advocates of limits-to-growth, the anti-nuclear movement, and legislative initiatives to break up integrated oil companies.[12]

The ideology of individualism, with its faith in the market, has had far different but no more consistent effects on energy issues. For those who subscribe to this view, the pulling and hauling of individual self-interests creates wealth best by letting price optimize the flow of goods. Government's only role is to mitigate failures and externalities, such as monopoly and environmental pollution. From this perspective, energy resources are not limited in an economic sense. Every commodity has potential substitutes that inevitably become available as prices rise. As long as price works freely, the supply of fuels would always equal demand. And as a bonus, self-interest supposedly creates opposing pressures that check excesses of economic or political power.

The clash of these two ideologies invariably muddled the issues of energy policy. In the face of a glut or foreign competition, subscribers to "free enterprise" scarcely paused before calling on government to help. And those who espoused collective goods would not accept higher prices and chafed at the callous power of bureaucrats.

These factors together – physical depletion, energy economics, and ideologi-

---

[11] For a thoughtful discussion of the impact of this perspective on energy issues, see Aaron Wildavsky and Ellen Tenenbaum, *The Politics of Mistrust* (Beverly Hills, Cal.: Sage Publications, 1981), pp. 20–48.

[12] See Barry Commoner, *The Closing Circle* (New York: Alfred Knopf, 1971) and *The Poverty of Power* (New York: Alfred Knopf, 1976); also, Amory Lovins, *Soft Energy Paths: Toward a Durable Peace* (Cambridge, Mass.: Ballinger Publishing Co., 1977).

cal conflict – were sources of continuity in the history of U.S. energy policy. The sources of change, on the other hand, were the interactions of business and government that have shaped the political economy.

The political economy – some propositions

The literature of political economy generally relies on three interpretative perspectives to explain the substance and process of business-government relations.[13] Various "private-interest" theories attribute public policy to the interplay of private groups, or to the capture of governmental authority by one or more such groups.[14] "Public-interest" theories hold that policy derives from constitutional checks on private power, or attempts by government to alleviate failures of the market.[15] A third perspective focuses on the organization and behavioral characteristics of bureaucracies, with their institutional and informational constraints, to explain the outcomes of public policy.[16] Each of these perspectives has something to contribute to our historical understanding of energy policy.

The history, however, shows limitations to each. Private-interest theories, at best, make sense for conditions of surplus. Public-interest theories seem more

---

[13] For useful surveys of the theoretical literature on regulation, see Paul L. Joskow, "Regulatory Agencies by Government Activities," December, 1975 (No. 171 in Working Papers of the Department of Economics, Massachusetts Institute of Technology); Thomas K. McCraw, "Regulation in America: A Review Article," *Business History Review*, Vol. XLIX, No. 2 (Summer, 1975), 159–183; Peter Navarro, "Theories of Government Regulation: A Survey and Synthesis," unpublished working paper, Harvard University, January 1982; Barry M. Mitnick, *The Political Economy of Regulation* (New York: Columbia University Press, 1980); and Michael D. Reagan, "The Politics of Regulatory Reform," *The Western Political Quarterly*, March 1983, 149–167.

[14] For the pluralist perspective, see Gerald Nash, *U.S. Oil Policy, 1890–1964*; Lee Benson, *Merchants, Farmers, and Railroads: Railroad Regulation and New York Politics, 1850–1887* (New York: Russell and Russell, 1955); and K. Austin Kerr, *American Railroad Politics, 1914–1920* (Pittsburgh: University of Pittsburgh Press, 1968). For critiques of pluralism, see Grant McConnell, *Private Power and American Democracy* (New York: Alfred Knopf, 1966), and Theodore Lowi, *The End of Liberalism* (New York: Norton, 1969). For theories of capture, see Marver Bernstein, *Regulating Business by Independent Commission* (Princeton: Princeton University Press, 1955); Gabriel Kolko, *The Triumph of Conservatism: A Reinterpretation of American History, 1900–1916* (New York: Glencoe, 1963); George J. Stigler, "The Theory of Economic Regulation," *Bell Journal of Economics and Management Science*, Vol. 2, No. 1 (Spring, 1971), 3–21.

[15] See William Baumol, *Welfare Economics and the Theory of the State* (Cambridge: Harvard University Press, 2nd edn., 1965); Mancur Olson, *The Logic of Collective Action: Public Goods and the Theory of Groups* (Cambridge: Harvard University Press, 1965); and Kenneth Arrow, "The Organization of Economic Activity: Issues Pertinent to the Choice of Market Verses Nonmarket Allocation," in R. H. Haveman and J. Margolis, eds., *Public Expenditure and Policy Analysis* (New York: Rand McNally, 1977), 67–81.

[16] Douglas D. Anderson, *Regulatory Politics and Electric Utilities* (Boston: Auburn House, 1981); Michael Porter and Jeffery Sagansky, "Information, Politics, and Economic Analysis: The Regulatory Decision Process in the Air Freight Cases," *Public Policy*, Vol. 24, No. 1 (Spring, 1976), 263–307; and Barry Mitnick and Charles Weiss, Jr., "The Siting Impasse and a Rational Choice Model of Regulatory Behavior: An Agency for Power Plant Siting," *Journal of Environmental Economics and Management*, Vol. 1 (1974), 150–171.

applicable to periods of shortages, or the perception thereof. Bureaucratic shortcomings and misinformation have been prevalent throughout.

The history of U.S. energy policy is rich and diverse enough to suggest a reasonable synthesis of these interpretative views. The following propositions, derived from that history, are intended to provide a frame of reference for better understanding the American political economy.

Proposition 1. Market disequilibria, in the form of supply-demand imbalances and price changes, precipitate policy issues and subsequent government initiatives.

Not surprisingly, the intensity of political conflict has usually been proportionate to the severity and persistence of the imbalance. The significance of this is that the character of business-government relations and the nature of the particular political process depend, in large measure, on whether the disequilibrium is one of scarcity (inadequate marketable supply and rising price) or over-abundance (excess capacity and declining price).[17]

The perception of scarcity has inspired all sorts of public pressures for price controls, allocation of resources based on equity criteria, redistribution of economic rents, structural reform of integrated firms, forced product substitution, and public subsidy of technological remedies. Surplus, on the other hand, gave rise to different issues. By 1945, vigorous enforcement of the antitrust laws had substantially reduced the feasibility of horizontal combination or cooperative arrangements as strategic options for managing excess capacity.[18] Since that time, administrative or regulatory intervention by government has been the only practical alternative for allocating limited markets, supporting prices, and moderating the disruptive effects of changing market share. Rarely since 1945 have producers, consumers, or their political representatives been willing to rely on price for the restoration of equilibrium.

Proposition 2. The political process and the participants involved differ according to prevailing conditions of supply and price.

One can discern four types of political conflict in the postwar history of U.S. energy policy. There is "intrafuel politics" – contention among firms and segments of a particular industry to contrive public policies that will enhance or protect one firm's income or market share relative to others in the same industry. "Interfuel politics" pits industry against industry (for example, coal versus natural gas) in efforts to use government to bestow or revoke competitive advantages on one or the other. "Intragovernmental politics" characterizes the

---

[17] An economist might argue that disequilibria are fleeting in the absence of friction, imperfect competition, or administrative intervention. That may be true, but during the twentieth century, they have been present in most major industries, at one time or another.

[18] Prior to 1945, and outside the United States, structural and cooperative solutions for rationalizing excess capacity were still realistic options. For an analysis of the link between excess capacity and industrial structure, see Alfred D. Chandler, Jr., "Industrial Groups, American Style: The Multidivisional Form" (unpublished working paper, Harvard University, January 1982). On the relationship between excess capacity and the antitrust movement, see Thomas McCraw, "Rethinking the Trust Question," in T. McCraw, ed., *Regulation in Perspective* (Boston: Harvard Business School, Division of Research, 1981), 1–55.

process when policy issues affecting industry are principally defined by conflicting positions among branches or agencies of the federal government (and occasionally between federal and state governments). Finally, there is a broad-based type of politics in which non-business interest groups, widespread public opinion, or partisanship create pressures for government to entertain policies that would affect an entire industry. For lack of a better term, this might be called the "politics of business reform." These four types of political interaction can, and frequently do, overlap and commingle. Over time, the dominant type often shifts as the political-economic context changes, or as the unintended effects of past policy become apparent.

The intrafuel and interfuel types of conflict tended to dominate the policy process in times of surplus capacity. Allocation of market share and price stabilization were the problems at issue. Intrafuel politics was more prevalent in the oil industry, because of its functional segmentation and its diversity in size of firms and sources of crude oil. During the 1950's, for example, the issue of import quotas was fought among small domestic producers, independent refiners, and vertically integrated, multinational oil companies. Intrafuel politics has several characteristics: It is less intense at the stage of policy formation than during protracted implementation; there is infighting on highly technical issues; and the contestants tend to be small sub-groups of the industry or individual firms, rather than major trade associations that must avoid internecine frictions. Energy policies determined in this area are particularly important to the line operations of firms, and are usually of less interest to the general public.

Interfuel politics has involved larger aggregations of business interests, trade associations, and occasionally labor unions. In these controversies, the coal industry has generally been the loser to oil, natural gas, and nuclear power. Despite broader participation, these interfuel issues rarely attained widespread public recognition but did at times polarize the Congress along regional lines. Since the mid-1960's, interfuel politics at the level of primary producers has moderated because of the oil industry's diversification into other fuel industries.

In periods of lagging supply and rising price, intragovernmental politics and the politics of business reform have dominated the policy process. Intragovernmental politics affects policy-making and implementation through a multilateral process. This typically has involved high-ranking bureaucrats, contending for the president's support. Influential congressmen and industry leaders frequently participated informally, through consultation. Eisenhower's workout of the Iranian crisis in 1954 and Nixon's Cabinet Task Force on Oil Import Controls in 1969 are examples. Occasionally this type of politics has escalated into the business-reform variety, where Congress and the president take center stage.

When there are energy crises or issues of propriety, the scene is set for the politics of business reform. In these circumstances, broad segments of an energy industry do battle with Congress, the White House, or both. This process is quite different in its dynamics from the other three. At stake are distributive effects on large numbers of citizens. Ideologies clash. Questions of monopoly power, the public domain, and fairness are amplified by the news media and tend to obscure rational debate and stimulate political rhetoric. After prolonged political struggles, the policy determined by compromise is unlikely to contribute to economic efficiency, and is just as unlikely to serve the national interest, however defined. This process can help unify an industry temporarily, but it tends to damage or destroy existing channels for cooperation between business and government.

Proposition 3. The influence of business on public policy is limited by its structural diversity, and that of the government. Neither business nor government is apt to be unified or coherent in its objectives or political actions.

Misguided stereotypes have abounded in the history of economic policy, especially in the energy sector. It is rarely accurate to speak of the oil industry's "position" on any major policy issue, whether it is oil price controls, import quotas, antitrust prosecution, or taxation. There have been exceptions, such as the oil depletion allowance, but even there, industry consensus finally broke down under fire in the early 1970's. The same is true for the natural gas and coal industries, except for brief periods of crisis or widespread public criticism, such as the gas shortages and environmental movement of the early 1970's. This lack of coherence is scarcely surprising if we consider the complexity and diversity of these industries. Nor is it surprising in an immense federal establishment of agencies with conflicting statutory responsibilities. The point needs to be made, however, since it is essential to a clear understanding of business-government relations.

Proposition 4. Administrative allocation of resources by government usually encounters serious difficulties as a result of faulty design, bureaucratic limitations, or the imposition of contradictory criteria.

These problems in the history of energy policy have helped to widen the gap between administered allocation and the reality of the market. The Natural Gas Act of 1938 is an early example of faulty design. By defining the Federal Power Commission's objectives ambiguously, Congress set in motion decades of adjudicatory blundering and judicial intervention. In Chapter 6, we will see how non-relevant criteria of social welfare and foreign policy further made a mess of oil import quotas. Bureaucratic limitations will be all too apparent when we look at the Office of Coal Research and the Federal Energy Administration. These persistent problems raise some serious questions regarding the policy-making process.

Proposition 5. Over time, the federal government's intervention in industry seems to fluctuate within limits, rather than increase in any kind of linear fashion.

At least this has been the case in the fossil fuel industries. For certain functions, such as gas importation and environmental control, the degree of intervention has recently increased. For other activities, including oil importation and pricing, the role of government has subsided. Irrespective of political party or presidential philosophy, at no time since 1932 have the energy industries been free of controls or deprived of subsidies. The federal government has moved no closer to establishing the sorts of state-owned enterprise that are prevalent in most other industrial countries. The last attempt to do so – the proposal of Harold Ickes for a Petroleum Reserve Corporation in 1944 – failed miserably.

As mentioned briefly at the outset of this chapter, America's political economy imposes boundaries within which a relatively stable tension is maintained between market means and administrative means of allocating economic goods. In part, these boundaries derive from constitutional limitations, ideological balance, and the diversity of America's political institutions. But the market's own mechanisms for equilibrating are crucial. Price controls for natural gas could not survive the shortages they evoked. The price controls imposed on oil were similarly abandoned once their effects became intolerable. Projects to develop synthetic fuels came and went in cycles that paralleled the market.

In the American political context, market imbalances have contributed as much to extinguishing government intervention as they have to igniting it.

Part I. The transition to peace and fluid fuels, 1945–1958

It is difficult in the long run to envisage a national coal policy, or a national petroleum policy, or a national water-power policy without also in time a national energy resources policy. Such a broader and integrated policy toward the problems of coal, petroleum, natural gas, and water power cannot be evolved overnight.

Franklin D. Roosevelt, 1939

2. The foundations of postwar policy

"I have been impressed," wrote Harry S. Truman in May of 1946, "with the great contribution of government-industry cooperation to the success of the war petroleum program and feel that the values of such close and harmonious relations . . . should be continued."[1] Despite this predisposition, President Truman would find (or perhaps cause) those relations to be less than harmonious during the course of his administration. World War II had convulsed the economics and technology of energy supply and demand. It fell to Truman's lot to preside over a disorderly transition from wartime shortage to peacetime glut.

This reversal in energy markets created major policy problems for energy producers and the government alike. At issue were synthetic fuels, leasing policy for the outer continental shelf, regulation of natural gas and imported oil, foreign oil policy, and antitrust. None of these was resolved by the time Truman left office. Taken together, they were part of a more general realignment of business-government relations in energy. By confirming the importance of energy, World War II raised new questions about the manner and means by which industry and government should interact and share authority for the production, pricing, and distribution of fossil fuels.

The process of realignment did not start, of course, from a clean slate. The federal government had an established role in minerals leasing, taxation, and antitrust dating from World War I. The State Department was involved in foreign oil policy on behalf of U.S. firms from the early 1920's. An oil glut that began in the 1920's and worsened during the Great Depression had led to an abiding intervention by state governments, with federal support, in the management of domestic oil supplies. And finally, war itself had been the occasion for a successful experiment in cooperative decision-making by business and government. "We have never had a policy officially adopted by the American government," observed the president of Amerada Petroleum in 1949, but the policy "has evolved during the whole life of the American oil industry."[2]

---

[1] H. S. Truman to J. Krug, May 3, 1946, quoted in U.S. Congress, House, Judiciary Committee, Antitrust Subcommittee, *Hearings: WOC's and Government Advisory Groups* (84th Cong., 2nd Sess.), Pt.4, July 26, 1956, p. 2267.

[2] A. Jacobsen, quoted in National Petroleum Council, Meeting Transcript, January 13, 1949, Department of the Interior, National Petroleum Council files, Washington, D.C. (NPC/DOI), pp. 18–19.

15

Prewar energy policies

Before 1941, the federal government's role in energy extended to control of the public domain, taxation, and regulation of interstate commerce. This authority was not insubstantial. The Mineral Leasing Act of 1920 gave government some initiative and control over development of domestic oil, natural gas, and coal resources. (In 1953, Congress extended the principles of this Act to the outer continental shelf.) In the Revenue Act of 1916, the federal government adopted a policy of subsidizing oil and gas exploration with distinctive tax policies. And during the Great Depression, the federal government assumed a role in managing energy markets. The Connally Hot Oil Act of 1935 provided the federal sanctions necessary to enforce "market demand prorationing" of oil production by state governments. These three areas of public policy endured through World War II and served until the early 1970's as the foundation of U.S. energy policy.

Following is an overview of developments in each area – public domain, taxation, and interstate commerce – in each case beginning before World War II and continuing into the early postwar period.

The public domain

The Mineral Leasing Act of 1920 was a compromise between the interests of mineral development and conservation. It marked the end of a 50-year dispute over the government's responsibility for managing mineral resources in the public domain. Several issues were involved in the dispute: (1) the rate of mineral development, (2) monopolistic control of resources, (3) division of authority between federal and state governments, and (4) public revenues from mineral exploitation. Presidents Theodore Roosevelt and William H. Taft had forced the issue by withdrawing from claim-entry (under the General Mining Law of 1872) millions of acres containing oil, natural gas, and coal resources. Intense congressional debate over appropriate national policy lasted nearly a decade, pitting the interests of eastern conservationists and anti-monopolists against those of oil, coal, timber, grazing, and railroads in the West.[3]

By 1919, leasing appeared to be the only feasible solution if mineral development were not to be forever frozen. With the political forces on both sides of the issue holding their noses, a conference committee finally reported a bill that would "go a long way toward the development of the West and of the natural resources of the West and at the same time reserve to the Government the right to supervise, control, and regulate the same, and prevent monopoly and waste and other lax methods that have grown up." Woodrow Wilson signed the bill into law in February, 1920.[4]

The Mineral Leasing Act empowered the Secretary of the Interior to grant and administer leases of federally-owned mineral rights, either at the Secre-

---

[3] John Ise, *The United States Oil Industry* (New Haven: Yale University Press, 1928), pp. 317–340.
[4] U.S. Congress, House, *Report No. 1138* (65th Cong., 2nd Sess.), 1919, p. 19; also, Stat. 437 (1920), 30 U.S.C., 181.

tary's initiative, or that of prospective lessees. The Bureau of Land Management would conduct mineral leasing, with technical assistance from the U.S. Geological Survey for evaluating properties and supervising exploration. Both competitive and non-competitive leasing systems would be used to stimulate exploration and maximize federal revenue. State governments were to receive 37.5 percent of revenues from sales, bonuses, royalties, and rentals; 52.5 percent was earmarked for a federal reclamation fund, and the Treasury would keep the remaining 10 percent.[5]

Congress designed non-competitive leasing to stimulate wildcat exploration on properties that did not overlay "Known Geologic Structures" (identified by the U.S. Geological Survey). For oil and gas, the Act authorized 10-year leases of up to 2,560 acres, with a minimum royalty of 12.5 percent. A similar system applied to coal, except with larger exploratory leases and a minimum royalty of five cents per ton. The Act set generous limits on the total acreage that any individual or company could hold under lease (246,080 acres per state for oil and gas, except more in Alaska, and 46,080 acres for coal), and did not explicitly require diligent development.[6]

During the first 50 years under this system, about 90 percent of all oil and gas leases and 50 percent of the coal leases were the non-competitive variety.[7] By the 1970's, the cumulative effects of this non-competitive leasing had come under widespread attack. Critics alleged that in the absence of competitive bonus-bidding, giant oil-energy companies had monopolized hydrocarbon reserves, withheld them from development, and enjoyed windfall gains at the expense of the public. The evidence and rationale for such behavior, however, were subject to debate.

For properties containing known geologic structures, the Mineral Leasing Act provided a system of competitive bidding. From time to time, usually at the behest of would-be lessees, the Secretary conducted lease sales either by oral auction, sealed bid, or a combination of the two. Although acreage limitations were smaller and rental prices higher, the big difference was a competitive bonus bid (a lump sum payment for the franchise to explore). The purposes of the bonus bid were to capture economic rents for the government, induce competition, and make resources widely available along a time path determined by market demand. Other competitive methods of leasing, such as bidding on rents, royalties, profit shares, and work commitment, were not tried and were not seriously considered until the early 1970's.[8]

The competitive lease system that was used had mixed results. Although the

---

[5] James Olson, "History of Public Land Mineral Policy," in U.S. Congress, Senate, Committee on Interior and Insular Affairs, *Report to the Federal Trade Commission on Federal Energy Land Policy: Efficiency, Revenue, and Competition* (94th Cong., 2nd Sess.), Committee Print, 1976, pp. 59–63.
[6] Calvin Roush, "Onshore Oil and Gas," and Martha Brand and Arnold Baker, "Coal," *Ibid.*, 429–433, 576–588.
[7] *Ibid.*, 434, 461–463, 613–616. Production from non-competitively leased coal properties was low partly because the location of coal reserves was better known than oil and gas, and because there was a spurt of non-competitive coal leases late in the 1960's.
[8] For a thorough discussion of leasing economics, see Stephen L. McDonald, *The Leasing of Federal Lands for Fossil Fuels Production* (Baltimore: RFF/Johns Hopkins University Press, 1979).

cumulative revenue from bonus payments was insignificant until the early 1970's, the acreage provided was sufficient to meet the apparent exploratory needs of domestic energy companies. Competitive leasing does not appear to have caused damaging concentration of reserve ownership or significant disadvantage to small producers. Even by the early 1970's, control of producing onshore oil and gas leases was still widely dispersed. Coal holdings, although more concentrated, were anything but monopolized.[9]

As for offshore oil and gas resources, commercial interest did not develop until the period of shortages during and immediately after World War II. But when it did, the controversy over leasing policy was at least as intense as it had been in 1920. The outer continental shelf is an extension of the continent seaward an average of 8 miles from the Pacific coast and 59 miles in the Gulf of Mexico. By the end of the war, a few states had granted leases within their historic boundaries (3.5 miles for California and Louisiana, and 10.5 miles for Texas). Limited drilling in shallow waters already indicated a potential of 15 billion barrels of oil.

Harold Ickes, Secretary of the Interior, doubted the validity of the states' title. In September 1945, he convinced President Truman to sign a proclamation asserting federal jurisdiction over submerged lands. The Justice Department promptly brought suit against California to test the constitutionality of this claim.[10] Ickes' initiative sparked a major political battle, with coastal states, the oil industry and advocates of states' rights on one side, and the Truman administration, northern oil-consuming states, and spokesmen for consumers and taxpayers on the other. When Congress passed a joint resolution yielding title to the states, Truman vetoed it. When the Supreme Court upheld the federal government in 1947, the struggle began in earnest.[11]

The oil industry's role in this contest was relatively passive, although it was clearly on the side of the coastal states. State control of offshore mineral rights held an immense revenue potential for Texas, Louisiana, and California, and oilmen had no reason to side with the President against such patrons as Tom Connally, Russell Long, and Lyndon Johnson. Moreover, as an Ickes initiative, Washington's claim on the outer continental shelf was viewed as another of his attempts to control and possibly nationalize the oil industry. Then too, the industry could reasonably presume that state lessors would likely impose easier terms than the Interior Department. But the industry wisely maintained a low profile to avoid inflammation of the "monopoly power" issue that Truman and

---

[9] C. Roush, "Onshore Oil and Gas," pp. 451–462, and M. Brand and A. Baker, "Coal," pp. 616–640.

[10] H. L. Ickes to H. S. Truman, July 17, 1945, and Presidential Proclamation 2667, October 2, 1945, White House Official File, Box 273, File 56F "Tidelands Oil," Harry Truman Presidential Library, Independence, Missouri.

[11] For the two most complete accounts of the OCS controversy, see Hubert Marshall and Betty Zisk, *The Federal–State Struggle For Offshore Oil*, No. 98, Inter-University Case Program (Indianapolis: Bobbs-Merrill Co., Inc., 1966), and Ernest R. Bartley, *The Tidelands Oil Controversy* (Austin: University of Texas Press, 1963).

his supporters tried to invoke. When the Interior Department asked the National Petroleum Council to make recommendations on the issue in 1947, the Council's agenda committee declined, noting the political sensitivity of the issue. Again in 1949, when Secretary Julius Krug urged the Council to cooperate, a few members agreed but the leadership steadfastly refused.[12]

By 1952, Congress had made little progress toward resolution of the "tidelands issue."[13] The entire state-federal conflict was shattering to Democratic Party unity, with southern Democrats increasingly resentful of President Truman's stubbornness. The Supreme Court, meanwhile, had upheld the federal government's claim in two additional cases involving Texas and Louisiana. The Texas case was crucial, since that state had claimed 10.5 miles of the continental shelf in its original constitution as a republic, prior to statehood.[14] Four months before the election, President Truman again vetoed a joint resolution granting the states title to the tidelands. Louisiana's Democratic governor bolted the national ticket to support Eisenhower, and the Republican candidate carried both California and Texas. On the eve of Eisenhower's inauguration, Harry Truman signed an executive order to set aside all offshore lands as a naval petroleum reserve – an act of either desperation or "personal spite."[15]

Even though Eisenhower and his party had endorsed the states' claim to submerged lands, the issue was still not easily settled. Once Democratic liberals took the federal-control position as a foil to a Republican "giveaway," the President would not rescind his predecessor's order. Only after several more months of debate was a compromise finally reached. In May 1953, Eisenhower signed the Submerged Lands Act, granting title to submerged lands within historic boundaries to coastal states. In September, he signed the Outer Continental Shelf Lands Act, providing federal jurisdiction over lands beyond the states' boundaries. The Act authorized the Secretary of the Interior to administer OCS properties, set conservation rules and determine leasing schedules, and grant leases of oil and gas properties by sealed, competitive bids on the basis of a cash bonus and a fixed royalty.[16]

With these laws in place, federal leasing policy did not change again until 1969, when Congress passed the National Environmental Policy Act.

[12] M. Ball to W. S. Hallanan, October 2, 1947, and "Report of the Agenda Committee," in NPC Meeting Transcript, October 9, 1947, NPC/DOI, 1947, pp. 63–68; also, J. Krug, in NPC Meeting Transcript, April 27, 1949, NPC/DOI, 1949, p. 37.
[13] For details of the congressional debate, see U.S. Congress, Senate, Committee on Interior and Insular Affairs, *Hearings on Submerged Lands* (81st Cong., 1st Sess.), October 1949, and *Hearings on Submerged Lands* (82nd Cong., 1st Sess.), March–April, 1951.
[14] *United States v. Louisiana*, 339 U.S. 699, June 5, 1950, and *United States v. Texas*, 339 U.S. 707, June 5, 1950.
[15] Truman persisted, on grounds of national security, equity, and public finance, that "it would be the height of folly for the United States to give away the vast quantities of oil contained in the Continental Shelf." It was Senator Daniel Price (D-Tx) who called the order "a pure and simple act of personal spite and political revenge." See H. Marshall and B. Zisk, *The Federal-State Struggle for Offshore Oil*, p. 32.
[16] S. McDonald, *The Leasing of Federal Lands*, pp. 16–20.

Taxation

Like its leasing policies, the federal government's tax policies for energy industries originated during World War I and remained relatively stable until 1969. Since minerals of all kinds were acknowledged to be "wasting assets," Congress had difficulty choosing appropriate procedures to make allowance for capital consumption.[17] The Revenue Act of 1916 provided that newly discovered mineral assets should be valued at cost for purposes of depreciation (depletion), unless discovered prior to 1913, in which case "fair market value" was an appropriate basis. Then, in 1918, with Congress under wartime pressure to provide larger incentives for oil production, Boise Penrose, a Pennsylvania Republican and chairman of the Senate Finance Committee, got Congress to modify the Revenue Act, making the "discovery value" basis for depletion a permanent feature of the tax code. Senator Robert LaFollette of Wisconsin spoke out against the measure, but only six other senators were listening.[18]

For several years, this issue remained up in the air. Oil producers and the Bureau of Internal Revenue could not agree to a definition of discovery value. Meanwhile, tax write-offs were approved that could amount to several times the actual cost of a well. A congressional conference committee finally compromised on a rule-of-thumb in the Revenue Act of 1926. Discovery value was defined as 27.5 percent of gross income, up to a ceiling of 50 percent of net income, for producing oil and gas properties. This amount of revenue would be tax-free to oil producers. Coal and other minerals received substantially lower allowances, technically because the risks associated with exploration were smaller. But Congress also extended the depletion allowance to all oil and gas properties, including those acquired by purchase or developed for proven production.[19]

The percentage depletion allowance was not the only unusual tax break for the oil industry. Pursuant to the Revenue Act of 1916, the Bureau of Internal Revenue ruled in 1918 that "intangible" drilling costs, including dry holes, could be expensed against current income, rather than capitalized for recovery through depreciation. This ruling, with a generous definition of "intangible," was confirmed by the courts and by Congress in 1954.[20]

The revenue loss to government from these two tax policies has been estimated at $400 million to $2.5 billion annually over the fifty years they were in effect.[21] Congressional attempts to reduce or revoke them failed repeatedly

---

[17] See U.S. Congress, Joint Committee on Internal Revenue Taxation, *Legislative History of Depletion Allowances* (81st Cong., 2nd Sess.), Committee Print, 1950; also, J. Lichtblau and D. Spriggs, *The Oil Depletion Issue* (New York: Industrial Research Foundation, 1958).

[18] Ronnie Dugger, "Oil and Politics," *Atlantic Monthly*, September 1969, pp. 66–90.

[19] Stephen L. McDonald, *Federal Tax Treatment of Income from Oil and Gas* (Washington: The Brookings Institution, 1963), pp. 11–14; also Gerald Nash, *United States Oil Policy, 1890–1964* (Pittsburgh: University of Pittsburgh Press, 1968), pp. 85–86.

[20] John Blair, *The Control of Oil* (New York: Pantheon Books, 1976), pp. 192–193.

[21] Nash cites a Treasury Department memorandum that estimated the cost of the depletion allowance at $400 million in 1947. Blair cites an estimate of $2.35 billion for 1972. See, G. Nash, *U.S. Oil Policy*, p. 198, and J. Blair, *Control of Oil*, p. 193.

until 1969 (see Chapter 9). Despite many drawbacks, these two deductions did stimulate more exploration and production than would otherwise have occurred. This, of course, was their purpose at a time (1916–1926) when the United States was thought to be running out of oil. But after 1926 (except during World War II), they only aggravated the problem of excess capacity. By reducing taxable income so much, they propped up thousands of marginal wells artificially. Not only did this reduce economic efficiency, but it forced authorities that prorated oil production to support domestic prices at higher levels than would otherwise have been necessary.[22]

Prorationing

Prorationing – the restriction of oil production among all producers in proportion to their rated capacities – started out as a conservation measure well within the purview of traditional government authority. In the face of an immense petroleum surplus during the Great Depression, this function was transformed into an administrative system for managing the domestic petroleum market. Prorationing, like the depletion allowance, endured well beyond the immediate circumstances that evoked it. Its durability and effectiveness, in part due to its conservationist origins, contrast sharply with the failure to devise and maintain a similar system for stabilizing competition in the coal industry.

By the late 1920's, substantial excess production capacity existed in petroleum and coal. In the case of coal, high prices during World War I had stimulated an immense expansion of mines, to the point where Commerce Secretary Herbert Hoover estimated idle capacity at 300 million tons (against annual production of 564 million tons) in 1922.[23] In oil, the first price break came in 1927 after a large discovery in Oklahoma. Major discoveries in California in 1928 and 1929 added to the surplus. Then in 1930, with the discovery of the giant East Texas field, the bottom fell out of the petroleum market.

Herbert Hoover, while Secretary of Commerce, was the only prominent advocate of government help for rationalizing excess capacity in these industries. But Hoover's initiatives made little headway. His ideas for limited cooperation between business and government seemed politically ill-suited to the atomistic coal industry. Even for oil, it took nearly a decade to work out a practical means of stabilizing markets. With the help of Henry Doherty, the maverick founder of Cities Service, Hoover convinced President Coolidge in 1924 to create a cabinet-level committee – the Federal Oil Conservation Board – to report on conditions of physical waste in the oil industry.[24]

---

[22] By making crude oil the profit center of the petroleum industry, the depletion allowance (in conjunction with prorationing) may also have stimulated concentration and reduced competition in the refining, transportation, and marketing sectors of the petroleum industry. See Alfred Kahn and M. DeChazeau, *Integration and Concentration in the Petroleum Industry* (New Haven: Yale University Press, 1959).

[23] Ellis W. Hawley, "Secretary Hoover and the Bituminous Coal Problem, 1921–1928," *Business History Review*, XLII, No. 3 (Autumn, 1968), p. 250.

[24] Norman Nordhauser, *The Quest for Stability: Domestic Oil Regulation 1917–1935* (New York: Garland Publishing, 1979), pp. 1–18.

At the time, waste was a real problem. Self-interest and the antitrust laws had so far prevented attempts to "unitize" the flush oil fields of the southwest. (Unitization refers to the organization of wells on separately-owned properties in an oil field as a single unit of production.) Since oil from a common pool belonged to whichever well-operator brought it to the surface ("rule of capture"), most oil fields were over-pumped, regardless of market conditions, resulting in physical damage to the field and permanent loss of 30 to 50 percent of the field's potential. Agencies established in the individual producing states after World War I had failed to implement conservation practices that could withstand judicial review of the political resistence of local producers.[25]

It did not take long for the Federal Oil Conservation Board to realize that the management of physical waste was virtually inseparable from "economic waste." In its 1926 report, the Board commented that "if the several oil-producing states should protect property rights in the oil produced from a common underground supply, it undoubtedly would have some effect in the direction of stabilizing production" and "of retarding development whenever economic demand does not warrant." Legislation could not accomplish this without "freeing owners and operators from the present pressure of a competitive struggle."[26] As the oil glut worsened, executives of some major oil companies admitted this implication and endorsed the need for production controls, preferably voluntary and self-administered. In 1929, an advisory committee to the Conservation Board recommended that Congress waive the Sherman Act so that oil companies could make agreements to curtail production. A month later, the American Petroleum Institute (a trade association representing the major integrated companies) recommended a larger set of agreements to stabilize production throughout the world.

These proposals, however, were too extreme for President Hoover; his Attorney General rejected them both. Instead, he authorized the Bureau of Mines to publish semi-annual demand forecasts, presumably in the hope that rational operators would voluntarily adjust their production schedules accordingly.[27]

Meanwhile, in the oil fields of Texas and Oklahoma, political and economic tensions actually threatened civil order. Independent oil producers intensely resented pressures from the major integrated companies to curb output through regulation. In Texas, where the Railroad Commission was charged with prorating production to avoid physical waste, independents used the courts and the

---

[25] On the early problems of petroleum conservation, see Blakely M. Murphy, ed., *Conservation of Oil and Gas: A Legal History, 1948* (Chicago: American Bar Association, 1949); and Erich Zimmermann, *Conservation in the Production of Petroleum: A Study in Industrial Control* (New Haven: Yale University Press, 1957).

[26] *Report of the Federal Oil Conservation Board to the President of the United States, September 1926* (Washington: GPO, 1926), p. 14.

[27] *Report of the Federal Oil Conservation Board to the President of the United States, February 1929* (Washington: GPO, 1929), p. 17; U.S. Congress, Senate, Select Committee on Small Business, *The International Petroleum Cartel: Staff Report to the Federal Trade Commission* (82nd Cong., 2nd Sess.), Committee Print No. 6, pp. 210–212; also, E. Zimmermann, *Conservation in the Production of Petroleum*, pp. 124–130.

legislature to thwart any attempt by the Commission to tie its prorationing orders to market demand. As pressure intensified for each operator to capture his share of oil, the orders were ignored. Hundreds of thousands of barrels per day were shipped out of the state illegally. Since more than 5,000 wells were drilled in East Texas between 1930 and 1932, production from that field alone was equivalent to one-third of U.S. demand. Crude oil prices fell from $1.05 to $.25 per barrel. In the summer of 1932, the governor of Texas declared martial law and used the national guard to shut down the oil fields (Oklahoma had already done so).

Finally, in November, a special session of the Texas legislature approved the Market Demand Act, which broadened the Railroad Commission's definition of waste to include "production of crude petroleum in excess of transportation or market facilities or reasonable market demand." Although the independents were still opposed in principle, they thought it at least preferable to federal control or compulsory unitization.[28]

Even after several states followed the lead of Texas, prorationing could make little progress toward stabilizing markets without interstate coordination or federal sanctions. The governors of Texas, Oklahoma, and Kansas formed an Oil State Advisory Committee, but it had no authority without congressional approval. By March 4, 1933, all but the most obstinate of independents realized that some sort of federal control would be necessary.

So did President Franklin D. Roosevelt, and the National Industrial Recovery Act seemed to provide the least offensive mechanism. The petroleum industry was the first to adopt a code of fair practice under the NIRA. Its code, adopted in July of 1933, involved a system of regional committees organized by the American Petroleum Institute to control production, refining, and wholesale marketing of petroleum. Only the issue of price-fixing remained unsettled among the integrated majors and the independents. Interior Secretary Harold Ickes, whom FDR appointed to administer the oil code, wanted and threatened to use price controls, but never succeeded before the Supreme Court declared the NIRA unconstitutional.[29]

Even before the *Schechter* decision invalidated the National Recovery Administration's codes, violations of the codes and the problem of "hot oil" (oil produced in excess of prorationing orders) were severe enough to provoke a variety of proposals for more comprehensive controls. In 1935, Congress put an end to interstate shipments of non-prorated oil by passing the Connally Hot Oil Act.[30] A few months later, it approved an Interstate Oil Compact Commission, with permanent staff and the authority necessary to coordinate prorationing by

[28] For the most complete and thoughtful analysis of this episode, see Barbara T. Day, "The Oil and Gas Industry and Texas Politics, 1930–1935" (Houston: Rice University Doctoral Thesis, 1973); also, D. F. Prindle, *Petroleum Politics and the Texas Railroad Commission* (Austin: University of Texas Press, 1981).
[29] G. Nash, *U.S. Oil Policy*, pp. 128–156; N. Nordhauser, *The Quest for Stability*, pp. 116–159.
[30] For the details of this legislative battle, see Samuel Pettenbill, *Hot Oil: the Problem of Petroleum* (New York: Economic Forum Co., 1936).

the states. With that, stabilization was achieved. However complicated, this mesh of state and federal controls constituted an effective administrative system for managing domestic petroleum output until 1972.

The New Deal also brought administrative stabilization to the coal industry, but through different institutions and control mechanisms that did not survive World War II. By 1932, the coal industry was in terrible shape, already having endured a decade of severe excess capacity and cutthroat price competition. At least 4,000 companies had failed, and of the 1,864 companies still reporting to the Bureau of Internal Revenue, 84 percent reported no net income. The number of miners employed had fallen from 700,000 to 400,000, and for those still working, hours worked were down 25 percent and wages, 38 percent. In September 1933, after months of wrangling, coal operators agreed to adopt an NRA code.[31]

The code for coal was based on "fair market prices," instead of production controls like the code for petroleum. Several organizations were created to administer it: a National Bituminous Coal Industrial Board, chaired by Hugh Johnson, the NRA administrator; five regional Code Authorities controlled by operators; and a Labor Board to stabilize wages and working conditions. Coordination among these authorities proved totally inadequate, and by the time the NIRA was struck down, violations of the minimum price structure were pervasive.

Congress moved swiftly to replace the coal code with a separate regulatory system (Bituminous Coal Act of 1935) to set minimum wages and prices and collect a rebatable production tax as a means of enforcement. But because of its labor provisions, this first Coal Act was held unconstitutional by the Supreme Court even before its provisions became fully operational.[32]

Congress passed another Bituminous Coal Act in 1937. The labor standards, to which the Court had objected, were omitted, and the enforcement tax was modified. The new law sought to establish minimum prices based on a determination of average costs (including a fair return to capital) and prevent unfair methods of competition. It reestablished regional authorities to recommend and supervise minimum prices. But in this Act, power was centralized in a seven-member, National Bituminous Coal Commission, appointed by the President. The Commission was responsible for promulgating the code, calculating average costs, formally setting minimum prices, passing on marketing rules and regulations, and settling complaints of violations. Its enforcement powers included cease-and-desist orders and the right to impose a 19 percent tax on violators and non-participants in the code.[33]

The Coal Commission operated for six years as a hybrid between an NRA

---

[31] This section on coal stabilization is derived largely from two excellent books: Waldo Fisher and Charles James, *Minimum Price Fixing in the Bituminous Coal Industry* (Princeton: Princeton University Press, 1955), and James P. Johnson, *The Politics of Soft Coal* (Urbana: University of Illinois Press, 1979).

[32] Ellis W. Hawley, *The New Deal and the Problem of Monopoly* (Princeton: Princeton University Press, 1966), pp. 205–210.

[33] W. Fisher and C. James, *Minimum Price Fixing in Bituminous Coal*, pp. 31–49.

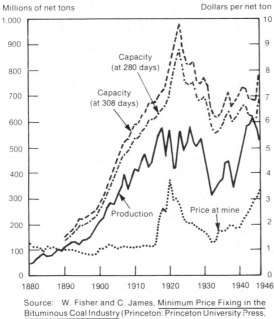

Chart 2-1
Annual Capacity, Production, and Mine Price in the
Bituminous Coal Industry, 1880-1946

Source: W. Fisher and C. James, Minimum Price Fixing in the
Bituminous Coal Industry (Princeton: Princeton University Press,
1955), p. 7.

code authority and an independent regulatory commission. In terms of its
administrative procedures, it was a success. The Commission developed sophisticated methods for determining costs and setting minimum prices, similar
to area rate-making for natural gas developed by the Federal Power Commission during the 1960's. But its success in stabilizing coal markets and strengthening the industry were at best modest, and difficult to discern from the effects
of war-induced recovery. In 1940, prices were still about equal to, or slightly
below, computed average costs. Sixty-two percent of all coal companies still
reported no net income.[34] As Chart 2-1 indicates, significant recovery of coal
prices and production occcurred only after the outbreak of war. In 1943, with
conditions in the coal industry apparently improving, and with production allocation in the hands of the Solid Fuels Administration, Congress allowed the
statutory authority for the Commission to lapse.

Shortly after the war, the coal industry slumped back into its perennial state
of "sickness." Nothing permanent had been accomplished to rationalize its
fragmented structure. Where natural gas was deemed a public utility to be
managed by an independent regulatory commission (discussed in Chapter 4),
and oil controls were technically decentralized and excused as conservation,

[34] Ibid., 316–332.

stabilization of the coal industry had relied on dubious minimum prices, justified as an emergency measure. As such, the Bituminous Coal Act of 1937 was neither politically nor institutionally stable. Once the emergency ended, the coal industry, unlike petroleum and natural gas, faced the harshness of the market without benefit of stabilizing public policies.

U.S. foreign oil policy

The foreign oil policy of the United States has long been an important part of national energy policy, but of little visibility prior to World War II. It has been a story of surpluses and market stabilization, administered privately by a handful of international oil companies. Before and after World War II, proved reserves of petroleum generally exceeded worldwide demand. This condition of surplus, periodically exacerbated by large discoveries in the Middle East, naturally put downward pressure on prices and posed a constant competitive threat to crude-short major companies, high-cost producers (especially in the United States), and other more costly fuels.

Three companies dominated the worldwide petroleum business. Anglo-Persian Oil (now British Petroleum) and Royal-Dutch Shell, a trading and transportation group, controlled most oil production in Asia and the Middle East. Standard Oil of New Jersey (now Exxon) shared their European and Asian markets, but relied on Venezuela for its crude oil. Throughout the 1920's, these three giants had repeatedly engaged in destructive price wars, with little effect on relative market shares. Meanwhile, four other American firms – Standard of New York (now Mobil), Gulf Oil, Standard of California (SoCal), and Texaco – had begun penetrating foreign markets and searching for foreign crude supplies.

Early in the 1920's, when it appeared that the United States would soon exhaust its domestic oil supplies, Congress, the State Department and the American Petroleum Institute had been concerned that the British were intentionally excluding American interests from access to the Middle East. Walter Teagle, president of Standard Oil of New Jersey, prodded the State Department to bring pressure on the British for an "open door" in Mesopotamia (Iraq). Bilateral discussion of this issue dragged on for several years.[35]

By 1928, petroleum was a glut on the world market. Thus, the challenge for the American firms was to gain access to the Middle East for long-term supplies without disrupting foreign markets already saturated in the short-term. In April of that year, Teagle's efforts bore fruit; the Turkish Petroleum Company was reorganized as the Iraq Petroleum Company (IPC), with an American group (Near East Development Corporation) receiving 23.75 percent of the stock. Although five American companies originally participated in the consor-

---

[35] "History of Negotiations Leading to Participation of American Companies in Iraq Petroleum Company," in U.S. Congress, Senate, Committee on Foreign Relations, Subcommittee on Multinational Corporations, *Multinational Corporations and United States Foreign Policy* (93rd Cong., 2nd Sess.), Pt. 8, pp. 508–517.

tium, three were shortly bought out by Standard of New Jersey and Mobil.[36] Anglo-Persian, Shell, and Compagnie Francaise des Petroles each received 23.75 percent. Mr. C. S. Gulbenkian, a Syrian entrepreneur who put the deal together, retained 5 percent. This agreement has been called the "Red Line Agreement" for a line Gulbenkian supposedly drew on a map of the Ottoman Empire, encompassing Turkey, Jordan, Syria, Iraq, and Saudi Arabia. No party to the agreement would be allowed to develop any concessions within that area independently of their joint venture, the Iraq Petroleum Company. This provision, the so-called "self-denying clause," was the cornerstone of an administrative system for controlling Middle East oil, and of subsequent antitrust investigations.[37]

In 1933, Gulf Oil and British Petroleum negotiated an exclusive concession in Kuwait, and British Petroleum's concession in Iran was reorganized as the Anglo-Iranian Oil Co., in which Shell held 22 percent. Although Kuwait and Iran were outside the Red Line, oil production from those countries was linked by long-term offtake agreements to Standard of New Jersey and Mobil, in such a manner that none of the five companies could use excess production to undercut the market position of any other.[38]

The only loose end in this system of production control was the Saudi Arabian concession that Standard of California acquired with the help of the State Department in 1933. SoCal, which had neither the capital nor market outlets necessary to develop the petroleum potential of Saudi Arabia, brought in Texaco as a partner to form the Arabian-American Oil Company (Aramco). With immense reserves of inexpensive crude oil, Aramco would pose a significant threat to the market positions of the IPC partners after World War II.[39]

With the ink scarcely dry on the Red Line agreement, Walter Teagle of Standard, Sir Henry Deterding of Shell, and Sir John Cadman of Anglo-Persian met in September of 1928 at Achnacarry Castle in Scotland. There the three giant companies entered into a pool association, called the "As Is Agreement." They agreed on guidelines for fixing each company's sales volume at the prevailing parity. They also agreed to share existing facilities, add new facilities only as demand expanded, and prevent surpluses in one area from upsetting the price structure in any other. Through a series of addenda during the next six years, other big American oil companies were brought into the arrangement, and its terms were elaborated to provide for sales quotas, price fixing, and buyouts of non-participants.[40]

---

[36] Pan-American Petroleum and Atlantic Refining sold their shares of NEDC in 1930, and Gulf Oil did likewise in 1934; see U.S. Congress, *The International Petroleum Cartel*, pp. 47–54.

[37] *Ibid.*, 56–61. This clause, retained from the Turkish Petroleum Company's original concession, was opposed by the American participants until 1927, when French insistence on it appeared to threaten a collapse of the negotiations.

[38] J. Blair, *The Control of Oil*, pp. 42–44; also, U.S. Congress, *The International Petroleum Cartel*, pp. 129–134.

[39] Irving H. Anderson, *Aramco, the United States, and Saudi Arabia: A Study in the Dynamics of Foreign Oil Policy, 1933–1950* (Princeton: Princeton University Press, 1981).

[40] U.S. Congress, *The International Petroleum Cartel*, pp. 198–214.

Technological competition was the remaining threat to the stability of international petroleum markets. During and just after World War I, the field of hydrocarbons chemistry took off in a series of revolutionary discoveries. Through catalytic cracking in the United States and hydrogenation in Germany, scientists could use petroleum or coal to synthesize explosives, fertilizer, alcohol, solvents, plastic, rubber, and hundreds of other industrial chemicals. For the Germans, hydrogenation provided a means of converting their indigenous coal to synthetic liquid fuel. I. G. Farbenindustrie A. G., which was created by mergers in 1925, became the largest chemical company in the world, controlling hundreds of key German patents.

In March 1929, a meeting took place at Standard's boardroom in New York between senior executives of Standard and I. G. Farben. The group discussed the incipient conflict if Standard entered further into the chemicals business or if I. G. Farben moved into energy fuels. All agreed that the wiser course would be a patent pool between the two firms, with Standard refraining from competition in chemicals worldwide (except in the United States) and I. G. Farben refraining from competition in fuels (except in Germany), especially with synthetic liquids from coal. Teagle added that Shell would have to be included on fuels, since at the Achnacarry meeting, he had promised Deterding "that if we made a world agreement with the I. G., we should hold the door open to him."[41] The Germans were amenable to this and agreed with Standard to pool nearly 2,000 patents in an arrangement for avoiding worldwide competition in either chemicals or energy. The risk that coal-derived liquid fuels might further destabilize already-glutted petroleum markets was thereby eliminated.[42]

In conjunction with market-demand prorationing in the United States, the Red Line, As Is, and patent pool agreements constituted a rational attempt to cartelize the world oil industry in the face of an immense surplus. But despite the elaborate administrative procedures and interlocking joint-ventures designed to implement these agreements, their effectiveness was limited by the absence of sovereign authority. Only prorationing within the United States proved to be durable, comprehensive, and enforceable. The Red line Agreement was unable to keep non-participants from opening up Saudi Arabia. As Is achieved some stabilization of European markets, but too many outsiders kept scrambling to expand their operations by cutting prices. The patent pool did prevent competition between Standard and I. G. Farben, but rapid technological developments by others either circumvented the pool or forced expansion of its membership to the point of meaninglessness.

For its American participants, this private system of market stabilization obviously conflicted with the antitrust laws of the United States. Those laws – the Sherman and Clayton Acts – merely accounted for the covert nature of the system, not its demise. As we shall see further on in this chapter, enforcement of those laws came only after the fact. Rather, it was the outbreak of world war

[41] Exhibit No. 373, "Memorandum of Meeting, March 21, 1929," *United States v. Standard Oil Company of New Jersey*, in U.S. Congress, Senate, *Investigation of the National Defense Program* (77th Cong., 1st Sess.), pt. 11, "Rubber," March–April 1942, pp. 4591–4593.
[42] *Ibid.*, Exhibit Nos. 360 and 362, pp. 4561–4573.

that brought an end of this system by relieving the problem of surplus and confirming the geopolitical importance of Middle East oil.

In May 1941, President Franklin D. Roosevelt created the Office of Petroleum Coordinator for National Defense (predecessor of the Petroleum Administration for War). At the same time, he appointed Interior Secretary Harold Ickes to serve as Coordinator. This agency, noted its historians, was "dedicated to the proposition that cooperation, rather than coercion, was the formula by which the forces of Government and industry could best be joined in the service of the Nation."[43] Although generally accurate with respect to domestic petroleum, this eulogy did not extend to Harold Ickes' vision of postwar oil policy in the Middle East.

As the war intensified, Ickes and the leadership of the petroleum industry grew concerned by the decline of domestic crude oil reserves. Anticipating rapid postwar growth in the demand for oil, industry leaders were already predicting that the United States would become partially dependent on foreign sources. In December 1943, the Petroleum Industry War Council, a broad-based advisory group that linked the Petroleum Administration to industry, recommended that "the national oil policy of the United States should aim at securing for American nationals access to the world's oil resources." But "any direct participation by the Government," said the War Council, "will discourage private enterprise" and "retard the orderly development of the world's oil resources."[44]

Ickes thought otherwise. The Saudi Arabian concession was too big and too important an oil reserve for America's future to be left to management by private firms. Participation of "a sovereign character" was necessary to secure it from foreign companies in which foreign governments exercised direct control.[45]

Ickes seized on a proposal for a government-owned Petroleum Reserve Corporation, originally conceived by Herbert Feis in the State Department, to buy options on foreign oil produced by American firms. The idea initially was to relieve some of the pressure from host governments on their concessionaires while getting some secure oil for military purposes in return for the lend-lease aid that the United States was providing. But Ickes convinced Roosevelt that the federal government should acquire proprietary and managerial control of foreign operating companies, such as Aramco or Gulf's interests in Kuwait Oil, Ltd. Public ownership in the oil industry would fulfill a longstanding New Deal vision.

Not only did SoCal, Texaco, and Gulf rebuff Ickes' offers, but the entire oil industry was alarmed at the prospect of "nationalization." Even small domestic

[43] John Frey and H. Chandler Ide, *A History of the Petroleum Administration for War, 1941–1945* (Washington: GPO, 1946), p. 1.
[44] Petroleum Industry War Council, Foreign Operations Committee, "Report on Foreign Oil Policy," December 8, 1943, *Ibid.*, Appendix 8, p. 391.
[45] Stephen J. Randall, "Harold Ickes and United States Foreign Petroleum Policy Planning, 1939–1945," *Business History Review*, vol. LVII, no. 3 (Autumn, 1983), 367–387; also, Michael B. Stoff, *Oil, War, and American Security* (New Haven: Yale University Press, 1980), pp. 73–88.

producers, with little sympathy for the international majors, viewed Ickes and the Petroleum Reserve Corporation as a threat to "free enterprise." FDR was only mildly supportive, and the State Department was ambivalent. When the oil companies refused to sell out after protracted negotiations, the venture was quietly abandoned.

The Anglo-American Oil Agreement, which met a similar fate, was a bilateral effort to provide for orderly and cooperative development of oil resources in the Middle East. Negotiations with the British got started in mid-1944 under the leadership of Ickes and Cordell Hull, the Secretary of State. The talks, in which a few oil executives from both countries participated, resulted in a draft treaty that proposed a Joint Petroleum Commission to settle concession disputes, collaborate on pipelines, and manage overall output. President Roosevelt endorsed the treaty and sent the draft to Congress.[46]

Domestic oil producers, especially small independents, lobbied hard against the treaty. Many thought it was nothing but a scheme by the international companies to flood domestic markets with cheap imported oil. The government's motives, which appeared to involve the forced shut-in of one million barrels a day of domestic capacity for national security purposes, were even worse in their view. "The ultimate aim," said a spokesman for Texas producers, "is for international and national control and regulation of the oil industry."[47] The Petroleum Industry War Council, the Texas Railroad Commission, and the congressional leadership of Texas and Louisiana shared this view. In the face of this intense opposition, President Truman eventually abandoned the treaty as "obsolete," preferring to expend what political capital he had on more pressing issues such as natural gas regulation and offshore oil.

Restoration of peace and worldwide economic recovery created an immense demand for petroleum. The major integrated oil companies faced this prospect from widely different positions. Standard of New Jersey and Mobil had extensive marketing networks and refining capacity, but still did not control enough crude oil. Their dependence on Venezuela and restricted involvement in the Red Line area, would not be enough to meet market demand in Europe once it recovered. SoCal and Texaco, on the other hand, had a huge potential for producing low-cost oil from their Arabian concession, but lacked the market outlets and working capital necessary to develop it quickly. A merger appeared an ideal solution if the State Department would help get Standard and Mobil released from the Red Line Agreement's self-denying clause over certain opposition from the British government.[48]

For its part, the State Department viewed such a merger as a private means for assuring U.S. control over the Saudi Arabian concession and for achieving stability in international petroleum markets. With Standard and Mobil involved in Aramco, Saudi Arabia would be assured adequate outlets for its crude oil,

[46] M. Stoff, *Oil, War, and American Security*, pp. 151–195.
[47] H. J. Porter, president, Texas Independent Producers and Royalty Owners Association, in NPC Transcript, Janaury 21, 1947, NPC/DOI, 1947, pp. 19–24.
[48] U.S. Congress, Senate, *The International Petroleum Cartel*, pp. 120–122.

and thus enough revenue to satisfy King Ibn Saud. At the same time, Aramco's oil production could be fitted into an orderly pattern of Middle East oil development, without potentially disruptive price wars. State Department officials, no doubt pleased that it would further erode British hegemony, agreed that a merger would serve the U.S. national interest.[49]

The Aramco merger was consummated in 1947. Attorney General Tom Clark expressed no opposition, and the State Department helped Standard of New Jersey and Mobil vacate the Red Line agreement. A year later, Aramco raised its price, which had previously been discounted, to the world level. The world petroleum market was effectively stabilized.[50] In this manner, SoCal and Texaco joined the ranks of the "seven sisters," with the tacit blessing of the Truman administration.

Converting Aramco into a profit center, however, had an unanticipated effect of inciting King Ibn Saud to demand a greater share of the oil revenues. Saud's royalty rate of 12.5 percent yielded revenue of about 21 cents per barrel at a posted price of $1.75. After 1946, this paled in contrast to Venezuela's 50 percent income tax on the difference between price and production cost. Ibn Saud demanded a larger royalty until a U.S. Treasury official reportedly explained to him the Internal Revenue Service provision for foreign tax credits. After extensive consultations between Aramco partners, officials of the State and Treasury Departments, and the U.S. Ambassador to Saudi Arabia, it was agreed that Aramco would be allowed to credit a Saudi income tax of 50 percent against its U.S. income tax liabilities. A recommendation from the National Security Council apparently clinched the deal, since any of the alternatives posed a greater threat to the stability of U.S. influence in Saudi Arabia. The Saudi tax took effect in November 1950, and quickly spread to the other oil concessions in the Middle East.[51]

---

[49] R. C. Stoner to R. G. Follis, June 10, 1946, in U.S. Congress, Senate, *Multinational Corporations and United States Foreign Policy*, pt. 8, pp. 84–89; also, pp. 111–112. Besides immediate cash benefits from the transaction, a merger with Standard of New Jersey and Mobil would presumably benefit SoCal and Texaco by vastly expanding the market for Aramco's oil. As 60 percent owners, SoCal and Texaco would have a smaller cut of a much larger pie (Standard was to get 30 percent and Mobil, 10 percent). Most of SoCal's directors appreciated the benefits of "better stabilization of World Markets," reduction of "political, commercial, and economic risks," and greater assurance of U.S. government support. But at least one of them, Ronald Stoner, opposed the merger because it would foreclose any possibility that SoCal could ever improve its competitive position vis-à-vis Standard, Mobil, Shell, or BP (since they all had production sharing agreements). Stoner saw a tremendous opportunity to supply crude-short independent refiners in the United States, taking market share from the other majors there as well as in Asia and Europe. But Stoner was overruled.
[50] Standard attorneys used a legal technicality to force SoCal and Texaco to raise Aramco prices from a cost basis (where transfer pricing let the parent companies earn profits through downstream sales) to the world level (where Aramco itself became the profit center). This pricing arrangement prevented SoCal and Texaco from shaving margins to expand volume sales at Standard's expense, since Standard and Mobil would share the production revenues.
[51] For discussion and analysis of this foreign tax credit issue, see U.S. Congress, Senate, *Multinational Corporations and United States Foreign Policy*, pt. 4, pp. 12–119; U.S. Congress, House, Committee on Government Operations, *Foreign Tax Credits Claimed by U.S. Petroleum Companies* (95th Cong., 1st Sess.), 1977; also, John Blair, *The Control of Oil*, pp. 193–204.

By providing large transfers of revenue from the U.S. Treasury to those of Saudi Arabia and other Middle East producers, the allowance of a foreign tax credit served as tacit foreign aid. Together with the Aramco merger, it constituted a second leg of U.S. stabilization policy for Middle East oil. The third leg involved Iran, where restoration of stability called for more explicit cooperation between the oil industry and government.

Until 1951, the Anglo-Iranian Oil Company, controlled by British Petroleum and Royal-Dutch Shell, had the exclusive concession to oil production in Iran. After World War II, however, the Iranians had become less and less satisfied with their share of the oil revenues. Dr. Muhammed Mossadeqh, chairman of the Iranian Parliament's oil commission, took the lead in efforts to renegotiate the terms of the 1933 concession. After more than a year of deadlocked discussions with British Petroleum, the Parliament nationalized the oil company and elected Mossadeqh to prime minister. The British refused to accept the nationalization, and threatened other oil companies with legal action if they purchased any oil from the newly organized National Iranian Oil Company (NIOC). Effectively boycotted, Iran's oil production ground to a halt, throwing the country into further political and economic turmoil.[52]

At this point, in June 1951, President Truman accepted the advice of his National Security Council to "bring [U.S.] influence to bear in an effort to effect an early settlement of the oil controversy." This position reflected the Administration's concern that economic destabilization would enhance the Soviet Union's influence in Iranian politics. When efforts failed to restore British Petroleum as sole concessionaire, the State Department decided that participation by American firms would be necessary. But James McGranery, the Attorney General, warned that such an approach would conflict with pending antitrust litigation if it involved cooperation among the American international majors. (This antitrust issue is discussed in the next section of this chapter.)[53]

The impasse between Iran and British Petroleum eventually led to financial crisis and revolution. In the summer of 1953, the Shah of Iran tried to oust Mossadeqh, but was himself deposed. Demonstrations and rioting in Tehran turned violent as the military moved effectively to restore the Shah to his throne. After his return, the State Department stepped up its efforts to provide oil revenues necessary to stabilize the Iranian government. Undersecretary Herbert Hoover Jr. first convinced the British to accept the idea of an expanded consortium in which the five major American companies would participate. Enlisting support from the five companies was easier. As Orville Harden of Standard coyly noted, "from the strictly commercial viewpoint, our company has no particular interest in entering such a group, but we are very conscious of the large national security interests."[54] The Departments of State, Defense,

---

[52] For more detailed background on these developments and subsequent events, see Robert B. Stobaugh, "The Evolution of Iranian Oil Policy, 1925–1975," in George Lenczowski, ed., *Iran Under the Pahlavis* (Stanford: Hoover Institution Press, 1978), pp. 201–252.

[53] NSC 107/2, quoted in U.S. Congress, Senate, Committee on Foreign Relations, Subcommittee on Multinational Corporations, *Report on Multinational Oil Corporations and U.S. Foreign Policy* (93rd Cong., 2nd Sess.), Committee Print, January 2, 1975, p. 58.

[54] O. Harden to J. F. Dulles, December 4, 1953, in U.S. Congress, Senate, Committee on

and Interior, as well as the National Security Council, had in mind an Iranian Consortium composed of the five largest American oil companies, British Petroleum, and Shell. Their rationale was that only those companies had the technical skills, tanker fleets, and distribution channels necessary to restore Iranian oil production in a major way.

In promoting a start-up of Iranian oil exports by American multinationals, the State Department dared not alienate congressional spokesmen for the U.S. domestic oil industry. Domestic producers had enjoyed vigorous demand and rising prices during the Korean War, especially in the absence of imported oil from Iran. After attending a meeting with Vice-President Nixon and various members of the National Security Council, Senator Lyndon Johnson of Texas expressed concern to Secretary Dulles whether sufficient "care was to be taken to see that this oil did not serve to jeopardize the position of American independents." In reply, Undersecretary Hoover assured him that no importation was anticipated, and that the five international majors were chosen precisely because they "could and would absorb the Iranian production without unsettling world markets."[55]

The only obstacle was the Justice Department, which claimed that there was no national security exemption to the Sherman Act. To mollify this concern, Hoover convinced the five American majors to relinquish one percent each of the proposed consortium. Collectively, that 5 percent was awarded to Iricon, a joint venture that represented 12 smaller American companies. This arrangement would leave 8 percent each for Gulf, SoCal, Texaco, Standard of New Jersey, and Mobil; 40 percent for British Petroleum, 14 percent for Shell, and 6 percent for the French firm, CFP.

This ownership pattern was designed to provide a countervailing balance between American and non-American firms and between crude-long and crude-short firms in control of the Consortium's decisions regarding production and pricing. In this manner, Iran's future oil output would be integrated with that of the Iraq Petroleum Company, Kuwait, and Aramco.[56] If managed adroitly, the growth rate of Iranian output would match the growth rates of production in each of the other Middle East concessions, and the sum would presumably match the growth of worldwide demand. But to accomplish this third piece of postwar stabilization, the Justice Department was forced to abandon its belated antitrust prosecution of the prewar cartels as well.

The antitrust legacy

Conflict between antitrust policy and the government's energy-related policies pre-dated President Truman's dilemma in the Iranian Crisis by at least two decades. Since the enactment of the Sherman Act in 1890, the Justice Depart-

---

Foreign Relations, Subcommittee on Multinational Corporations, *The International Petroleum Cartel, the Iranian Consortium and U.S. National Security* (93rd Cong., 2nd Sess.), Committee Print, February 1974, p. 58.
[55] Quoted in U.S. Congress, Senate, *Report on Multinational Oil Corporations*, p. 73.
[56] U.S. Congress, Senate, *Report on Multinational Oil Corporations*, pp. 65–74.

ment has been responsible for regulating competition. Its scrutiny of monopolistic and non-competitive practices in the oil industry has been almost continuous, but not often successful. At the very least, this record helped create an
unusually virulent and mutual distrust between government and the oil industry.

The tone for antitrust policy in oil was first set in 1911, when the Supreme
Court broke-up the Standard Oil Trust.[57] It was not until 1929, however, that
the Justice Department clashed with other government interests on matters of
oil policy. The issue, as discussed earlier in this chapter, was a plan devised by
the Federal Oil Conservation Board and modified by the American Petroleum
Institute for voluntary curtailment of oil production. When asked for his opinion, Attorney General William Mitchell said that formal production controls
would conflict with the Sherman Act, and would likely be challenged. The
proposal and the Board were abandoned, eventually replaced by the apparatus
of state prorationing and the codes of fair practice under the National Recovery
Act.

The petroleum industry's enforcement of its NRA codes led to a worse clash
in the so-called Madison cases of 1936. Under its code of fair competition, the
American Petroleum Institute had formed a Planning and Coordination Committee to administer a program of price and production stabilization. After the
Supreme Court overturned the NRA, this Committee's marketing sub-group
continued to function in a modified form under the direction of Charles Arnott,
vice-president of Socony-Vacuum Oil Co. In May 1936, a federal grand jury
was empaneled in Madison, Wisconsin, to investigate the "Gasoline Buying
Program" that Arnott's committee had administered. Later that year, the grand
jury issued criminal indictments against 56 oil company executives and two
dozen companies for allegedly buying oil from independent refiners to prevent
cut-rate sales, and for fixing jobbers' margins (as they resold it wholesale).[58]
Despite the oilmen's defense that they had operated with approval of the NRA
and the Interior Department, most were criminally convicted in a decision later
upheld by the Supreme Court.

In 1940, after a series of other regional price-fixing cases, the Justice Department launched what has subsequently been called a "shared monopoly" suit.
The Mother Hubbard Case, as it was called, alleged that the American Petroleum Institute, its 22 largest corporate members, their subsidiaries and principal officers so dominated the industry through their size, integration, and
price leadership as to constitute a monopolistic combination in restraint of
trade.[59] The case, suspended with the outbreak of war, was briefly restored to
the docket in 1946, but then removed again in favor of separate actions against
smaller groups. Still, it had put the oil industry on notice that its every action
was subject to question by the Attorney General of the United States.

[57] *United States vs. Standard Oil Company of New Jersey*, 173 Fed. Rep. 183.
[58] *United States vs. Socony–Vacuum Oil Co.*, 310 U.S. 150,221 (1940), and *United States vs. Standard Oil Company of Indiana et al.*, (January 21, 1938, No. 11,365 in the Western District of
Wisconsin).
[59] *United States vs. American Petroleum Institute*, Civil Action No. 8524 (Dist. of Columbia, 1940).

During the war, the Justice Department generally relieved the petroleum industry from risk of antitrust prosecution if its cooperative actions were performed under the auspices of the Office of Production Management (and subsequently the Petroleum Administration for War).[60] For the duration, at least, members of the Petroleum Industry War Council and its subordinate and affiliated advisory committees were relatively safe. But advisory committees assisting in demobilization would have to be more careful. Attorney General Francis Biddle ordered that "each specific plan" involving cooperative endeavors by oil industry groups be submitted to him "for advice and individual clearance."[61]

His successor, Tom Clark, took a similar position in 1946 when asked his views on a National Petroleum Council that would replace the Petroleum Industry War Council as a liaison between business and government in peacetime. Against the advice of some independent oilmen, Attorney General Clark approved the Council in principle. He specified, however, that it must not initiate any actions or advice prior to a request from the Interior Secretary, and that all groups within the oil industry should be represented on the Council.[62]

The petroleum industry was so diverse that its various sectors could, and usually did, have divergent interests in most policy issues. Seven companies, of which five are American-owned, were in a class by themselves – vertically integrated with widespread international operations. Besides these, there were approximately 20 other vertically integrated domestic companies, referred to throughout this book as "majors." By the 1970's, most of these had developed foreign operations. "Independent refiners," which numbered between 100 and 200 in the postwar period, are companies that refine petroleum, but generally do not produce it or sell refined products at retail. Independent oil producers, or "independents," are the thousands of individuals or companies in the business of finding or producing crude oil or natural gas in the United States – but not transporting or refining it. (In the chapters on natural gas, "independent producer" refers to any company, including a major, that produces gas but is not an interstate pipeline company.) In the distribution sector of the oil industry, there are hundreds of terminal operators, pipeline companies, tanker fleets and wholesale jobbers, and thousands of independently-owned service stations.

Finding appropriate members to represent the major companies on the new Council was a problem all around. The most likely candidates were the very executives who had been prosecuted in Madison or were defendants in the Mother Hubbard suit. Not surprisingly, they too were wary when invited by Interior Secretary Julius Krug to participate in a peacetime "experiment" in cooperation between business and government. When Clark reviewed the candidates that Krug was considering for the National Petroleum Council, he

---

60 Robert H. Jackson, Attorney General, to John Lord O'Brian, General Counsel, Office of Production Management, April 29, 1941, Attorney General Correspondence File (1946), in Administrative Files of the Office of Oil and Gas, Department of the Interior, Washington, D.C.
61 Francis Biddle to John Lord O'Brian, July 6, 1944, *Ibid.*
62 E. M. Callis, president of Petrol Corporation, to Tom. C. Clark, May 20, 1946; Julius Krug to Tom C. Clark, May 24, 1946; Tom C. Clark to Julius Krug, May 27, 1946, *Ibid.*

found that more than half had either been convicted of criminal antitrust violations, pleaded nolo contendere, headed companies that had been convicted, or were still under indictment.[63] As we shall see in the next section of this chapter, caution and rigorous self-control would dominate the Council's procedural organization and early activities if the experiment were to survive, let alone succeed.

At about this time, the Federal Trade Commission reactivated an investigation of monopolistic practices in the international oil business that it had begun before the war. Its report, completed in 1951, remained unpublished for reasons of national security until 1952. At that time, Senator John Sparkman, chairman of the Select Committee on Small Business, ordered it published as a committee print entitled, "The International Petroleum Cartel." The report documented the Red Line Agreement, the As Is Agreement, restrictive offtake agreements, and a half-a-dozen other international combinations involving 21 American firms. President Truman ordered the Justice Department to empanel a grand jury and prosecute for criminal conspiracy.[64]

It was at this point that U.S. antitrust policy and foreign oil policy reached a loggerhead. The Iranian crisis had begun, and by January 1953, the State Department had decided that a settlement could only be achieved with participation of the very companies under grand jury investigation. At the National Security Council's meeting on January 9, 1953, the Departments of State, Defense, and Interior recommended that the investigation be dropped. Because the Soviet Union bordered on Iran, and because the major American companies supplied western Europe with critical oil, the State Department argued that "we cannot afford to leave unchallenged the assertions that these companies are engaged in a criminal conspiracy for the purposes of predatory exploration." The Justice Department refuted this recommendation, arguing that prosecution of a world oil cartel in place since 1928 was paramount in the national interest.[65]

Two days later, President Truman summoned the government's prosecutor in charge of the case and ordered him to abandon the criminal suit. It should be pursued, said Truman, but only as a civil suit. But to convince the American companies to participate in the consortium, President Eisenhower had to order the Justice Department to drop the production aspects (the Red Line Agreement) from the civil charges in August, 1953. In that attenuated form, the cartel case dragged on for another decade, when it was finally settled by an innocuous consent decree. This would not be the last time that antitrust standards were at odds with the government's energy policies.

---

[63] Tom Clark to Julius Krug, June 6, 1946, and Ralph K. Davies to Tom Clark, Telephone Memorandum, June 7, 1946, *Ibid.*
[64] For a complete discussion of the cartel case, see Burton Kaufman, *The Oil Cartel Case: A Documentary Study of Antitrust Activity in the Cold War Era* (Westport: Greenwood Press, 1978); also, U.S. Congress, *Report on Multinational Corporations and United States Foreign Policy*, pp. 57–74.
[65] Appendices C and D, in B. Kaufman, *The Oil Cartel Case*, pp. 137–157.

Experiment in cooperation

The advisory council mechanism, as a means for coordinating the oil policies of business and government, attained its highest form in the petroleum sector during World War II. The Petroleum Administration for War, as previously mentioned, was the principal agency for coordinating the activities of the petroleum industry. Ralph K. Davies, formerly a vice-president of Standard Oil of California, was its Deputy Administrator. To facilitate the Administration's directives and provide necessary communications, Ickes designated 66 oil industry executives to serve as a Petroleum Industry War Council (PIWC). It eventually organized 83 functional sub-committees to administer domestic activities, and a Foreign Operations Committee to coordinate the work of 27 other sub-committees. Amidst both praise and criticism of this system after the war, the Petroleum Administration's official history explained that it was "frequently difficult to distinguish between the activities of PAW on the one hand, and the industry committees on the other. So closely and continuously did they work together," that it was "all but impossible to say where one left off and the other began."[66]

At the war's end, Ralph Davies was a vocal advocate for continuing a scaled-down version of this administrative system. "Similar benefit will flow," he told a senate committee, "from having a similar relationship between the industry forces and the Government forces in time of peace."[67] Davies was concerned that the government might assert new controls over the energy sector. He tried to convince other oilmen, who wanted nothing more to do with government, that a strong advisory council would "best protect the industry's continued independence."[68]

Despite critics in Congress, in other bureaucracies (notably the Federal Power Commission and Department of Commerce), and especially among independent oil producers and gasoline retailers, Davies succeeded in convincing President Truman that his idea was worth a try. So when he abolished the Petroleum Administration and its War Council in 1946, Truman ordered Secretary Krug to create an office within the Interior Department "to serve as a channel of communication between the Federal Government and the petroleum industry." That office would be accompanied by "an industry organization to consult and advise with."[69] Accordingly, Secretary Krug established an Oil and Gas Division to gather and analyze data, coordinate government policy, and administer the Hot Oil Act. At the same time, he created the National Petroleum Council.

Once Secretary Krug worked out the antitrust ground rules with Attorney

---

[66] J. W. Frey and H. C. Ide, *A History of the Petroleum Administration for War*, p. 2.
[67] U.S. Congress, Senate, Special Committee Investigating Petroleum Resources, *Hearings on the Oil and Gas Division of the Department of the Interior* (79th Cong., 2nd Sess.), June 17, 1946, pp. 7–8.
[68] R. K. Davies to J. Krug, April 5, 1946, File 1–322, Administrative Pt. 1, Box 3177, Office of the Secretary, Central Classified Files, Record Group 48, National Archives, Washington, D.C.
[69] *Supra* Note 1.

General Clark, he appointed 85 members to the Council, 55 of whom had served on the War Council. All members were chief operating officers of firms or trade associations. The membership included representatives of the natural gas transmission industry, independent oil producers, refiners and retailers, 21 trade associations, and 22 executives from the major integrated oil companies.[70]

Walter Hallanan, president of the Plymouth Oil Co., was elected chairman of the Council. Hallanan, a Republican national committeeman from West Virginia, had no record of antitrust violations and evidently satisfied the major companies and the independents. Under Hallanan's leadership, the Council's first order of business was to develop by-laws that would keep the Council out of trouble and give it control over the Oil and Gas Division.

The Council's first principle was that it would only act upon a direct request from the Secretary of the Interior, although members could suggest a request informally through the Oil and Gas Division. The Council reserved the right to turn down any request for an informational study or a recommendation of policy. Council meetings were to be closed, except for invited guests, although a verbatim transcript would be kept. Two 11-member committees, elected annually, would oversee the Council's activities. An Agenda Committee, first chaired by George Hill of the Houston Oil Company, was responsible for accepting or rejecting assignments from the Interior Secretary and for approving all matters to be discussed or acted on at Council meetings. An Appointment Committee, chaired by Alton Jones of Cities Service, chose NPC members to serve on the various task-oriented committees that performed the Secretary's advisory assignments. Majority vote would determine substantive actions by the Council and each committee. Operating expenses were paid by voluntary contributions from its members' firms.[71]

The official functions of the National Petroleum Council – to provide data and make policy recommendations to the Interior Secretary – were not necessarily its most important. The Council was a forum in which industry leaders could meet and discuss issues of public policy among themselves and with key personnel from the federal bureaucracies involved in petroleum-related matters. In this manner, the Council's quarterly meetings in Washington, and those of its committees, provided opportunities for consensus-building, within the industry and between business and government. As Ralph Davies explained in 1947, "we need at least this as a unifying arrangement in respect of the oil industry, with so many highly competitive individual units."[72]

Maintaining the symbolism of cooperation was among the Council's chief functions. In his acceptance speech, Walter Hallanan alluded to this aspect: "We shall be charting new courses in this unique peacetime cooperative effort

---

[70] National Petroleum Council, "Membership List," NPC/DOI, 1946–47; also, J. W. Frey and H. C. Ide, *PAW History*, Appendix 4, p. 327.
[71] National Petroleum Council, "Report of the Committee on Organization to the National Petroleum Council, September 26, 1946," By-laws file, 1946; also, NPC, "Articles of Organization (As Amended) of the National Petroleum Council," March 22, 1963, file 106, 1963, NPC/DOI.
[72] National Petroleum Council, Meeting Transcript, July 10, 1947, NPC/DOI, p. 183.

between Government and the industry we represent." By the beginning of the Eisenhower administration, the Council had become the model for effective business-government relations. Addressing its members in 1953, Secretary Douglas McKay attested to unqualified support of the Council; he thought that "the whole future of the country depends upon cooperation among our people." His Assistant Secretary for Minerals, Felix Wormser, wanted to copy the council "for copper, lead, coal, or what have you."[73]

The National Petroleum Council achieved this stature despite serious frictions between the industry and the Truman administration over natural gas, offshore minerals leasing, antitrust policy, and synthetic fuels. It did so through circumspect responsiveness to the government's requests for data, for help with the fuel shortage of 1947–48, and for coordinating the oil industry's mobilization during the Korean War. In return, the Council had considerable influence on some domestic energy policies, and probably did prevent initiatives for more forceful regulation by government.

Information was the Council's stock-in-trade. During the late 1940's, the Interior Department requested studies from the Council every few months. Studies were done of domestic oil and gas reserves, productive capacity, steel requirements, fuels for military aircraft, tank car shortages, mineral leasing rules, oil imports, the Soviet Union's productive capacity, and a dozen other subjects. Apart from mere statistical data, which was already gathered by the Bureau of Mines and the Geologic Survey, these NPC studies provided the only expert basis that Congress, the Interior Department, or defense planners had for making decisions about postwar energy policy. Committees appointed by the Council used the technical staff of their members' firms to compile and assess the relevant data and prepare comprehensive reports. Among other things, this prevented the need for an autonomous government agency to fulfill this function. The Oil and Gas Division, whose employees were generally recommended by the Council, remained a small staff entity, with no power other than that which it derived from the Council.

These reports often concluded with recommendations of policy representing the petroleum industry's consensus view. For example, in an early report on the Bureau of Land Management's administrative regulations for mineral leasing, the NPC criticized ten specific rules and proposed changes for each. Max Ball, who replaced Davies as Director of the Oil and Gas Division, subsequently reported that "the Leasing Act regulations were modified to meet every one of the recommendations of the committee [NPC] except one."[74]

The Council's influence on more important issues was hardly so decisive. On the problem of oil imports, which is treated at length in Chapters 5 and 6, the National Petroleum Council managed, with difficulty, to articulate a consensus view. Although necessarily vague to satisfy both domestic and international producers, it did seem to provide a framework for policy that prevailed from

[73] NPC, Meeting Transcript, Janaury 21, 1947, NPC/DOI, p. 17; NPC, Meeting Transcript, February 25, 1953, NPC/DOI, p. 57; NPC, Meeting Transcript, May 28, 1953, NPC/DOI, p. 47.
[74] NPC, "Report of Subcommittee of National Petroleum Council: Regulations Under Federal Mineral Leasing," December 6, 1946; NPC, Meeting Transcript, July 10, 1947, NPC/DOI, p. 21.

1949 until 1959.[75] On the issue of federally funded synthetic fuels, as discussed in the next chapter, the Council had a major impact, but only after a Republican captured the White House. On the other hand, the NPC's views on natural gas regulation and submerged lands had virtually no effect on the Truman administration's policies.[76]

The Council's first action-oriented assignment came shortly after it was organized, during the energy crisis in the winter of 1947–48. Demand for all fuels, and especially home heating oil, had increased sharply during the postwar economic recovery, but sources of supply lagged due to depleted reserves, materials shortages, inadequate refinery capacity and a tanker shortage. As early as April, 1947, Max Ball raised the prospect of a wintertime shortage at a meeting of the Council, warning that "if we ever go to allocation or distribution by government in peacetime this industry is just headed for government control, which is certainly a thing that we all abhor."[77]

At first, the Agenda Committee refused to study the situation since it raised issues of price and competition. Even after Secretary Krug formally requested the Council's help in October, the Agenda Committee declined to make recommendations involving "concerted industry action" until the Justice Department had given its blessing. In December, the Council did suggest a series of actions that government, consumers, and individual oil companies could take to alleviate the pending emergency.[78] By that time, midwestern refiners were already rationing product supplies, and retailers were claiming that the majors were creating a shortage to force up prices.

In January 1948, after Congress had passed the Anti-Inflation Act of 1947 (allowing voluntary agreements by industries to allocate goods without driving up prices), Secretary Krug succeeded in convincing the Council to formulate an allocation plan. After the Attorney General grudgingly granted antitrust immunity, the NPC went ahead with a voluntary program to allocate petroleum products.[79]

By June, although the crisis had passed, the reprobations had begun. The Select Committee on Small Business held well-attended hearings on Monopolistic Practices in the Petroleum Industry. Featured at those hearings were independent retailers and wholesale jobbers who aired bitter complaints of abuses by the major companies under the voluntary allocation program.[80] Al-

---

[75] National Petroleum Council, *A National Oil Policy for the United States* (Washington: NPC, 1949), p. 19; NPC, "A Report of the Committee on Petroleum Imports, January 26, 1950"; NPC, Report of the National Petroleum Council's Committee on Petroleum Imports," May 5, 1955, NPC/DOI.

[76] NPC, *A National Oil Policy*, pp. 12, 15–16.

[77] NPC, Meeting Transcript, April 22, 1947, NPC/DOI, pp. 80–85.

[78] J. Krug to W. Hallanan, October 17, 1947, Correspondence File, 1947; NPC, "Report of the National Petroleum Council's Committee on Petroleum Products Supplies and Availability, December 1, 1947," NPC/DOI.

[79] NPC, "Report of the National Petroleum Council Committee on Voluntary Petroleum Allocation Agreements," January 22, 1948; J. Krug to T. Clark, exchange of correspondence, Jan. 28 – Apr. 30, 1948, File 016.2 (Attorney General Correspondence), 1948, NPC/DOI.

[80] U.S. Congress, Senate, Select Committee on Small Business, *Hearings: Investigation and Study of Monopolistic Practices in the Petroleum Industry* (80th Cong., 2nd Sess.), June, 1948.

though nothing more punitive than adverse public relations resulted from those hearings, the Council's role in the allocation program would be cited in subsequent challenges to the legitimacy of business advisory committees.[81]

Two years after the energy crisis, when the Korean War posed a different sort of emergency, the government was better prepared. In 1949, the National Petroleum Council had produced recommendations for the organization of a Petroleum Administration for Defense. The Council had specified that this organization should be specialized vertically, "to deal with the internal problems of the petroleum industry," rather than part of a cross-industry bureaucracy. It would thus be independent of the general mobilization machinery, reporting directly to Oscar Chapman, the new Secretary of the Interior. The idea was to give the petroleum industry a unique organizational status, reproducing conditions of World War II.[82]

With these careful preparations, the Petroleum Administration for Defense was activated swiftly, under provision of the Defense Production Act of 1950. Bruce K. Brown, a NPC member who also chaired the Military Petroleum Advisory Board (established by Krug in 1947 at the NPC's recommendation), assumed the position of Deputy Administrator. The NPC immediately organized a committee to identify and recommend personnel from the oil industry to staff the Petroleum Administration. It was operational by December 1950. Meanwhile, another NPC committee drew up plans by which regional and functional committees of the Council would take domestic operational responsibilities, similar to those of the old Petroleum Industry War Council. A Foreign Petroleum Supply Committee, also recommended by the NPC, was subsequently created to deal with international supply dislocations caused by the shutdown of Iran. This committee operated for the duration of the war under a provision of the Defense Production Act.[83]

The National Petroleum Council's plans for working with the Petroleum Administration did not easily gain approval. Despite mobilization, the Justice Department had decided that business advisory committees were getting out of hand, particularly in the petroleum sector. Attorney General Howard McGrath took the opportunity of general mobilization to issue new rules for the organization and activities of advisory committees. To "minimize the possibility of antitrust prosecution," McGrath suggested that the agenda for all advisory committees be formulated by government, that their chairmen be government officials, and that the functions of committees remain purely advisory.[84]

Oscar Chapman was unwilling to accept these limitations without a fight. His experience in the Interior Department since 1945 had taught him that "you have to have success in these councils [for] the success of the country. There is

---

[81] See, for example, U.S. Congress, House, Judiciary Committee, Subcommittee on Antitrust, *WOC's and Government Advisory Groups* (84th Cong., 1st Sess.), 1955, Pt. IV, pp. 2404–2494.
[82] NPC, Meeting Transcript, September 28, 1950, pp. 140–142, 176–177; also, NPC, "Report of the National Petroleum Council's Committee on Government Oil and Gas Organization," December 3, 1953, NPC/DOI, pp. 4–5.
[83] NPC, Meeting Transcript, December 5, 1950, NPC/DOI, pp. 18–23.
[84] Peyton Ford to Oscar Chapman, October 19, 1950, in Antitrust and Advisory Council File, 1955, NPC/DOI.

no other way." Like others, Chapman had once "stood in fear of the great oil industry's doing this or that" to the economy or the government. But as he told the Council, "you kind of learn as you go along."[85] Accordingly, Chapman sent McGrath his own guidelines for the operations of the National Petroleum Council that varied "in certain minor particulars" from those outlined by the Attorney General. The Council and its committees would not be chaired by a government official, although one would be present at all meetings. The Council's Agenda and Appointment Committees would continue their traditional functions, although their decisions would require the Deputy Administrator's *pro forma* approval.[86]

The Attorney General flatly rejected these "minor" variations. Furthermore, he launched into a wideranging criticism of the activities of petroleum advisory committees during and since World War II. He documented a great many complaints of abuses from independent companies, concluding "that the root of most complaints" was the "intermingling of government functions with private groups" that characterized Chapman's proposal.[87]

Secretary Chapman, who "was shocked and surprised" by these criticisms, decided to go directly to the President in defense of the National Petroleum Council's unique stature.[88] In a private meeting, Chapman apparently convinced Truman that the NPC should maintain the operating status that he had originally approved in 1946. The President made this clear to the Attorney General during a cabinet meeting three days later. The Justice Department did not exactly give up its reform campaign, which continued 18 months longer and refocused on removal of trade association personnel from advisory councils.[89] But the National Petroleum Council, alone among all of the government's business advisory committees, continued to exist and function by its own rules, with its own chairman and agenda, until the early 1970's.[90]

---

[85] NPC, Meeting Transcript, May 9, 1951, pp. 38–40.

[86] O. Chapman to H. McGrath, January 29, 1951, Antitrust and Advisory Council File, 1955, NPC/DOI.

[87] P. Ford to O. Chapman, February 16, 1951, and H. G. Morison to O. Chapman, March 15, 1951, *Ibid.*

[88] Interior Secretary Chapman was not nearly as protective of other advisory councils. A Gas Industry Advisory Council, created in 1950 to advise the Petroleum Administration for Defense, did have to conform with the Justice Department's guidelines. And the coal industry lost out entirely. In 1948, Krug had created the National Bituminous Coal Advisory Council when coal executives complained that the NPC afforded the oil industry unique access to government. Although this coal council had accomplished little of substance since then, it too wanted Chapman to obtain an exemption from the new rules similar to that of the petroleum council. In 1952, when Chapman was "unable" to do so, the coal council was dissolved rather than operate under more restrictive rules than the NPC. See, Bureau of Mines, File 11–34, Minerals/Coal, pts. 1–7; especially L. E. Tierney to O. Chapman, October 17, 1951 (pt. 6), and Department of the Interior Order No. 2698, August 8, 1952 (pt. 7), Record Group 70, National Archives, Washington, D.C.

[89] O. Chapman to H. S. Truman, May 18, 1951, and continuing correspondence between Secretary Chapman and the Justice Department, May 1951 to November 1952, in Antitrust and Advisory Council File, 1955, NPC/DOI.

[90] In 1961, President Kennedy initiated a new round of reforms for advisory committees, but the NPC maintained a special status. The Council refused to meet for a year until Kennedy compromised by allowing it to have its own chairman plus a "co-chairman" from government. In that hybrid form, the National Petroleum Council continued to operate effectively for another decade.

A conventional balance

In the aftermath of war, energy policy and the government's relationship with business were in a state of flux that mirrored conditions in energy markets. With the balance between supply and demand so volatile and uncertain for all three fossil fuels, questions of government promotion and control were raised and debated, but not easily answered. In the next three chapters, we will see how the most important of these – synthetic fuels from coal, natural gas prices, and oil imports – were resolved only as the energy glut became increasingly apparent.

But the past policies and institutional relations described in this chapter would constrain those choices, and the manner in which they were made. Three basic policies of an earlier age – minerals leasing, the depletion allowance, and market-demand prorationing – carried over into the postwar period with little change. The first two of these gave private firms the opportunity and incentive to develop immense reserves of petroleum, natural gas, and to a lesser extent, coal. In the face of such surpluses, prorationing had already become necessary politically to keep prices from falling and protect the least efficient producers. But with these policies still in place after the war, natural gas inventories would appear deceptively large, cheap foreign oil could easily penetrate U.S. markets, and commercial demand for synthetic fuels would not likely materialize.

In its foreign oil policy, hegemony and stability in the Persian Gulf appeared to be the government's strategic objectives. To achieve them, the State Department enlisted the American multinationals in a tacit relationship of mutual benefit. The system of interlocking joint ventures, arranged and approved in the postwar decade, worked well until the late 1960's. But it wasn't airtight, and the spillover of foreign surpluses into U.S. markets was enough to hurt coal and undermine the effects of prorationing in oil. American industry would get an early taste of interdependence in a global market, and learn the problems of attempting insularity the hard way.

Except for the National Petroleum Council, relations between business and government were tentatively restored after the war to their conventional balance. The Council was a unique experiment that might have been extended to other energy sectors had it contributed more to sound policy. While it did provide data and help with emergencies, it was constrained by antitrust scrutiny and the limits of internal consensus. Its members' advocacy of their own private interests denied even the legitimate responsibilities of government. In its own view, the Council had "moved out ahead to blaze a bright new trail in demonstrating that industry and government can work together in the public interest without surrender by either of one iota of sovereignty."[91] The point on sovereignty was accurate enough, but the comment on public interest was myopic.

[91] National Petroleum Council, "The NPC: A Unique Experience in Government–Industry Cooperation, The First Seven Years" (Washington: NPC, 1961), NPC/DOI, p. 80.

3. "Stepping right out" with synthetic fuels

In 1980, when Iranian oil exports were shut down by revolution and OPEC oil prices were doubling again, Congress created a Synthetic Fuels Corporation.[1] This "independent federal entity" was authorized to spend $88 billion to facilitate development of a commercial synthetic fuels industry by 1992. Major oil and gas companies expanded their research and development programs and planned a score of huge projects to liquefy and gasify coal and to produce oil from shale.

A push of the same sort, more than three decades earlier, had all but faded from the nation's memory. In 1948, the *New York Times* had reported that "the United States is on the threshold of a profound chemical revolution. The next ten years will see the rise of a massive new industry which will free us from dependence on foreign sources of oil. Gasoline will be produced from coal, air and water."[2] During World War II, the federal government had begun a program to develop synthetic fuels, and the Truman administration considered them to be nearly commercially feasible. How and why that program came into being – and then was abandoned – tell something about the making of public policy in the United States.

In the judgment of John O'Leary, an experienced energy bureaucrat, the effort was abandoned "when the Eisenhower administration came into office, largely because of the representations of the petroleum industry." Had the program continued and expanded like nuclear power, O'Leary told Congress in 1975, "we would have had an orderly transit from our dependence on natural liquid and fuels to synthetic fuels sometime in the 1960's."[3]

The oil industry's opposition to federal development of synthetic liquid fuels

---

[1] Portions of this chapter were previously published as an article: Richard Vietor, "The Synthetic Liquid Fuels Program: Energy Politics in the Truman Era," *Business History Review*, vol. LIV, 1 (Spring 1980), pp. 1–34.

[2] *New York Times*, September 12, 1948.

[3] U.S. Congress, Senate, Committee on the Judiciary, Subcommittee on Antitrust and Monopoly, *Hearings on Interfuel Competition* (94th Cong., 1st Sess.), June–October 1975, pp. 89–90. O'Leary, a consultant at the time, had held high-level appointments in the Bureau of Mines, the Department of the Interior, the FPC and the AEC, the Federal Energy Administration, and the Department of Energy. See Richard Corrigan, "Energy Focus, the Man Who's Done it All," *National Journal*, January 29, 1977, p. 181.

did indeed contribute to the program's demise in the 1950's. But O'Leary's observation is only part of the story. The prevailing rationale for government involvement in synthetic fuels was undermined by a dramatic shift from a shortage to a surplus of crude petroleum. This stretched the time frame of national security planning into the indefinite future. The oil industry's opposition was also part of the broader political issue of redefining appropriate relations between business and government. Thus, the government's role in synthetic fuels fell victim to Eisenhower's more general recision of wartime programs. Finally, the coal industry, which was falling apart at the time, had neither the financial nor organizational resources to mount an effective counter-offensive against the oil industry's National Petroleum Council.

The synfuels potential

The term "synthetic fuel," or "synfuel," usually means the artificial gas or substitute petroleum derived by heating coal, lignite, or oil shale in the presence of water vapor.

The U.S. Geological Survey has estimated that recoverable reserves of bituminous coal and lignite in the United States amount to 1.2 trillion tons. In the late 1940's, production of as much as 400 billion tons was thought to be commercially feasible. With coal production at a record level of 630 million tons in 1947, the reserve base could obviously sustain large production increases for synthetic fuels. The dispersion of coal deposits across the country in more than twenty states meant that coal-derived liquids could be processed regionally to minimize transportation costs.

Oil shale held even greater promise. Oil shale is a fine-textured sedimentary rock containing organic matter called "kerogen," which is released as a liquid by heating. Low-grade oil-shale deposits occur in 30 states. The world's richest concentration of high-grade shale (that is, yielding at least 15 gallons of oil per ton of shale) is the Green River Formation, covering 17,000 square miles where Colorado, Utah, and Wyoming intersect. The high-grade deposits there contain approximately 1.2 trillion barrels of liquid, of which 480 billion barrels have been considered technologically accessible.[4] This amounts to two-thirds as much as the total proved petroleum reserves of the free world.

Synthetic fuels have a fairly long history. In Europe as early as the 1760's, and in America before the Civil War, gas was produced from coal and kerogen from oil shale.[5]

In the United States the Oil Placer Act of 1872 permitted private parties to file claims on shale lands, and thousands did. But when studies of the Geological Survey and Bureau of Mines in 1914 and 1915 revealed the immensity of shale reserves, President Woodrow Wilson hastened to foreclose additional placer claims by establishing Naval Oil Shale Reserves on 45,000 acres in

[4] U.S. Department of the Interior, *Prospects for Oil Shale Development* (Washington: DOI, 1968), p. 15.
[5] For a general history of oil shale, see Chris Welles, *The Elusive Bonanza* (New York: E. P. Dutton, 1970).

Colorado and 87,000 acres in Utah. The Mineral Leasing Act prohibited further claims on publicly owned shale lands, and President Coolidge added more acreage to the reserves. In all, the federal government controls 72 percent of the Green River shale, including most of the higher-grade deposits.

The scarcity of petroleum during and immediately after World War I sparked a flurry of commercial interest in shale. During the twenties, several major oil companies acquired private shale properties, but Union Oil of California was the only one to develop a pilot plant for shale oil. This project, and other minor ones, were all abandoned after the oil glut returned in the 1930's. The Bureau of Mines did begin some experimental work in the late 1920's that eventually produced laboratory techniques for extracting and refining shale oil.

During this same period in Western Europe, where there were few natural occurrences of petroleum liquids, technologies for coal liquefaction attracted great commercial interest. By 1928, German scientists had developed three sophisticated processes for synthesizing oil and gas from coal: The Lurgi process for carbonizing coal at low temperatures, the Fischer-Tropsch process using metal catalysts, and the Bergius process of hydrogenation.[6] Hitler's autarky program encouraged large-scale development of all three techniques, and by 1942 Germany was synthesizing about half of its gasoline, diesel oil, and aviation fuel from coal.[7]

In 1941, the Justice Department entered an antitrust suit against Standard Oil of New Jersey and several other American oil companies for their participation in the patent pool with I. G. Farben. Although Standard agreed in a consent decree to license the patents freely to other firms, existence of the pool at the outbreak of war had already allowed the Alien Property Custodian to vest Farben's share of the patent-holding company on behalf of the U.S. government.[8] As a result, the Bureau of Mines was able to develop and improve the German synfuel processes without any proprietary commitment to Standard. Moreover, to Interior Secretary Harold Ickes and many others, the history of the pool suggested the need for government to lead the development of synthetic fuels, since the oil companies apparently lacked the incentive to do so.[9]

Shortages and the national security climate

The experience of mechanized war between 1941 and 1945 convinced American policy-makers not only that petroleum was the *sine qua non* of military

[6]   Kenneth S. Mernitz, "Progress at a Price: Research and Development of Liquid Motor Fuels in the United States and Germany, 1913–1933," (University of Missouri/Columbia: unpublished doctoral dissertation, 1983); also, Thomas Hughes, "Technological Momentum: Hydrogenation in Germany, 1900–1933," *Past and Present*, 55 (August 1969) pp. 106–132.
[7]   Arnold Krammer, "Fueling the Third Reich," *Technology and Culture*, July 1978, pp. 394–422.
[8]   Vesting Order No. 1, 7 F.R. 2417 (March 31, 1942); Supplemental Order No. 1, 9 F.R. 5613 (May 25, 1944).
[9]   H. L. Ickes to M. Straus, January 29, 1943, in National Archives Record Group 48, Department of the Interior, Central Classified Files, 1937–1953, Box 3762, File No. 11–34, "Synthetic Fuels," pt. 3. Ickes' very first response to Straus' proposal of a synfuels program was concern about oil company opposition.

victory but that it was a wasting asset which could not be counted on indefinitely. The synthetic fuels program sprang from those convictions.

In January 1943, Michael Straus, director of the War Resources Council, conceived the synfuels program when he told his superior, Secretary Ickes, that "our eyes are in the dust instead of on the stars in attempts to realize on the hydrogenation of coal." Straus was tired of "piddling around" with the small appropriations that the Bureau of the Budget had been allowing the Bureau of Mines for modest laboratory research on coal synthesis since 1925. Supported by R. R. Sayers, the Bureau of Mines director, and Oscar Chapman, an assistant secretary of Interior, Straus suggested that the Interior Department skip over the pilot-plant stage of development altogether: "I recommend we raise our sights and dramatize this possibility by the Department's stepping right out and asking authorization and appropriation legislation to build a small commercial-size plant (possibly $20,000,000) for obtaining gasolines, kerosenes, and oils from coal." But he cautioned that the department "not even purport to justify a commercial plant on a dollars bookkeeping basis." Instead, it should appeal to the Budget Bureau's responsibility for national security, presenting synfuels as "essential insurance to the future welfare of the Nation."[10] And it was just that distinction that would remain the heart of the controversies over government development of synthetic fuels for the next 40 years.

Straus embellished his proposal with an appeal to Ickes' well-known fondness for expanding his bureaucratic authority. He said Ickes, "as supervisor of the Bureau of Mines, Solid Fuels Coordinator, Petroleum Administrator for War, Secretary of the Interior, not to mention 'Spark Plug,'" had an opportunity "to surpass your splendid record for public interest and foresight."[11] Ickes agreed, although he worried that the oil industry would oppose it and that Interior would be unable to convince the Budget Bureau. Nonetheless, he told Straus to "see what support can be built up" in the Congress, and he urged his staff to "pursue it vigorously."[12]

Straus undertook a three-pronged strategy to alleviate potential opposition from the oil industry, gain approval from other agencies, and develop the active support of coal interests in Congress. To clear the first hurdle, he assured Ralph Davies, the Deputy Petroleum Administrator for War, that the government did not intend "to take up the national petroleum trade."[13] As long as the project would not be "competitive with the petroleum industry," said Davies, "it should have the hearty support of the petroleum industry."[14] War Department officials were enthusiastic when the Bureau of Mines demonstrated an Army tank fueled by "liquid coal." The Army Corps of Engineers liked the prospect of gathering German technical data, surveying potential plant sites,

[10] M. Straus to H. Ickes, Janaury 28, 1943, Box 3762, NA/RG48.
[11] *Ibid.*
[12] H. L. Ickes to R. R. Sayers, September 9, 1942; also, H. L. Ickes to M. Straus, Janaury 29, 1943, Box 3762, NA/RG48.
[13] M. Straus to R. K. Davies, February 1, 1943, Box 3762, NA/RG48.
[14] R. K. Davies, quoted in U.S. Congress, Senate, Interior Committee, Subcommittee on Public Lands, *Hearing on Synthetic Liquid Fuels* (78th Cong., 1st sess.), August 1943.

and perhaps even building some dams to provide the water necessary for hydrogenation.[15] And for the Department of Agriculture, Straus proposed a small share of the research funds for the distillation of alcohol from crop wastes.

To organize congressional support, Straus and Ickes enlisted Senator Joseph O'Mahoney, Democrat of Wyoming (the state with the greatest coal reserves), who chaired the public lands subcommittee of the Senate Interior Committee. By April 1943, Straus could report to Ickes that O'Mahoney was on board and planned to hold "full-dress public hearings to dramatize this possibility." To manage the proposal in the House, Ickes tapped Jennings Randolph of West Virginia (the state with the largest annual coal production), chairman of the House Appropriations subcommittee on mining.[16] Senator O'Mahoney introduced a bill that would authorize the Bureau of Mines to spend $30 million on synfuels research in a project that would culminate in demonstration plants to determine the cost of producing gasoline and oil from various raw materials and encourage "expansion of a process to full commercial scale."[17]

At hearings in cities across the country, more than seventy witnesses endorsed the plan. Although oil company officials expressed a preference for more laboratory work, they did not seriously object to the bill. According to Straus, "the hearings and proposal snowballed with increasing scope and velocity." He told Ickes that "the whole transcontinental hearing had an accelerating effect, and widespread, highly favorable publicity was a byproduct."[18] The Synthetic Liquid Fuels Act with its $30 million authorization became law in April 1944 after passing the Senate unanimously and the House by a wide margin.

Interior officials had underestimated the difficulties and cost of starting a new energy industry. For the first few years, technical and legal problems plagued the program. It took some time for the Bureau of Mines to gain clear title to the relevant patents and engineering data necessary to build a liquefaction plant. The Alien Property Custodian contributed his patent holdings, however, and in 1945 the Bureau sent nine of its people to Germany as part of a technical oil mission.[19] That group, headed by W. C. Schroeder, examined the remains of German synfuel plants and gathered technical documents. Meanwhile, Straus struggled to convince procurement officials in Washington that the synfuels project was worthy of scarce construction materials. With help from Julius Krug, then chairman of the War Production Board, the Bureau finally got the steel and other materials needed for its pilot plants.[20]

[15] H. L. Ickes to G. Lloyd, April 5, 1943, Box 3762, NA/RG48.
[16] M. Straus to H. L. Ickes, April 3, 1943; and H. L. Ickes to C. O. Brooks, May 14, 1943, Box 3762, NA/RG48.
[17] M. Straus to J. Guffey, January 27, 1944, Box 3762, NA/RG48.
[18] M. Straus to H. L. Ickes, August 20, 1943, Box 3762, NA/RG48.
[19] Solicitor to M. Straus, September 9, 1944; H. H. Sargent to M. Straus, October 10, 1944; M. Straus to H. H. Sargent, November 7, 1944, Box 3762, NA/RG48; also, U.S. Congress, Senate, Interior Committee, *Hearings on Synthetic Liquid Fuels: S134* (80th Cong., 2nd Sess.), January 1948, p. 60.
[20] M. Straus to H. L. Ickes, July 7, 1945, Box 3733, NA/RG48. Straus had even more difficulty finding exotic gasification equipment. He finally submitted an order to the Army's occupation

In compliance with the Act, the Interior Department had to appoint an advisory committee to oversee the synfuels program. When Straus reviewed a list prepared by Bureau of Mines Director Sayers, he balked at "its appearing to be so loaded with major oil companies." Straus, who wanted to see the program on a solid footing before giving up his command, feared that a committee dominated by Standard Oil, Texas, and Gulf might "bring emotional and political criticism." Nonetheless, when the Synthetic Liquid Fuels Technical Advisory Group met in April 1946, its 18 members included 13 from the oil companies.[21] Their scrutiny of the Bureau's progress eventually contributed to a dispute between the Bureau of Mines and the National Petroleum Council.

Slowly the synthetic fuels program showed signs of progress. The Bureau divided the project into three parts: coal hydrogenation, gas synthesis and the mining and processing of oil shale. Bench-scale work began at several of the Bureau's laboratories where engineers experimented with various approaches to hydrogenation on different types of coal. At the naval oil-shale reserve near Rifle, Colorado, the Bureau started a demonstration plant for extracting and refining kerogen from the extremely rich "Mahogany Ledge" formation. In the town of Louisiana, Missouri, the Bureau acquired an Army surplus ammonia plant as the site for two large demonstration units, one for direct coal hydrogenation and one for coal gasification by the Fischer-Tropsch process. These two units, designed for capacities of 200 and 100 barrels per day respectively, would be larger than anything operated outside of Germany. Although oil industry spokesmen belittled the usefulness of large demonstration units, Bureau engineers persisted in the conviction that the Missouri plants were the minimum size needed to derive cost estimates that would be commercially realistic. Construction of the hydrogenation unit began in 1947, but the War Department's decision to reactivate part of the plant for ammonia production delayed work on the Fischer-Tropsch facility until early 1949.[22]

While the Bureau's demonstration program moved ahead, conditions in the domestic energy market actually worsened as the postwar economic recovery accelerated. Most of President Truman's energy advisors, including Julius Krug, who had succeeded Ickes as Secretary of the Interior, were convinced that a serious domestic petroleum shortage was emerging. They believed that the national security dictated a commercial synfuels program on a far larger

command in Europe for eighteen pieces of captured hydrogenation equipment, including a 125-ton gasifier and an entire Fischer-Tropsch pilot unit: M. Straus to Army Intelligence, October 25, 1945, Box 3763, NA/RG48.
[21] M. Straus to R. R. Sayers, August 6, 1945, and R. R. Sayers to J. Krug, July 3, 1946, Box 3763, NA/RG48. Several of the members of this advisory group eventually served as well on the National Petroleum Council's synthetic Liquid Fuels Committee. In particular, E. V. Murphee, the research director of Standard Oil of New Jersey, chaired the Petroleum Council's subcommittee on synfuel production costs.
[22] For descriptions of the Bureau's progress between 1946 and 1948, see U.S. Bureau of Mines, *Synthetic Liquid Fuels, Annual Report of the Secretary of the Interior* (Washington: GPO, 1949), Pub. No. R. I. 4456, pp. viii–xvi; also, James Boyd, "Summary of Appropriations Requests, Appropriations Made, Obligations and Expenditures for Synthetic Liquid Fuels Funds," in U.S. Congress, Senate, *Synthetic Fuels* (1948), pp. 25–65.

scale than the demonstration projects. In January 1947, a special committee on petroleum, chaired by Senator O'Mahoney, made its report after three years of hearings. The committee urged "bold steps" toward synthetic production. "Until such time as synthetic production costs are not in excess of those of production from crude oil, there will be a natural temptation in peacetime to meet domestic deficiencies with imported petroleum," said the committee, adding that "synthetic production will fail to emerge through private invest-ment." The committee concluded that even in time of peace, "a nation, to maintain a first-class rating in the trade and commerce of the modern world, must have access to an abundant supply of oil."[23]

The heating oil shortage and voluntary allocation program in the winter of 1947–48 created an atmosphere of crisis that was conducive to synfuels. James V. Forrestal, Truman's new Secretary of Defense, forced the issue in January 1948 by recommending to Congress an $8 billion synthetic-fuel program to assure the national security. Krug added his voice, calling for a government-sponsored, 10-year program to begin immediately with construction of three prototype plants capable of producing 30,000 barrels per day of gasoline.[24] In another significant development, Representative Charles A. Wolverton of New Jersey, chairman of the House Commerce Committee, introduced a bill that would authorize the Reconstruction Finance Corporation to lend as much as $400 million to anyone willing to build a coal or oil-shale liquefaction plant that would produce 10,000 barrels of oil per day.[25]

Heretofore the petroleum industry had been cautiously optimistic regarding the commercial feasibility and prospective need for synthetic fuels.[26] Public and private estimates of the costs of synthetic fuels differed little as late as 1948, generally in the range of 10 to 18 cents per gallon of gasoline. The wholesale price of gasoline from natural petroleum, at the refinery, was about 12 cents per

[23] U.S. Congress, Senate, Special Committee Investigating Petroleum Resources, *Report No. 9*, "Investigation of Petroleum Resources in Relation to the National Welfare" (80th Cong., 1st sess.), January 31, 1947, pp. 15, 30–31; also, J. Krug to J. O'Mahoney, December 27, 1946, File 1–322, pt. 1, Box 3177, NA/RG48.
[24] *National Petroleum News*, 40 (January 21, 1948), 11; and (January 28, 1948), 19. Krug and Secretary of War Robert Patterson had previously discussed a plan for the production of 1,000,000 barrels per day of synthetic oil; R. Patterson telephone memo to J. Krug, July 2, 1947, and R. R. Sayers to H. C. Wolfe (Army Eng. Corps), July 11, 1947, File 11–34, Pt. 4; Box 3763, NA/RG48.
[25] U.S. Congress, House, Commerce Committee, *H. R. 5475: Committee Print*, March, 1948.
[26] B. H. Weil, Gulf R&D Co., wrote in 1943 that shale oil was nearly competitive with petroleum and was "approaching an era where large-scale use may be possible," in "Oil Shale and Shale Oil – A Survey, Part II," *Oil and Gas Journal*, April 29, 1943, pp. 73–79. In a 1944 briefing paper to the Navy Department, Robert Wilson, president of Pan American Petroleum, estimated that gasoline could by synthesized from coal or oil shale for less than 5 cents per gallon above present gasoline costs from crude petroleum. However, he noted that the oil industry would only be interested if crude oil prices showed "a gradual up-trend" after the war. Otherwise, "from the view-point of broad national interest, it would be foolhardy not to get started on a substantial program well in advance of any certainty as to the need therefor." R. Wilson, "The Technical and Economic Status of Liquid Fuel Production from Non-Petroleum Sources, with Recommendations as to a Research Program," July 12, 1944, File labelled Post-War Army and Navy, July 1–12, 1944, Compton-Killean Papers, Institute Archives, M.I.T., Cambridge, MA.

gallon at the time.[27] It was not until the National Petroleum Council entered the debate in 1950 that a significant gap developed between the estimates of the government and the industry.

Bruce K. Brown, vice-president of Standard Oil of Indiana and chairman of the Military Petroleum Advisory Committee, opened the oil industry's campaign against any expansion of the federal synfuels program.[28] Before the House Armed Services Committee, Brown challenged the claims of Forrestal and Krug and criticized them for sponsoring a forced-draft program of subsidized synfuels that would drain off scarce steel and investment capital needed for the exploration and development of petroleum. He assured the committee that when crude supplies grew scarce enough, the oil industry itself would see that "all of the liquid hydrocarbon fuels that are really needed" would be synthesized from natural gas and coal.[29]

The oil industry opposed Representative Wolverton's bill as well as the Krug-Forrestal proposal. Eugene Ayers (Gulf) and E. V. Murphee (Standard of New Jersey), two of the industry's foremost experts on synfuels, told the House Interior Committee that neither the state of technology, nor supply conditions, nor costs yet warranted demonstration plants, let alone commercial operations. Six members of the National Petroleum Council flatly opposed the bill, and nine others complained that the program was too large, that pilot-plants and laboratory work would suffice, and that if truly required for national security, then the entire project should be a joint venture conducted by a group of oil companies.[30]

In 1948, although Congress did extend the 1944 Synthetic Liquid Fuels Act and authorize an additional $30 million, the Wolverton bill languished in the House. In part, this was due to the Truman administration's preference for a

[27] In 1943, W. S. Farrish, president of Standard Oil of New Jersey, estimated that gasoline could be produced by coal hydrogenation at a cost of 15.9 cents per gallon. F. Dennig, president of Koppers Co., cited a figure of 18.2 cents per gallon with the Fischer-Tropsch process. The Bureau of Mines estimated 10.7 cents per gallon for gasoline produced from oil shale. See, U.S. Senate, Public Lands Subcommittee, *Hearings on Synthetic Liquid Fuels,* pp. 51–59, 238–247, and 303–318. B. H. Weil of Gulf Oil estimated a cost of 12 cents per gallon; *The Oil and Gas Journal,* April 29, 1943, pp. 73–79. E. V. Murphee, president of Standard Oil Development Co., estimated in 1948 that gasoline from oil shale could be produced for 16 cents per gallon, and for slightly more by Fischer-Tropsch gasification; in U.S. Congress, House, Interior Committee, *Hearings on Synthetic Liquid Fuels* (80th Cong., 2nd Sess.), March 1948, p. 88.

[28] Brown's committee, whose members were appointed by the National Petroleum Council, would subsequently be the only security agency to oppose large-scale development of synthetic fuels. See Bruce K. Brown to Walter S. Hallanan, Chairman, National Petroleum Council, May 8, 1950, File 017, "NPC Committee on Synfuel Liquefied Fuels Production Costs," 1950, NPC/DOI.

[29] Quoted in *National Petroleum News,* 40 (February 4, 1948), 20–B, and February 25, 1948, 21.

[30] U.S. Congress, House, *Hearings on Synthetic Fuels.* pp. 5, 37–39, 53, 61, 86–103. Union Oil of California and Southeastern Oil were exceptions. Union Oil did not have foreign petroleum supplies and was frequently short of crude for its refineries. It had acquired significant oil shale properties, done research, and believed that a shale oil refinery would be profitable if the federal government would subsidize the cost of transporting the product from Colorado to California. Gordon Duke, president of Southeastern Oil, favored synfuels as an alternate source of supply for independent oil refiners. Duke urged that any synfuels project should include participation by independents.

bigger program that would authorize the construction of government-owned plants if private industry failed to make use of the proposed subsidies.[31] But even after Wolverton came to terms with the administration, the legislative prospects for a massive, national synfuels program failed to improve. In every legislative session between 1948 and 1953, Wolverton and Senator Pat McCarran (D–NV) introduced bills to promote a synfuels industry. And throughout that period, the White House, Interior Department, Bureau of the Budget, Defense Department, National Security Resources Council, and the Council of Economic Advisers all supported the initiatives, but to no effect.[32] The oil industry was dead set against any wider role for government.

Had energy shortages continued, that opposition might have failed. But after 1948, the oil industry increasingly had the weight of the market behind it. Energy crisis gave way to fleeting equilibrium and then to indefinite glut.

Energy glut and the costs dispute

Harry Truman had scarcely declared an energy emergency in the spring of 1948 before it was over. In a matter of months, domestic crude oil stocks began rising, natural gas became more widely available in urban and industrial markets, capacity utilization in the coal industry started its long decline, and most critically, the United States became a net importer of cheap foreign crude and residual oil. Except for a few months of tight markets at the height of the Korean War and during the Suez Crisis, this energy surplus continued for the next 20 years.

Market changes in the natural gas and petroleum industries will be discussed in Chapters 4 and 5. Here, in connection with synthetic fuels, a quick summary will be enough. With the lifting of wartime price controls in 1946–47, the price of crude oil more than doubled, from $1.19 to $2.61 per barrel, setting off a dramatic boom in domestic exploration. As demobilization progressed, drilling equipment and construction materials became more readily available, alleviating bottlenecks and allowing rapid expansion of pipelines and refinery capacity. These developments facilitated the commercial use of natural gas as well. Large-diameter interstate pipelines made gas available to the large markets in the Northeast.

Meanwhile, the coal industry enjoyed a similar boom. After the war, the price of coal increased from $3.06 to $4.99 per ton, and the number of mines jumped from seven to nine thousand. Coal output climbed to a record level of 630 million tons by 1947, reflecting a 47 percent share of the domestic energy market.

[31] W. L. Ware to J. A. Krug, December 12, 1948, File 11–34, pt. 5, Box 3763, NA/RG48.
[32] C. A. Cogan to J. Steelman, March 18, 1949, File 56-E (1948), Box 273, Official File, Harry Truman Presidential Library, Independence, Missouri; Bureau of the Budget to W. J. Hopkins, September 21, 1950, Box 79, White House Bill File, HTPL; also, James Boyd, Director of the Bureau of Mines, "Synthetics in Defense," a speech delivered November 15, 1950, to the American Petroleum Institute, Los Angeles, California, Box No. 13, Speeches and Statements File, James Boyd Papers, HTPL.

But when economic growth turned to recession in 1949, it became clear that expansion of energy productive capacity had been excessive, and fears of a lasting shortage premature. The coal industry was the most overextended, for its immense capacity could not sustain new interfuel competition from cheap natural gas and imported oil. By 1954, coal production had plummeted to 391 million tons. Industry profits were negligible, and 3,000 mines had closed.[33]

Domestic oil producers were also overextended, because, as Senator O'Mahoney had predicted, cheap imported oil from Venezuela and the Middle East had met "domestic deficiencies" – and then some. Oil imports increased 65 percent from 1948 to 1950, easily penetrating domestic markets and putting a lid on further domestic price increases.

Here was the crux of the synfuels dilemma. Once foreign oil became continuously available to meet or exceed domestic demand growth, any potential market demand for synthetic fuels was foreclosed. Several major oil companies canceled their synfuel experiments in 1949 and 1950.[34] When foreign oil displaced higher-cost domestic oil, prorationing created spare domestic capacity that served as an effective strategic reserve. Thus, even the short-term security rationale for synfuels was undermined. And with so much spare capacity, domestic independent producers and the international majors were united in political opposition to public development of synthetic fuels. Even the federal demonstration program was at risk if it could not be justified on a cost-effective basis.

But the government was nowhere near ready to surrender. At the dedication of its liquefaction units in 1949, the Bureau of Mines described them as "forerunners of a new basic industry that ultimately may free the United States from dependence on foreign oil."[35] The gas-synthesis unit was not actually completed, but the coal-hydrogenation unit had been tested successfully and was steadily improved during the next two years. At Rifle, Colorado, the Bureau reported doing impressive work on new methods for mining and refining oil shale.[36] Based on these initial efforts, very favorable cost estimates were being discussed informally within the Interior Department.[37]

---

[33] National Coal Association, *Coal Facts 1978–1979* (Washington: NCA, 1980), pp. 54–57; also, U.S. Congress, House Interior Committee, Special Subcommittee on Coal Research, *Coal* (85th Cong., 1st Sess.), March 1957, pt. 2, pp. 571–573.

[34] Standard Oil (N.J.) terminated its joint project with Consolidation Coal on a coal-hydrogenation pilot plant, and Union Oil curtailed work on oil shale. H. G. Slusser to O. Chapman, June 26, 1950, and A. C. Rubel to W. C. Schroeder, March 28, 1950, File 11–34, pt. 6, Box 3763, NA/RG48.

[35] U.S. Bureau of Mines, *Annual Report of the Secretary of the Interior, 1949* (Washington, 1950), p. 143.

[36] The hydrogenation unit was run continuously for a two-month period. In one run, it converted 2,600 tons of coal into 336,000 gallons of synthetic oil. The Bureau also reported significant improvements in equipment and the innovative use of iron catalysts. At the shale facility, the Bureau reported mining 29,000 tons at a direct cost of 32.9 cents per ton. See, U.S. Bureau of Mines, *Annual Report of the Secretary of the Interior, 1951* (Washington, 1951), pp. 17–19.

[37] Gasoline from coal-hydrogenation was put at 12 to 14 cents per gallon, and synthetic oil from shale at $2.50 per barrel. Secretary Krug actually reported to the White House that oil-shale costs had achieved parity with petroleum. Robert Friedman, from the Oil & Gas Division, balked at this

In August 1949, the Bureau of Mines published, for the first time, a formal and detailed report entitled, "Estimated Plant and Operating Cost for Producing Gasoline from Coal Hydrogenation."[38] The report concluded that gasoline could be produced from coal at a cost of 11 cents per gallon. In effect, the federal government's most respected research organization was asserting officially that synthetic liquid fuels had attained commercial status and were nearly competitive with natural petroleum.

The oil industry disagreed. Industry leaders generally felt that synthetic fuels were far too risky to justify private investment. Moreover, the Bureau's report seemed to insinuate that the oil companies themselves should already be developing synthetic fuels. For the Bureau of Mines, the worth of its demonstration program was at stake. And for the Interior Department, and various congressional promoters of coal and shale, the issue was whether the cost premium for producing synthetic liquid fuels was small enough to justify a government program for subsidizing prototype commercial plants. All these perspectives fostered different assumptions regarding rate of return, interest on invested capital, risk, equity, and other major factors of cost.

Acrimonious debate over synfuels was a serious and unpleasant problem for Oscar Chapman. Chapman succeeded Julius Krug as Secretary of the Interior in the spring of 1950. Until then he had maintained relatively harmonious relations with the petroleum industry and had subscribed to the concept of business-government cooperation embodied in the National Petroleum Council. But now he was responsible for the Truman administration's energy policies, including the development of synthetic fuels, which Chapman personally supported. Right away he asked the National Petroleum Council to establish a committee to (1) review the cost estimates made by the Bureau of Mines; (2) prepare independent cost estimates; and (3) make recommendations for improvement of future cost estimates.[39] The Council agreed, and Oscar Chapman got more than he bargained for. The Council's studies only exacerbated the controversy and eventually led to the program's termination in 1953.

The National Petroleum Council chose W. S. S. Rodgers of the Texas Company to direct the synfuels study. His coordinating committee included chief executives of several major oil companies, Max Ball, the past director of the Oil & Gas Division, and Bruce K. Brown. To conduct the substantive work, Rodgers appointed a subcommittee on production costs for which Brown recommended several people previously on record as opposing synfuels.[40] Other

statement and suggested that "the Department should be more cautious in its assertions as to costs." However, James Boyd and Robert Day (Krug's secretary) overrode Friedman's advice, assuring Krug that "we can back up the statements made." See J. A. Krug to K. Wallgren (draft), February 9, 1949; R. Friedman to R. Day, February 23, 1949, and R. Day to J. A. Krug, February 24, 1949, File 11–34, pt. 4; W. L. Ware to J. A. Krug, August 9, 1949, pt. 6, Box 3763, NA/RG48.

[38] U.S. Bureau of Mines, *Report of Investigations, 4564* (Washington, 1949).

[39] O. Chapman to W. S. Hallanan, April 21, 1950, File 106.61, NPC/DOI, 1951.

[40] B. Brown to W. S. S. Rodgers, June 27, 1950, File 017, NPC/DOI, 1950. Three months after making his recommendations, Brown resigned from the NPC Synfuels Committee to become deputy administrator of the Petroleum Administration for Defense. In that capacity, he continued to oppose the development of synfuels by blocking authorization of federal loan funds.

subcommittees on raw materials, economics, processes, and engineering eventually contributed to the study. In all, 49 subcommittee members aided by 150 technical personnel reportedly spent more than $500,000 to prepare the study. The purpose of this immense undertaking, as A. P. Frame of Cities Service put it, was to produce "an authoritative evaluation" of value to government and industry, "indicating the probable future course of synthetic liquid fuels."[41]

Cost estimates for three basic processes were at issue: coal hydrogenation, oil shale, and Fischer-Tropsch gas synthesis. For coal hydrogenation, both the Council and the Bureau made estimates based on separate designs for a single plant in Wyoming and for a multi-plant industry. For oil shale, the Council agreed to use the same basic design data for two hypothetical cases: a single oil-shale plant in Rifle, Colorado, producing 39,700 barrels a day, and a five-plant industry in Colorado with a capacity of 201,230 barrels a day. For gas synthesis, the Bureau of Mines had no detailed data, so the Council's design stood uncontested.[42] Table 3-1 summarizes the two designs for a coal hydrogenation plant and the joint design for oil shale.

The cost estimates for oil shale caused disagreement, but not much political controversy. The Bureau estimated 11.5 cents per gallon of gasoline, compared with the Council's 16.2 cents. Since the wholesale price of gasoline was about 12 cents, the Bureau concluded that oil shale was commercially feasible while the Council thought it was not.[43]

The case of coal hydrogenation was a different matter. Something was obviously wrong with the immense margin between the Bureau's estimate of 12 cents a gallon and the Council's estimate of 41 cents. Furthermore, the Council's report on hydrogenation was very critical of the Bureau's assumptions, methods, and computations. Hydrogenation was the most technically advanced of the three processes under investigation and the most politically salient in view of the coal industry's imminent decline. In a futile effort to arbitrate the dispute, Secretary Chapman eventually hired Ebasco Services, an engineering firm experienced at designing power plants, to provide an independent review of the Bureau's estimates. Table 3-2 summarizes all three sets of cost estimates.

The disputed costs fell into four categories: capital costs, operating costs, by-product credits, and finance charges. In each category, problems of perception accounted for the difference between estimates. For capital costs, the NPC's estimate exceeded the Bureau's by $48 million for plant facilities, $55 million

[41] NPC, Meeting Transcript, December 5, 1950, NPC/DOI, 1950, p. 80.
[42] The NPC estimated that a single Fischer-Tropsch plant would have a capital cost of $380 million and would produce gasoline for a unit cost of 29.4 cents per gallon; NPC, "Final Report of the NPC's Committee on Synthetic Liquid Fuels Production Costs," February 26, 1953, File 106.61, NPC/DOI, 1953, p. 8.
[43] U.S. Bureau of Mines, "Comments on Reports of the NPC Subcommittee on Synthetic Liquid Fuels Production Costs for Oil Shale," October 25, 1951, and NPC, "Report of the NPC's Committee on Synthetic Liquid Fuels Production Costs," in Synthetic Fuels File, NPC/DOI, 1951.

Table 3-1. *Summary data from 1951 designs for coal-hydrogenation and oil-shale plants*

	National Petroleum Council's hydrogenation plant	Bureau of Mines hydrogenation plant	Joint design for oil-shale plant
Coal or shale input (tons per day)	12,960	14,800	76,800
Products (barrels per day)			
gasoline	19,490	18,600	25,380
liquefied petroleum gas	6,390	7,100	1,780
other fuels	—	—	12,540
total liquid fuels	25,880	25,700	39,700
Chemicals (barrels per day)	1,120	3,960	—
Ammonia (tons per day)	—	359	92
Sulfur (tons per day)	—	47	43
Construction materials steel (tons)	220,000	217,130	178,000
Investment capital (millions of dollars)	533	400	333
Cost per gallon of gasoline with 6 percent return on equity investment (in cents)	41.4	11.0	16.2 (NPC) 11.5 (BOM)

Sources: Compiled from National Petroleum Council, "Report of the National Petroleum Council's Committee on Synthetic Liquid Fuels Production Costs," October 31, 1951, Synthetic Fuels File, NPC/DOI, 1951.

Table 3-2. *Summary of unit-cost estimates for producing gasoline by coal hydrogenation*

	National Petroleum Council (10/31/51)	Bureau of Mines (10/25/51)	Ebasco Services (March 1952)
Operating costs	25.3	17.7	19.5
Housing costs	2.6	—	—
Finance charges	19.0	8.2	22.0
Total process costs	46.9	25.9	41.5
Less by-product revenue	−5.5	−14.9	−13.4
Total costs	41.4	11.0	28.1

Note: Cents per gallon.
Sources: National Petroleum Council, "Interim Report of the NPC's Committee on Synthetic Liquid Fuels Production Costs," July 25, 1952, file 106.61, NPC/DOI, 1952, p. 8.

for housing, and $19 million for working capital and start-up expense.[44] Of the plant facilities, the power plant accounted for the biggest single discrepancy. On that, Ebasco sustained the Bureau.[45] The housing issue was entirely subjective. Since the oil industry did not ordinarily subsidize housing for its refinery employees, the Bureau did not feel obligated to do so for its hypothetical hydrogenation plant. On the other hand, the NPC's estimate for working capital seemed a closer approximation of the industry's average (as a percent of gross property) than the Bureau's far smaller figure.

For operating costs, the Bureau's figures were 40 percent below those of the Council. The Synfuels Committee complained that the Bureau's procedure for estimating the ratio of maintenance labor to operating labor was inconsistent with industry practice. The Bureau countered by claiming that the Council had grossly overestimated the number of operators needed per shift for the power plant, oxygen plant, and water system.

The two estimates differed grossly with respect to the credits assigned to by-products. The NPC committee disagreed with the Bureau's view that revenues from by-products should be charged against gasoline costs. Although it grudgingly agreed to do so, its plant design intentionally minimized chemical output on the grounds that demand would be saturated after two or three plants went on line. According to the Bureau, however, the demand for benzenes, phenols, and creosols had risen phenomenally during the five years prior to 1951, and would continue to do so for another decade. Since chemicals were more valuable than gasoline, the Bureau maximized chemical output in its design.[46]

[44] NPC, "Interim Report of the NPC Committee on Synthetic Liquid Fuels Production Costs," January 29, 1952, Synthetic Fuels File, NPC/DOI, 1952.
[45] NPC, Meeting Transcript, July 29, 1952, Synthetic Fuels File, NPC/DOI, 1952, p. 155.
[46] U.S. Bureau of Mines, "Cost Estimate for Coal Hydrogenation," October 25, 1951, Synthetic Fuels File, NPC/DOI, 1951, pp. 11–16.

Different methods of assigning finance charges were the most critical factor in the gap between cost estimates. The National Petroleum Council, arguing the risky nature of a synfuels venture, chose to calculate those charges based on 100 percent equity financing. At a rate of return of 6 percent on equity after taxes, the NPC calculated the daily cost of capital at $78,000, or 11 cents a gallon more than the Bureau. The Bureau based its estimate on 60 percent funded debt (at a market interest rate of 3.5 percent) and 40 percent equity, arguing that a synfuels plant would involve less risk than the NPC anticipated.[47] According to the Bureau, a hydrogenation plant was actually more stable and lasted considerably longer than an oil field; it avoided the risks of exploration; and, it was far more flexible in meeting shifts in product demand than a conventional refinery. Bureau staff vehemently insisted that oil companies never used 100 percent equity financing, even for projects that did involve unique technology or unusual risk.

Several other issues aggravated this controversy indirectly. One issue was steel requirements. The oil industry, and Bruce Brown in particular, opposed steel allocations for synfuels plants in the face of postwar shortages. But even taking into account coal production, transportation, and then liquefaction, the steel requirements for the hydrogenation plant (approximately the same for the Council and the Bureau) amounted to 2.78 pounds per annual barrel of gasoline. That was far less than the 4.55 pounds of steel required for an annual barrel of refined petroleum.

Tax treatment was another sore point. The NPC insisted on calculating income taxes at 50 percent. Although the Bureau did the same, it felt that was unfair, since the petroleum industry almost never paid an effective rate higher than 25 percent. Moreover, natural petroleum benefited from a depletion allowance of 27.5 percent – more than double the allowance for liquefied coal or shale oil – and a first-year write-off on intangible drilling expenses as well.

Profitability was also a contentious issue. The National Petroleum Council argued that at least a 15 percent return on investment would be necessary to justify a commercial plant (although it submitted to using a 6 percent return for its cost study). But the Bureau of Mines and the Interior Department were not oriented to a market rate of return. Their interest was to justify a federal loan program for prototype plants, with a public-policy objective of U.S. energy independence. For that purpose, a 6 percent rate of return seemed adequate for estimating costs.

The Ebasco study, released in March 1952, added more heat than light to the controversy. Ebasco concluded that the Bureau's hydrogenation plant could not be financed "with private capital under conditions prevailing" in 1951.

Both the National Petroleum Council and the Bureau of Mines felt vindicated by the Ebasco report. Although the Council was critical of the Interior Department's contract that prevented the engineering firm from considering all factors, it felt that Ebasco's estimate of total process costs (41.5 cents a gallon) was far closer to its own than to the Bureau's. Bureau officials, however, noted

[47] NPC, Meeting Transcript, October 31, 1951, NPC/DOI, 1951, pp. 49–50.

that Ebasco's estimates for operatng costs, housing costs, and by-product reve-nue came closer to its own estimates.[48] Indeed, 14 cents of the 17-cent dif-ference between the Ebasco and Bureau of Mines estimates was accounted for by finance charges. For synfuels boosters in government, that indicated that coal hydrogenation was competitive with natural petroleum on a *cost* basis although not by a market standard of net present value. This view granted that while oil companies had good reason to delay making synfuel investments, the government was not acting rashly by promoting large-scale coal liquefaction on grounds of national security and energy self-sufficiency.[49]

In February 1953, just a month after Dwight Eisenhower's inauguration, the National Petroleum Council released its final report on synfuel costs. After all the reviews, debate, conflicting studies, and considerable acrimony, its conclu-sion had not varied since 1950. Said the report: "As shown by this extensive and conclusive study, all methods of manufacturing synthetic liquid fuels pro-posed by the Bureau of Mines are definitely uneconomical under present con-ditions." The NPC continued: "The need for a synthetic liquid fuel industry in this country is still in the distant future. Since new techniques may be available then, we question the wisdom of the Government financing large-scale demon-stration plants."[50]

Time had run out for both the Truman administration and its alternative to petroleum dependency.

Conflicting premises and the abandonment of synfuels

When Representative James Wolverton stubbornly prepared to introduce his synfuels bill for the sixth time in 1953, the *National Petroleum News* accurately predicted that his efforts "will stand less chance in a Republican-dominated Congress that will want even less Government intervention in private enter-prise."[51] When the House Appropriations Committee opened hearings on the budget in March, it seemed as if no one in the new administration wanted to continue the synfuels demonstration program, let alone permit RFC loans for synfuels commercialization. In the general Republican drive to reduce federal expenditures, the new Interior Secretary, Douglas McKay, cut $2 million from the funds earmarked for the demonstration plants at Louisiana, Missouri. The

---

[48] Bureau of Mines Press Release, March 31, 1952, Program Staff Central Files, 1947–1953, Box 51, NA/RG48.

[49] At the time, there was one other source of cost data relevant to the synfuels controversy. Shortly after the Ebasco study appeared, the Paley Commission (President's Materials Policy Commission) released its report, in which it forecast a tremendous increase in oil imports and offered surprisingly low cost estimates for synfuels. Based on a Koppers Company study, the Commission pegged the cost of synthetic gasoline at 12.6 cents a gallon from oil shale, 17.3 cents a gallon from coal hydrogenation, and 26.6 cents a gallon from Fischer–Tropsch synthesis. See, Koppers Company, "Coal Products as Raw Materials for the Chemical Industry," a report prepared for the President's Materials Policy Commission, September 1, 1951, Box 37, File, "Executive Secretary Mis-cellaneous Reports and Studies," PMPC Papers, HTPL, pp. B–8, B–9.

[50] NPC, "Final Report," February 26, 1953, pp. 10–11.

[51] *National Petroleum News*, 44 (December 17, 1952), 7.

new leaders of the Bureau of Mines, explaining the proposed curtailment to Homer Budge (R-Idaho), chairman of the appropriations subcommittee for the Interior Department, said, "We have learned what we need to know about these older types of operations." Since "the petroleum industry said it would cost 47 cents a gallon to make gasoline by hydrogenation," the Bureau had concluded that it could "put this plant on standby basis."[52]

Budge agreed and went further. His subcommittee promptly cut the Bureau's budget by $9 million, terminating the entire synfuels program. The Senate Appropriations Committee, however, in deference to Senator Eugene Millikin (R-Colorado), restored the oil-shale funds; Representative Wayne Aspinall (D-Colorado), the ranking Democrat on the House Appropriations Committee, convinced Budge to agree.[53]

During debate on the 1953 appropriations bill, coal-state congressmen, most of whom were Democrats, objected vehemently to the curtailment of the synfuels program. Paradoxically, the House Appropriations Committee defended its cuts on the basis that great progress had been made – "they had come within a couple of cents of the commercial costs of producing gasoline from petroleum." Representative Melvin Price of Illinois, like many others representing the beleaguered coal fields, concluded that the reason for killing the synfuels projects was that "they have been very successful operations." Senator Estes Kefauver of Tennessee believed that shutting down the synfuel plants "was part of the general pattern," along with gas deregulation and the submerged lands act, "to effectuate an all out giveaway program." According to Kefauver, the oil companies "do not want the competition of oil from coal" and "it now appears that the big interests have prevailed." Emanuel Celler of Brooklyn was especially sensitive to the implications for competition. "Big oil companies," said Celler, "do not want this type of competition. They are powerful enough, apparently, to pressurize the scuttling of the plan." And just before the Speaker closed off House debate, Representative Carl Perkins of Kentucky pinned the blame squarely on the National Petroleum Council. "Walter S. Hallanan's Petroleum Council," said Perkins, "recommended in February of this year that the coal-to-oil plant at Louisiana, Missouri, should be closed down." Noting that Hallanan was a Republican national committeeman from West Virginia, Perkins concluded that "we have a process that has been proved successful and has reached the point of being commercially competitive with crude oil. Yet, because of that fact, we want to destroy that process in favor of the oil lobby."[54] Congress upheld the cuts, and in 1954, the federal government shut down the synfuels plants at Louisiana, Missouri.

The oil-shale facility in Colorado survived a bit longer, until the Interior Department asked the National Petroleum Council to re-evaluate it and make

[52] U.S. Congress, House, Committee on Appropriations, *Hearings on Interior Department Appropriations for 1954* (83rd Cong., 1st Sess.), March 11, 1953, pt. 2, p. 627.
[53] *Ibid.*, 628, 1006.
[54] *Congressional Record*, 1953, vol. 99, pt. 3, pp. 3355, 4022–4026, 4120, 4145.

further recommendations regarding its future. Although some members of the Council seemed impressed with the technical work of the Bureau of Mines, they were more concerned with the larger issue of government intervention.[55] In 1955, the Council recommended that "there is no need for further government effort along these lines." It noted that petroleum reserves and production capacity were more than ample, and that various companies were experimenting with oil shale. The Council felt that these companies and others would "undoubtedly continue to carry on such work to the degree warranted by present and future circumstances."[56] Although it "generated quite a bit of hostility," the Interior Department accepted the Council's recommendation and passed it along to Congress. Congress terminated the funding, and ordered that the oil-shale facility be mothballed in 1956.

There seems little doubt that in the early fifties, synthetic liquid fuels from coal or oil shale were not price-competitive with products refined from crude petroleum. Moreover, American oil companies, both domestic and international, controlled ample, indeed excessive, reserves of petroleum. Certainly, neither cost nor supply justified the risk of private investment in a commercial synfuel venture. But that was not exactly at issue, although members of the National Petroleum Council acted as if it were.

The issue was one of relative costs as they related to the public policy objectives of the Truman administration. If the cost of producing synfuels were not too far above the price of natural petroleum products, then the opportunity costs of a public investment would not be unreasonable.

The data suggest that a reasonable estimate for gasoline from oil shale would be 13.6 cents a gallon (the Bureau's estimate of 11.5 cents plus the NPC's estimate of 2.1 cents a gallon for housing costs). For coal hydrogenation, if we accept Ebasco's estimate minus the excess of finance charges (13.8 cents) above the Bureau's estimate, a reasonable estimate of unit cost might be about 15 cents a gallon.[57] Compared to the 12 cents-a-gallon wholesale price of gasoline, these numbers suggest that the government could have financed commercial plants with subsidies of 2 to 3 cents a gallon, and still returned 6 percent on the public investment. At that rate, a 25,000-barrel-a-day plant

---

[55] R. A. Cattell to J. J. Forbes, October 5, 1954, File 106.6 (Shale Oil Policy Committee Correspondence), NPC/DOI, 1954.

[56] NPC, "Report of the National Petroleum Council's Committee on Oil Shale Policy," January 25, 1955, File 106.61 (NPC Shale Oil Policy Committee Reports), NPC/DOI, 1955, p. 2. In an unusual development, three council members, none of whom was associated with a major oil company, voted against the Council's recommendation; NPC, Meeting Transcript, May 5, 1955, NPC/DOI, 1955, pp. 59–60.

[57] In a 1962 study, economist Henry Steele estimated the cost of producing synthetic crude oil from shale at $1.68 per barrel, or approximately 4 cents per gallon (before refining); Henry Steele, "The Prospects for the Development of a Shale Oil Industry," in U.S. Congress, Senate, Committee on the Judiciary, Subcommittee on Antitrust and Monopoly, *Competitive Aspects of Oil Shale Development* (90th Cong., 1st Sess.), April–May 1967, pp. 542–558; also, Henry Steele, "The Economic Potentialities of Synthetic Liquid Fuels from Oil Shales" (Cambridge: unpublished M.I.T. dissertation, 1957).

would have required an annual subsidy of $12 million, if the nominal price of oil held constant.

The Truman administration had a variety of reasons for supporting programs to develop synthetic fuels. The least commendable of these was the Interior Department's bureaucratic impulse to expand its authority. Support for the declining coal industry and the government's general responsibility to foster research and development were also relevant. But the most legitimate rationales were national security and long-term energy self-sufficiency. Nearly all resource analysts agreed that domestic petroleum reserves would be inadequate sometime after 1960. Immense reserves of coal and oil shale represented a hedge against the political and military risks of eventual dependence on foreign oil. For many officials in the Truman administration, a subsidy for commercial synfuels plants offered a strategic alternative to petroleum liquids.

For the petroleum industry, however, commercial development of synthetic fuels was premature in every respect. At the very least, it would worsen the problem of managing surplus oil. With import restrictions already being discussed, and with prorationing squeezing down on allowable production in Texas, the industry was nearly unanimous on this point. For many executives in the oil industry, the Bureau of Mines' demonstration plants, much less subsidies for commercial plants, raised the specter of statism.

From the government's perspective, the synfuels issue seemed ideally suited to study and recommendations by the National Petroleum Council. It had both the expertise and resources necessary to address the technical and financial questions involved. But the Council's advice, whether or not its effects were sound in hindsight, appears to have been ideologically biased and ill-suited to the premises of the public policy issue. What was needed was a technical cost analysis that assumed some reasonable public discount rate, rather than private standards of profitability. Instead, the Council chose to define its task narrowly, as a commercial feasibility study that maximized every potential cost item.

Perhaps the Interior Department was at fault for not defining appropriate premises or articulating a rationale for the program against which costs and benefits could be measured. Perhaps it erred by not interpreting the Council's report when it passed it on to the Congress. If a public bureaucracy acts as a mere pipeline, rather than a filter, for advice from the private sector, then it is not fulfilling its own institutional responsibilities that are necessary to make the advisory-council mechanism work.

The synfuels story during the Truman era exemplifies several of the propositions stated in Chapter 1. In the broadest sense, energy-market conditions framed the public policy issue. The demonstration program was undertaken in a period of shortages and terminated as a glut was emerging. A mix of intra-governmental and interfuel politics characterized the political process. Bureaucratic mismanagement was certainly in evidence, to the extent that the Bureau unnecessarily minimized its cost estimates and the Interior Department provided inadequate direction.

The Truman administration stood at a kind of energy-policy crossroads, contemplating a variety of paths leading to different energy futures. In the case of synfuels, it relied on its institutional experiment for cooperating with the oil industry. When the industry's leadership chose to define the national interest in its own terms, a future of reliance on foreign oil was accepted as the price of limiting the role of government.

4. Regulating natural gas in the absence of economics

In the forties and fifties, a relatively new source of energy spread rapidly to all regions of the United States. This was natural gas. Earlier, it has been used locally, in the Southwest; now it became the basis of a national industry. The public interest seemed to require that this emerging industry be regulated, but regulated how? The attempt was fraught with complications. Among these were jurisdictional disputes between state and federal authorities, frictions among regions, clashes of ideology, issues of conservation and end-use, and the crucial question of whether wellhead prices would be determined by government or the market. Resolution of these problems proved to be intensely controversial, illogical, and eventually elusive. The result was a gas crisis more than two decades later.

Prior to World War II, natural gas was a by-product of the search for petroleum. Exploratory wells that yielded only gas were considered commercial failures. To the extent that gas was often found with petroleum, it was either reinjected to enhance petroleum recovery, used as a power source in the oil fields, or sold to produce heat and light in adjacent communities. (The gas used for lighting in eastern cities was manufactured by a simple but inefficient process of cooking coal.) Otherwise, natural gas was flared (burned off) as an effluent. As late as 1944, less than half of gross gas production was marketed to transmission lines. The worst waste occurred when gas released by oil production (referred to as "associated" or "casinghead" gas) was inadequate to justify the expense of gathering and processing. "Dry" or "non-associated" gas, which was found separately in fields without petroleum, was less of a conservation problem, since the wells could at least be capped and left for future development.

At first, commercial development of natural gas was a gradual process. Regional entrepreneurs built small-guage pipelines connecting gas fields to the municipal utilities of nearby cities and towns. As the technology for large-diameter, long-distance pipelines improved, these small systems expanded rapidly. Natural gas was a clean, safe, and reliable source of energy, and a good deal cheaper than the coal-gas most municipalities had relied on.

World War II not only stimulated demand for natural gas, but subsidized construction of long-distance pipelines. By 1945, the total gas pipeline system, including lines for gathering, transmission, and distribution, had grown to 218,000 miles. Almost 90 companies were in the business of transmitting natural gas interstate to serve 12 million end-use customers. Still, the return to peacetime found the gas industry in an unusual circumstance; it had both excess product and unrequited demand. A far larger network of transmission facilities would be necessary to balance the two.

The natural gas industry was less integrated vertically than the petroleum industry. There were several reasons for this. Since the technology was less complicated and the supply more stable, vertical integration in natural gas offered less potential for cost savings or economies of scale. Oil companies that discovered and produced 75 percent of the gas sold in interstate commerce did not integrate forward because interstate transmission was a regulated, public-utility function after 1938, as was all retail distribution. Although pipeline companies did integrate backward into gas production, this trend was limited by the established presence of oil companies and by adverse regulatory decisions. The distribution companies did not integrate backward into interstate transmission because they were restricted from doing so by the Public Utility Holding Company Act of 1935. Thus for the most part, the natural gas industry remained segmented in three parts: production, transmission, and distribution (see Chart 4-1).

Because of this segmentation, the natural gas industry was not especially concentrated, at least on a national basis. As of 1953, the 30 largest gas producers, most of which were oil companies, controlled less than half of all proved gas reserves, and accounted for only one-third of sales to interstate pipelines. The 13 largest pipeline companies, although they did account for three-fourths of the total trunk mileage and interstate sales volume, controlled only 12 percent of gas reserves.[1] Within any individual gas field, however, the level of concentration for both producers and pipeline companies was often considerably higher. It was this localized concentration that gave rise to periodic antitrust scrutiny and provided the rationale for federal control of wellhead prices.

One reason why the regulation of gas pipeline companies would prove to be so difficult was that they were not common carriers, like oil pipelines or railroads. Although primarily in the transportation business, they purchased gas from producing and gathering companies. Then they delivered it across state boundaries and resold it to industrial customers and to wholesale and retail distributors. Thus, as sellers, their gas was a product, but as shippers, it was an operating cost. To complicate matters, the regulated pipelines produced 23 percent of their own sales volume.[2] This captive production was a means for expanding their assets, for diversification, and for providing a source of gas whose flow the pipelines could use flexibly to balance their seasonal load variations. But on what basis were regulators to expense this gas? Precedent offered little help.

[1] Edward J. Neuner, *The Natural Gas Industry: Monopoly and Competition in Field Markets* (Norman: University of Oklahoma Press, 1960), pp. 10, 14, 30.
[2] Federal Power Commission, *Statistics of Natural Gas Companies, 1946* (Wash., D.C.: FPC, 1947), vi.

Chart 4-1

The Natural Gas Industry

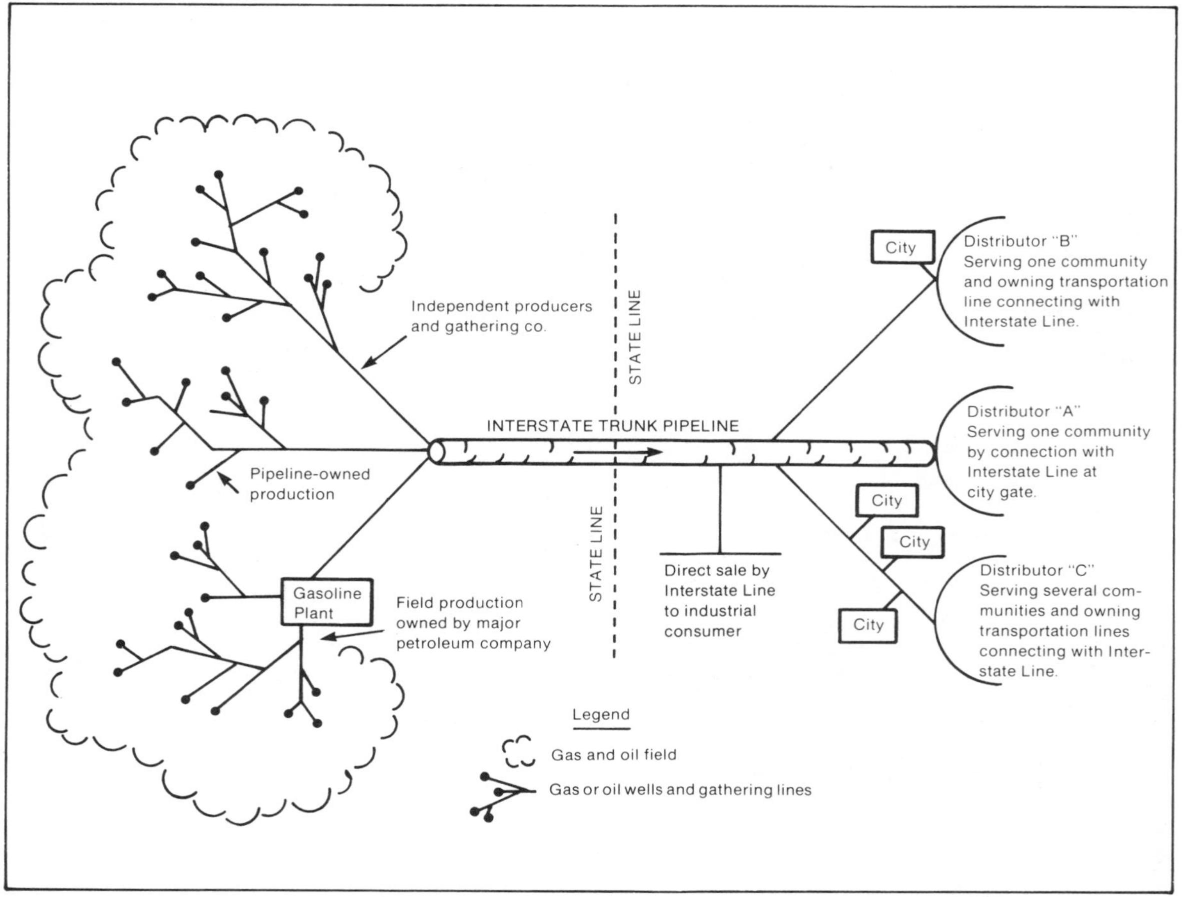

Distributor "B"
Serving one community and owning transportation line connecting with Interstate Line.

Distributor "A"
Serving one community by connection with Interstate Line at city gate.

Distributor "C"
Serving several communities and owning transportation lines connecting with Interstate Line.

City

City
City
City

INTERSTATE TRUNK PIPELINE

STATE LINE

STATE LINE

Direct sale by Interstate Line to industrial consumer

Independent producers and gathering co.

Pipeline-owned production

Field production owned by major petroleum company

Gasoline Plant

Legend

Gas and oil field

Gas or oil wells and gathering lines

Source: U.S. Congress, House, Committee on Interstate and Foreign Commerce, Hearings — Amendments to the Natural Gas Act (80th Cong., 1st

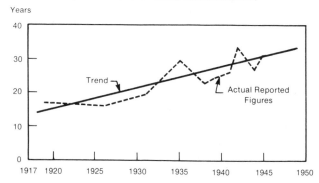

Chart 4-2
Trend of Reserve Life Index for Natural Gas
(Proved Reserves Divided by Annual Production)

Source: FPC, Natural Gas Investigation (Report of Commissioners Smith and Wimberly), Wash., D.C.: 1948, p. 47.

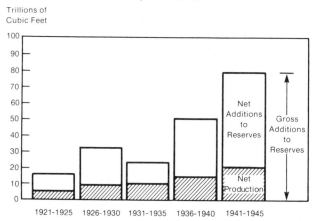

Chart 4-3
Additions to Reserves vs Net Production of Natural Gas
by 5-Year Periods

Source: FPC, Natural Gas Investigation (Report of Commissioners Smith and Wimberly), Wash., D.C.: 1948, p. 47.

The natural gas industry, after its wartime expansion, was poised for years of unprecedented growth. Proved uncommitted reserves as of 1946 amounted to 144 trillion cubic feet. With annual marketed production at only 4 trillion, these reserves implied a reserve-life (at existing consumption rates) of more than 30 years (see Chart 4-2). Annual new additions to reserves were exceeding production, and by a growing margin (Chart 4-3). The fact that oil discovery ratios

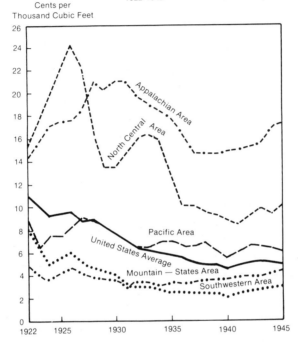

Chart 4-4
Average Wellhead Price
of Marketed Natural Gas

By Areas and for the United States
1922-1945

Cents per
Thousand Cubic Feet

Source: FPC, Natural Gas Investigation (Report of Commissioners
Smith and Wimberly), Wash., D.C., 1948, p. 179.

(per wells drilled) had begun to decline was actually good news for gas reserves. "As the drill bores deeper and deeper into the earth," explained one geologist, "the proportion of gas to oil which is found increases."[3] Thus, while conservationists decried the wastage of gas resources, industry spokesmen claimed that reserves were more than adequate until eventually supplemented by coal gasification.[4]

Because of these immense reserves, the price of natural gas stayed extremely

---

[3]   Quoted in Federal Power Commission, Docket No. G-580; *Natural Gas Investigation*, Report of Commissioners Nelson. L. Smith and Harrington Wimberly (Wash., D.C.: GPO, 1948), p. 41. Hereafter, unpublished materials pertaining to the Natural Gas Investigation will be cited as part of *Docket No. G-580;* the two reports will be cited as *Natural Gas Investigation* (Smith and Wimberly) or (Olds and Draper).

[4]   *Docket No. G-580*, "Statement of Position and Recommendations of Independent Petroleum Association of America," October 15, 1946, pp. 26–29; also, "Brief and Recommendations of Natural Gas Industry Committee," October 15, 1946, pp. 12–13.

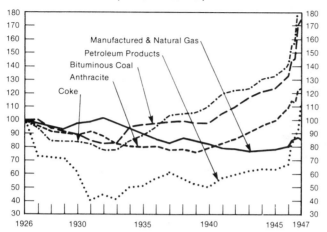

Chart 4-5
Wholesale Price Trends for Competitive Fuels
(Indexes — 1926 = 100)

Note: The indexes shown represent annual averages except that for 1947 they are monthly figures for March, June, September, and December.

Source: FPC, <u>Natural Gas Investigation</u> (Report of Commissioners Smith and Wimberly), Wash., D.C., 1948, p. 342.

low after the war. The average price of natural gas was about 5 cents per thousand cubic feet – less than half what it had been in 1920 (Chart 4-4). In the huge fields of the Southwest, it was a mere 3 cents. At this low level, gas production was a marginally profitable enterprise. The price simply did not justify the expense of gathering lines and treatment plants (to remove liquids and impurities), except for the richest, largest deposits. But low prices did give natural gas an advantage in interfuel competition (Chart 4-5). After the war, coal and oil prices increased sharply, to a point where gas cost half as much as the Btu-equivalent of coal (the British thermal unit is a standard measure of calorific content), and three-fourths as much as oil. Although the gap in delivered costs was smaller because the capital costs of pipelines were large, the difference would remain a significant advantage.

The problems of gas regulation

Under the doctrine of a case known as *Munn v. Illinois* in 1877, the interstate distribution of natural gas had long been acknowledged as a business "affecting the public interest," and was therefore regulated by state authorities.[5] But the interstate pipelines, as they expanded in the 1930's, exceeded local regulatory jurisdiction. When this had happened with electric power transmission a dec-

---

[5] *Munn v. Illinois* 94 U.S. 113 (1877).

ade earlier, Congress created the Federal Power Commission to fill the regulatory void. In the Natural Gas Act of 1938, Congress extended the FPC's authority to include interstate commerce in gas.

Although the Natural Gas Act passed without dissenting votes in either house, its legislative history did involve considerable discussion of the FPC's jurisdiction and its method and criteria for rate regulation.[6] The Commission would certainly regulate the construction of interstate pipelines, any extensions or abandonments thereof, and the companies' prices and rates of return. The lawmakers, however, could not easily agree whether the FPC's jurisdiction should extend forward to wholesale distributors or whether it should extend backward to production and gathering.[7] When the House held hearings on the bill, several congressmen pursued this point with extreme care. One congressman asked, "Does this bill give anywhere the Commission power over the sources of natural gas in the different fields?" An FPC solicitor responded in the clearest of terms: "It does not; no. It does not attempt to regulate the gathering rates or the gathering business."[8] During Senate debate, Burton Wheeler (D-Montana) addressed the same issue as chairman of the Commerce Committee. "It does not attempt to regulate the producers of natural gas," he said. "It is limited to transportation in interstate commerce."[9]

Despite these obvious intentions to exempt gas producers from the FPC's jurisdiction, the key provision of the law was still ambiguous. Section 1 (b) of the Act was as follows:

The provisions of this act shall apply to the transportation of natural gas in interstate commerce, to the sale in interstate commerce of natural gas for resale . . . and to natural gas companies engaged in such transportation or sale, but shall not apply to any other transportation or sale of natural gas or the local distribution of natural gas or to the facilities used for such distribution or to the production or gathering of natural gas.

Standing alone, the second half of this passage would seem clear enough in exempting production from federal regulation. But as a qualifier to the first half of the passage, this construction would cause no end of debate and deliberation by the courts, the FPC, and the Congress.

Even where the FPC's jurisdiction was certain, the language of the Act failed to specify how rates should be set. The statute simply mandated that rates be

---

6   *Public Law No. 688* (Chapter 556, U.S. Codes); for the legislative history of the Natural Gas Act, see J. C. Jacobs, "Legislative History of the Natural Gas Act," *Georgetown Law Journal*, vol. XLVI, No. 4 (1956), 695.
7   U.S. Congress, House, Committee on Interstate and Foreign Commerce, *Hearings – Natural Gas* (75th Cong., 1st Sess.), March 1937, p. 11.
8   U.S. Congress, House, Committee on Interstate and Foreign Commerce, *Hearings – Natural Gas* (74th Cong., 2nd Sess.), April 1936, p. 34.
9   *Congressional Record*, vol. 81, pt. 8, August 19, 1937, p. 9312. It should be noted that the 1937 House Report on the Lea bill (which became the Natural Gas Act) introduced a contradictory element that became significant to subsequent court interpretation of the Act. In elaborating the appropriate areas of FPC jurisdiction, the Report included, in a parenthetical phrase, "for example, sales by producing companies to distributing companies. . ." See, U.S. Congress, House, Committee on Interstate and Foreign Commerce, *House Report No. 709* (75th Cong., 1st Sess.), June 1937.

"just and reasonable" and that the Commission determine the "actual legitimate cost of the property of every natural-gas company," and any other facts "which bear on the determination of such cost or depreciation and the fair value of such property." Companies were also required to file a statement of the "original cost" of their assets. Thus, it appeared that Congress intended the gas production properties of pipeline companies to be included in the rate base for purposes of regulation. But the methods of doing this were left uncertain.

To appreciate the importance of this statutory vagueness, it is worth digressing briefly into the principles of cost-based utility rate-making. The concept itself was relatively simple. To be "just and reasonable," rates on a given volume of sales had to yield sufficient revenue to cover the regulated company's cost of operations and provide a "fair" rate of return. In practice, the process of determining both costs and rate of return was exceedingly complex and provided limitless opportunities for contention over definitions and computations. Although this "cost-of-service" regulatory concept was generally applicable to any utility, it evolved through specialized application in each different industry. With respect to natural gas, a huge body of Commission and court precedent accumulated during the 1940's and 1950's. These decisions haltingly translated the concept into an administrative procedure for rate regulation that rested on three distinct legs: cost of operations, rate base, and rate of return.

Calculating the regulated firm's cost of operations was the starting point in the rate-setting process. This had three components: direct and indirect operating expenses, depreciation, and taxes. Gas purchases, and the cost of any gas produced by the pipeline company itself, were the largest components of operating expense. Others were storage, maintenance, pipeline operations, royalties, and administrative overhead. Some items proved extremely difficult to calculate. Depreciation expenses, for example, could be computed by various methods depending on the asset. And taxes, which might appear straightforward, were complicated by special provisions for rapid amortization, rapid expensing of intangible drilling costs, and the percentage depletion allowance. Rarely did the regulated firm, its customers, and the Commission agree easily on these items.

The second step in this process was the determination of the so-called "rate base" – the assets on which a rate of return would be allowed. The Commission had to determine which properties should be included in the rate base. For diversified firms, this was not at all clearcut. For example, what portion of a natural gas treatment plant, which produced saleable liquid by-products, should be credited to the rate base? Property valuation was even more difficult. It was a matter of intense legal controversy whether the appropriate standard was the depreciated original cost or the current "fair market value." If assets were valued at original cost, then earnings would likely be inadequate to finance new investment at inflated replacement costs. "Fair value," on the other hand, was nearly impossible to determine in the absence of a market mechanism. The Supreme Court had ruled in 1898 that regulators must determine the "fair market value" of assets. But the Court appeared to reverse that standard in 1944 when it ruled against the Hope Natural Gas Company which had urged a valuation of its rate base according to "reproduction costs." The Court, in an opinion written by Justice William O. Douglas, upheld the FPC's rejection of that method and agreed that depreciated original cost should be the criterion *in that instance*.[10] The *Hope* case had broad implications to be discussed presently.

The third step in the process of rate regulation was determining the rate of return. This was a percentage of the rate base deemed sufficient to cover debt service, dividend obligations on preferred stock, and a reasonable return to common equity. Given any particular rate of return on the rate base, the portion left for yield on common equity was a function of the regulated firm's capital structure, that is, the ratio of debt to equity. Between 1945 and 1960, the rate of return generally allowed by the FPC ranged from 5.7 to 6.5 percent. As Alfred Kahn has noted, determination of this rate "inevitably reflected a complex mixture of political and economic considerations." Or to put it more plainly, "an acceptable compromise between the interests of investors on the one hand and consumers on the other."[11]

Once the Commission determined these three factors – cost of operations, rate base, and rate of return – it could compute the overall revenue require-ment of the pipeline company by multiplying the rate of return by the rate base and adding the cost of operations. That sum, divided by the estimated volume of gas to be delivered during the relevant rate period, yielded the average charge per unit of gas (as in the example below).

Simple formula for cost-based rate determination
rate base × rate of return + cost of operations = revenue requirement
revenue requirement ÷ estimated gas sales = average rate
Hypothetical Example
$549.6 million × .06 + $160.7 million = $193.6 million
$193.6 million ÷ 625 billion cubic feet = $.31 per thousand cubic feet

The Commission's final, contentious chore was then to allocate those rates (or rate increases) among the different categories of customers.

The FPC's task of rate-setting in natural gas was hampered by limited resources, inefficient adjudicatory procedure, and nebulous statutory authority. Five commissioners (appointed by the president) and a professional staff of 700 had to absorb regulatory authority for the gas industry without a significant increase in budget.[12] Each case seemed to raise circumstantial problems that were exceedingly complex. The Commission generally relied on case-by-case decisions which, through the appellate process, would eventually yield a body of precedent that defined the FPC's authority.

For unprecedented questions of broad policy, the case-by-case method was

[10] *Smith v. Ames* 169 U.S. 466 (1898), and *FPC v. Hope Natural Gas Company* 320 U.S. 591 (1944).
[11] Alfred Kahn, *The Economics of Regulation: Principles and Institutions* (New York: John Wiley & Sons, 1970), vol. I, p. 42.
[12] Federal Power Commission, *Thirty-third Annual Report*, 1953 (Wash., D.C.: GPO, 1954), pp. 156–161.

inadequate. To deal with those, the FPC undertook a wide-ranging investigation of the industry in 1944. This Natural Gas Investigation, which took three years, was supposed to clarify the issues and recommend rational legislative solutions.

But the Investigation, together with several court decisions during the period, only made matters worse. Industry leaders, consumers, state regulators, and congressmen held widely different views of the problems and the appropriate solutions. So did the FPC commissioners, as it turned out. The entire process reportedly caused "fear, distrust, and confusion" to spread among oil and gas producers, especially because of "those in Government who openly advocate Federal control and regulation of oil and gas production as a public utility."[13]

Federal control over wellhead prices was the most controversial issue. It has two separate, but related, dimensions. One was the question of control over gas producers that were not pipeline companies. The other was the method of price control for pipeline companies that also produced natural gas.

The FPC addressed the first question in 1940, in a case involving the Columbia Fuel Corporation. The Commission held that it had no authority over sales of natural gas made as incident to production and gathering. At the time, Commissioner Leland Olds concurred in the majority's opinion.[14] Though a majority of the Commission never waivered from this view, subsequent interpretations by the Supreme Court injected ambiguities that fed the industry's fears. In a case involving the Interstate Natural Gas Company, the FPC ruled in 1945 that Interstate's prices were subject to its regulation. The company produced and gathered its own gas, mixed it with gas purchased from other producers, and transmitted it by a trunk pipeline, entirely within one state, for delivery to three interstate pipeline companies.[15] When the Supreme Court affirmed this decision in 1947, oil and gas trade groups concluded that judicial interpretation of the Natural Gas Act was on the verge of authorizing FPC control over production and gathering.[16]

For pipeline companies that produced gas, the *Hope* decision was the point of departure. There were two arguments in support of cost-based wellhead pricing. One, which motivated Justice Douglas in his *Hope* opinion, was that costs plus reasonable return was the only appropriate method for complying with the "just and reasonable" mandate of the Act. To merely rubber-stamp the market price, he noted, was scarcely a legitimate regulatory procedure. The other rationale, to which Commissioners Leland Olds and Claude Draper subscribed, was that "fair field price" was impossible to certify since it required

[13] U.S. Congress, House, Committee on Interstate and Foreign Commerce, *Amendments to the Natural Gas Act* (80th Cong., 1st Sess.), April–May, 1947, p. 115.

[14] *In the Matter of Columbia Fuel Corp.*, 2 FPC 200 (1940). A dissent by Commissioner John W. Scott in this case was widely quoted in subsequent debate. Scott argued that the exemption in the Act only prohibited the FPC from interfering with the *physical activity* of production and gathering, but not from regulating the sale price of gas intended for interstate commerce.

[15] *Interstate Natural Gas Company v. Federal Power Commission*, 156 F. 2d 949 (1946).

[16] *Docket No. G-580*, IPAA Brief, pp. 21–22, and Natural Gas Industry Committee Brief, pp. 18–19.

that true competition, rather than oligopoly, prevail. Since they believed that concentration in many gas fields was excessive, the fair field price would, in their view, "protect the monopoly position of the industry."[17]

Justice Robert H. Jackson's landmark dissent in the *Hope* case became the gospel of the gas industry's opposition to cost-based wellhead pricing. "A rate base is little help in determining reasonableness of the price of gas," wrote Jackson. "The service one renders to society in the gas business is measured by what one gets out of the ground, not by what one puts into it, and there is little more relationship between the investment and the results than in a game of poker."[18] In the first test of the *Hope* doctrine that applied to gas producing properties of a pipeline company, the Commission chose original cost over fair field price as the basis for asset valuation. When the Supreme Court upheld the FPC's choice by a 5–4 decision in 1945, Justice Jackson reiterated his view that the application of cost-based rate making to gas production was "little better than to draw figures out of a hat."[19]

Gas producers offered a host of other arguments against cost-based pricing: (1) Exploration was not a utility function, thus a cost criterion would stifle discovery incentive as well as prudent risk aversion; (2) Cost-based pricing would result in many different prices for the same commodity; (3) Producers would be encouraged to avoid interstate markets in favor of unregulated sales in intrastate markets; (4) A cost-based price would stimulate demand and dampen supply; and (5) Prices based on original costs were illsuited to a depleting resource, since replacement costs could never be attained in the long run. R. H. Hargrove, the vice-president of United Gas who made these points, concluded his testimony by warning that cost-based valuation was not only "unfair" and "illogical," but could only drive pipeline companies out of exploration and production, to the long-run detriment of gas consumers.[20]

Waste, although less controversial, played a prominent role in the emerging policy debate. "Conservation" meant different things to different people; it had both physical and economic connotations.

Nearly everyone deplored the real, physical waste of casinghead gas by flaring. But there was little agreement over methods for achieving conservation. State officials felt that mandatory conservation measures, such as field unitization or prorationing (called "rateable take" when applied to gas), fell exclusively within their jurisdiction. In addition to the "separation of powers" argument, state officials pointed to the need for local flexibility, presaging an argument that was applied to strip-mining control three decades later. A former Kansas governor who had chaired the Interstate Oil Compact Commission, explained that "the problems of conservation vary so widely from one area or section to

[17] *Natural Gas Investigation* (Olds and Draper), pp. 1–2, 11, 144. The argument that concentration was worsening was based on the fact that 25 firms had come to control 77 percent of the acreage in the Panhandle and Hugoton fields.

[18] *FPC v. Hope Natural Gas Co.*, 320 U.S. 645–647 (1944).

[19] *Colorado Interstate Gas Company and Canadian River Gas Company v. FPC*, 324 U.S. 581 (1945).

[20] Quoted in *Natural Gas Investigation* (Smith and Wimberly), pp. 217–218.

another that the whole Nation could not or should not be 'straight jacketed' under one absolutely uniform treatment."[21]

But the states had yet to put an end to flaring, and federal authorities were impatient. The FPC commissioners felt that "three years at most" should be allowed "to eradicate every significant instance of gas wastage to the air." Industry officials were nearly as impatient, for they knew that if state authorities could not stop the waste, then federal regulators would.[22]

The real problem, from the industry perspective, was not inadequate regulation, but rather the inadequate price structure. "Why expect a producer to conserve," asked Everette DeGoyler, a prominent geologist, "when the cost of doing so is greater than the low and inadequate value which the buyer puts upon it?" Ernest Thompson, chairman of the Texas Railroad Commission, ironically held a similar brief for the market mechanism. "An increased field price for gas," he said, "would be the greatest conservation measure that could be adopted." The pipeline companies more or less agreed, but with reservations. They opposed greater control by the FPC, but also relied on low prices to penetrate markets in interfuel competition.[23]

The consumerist approach to gas conservation was not at all price-oriented. From the user's perspective, "conservation" meant using less of a resource, not using it more efficiently. Consumerist spokesmen, like Leland Olds, were critical of the "narrow" definition of conservation held by Thompson and others who sympathized with the industry. The way to achieve conservation in Olds' opinion was through direct federal control of production and end-use.[24]

"End-use controls" on natural gas was another contentious issue. This usually meant some form of constraint, but not price controls, on industrial consumption, particularly by electric utilities, where coal would suffice. For the quantity-oriented conservationist, the combustion qualities of natural gas were "superior" to those of other fuels. By this logic, gas should be reserved for residential consumption and specialized uses, such as brick-making. Since the price mechanism apparently failed to make this distinction, administrative allocation was deemed necessary.

The coal industry, of course, thought this was a great idea. Coal producers outdid their oil and gas counterparts in complaining that the price of gas was beneath its "intrinsic" value. Noting that gas was invading coal's traditional industrial markets by "cutthroat competition," the National Coal Association did not hesitate to call for end-use controls.[25]

Not surprisingly, gas producers and pipeline companies adamantly opposed federal end-use controls. So did state regulators, who feared Washington's intrusion into their bailiwicks. These interests actually reversed the conservationist arguments, claiming that end-use controls would worsen the problem of

---

[21] Andrew Schoeppel, quoted in *Natural Gas Investigation* (Smith and Wimberly), p. 149.

[22] *Natural Gas Investigation* (Smith and Wimberly), pp. 151–153.

[23] Quotes from *Natural Gas Investigation* (Smith and Wimberly), pp. 177, 190.

[24] *Natural Gas Investigation* (Olds and Draper), pp. 12, 80.

[25] *Natural Gas Investigation* (Smith and Wimberly), pp. 301–302.

waste in the field by widening the breach between demand and the present over-supply.[26]

All of these issues of public policy related to a central dilemma; how to balance short-term circumstances of over-supply with the long-term inevitability of depletion. Existing regulatory concepts could not maximize economic efficiency and at the same time balance conflicting institutional interests. It remained to be seen if Congress had the answer.

Regulation: the Truman fight

Early in 1947 the gas industry, without waiting for the Supreme Court's decision in the *Interstate* case, nor for the Commission's report on its Natural Gas Investigation, began a campaign to amend the Natural Gas Act. Two Oklahoma Republicans, Representative Ross Rizley and Senator E. H. Moore, introduced the necessary legislation. The Rizley-Moore bill addressed all of the major policy problems that threatened the industry. It sought to exempt non-pipeline gas producers from wellhead price regulation. To ensure against federal intrusion in conservation matters, it would also exempt "the producing, gathering, treating, or processing facilities" from FPC jurisdiction. To block the threat of end-use controls, the bill exempted "local distribution" and ordered the FPC not to restrict gas sales "for utilization for any purpose."[27]

These proposed restrictions were obviously aimed at preventing any prospective expansion of FPC jurisdiction. As such, they were preemptive, since the Commission had never exercised such controls. But Rizley-Moore would also reverse existing regulatory policy toward gas produced by pipeline companies. As told earlier, the Commission and the Court had established the principle of cost-based valuation for production properties of pipeline companies within FPC jurisdiction. Rizley-Moore not only sought to overturn this concept, but to provide gas pipeline companies with the best of both worlds. The bill said that "if the gas is produced by a natural-gas company or purchased from a subsidiary or affiliate," the Commission should allow "the prevailing current market price in the field or fields where produced." But if market competition was too tough for pipeline companies with more costly production, then they could elect to have their production properties included in their overall rate base and receive a cost-based valuation from the FPC.[28] This modification seemed worse to its critics than no regulation at all. They viewed Rizley-Moore as a blatant attempt to shackle the government's prerogatives in service to the industry.

All of the industry trade groups, representing integrated majors, independent

---

[26] *Docket No. G-580*, "Brief of the Mid-Continent Oil & Gas Association," September 30, 1946, p. 19.

[27] H.R. 2185, 80th Cong., 1st Sess., in U.S. Congress, House, *Amendments to the Natural Gas Act* (1947), p. 1.

[28] *Ibid.*, 2–3. In his testimony (p. 32), Rizley justified this optional device as a necessary protection for Appalachian gas producers whose costs exceeded those in the Southwest by as much as 400 percent.

producers, and pipeline companies, endorsed the Rizley-Moore amendment and lobbied for it in earnest. Hines Baker, executive vice-president of Humble Oil, admitted that the oil and gas industry was "interested broadly and primarily in preventing the exercise of authority or power by the Federal Power Commission."[29] Regulatory officials from most of the gas-producing states likewise supported Rizley-Moore. Among industry interests, only the National Coal Association dissented, preferring a different amendment that would have extended FPC jurisdiction to both production and end-use controls.

Undaunted, the Federal Power Commission took the position that such drastic legislation was at best premature. Chairman Nelson Lee Smith urged Democratic congressional leaders to await the Commission's report on its three-year investigation. With President Truman's approval and the Commission's help, Representative J. Percy Priest from the coal state of Tennessee introduced a substitute bill that would exempt non-pipeline gas producers from federal rate regulation but do nothing else.[30] Such a measure would presumably satisfy the most pressing fears of the gas-producing sector, the base of Democratic political power in the Southwest, without alienating big-city Democrats in the eastern consuming states.

But the timing was wrong, at least in the House. The industry and its congressional supporters preferred to stick with the Rizley bill and the prospect of total victory. The House rejected two attempts at substitution, and then passed the Rizley bill by a voice vote. In the Senate, however, the administration succeeded in blocking a favorable committee report.[31]

Once it was evident that the bill would not clear the Senate, the FPC decided to take the unusual step of issuing an administrative resolution (Order 139) to clarify the confusion. Only Claude Draper dissented from the statement, which said that independent producers could sell "at arm's-length" to interstate pipelines "without apprehension that in doing so they may become subject to assertions of jurisdiction by the Commission."[32] Both Leland Olds and Harry Truman would later regret their approval of this position.

Now, at long last, the Natural Gas Investigation came to an end. When the Eightieth Congress reconvened in 1948, the Commission presented, to the amazement of both houses, two separate and contradictory reports. Commissioners Nelson Lee Smith and Harrington Wimberly subscribed to one, and Leland Olds and Claude Draper wrote the other. Since there was a vacancy on the Commission, neither report represented a majority. This split threw the controversy over gas regulation into complete confusion.

The Smith-Wimberly report reviewed the major issues, weighing the pros and cons on each point as they had emerged from the hearing testimony. In

[29] Ibid., 143.
[30] N. L. Smith to H. Truman, March 10 and April 3, 1947, and Robert Kerr to H. Truman, August 12, 1949, Box 636, file 346, Harry Truman Papers, Official File, Truman Library, Independence, Missouri.
[31] Anne H. Morgan, Robert S. Kerr: The Senate Years (Norman: University of Oklahoma Press, 1977), p. 58.
[32] Quoted in Natural Gas Investigation (Smith and Wimberly), pp. 126–127.

cautious and qualified terms, Commissioners Smith and Wimberly recommended amendatory legislation to clarify the FPC's jurisdiction. The regulatory exemption for independent producers should be made explicit. For gas produced by pipeline companies, they urged Congress to provide "a standard of reasonable commodity value, subject to necessary safeguards against abuse." Waste and end-use problems, despite their seriousness, did not require federal regulation.[33]

The Olds-Draper report differed entirely in tone, purpose, and conclusions. It made no pretense of scientific rigor or adjudicatory balance; it was a vigorous political brief against big business, sounding the alarm that the foxes were about to raid the chicken coop. The Olds-Draper argument followed a line of reasoning that anticipated another gas policy debate in the early 1970's. Since reserves were sufficient in the short-run, prices should be stable. But they were rising – a sure sign that monopoly was prevalent. In order to protect the consumer, the FPC needed authority to set rates based on cost and to scrutinize and possibly regulate sales prices between producers and pipelines. Over the longer term, however, gas reserves were both finite and inadequate. Conservation and control of end-uses were therefore needed. The report used data on gas reserves creatively to sustain these two arguments.

A large part of the Olds-Draper report was devoted to analysis of industry structure. It concluded that levels of concentration in production, distribution, and control of reserves, were rising dangerously. This illogically suggested that in the midst of glut, field prices were determined by monopolistic or oligopolistic behavior among dominant producers. According to Olds and Draper, the last thing the public interest needed was amendatory legislation that would weaken the Commission. Rather, they urged the Commission to redouble its surveillance of "the field price situation to determine when the trend toward concentration of control of gas reserves reaches a point where effective competition is destroyed." Should such a situation develop, they felt there would be "no recourse but Federal regulation of all sales of gas in interstate commerce."[34]

The views of Commissioners Olds and Draper not only alarmed the industry but transformed a technical issue of economic policy into a broader question of the public interest. The language of the report cast the entire debate in the light of public-private conflict, ascribing nothing but base motives to those who would amend the Act. The very notion that the act was unsatisfactory and required drastic overhauling was "a brain child of the oil and natural gas interests" and was fostered and supported by well-organized propaganda, they said. "Its objective was the objective of practically all big industries affected with a public interest, viz, to render regulation a hollow formality."[35]

Since 1948 was an election year in which Democratic succession would be seriously challenged, this politicization of the gas regulation issue brought con-

33 *Natural Gas Investigation* (Smith and Wimberly), pp. 26–27.
34 *Natural Gas Investigation* (Olds and Draper), p. 13.
35 *Ibid.*, 1.

gressional action to a temporary halt. Consumer-state politicians of either stripe were unwilling to give support to any legislation that might make them enemies of the people. Even Ross Rizley suffered in his Oklahoma campaign when his Democratic opponent, Robert S. Kerr, a founder of the Kerr-McGee Oil Company, cynically attacked the Rizley bill for favoring "the interests."[36] Harry Truman also heard the public outcry and withdrew his nomination of Burton Behling (a staff director of the Natural Gas Investigation) to the Commission, nominating instead Thomas Buchanan, a Pennsylvanian who favored wellhead price regulation. The strong anti-monopoly theme that ran through President Truman's campaign platform – a fair deal for the little man – emerged as a continuing factor in the gas regulation controversy.

But the Democratic Party did retain the presidency, and gained majorities in both the House and the Senate. Thus in 1949, Robert Kerr entered the Senate along with Lyndon B. Johnson of Texas. In the House, Oren Harris, Democrat of Arkansas, became chairman of the Subcommittee on Petroleum and Federal Power, and Sam Rayburn of Texas took over the Speakership. From the perspective of the oil and gas industry, these were welcome developments in light of the prevailing atmosphere of animosity toward their industry. The previous winter's oil shortages had caused widespread criticism; the Federal Trade Commission was completing its investigation of the international oil companies; the percentage depletion allowance was under attack from a coalition of northeastern congressmen headed by Senator Paul Douglas, and the press was characterizing the issue of offshore mineral rights as another battle between the people and the interests.

In these circumstances, the gas industry and its supporters realized that legislation on the order of Rizley-Moore was no longer feasible. "There was a limit," wrote Lyndon Johnson to one constituent, "as to how far we could go as a practical matter."[37] At the same time, with Truman's nomination of Buchanan to the FPC, the threat of wellhead price regulation had worsened. A lawyer for Phillips Petroleum proposed that Senator Kerr introduce a more limited bill that would simply exempt independent producers from FPC jurisdiction. This, after all, was the principal concern of Kerr's constituents. The more complicated technical issue of cost versus fair field price in rate-setting was of interest chiefly to the interstate pipeline companies which, by themselves, had no significant political leverage. Kerr was assured that the pipeliners were willing to stand aside and let the producers solve their problem separately, as a first step toward an improved regulatory environment.

Accordingly, Senator Kerr and Representative Oren Harris introduced identical bills drafted by the Phillips attorney.[38] Representative John Lyle, Democrat of Texas, separately introduced a similar measure. The strategy was to emphasize the difference between this legislation and that of Rizley-Moore,

---

[36] Morgan, *Robert S. Kerr*, p. 59.
[37] L. B. Johnson to R. L. Clark, June 30, 1949, in LBJ Papers, U.S. Senate Legislative Files, Box 216, file entitled, "Amendments of the Natural Gas Act," Lyndon B. Johnson Presidential Library.
[38] Morgan, *Robert S. Kerr*, p. 59.

which had failed in the Senate. According to Kerr and Harris the new bill was substantively the same as the Priest bill which the Commission and the President had supported. It attempted only to preclude expansion of Commission jurisdiction, not undo any existing authority or activity.[39]

Oil and gas producers, of course, supported the new initiative, and the pipeline companies generally remained quiet.[40] The sticking point was the split Commission, particularly the crusading Mr. Olds. Although Smith and Wimberly supported the Kerr-Harris bill, the new majority of Olds, Draper, and Buchanan opposed it. In his long and contentious testimony to the Senate Commerce Committee, Leland Olds represented himself as the consumer's champion, fighting to prevent a $500 million raid by the interests on the pocketbooks of midwestern farmers and northeastern homeowners. Several senators appeared mystified and considerably irritated by Leland Olds' change of heart. He had, after all, endorsed the Priest bill and concurred in the FPC's Order 139, reassuring the independent producers. When Olds said he believed that the chief proponents of the bill "are interested in higher field prices for natural gas," an exasperated Senator Kerr made a candid retort that proved to be disastrous politically. "That will be admitted," he said.[41]

Once the press publicized the bill's hypothetical effects on price, the legislative campaign became an uphill battle that the President wanted nothing to do with. The Truman White House was already wary, since the Bureau of the Budget had warned that Kerr's bill "strongly suggests an attempt to weaken the Administration's present policy toward the industry."[42]

In August 1949, when the President told Kerr that he opposed the bill, the Oklahoman could not understand the administration's trepidation. In view of Truman's prior approval of the Priest bill and Order 139, Kerr concluded that "opposition to these bills is tantamount to endorsement of regulation for regulation's sake alone." In his correspondence with the President, Kerr blamed the controversy primarily on the recalcitrance of Leland Olds. He complained that Olds would even disregard existing contracts and have the Commission force producers to sell their gas at any mandated price.[43] In the face of presidential intransigence, it is perhaps understandable that Senator Kerr and his colleagues from the Southwest decided to purge the source of apostasy. And since Truman had decided to renominate Olds to a fourth term on the Commission, the opportunity was at hand. Senate approval was required.

[39] U.S. Congress, House, Interstate Commerce Committee, Subcommittee on Petroleum and Federal Power, *Natural Gas Act Amendments (Production and Gathering)* (81st Cong., 1st Sess.), April 1949, pp. 5, 19.
[40] At the hearings, only Panhandle Eastern complained that the exemption for independent gas producers would discriminate against pipeline companies that were also producers; U.S. Congress, Senate, Subcommittee of the Interstate Commerce Committee, *Amendments to the Natural Gas Act* (81st Cong., 1st Sess.), May–June 1949, p. 453.
[41] *Ibid.*, 220.
[42] W. G. Fritz to E. B. Staats, February 21, 1949, and F. Pace to H. Truman, July 22, 1949, Box 636, file 346, Official File, HTPL.
[43] R. Kerr to H. Truman, August 11 and August 12, 1949, Box 636, file 346, Official File, HTPL.

The story of the Olds reappointment fight has been capably told elsewhere.[44] It was a dramatic struggle between the executive and legislative branches of government and between two wings of the Democratic Party. It included a scurrilous, McCarthy-style attack on Olds' early career as a journalist who preached socialism. Representative Lyle led the attack, while Lyndon Johnson and Robert Kerr managed the process. Throughout the confirmation hearings, regulatory concepts and problems of the gas industry were scarcely mentioned, and the industry wisely stayed out of it.[45] Truman was so determined to prevail that he went to the extreme of mobilizing the power of patronage right down to the country level. But with Republicans relishing the Democrats' feud, and with the Dixiecrats like Kerr and Johnson frustrated beyond compromise, the President's efforts were not enough. In October 1949, the Senate rejected Olds' appointment by 53–15.

The Leland Olds affair made him a martyr on behalf of consumerist opposition to the gas legislation. By doing so, it further obscured the substantive regulatory issues. Senator Paul Douglas succeeded Olds as the consumers' champion and headed opposition to Kerr-Harris in 1950. He developed his argument along the same lines as had Olds, but with greater oratorical skill. "Should the field price of natural gas," he asked, "be allowed to rise to the full extent of what the domestic and industrial markets for gas will bear?" Or should it be subject to regulation? Douglas told the Senate the question was "whether we should allow these concentrated gains to fall into the hands of the small groups of big and wealthy oil companies and oil men" or whether these advantages "should be shared with the 40 million and more consumers."[46]

Despite its eloquence, this appeal had little impact on Congress. Both houses passed the legislation by narrow margins. But the White House was flooded with negative mail. Big city mayors, organized labor, the National Farmers' Union, and most major newspapers demanded a veto in the name of Franklin D. Roosevelt, Thomas Jefferson, and all the principles for which the Democratic Party stood.

On April 15, 1950, Harry S. Truman vetoed the bill, determined to prevent "windfall profits to gas producers." The gas issue had become a matter of equity.[47]

The political fight over amendments to the Natural Gas Act and its resolution by presidential veto had some interesting effects. For one, it turned the issue on its head. The presidential veto appeared to protect and reaffirm a kind

---

[44] Joseph B. Harris, "The Senatorial Rejection of Leland Olds: A Case Study," *American Political Science Review*, Vol. 45, No. 3 (September 1951), 674–692; also, Morgan, *Robert S. Kerr*, Chapter 3.
[45] U.S. Congress, Senate, Interstate and Foreign Commerce Committee, Subcommittee on the Nomination of Leland Olds, *Hearings on the Reappointment of Leland Olds to the Federal Power Commission* (81st Cong., 1st Sess.), 1949.
[46] Speech of Senator Paul H. Douglas, U.S. Senate, March 21, 1950, p. 3, in Box 636, file 346, Official File, HTPL.
[47] H. Truman, "Presidential Message on Natural Gas Bill," April 15, 1950, Box 636, file 346, Official File, HTPL.

of regulatory authority that the federal government did not yet have nor had ever exercised. Thus, when the Commission failed to extend its jurisdiction over independent producers in the years following Truman's veto, it appeared to consumers that the FPC was not enforcing the law. This perception encouraged litigation. But the lengthy controversy had done nothing to resolve the substantive problems of regulating natural gas. So failure to legislate a clarification of the Commission's mandate only foisted the complex issues off onto the courts, which were ill-suited to the task of making rational and efficient economic policy.

Policy by default: the Phillips and Panhandle cases

Throughout the legislative fight, the FPC's case-by-case interpretation of regulatory policy ground on. To test the question of jurisdiction over gas producers that were not pipeline companies, the Commission chose Phillips Petroleum, which was the largest gas producer in the United States, but which had no interstate transmission facilities whatsoever. Phillips produced and gathered natural gas in several different fields, processed it in its own facilities, and sold it, at the processing plant exit, to several interstate pipeline companies. The case did not involve any question of whether Phillips' prices were "just and reasonable." The Commission limited its investigation solely "to determine whether Phillips Petroleum Co. is a 'natural gas company,' as that term is defined in the Natural Gas Act."[48] Phillips even conceded, and the Commission accepted, that its sales were sales "in interstate commerce" within the affirmatively stated coverage of the Act's section 1(b), quoted earlier in this chapter.

The Commission delivered its opinion in August 1951. A majority of four Commissioners held that Phillips was not a "natural-gas company" within the meaning of the Act and that its sales from production and gathering activities were thus exempt from regulation by the FPC. It should be noted that the FPC staff disagreed on the grounds that Phillips transmitted raw gas through large-diameter pipes from various gathering points to central processing facilities. But the Commission concluded that regulation of sales from production and gathering would constitute "substantial interference" with state conservation efforts because "there is a direct relation between price and conservation."[49]

Commissioner Buchanan, the dissenter, pointed to President Truman's "resounding veto" of the Kerr-Harris bill as evidence that exempting independent producers conflicted with the national interest.[50] But the majority rejected any blame for having chosen to limit its jurisdiction to interstate pipelines. It was the Congress that had defaulted on its responsibility: "If such authority be deemed insufficient to afford adequate protection to the consuming public, the appro-

[48] Federal Power Commission, *Opinion No. 217*, "In the Matter of Phillips Petroleum Co.," 10 FPC 246 (August 1951).
[49] The principal producing states of Texas, Oklahoma, and New Mexico had intervened in the case to oppose producer regulation on that basis.
[50] *Ibid.*, 284–285.

priate remedy is through amendatory legislation by the Congress."[51] The Commission encouraged any dissatisfied intervenors to seek judicial review.

The gas-consuming State of Wisconsin took this offer seriously and sued the Commission. The circuit court reversed the FPC, and Phillips Petroleum appealed the case to the Supreme Court. In June 1954, the Court, with three justices dissenting, upheld the circuit court and concluded that Phillips was indeed a "natural-gas company" whose sales were subject to the FPC's jurisdiction. In its opinion, the Supreme Court relied heavily on the *Interstate* case of 1947, emphasizing the importance of the direct link between Phillips' sales and interstate commerce. As the Court put it , "the rates charged may have a direct and substantial effect on the price paid by the ultimate consumers. Protection of the consumers against exploitation at the hands of natural-gas companies was the primary aim of the Natural Gas Act."[52]

By this decision, the Supreme Court established federal price controls over the entire natural gas industry and the several thousand companies that produced natural gas for sale to interstate pipelines.

Two months earlier, the FPC had issued an opinion in another case that could have neutralized the effects of the *Phillips* decision. In that case, The Panhandle Eastern Pipeline Company had petitioned the Commission to accept a valuation of the gas it produced for itself based on "fair field price" rather than depreciated original cost fitted in to its overall rate base. Panhandle contended that the natural gas it produced should be accorded its value as a commodity, "the same as similar gas which it purchases from others." This would yield Panhandle 1.3 cents per thousand cubic feet more than would the cost-based method.[53] A majority of the Commission approved Panhandle's request and acknowledged that its decision was a departure from the traditional approach, necessitated by economic rationality.

"The time has come," spoke the majority, "when the practice heretofore followed by the Commission should be re-examined in light of its economic impacts." Quoting extensively from Justice Jackson's dissent in the *Hope* case, the Commission explained the short-term irrationality and long-term ill effects of continuing with the cost-based method. In the short term, this was "a situation of multiple pricing of gas from the same wells and going to the same consumers which just does not make economic sense." And from a longer perspective, "an arbitrary depressed price, related to what may truly turn out to be a 'vanishing rate-base,' would tend to accelerate the consumption and fail to encourage the discovery and development of this limited and irreplaceable natural resource."[54] These insights into the economic effects of cost-based regulation marked an extraordinary intellectual departure from precedent. Unfortunately, they were not to re-emerge again until the late 1960's, by which time it was nearly too late to benefit from their prophetic quality.

[51] *Ibid.*, 280.
[52] *Phillips Petroleum Company v. State of Wisconsin*, 374 U.S. 672.
[53] Federal Power Commission, *Opinion No. 269*, "Panhandle Eastern Pipeline Co., et al.," 13 FPC 53 (April 1954), 61–63.
[54] *Ibid.*, 71–74.

Had this decision to allow a fair field price withstood judicial review, it would have meant that FPC regulation of independent producers under the *Phillips* doctrine could have proceeded with little disruption; a controlled analogue for competitive markets. But the City of Detroit, along with other Panhandle customers, objected to the new regulatory rationale and sued the FPC. In mid-1955, an appellate court overturned the Commission and held that costs must remain the "point of departure" for federal rate regulation. In ambiguous language, that court did not rule out a commodity method of regulation, but held that if costs were abandoned, "the whole experience under the Act is discarded and no anchor, as it were, is available by which to hold the terms 'just and reasonable' to some recognizable meaning."[55] When the Supreme Court declined to review the case, it effectively closed the circle of judicial policy-making that would stand as law of the land unless Congress intervened.

Deregulation: the Eisenhower fight

In response to the Supreme Court's pronouncement in the *Phillips* case, the Federal Power Commission ordered all gas prices frozen in July 1954, unless a petition were filed to justify an increase.[56] By mid-1955, the Commission had received 6,000 new applications for certification from independent gas producers and 11,000 rate filings. This flood more than quadrupled the Commission's workload, and its only recourse was to approve the vast majority of the rate requests, pending formal determination of "just and reasonable" rates, or congressional intervention.[57]

In the meantime, the *Phillips* decision plunged the American polity into another round of legislative conflict over regulation of natural gas. This second battle, however, bore only a superficial resemblance to the Truman fight. The Supreme Court had reversed the momentum, so the issue had become whether to deregulate, rather than whether to avoid regulatory encroachment. Consumer activists and their congressional advocates were loath to see their victory come unravelled at the hands of the so-called interests. Conditions in the gas industry and in energy markets generally had also changed dramatically, and those changes altered the policy issues and the political objectives of various industry sectors. The Eisenhower fight in the mid-1950's would involve intra-fuel politics, interfuel politics, and the politics of business reform – an incredibly complex situation.

To appreciate these changes, it is necessary to go back a few years to review new developments in domestic energy markets. Between 1947 and 1954, interstate pipelines had expanded rapidly into the northeast, midwest, and far west to bring natural gas to the very large urban markets. As they did, demand simply multiplied, and the pipeline companies had to scramble to obtain long-term commitments of gas reserves. From a condition of glut and waste prior to 1947,

---

[55] *City of Detroit, Michigan v. Federal Power Commission, et al.*, 230 F. 2(d) 810 (D.C. Cir. 1955); cert. den. 352 U.S. 289 (1956).
[56] Federal Power Commission, *Order No. 174*, 13 FPC 1195 (July 16, 1954).
[57] Federal Power Commission, *1955 Annual Report* (Wash., D.C.: GPO, 1956), pp. 88, 106–112.

the field market for natural gas had reversed by 1954. With pipeline companies bidding vigorously against one another, a seller's market prevailed. The average wellhead price nearly doubled, and new contract prices reached 20 cents per thousand cubic feet.[58]

Rising prices and the advent of a seller's market gave gas producers new leverage in the type of price escalators they could demand in their long-term sales contracts with pipeline companies. Price escalation clauses had traditionally contained increases of a fixed amount – something like 1 cent per thousand cubic feet every fifth year. But with prices rising, sellers demanded "indeterminate" escalators that linked sales contracts to the price terms of other contracts entered subsequently by the same pipeline company (a two-party clause) or even by any pipeline in a particular gas field (a "most-favored nation" clause). With these provisions, gas producers received future price increases that could not be determined at the time of the initial contract.[59]

These new price escalators had several political consequences. Consumer activists claimed that indeterminate escalators artificially pushed gas prices higher than necessary and reduced competition among producers within each gas field. The distribution companies were no longer able to plan their investments on the basis of their gas purchase contracts. And neither the Federal Power Commission nor the state public service commissions knew how to treat the constant requests for rate increases caused by the escalators. By 1955, these developments had caused divisiveness between producers, pipeline companies, and distributors that had previously been united on the issues of regulation.

With the emergence of a seller's market, the *Phillips* decision caused a more negative reaction among independent producers than would otherwise have occurred. Particularly among the small operators and royalty owners, there was a sincere ideological reaction. Big government seemed simultaneously to be attacking the honored principles of states' rights and free enterprise. The FPC's price freeze scarcely helped the situation. This action, complained one small producer to Lyndon Johnson, was "confiscatory to both state and individual rights." Another told the Senator that the FPC was "the first step toward government control of the oil business." Pretty soon, he added, the United States would be well along the road that Great Britain had traveled.[60] Throughout Oklahoma, Louisiana, Texas, and Arkansas, the cry went up for Congress to curb the Commission and overturn the Supreme Court.

Remembering the lessons of the Truman fight, Senator Lyndon Johnson

---

[58] U.S. Congress, Senate, Committee on Interstate and Foreign Commerce, *Amendments to the Natural Gas Act* (84th Cong., 1st Sess.), May–June, 1955, p. 1266; Neuner, *The Natural Gas Industry*, pp. 51–64; and U.S. Congress, House, Committee on Interstate and Foreign Commerce, *Natural Gas Act (Exemption of Producers)* (84th Cong., 1st Sess.), March–April, 1955, pp. 362–363.
[59] For detailed discussion of the various price escalators, see Neuner, *The Natural Gas Industry*, pp. 81–111; J. C. Jacobs, "The Gas Purchase Contract," in Alfred M. Leeston et al., *The Dynamic Natural Gas Industry* (Norman: University of Oklahoma Press, 1963), pp. 309–336; and Statement of D. T. Searls, in U.S. Congress, Senate, *Natural Gas Amendments* (1955), pp. 98–102.
[60] H. F. Heep to L. B. Johnson, July 19, 1954, and H. H. Allen to L. B. Johnson, August 11, 1954, LBJ Papers, Box 252, "Natural Gas File," U.S. Senate Legislative Files, LBJ Library, Austin, Texas.

responded to the pressure from his constituents by asking the Republican president to commission a blue ribbon panel on the problems of gas regulation. The Senator indicated that the oil and gas industry would support this proposal.[61] He also urged the FPC to delay implementation of new price regulations until such a study was completed.

Since President Eisenhower had already planned a similar commission to study the coal industry's problems, he needed only to expand its scope. In July 1954 he appointed Arthur Flemming, director of the Office of Defense Mobilization, to chair a Presidential Advisory Committee on Energy Supplies and Resources Policy. Its other members were the secretaries of Interior, Defense, Commerce, Labor, State, and Treasury, and the Attorney General.

This Cabinet Committee released its report in February of 1955. There were recommendations on oil imports and other energy matters outside the scope of this chapter. With regard to gas regulation, the committee recommended that (1) the federal government "should not control the production, gathering, processing or sale of natural gas prior to its entry into an interstate transmission line," and (2) in evaluating applications for increased rates, the commission should consider whether the contract prices of the natural gas "are competitively arrived at and represent the reasonable market field price."[62]

These two points were accepted by producing-state congressmen as the basis for legislative compromise that would protect the interests of both producers and consumers. As such, it satisfied neither group, and only pleased the interstate pipeline companies.

With indifferent support from the Eisenhower administration, the Arkansas team of Senator J. William Fulbright and Representative Oren Harris promptly introduced a bill to exempt independent producers from *direct* federal regulation. The Fulbright-Harris bill stated this explicitly, but limited the exemption by authorizing the FPC to reject new contracts or rate increase petitions by pipeline companies that exceeded what it deemed to be the "reasonable market price."[63] Initially undefined, that expression was subsequently qualified to give the FPC some flexibility to consider, "among other things," (1) whether the price was competitively arrived at, (2) its effect on the assurance of supply, and (3) its reasonableness with respect to existing or future prices.[64] The bill also provided that the same standards be applied to gas produced by affiliates of pipeline companies for themselves. By replacing the rate-base, cost-related method with these new "reasonable market" standards, the bill would enable the pipelines to achieve their long sought goal of being on the same footing with

[61] L. B. Johnson to D. D. Eisenhower, June 14, 1954, LBJ Papers, Box 252, Senate legislative files, LBJPL.
[62] "The White House Report on Energy Supplies and Resources Policy," February 26, 1955, p. 2, in White House Official File, Box 684, file 134-H, Dwight D. Eisenhower Presidential Library, Abilene, Kansas.
[63] U.S. Congress, House, *Report No. 992*, "To Amend the Natural Gas Act" (94th Cong., 1st Sess.), June 28, 1955, pp. 42–44.
[64] U.S. Congress, Senate, *Report No. 1219*, "Amendments to the Natural Gas Act" (84th Cong., 1st Sess.), July 28, 1955, p. 6.

independent producers. Further, by eliminating the cost-based rate method, the bill would relieve the FPC of an otherwise impossible regulatory mission that the recent court decisions had imposed on it.

The fragile nature of this compromise was severely tested during extensive hearings on the Fulbright-Harris bill. In fact, from the very beginning, Senator Fulbright seemed embarrassed by his own proposal: "It may be that the measure goes too far in compromising the various conflicts within the gas industry itself." When pressed by colleagues to explain how the provisions for contract rejection and "reasonable market price" were substantively different from regulation, Fulbright admitted that it was a kind of indirect supervision. "I regret we felt it necessary to accept supervision to this extent," said the Senator. But "the impetus behind this," he explained, "are the people from Boston, New York, Richmond, and so on – the big cities. We would not be here if it were not for them."[65]

The pipeline companies endorsed Fulbright-Harris with enthusiasm.[66] The *Phillips* decision threatened to disrupt all their existing contracts and to force producers to withdraw into the intrastate markets. The *City of Detroit* decision (in the *Panhandle* case) had affirmed their subjugation to cost-based regulation of their own gas production. But the proposed legislation would alleviate those problems and might even curtail the worst of the indefinite escalators demanded by large producers. What more could they ask?

The independent oil and gas producers were barely satisfied with the Fulbright-Harris proposal. On behalf of the Independent Petroleum Association of America, Russell Brown urged Congress to consider the issue as a matter of principle and not be content to go halfway. The provision that authorized the FPC to supervise contract prices presented a serious threat. Brown favored its deletion. With true insight on the nature of regulation, he warned that "once you get a start on control, I don't know how you can escape enlarging it as you go on."[67]

But there was no hope of deleting that provision. Even as it stood, it dissatisfied the gas distributors and the consumers they served. The distributors had defected from the industry coalition, leaving the issue of regulation more than just polarized. As a spokesman for Consolidated Edison of New York explained, there were now a range of positions. Producers desired "complete freedom of any control." Public service commissions and municipalities favored "imposition of the same stringent type of regulation" that had long been applied to the distributing companies. The position of the distributors "lies between these two extremes."[68]

J. French Robinson, chairman of the Consolidated Gas Co. of Pittsburgh, represented this position. Because of his record of leadership in the public affairs of the gas industry, Robinson spoke with authority. In 1947, he had

[65] U.S. Congress, Senate, *Natural Gas Amendments* (1955), pp. 13, 17.
[66] U.S. Congress, House, *Natural Gas Act* (1955), pp. 394–400.
[67] U.S. Congress, Senate, *Natural Gas Amendments* (1955), pp. 275–280.
[68] U.S. Congress, House, *Natural Gas Act* (1955), p. 685.

actively supported the Rizley-Moore bill, but like Leland Olds, was forced to change his views. Then he believed "that true competition" would result in reasonable field prices. But in 1955, he testified that "events since that time had proven otherwise." He opposed the Fulbright-Harris bill as written because he thought it would "preserve existing and future contracts made by producers, whatever their terms, and whether or not they may be harmful to the public interest." Robinson urged Congress to give the FPC authority to control escalator clauses; otherwise, it would be better to "leave the Natural Gas Act as it now stands."[69]

The municipalities and state public service commissions did prefer cost-based rate regulation for the entire gas industry. The courts had provided for such regulation, and these spokesmen for the perceived consumer interest were nearly unanimous in their opposition to any legislative amendment of the Act. At the heart of this coalition was a Mayor's Committee of 50 big-city mayors that included New York's Robert Wagner and Chicago's Richard Daley. These urbanites were backed by many of their congressmen as well.[70]

The interests of coal-producing states represented still another position. Senator Harley Kilgore of West Virginia sponsored an amendment that would require end-use controls on natural gas. This had the support not only of the coal industry, but of eastern railroads and organized labor. Despite this coalition, coal seemed not to have an effective voice.

The Commerce committees of both houses made several changes in the Fulbright-Harris bill to address the concerns of distributors. But these only alienated independent producers and did little to mitigate the opposition of consumer advocates. The lengthy and emotional floor debates again focused on charges of "giveaway" and "special interests." The bill's opponents claimed that its passage would defeat Democrats in the 1956 elections. Nonetheless, early in 1956, a slim majority of Republicans and southern Democrats passed the Fulbright-Harris bill in both houses, accepting it as the only reasonable compromise.

On the day of the Senate vote, Francis Case, Republican of North Dakota, made a statement that precipitated a presidential veto. According to Case, a lobbyist for the oil industry had tried to bribe him with a $2,500 cash campaign contribution. The lobbyist, working for the bill's passage, had learned that Case was undecided and he apparently hoped to tip the balance.[71] This revelation evidently stirred real concern in the White House. Eisenhower had never explicitly endorsed the Fulbright-Harris bill, much less lobbied for it. In general terms, however, he had supported the need for legislation "of that type" that would be consistent with the recommendations of his Cabinet Committee. Case's charges further excited the bill's opponents. The President, in a discus-

69 U.S. Congress, Senate, *Natural Gas Amendments* (1955), pp. 1266, 1273. The schism between distributors and producers explains why the American Gas Association, with members in both camps, did not participate in the deregulation controversy.
70 U.S. Congress, House, *Natural Gas Act* (1955), p. 323.
71 For a thorough discussion of this affair, see Robert Engler, *The Politics of Oil* (Chicago: University of Chicago Press, 1961), pp. 405–412.

sion with his cabinet, sought assurances that the bill would adequately "protect the consumer." Although his advisors disagreed on that point, there was a consensus that given the circumstances, the Administration should veto the bill in order to avoid demagogic recriminations of the Republican Party as the party of "Big Business."[72]

The President delivered his veto on February 17, 1956. In a brief, carefully worded statement, he noted his agreement with the bill's "basic objectives," but also remarked that any new legislation "should include specific language protecting consumers in their right to fair prices."[73] During the next five years, however, the Eisenhower administration never did sponsor natural gas legislation and only maintained a vague commitment to legislation "reconciling the interests of producers and suppliers with those of consumers."[74] Unless urban consumers plainly needed deregulation, it scarcely made sense for the Republican Party to take the blame.

The absence of economics

The Fulbright-Harris bill and its veto by President Eisenhower marked the last substantive effort by Congress to resolve the problems of gas regulation until crisis was at hand in 1976. In the interim, the failings of regulation by the Federal Power Commission were certainly not due to an earlier generation's ignorance that serious problems and inherent contradictions existed. In the decade between Ross Rizley's first bill and Eisenhower's veto, every branch of the federal government and every sector of the industry had investigated and debated the issues of gas regulation nearly to exhaustion. Why, then, could no rational solution be obtained? That the problems were truly difficult is scarcely an adequate answer, nor does it suffice to conclude that the interests of producers and consumers were irreconcilable. To the extent that there is an answer, it is obviously a complex one that would seem to include problems of economics, ideology, and the political process.

What about economics? It is worth noting that academic economists were absent throughout the entire regulatory controversy. Hindsight suggests that their presence would not necessarily have added clarity or hastened resolution of the issues. But their absence is indicative of the rudimentary state of understanding that prevailed with regard to the economics of both regulation and of non-renewable resources. Indeed, there were scarcely any empirical data on the effects of cost-based pricing for pipeline-producers or overall field prices, or

[72] Minutes of the Cabinet Meeting, February 13, 1956, Box 6, Whitman File, Cabinet Series, DDEPL.

[73] "Presidential Message, February 17, 1956," Box 726, file 140–C, White House Official File, DDEPL.

[74] Acting Secretary of the Interior to Oklahoma Independent Petroleum Association, March 11, 1960, Box 726, file 140–C, White House Official File, DDEPL. Also, in 1957, the Administration urged that another Harris bill be amended to include explicit controls of indefinite escalators and clearer authority for the FPC to determine and use the "reasonable market price" provision. On this point, see U.S. Congress, House, Committee on Interstate and Foreign Commerce, *Natural Gas Act – Regulation of Producers' Prices* (85th Cong., 1st Sess.), May 1957, pp. 29–89.

the relationship between rate of return and investment, or the effects of regulatory lag with respect to interest rates and inflation. There were arguments, but no hard data, on the effects of price regulation on demand for gas or on interfuel substitution. The notions of marginal cost and marginal pricing were completely missing from both the regulatory and legislative dialogues.

Worse still, there was no clear understanding, much less consensus, on the economic *purpose* of regulation. Everyone agreed that regulation was necessary to "protect" consumers in the absence of pure competition, but to what end? In the case of gas producers, should it seek to duplicate the market mechanism, or strive for maximum technical efficiency, or merely backstop to protect against obvious abuses? Few participants in the controversy sincerely believed that independent producers really were utilities, but many still demanded that cost-based regulation be applied to them.

Conflicting ideologies, nearly as muddled as the economics, also contributed to the political morass. Businessmen in the oil and gas industry constantly touted the merits of "free enterprise," but sometimes seemed to forget its meaning. Industry's idea of free enterprise did not encompass price cutting in times of excess supply, or the contractual demands of sellers in a seller's market, or for that matter, prorationing. At the other extreme, consumers and their advocates were unwilling to accept any link between supply and price. They viewed natural gas as a physical endowment and treated its price as an independent variable that merely reflected the greed and profitability of big business.

Economic and ideological confusion was aggravated by the relationship between business and government in this political process. In both the Truman and Eisenhower episodes, aggressive industry strategies contributed to the escalation of conflict beyond relatively contained disputes of the intrafuel and intra-governmental varieties to heated and irrational disputes pitting business against the public. In the first instance, the relatively united gas industry went for "all the marbles" in the Rizley-Moore bill, offering no solace for consumers, conservationists, or the coal industry. When that evoked limited opposition, the mistake was compounded by the heavy-handed response of destroying the career of Leland Olds. After that, compromise was no longer feasible as important regulatory problems got lost in the larger contest between the "people" and the "interests." In the Eisenhower period, the fight over deregulation was tinged from the start by the residue of previous animosity. This time the gas producers recognized the need for compromise, but held fast to their escalators and thus alienated the distribution sector. Its opposition gave renewed strength to the consumer advocates and again the issue escalated into the politics of business reform.

Since the natural gas industry, its customers, and their legislative representatives were unable to make the process of policy work, the responsibility for solving the problems of gas regulation again devolved onto the adjudicatory mechanisms of the Commission and the courts. By that default, the perceived problems of price and distributive equity were soon to become real problems of supply.

5. Oil imports: the failure of voluntarism

The postwar availability of foreign oil at nearly half the price of domestic supplies caused a major disruption to existing energy markets. Not only did it foreclose the potential market for synthetic fuels, but beginning in 1949, and for the next 20 years, it created a dilemma for the American political economy.

Since foreign oil was so much cheaper than domestic, it served the short-term interests of American consumers. Dependence on foreign oil, however, posed a problem for national security. In the long run, it could foster conservation of domestic reserves. But in the short-run event of geopolitical or military crisis, would domestic production capacity then be adequate? The perceived need for a U.S. presence in the Middle East and reasonable control of its oil resources by U.S. multinational firms confounded the dilemma. Since retention of their concessions depended on constantly increasing their output, those companies were invariably under pressure to increase deliveries of oil to the United States, the world's largest and fastest growing market.

As real as this dilemma was, it amounted to an allegory for a protracted conflict among interest groups that were competing for market share during a period of energy glut and declining prices. While cabinet task forces, the Office of Defense Mobilization, and the White House deliberated over the security implications of growing oil imports, *ad hoc* coalitions of independent producers, wholesale and retail jobbers, crude-long and crude-short domestic majors, the international companies, and the coal industry jockeyd for policies that would ensure market share and price maintenance. It was this process, rather than security planning, that determined the public policy outcome.

The interplay between the national security debate and the interest group conflict precipitated several attempts at voluntary cooperation on oil imports. But because of intense intra-industry differences, the normal mechanisms by which business and government interacted, such as the National Petroleum Council and the American Petroleum Institute, were unable to resolve the problem. Instead, government provided a coordinating function that became increasingly structured and which, after each successive failure of voluntarism, took on more and more of the attributes of regulation. That is what this chapter is about.

91

The postwar surge of foreign oil

This was not the first time oil imports had become enough of a problem to warrant intervention by the federal government. In 1932, the domestic oil industry, deep in a recession caused by stagnant demand and the vast discoveries in East Texas, convinced the government to impose a tariff of 21 cents per barrel. That tax brought an immediate reduction of oil imports and incidentally hastened Mexico's nationalization of its American-owned oil industry.

Although oil supplies were tight during World War II, domestic producers remained wary of imports, concerned that the end of the war would bring about a resurgence of them. In 1945, the Petroleum Industry War Council adopted a "Petroleum Policy for the United States" that anticipated the import problem. Its carefully worded resolution, an effort to satisfy the interests of domestic and international producers – as well as those of national security – remained the industry's official policy for the next two decades. The resolution said that "it should be the policy of this nation to so restrict amounts of imported oil so that such quantities will not disturb or depress the producing end of the domestic petroleum industry." Imports should be limited to the amount "absolutely necessary to augment our domestic production when it is produced under conditions consonant with good conservation practices."[1]

Ironically, a severe shortage of marketable petroleum, as mentioned earlier in connection with synfuels, plagued economic recovery during the first three years after the war. Tankers, drilling equipment, pipelines, and construction materials were scarce. As a result, it was difficult for oil producers to repair and expand output that had been depleted by overproduction during the war. This supply condition had some immediate effects that precipitated the oil import "problem." After wartime controls were lifted, oil prices doubled. This stimulated an increase in exploratory drilling and development of domestic production capacity; domestic production jumped 16 percent between 1946 and 1948.[2] Meanwhile, the Truman administration had asked the international oil companies to increase their imports to the United States as quickly as possible. They did so willingly, entering into long-term tanker contracts and expanding east coast refineries.[3] These actions helped alleviate the heating oil crisis, but

[1]   Petroleum Industry War Council, "A Petroleum Policy for the United States," October 24, 1945, (Wash., D.C.: n.p., 1945), p. 3.
[2]   U.S. Congress, House, Select Committee on Small Business, *Hearings: Aspects of Foreign Oil Imports on Independent Domestic Producers* (81st Cong., 2nd Sess.), April 1950, pt. 3, p. 670.
[3]   U.S. Department of the Interior, Oil and Gas Division, "Report on the Supplies of Coal and Petroleum Products in the U.S. with Suggestions for Government Action to Make Proper and Necessary Supplies Available," April 1948, in Office of the Secretary of the Interior, Central Classified Files, 1947–1953; Box 3177, File 1-322, pt. 5, Record Group 48, National Archives, Washington, D.C. Also, J. F. Drake, chairman, Gulf Oil Corporation, "Statement on Oil Imports at Meeting of National Petroleum Council, January 26, 1950," in Department of the Interior, National Petroleum Council files, file 017, 1950, pp. 3–5. Drake describes how the Committee on Military and Government Petroleum Requirements agonized over the need for additional crude oil during 1947–48, and that representatives of the Army, Navy, and Air Force "emphasized the urgency of their needs." In response, Gulf committed itself to a 30,000-barrel-per-day enlargement of its Philadelphia refinery and signed orders for $40 million worth of tankers.

left a residue of permanently expanded imports which shortly came to plague domestic producers.

The period of fuel shortage had punctuated a general preoccupation with preparedness that was a legacy of the recent war and a growing concern of Cold War mentality. In January 1947, the Special Committee Investigating Petroleum Resources, headed by Senator O'Mahoney, issued its report on the situation. This was the same report that urged bold action on synthetic fuels. The committee concluded that "the reserves within our own borders are more likely than not to constitute the citadel of our defense." It followed that "nothing should be done to weaken the productive capacity" of the domestic petroleum industry.[4] A year later, the National Security Resources Board produced a draft position-paper that suggested the need to maintain a hemispheric production capacity equal to the anticipated requirements for military and civilian purposes. To do so, Venezuela, Mexico, and Canada would have to cooperate with U.S. producers and prorationing authorities to restrict oil output "to a rate lower than the most efficient rate." This would create "a military stockpile in the ground" of one million barrels per day of spare capacity. This paper was never published, however, for when domestic producers learned of it, they were appalled by its financial and political implications. Indeed, such a policy would have been extremely costly for the producers and would have imposed U.S. security obligations on hemispheric neighbors.[5]

Another entrant in the policy debate was Yale's Eugene Rostow, who published a widely read and controversial study entitled, *A National Policy for the Oil Industry*, early in 1948. Rostow's thesis was that the oil industry was monopolistic and in need of radical restructuring. He proposed that market-demand prorationing be abolished and that importation of foreign oil be encouraged as a means of putting competitive pressure on the domestic price structure.[6] This proposal evoked considerable sympathy among independent jobbers and retailers, not to mention consumer advocates. But it shocked and angered the oil establishment.[7]

With the issue of oil policy open to public debate, Julius Krug, the Secretary of the Interior, decided to involve the National Petroleum Council, to obtain "the wisdom and experience of the industry."[8] The Council agreed to make a

[4] U.S. Congress, Senate, Special Committee Investigating Petroleum Resources, *Investigation of Petroleum Resources in Relation to the National Defense: Final Report* (80th Cong., 1st Sess.), Report No. 9 (Wash., D.C., 1947), p. 28.

[5] George A. Hill, Jr. to Alfred Jacobsen, October 9, 1948, file 019, "Committee on National Oil Policy," NPC/DOI, 1948.

[6] Eugene V. Rostow, *A National Policy for the Oil Industry* (New Haven: Yale University Press, 1948).

[7] During the National Petroleum Council's meeting in April 1948, Rostow's book was subjected to vehement criticism. Barney Majewski, an executive of a large midwestern independent oil company, noted that "every time a louse grows up he comes from the East." Although Majewski and others urged that the Council attack Rostow, cooler heads agreed that it was beyond the NPC's charter to do so, and that the American Petroleum Institute should take care of it; NPC, Meeting Transcript, April 15, 1948, NPC/DOI, 1948, pp. 90–96.

[8] J. Krug to W. Hallanan, July 3, 1948, file 019, Committee on National Oil Policy, NPC/DOI, 1948.

Table 5-1. *Oil imports into the United States, 1949*

Crude oil	Barrels per day
Colombia	31,364
Curacao and Aruba	10,934
Iran	3,033
Iraq	934
Kuwait	52,269
Mexico	16,529
Saudi Arabia	43,406
Venezuela	265,975
Total	424,444
Refined products	
Distillate fuel oils	4,712
Residual fuel oils	203,261
Other	8,038
Total	217,001

Source: U.S. Congress, House Select Committee on Small Business, *Hearings – Effects of Foreign Oil Imports on Independent Domestic Producers* (81st Congress, 1st Sess.), May 1949, pt. 1, p. 16.

general study of oil policy, knowing that internal consensus might be difficult to achieve. The 24-member subcommittee responsible for producing the report reflected an unusual balance among international and domestic producers, majors and independents, and wholesale and retail jobbers. Its statement said that "the nation's economic welfare and security require a policy on petroleum imports which will encourage exploration and development efforts in the domestic industry." Together with other pertinent factors, "the availability of petroleum from domestic fields produced under sound conservation practices" should determine "if imports are necessary and the extent to which imports are desirable."[9]

Notwithstanding this agreement, oil imports rose so dramatically that the United States became a net importer for the first time in the very year the Council published its report. Charles Roester, a Texas independent, cynically commented that the majors had put forward a "fine, sound, statesmanlike problem – but they exceeded that program to the point that it was necessary for the State of Texas on January 1st [1949] to cut its production 700,000 barrels a day."[10]

[9] National Petroleum Council, *A National Oil Policy for the United States* (Wash., D.C., 1949), p. 19.
[10] National Petroleum Council, Meeting Transcript, April 27, 1949, NPC/DOI, 1949, p. 40.

Table 5-2. *U.S. imports of crude oil and refined products by 11 principal importing companies, 1948 and 1950 (estimated)*

Importing company	Average year 1948	Average second six months, 1950 (estimated)	Percentage change
Standard Oil Co. (New Jersey)	184,300	236,500	+28
Gulf Oil Corp.	83,045	105,000	+26
The Texas Co.	16,977	66,000	+289
Socony-Vacuum Oil Co.	57,261	73,000	+27
Shell Caribbean Petroleum Co. (formerly Asiatic Petroleum Corp.)	9,798	82,200	+739
Atlantic Refining Co.	24,482	62,515	+155
Standard Oil Co. (Indiana)	25,414	45,417	+79
Sinclair Oil Corp.	24,595	50,683	+106
Standard Oil Co. (California)	13,273	32,979	+148
Shell Oil Co.	5,947	13,835	+132
Cities Service Co.	18,446	13,295	−28
Total 11 Companies	463,538	781,424	+69
All other imports	50,462	50,148	−1
Total imports	514,000	831,572	+62

Note: Barrels per day.
Source: U.S. Congress, House Select Committee on Small Business, *Hearings – Effects of Foreign Oil Imports on Independent Domestic Producers* (81st Congress, 1st. Sess.), May 1949, pt. 1, p. 27.

Mr. Roester did not exaggerate much. As of January 1949, oil imports were increasing at a rate of 25 percent a year. Declining exports amplified the net effect of this development, resulting in an excess of supply over domestic demand of some 300,000 barrels per day. Ernest Thompson, chairman of the Texas Railroad Commission, noted that the daily average import volume of 643,000 barrels in May of 1949 corresponded "almost exactly with the reduction of Texas allowables" during the preceding six months.[11] Seven countries and 11 companies were responsible for most of this inflow (see Tables 5-1 and 5-2). These developments not only caused a temporary revenue loss for domestic producers, but would allegedly contribute to a lasting transfer of market share from independent producers to the international majors – a sure sign of concentration and monopoly.[12]

[11] U.S. Congress, House, Select Committee on Small Business, *Hearings: Effects of Foreign Oil Imports on Independent Domestic Producers* (81st Cong., 1st Sess.), May 1949, pt. 1, p. 958, and *Aspects of Foreign Oil Imports*, pp. 7, 46.
[12] U.S. Congress, House, *Effects of Foreign Oil Imports*, p. 94.

In a theoretical market economy, the normal response to excess supply would be a decline in price and curtailment of marginal producers. But in the political economy of the United States, the sequence of events was quite different. First, state prorationing agencies reduced allowable production so that imports might be absorbed without affecting the price structure. This was the action to which Thompson alluded. Then, domestic producers, whose legal production rate was thereby reduced to only 17 days a month, raised an immediate hue and cry for their representatives to do something about the situation. Mail and telegrams from independent operators, lawyers, chambers of commerce and various hangers-on swamped the offices of Senators Lyndon Johnson and Tom Connally, Congressmen Lindley Beckworth, John Lyle, and Wright Patman, and of course, President Harry S. Truman.[13]

The correspondence sizzled with discord in the oil industry – the independents' deep distrust of the major companies. For example, Tex Willis, an oil geologist from Dallas, asked if Senator Johnson were "going to be able to do anything for us independent oil suckers on that foreign oil that has destroyed the market for two billion dollars worth of Texas independent oil this year?" Tex felt there was "no sense in bankrupting every independent oil man in Texas for a few Arabian princes and because Gene Holman's Standard Oil of New Jersey claims they need the money."[14] Alf Landon, the Republican governor of Kansas and an oilman who had run for president against Franklin D. Roosevelt in 1936, urged President Truman to clamp an immediate quota on imported oil. It would not be healthy, warned Landon, "if crude oil imports into this country are allowed to reach a volume which breaks the present price of domestic crude."[15]

Of all the groups demanding relief from oil imports, the Independent Petroleum Association of America (IPAA) was probably the most influential. Although its concern was the same as Landon's – that foreign oil "would break our prices" – the IPAA couched its position in the rhetoric of national security and monopoly. "We came out with a strong statement," explained the Association's president, that "Middle East oil could not be defended in time of war, that these fields were only six hours bombing time from Russia, and that the companies who owned these fields were in effect a monopoly."[16] On this basis, the IPAA formed an Import Policy Committee to lobby the Senate for an amendment to the Reciprocal Trade Agreement Act, which was pending in Congress. The amendment would limit oil imports to five percent of domestic consumption. In the meantime, IPAA officials went to New York to discuss voluntary import reductions with the major companies.

---

[13] Collections of these letters can be found in LBJ Papers, U.S. Senate Legislative Files, Boxes 216–217, 252, 260, and 289, LBJPL; Harry Truman Papers, Official File, Box 273, HTPL; and Box 3177, NA/RG48.

[14] H. P. Willis to L. B. Johnson, September 7, 1949, Senate Legislative File, Box 217, LBJPL.

[15] A. Landon to H. Truman, February 2, 1949, Official File, Box 273, file no. 56, HTPL.

[16] Fred Shields, president, Independent Petroleum Association of America, "Remarks Before the Mid-Year Meeting of the West Central Texas Oil and Gas Association," Cisco, Texas, June 29, 1949, p. 3.

Neither strategy proved very successful. Only Shell and Jersey Standard agreed to curtail their imports, but maintained their commitment for less than three months. The Senate passed the trade bill without the amendment.[17] The Truman administration had little sympathy for this first wave of protectionism from the domestic petroleum industry. The White House was still preoccupied with resource and material shortages at home, and abroad, with the reconstruction of Europe and Cold War diplomacy. Maintenance of a healthy domestic industry was important, but so were free trade and diplomatic obligations to American allies. In this context, restrictive amendments to the trade act were deemed counter-productive.[18]

Despite the Administration's studied indifference, the oil import "problem" wouldn't go away. Throughout 1949 and 1950, the total volume of imports rose dramatically while the regulated output of domestic producers continued to decline. In a 1950 report, the National Petroleum Council acknowledged that oil imports were indeed hurting domestic producers. Its members subscribed to a policy that imports should "supplement" but not "supplant" domestic output.[19] But how was that to be achieved?

The international companies, meanwhile, cast the problem as a temporary phenomenon. A brief recession had caused domestic demand to level off, while European markets were absorbing less oil than expected because of the United Kingdom's sterling-dollar crisis.[20] And in defense of imports, the international companies turned the national security argument on end. Given the rate of domestic depletion, imports would be needed in the long run. If depletion were to continue unchecked, argued the chairman of Texaco, "our national security would certainly be put in jeopardy."[21] By extension, this long-run viewpoint led

[17] *Ibid.*, 3–4, 9–10.
[18] J. Krug to T. Connally and to L. B. Johnson, February 1949, and to L. Beckworth, March 29, 1949, Box 3177, file 1–322, pt. 7, NA/RG48; also, Staff Memorandum for the President, "Governor Landon's Letter of February 2 on Petroleum Imports and Domestic Petroleum Development," May 1949, Official File, Box 273, file no. 56, HTPL.
[19] National Petroleum Council, "A Report of the Committee on Petroleum Imports," January 26, 1950 (Wash., D.C., 1950), p. 5.
[20] The U.K. had too little foreign exchange to support the value of the Pound Sterling. The British, therefore, discriminated against buying from American oil companies in favor of Shell and British Petroleum. So serious was the foreign exchange situation that the Economic Cooperation Administration, the agency which managed Marshall Plan funds, actually cooperated in the discrimination, exacerbating the distrust of U.S. foreign policy by independent domestic producers. Walter Levy, "Address to the National Petroleum Council," April 27, 1949, in Meeting Transcript file, NPC/DOI, 1949. In a discussion following Levy's presentation, A. Jacobson, the president of Amerada Petroleum, expressed the independent's view of the ECA and the sterling-dollar problem as follows: "Here is a man in Europe who has a nice little five-room house, and the house was destroyed by war. Then we say, that is a shame, and we ought to help you. We will fix it up. We will restore your house. But we don't build him a nice little five-room house. We build him a 30-room mansion instead." In helping develop Europe's oil capacity, Jacobson complained, "We are giving her so much that we are really placing them in a preferred position as against the American companies who have to operate abroad at their own expense" (transcript, p. 70).
[21] Quoted in U.S. Congress, House, Select Committee on Small Business, Subcommittee on Imports, *Report No. 2344*, "Effects of Foreign Oil Imports on Independent Domestic Producers" (81st Cong., 2nd Sess.), June 1950, p. 62.

Table 5-3. *U.S. petroleum reserves, productive capacity, production, total demand, reserve capacity, and imports*

Year	Proved reserves of petroleum liquids at year end (millions of bbls.)	Productive capacity of all petroleum liquids	Production of all petroleum liquids	Total demand	Total imports	Ratio of capacity to production	Ratio of capacity to demand
1940	21,150	4,945	3,849	3,981	229	22.2	19.5
1946	24,037	5,230	5,068	5,331	377	3.1	-1.9
1947	24,742	5,590	5,450	5,902	437	2.5	-5.6
1948	26,821	5,950	5,921	6,143	514	0.5	-3.2
1949	28,378	6,460	5,476	6,130	645	15.2	5.1
1950	29,536	6,980	5,906	6,812	850	15.4	2.4
1951	32,193	7,500	6,719	7,475	844	10.4	0.3
1952	32,958	7,950	6,867	7,712	952	13.6	3.0
1953	34,383	8,471	7,112	8,005	1,034	16.0	5.5
1954	34,805	9,096	7,027	8,108	1,052	22.7	10.7
Change 1948–1954	7,984	3,146	1,106	1,965	538		
Average annual % change	4.4	7.3	2.9	4.7	12.7		

Note: Thousands of barrels per day.
Source: National Petroleum Council, "Report of the NPC's Committee on Petroleum Imports," May 5, 1955 (NPC/DOI, 1955), p. 8.

logically to the importance of maintaining the foreign concessions controlled by American companies. And this could not be done, warned Gulf Oil's president, "if ours were a policy of turning oil imports on and off like a faucet."[22]

As a fall-back position, all of the international majors agreed that if imports were indeed excessive, the only sensible way to control them was by voluntary action among importers. Government intervention of any kind could only result in bureaucratic inefficiency and market distortions.

Gulf Oil, the second largest importer, took the initiative by announcing a voluntary reduction for the first quarter of 1950 of 12,000 barrels per day beneath its crude oil import volume for the last quarter of 1949. If others followed suit, Gulf would plan future increases according to the growth of total domestic demand.[23] This at least offered some encouragement to those industry leaders who eschewed an adversarial solution to the import problem. "There is an answer," said William Boyd, president of the American Petroleum Institute. "It is a question of statesmanship and doing something before the door is opened, and the horse gets away and something else happens."[24] This sentiment was widely shared, even by critics of the oil importers. Representative Wright Patman's committee on small business, in its exhaustive investigation of the import problem, concluded that the best solution would be a balance achieved by the "independent intelligence" of the oil community, rather than imposition by Congress of "crippling limitations" that could sap the vitality of an essential industry.[25]

But this experiment in voluntarism was not put to a test for another three years. When North Korean troops crossed the 38th parallel to invade South Korea in June 1950, the oil import problem was suspended. The Korean War stimulated both military and domestic demand for fuels, especially diesel oil, gasoline, and aviation fuel. As early as August 1950, the Texas Railroad Commission raised production allowables, Congress approved the organization of a Petroleum Administration for Defense, and the international majors were scrambling to increase foreign production and to find as many tankers as possible.

Oil glut and interfuel protectionism

Mobilization for the Korean conflict initially did absorb some of the spare capacity that had so agitated domestic oil producers. But it also stimulated a spurt of domestic exploration and a permanent increase of oil imports. Excess capacity was on the rise again by 1952, and prorationing authorities began reducing allowable production. Table 5-3 summarizes the relative growth rates of demand, domestic production, and imports. Two figures stand out as obvious sources of political conflict; the growth of imports exceeded that of do-

22 U.S. Congress, House, *Aspects of Foreign Oil Imports* (November 1949), pt. 2, pp. 342–343.
23 J. F. Drake, "Statement on Oil Imports," January 26, 1950.
24 NPC, Meeting Transcript, January 26, 1950, NPC/DOI, 1950, p. 67.
25 U.S. Congress, House, *Report No. 2344*, p. 148.

Table 5-4. *Postwar economic effects of foreign residual oil imports, 1942–1952*

Year	Residual imports (millions of coal-equivalent tons)	Bituminous coal revenue loss	
		Value per ton	Amount (millions)
1946	10.6	$3.44	$36.9
1947	13.0	4.16	54.2
1948	12.8	4.99	63.8
1949	17.9	4.88	87.3
1950	28.8	4.84	139.4
1951	28.6	4.92	140.7
1952	30.8	4.88	150.5

Source: National Coal Association, "Submission to the President's Commission on Foreign Economic Policy," November 1953, Box No. 25, Hearing Presentation File, Dwight D. Eisenhower Library, Abilene, Kansas, p. 21 and Appendix 1.

mestic production by a factor of six, and spare productive capacity, already high in 1952, doubled by 1954. By the end of that year, Texas wells were allowed to produce only 14 days each month.

Crude oil imported from the Middle East was the newest problem, but not yet the worst. Residual oil, imported for the most part from Venezuela, had begun to penetrate industrial markets on the East Coast. This fuel, the heaviest fraction in the refining process, competed directly with bituminous coal. Because of its low value relative to transportation costs, it was not competitive in European markets. But distributors on the east coast of the United States were an ideal market for refineries in Venezuela to dump their residual for some marginal gain. This development occurred in the midst of the coal industry's collapse.

Since 1947, domestic coal output had declined 6.6 percent annually, primarily because of competition from cheap natural gas and the loss of railroad and shipping markets to dieselization. Table 5-4 indicates the coal industry's view of how residual imports were contributing to this disaster. As early as 1950, the National Bituminous Coal Advisory Council had completed a study of oil imports for the Secretary of the Interior. That report alleged that imported residual was being dumped intentionally, as evidenced by its 50 percent drop in price during 1949, and its successful invasion of coal's industrial markets. Drawing on the national security argument, the coal council warned that in the event of war, east-coast industries would be cut off from their fuel supplies, and the coal industry could not be mobilized quickly enough to replace it.[26]

[26] National Bituminous Coal Advisory Council, "Report of Petroleum Imports Committee," March 1, 1950, in NPC Meeting Transcript File, January 1, 1950, NPC/DOI, 1950, pp. 13–17.

Here then, were grounds for a powerful protectionist alliance between the Southwest and Appalachia, and the legislative opportunity was at hand. In 1953, the Reciprocal Trade Agreements Act again came before Congress for renewal.

The Republican Party had historically opposed reductions of tariff barriers. Since 1934, when Congress enacted the Reciprocal Trade Agreements Act, Republican opposition had been especially vocal. But Eisenhower, the first Republican president since Hoover, was determined to reverse this tradition. He stated this goal clearly in his first State of the Union message. "Trade, not aid," described the new Administration's foreign economic policy. This role reversal, however, was easier said than done; Democrats from oil and coal-producing states, along with conventional Republicans, were determined to raise some barriers.[27]

In the protracted battle that ensued, the question of imported oil was central. Richard Simpson, a Republican from Pennsylvania and a ranking member of the House Ways and Means Committee, introduced an amendment to the trade act that would put a quota on imported oil, limiting it to 10 percent of domestic production. Despite their potential, coal interests failed to mobilize their political resources effectively. Wholesale and retail marketers of residual oil were far better prepared. The New England congressional delegation was vigorously lobbied by these merchants, as well as by Venezuelan government officials, their allies in the State Department, and the oil importers themselves.[28] With this support, the Administration managed to defeat the Simpson amendment, but only by making a number of other compromises.

President Eisenhower agreed to appoint Clarence Randall, a retired steel executive, to head a blue ribbon panel on trade problems. Leaders of the coal industry, meanwhile, had learned from their experience and were better prepared to present their case to the Randall Commission. Under the leadership of Tom Pickett, a vice-president of the National Coal Association, a coalition of coal producers, railroads, and organized labor formed the Foreign Oil Policy Committee and presented a well-documented and broad-based brief against excessive importation of residual oil.

According to the Foreign Oil Policy Committee, there was a double standard for oil-product imports. The tariff on gasoline was 51 cents per barrel, but only 5 cents for residual oil. Thus, while imports of residual had increased 136 percent, imports of more valuable distillates had actually declined 18 percent. It appeared that the oil industry's doctrine of not "supplanting" domestic production did not extend to the coal industry. The coal alliance claimed that residual

---

27 This contest over trade policy is documented exhaustively in R. Bauer, I. Pool, and L. A. Dexter, *American Business & Public Policy* (Chicago: Aldine/Atherton, Inc., 1963).
28 The National Oil Jobbers Council and the Independent Oil Men's Association of New England took the lead in opposing the coal lobby. See, for example, U.S. Congress, Senate, Committee on Interior and Insular Affairs, *Hearings: Stockpile and Accessibility of Strategic and Critical Materials in the U.S. in Time of War* (83rd Cong., 1st Sess.), pt. 6, "Petroleum, Gas, and Coal," November 1953, pp. 1270–1277; also, D. M. Sullivan to S. Adams, October 26, 1954, Box 681, Official File 134–F, file F–2 Fuel Oil, DDEPL.

imports had caused job losses in the coal industry of 30 million man days; lost wages amounted to $340 million, with about the same amount lost in rail-freight revenues. The situation was so serious, claimed the coal people, that a higher tariff wouldn't help. There had to be a volumetric quota to stop foreign oil producers from their "cutthroat" ways.[29]

The petroleum industry – even the domestic sector – was still not united in its stance on oil imports. Domestic producers agreed that imports were excessive, but could not agree on the appropriate course for public policy. Most independent oilmen believed themselves committed to a "free enterprise system," in which direct intervention by the federal government was anathema. Furthermore, the larger and more secure of the independent producers were loath to call for federal controls in the fear that they might be extended to the domestic sector as well. And they hesitated to confront the international majors, to whom many of them sold their oil. Because of these various tensions, the Independent Petroleum Association of America purposely made a vague recommendation to the Randall Commission. The trade act should be modified, it said, to ensure that oil imports "will supplement U.S. oil production in a fair and equitable relationship to U.S. oil demands."[30]

The international majors flatly opposed any kind of legislated restrictions on oil imports, although they too disagreed among themselves as to the best course of action. Standard Oil of New Jersey took a relatively hard line, even suggesting that spare domestic capacity was a good thing for military security.[31] Others took a more compromising position. Sidney Swensrud, chairman of Gulf Oil, offered a "share-the-growth" formula that revealed a clear sense of the market's dynamic. "If the import curve is to serve as a *balance wheel* [emphasis added], the importers must be guided by the trend of demand." This could only be done, Swensrud concluded, "by sensitivity and awareness on their part, in the presence of similar qualities of sensitivity and awareness on the part of domestic producers and the regulatory bodies."[32]

As long as the oil industry was willing to pursue voluntary solutions, the coal industry would fail to get a quota. In 1955, when Congress again reviewed the Reciprocal Trade Agreement Act, Senator Matthew Neely, a Democrat from West Virginia, introduced an amendment identical to the Simpson bill. The

[29] National Coal Association, "Submission to the President's Commission on Foreign Economic Policy," November 1953, in Box 25, Series on Commission on Foreign Economic Policy, hearings presentation file – coal, DDEPL pp. 3, 24, and appendix pages 1, 2, and 9; also, Foreign Oil Policy Committee, Statement for the Commission on Foreign Economic Policy, Box 32, p. 11. Separate briefs in support of quotas on residual oil imports were submitted by the Norfolk & Western Railway Company, the Pennsylvania Railroad, and the United Mine Workers of America.
[30] C. H. Lyons to Clarence Randall, "IPAA Statement," December 31, 1953, Committee on Foreign Economic Policy, Box 32, hearing presentations file no. 3, DDEPL, p. 6.
[31] "A Presentation by Standard Oil Company of New Jersey to the Commission on Foreign Economic Policy," November 17, 1953, Committee on Foreign Economic Policy, Box 32, hearings presentations petroleum file no. 1, DDEPL, pp. 4, 13.
[32] Sidney Swensrud, "The Dynamics of Oil," an address delivered before the New Mexico Oil & Gas Association in Albuquerque, New Mexico, December 2, 1953 (Gulf Oil Co., corporate files, Pittsburgh, Pa.), p. 8.

Neely amendment was defeated by a narrow margin, although it did result in a significant compromise. The Office of Defense Mobilization was empowered to keep track of oil imports. If it found that national security was being injured, it could recommend that the President impose quotas.

"Industrial statesmanship"

Voluntary solutions to the problem of oil imports, said Interior Secretary Douglas McKay, required "industrial statesmanship."[33] From 1954 until 1957, various forms of industrial statesmanship were tried as alternatives to formal protectionism. But unlike a fixed quota, industrial statesmanship was a highly subjective notion.

In the fight over the trade act, the Independent Petroleum Association had not supported quotas, in part because its directors were still "hopeful that some branch of the government might call the importing companies together and ask the Attorney General's Department to give the immunity to sit down and work with each other and with the domestic producers to try to solve this problem." After all, that was the solution in the Iranian situation.[34] Lyndon Johnson commended this approach, but noted that the analogy was flawed. In the case of Iran, the cooperative solution served the interest of the international companies as well as the State Department. But in this instance, antitrust immunity would not be forthcoming, and the cost of reduced imports to each company would appear large compared to the collective benefit.[35] The senator also realized that pressure would be necessary to win the importers' cooperation. This was applied in a letter from Ernest Thompson to the presidents of the international companies and by circulation of rumors that the independents were ready to ask for a tariff.[36]

While the coal industry pressed for quotas and the oil industry tried voluntarism, the Eisenhower administration created the Cabinet Committee on Energy Supplies, already mentioned with regard to natural gas. Both the President and Secretary of State Dulles had hesitated, for fear that a cabinet review might foreshadow quotas or tariffs that would "create panic in South America" and possibly upset the Iranian settlement. Arthur Flemming, the director of the Office of Defense Mobilization, had originated the plan and assured them not to worry.[37]

Flemming was as good as his word. The committee report, released in February 1955, explicitly renounced any need for government intervention. Although it did conclude that imports of crude and residual oil should not exceed their respective proportions to domestic production as of 1954, it recommended continued voluntarism. "It is highly desirable," reported the committee, "that this be done by voluntary, individual action of those who are importing or those

33 NPC, Meeting Transcript, May 29, 1953, pp. 39–40.
34 F. W. Shield to L. B. Johnson, May 6, 1954, Senate Legislative Files, Box 252, LBJPL.
35 L. B. Johnson to F. W. Shield, May 12, 1954, Senate Legislative Files, Box 252, LBJPL.
36 M. Nixon to L. B. Johnson, June 21, 1954, Senate Legislative Files, Box 252, LBJPL.
37 Minutes of the Cabinet Meeting, July 29, 1954, Whitman File Cabinet Series, DDEPL, p. 2.

who become importers."[38] This official sanction gave industrial statesmanship a needed boost, and gave domestic producers a concrete standard on which to base their continuing private negotiations with the importers.

Officials of the Independent Petroleum Association undertook to call on each of the importing companies in person, urging "an orderly reduction of imports without the necessity of resorting to Governmental aid or legislative action."[39] Although several large importers promised to comply with the standard suggested by the President's committee, some of them worried that their current reductions might jeopardize their future market share relative to other less compliant importers.[40]

Secretary McKay, who was growing impatient with the dubious results of these private negotiations, asked the National Petroleum Council to take another look at the problem and recommend a solution. By this time, however, the import problem was too severe for the Council to fashion a consensus. In May 1955, the Council reported that domestic producers were being hurt and that the growth of imports was exceeding the growth of domestic demand.[41] The drafting committee could only urge council members to refer to the conclusions of the Cabinet Committee on Energy Supplies. Worse still, several independent producers and one international major voted against the report, and for the first time in the Council's experience, a minority report was issued (by the National Oil Jobbers Council). A disappointed Interior Secretary warned "that the oil industry, the importers, are just asking for trouble."[42]

Under the new provisions of the 1955 trade act, Arthur Flemming informed the major oil importers that they were still exceeding the "formula" recommended by the Cabinet Committee. He asked them to submit data on their current imports, together with a statement of intentions through mid-1956.[43] With this monitoring activity, Flemming hoped to provide enough pressure to encourage voluntary control efforts on the part of the importers. He started a letter-writing campaign, trying to intimidate free riders from undercutting the voluntary cutbacks of others. Next, the Office of Defense Mobilization inaugurated a system of monthly reports that gave details of the imports situation.[44] Flemming began to focus his importunacy on specific sources (e.g., Canada and the Middle East) and on particular problem markets, such as the West Coast and New England.[45]

By August 1956, it was evident that industrial statesmanship was not getting

---

[38] Cabinet Paper, "Energy Supplies and Resources Policy – Final Report of the Presidential Advisory Committee," February 26, 1955, Whitman File Cabinet Series, DDEPL, p. 3.

[39] W. Vaughey, President of the IPAA, to S. Swensrud, February 2, 1955, Gulf Oil Co. files.

[40] S. Swensrud to W. Vaughey, December 28, 1954, Gulf Oil Co. files.

[41] NPC, "Report of the National Petroleum Council's Committee on Petroleum Imports," May 5, 1955, NPC/DOI, 1955, pp. 13–14.

[42] NPC, Meeting Transcript, May 5, 1955, NPC/DOI, 1955, pp. 48, 81–91.

[43] A. S. Flemming to W. K. Whiteford, August 5, 1955, Gulf Oil Co. files.

[44] A. S. Flemming to W. K. Whiteford, September 12, 1955, October 29, 1955, and November 16, 1955, Gulf Oil Co. files.

[45] Office of Defense Mobilization, "Staff Memorandum on Oil Imports," May 7, 1956, Gulf Oil Co. files.

Table 5-5. *U.S. petroleum imports, domestic demand, and production*

Year	Total petroleum imports	U.S. domestic demand	U.S. petroleum production	Imports % of U.S. domestic demand	Imports % of U.S. production
1949	.65	5.80	5.48	11.1	11.8
1954	1.05	7.76	7.03	13.6	15.0
1955	1.25	8.46	7.58	14.8	16.5
1956	1.43	8.76	7.94	16.3	18.0
1957	1.53	8.80	7.98	17.3	19.1

Note: Millions of barrels daily.
Source: From API Statistical Bulletin, U.S. Bureau of Mines, and Platt's Oilgram News Service, in R.O. Rhodes to Wilbur Mills, February 27, 1958 (Gulf Oil Co., Pittsburgh, PA).

the desired results. The volume of imported oil had increased another 40 percent in less than two years, and the ratio of imports to domestic production had jumped to nearly 18 percent (see Table 5-5). Flemming was forced to request a 7 percent cut in the volume of imports from the Middle East. Although several of the major importers appeared to be cooperating, others continued to exceed their apportionments. New participants in the Iranian concession were trying to export more to the United States, and several third parties had begun buying "distress" oil from Middle East producers, importing it under their own logos. Canadian imports, exempted from the guidelines for diplomatic reasons, were growing very rapidly as major discoveries in Alberta had created a glut in Canada too.

It was even possible that the activities of the Office of Defense Mobilization were aggravating the situation. At least one importer suggested that Flemming's program "may have lessened the normal forces of self-control and self-discipline on the part of importers." In the absence of enforcement and publicity of non-compliance, guidelines and pressure from the government might have pushed importers "to step up their imports in order to increase their base as a protection against the possible subsequent imposition of involuntary quotas."[46] Events would confirm that this sort of hedging against future policy was the critical aspect of the free-rider problem.

Shut-in domestic oil capacity had reached two million barrels per day, and well abandonments in Texas were at record levels. With crude prices showing signs of slippage, the domestic producers finally turned their backs on industrial statesmanship. They would no longer "rely on the individual and voluntary actions of importing companies," since they "necessarily are guided in part by economics." Now, it was "the responsibility of the government to affirm and

[46] "Gulf Oil Corporation Statement Filed with the Director of the Office of Defense Mobilization in Connection with its Hearings on the Petition, dated August 7, 1956, of the Independent Petroleum Association of America, et al.," October 24, 1956, Gulf Oil Co. files, p. 15.

enforce whatever oil import policy is necessary to the national security." A coalition of 19 state and regional oil trade associations, headed by the IPAA, petitioned the Office of Defense Mobilization to take formal action on oil imports, under the national-security amendment to the 1955 Trade Act.[47]

The national securizy debate

The Suez Crisis, although it delayed action on the oil producers' petition, had a more symbolic than substantive effect on the controversy over oil imports policy. In October 1956, when fighting broke out between Israel and Egypt, the Suez Canal was closed by bomb damage. At the same time, a major crude oil pipeline in Syria was sabotaged. Although the flow of oil to Western Europe was briefly reduced by 60 percent, a quick cease fire and rapid repairs ended the emergency in less than six months. In the United States, oil imports began rising once again in April 1957.

The real impact of the Suez Crisis was to highlight the political instability of the Persian Gulf. The disruption it caused in world oil markets underscored the strategic risks of energy dependency. But the lessons of the crisis cut both ways. Oil importers cited the incident as evidence of the Middle East's importance to the United States and the need to control the oil reserves of Saudi Arabia, Kuwait, Iran, and Iraq. The Suez Crisis, coming as it did during the IPAA's petition, magnified the security implications of international oil flow.

The national-security amendment to the trade act offered no standards for measuring a threat to the national security. It merely said that if imports looked threatening, the director of defense mobilization should inform the President. If the President agreed, he was to initiate an investigation and take action appropriate to its findings. Gordon Gray, the new director of Defense Mobilization, reviewed the crude oil import data in April 1957. He reported that the amounts that importers planned to import during the remainder of the year posed a threat to national security. President Eisenhower appointed six cabinet members to serve as another Special Committee to Investigate Oil Imports.

The committee's purpose was to clarify the security issues of U.S. oil policy, not resolve the economic issues of intrafuel competition. How strong a domestic oil industry was necessary, both in the short run and for the longer term? How much spare production capacity was desirable? To what extent should oil imports contribute to stretching-out the depletion of America's domestic reserves? Were Western Hemisphere oil sources more secure than others, and how reliable were the concessions in the Middle East? Overall, what level of oil imports would maximize national security and how could that level be attained? The Special Committee discovered little if any consensus on the answers to most of these questions.

No one disagreed that a "healthy" domestic oil industry was desirable; but

---

[47] Independent Petroleum Association of America et al., "Statement of the relationship of U.S. Oil Imports to Domestic Oil Production," submitted to the Advisory Cabinet Committee on Energy Supplies and Resources Policy, August 13, 1956, in Department of the Interior, Oil and Gas Division, 1956 Administrative Files (Department of the Interior, Washington, D.C.), p. 46.

no one could agree on how "healthy" was defined. As evidence of their problems, domestic producers pointed to shut-in capacity, the growth of imports
relative to domestic production, and the need for prices to stay ahead of rising
production costs in order to encourage exploration and development. Domestic
producers generally conceded that they could "maintain operations ranging
down to roughly 85 percent of maximum efficient rates of production." This
meant that imports should not exceed 15 percent of domestic production.[48]

Oil importers cited production statistics as evidence of the domestic industry's good health. Since 1954, domestic production had increased at an annual
average rate of 6 percent. In the first three quarters of 1956, nearly nine
thousand wildcat wells had been drilled. Both of these figures represented
higher growth rates than for domestic demand.[49] Importers tried to redirect the
national security debate to the long-term problem of depletion. If there was a
performance problem in the domestic oil industry, it did not involve the rate of
activity, but declining yield. Although more wells were being drilled, net new
reserves were no longer increasing because less oil was discovered per well.
The average addition to crude reserves per oil well completed had declined 31
percent since 1948.[50]

Part of the national security puzzle involved the desirability of maintaining
special access to oil sources in the Western Hemisphere. Given the intermina-
ble political instability of the Middle East, military planners and State Department officials gave priority to imports from Canada, Venezuela, and Mexico.
But this policy had encountered two problems by 1957. Since imports from
Canada and Venezuela were growing so fast, domestic producers were opposing an exemption. Furthermore, the international companies with large concessions in the Middle East complained that such a policy was discriminatory and
short-sighted. As a spokesman for Gulf Oil put it, "The proud and newly
awakened nationals of Middle Eastern countries are certain to take offense at
any discrimination. This could lead to the loss of our strategic position in the
Arabian Peninsula."[51]

With considerable insight, the importers argued that the price of protectionism in the fifties might well be an energy crisis in the seventies. A
spokesman for Gulf made the following statement:

Presently, the oil industry is in a period of surplus supply of crude oil. Ten to twenty
years from now, however, the demand for petroleum products will have become so great
that a new crisis may very well develop – a crisis of world-wide oil shortage. If we do not
now establish firm, long-range commitments for crude oil with other nations, we will be
not only a "have not" but a "can't get" nation. Such a catastrophe might well relegate us
to the category of a "has been."[52]

---

[48] IPAA et al., "Statement of the Relationship of U.S. Oil Imports to Domestic Oil Production,"
p. 34.
[49] S. A. Swensrud to A. S. Fleming, September 18, 1956, Gulf Oil Co. files, pp. 8–9; also, David
T. Staples, "Statement of Tidewater Oil Company to the Office of Defense Mobilization," October 15, 1956, Fred Seaton Papers, Box 4, Oil Import Clipping File, DDEPL, pp. 7–8.
[50] *Ibid.*, 12.
[51] R. O. Rhoades to H. Boggs, November 12, 1957, Gulf Oil Co. files, p. 10.
[52] R. D. McGranahan, vice president, Gulf Oil Co., "Address on the Importance of the Reciprocal Trade Agreements Act," March 9, 1958, Gulf Oil Co. files, p. 13.

The importers' arguments for a long-run view fell on deaf ears. The Special Committee considered and discarded the idea of a national storage system to stockpile imported oil as too impractical. It rejected the idea of government subsidies for shut-in domestic capacity as too costly. And it dismissed the simple alternative of encouraging imports as a means of conserving domestic resources.

Concern for rapid mobilization in the event of a short-term, military emergency prevailed. Under any of the alternatives, according to the committee, the nation would suffer "delays, waste, and inefficiency," the liabilities of a static mobilization base. Since the Committee recognized that the import problem had "important foreign policy" aspects, it concluded that the "national security requires the maintenance of some reasonable balance between imports and domestic production." This was a foregone conclusion.[53]

The real issue was the definition of "reasonable."[54] The Special Committee recommended to President Eisenhower that crude oil imports be formally but "voluntarily" restricted to 12 percent of domestic production except for the West Coast, where they should be restricted to the difference between demand and local supply. This ratio was based on the average level of crude imports between 1954 and 1956. It exceeded the level sought by some domestic producers, but was less than what importers had planned to bring in during the second half of 1957. The international majors with concessions in the Middle East could take solace from the fact that Canada and Venezuela were no longer to receive preferential treatment.

In July 1957, the President accepted this plan as the best solution to the national security dilemma. He ordered the Secretary of the Interior and the Office of Defense Mobilization to implement the plan as rapidly as possible. The Committee pointedly cautioned that mandatory controls would become necessary if voluntary compliance were not promptly attained.[55]

Last chance for voluntarism

With the national security debate presumably settled, the issue reverted to the problems of distributing market share by administrative rather than competitive means. The normal free-rider problems of cheating and non-compliance immediately reasserted themselves.

[53] Sinclair Weeks to Dwight D. Eisenhower, "Transmittal of Recommendations of the Special Committee to Investigate Crude Oil Imports," July 29, 1957, and Special Committee to Investigate Oil Imports, "Findings and Recommendations," in Fred Seaton Papers, Box 4, Oil Imports, Memos (4), DDEPL.

[54] Industry views varied widely on this point. The smallest independent producers favored something less than 10 percent of domestic production; the IPAA would accept 15 percent, and the major importers asked for 18 percent or more. See, D. Proctor to G. Gray, June 26, 1957, Gulf Oil Co. files, and P. R. Schultz, president of the Oklahoma Independent Petroleum Association, to S. Weeks, July 19, 1956, in Fred Seaton Papers, Box 5, Oil Imports, Memos (3), DDEPL, pp. 2–3.

[55] D. D. Eisenhower to Secretary of the Interior, July 29, 1957, and Special Committee, "Findings and Recommendations," pp. 12–14, Fred Seaton Papers, Box 4, Oil Imports, Memos (2), DDEPL.

Formalization of the government's role injected the program with a new subjective criterion of equity. Given prevailing suspicions that the seven biggest international companies already monopolized world crude oil production, the federal government could scarcely condone, much less regulate, a cartel for a few oil importers. It would have to provide generously for "new" importers. And since the price differential between foreign and domestic crude oil already exceeded $1.00 per barrel, there would be no end to the number of potential "new" importers. They could only be accommodated by reducing disproportionately the allotments of the "established" importing companies. If that weren't enough to ruin the program, it would at least stimulate so many exemptions and special rules that the Voluntary Oil Import Program would effectively be transformed into formal regulation, lacking only enforcement.

Most of the importers had anticipated the problem of allocating imports between new and established. New importers, like Tidewater, vigorously opposed even voluntary controls, since their limit would likely be frozen at a relatively low level. Several of these firms had recently constructed coastal refineries in an effort to establish themselves as legitimate importers before the regulatory die was cast.[56] Such strategies, of course, only hastened the onset of more formal controls. For the bona fide importers with large foreign concessions and production investments, the prospect of controls posed the opposite problem. They did not want to be penalized for their previous gestures of industrial statesmanship. So they urged that any control system be tied to "historical" (e.g., 1954) import proportions. Room for new importers, they argued, should be made from growth increments rather than out of existing import volumes. In the formula proposed by Gulf, for example, the annual increment was to be divided equally between new importers and old.[57]

The Special Committee had also anticipated this problem and recommended a formula with little sympathy for the vested interests of established importers. In order to hold imports to 12 percent of domestic production, the Committee suggested that established importers be requested to cut back their imports for 1957 by 10 percent of their average for 1954–1956. This was necessary so that small importers (as of 1954) and new importers would "have the opportunity to participate in the United States market on a basis more equitable than if the above cutback were applied to them." These companies would be allowed to import the amounts they had scheduled for the second half of 1957, if the increase didn't exceed their 1956 imports by more than 12,000 barrels per day. Importers on the Pacific Coast were allowed the amounts that each had already scheduled for the coming year.[58]

Matthew Carson, a Navy captain appointed by Interior Secretary Fred Seat-

[56] D. T. Staples, president of Tidewater Oil Co., to F. Seaton, July 10, 1957, Fred Seaton Papers, Box 5, Oil Imports, Memos (3), DDEPL. Most of these coastal refineries were designed to run according to the physical characteristics of specific foreign crude oils. This gave new importers a technical, as well as economic, excuse for demanding sufficient import allocations.

[57] D. Proctor to G. Gray, June 26, 1957, Gulf Oil Co. files.

[58] Special Committee to Investigate Crude Oil Imports, "Findings and Recommendations," pp. 11–12.

Table 5-6. *Permissible crude oil imports to United States, east of California, under cabinet committee rules published July 30, 1957*

Company	Actual imports 1956	Imports 1st half 1957	Planned imports 2d half 1957	Permissible imports 2d half 1957	Difference between planned and permissible imports
Established importers					
Atlantic	69.4	55.7	75.7	58.9	−16.8
Gulf	129.0	96.4	153.0	116.6	−41.4
Sinclair	73.5	71.5	74.6	62.2	−12.4
Socony	65.0	58.8	78.9	67.1	−11.8
Std. of Calif.	75.3	58.7	86.0	66.8	−19.2
Std. of N.J.	79.9	62.9	87.0	72.0	−15.0
Texas	64.2	56.5	74.9	54.5	−20.4
Subtotal Estab.	556.3	460.5	630.1	493.1	−137.0
New importers					
Cities Service	25.8	21.2	32.6	32.6	0
Eastern States	18.6	4.5	18.3	18.3	0
Gabriel	5.7	3.0	7.5	7.5	0
Great Northern	21.1	24.0(E)	33.0	33.0	0
International Ref.	9.2	10.0(E)	10.9	10.9	0
Lakehead	0.3	0.3(E)	0.3	0.3	0
Lake Superior	5.0	4.4	5.0	5.0	0
Northwestern	6.0	7.0(E)	10.0	10.0	0
Phillips	11.1	11.8	12.0	12.0	0
Shell	0.8	0	7.5	7.5	0
Std. of Indiana	17.8	43.3	49.4	29.8	−19.6
Std. of Ohio	1.9	0.8	8.2	8.2	0
Sun Oil	38.4	17.9	58.4	50.4	− 8.0
Tidewater	22.2	63.6	84.6	34.2	−50.4
Southwestern	2.1	1.3	2.9	2.9	0
Subtotal	186.0	213.1	340.6	262.6	−78.0
Subtotal named importers	742.3	673.6	970.7	755.7	−215.0
Miscellaneous	12.7	15.0(E)	15.0(E)	15.0(E)	
Total all importers	755.0	688.6	985.7	770.7	
West Coast	179.0	224.0	275.0	275.0	
Total U.S.	934.0	912.6	1280.7	1045.7	

Note: All figures are in thousands of b/d.
E = Estimated.
Source: Gulf Oil Co. "Abstract of the Special Cabinet Committee's Plan for the Control of Petroleum Imports," August 2, 1957 (Pittsburgh, PA), p. 4.

on to administer the voluntary program, sent out telegrams to each importer, explaining its allotment and requesting "voluntary" compliance. "Your cooperation is essential," read the message, "if such a voluntary program is to succeed and thus render consideration of other means unnecessary."[59]

Few of the recipients were pleased with their allocations. Table 5-6 shows the impact of the proposed program on each of the 22 participants. The seven established importers were no doubt dismayed that Cities Service, Sun Oil, and Standard of Indiana had been granted "new importer" status, even though they had been substantial importers since the early 1950's.[60] The data indicate that established importers had borne the brunt of prior voluntary reductions. Those that had cooperated most had damaged themselves by lowering the average on which allotments were now based. Among the new importers, Standard of Indiana and Tidewater stand out as the free riders that contributed most egregiously to the failure of industrial statesmanship. Those two, along with Sun Oil, had programmed increases in excess of the committee's limit, and would most likely resist compliance. Finally, if one compares the allotments under the new program with actual imports as of 1956, it is apparent that the formula would redistribute 10 percent of import market share from the 7 established companies to the 15 new entrants.

"Any program designed to restrict oil imports," commented one importer philosophically, "would of necessity give rise to inequities and hardship."[61] Although most of the companies agreed to comply with the Administrator's request, several appealed their initial allocation on grounds that it was discriminatory, caused particular production hardships, or penalized the company unjustly for its voluntary reductions in the base period.[62] Except for a few obvious oversights, Carson rejected these appeals because of the intense pressure from those firms that were cooperating. "Any decision permitting substantial increases," warned a spokesman for Gulf, "can only result in a chain reaction." This would force Gulf, and certainly the other majors, "to re-evaluate its earlier decision to comply with the program."[63]

The voluntary program appeared to have worked reasonably well at first. Captain Carson reported that imports, except on the West Coast, had been reduced 17 percent below the amounts originally programmed by the com-

---

[59] M. V. Carson to W. K. Whiteford, August 2, 1957, Gulf Oil Co. files.

[60] The Special Committee had defined new importers as any company that imported less than 20,000 barrels per day in 1954. Cities Service, Standard Oil Indiana, and Sun Oil had made their rapid increases in imports between 1955 and the first half of 1957.

[61] D. Proctor to M. V. Carson, September 13, 1957, Fred Seaton Papers, Box 5, Oil Imports, Memos (3), DDEPL.

[62] P. H. Bohart to W. K. Whiteford, August 21, 1957, "Memorandum Summarizing Responses to Captain Carson's Telegram," Gulf Oil Co. files. Among the established importers, Atlantic and Sinclair complained of being hurt by their previous voluntary reductions. Of the new importers, Phillips, Standard of Ohio, and Standard of Indiana complained of specific discrimination. Standard of Indiana, for example, had recently completed a coastal refinery designed to run low gravity, Venezuelan crude. It claimed to have done so on the basis of the previous policy that exempted imports of Venezuelan oil from voluntary controls.

[63] D. Proctor to M. V. Carson, September 13, 1957, Gulf Oil Co. files.

panies. This fell short of the government's goal by just 3 percent. Only 3 of the 24 participating firms had failed to cooperate, a "remarkably successful" compliance rate in Carson's view. Sun Oil had flatly refused to participate because of the program's alleged antitrust implications.[64] Tidewater exceeded its allocation by more than 100 percent without offering justification, and Eastern States imported 6,500 barrels per day too much because of a long-term purchase contract from which it could not obtain relief.

But as Carson publicly commended the cooperating companies, he complained privately to the Special Committee that without some leverage over the few cheaters, the program threatened to break down. The Pacific Coast program, as originally constituted, had already failed and been reorganized into an allocation system similar to the main program.[65]

The Voluntary Program's initial success proved to be short-lived. Throughout 1958, the domestic oil glut worsened because of a domestic recession. Domestic crude oil demand was running nearly one million barrels per day behind what it had been a year earlier. Allowable production in Texas was reduced to a mere eight days per month, leaving shut-in capacity of more than three million barrels per day. Domestic producers concluded that the voluntary quotas, based on a percent of average production during the 1954–56 base period, were too high. They urged that further reductions be made in order to re-establish the 1954 parity.[66] In March 1958, Eisenhower himself warned that "if voluntary controls do not increase allowables in Texas," the government "must go to mandatory controls."[67] These external pressures made the program's internal problems all the more unmanageable.

Even to maintain the aggregate ratio of imports to production at 12 percent, the Special Committee found it necessary to recommend another 9 percent reduction of allowable imports for the second quarter of 1958. The reduction was prorated among all of the importing companies. Additional reductions, amounting to 4 and 2 percent, were subsequently announced for the third and fourth quarters respectively.[68] To help encourage compliance, President Eisenhower signed an executive order applying the Buy American Act to the program. Companies which failed to comply would be ineligible for government contracts.[69]

---

[64] Arthur M. Johnson, *The Challenge of Change: The Sun Oil Company, 1945–1977* (Columbus: Ohio State University Press, 1983), pp. 99–124.
[65] Administrator, Voluntary Oil Import Program to Chairman, President's Special Committee to Investigate Crude Oil Imports, "Memorandum on the Status of the Voluntary Oil Import Program," January 31, 1958, in Fred Seaton Papers, Box 4, Oil Imports, Memos (1), DDEPL, p. 2.
[66] M. J. Davis, president, Humble Oil, to S. Weeks, February 11, 1958, Fred Seaton Papers, Box 4, Oil Imports, Memos (2), DDEPL.
[67] H. Chilson to F. Seaton, March 29, 1958, Fred Seaton Papers, Box 4, Oil Imports, Memos (2), DDEPL.
[68] Gulf Oil Company, "Petroleum Import Statistics Under Oil Import Control Programs by Import Periods Through 1972," July 1972, Gulf Oil Co. files, p. A–1.
[69] U.S. Department of the Interior, Oil Import Administration, "Brief History and Description of Oil Import Program," in Records of the Oil Import Administration, accession no. 72A–6599, Group 3, Box 81, U.S. Federal Records Center, Suitland, Maryland, p. 5.

More cuts made it nearly impossible to find room for newcomers and to force those importers that were not complying into line. Pressure on cooperating firms to make third-party sales and to take advantage of the program's loophole for "semi-refined" products increased. By mid-year, Carson had granted allocations to 13 newcomers, amounting to 45,000 barrels per day. Reductions of 69,000 barrels per day to offset the decline in domestic production meant a further cut of 15 percent in the allocations of older importers.

These deeper cuts created various operating pressures on the established importers. It became difficult for some to keep costly tanker fleets active and to maintain the capacity utilization of their coastal refineries at a break-even level. For the international majors with concessions in the Middle East, the cuts made it even more difficult to meet the production demands of their host governments. To relieve these pressures, several of the large companies increased their imports of "unfinished oils," a product category not covered by the Voluntary Program (this included naphtha and other distillates that required further processing), and even residual oil to be used as a feedstock for further refining in the United States. Covert sales of crude oil to some of the "newcomers" also increased.[70]

The combined effect of these external and internal pressures compelled the Special Committee and the program's administrator to promulgate increasingly elaborate "guidelines" in a vain effort to seal the cracks spreading through the dike. In June 1958, Carson issued quotas for various categories of "unfinished oil." In July, allocations for the West Coast were adjusted to make room for newcomers there too. Carson's staff conducted appeals hearings on a fortnightly basis.[71]

Still the pressure intensified. Twenty of the older importers were requesting increased allocations that amounted to 316,000 barrels per day, while 70 potential newcomers had applied for allocations totalling 491,000 barrels per day. If granted in full, these applications would result in an increase of 113 percent over the existing total of permissible imports. Even worse, noted Carson gloomily, there was no prospect of an immediate increase in domestic production.[72]

With the Voluntary Program falling apart after little more than a year, Carson, consulting the Special Committee, tried to restructure the entire program in a last-ditch effort to save it. His plan was designed to address two of the most serious political problems: The desire for administrative simplicity, and relief from the intense pressure by domestic refiners to gain access to the cheap foreign oil that was giving their competitors a significant cost advantage.[73] The proposed scheme would redistribute import quotas to every U.S. refiner in proportion to the average daily crude runs of each. The aggregate volume of permissible imports would be computed on the basis of domestic demand,

[70] *Ibid.;* also, R. O. Rhoades to M. V. Carson, November 5, 1957, Gulf Oil Co. files.
[71] Department of the Interior, "Governmental Actions Relating to Imports of Oil," n.d., Fred Seaton Papers, Box 4, Oil Imports, Memos (1), DDEPL, p. 6.
[72] M. V. Carson, Working Draft of Proposed Import Plan, September 4, 1958, Fred Seaton Papers, Box 4, Oil Imports, Memos (2), DDEPL, p. 3.
[73] *Ibid.,* p. 5.

rather than production. The Bureau of Mines would make the estimate semi-annually, and 10.1 percent of that amount would be authorized for imports and prorated among all refiners. If the total volume needed to be raised or lowered, the change would simply be distributed across-the-board. Unfinished oils would be included and the whole system would be phased-in over 18 months. The same system, but with a different aggregate percentage, would apply to the West Coast. Since this program would give inland refiners the right to import, the quotas were made non-transferrable, but the imported oil itself could be sold before actually being refined.[74]

When this proposal appeared in the September 12th *Federal Register*, with a request for comments from interested parties, the established importers were outraged. The proposal totally ignored the historic importing activities of the major international companies, along with their immense investments in tanker fleets, in foreign exploration and production, and in coastal refineries. The plan, which disregarded its original national-security rationale, seemed "primarily concerned with regulating the economics of refining and with the arbitrary realignment of competitive conditions."[75] Its objective of administrative simplicity appeared misguided to the importers. The idea of providing import allocations for inland refiners had no economic basis whatever. Most of them could not transport the crude to their refineries, and their refineries weren't designed to handle foreign crude oils anyway. Few of those inland newcomers had any intention of refining what they were permitted to import. They would merely trade it for domestic oil to those with facilities that could process it, but were restricted from importing what they needed. "The quotas," said one large importer, "would not be 'oil quotas,' but 'dollar quotas' – a subsidy from some refiners at the expense of others."[76] The plan would mean further reductions of nearly 50 percent for most of the established importers. As a voluntary program, it stood little chance of success.

When the Special Committee reviewed these comments, it realized that intrafuel conflict was too intense and fragmented for voluntary resolution. Accordingly, the Committee recommended that the Office of Defense Mobilization once again investigate the national security implications of oil imports.[77] While this investigation was under way, the Committee asked the Attorney General for his comments on the antitrust implications of various recommendations for a mandatory allocation plan.

Leo Hoegh, then director of defense mobilization, completed his investigation late in February 1959. He advised the President that crude oil and its derivatives were being imported in quantities sufficient "to impair the national security."[78] Ten days later, President Eisenhower promulgated a system of mandatory oil import quotas that remained in effect for 14 years.

[74] *Ibid.*, pp. 6–10.
[75] "Statement of Gulf Oil Corporation on Proposed Revision of Voluntary Oil Import Program," October 6, 1958, Gulf Oil Co. files, p. 1.
[76] *Ibid.*, p. 4.
[77] Department of the Interior, "Government Actions Relating to Imports of Oil," pp. 6–7.
[78] Leo Hoegh, "Memorandum for the President," February 27, 1959, in Fred Seaton Papers, Box 4, Oil Imports, Memos (1), DDEPL, p. 6.

In explanation, Eisenhower commended the "great majority" of the industry that had cooperated with the government to restrict imports. But he placed the blame for the failure of voluntarism squarely on "the actions of some in refusing to comply."[79] This explanation was politically palatable, if not entirely accurate. Still, the President's personal regret seemed sincere. For nearly a decade, Eisenhower, his predecessor, and most of the oil-industry leadership had repeatedly opted for voluntary solutions to the problem of oil imports. But voluntarism had repeatedly failed.

Apart from the national security issues, there were two fundamental problems, one economic and the other political, that ruined the succession of voluntary programs.

The real impetus for controlling oil imports came from high-cost domestic producers who tried to insulate themselves from the international market. Without controls, cheaper foreign oil would have forced down domestic oil prices and driven marginal producers out of business. Before foreign oil became available, the state prorationing agencies had managed output in order to avoid such circumstances. But once cheap oil was available anywhere in the world economy, it was irresistibly drawn into the market vacuum that prorationing had created in the United States. Maintenance of domestic prices at a level above long-run marginal costs just aggravated the problem. It stimulated domestic production and dampened demand. As long as there was a disequilibrium between domestic and foreign crude oil prices, competitive distortions would worsen.

The other critical problem, inherent in the government's involvement in the voluntary efforts, was the injection of non-economic criteria for distributive equity in the allocation process. As soon as the Office of Defense Mobilization became involved, it had to attune policy to address regional frictions, the relationship between big and small firms, and the balance between new and established importers. Once the program was formalized as a joint undertaking by business and government in 1957, these new political criteria shattered an already divided industry.

The adoption of mandatory quotas in March 1959 was the single most important energy policy in the postwar era. It ushered in a decade of stasis in policy that ignored continuing changes in energy supply and demand.

[79] White House Press Release, "Statement of the President, March 10, 1959," in Fred Seaton Papers, Box 5, Oil Import Program, DDEPL, p. 1.

Part II. Managing surplus through the politics of stasis, 1959–1968

I have today issued a Proclamation adjusting and regulating imports of crude oil and its principal products into the United States. . . . The new program is designed to insure a stable, healthy industry in the United States. . . . In addition to serving our own direct security interests, the new program will also help prevent severe dislocations in our own country as well as in oil industries elsewhere. . . .

Dwight D. Eisenhower, 1959

6. Oil import quotas

Few other regulatory schemes in America's history can match the Mandatory Oil Import Program for labyrinthine complexity, or for the distortion of markets and interest-group dissension that it caused. While managers and bureaucrats were preoccupied with the tactical politics of allocating the surplus, it simply slipped away.

This chapter examines political relationships in this major regulatory program.[1] It is not a story of a simple bilateral relations between agency and industry. Oil import regulations were determined by a host of multilateral frictions: among sectors of the industry and individual firms, between them and the Oil Import Administration (the agency that ran the program), and among various cabinet departments and congressional interest-groups that cared about the program's policies. Intrafuel and intra-governmental politics commingled to create detailed rules that affected not just the financial, logistical, and operating decisions of the companies, but in many instances, their basic corporate strategies. Each rule seemed to precipitate a score of side effects and political repercussions which, like a tar baby, resulted in a longer, more complicated chain of regulations as time went on.

From 1959 to 1973, the Mandatory Oil Import Program evolved through three phases of policy controversy. Start-up problems, and their distributional impact on different sectors of the oil industry, dominated the first phase through 1964. The focus of political conflict shifted in 1965 to quota exemptions for individual firms and the program's unanticipated effects. This lasted three years, during which the program, in the words of a White House aide, turned into "an administrative nightmare."[2] Phase three began in 1968, when widespread and intense criticism of the program forced Congress and the

---

[1] For other studies of the Mandatory Oil Import Program, see Douglas R. Bohi and Milton Russell, *Limiting Oil Imports: An Economic History and Analysis* (Baltimore: Johns Hopkins University Press, 1978); also, Kenneth Dam, "Implementation of Import Quotas: The Case of Oil," *The Journal of Law and Economics*, vol. 4, April 1971, pp. 1–60. See also, Edward H. Shaffer, *The Oil Import Program of the United States: An Evaluation* (New York: Frederick A. Praeger, Inc., 1968), and Yoram Barzel and Christopher D. Hall, *The Political Economy of the Oil Import Quota* (Stanford: Hoover Institute Press, 1977).
[2] DeVier Pierson to the President, March 23, 1968, Lyndon B. Johnson Papers, Executive, Box 19, File TA6/Oil, LBJPL.

White House to reassess it. Although President Nixon chose to maintain the quota system after 1970, he acceded to market pressures by gradually liberalizing its controls until 1973, by which time they were irrelevant anyway.

Ike's mandatory quota program

When President Eisenhower instituted mandatory oil import quotas on March 10, 1959, their stated purpose was to preserve a "vigorous, healthy petroleum industry in the United States," to insure the national security.[3] This was the same objective that had previously motivated the voluntary program. In fact, according to the President's statement, the only significant change was that the government had assumed the authority necessary to enforce compliance.

Only at the aggregate level did the Mandatory Program resemble its voluntary predecessor. The President delegated authority for import controls to the Interior Secretary who would manage the program through an Oil Import Administration within his Department. This agency would set quotas every six months for imports of crude and unfinished oils, residual oil, and refined products. Quotas were fixed separately for each of three regions. Petroleum imports into Districts I–IV, the continental United States except for the West Coast, could not exceed 9 percent of demand. (That aggregate ceiling was subsequently modified to 12.2 percent of *production*.) Within this limit, imports of refined products could not exceed their 1957 levels. The same applied to residual oil, although it was not included in the aggregate ceiling. The quota for District V, the West Coast, would be an aggregate of crude oil and refined products sufficient to fill the gap between local demand and available domestic supply. Puerto Rico, at the Oil Import Administration's discretion, would be allowed whatever imports it needed for domestic demand and export to foreign areas.

On a firm-by-firm basis, it was evident that the government's new authority had vested the quota with a tangible dollar value. To achieve "fair and equitable distribution," quotas for crude and unfinished oils were to be allocated only to refiners in proportion to their average refinery runs. Initially no company was to receive less than 80 percent of its last allocation under the Voluntary Program.[4] This scheme attempted a delicate compromise among established importers, newer importers, and refiners that had yet to import but were allegedly disadvantaged by their reliance on higher-cost domestic crude oil. It was the inland refiners that received the real windfall – quota "tickets" worth more than a dollar a barrel. Quota tickets could be traded, but not sold, evidently in the hope that barter would mask the value of the quota as well as the economic absurdity of granting it to inland refiners.

Experience with the voluntary program had convinced President Eisenhower

---

[3] Presidential Proclamation 3279, "Adjusting Imports of Petroleum and Petroleum Products into the United States," 24 *Federal Register* 1781–84, March 12, 1959.
[4] "Report of the Special Committee to Investigate Crude Oil Imports," March 6, 1959, Fred Seaton Papers, Box 5, Oil Import Program, DDEPL, p. 3.

that mandatory controls would need to be "flexibly administered." This insight was understated, to say the least. To ensure such flexibility, the Interior Secretary was allowed considerable discretion to make and modify allocations of crude oil "subject to such conditions as he may deem appropriate." To make the program responsive to hardship, error, or "other special consideration," the President created an Oil Import Appeals Board comprised of sub-cabinet representatives from the Departments of Interior, Commerce, and Defense. Besides adjusting existing allocations, the Appeals Board could grant special quotas to parties not otherwise eligible, as long as they were encompassed by the aggregate ceiling on imports.[5]

It is worth noting a number of things for which the quota program did not provide. Although the rules for crude oil seemed flexible enough, the limits on finished products and residual oil were explicit and absolute. It made no provision for independent jobbers and retailers who might wish to import their products. Industrial firms that used petroleum were not recognized as eligible importers, nor were electric utilities that had not previously imported residual oil. The criterion for prorating crude oil quotas according to refinery capacity made no special provision for small refiners that lacked economies of scale. And finally, the Program made no distinction among countries of origin. The only indication of a hemispheric preference was in the White House press release, which mentioned "informal conversations with Canada and Venezuela looking toward a coordinated approach to the problem of oil."[6]

Quotas for distributive equity

Controversies over the major distributive policies of the mandatory program dominated its implementation between 1959 and 1964. These issues generally pitted different segments of the oil industry against one another according to characteristics of region, function, timing, and size as they related to the competitive effects of the Program. Five such issues involving the government's secondary objectives were especially divisive: (1) maintaining historical quotas, (2) quota exchanges by inland refiners, (3) the sliding scale, (4) hemispheric preference, and (5) quotas for residual oil. Problems regarding these issues caused frictions between government and the oil industry to intensify, but did not break into open hostility until near the end of the 1960's. The domestic producers, although persisting in legislative efforts to reduce aggregate imports, were repeatedly forced to accept the Program's existing levels as a sufficient compromise.[7] The larger consuming public did not get involved as long as the surplus of oil kept prices constant.

[5]   *Ibid.*
[6]   White House Press Release, "Statement by the President," March 10, 1959, Fred Seaton Papers, Box 5, Oil Import Program, DDEPL, p. 1.
[7]   As part of its broader goal of trade liberalization, the Kennedy administration was determined to get a "clean" renewal of the Reciprocal Trade Agreements Act in 1962. However, domestic independent producers, organized by TIPRO and the IPAA, lobbied hard to attach the Steed–Moore amendment (also supported by the coal industry) which would restrict crude and residual oil

1. *Historic quotas*

For the dozen or so oldest and largest importing companies, loss of import market share through the programmed erosion of their historical positions was the program's worst transgression. After their experience with the Voluntary Program, none of these major importers expected to receive an exclusive franchise. The most they had hoped for was that quotas for newcomers would come out of new demand without disturbing their last allocations prior to 1959. The worst they could imagine was the proposal of late 1958 which would abandon historical positions altogether by substituting a straight allocation to refinery runs. The outcome was a compromise. The Program allowed established importers to start with 80 percent of their historical allotment. To make room for newcomers and certain exempt imports, their share would be reduced gradually until it equalled, for each company, a level proportionate to its refinery runs. At that point, the company would shift to the same standard as all other importers.

Since the alternatives advocated by the majority of their competitors were worse, most of the established importers acceded to the compromise, with varying degrees of bitterness. Under the Voluntary Program, the 7 largest historical importers, responsible for 95 percent of foreign production, had already tolerated a decline of their import share from 87 to 54 percent. The Mandatory Program's initial 20 percent cut further reduced their share to 43 percent.[8] Since Gulf Oil (in Districts I–IV) and Standard of California (in District V) were the two largest importers, they were the most aggrieved.

Gulf did not fight what was done, but vigorously opposed further reductions of its historical quota. The company cited legislative and judicial precedent from wartime and depression experiences; it even appealed to the government's sense of fairness and equity. To ignore historical positions, urged one Gulf executive, "is tantamount to a confiscation of the rights and property of those who have spent their efforts and risked their capital in finding and importing oil over many years past." Such a system would be contrary to the "principles of equity and justice upon which the traditional American method of rewarding free enterprise is based."[9] Coming from one of the Seven Sisters, this plea evoked little sympathy.

R. G. Follis, chairman of Standard Oil of California, earned a bit more sympathy by a personal plea to President Eisenhower, but to no substantive effect.[10] Secretary Seaton, in response to his complaints, chided Follis for

imports by statute to lower levels than allowed by the Mandatory Program. That effort failed in the House of Representatives by a vote of 253 to 171. Minor Jameson, vice president of the IPAA, credited the defeat to the fact that some oil state congressmen had received assurances from Kennedy officials that "administrative action would be taken to meet the oil import problem." See, Minor Jameson, Memorandum to the Members of the Independent Petroleum Association of America, June 29, 1962, Feldman Papers, Box 23, John F. Kennedy Library, Boston, Massachusetts.

[8] "Testimony of Gulf Oil Corporation," Import Hearings, Department of the Interior, Washington, D.C., May 10–11, 1961 (Gulf Oil Co., Pittsburgh, Pa.), p. 6.

[9] *Ibid.,* 8.

[10] D. D. Eisenhower to Secretary of the Interior, July 6, 1959, Whitman File, Administrative Series, Box 36, Fred Seaton (1), DDEPL.

Table 6-1. *Competitive effects on policy positions: phasing-out the historical preference*

Eleven largest East Coast refiners	Refinery capacity (1)	Quota criterion as of 1964 (2)	Difference between historical quota and refinery run criterion (2)	Policy position on historical preference (1965) (3)
Standard Oil of N.J.	804	runs	—	Abolish
Standard of Indiana	632	runs	—	Abolish
Texaco	573	runs	—	No position
Socony Mobil	463	historical	-5.5	Abolish
Gulf	443	historical	-27.7	Retain
Sinclair	403	historical	-5.3	Retain
Cities Service	260	runs	—	Abolish
Sun	201	historical	-7.2	Retain
SoCal[a]	197	historical	-18.3	No position
Atlantic	194	historical	-15.2	Retain
Tidewater	110	historical	-7.2	Retain

Note: Thousands of barrels per day.

[a] Standard Oil of California was ambivalent. It preferred the refinery runs criterion because of its dominant position in District V of a capacity of 332,000 bbls./day, but for Districts I–IV, it benefited from historical preference.

Sources: (1) U.S. Congress, Senate, Select Committee on Small Business, *Oil Import Allocations* (88th Cong., 2nd Sess.), August, 1964, p. 177; (2) Statement of Byron Milner, Atlantic Refining Co., in *Oil Import Allocations*, p. 104; (3) Gulf Oil Company, "Analysis of Transcript of Import Hearings, March 10–12, 1965" (Gulf Oil Co., Pittsburgh, PA).

disregarding antitrust pressures. "It is quite apparent," said Seaton, "that we could not support a program confining the privilege of importing crude oil to a special class of refiners." When Follis raised the issue of foreign investments, the Secretary admitted that the Program would inhibit them, but that was irrespective of the method of allocation. Finally, Seaton none-to-subtly reminded Follis of the considerable political pressure from domestic refiners who opposed any consideration of historical positions.[11]

Both the Kennedy and Johnson administrations continued the policy of gradually reducing the established importers' historical advantage. Had it not been for certain diplomatic considerations, this phasing-out process would likely have been accelerated.[12] Besides this policy's obvious competitive effect of shifting the cost advantages of imports from the real importers to domestic refiners, it also distorted competitive relationships among the established importers. This effect was apparent in the fact that some of them stopped supporting the historical allocation and eventually opposed it. Table 6-1 shows the relationship between refinery capacity, allocation criteria, and policy stance for the eleven largest importers on the East Coast. By 1965, those whose refinery capacities were largest relative to their historical quota positions had already shifted to the criterion of refinery runs. Since they no longer could benefit from the historical preference, they generally advocated its abolition in hopes of eliminating their competitors' remaining quota advantage. Companies like Gulf, Sinclair, and Atlantic, whose refinery capacities were low relative to their historical quota position, found themselves increasingly isolated in defense of the historical criterion.

2. Quota exchanges

Once the Eisenhower administration decided to extend import quotas to inland refiners, it couldn't avoid a policy of phasing-out the historical quotas of established importers. Otherwise, the Oil Import Administration could not maintain the aggregate ceiling while making room for the 100 or so inland refiners not previously involved in petroleum imports. Indeed, this was the fundamental

---

[11] F. Seaton to R. G. Follis, July 10, 1959, Whitman Files, Administrative Series, Box 36, Fred Seaton (1), DDEPL.

[12] M. Feldman to the President, December 14, 1961, Feldman Papers, Box 24, Residual Oil Imports, JFKL. The State Department opposed any acceleration of the phase-out of the historical quota preference. State was generally conscious of production pressures from Persian Gulf governments on the historic importers and was particularly sensitive to the concerns of Venezuela. As Meyer Feldman explained to President Kennedy, "Venezuela is a relatively high cost producer today and can only retain its position in the United States market because of the provision in the import program which largely confines allocations to historical importers, principally those with refineries in Venezuela." This applied to both crude and residual oil. If the preferential quotas for historical importers were terminated, their imports from Venezuela would be displaced by lower-cost oil acquired by newcomers from the Middle East. President Betancourt subsequently urged a U.S. delegation headed by Feldman to slow the phasing-out of historical quotas as one of several demands relating to the Mandatory Program. See, M. Feldman, "Report on Discussions with President Betancourt on the United States Oil Import Program," Caracas, Venezuela, December 29–30, 1962, Presidential Office Files, Box 104, Oil Imports/Foreign Nations, JFKL.

redistributive choice of the whole mandatory program. It was primarily a response to political pressure from domestic refiners, justified by a perverse obeisance to free enterprise. In an argument accepted by the government, the inland refiners asserted that if imports were limited to the real importers, their cost advantage would allow them to penetrate the markets of inland refiners and drive them out of business. The right to trade quotas to real importers in exchange for domestic oil was a paper transaction – as an editorial in *Petroleum Week* described it, "nothing more than industry subsidizing industry by government sanction."[13]

The eleven companies that actually imported and refined the foreign crude oil objected strenuously and consistently to this practice of quota trading. They had to participate in it since their own quotas were insufficient to supply their coastal refineries. In response to the argument of market penetration, Gulf argued that if it were "feasible to move the products from coastal refining areas," it was "also feasible to move the crude and run it."[14] A spokesman for Atlantic Refining calculated that the profits from quota exchanges amounted to an intra-industry subsidy of $135 million by 1964. Sun Oil complained that the Mandatory Program "was never meant to support or protect from competition any particular segment of the industry at the expense of another segment."[15] But of course, it was. This objective, although secondary, was nonetheless real and inherent in the government's involvement.

3. *The sliding scale*

Regardless of the economic irrationality of quota exchanges, domestic refiners continued to press for even larger allocations in the name of "fairness." The device for this was the sliding scale, established by the Oil Import Administration in its first administrative order. Similar in form and purpose to the graduated income tax, the sliding scale allotted disproportionately large quotas to small refiners. Each refiner received an allocation of 11.1 percent of its first 10,000 barrels of capacity. For each increment of capacity, that percentage declined, so that any capacity above 300,000 barrels per day would merit an allocation of only 3.7 percent. The sliding scale, explained Interior Secretary Stewart Udall, was "designed to prevent the lion's share of economic advantage from accruing to the very large refining companies." As such, it was "a measure for the preservation of the economic health of the refining industry as a whole."[16] That was precisely what the major importers objected to, particularly Standard Oil of New Jersey, the largest refiner. Were the sliding scale replaced by a proportionate allocation, Standard's quota would have increased from

---

[13] *Petroleum Week*, November 11, 1960.
[14] "Testimony of Gulf Oil Corporation," May 1961, p. 3.
[15] U.S. Congress, Senate, Select Committee on Small Business, *Oil Import Allocations* (88th Cong., 2nd Sess.), August 1964, pp. 99, 363.
[16] Stewart Udall, "Affidavit in Support of Defendants' Motion for Summary Judgment," *Standard Oil Company(N.J.) v. Stewart Udall*, Civil Action No. 2496–61, U.S. District Court for the District of Columbia, in U.S. Congress, *Oil Import Allocations*, p. 171.

43,000 to 78,000 barrels a day. Standard sued the Interior Department in an attempt to overturn the sliding scale.

Not only did Standard's litigation fail, but the domestic refiners succeeded in pressuring the Oil Import Administration to make periodic adjustments toward even steeper graduation of the scale. By the time the Program ended, the quota for a small refiner's first 10,000 barrels of capacity was 22 percent. Several factors accounted for the political effectiveness of the domestic refiners.

First, there was the small business ethos that permeated the American polity. Ninety-six refiners, with refinery capacities under 30,000 bbls./day, qualified as small businesses eligible for the special support of the Small Business Administration and the Small Business Committees of Congress. Prior to the establishment of the Mandatory Program, the casualty rate among small refiners had risen sharply because they couldn't compete with larger, integrated oil companies that produced and imported foreign crude oil. In a non-oil, non-politicized world, such casualties and low margins would be viewed as a healthy shakeout – the natural result of inefficiency and competition. But in the political economy of oil, the problems of small refiners were automatically attributed to the oligopolistic power of the major international companies.[17]

Domestic refiners derived additional political influence from the notion that they were the guarantors of price competition in an otherwise oligopolistic oil industry. Ignoring the fact that the majors charged lower wholesale prices, Eugene Foley, head of the Small Business Administration, advised the government to "resort to every available means of strengthening existing refineries," because "the competition they present to the giants of the industry holds down the price."[18] Advocates of the sliding scale alleged that imports were causing concentration levels in the oil industry to rise. Thus, disproportionate preference for small refiners was "essential to prevent a monopoly trend favoring companies with higher import privileges."[19] In both the Kennedy and Johnson administrations, the Justice Department was a leading advocate of eliminating the historical preference and increasing the small refiner bias. By shifting more of the quota to small refiners, the Justice Department hoped to "have a significant impact upon the competitiveness of the gasoline market."[20]

As important as the ideology of smallness or the rhetoric of monopoly was the fact that the domestic refiners exercised traditional political influence derived from their large numbers, their economic impact on certain congressional districts, and their substantial financial resources. Unlike the major international

---

[17] See, for example, Statement of E. M. Stone, president, American Petroleum Refiners Association, in U.S. Congress, Senate, *Oil Import Allocations*, pp. 2–5.

[18] Statement of Eugene P. Foley, Administrator, Small Business Administration, in U.S. Congress, Senate, *Oil Import Allocations*, p. 263.

[19] Statement of W. E. Turner, executive vice-president, Texas Independent Producers and Royalty Owners Association, in U.S. Congress, Senate, *Oil Import Allocations*, p. 49.

[20] D. Turner to J. Califano, n.d., Robson–Ross Office Files, Box 14, Pricing Fuel Oils/1966, LBJPL; also, U.S. Senate, *Oil Import Allocations*, fn. 8, p. 278; also, "Justice, Low–Rates, 'Historic' Quotas," *Oil and Gas Journal*, May 20, 1963, p. 102.

oil companies, most small refiners related to the Democratic Party. In the 1960 election, they supported the Kennedy–Johnson ticket. Not surprisingly, the Kennedy Administration was favorably disposed to their needs with regards to oil imports. In November 1961, Mike Manatos, one of Kennedy's aides, attended a dinner with 40 representatives of the independent oil refiners in California. They sought Manatos' support for a change in the sliding scale for District V that would increase the allocation for the first 10,000 barrels a day of capacity from 39 percent (already much higher than that for Districts I–IV) to 50 percent.[21] This was "an ideal opportunity," Manatos reported, "to make real headway with the independent oil men on the West Coast by adopting one change in the present import program." Explaining the scheme to Larry O'Brien, President Kennedy's special assistant for congressional relations, Manatos suggested that the President could announce it "as an aid to 'small business.' " To clinch O'Brien's attention, Manatos added that Democratic fund raisers had assured him "that this one step . . . would open up new avenues of contributions in '64."[22]

Such a change was perfectly consistent with the more general direction of policy recommended by the Petroleum Study Committee, an inter-departmental staff group the President had formed to advise him on oil imports. Among other things, the Committee recommended that historical preferences continue to be phased-out gradually so that the sliding scale could be tilted more steeply toward small refiners.[23] For whatever combination of reasons, the Oil Import Administration did announce a change in the sliding scale in the spring of 1962. For West Coast refiners, the allocation for the first 10,000 bbls./day of capacity was raised from 39 percent to 52 percent. In practical terms, this meant an increase of $1,300 in the daily subsidy to California refiners with a capacity of 10,000 barrels a day or less. For the same category in Districts I–IV, the allotment was only raised from 11.6 to 12.0 percent.[24]

The independent domestic refiners would probably have received far fewer benefits from the Mandatory Oil Import Program had they not been backed by the considerable political influence of the independent producer interests. As Eugene Foley put it, "The relationship of the small refiners to the small producers is vital. In their respective localities they provide markets for small producers and sources of supply for countless small distributors."[25] Without the small independent refiners using their quota subsidies to cross-subsidize their local crude purchases, producers in many marginal oil fields would proba-

---

[21] P. Owens, president, MacMillan Ring-Free Oil Co., to M. Manatos, November 7, 1961, Feldman Papers, Box 23, JFKL.
[22] M. Manatos to L. O'Brien, November 8, 1961, Feldman Papers, Box 23, JFKL.
[23] Petroleum Study Committee, "Task Force Report" (Draft), August, 1962, Feldman Papers, Box 23, JFKL, p. 13.
[24] Gulf Oil Company, "Petroleum Import Statistics Under Oil Import Control Programs by Import Periods Through 1972," July 1972, Gulf Oil Co., Pittsburgh, Pa., pp. C–2, D–2. See also Note 13 *supra*.
[25] U.S. Congress, Senate, *Oil Import Allocations*, p. 263.

bly have failed since the majors had little need for such high-cost sources. With the Texas Royalty Owners and Independent Producers groups defending the sliding-scale bias, domestic refiners were indeed highly leveraged, politically.

4. Hemispheric preference

Just two months after establishing the Mandatory Program, the Eisenhower administration announced the first of many modifications. There would be a hemispheric preference after all, at least for "overland" imports. The President invoked the criterion of national security to exempt from controls oil that entered the United States over land.[26] The immunity of overland imports to submarine attack justified an allowance of special access to U.S. markets. Since only Canada and Mexico bordered the United States, and the latter had no pipeline link, this exemption was accurately viewed as a foreign policy initiative designed to strengthen U.S.–Canadian relations. Of course, it upset the governments of Mexico and Venezuela, and was subsequently modified to calm them. As usual, these special provisions caused distributive conflicts among oil importers, with domestic oil producers, and with the coal industry. The issues of hemispheric preference also caused trouble between the Departments of State and Interior, and between regional groups in the Congress.

For District V, Eisenhower's modification exempted Canadian imports from controls, but provided that they be included in the computation of the overall quota for that region. For Districts I–IV, Canadian imports were entirely exempted from controls. This meant that east of the Rockies, unrestricted oil imports from Canada displaced domestic oil rather than imports from other nations. With very substantial oil discoveries in Alberta, Canadian producers took full advantage of this opportunity. By 1962, Canadian imports had increased 178 percent, more than doubling their share of total U.S. imports.[27] As soon as this trend became apparent, domestic producers began pressuring the Interior Department through complaints to their congressmen, and added recission of the overland exemption to their shopping list for the Trade Act renewal of 1962.[28]

Secretary Udall proposed to modify the Program to include imports from Canada within the overall ceiling on imports, while leaving the Canadian imports uncontrolled. Canadian imports would thus displace quota imports from other nations, including Venezuela. The State Department objected to the plan because it would offend Venezuela and the Persian Gulf exporters. Secretary Dean Rusk preferred to rely on bilateral discussions with Canada, which were already under way.[29]

---

[26] 24 *Federal Register* 3527, May 2, 1959.
[27] Gulf Oil Company, "Pretroleum Import Statistics," p. M–1.
[28] See footnote no. 8 *supra.*
[29] Petroleum Study Committee, "Task Force Report" (Draft), p. 11. The Commerce Department was sensitive to Canada's large trade deficit with the United States, and Justice was concerned by the antitrust implications of further restrictiveness. Edward McDermott, Director of the Office of Emergency Planning, agreed with Defense that no formal restrictions should be placed on secure

Pressures from domestic oil producers evidently prevailed over diplomatic concerns. When the White House announced major revisions of the Mandatory Program late in 1962, the aggregate quota was recalibrated as a percentage of production, rather than demand, which would include overland exempt imports.[30] This doubly pleased domestic producers.[31] It not only meant that Canadian imports would displace restricted imports, but also that the aggregate ceiling would grow more slowly once decoupled from demand growth that included Canadian imports. Two weeks later, a delegation of State and Interior officials went to Ottawa where they negotiated a secret agreement by which the Canadians would hold oil exports constant for half a year, and then restrict growth to no more than the growth of U.S. production.[32] Subsequently, the Canadian government was either unable or unwilling to enforce this agreement, for imports from Canada continued to grow rapidly until President Nixon finally imposed a mandatory quota for Canada in 1970.[33]

The overland exemption, like most every regulation of the Mandatory Program, distorted competitive relationships among individual firms as well as among industry groups. One situation is worth mentioning as an example. Before the Mandatory Program, only five "Northern Tier" refiners were established importers of Canadian oil. Thus, when the mandatory program began, before overland imports were exempted, they became eligible for the historical allocation of quotas. Two months later, when President Eisenhower exempted overland imports, four of these firms retained their historical quotas, but no longer needed them for Canadian oil. This gave four of the companies a "double dip," but not the fifth since it had been acquired by Continental Oil which was not an established importer. This idiosyncrasy gave the four lucky companies a huge quota advantage over Continental and their other competitors in the upper Midwest.[34] They could exchange their quota tickets for domestic oil from North Dakota and Montana and, with a cost subsidy of $1.25 per barrel, could market their refined products at a lower price than their competitors.

One would think that such an obvious fluke could easily have been remedied by a simple adjustment of the regulations. However, such was not the case, even though Interior officials recognized the inequity of the situation. In May 1960, the Interior Department considered a rule change to eliminate this loophole, but when North Dakota politicians intervened, the revision was abandoned.[35]

Canadian oil. See, E. McDermott to K. Hansen, November 9, 1962, and W. Brubeck to M. Feldman, November 16, 1962, Feldman Papers, Box 24, JFKL.

[30] Proclamation 3059, 27 *Federal Register* 11985–88, December 5, 1962.

[31] M. Feldman to President, June 25, 1962, Feldman Papers, Box 23, JFKL.

[32] G. Griffith Johnson, "Report of the United States Delegation to the United States-Canadian Discussion of Petroleum Policies and Programs," Ottawa, Canada, December 13–14, 1962, Presidential Office Files, Box 104, JFKL.

[33] Proclamation 3969, 35 *Federal Register* 4321, March 10, 1970.

[34] The four Northern Tier companies with historical quotas were Murphy Oil, Dow Chemical, Northwestern Refining, and Great Northern Oil.

[35] Continental Oil Company, Position Paper, "Northern Tier Crude Oil Allocations under the Oil Import Program," April 1964, Continental Oil Co., Houston, Texas, p. 8.

Continental Oil commenced a five-year running campaign to get the regulations amended. The Kennedy administration considered the possibility of changing the quotas of the four unique refiners to the basis of refinery runs, but pressure from Senator Hubert Humphrey of Minnesota allegedly prevented that change.[36] As a palliative, the historical quotas of Northern Tier refiners were eventually reduced somewhat more rapidly than those of other historical importers. But that amounted to only a few percentage points as long as North Dakota and Minnesota kept pressuring the Johnson administration with leverage that apparently exceeded Continental's.[37]

Hemispheric preference with regard to Mexico was not a significant issue since that country was not a major oil exporter. But its peculiar situation exemplified the absurdity of some of the Program's rules. Although Mexico and the United States shared a border, there were no pipelines crossing it. For two years, a ludicrous system of transshipment was tolerated to maintain diplomatic goodwill. Mexican crude oil previously shipped by tanker directly to New Jersey was diverted to Brownsville, Texas. There, it was unloaded into tank trucks and driven twelve miles south to the border, in bond. After clearing customs, the trucks returned to Brownsville where the oil was reloaded in tankers and shipped to the Northeast, officially having entered "over land." When this "Brownsville Turnabout" or "Mexican Merry-go-round" began attracting ridicule in the trade press and congressional hearings, it was replaced by a special bilateral exemption that simply allowed Mexico a fixed import quota of 30,000 barrels per day.[38]

5. *Residual oil*

By defining hemispheric preference in terms of overland imports, U.S. policy appeared to have short-changed Venezuela. Indeed, the Venezuelan government protested the overland exemption until Kennedy's assistant, Meyer Feldman, explained to President Betancourt how that policy benefited Venezuelan exports to Canada.[39] Meanwhile, Venezuela still enjoyed a unique degree of access to U.S. energy markets because of the quota system for residual oil. Since Venezuelan oil had a low specific gravity, it yielded a disproportionate amount of residual when refined. But since production costs in Venezuela were relatively high, it could not have competed with Middle East sources in an uncontrolled market. Later in the sixties, when residual imports were effectively

---

[36] *Ibid.*, 11.
[37] W. L. Guy, Governor of North Dakota, to L. B. Johnson, December 23, 1963, LBJ Papers, Executive, Box 19, TA6/Oil, LBJPL. For the arguments of the Northern tier group of refiners, see J. J. Flynn, "Statement of the Great Northern Oil Co. in Reply to the Position Paper of Continental Oil Co., August 10, 1964," in U.S. Senate, *Oil Import Allocation*, pp. 335–39.
[38] Bohi and Russell, *Limiting Oil Imports*, pp. 132–134.
[39] Without the overland exemption, Canada would have been forced to build a crude oil pipeline from Alberta into its eastern consuming provinces in order to maintain domestic production. Had it done so, those provinces would no longer have needed imports for which Venezuela was the principal source. See M. Feldman, "Report on Discussion with President Betancourt," p. 6.

decontrolled, Venezuela's market share declined precipitously. Until then, however, the Venezuelan government stood behind the efforts of various domestic interest groups to prevent tighter restriction of imported residual oil.

As an industrial fuel used primarily to generate electric power and process heat, residual oil (also called No. 6 Fuel Oil) competed directly with coal. Domestic oil producers didn't care about residual imports since domestic refining yielded too little residual to fulfill domestic demand. But the coal industry cared deeply. The Mandatory Program failed to alleviate political conflict between the coal industry and importers of residual oil that had begun during the voluntary program. If anything, the conflict sharpened into a regional controversy between Appalachian congressmen and the New England delegation (with help from New York, New Jersey, Maryland, and Florida).

Somewhat short-sightedly, the original Eisenhower proclamation of 1959 had limited imports of residual oil to the absolute levels of 1957. This failed to allow for demand growth or pressure from potential newcomers. The Eisenhower administration realized this shortly and took the first steps toward liberalizing controls on residual late in 1959. The State Department proposed that the Secretary of the Interior be authorized to grant quotas for residual oil, in excess of the 1957 level. The rationale for this amendment was that it was necessary to put Venezuela on an equal footing with Canada and give President Betancourt a gesture that he could exploit politically at home. The State Department acknowledged that the coal industry would object, but argued that "the aspirations of that industry could not be satisfied unless imports of residual fuel oil were restricted to the point of increasing prices so as to make coal more competitive."[40]

The Interior Secretary objected adamantly to the State Department's proposal. The petroleum industry, he felt, "would consider effective decontrol of residual as the first sign of weakness in administration of the program," even though domestic producers would not be injured.[41] This time, the State Department prevailed; in December 1959, the Interior Department was forced to increase quotas for residual oil.[42] A year later, the residual policy was again modified to provide quotas to newcomers, particularly among the many terminal operators along the Atlantic coast.[43]

One of the more interesting results of the program for residual imports was the formation of specialized trade organizations designed to oppose or promote further liberalization. Two of these, the National Coal Policy Conference and the Independent Fuel Oil Marketers of America, became the principal lobbies around which the regional political fight was organized.

The coal group was created to "articulate the problems and the requirements

[40] "Liberalization of Imports of Residual Fuel Oil for Burning," August 21, 1959, Fred Seaton Papers, Box 4, Oil Imports, Memos (1), DDEPL, p. 4.
[41] F. Seaton to the President, September 14, 1959, Fred Seaton Papers, Box 5, Oil Imports/Residual Oil, DDEPL, p. 2.
[42] Proclamation 3328, 24 *Federal Register* 10133–34, December 16, 1959.
[43] Proclamation 3389, 26 *Federal Register* 507, January 20, 1961.

of coal to the legislative and executive branches and other institutions of the government," and to "assist in the formation and establishment of policy."[44] During the next decade, these objectives were enlarged to include research and development funding for synthetic fuels and regulation of air pollution, as well as oil imports. The National Coal Policy Conference was something of an innovation for organizing business power. Conceived as an inter-industry association, it represented coal producers, electric utilities, railroads, manufacturers of mining equipment, and the United Mine Workers of America. The Conference remained active as coal's most effective lobby until 1971. By then, interfuel conflict had moderated since major oil companies had acquired many of the largest coal producers.[45]

While the National Coal Policy Conference lobbied against residual imports, the Independent Fuel Oil Marketers fought the battle on the other side. They aligned themselves with the Kennedy administration's goal of trade liberalization, with consumers, and with the government of Venezuela.[46] When the quota increases were deemed inadequate, the Marketers attacked the Coal Policy Conference and complained to President Kennedy that "the coal industry has been pampered by your Administration and has benefited at the unjust expense of the consumer of residual fuel oil on the East Coast."[47]

The fight over residual imports peaked in March 1963, when the Office of Emergency Planning (which had replaced the Office of Defense Mobilization) completed an investigation on the security effects of residual oil. A coalition of consumer groups, their congressional delegates, and the coal industry had requested it. Imported residual did not threaten the national security, the study concluded. Indeed, it recommended a "meaningful relaxation of controls."[48] With this, the Fuel Oil Marketers redoubled their clamor for another large increase in the residual quota; the National Coal Policy Conference dug in its heels. Telegrams poured into the White House from the governors of coal producing states. Senator Jennings Randolph (D-WV), who had voted with the Administration in a recent fight on the trade bill because of its assurance that residual controls would continue, felt betrayed and blasted the Emergency Planning report on the floor of Congress.[49]

At this point, White House staff advised President Kennedy that he had four options: (1) eliminate residual controls, (2) tighten them, (3) hold them constant, or (4) adopt a new program of allocations to every bona fide applicant, relaxing controls gradually to "cause a gradual price decrease." To abolish

[44] National Coal Policy Conference, *NCPC, Purposes, Platforms, Objectives* (pamphlet, n.d.), p. 4.
[45] National Coal Policy Conference, "The Facts about Residual Fuel Oil Imports," 1962, Feldman Papers, Box 23, JFKL.
[46] Carlos Perez, Chargé d'Affaires, to J. K. Evans, director of IFOMA, January 10, 1963, Feldman Papers, Box 23, JFKL.
[47] J. K. Evans to J. F. Kennedy, November 8, 1962, Feldman Papers, Box 16, JFKL.; also, J. K. Evans to J. F. Kennedy, August 28, 1962, Feldman Papers, Box 23, JFKL.
[48] Office of Emergency Planning, "Memorandum for the President (Relating to the National Security Considerations in the Residual Oil Control Program)," February 13, 1963, cited in Bohi and Russell, *Limiting Oil Imports*, pp. 152–53.
[49] *Ibid.*

controls was politically too drastic. To tighten them was likewise unsatisfactory, as it would antagonize consumers and the Venezuelan government. To hold them constant would "disappoint everybody" and continue to subject the Administration to semi-annual attacks by the coal interests. The fourth choice – to relax controls substantially – would also incur the coal industry's wrath, but it was preferred because it would put the program on a regular basis that didn't rely on administrative discretion.[50]

President Kennedy adopted it as of April 1, 1963.[51] The coal industry would just have to adjust.

Learning to live with regulation

The program for controlling imports of residual oil exemplified, in microcosm, how market pressures continually pushed against the political barricade of economic regulation. The Interior Secretary's criterion for increasing quotas for residual was "demand." In principle, he allowed imports to supplement demand for domestic residual, but "demand" at what price? At any price below alternatives (coal, for example), demand would keep growing. Thus, at the beginning of each new allocation period, demand always appeared to have grown beyond the existing quota. With this criterion in force, the coal interests were caught in a vicious circle, and knew it.[52]

The oil industry had also begun to understand the economics of the Mandatory Oil Import Program. The lessons varied among the domestic producers, refiners, and major international companies. Domestic producers were discovering that the Program put a ceiling as well as a floor on the price of crude oil.[53] Until 1968, the Mandatory Program, in conjunction with prorationing, supported domestic prices at nearly double the level of "arm's-length" prices in the Middle East. By stimulating domestic productive capacity and dampening demand, this system maintained a surplus that prevented prices from rising. Independent refiners grew dependent on the Program from which they drew "tickets," knowing that without them they could not long compete with larger, integrated refiners running cheap foreign crude.

The economics lesson had a profound impact on the policies of the major international oil companies. These "established" importers, it will be recalled, had unanimously opposed mandatory import controls. And when it came to protecting their own share of the quotas, they continued through the 1960's to fight further reductions. As early as 1962, however, several of these companies began to realize that in their own balance sheets, there was a trade-off between increased imports and the profitability of their domestic operations. The more they imported, the less they were allowed to produce domestically by the state prorationing authorities. Not only was it costly to maintain spare productive

---

50 *Ibid.*
51 K. Hansen to M. Feldman, February 27, 1963, and J. Kelly to M. Feldman, March 3, 1963, attachment, "Possible Residual Fuel Oil Program," Feldman Papers, Box 24, JFKL.
52 R. Martin to M. Feldman, May 23, 1963, Feldman Papers, Box 5, JFKL.
53 Warren Davis, Gulf Oil Corporation, interview with the author, August 1980.

capacity, but the same price erosion that threatened domestic producers also threatened losses to the U.S. operations of international firms. For example, one of these companies studied the prevailing conditions of price, supply, and its own tax liability and found that by 1964, a reduction of imports no longer meant a net loss of revenue as it had in 1962, and by 1968 would actually cause a net gain.[54]

On the basis of such analyses, together with sincere concern for the impact of imports on national security and a growing sensitivity to the political costs of continued opposition, the international majors began, one by one, to support the Mandatory Program.[55] By 1965, all except for Cities Service (which preferred a tariff) had come to support the principle of mandatory controls if not the Program's particular distributive policies. This transformation was reflected in a 1966 statement by the National Petroleum Council, in which it finally endorsed federal import controls.[56]

For a time, the Mandatory Program appeared to have produced not only an artificial equilibrium in the oil market, but a political equilibrium as well. In part, this reflected the convergence of economic interests between the domestic and international sectors of the oil industry. But it also reflected the international sector's acquiescence in the political necessity of accommodating their domestic brethren. As if it were not clear enough from the record of experience, Senator Russell Long of Louisiana eloquently explained how politics worked to an audience of oil company executives. Senator Long said that those in Congress from the oil states "are especially interested in the domestic phases of the industry, because that is the part that gives employment to our people and means revenue to our state governments, and it is essential to our economy." But, added Long, "we would like you fellows that produce oil overseas to realize this, that when problems come up with regard to your tax credit overseas or even your depletion allowance overseas, or the special tax treatment to your employees that you have overseas, the fellows you are going to rely upon to protect your activities in that respect are the same people who are interested in the domestic production of oil here." Long continued: "I believe your industry would make a great mistake not to realize that; that as far as the government is concerned, as far as the fair treatment you are entitled to expect from your government is concerned, the people who will be your advocates are people who are very much interested in domestic oil." And so to his point: "It is very much to your advantage to have a very healthy domestic industry and do everything within your power to cooperate to that end."[57]

Evidently, distributive squabbles among importers were politically accept-

[54] "Reduction in Gulf Net Profit if Levels of Crude and Unfinished Imports in Districts I–IV are Reduced," internal memoranda, June 7, 1960 and March 26, 1964, Gulf Oil Company, Pittsburgh, Pa.

[55] Warren Davis, interview with author.

[56] National Petroleum Council, *Petroleum Policies for the United States*, March 1, 1966 (Wash., D.C.), p. 4.

[57] National Petroleum Council, Meeting Transcript, March 19, 1964 (NPC/DOI, 1964), pp. 26–28.

able, but the aggregate import ceiling was inviolable. Put another way, the politics of oil imports had hitherto consisted of "shotgun blasts," directed by one sector of the energy business at another. Henceforth, it would be more like "rifle shots," important on a firm-specific basis, but not aimed at an overriding enemy.[58] Ironically, that very fragmentation would seriously wound the Mandatory Program, hastening its reassessment and subsequent demise.

The chain of exemptions

When Lyndon B. Johnson succeeded John F. Kennedy in the White House, he tried to disassociate himself from the image of the oil industry's spokesman. He delegated substantive authority for matters of energy policy and remained aloof from controversies involving gas regulation, coal, and oil imports. And although the Mandatory Oil Import Program continued to generate problems for his Administration, it was scarcely at center stage. The Johnson administration was preoccupied by the Vietnam War, the legislative goals of the Great Society, and the economic problems of inflation and balance of payments that attended those two programs. With relatively free rein, Stewart Udall, continuing as Interior Secretary, allowed the Mandatory Program to be further diverted from its original objectives. Between 1965 and 1968, he condoned whatever changes and exemptions seemed helpful for achieving the Administration's broader goals.

But Udall was hardly alone in this dissipation of the Program. At every opportunity, his fellow cabinet members, congressmen, and oil industry managers sought to exploit the Program for some new purpose or other. The Council of Economic Advisors wanted to liberalize imports to help hold down prices. The State Department pursued policies to favor Canada and Venezuela. Commerce supported exemptions for the petrochemicals industry to shore up the balance of payments. The congressional delegation from New England applied constant pressure, first to get residual decontrolled, and then to promote an exemption for a foreign trade zone. California senators labored to block imports of refined products from Puerto Rico, while the Texas and Oklahoma delegations kept pressing for a reduction of total imports. Nearly every sector of the oil industry supported the Program in principle, but it was every firm for itself in carving-up the pie. Phillips Petroleum won an exemption to help Puerto Rico that Leon Hess duplicated for the Virgin Islands. Asphalt refiners had special problems as did electric utilities in polluted cities. The Mandatory Program cared for them all. The Oil Import Appeals Board, with its own allocation of imports to use for settling grievances, had a docket of small-company cases that required almost daily decisions.[59] As one exemption begot another, the Mandatory Program lost sight of its national security rationale and began to crumble under the weight of its fragmented agenda.

[58] Warren Davis, interview with author.
[59] Oil Import Appeals Board, Decisions and Importing Company Correspondence File, Boxes 67–99, Records of the Oil Import Administration (Acc. No. 72A–6599), FRC, Suitland, Md.

It is beyond the scope of this chapter to provide a thorough description of even the major exemptions and special quotas that were added to the Program during the Johnson years. A few examples will suffice to indicate how the policy process changed and how its cumulative effects undermined the legitimacy of the Program.[60]

Take the case of Puerto Rico. In Eisenhower's original proclamation, Puerto Rico was set apart as a separate district for the purpose of administering oil import controls. Historical quotas were allocated to the only two refiners there, Gulf Oil and Commonwealth Oil & Refining Company. From the start, those refiners generated some products that could not be absorbed by the Puerto Rican economy, so they exported them to the U.S. mainland through what other companies considered to be a minor loophole in the Program.

The Phillips project in Puerto Rico apparently originated in a conversation between Udall and Puerto Rican officials at the San Juan airport in 1961. In a general discussion of Operation Bootstrap, the island's postwar program for economic development, the Puerto Rican officials explored the prospects for development of a petrochemical industry.[61] The Puerto Rican Economic Development Administration spent the next three years promoting such a project to major oil and chemical companies. Because the project's commercial feasibility would depend on an exemption from the quotas, there were no takers until 1964 when an agreement was finally reached with Phillips Petroleum.[62] Phillips would invest $45 million in a core chemical facility and then reinvest the first $55 million of earnings on satellite plants. It also agreed to provide some equity participation to Puerto Rican investors and to try and attract other chemical companies to invest in collateral facilities. To make all this possible, Phillips applied for special allocations of 50,000 barrels per day of crude oil into Puerto Rico and 24,800 barrels per day of refined product into the U.S. east coast. The latter allocation had to come out of the overall ceiling, meaning a reduction of someone else's quota.

Nearly every domestic producer, refiner, or other importer opposed this expansion of the Puerto Rican loophole. Robert Anderson, chairman of the Atlantic Refining Company, warned President Johnson that such an exemption would have serious implications "because it confers a special privilege and an unfair competitive advantage on one company," and therefore "tends to undermine the entire oil import program."[63] Congressmen from oil-producing states felt certain that an exemption for Phillips would open a Pandora's box.[64]

Although they should have known better, both Udall and Johnson were so

---

[60] See Bohi and Russell, *Limiting Oil Imports*, Chapter 5, pp. 144–87.
[61] J. Cordell Moore to Senator Henry Jackson, December 15, 1965, Moore Papers, Chronological File, Box 2, LBJPL.
[62] Statement by Sergio Camero, Administrator, Economic Development Administration, Commonwealth of Puerto Rico, in U.S. Congress, House, Committee on Interior Affairs, Subcommittee on Mines and Mining, *Hearings: Mandatory Oil Import Control Program, its Impact upon the Domestic Minerals Industry and National Security* (90th Cong., 2nd Sess.), May 1968, pp. 262–67.
[63] R. O. Anderson to the President, August 6, 1965, LBJ Papers, Executive File, Box 19, LBJPL.
[64] M. Moroney to S. Udall, June 8, 1965, LBJ Papers, Executive File, Box 19, LBJPL.

committed to the War on Poverty that they believed they could contain the project as a unique exemption.[65] But even before they issued the quota to Phillips, two applications for similar projects were pending and others were being developed hastily by corporate planners. Union Carbide and Commonwealth Oil & Refining got additional Puerto Rican quotas in 1967, and the next year Sun Oil landed a huge exemption to import 30,000 barrels a day of refined products from Puerto Rico. Perhaps the most controversial exemption was the product quota awarded to Leon Hess to subsidize a refinery expansion in the Virgin Islands. Hess purportedly used his contacts with the Democratic Party to build support among influential congressmen.[66]

Besides undermining the Mandatory Program's political standing among major producers and importers, exemptions such as these had unanticipated ill effects on competitive relationships, even at the wholesale and retail level as far away as California. In the Los Angeles area, for example, an independent gasoline distributor named Walter Simas learned a bitter lesson about the political economy by exploiting a loophole in a Puerto Rican exemption.

Simas' company, Ashland Oil (not to be confused with Ashland Oil of Kentucky), distributed gasoline that it purchased from Coastal States Refining on one-year contracts, to several chains of cut-rate service stations. In 1966, Simas was contacted by a broker trying to peddle 10,000 barrels a day of gasoline that Commonwealth Oil & Refining couldn't sell in Puerto Rico or export to the East Coast. When Secretary Udall had approved the Phillips quota in 1965, he restricted other product imports from Puerto Rico into Districts I–IV, but his order made no mention of District V, presumably because no one considered it relevant.[67] After visiting the refinery in San Juan, Walter Simas signed a contract for Commonwealth to supply Ashland with 12 million gallons of gasoline per month for four years.

To market that much gasoline, Simas expanded his terminal facilities, reduced his prices, and expanded his customer base to 303 service stations. That activity displeased the major oil companies that operated in California and caused intense alarm among the independent refiners in District V. Fearing that the regional price structure would be damaged by Simas' aggressive marketing, these companies began petitioning their congressmen, senators, the Oil

[65] Governor Luis Munoz Marin to L. B. Johnson, December 8, 1964, LBJ Papers, Executive File, Box 19, LBJPL.
[66] D. V. Perry to J. C. Moore, April 17, 1967, and J. C. Moore to S. Udall, April 18, 1967, Moore Papers, Chronological File, Box 3, LBJPL. For contemporary critiques of these developments, see Allan Demaree, "Our Crazy, Costly Life with Oil Quotas," *Fortune*, June 1969, p. 105, and "Leon Hess Never Plays it Safe," *Fortune*, January 1970, p. 141. Evidently, there was a limit. Later in 1968, Secretary Udall rejected a Texaco proposal for Puerto Rico and a dubious scheme by Ed Carey of New England Petroleum for a refinery in the Bahamas.
[67] Proclamation 3693, 30 *Federal Register* 15459–61, December 16, 1965. Walter Simas alleged that the government may have intentionally failed to mention District V in order to give Commonwealth a break. For this and the general background of the Simas situation, see U.S. Congress, Senate, Judiciary Committee, Subcommittee on Antitrust and Monopoly, *Hearings on Governmental Intervention in the Market Mechanism* (91st Cong., 1st Sess.), The Petroleum Industry, Pt. 3, July 1969, pp. 1217–35.

Import Administration, Secretary Udall, and the President to terminate the Commonwealth deliveries to California.[68]

The most vigorous and determined attack came from one Harry Rothschild, the president of Powerine Oil Co., an independent refiner that most directly competed with Simas. Rothschild accused Commonwealth of dumping gasoline below cost in order to obtain a higher quota for crude oil into Puerto Rico. Allowing it to continue would "result in irreparable economic damage to the independent refiners of District V." Ironically, while pleading thus with Udall, Rothschild was petitioning the Appeals Board to expand his own allocation of imported crude from 6,300 to 11,000 barrels a day.[69]

On December 15, 1967, Stewart Udall announced that Commonwealth Oil would be allowed to ship an additional 10,000 barrels a day to the East Coast. "This increase," said Udall, "will substantially expand employment opportunities in Puerto Rico . . ." However, in the very next paragraph of his announcement, he added that Commonwealth's present shipments to the *West* Coast would be terminated.[70] When Simas read of this in the trade press, he was dumbfounded by its logic. Two days later, Commonwealth cut off Simas' supplies, a full month before the President signed the necessary proclamation.

The worst was still to come. Faced with financial ruin, Simas hurriedly solicited emergency supplies from every refiner on the West Coast. All of them, including Powerine, turned him down, claiming to have no available supplies. Thirteen days later, however, Rothschild sent telegrams to each of Simas' customers offering to supply them with gasoline. "It is our understanding," read the wire, "that you may be needing an additional supply of gasoline."[71] Subsequent petitions by Simas to the President were of no avail, although in 1971, the Oil Import Appeals Board granted him a quota for 800 barrels a day. In its decision, the Board noted that after Simas' terminals ran out of supplies, wholesale gasoline prices in the area were raised substantially.[72]

By Washington's standards, the case of Walter Simas was a relatively inconsequential quirk of federal regulation, no different from hundreds of other local reverberations caused by the Mandatory Program. But the chain of political and economic effects surrounding the Simas situation does exemplify the process that leads regulation to fail. The Phillips exemption had first order effects of angering Phillips' competitors and distorting competitive relationships among them. This evoked a landslide of similar applications and forced Common-

---

[68] J. C. Moore to J. W. Towler (Union Oil), April 28, 1966; J. C. Moore to W. P. Tavoulareas (Mobil), July 14, 1966; J. C. Moore to Sen. Carl Hayden (D–AZ), July 14, 1966, Moore Papers, Chronological File, Box 2, LBJPL; also, extensive correspondence between Cordell Moore, West Coast congressmen, and other oil companies in Office of the Secretary, Central File, Secretary's Correspondence, Oil Import Administration, Permits and Quotas, Pts. 6–7 (DOI, Wash. D.C.).
[69] H. Rothschild to E. Hoehn, April 22, 1966, and Powerine Oil Co. to OIA, August 7, 1967, Oil Import Administration, Correspondence Files, Box 77, FRC.
[70] Department of the Interior, Press Release, December 15, 1967, Oil Import Administration, Correspondence Files, Box 74, FRC.
[71] U.S. Congress, Senate, *Government Intervention in the Market Mechanism*, pp. 1231, 1496–1500.
[72] OIAB decision on Docket No. T–55, April 20, 1971, Oil Import Administration, Correspondence Files, Box 74, FRC.

wealth Oil & Refining to seek another outlet for its product. That led to the Simas affair, and eventually to Senate antitrust hearings in 1969, where the Simas story was one of dozens reviewed. As will appear later, those hearings marked the beginning of the end for the Mandatory Oil Import Program.

By 1968, the Mandatory Program bore little resemblance to the controls envisioned by Eisenhower nine years before. Besides the exemptions already described, the Interior Department had authorized special allocations for asphalt refiners, electric utilities, heating oil importers, petrochemical companies, and finally, for crude oil quotas into foreign trade zones from which refined products would presumably be exported.

Oil-industry leaders were tired of these exemptions and the political process they entailed. "Favors granted to special interests," wrote an executive of Standard Oil of Indiana, "have come close to emasculating the program."[73] Spokesmen for domestic producers and state prorationing agencies added their weight in opposition to the "haphazard" allowance of special allocations.[74] Fred Hartley, the president of Union Oil, advised President Johnson that responsible businessmen and political leaders of both parties were "demanding the elimination of the existing Oil Import Program and its replacement by a program consonant with the original objective of aiding our national security in an equitable manner."[75]

Although these warnings may not have reached the President directly in 1968, he did get them summarized in the clearest of terms by one of his special assistants. DeVier Pierson began a harshly candid memorandum to the President with the statement, "The oil import program is a mess." He elaborated: "We are already drawing heavy fire from all parts of the industry – and the administration of the program is not pleasing anyone. While 'scandal' is too strong a term, evidence of shoddy administration, poor coordination and questionable policy decisions is growing."[76] According to Pierson, Udall was only partly responsible: "The heart of the problem has been that the White House does not participate in oil decisions." Pierson identified two options: either an interagency study or "adopt the policy of 'don't rock the boat.'"[77] Lyndon Johnson chose the latter.

Fittingly, the catalyst for change was a proposal for one last, giant exemption by Armand Hammer, the extraordinary political entrepreneur who had founded Occidental Petroleum. In less than a decade, Hammer had transformed Occidental into a major international oil company. Toward that end, pioneering the development of crude oil in Libya was his greatest coup. But his Libyan production was so prolific that it had outstripped Occidental's marketing capacity.

---

[73] George V. Meyers to Stewart Udall, March 7, 1968, Office of the Secretary, Central File, OIA Permits and Quotas, Pt. 9 (DOI, Wash., D.C.).

[74] W. E. Turner to M. Watson, April 14, 1967, and P. Johnson to S. Udall, August 21, 1967, LBJ Papers, Executive File, Box 13, LBJPL.

[75] F. Hartley to the President, May 10, 1968, Office of the Secretary, Central Files, OIA Permits and Quotas, Pt. 9 (DOI, Wash., D.C.).

[76] D. Pierson to the President, May 1, 1968, LBJ Papers, Executive File, Box 6, LBJPL.

[77] *Ibid.*, p. 3.

Armand Hammer sorely needed a U.S. outlet, and the new exemption for foreign trade zones seemed an ideal opportunity.

Playing on the State of Maine's depressed economy and the New England delegation's political apparatus for intervening in the Mandatory Program, Hammer proposed to build a refinery in the coastal town of Machiasport that would process 300,000 barrels a day of Libyan crude oil.[78] A quota for the crude oil would be unnecessary since the refinery would be constituted a foreign trade zone. But to make it profitable, Hammer needed an exemption to allow 100,000 barrels a day of the plant's products to enter U.S. customs territory from the zone. In return for this immense subsidy (approximately $45 million per year), Hammer claimed the project would (1) provide jobs for Maine; (2) give $7 million annually to an oceanographic research foundation; (3) help the balance of payments; (4) provide a new source of low-sulfur residual oil for New England; and (5) reduce the cost of fuel to the Defense Department by 10 percent.[79]

As Hammer anticipated, his proposal mobilized the entire New England congressional delegation and six governors in its support.[80] But he apparently underestimated the extent to which his scheme would mobilize opposition throughout the oil industry and attract the scrutiny of the press to the entire oil import program. The loophole Hammer was trying to enter was so big and so patently obvious that his competitors were outraged and even embarrassed. For the first time in more than a decade, the American Petroleum Institute took a position on oil imports. Frank Ikard, its president, told President Johnson that the Machiasport project "would place our oil import program and national security in a very precarious position."[81]

With three weeks left in his term, President Johnson announced that he would defer to the next Administration a decision on the Machiasport project. By doing so, he symbolically dumped the entire problem of oil import controls on Richard Nixon. And given the critical publicity over Machiasport and the Program's complete loss of support within the oil industry, President Nixon would have little choice but to act.

Prying open the barn door: Nixon's cabinet task force

In February 1969, after only a month in office, President Richard M. Nixon "reassumed" authority for oil imports that Lyndon Johnson had delegated to Interior. The White House also announced that the President, through a Cabi-

---

[78] For a full account of the Machiasport project, see Peter Bradford, *Fragile Structures: A Story of Oil Refineries, National Security, and the Coast of Maine* (N.Y.: Harpers Magazine Press, 1975); also, Martin Lobel, "Red, White, Blue and Gold: The Oil Import Quotas," *Washington Monthly*, August 1970, pp. 8–18.

[79] A. Hammer to L. B. Johnson, November 8, 1968, LBJ Papers, Executive File, Box 19, LBJPL. See also, U.S. Congress, Senate, *Governmental Intervention in the Market Mechanism*, pt. 3, pp. 1645–1673.

[80] Thomas McIntyre et al. to the President, December 30, 1968, LBJ Papers, Executive File, Box 19, LBJPL.

[81] F. Ikard to the President, November 7, 1968, LBJ Papers, Executive File, Box 19, LBJPL, p. 3.

net Task Force, would undertake a "full review of the nation's oil import policies." The review would devote special attention to the Machiasport project.[82] Two political initiatives lay behind these decisions: the oil industry's dissatisfaction with the process of allocating quotas, and growing external criticism of the Mandatory Oil Import Program's cost to consumers and its effects on competition.

The oil industry almost unanimously opposed a continuation of the Program as a process of single-interest exemptions. Determined to force some changes, Michael Haider, chairman of Standard Oil of New Jersey and the American Petroleum Institute, met with Arthur Burns, President Nixon's top domestic affairs advisor, shortly before the Cabinet Task Force was announced. Haider wanted a comprehensive re-evaluation of the Program rather than a narrow investigation of Machiasport.[83] The major companies that dominated the API sought a reorganized program that would allocate quotas on a no-frills basis, directly proportionate to refinery capacity. Domestic independent producers supported this position.

While responding to these pressures, President Nixon no doubt hoped to preempt the initiative from liberal Democratic senators who were responding to entirely different sources of political agitation. In March 1969, Senators Phillip A. Hart of Michigan and Edward M. Kennedy of Massachusetts commenced lengthy and intensive hearings before their Subcommittee on Antitrust and Monopoly, chaired by Hart, on the effects of governmental intervention in the petroleum industry. The purpose of those hearings was to examine and publicize the consumer costs of federal oil policy and its effects on the structure and competition of the oil industry. For John Blair, the Subcommittee's chief economist, the hearings were a continuation of the antitrust crusade he had begun in 1951 as author of the FPC's cartel report.[84]

A distinctive feature of Senator Hart's hearings was the intense, analytic criticism of government oil policy by an impressive collection of academic economists. The petroleum industry's "three gimmicks" – prorationing, the percentage depletion allowance, and import quotas – had created a sheltered, highly profitable, non-competitive market for crude oil that was very costly for consumers. Cornell's Alfred Kahn was among those who attributed excess capacity and rising costs to the interaction of prorationed production controls and the investment stimulus of the depletion allowance. But, as Kahn pointed out, that domestic system "could not survive unless there were controls maintained on imports." John Lichtblau estimated that import controls had cost consumers about $3.3 billion in 1968, since Arabian light crude was selling for $1.25 per barrel, while domestic oil brought nearly $3.00.[85]

---

[82] *Platt's Oilgram,* February 24, 1969.
[83] *Platt's Oilgram,* February 19, 1969.
[84] John Blair subsequently published *The Control of Oil* (N.Y.: Pantheon, 1976), a valuable study of policy and competition based on his experience at the FPC and with the Subcommittee on Antitrust and Monopoly.
[85] U.S. Congress, Senate, *Governmental Intervention in the Market Mechanism,* pt. 1, pp. 139, 320–325.

Hence, if the President's review was to have any credibility, it would need both institutional prestige and an aura of impartiality. On the fourth day of the Hart hearings, President Nixon announced that George Shultz, the Secretary of Labor, would head a Cabinet Task Force, whose other members would be the secretaries of State, Treasury, Commerce, Interior, and Defense, and the Director of the Office of Emergency Preparedness. Officials from other agencies would participate informally. Phillip Areeda, a Harvard law professor, would direct the study, assisted by Professor James McKie as chief economist. These two appointments and the absence of experienced industrial personnel alarmed some oil industry spokesmen and prompted scattered congressional criticism.[86] This concern on the part of the industry proved to be well-founded.

Under Areeda's direction, the Task Force study of oil import controls was painfully thorough. It was not limited, as the industry had hoped, to a review of the Mandatory Program's mismanagement of quota allocations. That turned out to be a non-issue. Instead, the Task Force staff challenged the basic rationale for import controls – the validity of the national security premise, the Program's costs to consumers, the effect of import controls on other energy sources, and alternative policies for managing oil imports. It received 10,000 pages of comments from more than 200 firms, trade associations, government agencies, and politicians. It solicited position papers from two dozen scholars and multi-volume analyses from some federal departments. It prepared its own series of working papers. In effect, the Task Force staff of economic liberals seized control of the review process and neither the Interior Department nor the White House could recapture it.

Investigation of the Program's costs to consumers was the most sensitive and contentious issue. Interested parties could only agree to the general proposition that import controls did impose costs on consumers and on the economy of the nation. There was little agreement on the size of these costs or the degree to which they should be discounted by related savings and revenue effects. The Task Force staff estimated that the net cost to consumers was $4.5 billion for 1969, and with no change in policy, it would increase to $6.7 billion by 1980.[87] Indirect costs in lost efficiency and wasted resources, for which the Task Force presented no conclusions, were variously estimated to be as high as $13 billion.

Given the political implications of these startling estimates, spokesmen for the oil industry took pains to refute them. Calculations by several major companies put the annual gross cost of import controls to consumers at approximately $3 billion. Discounted for savings on lower-priced natural gas and gas liquids and government revenues from taxes and royalties, this amounted to net costs between $550 million and $1.4 billion.[88] Independent producers extended such analyses by estimating the revenue losses that would result from

[86] *Wall Street Journal*, April 9, 1969; *Platt's Oilgram*, April 22, 1969; and *Oil and Gas Journal*, April 28, 1969.
[87] Cabinet Task Force on Oil Import Control, *The Oil Import Question*, February 1970 (Wash., D.C.: GPO, 1970), pp. 259–262.
[88] Continental Oil Company, "Summary Statement on Oil Import Control," July 15, 1969 (Continental Oil Company, Houston, Texas), p. 11.

decontrol; the balance of payments effects, lost wages, private royalties and supplier incomes, and lost state and local taxes would total more than $6 billion, purportedly offsetting the consumer costs.[89]

The controversy over costs led logically to debate over the price elasticity of demand and the effect that decontrol would have on both domestic and world price. There was little disagreement that decontrol of oil imports would at least result in a short-run decline in domestic crude oil prices, perhaps by as much as 85 cents a barrel. The real issue was what effect import decontrol would have on aggregate demand for petroleum and on world oil prices. Most economists believed that the demand was highly inelastic and would therefore not increase when prices declined. And since they also believed in equilibria where price matched marginal costs, they felt certain that decontrol would cause the world price to decline. After all, Arabian oil was selling for nearly ten times its marginal cost of production. "If the United States imported much more than it does now," declared Adelman, "the result would be lower, not higher prices." According to theory, "every producer would be under the greatest inducement and pressure, and host governments would lower taxes to let companies cut prices." Because of the huge surplus of production capacity in the U.S. and the Middle East, Adelman felt it would be many years before marginal costs caught up with existing high prices and caused those prices to rise.[90]

The oil industry's analysts were less certain about the price inelasticity of petroleum demand and did not believe that import decontrol would cause world prices to decline. Several of the major companies advised the Task Force that terminating quotas would stimulate demand and hence price. The marginal cost concept had merit when applied to a manufacturing facility, but was less useful with respect to a depletable resource controlled by the governments of undeveloped countries. Those governments, argued Gulf Oil, "are aware of the depletable natures of their resource and that selling more oil now at a reduced price will reduce their overall income from this resource." To the contrary, Gulf felt "quite confident" that the producing nations "will try to obtain an increase in price."[91] The National Petroleum Council echoed this analysis with the warning that "some very large increases in petroleum costs would be possible and even probable" if the United States became dependent on foreign oil.[92]

Whether or not the governments of producing nations could effect a price increase or control output was a crucial question in the whole issue regarding the benefits to national security derived from import controls. Proponents of import decontrol did not take issue with the basic premise that excessive dependence on foreign energy was a security risk in the event of a general non-nuclear war of substantial duration. However, import disruptions for political

[89] U.S. Congress, Senate, *Government Intervention in the Market Mechanism*, pt. 2, p. 629.
[90] *Ibid.*, 10.
[91] Gulf Oil Corporation, "Rebuttal to Initial Submissions – The Cabinet Task Force on Oil Import Control," July 15, 1969 (Gulf Oil Co., Pittsburgh, Pa.), pp. 19–20; also, Continental Oil Company, "Summary Statement on Oil Import Control," p. 9.
[92] National Petroleum Council, *U.S. Petroleum Imports 1969*, A Report of the National Petroleum Council to the Secretary of the Interior, August 1, 1969 (Wash., D.C.), p. 47.

purposes, while not dismissed, were viewed as unlikely and of limited consequence.[93]

The oil industry, from domestic independents to international majors, took issue with this apparent complacency. Various industry spokesmen cited the supply disruptions caused by Middle East wars in 1956 and 1967 as evidence of the need to maintain adequate domestic production capacity and to limit dependence on imports. In support of higher, rather than lower domestic prices, they pointed to the alarming decline in exploratory drilling and new discoveries. "A reduction in the price of domestic oil," claimed John Swearingen, the chairman of Standard Oil of Indiana, "would result in the U.S. becoming dependent at an accelerating rate and to an intolerable degree on insecure sources." Those sources, he warned, "could be denied overnight because of Russian influence, anti-American sentiment or cartel-type economic collaboration."[94]

Throughout the review, members of the Task Force were subjected to intense pressure from individual congressmen, regional coalitions, and all sorts of interest groups.[95] The final report, issued in February 1970, reflects as much. The staff obviously preferred immediate decontrol of oil imports. The Task Force majority compromised to the extent of supporting gradual liberalization of import controls through a declining tariff that would replace the quota. Imports from Canada and Mexico would be totally exempt, but all other special privileges would be phased out. The Secretaries of Interior and Commerce, together with the Chairman of the FPC, refused to endorse the majority recommendation. In a separate report, they urged the President to maintain a quota on imported oil, improve its administration, and increase its ceiling gradually.[96] During the next three years, President Nixon would follow the minority recommendation, until shortages finally forced him to abolish the quotas.

The balance wheel

The Mandatory Oil Import Program was a policy of political compromise that maintained the level of oil imports at about 12 percent of domestic production for 11 years. A political stand-off among contending interest groups and between government agencies with conflicting agenda made the achievement of this stasis possible. If short-term energy security was really a preeminent goal, then the policy was a success. It preserved a margin of spare domestic capacity and postponed dependency on foreign oil. Likewise, if its purpose was to subsidize small refiners, marginal domestic producers, and the school systems of Texas and Louisiana, that too was accomplished. But these ends were only achieved at considerable costs – to consumers and to economic efficiency. Import controls delayed for a decade the structural and economic adjustments that depletion made inevitable.

[93] Cabinet Task Force, *The Oil Import Question*, pp. 125–26.
[94] J. E. Swearingen to G. P. Shultz, December 24, 1969, Office of the Secretary, Central Files, OIA Permits and Quotas, Pt. 9 (DOI, Wash., D.C.).
[95] Office of the Secretary, Central File, OIA Permits and Quotas, Parts 2–4 (DOI, Wash., D.C.).
[96] Cabinet Task Force, *The Oil Import Question*, pp. 128–39, 343–44.

Because of its fixed, proportionate character, the import quota was at once too little and too much. By supporting domestic oil prices at an artificial level, it prevented the market, both at home and abroad, from adjusting gradually to the growth of world demand and the depletion of U.S. reserves. In other words, just enough Persian Gulf oil was allowed into the United States to discourage commercialization of synthetic fuels or the development of higher-cost petroleum reserves. At the same time, the quota sufficiently restricted demand for foreign oil so that world prices fell. This increased the value of a quota ticket in the United States, and hence the pressure on individual companies to find a way of importing more. It also alienated Middle East producers and helped reorient them to seek price rather than production increases.

While business and government concentrated on the politics of quota allocations, the import and price stasis gradually caused a reduction of spare domestic production capacity. At the end of 1964, spare capacity was estimated at 4.2 million barrels per day.[97] By 1969, it had declined to 1.7 million barrels per day because domestic demand for crude oil had grown by 3 percent per year while proved reserves remained constant.[98] If spare capacity continued to decline at that rate, there would be none left by 1972, at least in the United States. This trend, with its implications for price and national security, was either not apparent or unimportant to both public and private policy makers at the time of the Task Force review.

The Mandatory Oil Import Program had several microeconomic effects as well. It prevented the international majors that developed foreign oil from gaining as much market share as would otherwise have resulted from their substantial comparative advantage. It allowed several dozen, relatively inefficient independent refiners to stay in business. Without quota tickets, they could not have competed with the major companies in any but the most isolated markets. By protecting independent refiners, the Program probably did help the development of independent distributors and marketers, self-service chains, and a greater degree of retail competition than would have occurred otherwise. With regard to interfuel competition, the Mandatory Program had mixed results. By not enforcing restrictions on imports of residual oil, it certainly accommodated the coal industry's loss of industrial markets in the Northeast. And by supporting the price of home heating oil above market-clearing levels, the Mandatory Program helped stimulate demand for natural gas, which was shortly to exceed available supply.

In 1953, the chairman of Gulf Oil had foreseen that oil imports could be the "balance wheel" of U.S. energy policy – and so they were for nearly two decades. But in the absence of a functional price mechanism, the policy wheel could not balance indefinitely the pent-up and contradictory pressures of physical depletion and economic growth.

---

[97] National Petroleum Council, "Factors Affecting U.S. Exploration, Development, and Production 1946–1965," January 31, 1967 (Wash., D.C., 1967).
[98] Cabinet Task Force, *The Oil Import Question*, p. 51; also, American Petroleum Institute, *Basic Petroleum Databook*, November 1976, section 2, table 2.

7. Formula for shortage: natural gas price controls

Shortly before John F. Kennedy took office in 1961, he received a report on regulatory agencies from James Landis, the retired chairman of the Securities Exchange Commission. Landis, amidst his general criticism of the state of government regulation, singled out the FPC for particularly harsh judgment: "The Federal Power Commission without question represents the outstanding example in the federal government of the breakdown of the administrative process. The complexity of its problems is no answer to its more than patent failures." He concluded that these "defects stem from attitudes, plainly evident on the record, of the unwillingness of the Commission to assume its responsibilities under the Natural Gas Act and its attitude, substantially contemptuous, of refusing in substance to obey the mandates of the Supreme Court of the United States and other federal courts."[1]

Landis was not alone in his dismay over the Commission's failure to implement the Supreme Court's dictum for rate regulation of natural gas producers. In the six years since the court's 1954 decision that Phillips Petroleum as a gas producer was subject to FPC rate-making, natural gas prices had nearly doubled. And Landis judged that the Commission had taken the side of "monopolistic and excessive rates."[2] Landis, as well as other critics, felt that the Commission and its procedures, rather than any conceptual problems, were the sources of disorder. Shortly after becoming a special White House assistant, Landis explained the problem to the new President as follows: "The incidence of this problem of rate backlogs could largely have been avoided. The FPC, however, trod water hoping that the Fulbright bill would eliminate all these cases by removing federal controls over rates of natural gas producers. After this was defeated, I believe that the FPC deliberately sought to prove that rate regulation of natural gas production was an administrative impossibility."[3]

The Kennedy administration settled on two solutions to the problem: reg-

---

[1] James M. Landis, "Report on Regulatory Agencies to the President-Elect," in U.S. Congress, Senate Judiciary Committee, Subcommittee on Administrative Practice and Procedure, Committee Print (86th Cong., 2nd Sess.), December 1960, pp. 54–55.

[2] *Ibid.*

[3] J. Landis to J. F. Kennedy, February 20, 1961, Box 78, Presidential Office File, John F. Kennedy Library, Boston, Massachusetts.

ulatory reform and the appointment of new commissioners. White House staff prepared legislative recommendations to restructure the FPC and its procedures, and to provide limited deregulation for small independent producers. The reorganization, based in part on recommendations of the American Gas Association, would increase the Commission's membership to seven, extend their tenure of office, and allow them to sit in investigative panels. It would also recommend budgeting for additional professional staff.[4] These proposals clearly departed from the Eisenhower objectives of reducing government involvement in business. For the Kennedy administration, better regulation seemed to suggest more regulation. The proposals made no significant progress in the Congress. Nonetheless, because of expirations and resignations, the President was able to appoint five new commissioners – the whole body – among whom was Joseph Swidler, as chairman succeeding Jerome K. Kuykendall. Landis hoped that under Swidler's activist leadership, the new FPC would "revitalize" natural gas regulation.[5]

One thing was clear: such a revitalization would depend on the successful development by the Swidler FPC of a new system of rate-making. The Commission had made little progress since the *Phillips* decision toward establishing an effective system of regulation for the field price of natural gas. The Commission, swamped by its intolerable load of cases, had investigated cost-based, company-by-company rate setting for several years and had recently announced its failure. This investigation and failure occurred mainly in a "Second Phillips Case," begun by the Commission in 1956 and concluded in 1960.

The Second Phillips Case

The Second Phillips Case came about as follows. In the mid-fifties, both the Commission and the gas industry were preoccupied by the pending Fulbright–Harris legislation, which offered a solution to the problem. The majority of the Commission endorsed deregulation of producers, not only to avoid the administrative nightmare, but because it believed that producer regulation was unwise and not intended by Congress in the Natural Gas Act. But when President Eisenhower vetoed the legislation in 1956, the attention of commissioners and producers shifted to finding a usable regulatory formula. Pipeline companies that produced some of their own gas were likewise interested in establishing a rate method that would return something more than costs. It should be recalled that in the *City of Detroit* case, the court had ruled in 1955 that field prices were not an acceptable basis for the rates of interstate pipeline companies.

Gas producers that were not pipeline companies hoped that the FPC would not apply the *City of Detroit* ruling to them. In their various rate petitions since 1954, producers had submitted only field price evidence, trying to persuade the Commission that the public interest would be better served "by the law of

4   C. Bolton-Smith to M. Feldman, October 27, 1961, Box 9, Feldman Papers, JFKL; also, American Gas Association, "Report of the Special Committee of Executives on Regulatory Affairs," March 7, 1961.
5   J. Swidler to M. Feldman, February 15, 1962, Box 489, White House Central File, JFKL.

supply and demand."[6] The producers lacked the criteria, the accounting basis, and the incentive to prepare and submit the kind of data the Commission needed to determine cost-based rates.

In December of 1956, the FPC issued an opinion in a case involving Union Oil, which was not a pipeline company. The Commission held that neither field price data nor evidence of "arm's-length" bargaining were sufficient to sustain the burden of proof as to "just and reasonable" rates.[7] That decision, although it did not dictate cost-based regulation, appeared to leave independent producers with no alternative but to develop cost-based data and work toward convincing the Commission to adopt sensible criteria.

Proceedings in the Second Phillips Case, which the Commission had commenced a few months earlier, became the principal forum in which the new methods of gas price regulation would be developed. In the first *Phillips* case, the only issue before the Supreme Court had been that of the FPC's jurisdiction over independent gas producers. Thus, in the second case, the Commission had to start from scratch to determine "just and reasonable" rates for Phillips Petroleum, as precedent for several thousand other producers. The critical issue was whether or not cost-based rate regulation could and should be applied on a company-by-company basis. The conclusion would depend on the net effect of various subordinate issues pertaining to cost allocation, tax treatment, rate of return, and administrative feasibility.

Besides Phillips and the FPC staff, thirty-two intervenors participated in the case. Among these were several major gas distributors, four interstate pipeline companies, the Mid-Continent Oil & Gas Association, various city and state governments, and the utility commissions of California, Michigan, Wisconsin, and New York. Most of these intervenors offered evidence and testimony on particular technical or informational points. But full-scale cost-of-service studies were presented by Phillips, the FPC staff, the Wisconsin Public Service Commission, and a group of large distributors (the Eastern Seaboard Intervenors).[8] Among the witnesses for the latter was the economist Alfred Kahn, whose testimony in subsequent cases would have a major impact on gas regulation.

The natural gas industry did not unanimously oppose cost-based regulation of wellhead prices. Although most producers and the pipeline companies did, the distribution sector thought company-by-company rate-making was possible and supported it. And Phillips Petroleum, if it had to be regulated, ironically favored a cost-of-service method over a field-price standard or any similar criterion based on "commodity value." At the time, this was not an illogical position on Phillips' part. The rate it claimed under its cost formula (18.7 cents per thousand cubic feet) was considerably higher than the market price of 10.1

---

[6] Federal Power Commission, Report of the Hearing Examiner, *Docket No. G-1148,* "In the Matter of Phillips Petroleum Company," 24 FPC 590 (April 1959), p. 602.

[7] Federal Power Commission, *Opinion No. 300,* "In the Matter of Union Oil Company of California," 16 FPC 100 (December, 1956); this opinion was subsequently upheld in *Bel Oil Corporation v. Federal Power Commission,* 255 F. 2d 548.

[8] FPC, Report of the Hearing Examiner, *Docket No. G-1148,* pp. 601–602, 778.

Table 7-1. *Cost-based rate recommendations in the Second Phillips Case*

Party	Rate of return (%)	Total cost of service	Average unit cost (cents/thousand cu.ft.)
Phillips	12[a]	$92,309,438	18.79
FPC Staff	9	42,024,180	8.55
Eastern Intervenors[b]	9	55,046,180	11.21
	12	60,489,832	12.31
Wisconsin PSC	7.75	48,647,832	9.90
Commission	11	55,548,054	11.30

[a]This rate, together with retention of special tax privileges, would have amounted to an effective rate of return of 18%.
[b]Eastern Intervenors offered two sets of figures without recommending one over the other.
Source: FPC, Report of the Hearing Examiner, *Docket No. G-1148,* "In the Matter of Phillips Petroleum Company," 24 FPC 590 (April, 1959), p. 617.

cents that prevailed in the base year of 1954.[9] This cooperative stance by Phillips went a long way toward mitigating, at least in the view of the FPC hearing examiner, most of the complaints about cost-based regulation from various intervenors.

The four major cost studies, although similar in design, relied on different assumptions, values, and methodologies that together yielded significantly different rate recommendations. Table 7-1 summarizes the different effects, together with the findings of the Commission itself. Not surprisingly, Phillips' study produced a rate nearly double that of the consumer-oriented Wisconsin Public Service Commission. The FPC staff recommended the lowest price, reflecting its commitment to conventional rate-making principles and its reluctance to acknowledge the investment risks to exploration or a causal link between price and discovery.

Allocation of costs for the cost-of-service formula was the worst technical problem. For an integrated oil company like Phillips, how were costs to be separated between oil and gas activities, between interstate and intrastate sales, and between processed dry gas and the natural gas condensates that were valuable by-products? From its experience with transmission companies, the FPC was at least familiar with the latter two. But the physical and managerial activities involved in the exploration and production of oil and gas were virtually inseparable. Like other producers, Phillips purchased leases based on the hope of finding oil and the expectation that hydrocarbon resources were present. Exploratory wells were unidirectional, at least in the 1950's, making no distinction between oil and gas. In most companies, the operating expenses for the exploration and production departments were recorded on a single set of books. The Commission had to admit that any method for separating these costs

[9]   Federal Power Commission, *Opinion No. 468,* 34 FPC 159 (August, 1965), p. 257.

would be arbitrary at best, and most likely "inexact, complex, unsatisfactory" and "fraught with controversy."[10]

For production costs, Phillips proposed a so-called "relative cost method" which the Commission accepted with modifications. For direct costs, Phillips looked at its operations that were devoted exclusively to natural gas production from dry gas fields. It did the same for operations devoted solely to oil production. By summing the direct costs of each separately and dividing by the outputs, it came up with a ratio of unit costs that it then applied to joint oil and gas producing operations. Indirect costs were apportioned by a similar method. Both the Wisconsin Public Service Commission and the Eastern Intervenors accepted this method, but the Commission staff did not. Making no effort at allocation, the staff simply calculated Phillips' costs for producing dry gas, and then imputed that unit cost to the volume of associated gas that was produced jointly with oil.[11]

If this procedure seems strained, then the various methods proposed for exploration costs require an act of faith. Though ingenious, they reveal the inherent irrationality of cost-of-service rate regulation as a plausible substitute for market economics.

Of six methods proposed, only two interested the Commission. Phillips offered a two-step method that allocated 62 percent of joint exploration costs to natural gas. To get this result, it divided exploratory costs between its Natural Gas Department and its Oil and Gas Production Department in proportion to each department's net investment in producing leases. Then, it further separated the amount assigned to the Oil and Gas Production Department in proportion to the Btu-value of the oil and gas produced by that department. Phillips reasoned that its exploratory activities represented a search for energy that "is useable in whatever form it is found."[12] All of the intervenors, however, rejected this Btu rationale out-of-hand. Benjamin Caplan, an economist for the Eastern group, argued that "to ignore the differences in characteristics between the joint products and to subsume them under a single unit of physical measurement is to fly in the face of the economic facts of life." His colleague, Alfred Kahn, thought it "most unlikely" that the field price of gas would ever equal the Btu-equivalent price of oil. Things would look different twenty years later.[13]

As an alternate method, the Eastern Intervenors suggested that joint exploration costs be apportioned according to the "relative commercial importance" of additions to oil and gas reserves through successful exploration. In a sense, this was a compromise between something based on realized revenues and something based on physical results. It would measure the value of exploration on the basis of annual discoveries rather than sales. This method attributed only 30

[10] Federal Power Commission, *Opinion No. 338* ("In the Matter of Phillips Petroleum Company"), 24 FPC 537 (September 1960), p. 544.
[11] FPC, Report of the Hearing Examiner, *Docket No. G–1148*, pp. 619–29.
[12] *Ibid.*, 639.
[13] Benjamin Caplan, *Ibid.*, 643; also, Alfred Kahn, "Economic Issues in Regulating the Field Price of Natural Gas," *American Economic Review*, 50 (May 1960), 513.

percent of exploratory costs to natural gas. While less than half what Phillips sought, it was half again as much as most of the other intervenors had advocated.

The Commission adopted the Phillips method for allocating production costs, but drastically revised its Btu approach to exploration costs. Phillips had used a standard Btu ratio of 6:1 between a barrel of oil and a thousand cubic feet of gas. The FPC pointed to the ratio of 33:1 between Phillips' oil and gas field prices in 1954. Since the trend of this ratio was downward, the Commission felt that a ratio of 24:1 in realized revenue was more realistic. That translated, by an admitted exercise of "adminstrative judgment," to a Btu ratio of 4:1. On that basis, the Commission allocated 33 percent of Phillips' exploration costs to natural gas.[14]

A less difficult, but equally controversial issue involved the proper treatment of special tax privileges that oil and gas producers traditionally enjoyed. Phillips, in its first brush with cost-based regulation, hoped and perhaps expected to retain the benefits of the percentage depletion allowance and the expensing of intangible drilling costs. For its gas operations alone, Phillips' tax savings from these two provisions amounted to $23 million, or more than 50 percent of annual earnings. In the traditional formula for determining pipeline rates, taxes as actually paid were treated as operating costs. Thus, any tax savings were simply passed through to the consumer as a reduction in the cost-of-service computation on which rates were based. In order to retain these special benefits within the new framework of rate regulation, Phillips tried to report a tax obligation that reflected the standard rate of 52 percent on corporate income, as if it had paid that amount. Were it allowed to charge such "phantom tax," as its critics called it, the result would have been an effective rate of return of 18 percent (12 percent on the rate base plus tax savings amounting to 6 additional percent).[15]

The Commission had recently ruled on this issue in another case that involved the El Paso Natural Gas Company. In that instance, the FPC allowed retention of special tax benefits in lieu of a separate return on gas-producing assets.[16] But after the record in the Phillips case was closed and before the decision was rendered, an appeals court overturned the FPC's opinion in the El Paso case, finding no justification for charging consumers with phantom taxes.[17] This obviously undermined Phillips' position, and the Commission rejected it.

The question of rate of return, like every other issue in the Second Phillips Case, was more controversial than previous cases pertaining to pipeline companies. No one considered Phillips Petroleum to be a public utility, and yet its earnings on natural gas had to be regulated. Still, the hearing examiner, the

[14] FPC, *Opinion No. 338*, pp. 560–561.
[15] *Ibid.*, 567–569.
[16] Federal Power Commission, *Docket No. G-4769*, "Brief of El Paso Natural Gas Company," February 26, 1957, pp. 45–48; and Federal Power Commission, *Opinion No. 326*, 22 FPC 260 (August 1959).
[17] *El Paso Natural Gas Company v. Federal Power Commission*, 281 F. 2d 567 (1960).

FPC staff, and the Wisconsin Public Service Commission looked to precedent to justify their recommendations. Cited most frequently were the Supreme Court's criteria in the *Hope* case; that the return should provide "enough revenue not only for operating expenses but also for the capital costs of the business," and that "the return to the equity owner should be commensurate with returns on investments in other enterprises having corresponding risks."[18]

Phillips argued that its risks as a business enterprise engaged primarily in exploration, production, and wholesale competition were greater than those of an interstate pipeline company. Thus, Phillips proposed a 12 percent rate of return, over and above the tax savings, based on the ratio of its earnings to the book value of its equity. The FPC staff urged a 9 percent rate of return, without the tax savings, based on the conventional criterion – the ratio of earnings to the price of common stock. The hearing examiner accepted this method because it avoided the circularity of Phillips' approach. "The ratio of earnings to book value," he said, "is the end product of rate-making and not its starting point."[19] Following no particular rationale, the Commission compromised between these two approaches and allowed Phillips an 11 percent rate of return (which translated to a 12 percent return on equity because of its low debt-to-equity ratio). "Some allowance must be made," said the Commission, "to promote the continued exploration for and production of gas."[20]

Putting all of these precedential pieces together, the Federal Power Commission fixed a wellhead price of 11.3 cents per thousand cubic feet for the natural gas sales of Phillips Petroleum. Though this was far less than Phillips had sought, it was about equal to the average new contract price for gas as of 1957. In fact, it amounted to a cost-of-service allowance of $55 million, or about 18 percent more than Phillips' gas revenues under existing negotiated contracts. This forced the Commission to the ironic conclusion that "regulation of production by a company-by-company rate base method will in all probability result in higher consumer prices than we would otherwise have." The reason was finally clear, at least to this outgoing Commission: "Natural gas has been, in almost all instances, substantially underpriced."[21]

The FPC's substantive findings in the Second Phillips Case were quite overshadowed by its broader conclusions and concurrent action regarding the feasibility of cost-of-service rate making for independent gas producers. In view of the extraordinary technical difficulties and the four-year duration of the case, the commissioners realized that, if nothing else, company-by-company rate making was not feasible. "If our present staff were immediately tripled," the Commission noted plaintively, "we would not reach a current status in our independent producer rate work until 2043 A.D. – eighty-two and one half years from now."[22]

The Second Phillips Case not only demonstrated the administrative difficul-

---

18 *FPC v. Hope Natural Gas Company*, 320 U.S. 603 (1944).
19 FPC, Report of the Hearing Examiner, *Docket No. G-1148*, p. 731.
20 Federal Power Commission, *Opinion No. 338*, pp. 546–547.
21 *Ibid.*, 546.
22 *Ibid.*

ties of company-by-company rate-making, but it dramatized some conceptual problems of cost-based rate regulation. The data had been distorted, the criteria arbitrary, and the findings had no apparent connection to the economic realities of the gas business. Thus the Commission, in an unusual display of bureaucratic recantation, concluded that effective regulation "must be on some more manageable plan than the rate base method." It would be better "to establish fair prices for the gas itself and not each individual."[23]

With that, the FPC terminated the Phillips proceedings in September 1960, established temporary price ceilings for natural gas in each of the major gas-producing areas, and announced the beginning of a new proceeding to determine "just and reasonable" rates on an area basis.

Area rates and two-tier pricing

The FPC chose the Permian Basin Area for its test case. The Permian Area, covering a large part of Texas, is one of six major gas-producing regions in the continental United States. Proceedings in the Permian case lasted five years, and the Commission's 1965 decision was not confirmed by the Supreme Court until 1968.

To fill the regulatory gap during its Permian deliberations, the FPC established ceiling-price guidelines for old (flowing) and new natural gas in each producing area. For flowing gas, the guideline was based on the average field price in each area, while the new gas ceiling reflected the highest contract price that the Commission had previously certified.[24] The guidelines for old gas ranged from 11 to 14 cents per thousand cubic feet; new gas was allowed from 14 to 18 cents. In the Permian Basin area, for example, the suggested ceiling for old gas was 11 cents, and for new gas, 16 cents. According to the Commission's cryptic explanation, this revolutionary two-tier pricing structure was necessary "by virtue of economic factors." The price differential was supposedly temporary, and would eventually dissipate "as subsequent experience brings about revisions." These rates were not definitive, but mere guidelines, to serve until "just and reasonable" area rates could be determined.[25] In the meantime, negotiated sales contracts could go higher, subject to refunds if the rate determined eventually were lower.

Apart from its methodological innovations, the Permian case was noteworthy because it focused on substantive economic issues that had been wholly ignored in previous cases. One reason for this injection of economic thought was the shift from company-oriented cost computation to commodity-based price setting. Another was the participation in the proceedings of several capable economists, including Charles Foster, Alfred Kahn, Otto Eckstein, and Bruce Netschert. A third reason was that the area case involved not one but dozens of

[23] *Ibid.*, 527.
[24] E. W. Kitch, "Regulation of the Field Market for Natural Gas by the Federal Power Commission," in Paul MacAvoy, ed., *The Crisis of the Regulatory Commissions* (New York: W. W. Norton & Co., 1970), pp. 160–170.
[25] Federal Power Commission, *General Policy No. 61–1*, 24 FPC 818 (September 1960).

major producers and distributors. The Commission encouraged these participants to pool their resources and present joint briefs that were rich in data and
sophisticated analysis.[26] Finally, there was widespread concern over market
conditions; although gas prices had risen prior to 1960, the reserve life index
had still declined from 32.5 in 1946 to 20.1 by 1960. This development raised
questions regarding the degree and effectiveness of field price competition, the
economic relationship between natural gas and petroleum, the price elasticity of
supply, the effects of average-cost pricing, and the impact of long-term contracts and committed reserves on supply and price. Interestingly, the technical
issue of "directionality" affected most of these economic questions.

By 1960, production of gas from gas wells had grown to 72 percent of total
output (up from 64 percent in 1948). The ratio of gas-well reserves to casinghead reserves (gas associated with oil) was about the same. According to the
producers, the development of "directionality" was responsible for this trend.
"Directionality" refers to the technical capability of a producer to explore for
and develop gas reserves separately from the search for oil. Whether or not this
capability existed and was utilized was relevant to the problem of cost allocation
and crucial to the issue of incentive pricing.

The FPC staff maintained that producers only discovered natural gas incidental to their search for petroleum. The major producers refuted this. They
presented some compelling evidence that directional capability had been developed only recently with advances in seismic research and the accumulation of
more and more geologic data. Their geologists had kept records of pre-drilling
predictions as to whether oil or gas would be found. The results showed a
degree of accuracy between 80 and 90 percent.[27] The Commission examined
recent trend data for the exploratory footage and revenues of natural gas relative to oil. Although new exploratory footage for dry gas had risen 68 percent
since 1950, the same measure for oil had fallen by 19 percent. This appeared to
correspond with an increase of gas revenues by 48 percent, and a decline of oil
revenues by 8 percent. Taken together, these data convinced the Commission
that directionality was real. Alfred Kahn, who had previously dismissed that
argument, now acknowledged that "clearly we are at or have already crossed
that threshold of a high degree of separability."[28]

Directionality led to price elasticity. Prior to 1960, the gas supply was generally thought to be price inelastic. That is, an increase in price had little or no
effect on eliciting a greater supply. This assumption, which depended on the
absence of directionality, undercut the producers' contention that higher prices

---

[26] Federal Power Commission, "Area Rate Proceedings, Docket No. AR61-1," *Opinion No. 468*,
34 FPC 159 (August, 1965). Most of the major oil and gas producing companies cooperated as the
"Joint Producer Respondents." About a dozen, however, including Gulf, Phillips, and Texaco,
chose to submit separate briefs and testimony. Three interstate pipeline companies that operated in
the Permian Basin participated, of which El Paso Natural Gas, with 73 percent of the total volume,
was the most important. There were several groups of distributors, state utility commissions, as well
as the State of Texas, the Texas Independent Producers & Royalty Owners, and the Independent
Petroleum Association of America.
[27] FPC, *Opinion No. 468*, pp. 326–327.
[28] *Ibid.*, 325–327.

were needed to stimulate greater exploration and development. It was also germane to the issue of competitiveness, since an inelastic supply "might cause even a competitive market to work badly."[29] The Commission explained this important relationship as follows: "If the producers can drill directionally for gas, the elasticity of supply will be substantially increased, because they will be able to direct their efforts toward gas when it is economic for them to do so." From this, it followed that "if prices will evoke a substantial supply response, it can be used as a reasonably effective instrument in eliciting supply."[30] With directionality providing causation, the Commission identified an effect in the relationship of price to exploratory activity. It concluded that after 1956, "the supply of gas was responsive to gas price to a considerable degree." This conclusion became the fundamental rationale for a two-tier price structure which, ironically, the producers themselves opposed.

Neither the producers nor the FPC staff wanted a price structure that permanently distinguished between old and new gas – but for opposite reasons. The producers felt that all gas should be priced at current contract levels, or at least on the basis of current exploration and production costs. The staff, which denied that costs had risen significantly or that the supply was elastic, held out for a rate based on the historical average cost of flowing gas.

It was the distributor group that propounded a system of two-tier pricing. The distributors had a contradictory interest in keeping their rates low enough to gain market share in interfuel competition, but high enough to give producers an incentive to ensure that future supplies would continue to flow to the interstate gas market. Their spokesman, Alfred Kahn, explained that separate pricing was necessary because increasing costs and regulatory lag "would otherwise leave companies with chronically inadequate cash and incentive to add to capacity or commit what they find to interstate markets."[31]

From the Commission's perspective, a two-price system seemed an ideal compromise for an impossible regulatory issue. A single price based on current costs "would result in windfall profits for all other gas" and had little bearing on "the logic of inducement." On the other hand, the Commission rejected the staff's brief for historical costs, since it believed that the gas supply had become elastic. It was easy and perhaps logical to conclude that "the two-price system thus holds out a reward to encourage producers to engage in further exploration and development while preventing excess and unnecessary revenues from the sale of gas developed at a period when there was no special exploratory activity directed to gas discovery."[32] Given the prevailing state of regulatory economics and the inherent difficulty of the trade-off between equity and efficiency, the two-tier price structure, or "vintaging" as it would soon be called, seemed like a good idea at the time.

This still left the question of what levels to set new and old prices. It was a foregone conclusion that some measure of costs would be the basis. Judicial

[29] A. Kahn, "Economic Issues in Regulating the Field Price of Natural Gas," p. 507.
[30] FPC, *Opinion No. 468*, p. 329.
[31] A. Kahn, "Economic Issues in Regulating the Field Price of Natural Gas," p. 510.
[32] FPC, *Opinion No. 468*, pp. 186–187.

Table 7-2. *Comparison of gas rate proposals and market prices in the Permian area rate proceeding*

Proponent	New gas	Old gas	Other
Producers			20.0 (single price based on new gas costs)
FPC staff			13.7 (gas well gas)
			9.0 (casinghead gas)
Distributors	14.5	12.0–13.5	9.0–10.5 (casinghead gas)
California PUC	13.5	11.9	9.0–10.3 (casinghead gas)
Commission	16.5	14.5	
TIPRO			17.0–21.8
National average			15.1
Wellhead price (1961)			
National average			18.2
New contract price (1961)			

Note: Cents per thousand cubic feet.
Sources: Federal Power Commission, *Opinion No. 468*, 34 FPC 159 (August 1965); American Gas Association, *Gas Facts* 1975 (Wash. D.C.: AGA, 1976), p. 110; P. MacAvoy and Robert Pindyck, *Price Controls and the Natural Gas Shortage* (Wash. D.C.: AEI, 1975), p. 14.

precedent, the experience of the Second Phillips Case, the doubtful competitiveness of the market, and the Swidler Commission's own regulatory tenets left little room for any alternate approach. The producer's brief for fair field prices was dismissed out-of-hand. To simply validate negotiated prices, said the Commission, "would amount to an abdication of our regulatory responsibility."[33] It only remained for the Commission to compute unit costs based on separate aggregated data for old and new gas.

With two exceptions, the determination of costs was relatively non-controversial since it was based on the methods developed in the Second Phillips Case. The exceptions involved treatment of income taxes and rate of return. The producers urged that average taxation be included in average cost of service. But the Commission had no data on actual taxes paid, and since the producers were unwilling to reveal that, there could be no allowance for taxation under prevailing judicial interpretation. As to rate of return, the Commission chose to allow 12 percent on an estimated unit rate base of 43 cents per thousand cubic feet. Both the rate and the rate base were considerably less than producers claimed.

Toward the end of the summer of 1965, the Federal Power Commission issued its historic ruling in the Permian Basin area rate case. It fixed the price of new gas at 16.5 cents per thousand cubic feet – the same level as the guideline it imposed five years earlier. Old gas would be allowed 14.5 cents. Further-

[33] *Ibid.*, 181–183.

more, the Commission ordered a moratorium of two-and-a-half years, during which it would not consider rate increases for the Permian Area.

Administrative feasibility and political compromise were the hallmarks of this new price system. The Commission's rates were about midway between the lowest, cost-based positions and the producers' high incentive claim (see Table 7-2). The separation of old and new gas prices would hopefully mollify distributors while still leaving producers with a profit margin on new exploration and development. And most of all, the area rate system seemed simple and workable. When the Supreme Court affirmed the Permian decision in 1968, even Justice Douglas, in his lone dissent, charitably acknowledged this achievement. Behind the majority's approval, he thought, "may be an unstated premise that the complexity of regulating the wellhead price of gas sold by producers is both so great and so novel that the commission must be given great leeway."[34]

The effects of cost-based rates

For a short time, the area rate system developed in the Permian proceedings appeared to usher in an era of stable regulatory policy, welcomed by many who were tired of dissonance and uncertainty. When the Commission completed the other area rate proceedings, all of which were in their final stages, it was hoped that a comprehensive system of rate regulation would begin working smoothly.

But the cure was worse than the disease. The Permian case changed the fundamental relationship between the Federal Power Commission and the natural gas industry. In the 1938 Act, Congress had charged the Commission to perform utility rate regulation in a narrow field of interstate commerce. But when the Supreme Court upheld the Permian decision in 1968, it sanctioned federal price control of a major primary industry.

The FPC's control policy, under the Swidler Chairmanship, was guided by "determination to hold the line against increases in natural gas prices."[35] The Permian rate structure, in conjunction with previous guidelines and the subsequent moratorium on rate increases, largely accomplished that objective. Neither average prices nor new contract prices rose more than 2 cents over the course of the sixties.[36] The Commission was proud that the Permian decision "will help to assure continuance of the FPC's successful program to stabilize producer prices as has been done in recent years."[37]

But the Commission's success was the gas industry's failure. A policy of static prices was unresponsive to continuing changes in domestic supply, demand, production costs, inflation, and interfuel competition. Long-range measures of gas supply during the 1960's contradicted the relative stability of price. The annual number of successful exploratory gas wells peaked at 912 in 1959, just before the FPC issued its area-price guidelines. By 1968 that number had

[34] 390 U.S. 841.

[35] Federal Power Commission, *1963 Annual Report* (Wash., D.C.: GPO, 1964), p. 15.

[36] Paul MacAvoy and Robert Pindyck, *Price Controls and the Natural Gas Shortage* (Wash., D.C.: American Enterprise Institute, 1975), p. 14.

[37] Federal Power Commission, *1966 Annual Report* (Wash., D.C.: GPO, 1967), p. 109.

Table 7-3. *The declining supply of U.S. natural gas*

Year	Production during year	Proved reserves at year-end	Net change in reserves during year	Indicated year's supply of year-end proved reserves
1959	12.4	261.2	8.4	21.1
1960	13.0	262.3	1.2	20.1
1961	13.4	266.3	3.9	19.9
1962	13.6	272.3	6.0	20.0
1963	14.5	276.2	3.9	19.0
1964	15.3	281.3	5.1	18.3
1965	16.2	286.5	5.2	17.6
1966	17.5	289.3	2.9	16.5
1967	18.4	292.9	3.6	15.9
1968	19.4	287.3	−5.5	14.8
1969	20.7	275.1	−12.2	13.3

Note: Trillions of cubic feet.
Source: American Petroleum Institute, *Basic Petroleum Data Book*, November 1976, Section XIII, Table 2.

dropped to 468. The number of total exploratory wells (for oil and gas) declined by one-third.[38] What's more, the proportion of successful exploratory wells declined from 11 to 8.5 percent, a sign of the increased risk and difficulty of finding oil and gas. And the rising number of dry holes was only one source of rising production costs during this period. The costs of drilling gas wells rose 4.4 percent annually between 1959 and 1968. This was above the general inflation rate of 2.6 percent, and triple the increase in new contract prices. In light of this dichotomy, the decline in exploratory activity is understandable.

Gross annual additions to proved reserves of natural gas continued to average about 19 trillion cubic feet throughout the 1960's (although largely because of exploratory activity in prolific offshore areas). It was primarily this figure that convinced advocates of gas price stabilization that their policies were not harming supply. Less attention was paid to the net changes in reserves – a measure that included the draw-down of reserves due to annual production. As shown in Table 7-3, production kept increasing at more than 5 percent annually. With reserve additions stable, this resulted in accelerating the decline in the reserve-to-production ratio from 21 in 1959 to only 13 by 1968. This trend was misinterpreted because of an earlier concern with the effects of huge committed reserves on prices.[39] Until the middle 1960's, the declining reserve-to-

[38] American Petroleum Institute, *Basic Petroleum Data Book*, April 1977, section 3, table 1.
[39] In the Permian Area rate proceedings, there was a general consensus among producers, pipelines, and distributors, that gas inventories, in the form of reserves committed to long-term contracts, were uneconomically large. The Commission had traditionally required a 12-year deliv-

Table 7-4. *Comparison of interstate and intrastate wellhead prices for natural gas, 1966–1970*

	Permian (1)			Southern Louisiana (2)		
	Interstate	Intrastate	Differential	Interstate	Intrastate	Differential
1966	17.6	17.0	− .6	20.0	19.6	− .4
1967	17.8	16.3	−1.5	21.0	19.6	−1.4
1968	16.8	17.2	+ .4	20.8	20.2	− .6
1969	16.8	18.4	+1.6	21.3	20.3	−1.0
1970[a]	17.5	20.2	+2.7	21.7	23.0	+1.3

Note: Weighted average of new contract prices for the Permian Basin and Southern Louisiana area. Cents per thousand cubic feet.
[a]First half of year.
Sources: (1) K.E. Wedemeyer, *Interstate Natural Gas Supply and Intrastate Market Behavior* (New York: Arno Press, 1979), pp. 143–44, 152; (2) Jensen Associates, "The Intrastate Gas Markets in Texas, Louisiana and Oklahoma," A Report to the American Gas Association, April 1974, p. 29.

production ratio was thought to reflect the economic tendency to seek an optimum reserve inventory.[40] It appears that the absence of a meaningful price mechanism allowed that decline to continue well beyond the "optimal" balance. This finally became obvious in early 1969, when the American Gas Association published its annual supply statistics for 1968. For the first time, the net change in reserves was actually negative, by 5.5 trillion cubic feet.

It's difficult to estimate what the market price for natural gas would have been during the 1960's in the absence of the area-price guidelines and subsequent area rates.[41] Prices in the unregulated, intrastate markets are at least useful indicators. Their changing relationship to the regulated, interstate price reveals an incipient problem that would seriously hamper the Commission's best efforts to alleviate the gas crisis once it began in the 1970's.

The wellhead price of gas in intrastate sales was normally lower than interstate prices, because of lower transportation costs, the absence of regulatory costs, and vigorous competition among many producers too small for the interstate pipelines to bother with. After 1968, however, this relationship reversed, at least in the Texas and Louisiana intrastate markets. Table 7-4 shows that in

erability as prerequisite for certification of a contract. Because deliverability declines after several years, this standard meant that the pipelines needed to maintain committed reserves 20 times larger than annual sales. Alfred Kahn, among others, argued that this situation not only raised costs (and thus the price to the consumer), but artificially reduced available supply in the form of uncommitted reserves, thereby pushing up wellhead prices needlessly. The hearing examiner in the Permian proceeding recommended that the Commission encourage a reduction in the reserve-to-production ratio to a level of 17.5 years. For discussion of these points, see 34 FPC at 314–320.
40 Federal Power Commission, *1970 Annual Report* (Wash., D.C.: GPO, 1971), p. 51.
41 For the best available econometric analysis of gas regulation, see Paul MacAvoy and Robert Pindyck, *The Economics of the Natural Gas Shortage (1960–1980)* (N.Y.: American Elsevier, 1975).

the Permian Basin, intrastate prices for new gas surpassed the interstate price in 1968, creating a gap that continued to widen thereafter. The same thing occurred eighteen months later in the southern Louisiana area. This suggests that demand for new gas by intrastate pipelines was exceeding available supply, with the logical effect of driving up prices. It further suggests that if demand were similar elsewhere, prices in the regulated interstate market were not responding adequately. If this trend continued, it would obviously cause producers to commit new reserves to the intrastate markets where they could obtain a better price.

In interfuel competition, the demand for natural gas is determined by consumer preference for its intrinsic physical properties as well as its price competitiveness with other fuels. From the mid-1960's on, air pollution problems in the Northeast stimulated the demand for gas, apart from its favorable price. The price of natural gas on a Btu basis was 75 percent below that of petroleum and 30 percent less than coal.[42] No wonder that both industrial and residential demand for gas continued to outpace that of other fuels and resulted in a steady increase in market share as far from the gas fields as Boston. Carl Bagge, who resigned as an FPC commissioner to become the president of the National Coal Association in 1970, commented bitterly that "artificial and discriminatory gas pricing policies" since the *Phillips* decision had resulted in "the displacement of coal from a broad range of industrial and commercial markets."[43]

It was evident in both the Second Phillips Case and the Permian proceedings that the gas distributors were the producer's true nemesis. They had persistently favored field price regulation at far lower rates than sought by the producers. Their thorough cost studies, careful briefs, and expert witnesses had been influential in both major cases on such key issues as cost allocation and two-tier pricing. Nonetheless, the distributors were the first to feel the tightening of supply and were quick to evaluate the problem. By late 1968, several of the large gas utilities were having difficulty contracting increases in long-term supplies from the interstate pipelines. When they realized that new reserves were still being dedicated to the intrastate market at higher prices, they concluded that interstate prices were inadequate.

Accordingly, on December 16, 1968, Morton Jacobs, president of the American Gas Association, wrote an important letter to Chairman Lee White, Joseph Swidler's successor. The Association, which represented 300 distributors and transmission companies, formally reversed its historical opposition to higher wellhead prices for natural gas. The letter urged the Commission to "take a new look at all principles and methods by which it arrives at area price levels for new gas, to insure that the prices resulting will in fact be sufficient to occasion the necessary exploration, development and devotion of gas to interstate com-

---

[42] American Petroleum Institute, *Basic Petroleum Data Book*, November 1976, Section VI, Table 7, and National Coal Association, *Coal Facts 1974–1975* (Wash., D.C.: NCA, 1976), p. 52.
[43] U.S. Congress, House, Interstate Commerce Committee, Subcommittee on Communications and Power, *Hearings – Natural Gas Act of 1971* (92nd Cong., 1st Sess.), September 1971, p. 209.

merce."[44] This statement, according to Commissioner John Carver, was one of the four major turning points in gas regulation (the other three being the two Phillips cases and the Permian Area rate case).[45] It meant that for the first time, all three sectors of the natural gas industry were united in support of the general proposition that wellhead prices were too low. Of course, it remained to be seen whether this consensus could withstand the divisive particulars of regulatory or legislative reform.

Compared to the policy controversies before 1957 and after 1968, this middle period in the evolution of gas regulation might seem mundane and static. But to conclude that little of substance actually happened would be a mistake. A process of intrafuel politics during these years produced a new regulatory relationship between business and government and an energy policy that was more a product of procedural concerns and regulatory philosophies than good economics.

In dealing with the conflicting contentions of producers, pipeliners, distributors, and state public service commissions, the FPC tried to fabricate a regulatory system that was tolerable to all, that fit the requirements of judicial precedent, and would somehow provide reasonable trade-offs between considerations of equity and efficiency. The producers were committed to the efficiency of the price mechanism, as they defined it. The distribution and pipeline companies had a determined interest in using regulation to enforce a buyer's market and ensure their continued advantage in competition with coal. Though not insensitive to considerations of supply or return on investment, they tended to be preoccupied by price, contract terms, and control over their suppliers. The FPC staff and the activist state utility commissions seemed oblivious to the inevitability of resource depletion and the peculiar economics of the oil and gas industry. Their focus was on distributive equity, which they defined by a commitment to the traditional process of rate regulation based on historical costs.

Neither "capture" nor "life-cycle" theories of regulation do much to explain the relationship between the FPC and the gas producers during this period. The area-wide, two-tier pricing system was shaped by pragmatism and compromise in which the behavior of the Federal Power Commission evinced some of the characteristics that Hilton, McKie, and Anderson have identified. The Commission's opinions in both the Second Phillips and Permian cases were carefully designed to incur, as George Hilton has called it, "minimal squawk." The two-tier pricing system in particular was an effort to pacify both producer and distributor constituents.[46] McKie's "tar-baby" effect was also evident, particularly in the transitions from field price to cost-based rate-making in 1956

---

[44] W. M. Jacobs to Lee White, December 16, 1968, reprinted in U.S. Congress, House, *Natural Gas Act of 1971*, p. 139.

[45] U.S. Congress, Senate, Interstate Commerce Committee, *Hearings – Natural Gas Regulation* (92nd Cong., 2nd Sess.), March 1972, p. 294.

[46] George W. Hilton, "The Basic Behavior of Regulatory Commissions," *American Economic Review Papers and Proceedings*, 62 (1972), pp. 47–54.

and from company-by-company to area price control in 1960.[47] And in both of these complicated and precedential rate cases, the bureaucratic imperatives that Anderson has highlighted were relevant, as the commissioners sought to maintain a fragile balance between external pressures and the traditional regulatory philosophies of their professional staff.[48]

Because energy supplies were generally abundant, the political contention among these interests remained safely within the adjudicatory arena for nearly thirteen years. Both domestic and imported oil were in excess supply, with prices stable or falling in real terms. Excess capacity plagued the coal industry so that its price stayed about as low as possible. The gas industry, however, made a peculiar transition. With prices relatively constant, its huge pipeline network developed into a drain through which cheap, pent-up gas reserves flowed quickly to quench pent-up consumer demand. The inventory accumulated in the forties and fifties was drawn down steadily during the sixties. Meanwhile, equitable distribution of revenue flows was perceived as the essential problem.

The regulatory policy that emerged from this political-economic environment was a hybrid of field market prices, cost-based, utility rate-regulation, and federal price control. As such, it was probably doomed to fail. The area rate system, worked out in the Permain proceedings, offered stability, coherence, and fairness, but not enough natural gas to fulfill the demand it perpetuated. Average cost pricing, even modified by a two-tier price system, left producers with inadequate incentives to invest and gave consumers the wrong signals about the real cost of more gas.

A charitable interpretation might lay blame for what followed on inflation and high interest rates, caused by the government's deficit spending after 1965. That would suggest that the area-price levels were sound, only the economic environment was not. Another, more distrustful interpretation, which is described in Chapter 11, would likewise conclude that the regulatory framework was fine, but was destroyed intentionally by an artificial crisis fabricated by greedy and powerful oil companies.

While self-interest and inflation were no doubt relevant to the problems that soon enveloped the gas industry, it would be wrong to lay the causes of shortage elsewhere than on the system of cost-based price controls and the polity from which it derived.

---

[47] James McKie, "Regulation and the Free Market: The Problems of Boundaries," *Bell Journal of Economics*, I (1970), pp. 6–26.
[48] Douglas D. Anderson, *Regulatory Politics and Electric Utilities* (Boston: Auburn House, 1981).

8. Synfuels revisited: nostrum for the coal industry

The government's second program to develop synthetic fuels from coal evolved from *ad hoc* initiatives; national security was not even an excuse. The program grew out of modest congressional efforts to resuscitate the coal industry and the Interior Department's vague stewardship for oil shale. But excess capacity in crude oil and natural gas, together with stable real energy prices, was an overwhelming impediment to commercial development of synfuels. Without clear signals from the market, the private sector balked at the risks. And since government was unwilling to assume any real responsibility, as it had for nuclear power, it failed to develop and support a bureaucracy that could manage large projects successfully. From beginning to end (1959–1968), the second synfuels program floundered for lack of an effective clientele or strategic definition.

Research – the cure for a "sick industry"

By 1956, coal was a "sick industry" in more ways than one. Coal production had declined 39 percent from its peak in 1947; three thousand mines had closed, and the number of mine workers fell by nearly half. Coal's share of the energy market had fallen by 18 percent, with no end in sight. Although insufficient research was not necessarily the coal industry's principal problem, it was the most amenable to political redress. The industry's real problems – interfuel competition, adverse energy policies, and structural fragmentation, were less tractable politically. Coal-state congressmen, organized labor, and some of the industry's leaders looked to federally-sponsored research in synthetic fuels as a means of relief.

The coal industry, as mentioned in previous chapters, was losing share to imported residual oil in the electric utility market; to natural gas in commercial, industrial, and residential markets; and to diesel fuel in its railroad and shipping markets. Coal producers were quick to point out that these losses could not be blamed on lagging productivity. Labor productivity had doubled since 1923, and combustion efficiency (for electric power generation) had tripled. But coal prices had also doubled between 1942 and 1948. Although they fell 9 percent in the early 1950's, coal was still not competitive on a Btu-basis after transportation, handling, and combustion costs.

Spokesmen for the coal industry attributed their interfuel disadvantages to government policies rather than market competition. Natural gas prices were held below market-clearing levels by the Federal Power Commission; a low-tariff policy facilitated dumping of imported residual oil; and domestic oil's depletion allowance, at more than double the rate for coal, provided an unfair subsidy to exploration and production. But coalmen were most alarmed by the federal government's research subsidies to nuclear power. In 1957, the Department of the Interior projected that nuclear electric-generating capacity would likely displace 43 million tons of coal by 1970, and 383 million tons by 1980.[1] According to Carter Manasco, chief lobbyist for the National Coal Association, the Atomic Energy Commission would spend more in 1957 than the entire profits of the coal industry since 1920. This seemed unfair. By spending billions of dollars to build hydroelectric dams and atomic reactors, "the Federal Government has done as much to hurt the coal industry," claimed Manasco, "as any competing fuel."[2]

The absence of either horizontal or vertical integration in the coal industry was a basic cause of non-competitiveness and political ineffectiveness. Coal was among the least concentrated and least profitable of primary industries. There were an estimated 4,000 concerns, of which less than 1,000 reported any net income. The average net income for reporting firms was $82,000 in 1950 and $26,000 in 1953. After-tax profits averaged $22,000 during that period. The 20 largest companies, responsible for 39 percent of total coal production, averaged a return on net worth of only 5.8 percent from 1950 to 1955. This compared unfavorably even with other fragmented industries, let alone the largest oil companies with an average return of 14.8 percent.[3]

Structural fragmentation and low profitability meant inadequate research and development. Individual firms were simply too small to support R&D programs, while low profitability precluded collective efforts of any consequence. "Unbelievable as it may seem," said one coal-industry executive, "the amounts spent for research by some of the industrial groups is about 10 times larger than the total amount of net profit made by our entire industry." This was an understatement. In 1953, the chemical industry's R&D budget of $361 million was 30 times larger than the coal industry's net earnings of $12 million.[4] Of the $17 million spent on coal research in 1955, coal producers (excluding captive operations owned by steel and utility companies) contributed only $2.4 million. The rest came from government sources, equipment manufacturers, and other industrial firms.

[1]   U.S. Congress, House, Interior Committee, Special Subcommittee on Coal Research, *Report No. 1263* (85th Cong., 1st Sess.), 1957, pp. 52–56.
[2]   U.S. Congress, House, Interior Committee, Special Subcommittee on Coal Research, *Coal* (85th Cong., 1st Sess.), February 1957, pt. 2, pp. 566–567.
[3]   U.S. Congress, House, *Report No. 1263*, pp. 34–35.
[4]   U.S. Congress, House, Interior Committee, Special Subcommittee on Coal Research, *Coal* (84th Cong., 2nd Sess.), June–July 1956, p. 38.

The absence of integration limited the potential for economies of scale to all but the seven or eight largest companies. Credit was more costly for smaller firms, and retained earnings were inadequate to finance the capital costs of new mechanized mines which had risen from $3 to $10 or $15 per annual ton. There was no hope for the thousands of small firms to attract managerial and engineering talent, let alone support the financial, legal, and marketing services necessary to compete with gas and oil in regional and national markets. And least of all, these profitless coal operators could ill afford to support effective trade associations or marshal sufficient resources to influence public policy.

 Efforts to involve government in the coal industry's resuscitation were begun hesitantly and ineffectively in 1954, the year in which coal production reached its nadir. A group of coal-company executives approached the Eisenhower administration for help.[5] They issued a statement calling for government financing of cooperative research, policies to facilitate industrial rationalization, and the creation of an advisory council.[6] Although the President responded to this plea in form, by creating an interdepartmental committee on coal, nothing of substance resulted from the initiative.[7] It was only in 1956 that the coal industry even managed to get a serious hearing.

Representative John Saylor of Pennsylvania got the ball rolling with a resolution to investigate research and development as a means of stimulating an "economic revival of the coal industry." Saylor had in mind a program of considerable magnitude, along the lines of the Atomic Energy Commission. The prospective research fields would include some with a potential for "expeditious results" in coal production, transportation and utilization, as well as longer-term development of synthetic fuels.[8]

At hearings on this subject in 1956 and 1957, dozens of witnesses testified to the coal industry's woeful condition and attributed much of the problem to inadequate research. Almost everyone in industry, government, and academe agreed that more research was desirable, but there were some differences of opinion in the definition of Federal responsibility. Speaking for the Administration, Felix Wormser, the Assistant Secretary of Interior for Mineral Resources, did not share Saylor's vision. He admitted that the Bureau of Mines' present work might be "redirected toward more productive lines," but observed that

5   J. S. Cooper to D. D. Eisenhower, May 21, 1954, Box 678, File 134-E., White House Official File, DDEPL.
6   "The Coal Industry – Its Position, Problems, and Areas of Possible Relief," undated, *Ibid.* Nowhere else in the policy discussions of the coal industry's difficulties was the issue of structural fragmentation addressed. In this document, the coal executive themselves urged the President to consider adopting "changes in administration policies and in the antitrust laws, which would have the effect of encouraging physical consolidations and mergers." (p. 10) The document also expresses a degree of bitterness regarding the oil industry's favored relationship to government by means of advisory councils. It noted that the coal advisory council was abolished as illegal, but that the National Petroleum Council continued to provide oil executives special access to the Departments of Interior, Commerce, and State (p. 11).
7   D. D. Eisenhower to J. S. Cooper, June 29, 1954, *ibid.*, and Office of Defense Mobilization, "Report of the Interdepartmental Committee on the Soft Coal Industry," October 7, 1960, Fred Seaton Papers, Box 2, Minerals – Coal Program, DDEPL.
8   H. Res. 400 (84th Cong., 2nd Sess.), U.S. Congress, House, *Coal* (1956), p. 1.

any larger effort would be subject to stringent budgetary limitations. When questioned critically about the termination of the synthetic fuels program in 1953, Wormser replied defensively that the Eisenhower administration felt "it had become too large a project," and that beyond the pilot-plant stage, "it was desirable for the Government to step out."[9]

The coal industry disagreed. The National Coal Association proposed a Coal Research Foundation with a full-time administrator and a board of directors appointed by the President. Its 15 members would include five representatives of the coal industry, two from mining machinery and equipment manufacturers, one from a public utility, two academics, and one representative each from the Department of the Interior, Department of Commerce, private research institutions, organized labor, and the public. Although the Foundation would do no research of its own, it would make contracts with public and private organizations, and disseminate the results. The coal association suggested an initial appropriation of $10 million, to be increased by increments of $10 million annually for five years, after which it would continue at $50 million annually unless Congress felt that further increases were warranted.[10] The industry obviously hoped to control a very large program in which the government would have a minimal role, relatively immune to political pressures. Even for a "sick industry," this was asking a lot.

In 1957, the coal-research subcommittee of the House Interior Committee reported its recommendations. It proposed an independent Coal Research and Development Commission, modelled along the lines of the AEC. The three-member commission would place research contracts with public and private organizations, conduct research in its own laboratories when necessary, and develop a technical information system. It would have advisory committees representing the coal industry and its industrial customers. Organizational autonomy was necessary, the committee reported, so that the program would "not be shackled and inhibited by such traditional approaches and restrictive policies as control the research activities of the Department of the Interior." Instead, the research agenda would concentrate on "promising short-range possibilities" for (1) new and more effective uses for coal, (2) reduction of mining and distribution costs, and (3) developments of particular value to smaller producers. The initial appropriation for this program would be $2 million. Coal-derived synthetic fuels were not mentioned.[11]

Several bills providing for an independent coal research commission were introduced in 1958. The Administration opposed the idea, but offered to create an Office of Coal Research within the Interior Department. This Office, however, would do no research of its own, and could let research contracts only to trade associations, universities, and state governments – not private companies. Even then, the Secretary would have to approve each contract.[12] "This departmental recommendation," complained Wayne Aspinall, a Colorado Democrat

[9] U.S. Congress, House, *Coal* (1956), pp. 10, 16.
[10] U.S. Congress, House, *Coal* (1957), pt. 2, pp. 548–549.
[11] U.S. Congress, House, *Report No. 1263*, p. 91.
[12] U.S. Department of the Interior, Office of the Secretary, Press Release, April 16, 1958, Box 678, File 134–E, White House Official File, DDEPL.

and ranking member of the House Interior Committee, "was little more than a 'self-defense' proposal offered as a counter to the proposal for an independent commission."[13] The Senate passed an independent-commission bill anyway, but Republicans in the House delayed it too long for floor action.

In 1959, when Aspinall became chairman of the House Interior Committee, he re-introduced the bill for an independent commission. The Interior Department still opposed it, and did not reiterate its offer to create a new office. "Existing agencies," wrote the Secretary, "provide for a more appropriate degree of control by the Congress and the Executive."[14] Although Aspinall and Saylor ignored this opposition, the Senate succumbed to pressure from the Administration and agreed to place the new agency within the Department of the Interior.[15] Both bills passed, but in conference committee, the House view prevailed. Language providing for an independent commission was restored. President Eisenhower promptly vetoed it on the grounds that creation of an additional agency would dilute the Interior Department's "established interest." He did agree, however, to sign legislation that would expand coal research within the Interior Department.[16]

Left with no alternative, Representative Saylor introduced compromise legislation in 1960 to establish an Office of Coal Research (OCR) within the Department of the Interior. Although the Department promised to support the new agency actively, its initial appropriation was a skimpy $1 million.[17] The Office was to establish technical advisory committees and make research contracts, but do no research of its own. This bill passed both houses by voice vote, and the President signed it July 7, 1960.[18]

The Coal Research and Development Act of 1960 meant different things to different people. It obviously put the federal government back in the business of cooperative coal research; but at what level, in what directions, and to what ends was uncertain. As long as conditions in the energy market remained stable, the OCR's organizational weaknesses would have a lot to do with those decisions.

Pilot-plant management

The government's new program for coal research got off to a very slow start. After a year, Wayne Aspinall complained that it was "similar to the history of a

[13] U.S. Congress, House, Committee on Interior and Insular Affairs, *Report No. 370* (86th Cong., 1st Sess.), "Coal Research and Development Act," May 20, 1959, p. 11; also, U.S. Congress, House, Committee on Science and Astronautics, Subcommittee on Science, Research, and Development, *House Doc. No. 91–137* (91st Cong., 1st Sess.), "Technical Information for Congress," April 25, 1969, pp. 301–302.

[14] R. A. Hardy to W. N. Aspinall, March 4, 1959, in U.S. Congress, House, *Report No. 370*, p. 13.

[15] U.S. Congress, Senate, Interior Committee, Subcommittee on Minerals, Materials and Fuels, *Coal Research* (86th Cong., 1st Sess.), June 1969.

[16] "Memorandum of disapproval of bill creating a Coal Research and Development Commission," September 16, 1959, in *U.S. Public Papers of the Presidents, Dwight David Eisenhower, 1959* (Wash.: GPO, 1959), p. 660.

[17] R. Hardy to Secretary, December 29, 1959, Box 678, File 134–E, White House Official File, DDEPL.

[18] U.S. Congress, House, Committee on Interior and Insular Affairs, *Report No. 1241* (86th Cong., 2nd Sess.), February 4, 1960; also, *Public Law 86–599*, 74 Stat. 336.

patient who died before the doctor, who lived in a building adjacent to him, knew where he was." As feared, the Department of the Interior had no commitment to "immediate action."[19] Only with pressure from interested congressmen did the Interior Secretary finally appoint George Lamb, an employee of Consolidation Coal, as Director of the Office of Coal Research, and pick a "blue ribbon" panel to serve as the General Technical Advisory Committee. But the OCR remained unstaffed and without political organization or a clear rationale.

According to the Act, the Advisory Committee was supposed to examine and evaluate the programs administered by the Office of Coal Research. Its membership included researchers and executives from coal companies, utilities, railroads, equipment manufacturers, and the United Mine Workers. There was considerable overlap between its members and the directors of the National Coal Policy Conference. This group, which was also involved in oil import issues, might have become a clientele organization for the Office of Coal Research. But it made only a modest effort that never came close to the kind of political influence exercised by its analogue, the Atomic Industrial Forum. The Technical Advisory Committee's impact on appropriations would reflect as much.[20]

The Advisory Committee first met in June of 1961 to adopt procedures and identify the OCR's research agenda. Although everyone there agreed that priority should be given to "short-range research systems which offer promise of substantial tonnage for the coal industry," there was no consensus on what projects would best serve that objective. The committee outlined seven project areas, only one of which involved synthetic fuels. The criterion for selecting a project, according to the OCR's director, should be its "prospects of providing a market expansion." And if a synfuels project held greater promise than a dozen smaller studies of coal chemicals, then the OCR should choose it first. Members of the Advisory Committee did not take issue with this approach.[21]

In a matter of months, a number of high-technology, coal-conversion projects had attracted the OCR's interest, as well as the attention of congressmen responsible for the OCR's appropriations. Two of the OCR's three divisions – Economics & Marketing and Mining & Preparation – were considering several smaller studies which together amounted to less than $1 million. But the Division of Utilization already had in mind six projects, five of which involved synthetic fuels from coal. If approved, the five were estimated to involve at least $22 million in budgetary obligations over five years.[22]

As soon as a few concrete projects were on the table, a dispute broke out

[19] U.S. Congress, House, Interior Committee, *Politics, Programs, and Activities of the Department of the Interior* (87th Cong., 1st Sess.), 1961, p. 171.
[20] National Coal Policy Conference, Inc., *Purposes, Platform, Objectives* (Washington: pamphlet, 1965); also, Office of Coal Research, *Annual Report 1967* (Wash.: GPO, 1967), pp. 1–2.
[21] Minutes of the GTAC Meeting, June 6, 1961, Box 1, General Technical Advisory Committee, Office of Coal Research, accession no. 48–74–12, Federal Records Center, Suitland, Maryland, p. 2.
[22] OCR Contract Information Projections, February 18, 1962, Box 17, OCR Budget File (FY 1963), Accession No. 71A-963, Federal Records Center, Suitland, Maryland).

among interested parties over the course of policy and the policy process. Should the OCR commit resources to synthetic-fuels pilot plants, or stick to short-term projects of immediate benefit to coal producers? And who should make those decisions? Although George Lamb had the technical initiative through his staff, he scarcely had the stature within government necessary to push through major projects. The Office of Coal Research, besides being new, was the smallest of four agencies under the Assistant Secretary of Mineral Resources within the Department of the Interior. Two of the others were old-line bureaucracies – the Bureau of Mines and the Geological Survey – and the Office of Oil and Gas was intimately linked to the powerful National Petroleum Council.

At this early stage of development, the Technical Advisory Committee might have asserted its authority by providing political support for the OCR's proposals. But its members could not agree on a research strategy. Coal producers tended to favor small, pragmatic projects, while spokesmen for labor, the electric utilities, and one large chemical company shared Lamb's enthusiasm for synfuels pilot plants.[23] Furthermore, Advisory Committee members remained confused about their role for several years; whether it was general advice and liaison with the industry, or some more formal decision-making responsibility. Perhaps for lack of experience, or simply its smaller scale, the Committee adopted none of the by-laws or other internal controls that so effectively guided the National Petroleum Council.

With no clear direction of its own, the Office of Coal Research was a target of opportunity for several interested congressmen. Robert Byrd of West Virginia, a member of the Senate Appropriations Committee and stalwart advocate of coal research, moved quickly in 1962 to assert his influence. He tried to boost the OCR's appropriation to $6 million, mostly earmarked for two pilot-plant projects in West Virginia. To do so, he lined up support from the White House, the National Coal Association, and the United Mine Workers. Although he succeeded in getting only $3.5 million, members of the Technical Advisory Committee immediately recognized that Byrd was a potential champion. Few of them balked at the program's change of course.[24]

Representative Wayne Aspinall, as chairman of the House Interior Commit-

---

[23] H. R. Charmbury to G. Lamb, Dec. 13, 1961, S. Lehner to G. Lamb, Dec. 13, 1961, P. Sporn to G. Lamb, Dec. 21, 1961, H. LaViers to G. Lamb, Dec. 21, 1961, F. S. Elrond to G. Lamb, Dec. 19, 1961, and W. H. Bigelow to G. Lamb, Dec. 13, 1961, in Box 1, GTAC Committee Correspondence, 1960–1962, and Speech by Michael Widman, Minutes of the GTAC Meeting, June 6, 1961, GTAC/OCR/FRC.

[24] Besides a half-dozen marketing studies and three small technical projects on coal chemistry and combustion, the OCR initiated three synfuels projects in 1962. The FMC Corporation got $1.2 million for Project COED, a technology for producing usable char and liquids from coal. For Project Gasoline, the OCR granted $444,000 to Ralph M. Parsons, an engineering consultant, to evaluate Consolidation Coal's design of a coal-to-gasoline plant which that company had been working to develop for years as the Consohio Project. Finally, Spencer Chemical Company received $1.2 million for its solvation process of treating coal to remove ash and other impurities. Office of Coal Research, "1966 Annual Report," Department of the Interior, Office of the Secretary, Procurement/OCR Files, Pt. 7, Mechanical Floor, Department of the Interior, Washington, D.C., pp. 9–16.

Table 8-1. *Office of Coal Research synthetic fuels pilot plants, 1962–1972*

Project	Prime contractor	Contract duration	Government funding level	Location
Project Gasoline	Consolidation Coal Co.[a]	8/63–3/72	$20,377,000	Cresap, WV
Project COED	FMC Corp.	5/62–2/74	19,332,000	Princeton, NJ
CO_2 Acceptor	Consolidation Coal Co.	6/64–9/73	16,606,000	Rapid City, SD
HY-GAS	Institute of Gas Technology	7/64–7/72	14,399,000	Chicago, IL
			2,384,000 (AGA Contribution)	
SRC				
Low ash coal	Spencer Chemical Co.[b]	8/62–2/65	1,240,000	
Solvent refined coal	Pittsburg & Midway Coal[b]	10/66–4/72	7,640,000	Ft. Lewis, WA
BI-GAS	Bituminous Coal Research Inc.[c]	12/63–2/71	3,438,000	Homer City, PA

[a]Consolidation Coal was acquired by Continental Oil Co. in 1966.
[b]The Solvent Refined Coal Project started out as Low Ash Coal. Pittsburg & Midway Coal was a subsidiary of Spencer Chemical. In 1963, both firms were acquired by Gulf Oil Corp.
[c]BCR, Inc. is the research subsidiary of the National Coal Association.
Source: Office of Coal Research, *Annual Report*, 1967 and 1972.

tee, evidently resented Byrd's intervention and the program's shift towards synthetic fuels. He and his committee had not been consulted.[25] In an effort to curb the influence of Senator Byrd and the OCR staff on the course of coal research, Aspinall tried to force greater responsibility on the General Technical Advisory Committee. His Interior Committee issued an advisory resolution to the effect that the Advisory Committee should approve each OCR project, and that the views of its individual members be recorded. Byrd vigorously opposed this idea on grounds that it would undermine the authority of the Interior Secretary. Given the importance of Senator Byrd's support for President Kennedy's social programs and foreign policy, Secretary Stewart Udall got the message. He gently rejected Aspinall's recommendation, but tried to mollify him by agreeing to seek "expressions of opinion" from the Advisory Committee.[26] Udall may also have thrown in a commitment to renew the development of oil shale, since the program originated at about this time. At any rate, it was on the basis of this fragile political compromise that the Office of Coal Research turned almost exclusively to long-term synfuels projects after 1963. Needless to say, this was not a sound organizational formula for an effective energy program.

With its course more or less recalibrated, the Office of Coal Research steadily expanded its program for developing synthetic fuels over the next five years. Progress was slow, however, due to the low starting point of its budgetary authority. Although its appropriations increased 45 percent annually, they had scarcely reached $14 million by 1969.[27] From at least 1965 on, OCR staff were constantly making trade-offs between authorizing a few new projects and nurturing those in progress. Since the costs of pilot-plant projects were inevitably underestimated at their outset, they absorbed an ever-larger portion of the OCR's budget as they progressed toward completion. By 1968, the Division of Utilization was managing $60 million worth of contracts, of which $53 million were synthetic fuels pilot plants. Only $4 million was devoted to Mining & Preparation, with $220,000 left over for Economics & Marketing.[28]

Six pilot plants eventually constituted the heart of the OCR's program to develop synthetic fuels. These are listed in Table 8–1, together with their location, funding level, and prime contractors. Two other synfuels projects were terminated prior to pilot-plant construction for want of funds in 1967–68. Of the six major projects, three each were devoted to coal gasification and coal liquefaction. The projects ranged in size from the 75-ton-per-day HYGAS plant in Chicago to the 100-pound-per-hour gasifier developed by Bituminous

[25] U.S. Congress, House, Interior Committee, Subcommittee on Mines and Mining, "Review of the Coal Research Program," March 25, 1963, 5 volumes, typescript, in Box 17, OCR Budgetary Material, OCR/FRC, vol. 1, pp. 18, 112–116, and vol. 2, pp. 212–235, 276–278, 345–348.
[26] OCR to R. Byrd, June 1963, and S. Udall to C. Hayden, June 11, 1963, Box 17, File-House Interior Committee Meetings, 1963, OCR/FRC; also, R. Byrd to S. Udall, Feb. 20, 1963, and S. Udall to R. Byrd, March 4, 1963, in U.S. Congress, Senate, Appropriations Committee, *Interior Department and Related Agencies Appropriations for 1964* (88th Cong., 1st Sess.), 1963, pp. 593–594.
[27] U.S. Congress, House, *Technical Information for Congress*, p. 306.
[28] Office of Coal Research, *Annual Report 1968* (Wash.: GPO, 1969), pp. 25–35.

Coal Research, Inc. in Pennsylvania. The six plants were based on substantially different technologies to produce a variety of synthetic fuels.

Of the three liquefaction technologies, the Solvent Refined Coal process was the least complicated. Its purpose was to remove contaminents from coal to facilitate cleaner combustion. In the SRC process, crushed coal was dissolved in an aromatic solvent. After filtration, the process yielded a heavy organic solid that was largely free of ash and sulfur. With further treatment, solvent-refined coal could be liquefied, although that was not the thrust of the OCR project.[29] Project COED, which stands for Char-Oil-Energy-Development, was conceptually similar to petroleum refining. Crushed coal was heated to successively higher temperatures at which different fractions of liquids and gases were released. This was done in fluidized beds, where circulating hot gases contributed to the heat supply and kept the coal particles fluid. Synthetic oil was recovered by condensation and the residual char was recovered for use as a powerplant fuel.[30] Project Gasoline was the most complicated of the projects – politically as well as technically. From coal to synthetic crude oil, this process required eleven steps. The most critical of these was direct hydrogenation at a very high temperature and pressure. A major part of the problem for this flagship project was the difficulty of getting all eleven stages to work in simultaneous integration.[31]

The three gasification plants entailed similarly complex chemical reactions, but did not have as severe problems of materials-handling. The CO_2 Acceptor Process was perhaps the most innovative, since it worked without either hydrogen or pure oxygen. At the Rapid City plant, built by the M. W. Kellogg Company and operated by Consolidation Coal, hot calcined dolomite was circulated through fluidized beds of lignite coal in the presence of carbon dioxide. The reaction created sufficient heat to decompose the lignite and release gas enriched with methane and hydrogen.

Selection, funding, and implementation of these large-scale public-private ventures was accomplished by an extraordinarily inept system of administrative resource allocation. Even after the program of coal research crystalized around synthetic fuels pilot plants, the weaknesses of the OCR's political organization insured continuing controversy. Three aspects of this problem were especially detrimental: (1) project choice, site selection, and appropriations were largely governed by traditional pork-barrel politics; (2) the OCR's only clientele organization, the General Technical Advisory Committee, had little influence either in Washington or the private sector; and (3) as a bureaucratic entity, the Office of Coal Research failed to develop a strong, positive relationship with any one congressional committee that could enhance its autonomy within the Department of the Interior. The program was so politicized under these organizational circumstances that effective management of individual projects was severely hampered.

[29] Office of Coal Research, *Annual Report 1972* (Wash.: Department of the Interior, 1973), pp. 48–50.
[30] *Ibid.*, 45–46.
[31] Office of Coal Research, *Annual Report 1967,* (Wash.: GPO, 1968), pp. 15–16.

A congressional "champion" was absolutely essential to the selection and continued support of a pilot-plant project.[32] Among the more visible of such champions were Representative Julia Hansen and Senator Henry Jackson of Washington for the SRC Project, Karl Mundt of South Dakota for Project Lignite (the CO2 Acceptor Process), and of course, Robert Byrd for Project Gasoline.

Julia Hansen, a ranking member of the House Appropriations Committee, was experienced with the pork barrel through her lengthy tenure on the National Rivers and Harbors Congress and Western States Highway Policy Commission. Even before the SCR Project was formally funded, Hansen was assured that it would be located in Tacoma, Washington – hardly a center of coal activity. With her support, and that of Henry Jackson on the Senate Interior Committee, the SRC pilot plant received funding in 1965, even though a majority of the Technical Advisory Committee and an *ad hoc* committee in the Interior Department initially opposed it.[33]

Karl Mundt played a similar role. In 1963, Senator Mundt added an amendment to the appropriations bill for the OCR, inserting an extra $375,000 "for planning and engineering a pilot plant in South Dakota for the production of gas from lignite."[34] Since the OCR did not even have a proposal for such a project, it had to go to its contractors and find someone willing to make a suggestion. When Mundt kept pressing for visible progress, the OCR director could only reply, "we are pushing this as fast as we can." Not surprisingly, the OCR turned to Consolidation Coal, the contractor with which its staff was most experienced, to come up with a proposal.[35]

Robert Byrd was more than a sponsor for Project Gasoline. As the leading Senate supporter of larger appropriations for the OCR, Byrd was champion of the entire program. Not only did he get the OCR's first and largest pilot-plant project, but he protected it later in the 1960's when operational difficulties and widespread criticism threatened its termination. In several tense meetings between officials of Continental Oil, the OCR, and the Department of the Interior, it was the Senator who smoothed over differences and deflected the finger-pointing as the project soured.[36] When it needed additional millions due to cost overruns, Senator Byrd invariably used his influence with the Senate Appropriations Committee to keep the project active.[37]

---

[32] Eric Reichl, retired, Conoco Coal Development, interview with the author, December 1980.
[33] GTAC Meeting Transcripts, January 27, and July 13, 1965, Box 1, GTAC/OCR/FRC, pp. 36–39 and 37–38 respectively.
[34] G. E. Larson to Director of Budget, Department of the Interior, July 2, 1963, Box 18, OCR Budget File (FY 1964), OCR/FRC.
[35] U.S. Congress, Senate, Appropriations Committee, Subcommittee on Department of the Interior Appropriations, *Interior Department and Related Agencies Appropriation for 1965* (88th Cong., 2nd Sess.), February 24, 1964, pp. 659–660.
[36] Minutes of Meeting with Senator Robert Byrd, March 21, 1969, Box 15, file Consolidation Coal-Project Gasoline, Office of Coal Research, Accession No. 48-73-11, Federal Records Center, Suitland, Maryland.
[37] GTAC Meeting Transcript, May 21, 1968, Box 2, GTAC/OCR/FRC, p. 67; also, H. Dole to R. Byrd, May 21, 1969, Equipment and Property Files, pt. 1, OCR/DOI.

In each of these instances, the existance of a congressional champion appeared to have been the single most important criterion for project choice and site selection. With regard to project choice, this obviously implied that the best and most fruitful projects were not necessarily funded, that duplication was not necessarily avoided, and that the most suitable contractor was not necessarily found. The same problems applied to site selection. Senator Byrd's insistence on Cresap meant that two other potential sites, with greater accessibility to skilled labor and engineering staff, were rejected.[38] Finally, design, construction, and operation of these pilot plants was significantly affected by the size of the appropriation that the project's champion could obtain. The likelihood that the sponsor's degree of political leverage matched the requirements of optimal design was remote.

The OCR's synfuels effort would not have had to rely solely on political champions had coal-related business interests asserted their own technical, economic, and political influence. But the General Technical Advisory Committee simply lacked the organizational coherence, and perhaps the motive, necessary to become an effective clientele group. The diversity of its members, which could have been a source of power, only resulted in fragmenting the Advisory Committee's influence and its ability to coordinate outside support from the industries it represented. The Committee was no closer to a common vision for synthetic fuels at the end of the decade than it had been when organized in 1961.

In its advisory capacity to the OCR, the Technical Advisory Committee was virtually a rubber stamp. To some extent this was due to its limited charter. Its members had no staff of their own, and met only in formal quarterly sessions. Unlike the National Petroleum Council, the Committee did no independent studies using the staff of member-firms. When it met, its members heard presentations from OCR staff that were designed for easy approval.

Officials of the Office of Coal Research really didn't want the benefit of expertise from the Advisory Committee anyway. Only pressure from Congress forced George Fumich, who replaced Lamb as OCR Director, to seek the Committee's advice at all. "We have received word from the Hill," he told the Advisory Committee in 1965, "that any time we come to a point of decision on some of our hardware projects we should break bread with our GTAC and receive their comments."[39] When members of the Committee did question the progress of some projects, Fumich reminded them that "you have to remember that everyone of these pilot plant programs has been approved by you before. If we come around and get too many negative points of view," he warned, "we might get into a little more trouble."[40] Nowhere in the 10-year record of the Advisory Committee is there any indication that the OCR ever rejected or terminated a project based on the Committee's opposition.

---

[38] E. Reichl, interview.
[39] GTAC Meeting Transcript, January 27, 1965, Box 2, GTAC/OCR/FRC, p. 9.
[40] GTAC Meeting Transcript, October 3, 1966, Box 2, GTAC/OCR/FRC, p. 43.

The General Technical Advisory Committee accomplished little more as a liaison between business and government. At least until 1968, its members acted as individuals, rather than as spokesmen for their industries able to mobilize broad-based constituencies for the synfuels program. In 1967, for example, the Johnson administration denied the OCR's request for increased budget authority as part of its effort to economize on deficits resulting from the Vietnam War. Alarmed by the prospect of a budgetary plateau, with so many pilot plants already underway, Fumich suggested that the Advisory Committee "be the catalyst to really push this thing through." The problem was not Congress, where the OCR had its champions, but "within the Administration," explained Fumich, "where we get our first strictions." The best the Committee could apparently manage was a letter to Secretary Udall on the importance of coal research.[41] When the OCR's budgetary constraints got even tighter in 1968 (under pressure from Project Gasoline's cost overruns), Fumich nearly begged the Committee for outside help – a resolution, lobbying, letters – anything. "We have a lot of money eggs in this basket," said Fumich. "It has been getting hotter than hell around here in recent months."[42]

Finally, in October 1968, the Advisory Committee formed a subcommittee to drum up pressure on the Administration. The subcommittee put together data highlighting the relative inadequacy of the OCR's budget and the potential accomplishments of its pilot-plant program. A flurry of letters went off to the Bureau of the Budget and the Department of the Interior, but to little avail. The two agencies so limited the OCR's authorization for FY1970 that there could be no new projects, and three existing projects had to be eliminated.[43] The Advisory Committee was still fuming about ways to organize political support when Fumich announced that at last, "we have found a champion" in the Department of the Interior. He was referring to Hollis Dole, the new Assistant Secretary, who wanted to double the OCR's budget.[44]

Since the Office of Coal Research was dependent on individual champions, without strong support from industry, it failed to develop the kind of bureaucratic linkages it needed to become a major federal program. To get anywhere, the OCR was continuously running what Fumich called an "obstacle course" of four congressional committees and two executive agencies, none of which became an institutional sponsor for the synfuels program until the energy crisis. Compared to the nuclear energy program, said John O'Leary, this institutional situation "cut into ribbons any effort on the part of the Government to develop the sound comprehensive balance in energy R&D policies." In the relationship between Congress and the Atomic Energy Commission, "you find a sort of

[41] GTAC Meeting Transcript, May 26, 1967, pp. 12–16, and GTAC Letter File, June 1967, Box 2, GTAC/OCR/FRC.
[42] GTAC Meeting Transcript, January 15, 1968, Box 2, GTAC/OCR/FRC, pp. 89–92.
[43] Minutes of Meetings, GTAC Ad Hoc Subcommittee, November 8, 1968, and May 8, 1969; also, G. Fumich to GTAC Members, December 2, 1968, Box 2, GTAC/OCR/FRC.
[44] GTAC Meeting Transcript, June 10, 1969, p. 139, and October 7, 1969, p. 8, Box 3, GTAC/OCR/FRC.

mutual reinforcement society." But in coal, said O'Leary, "we have hostile appropriations committees and we have hostile substantive committees."[45]

Project Gasoline's problems epitomized the collective failings of the OCR's synfuels program during a period of energy surplus. This project was the biggest (in dollar terms), most ambitious and politically controversial from the start of the coal-research program. The plant at Cresap, although designed as an integrated, coal-synthesis system, did not actually produce gasoline, but rather crude feedstock suitable for refining. The project was managed by Consolidation Coal, one of the only coal companies big enough to have its own research program, and the company whose technical personnel and management were most closely associated with the OCR and its General Technical Advisory Committee. It was no political accident that this flagship project was given to a coal company. Nor was it any less significant politically that a major oil company bought Consolidation Coal and was running the project at the time of its termination.

The OCR indulged in some hyperbole when it sold Project Gasoline to the Interior Department and Congress. Whether because of technical optimism or political salesmanship, the Office of Coal Research seriously underestimated the project's capital costs, construction schedule and shake-down time, mechanical problems, and the unit costs of its end-product. In 1963, the OCR entered a contract with Consolidation Coal for $9.9 million to build the plant in three years and operate it for five years testing various types of coal. At the time, an outside engineering consultant estimated that the project would cost $17.6 million, would require two additional years, and recommended that it be built in Pennsylvania rather than Cresap, West Virginia. OCR officials rejected this assessment and stuck with their own estimates.[46] As it turned out, the construction took four years, shake-down operations lasted three years instead of 6 months, and when the project was shut down in 1970 for lack of results, $20.4 million had been expended by the government.

The estimated unit cost of synthetic gasoline from the project was the salient number, politically. On this point, optimism seemed not only excessive, but apparently infectious. In its preliminary analysis, the Ralph M. Parsons Company estimated that on a commercial scale, the process could produce 100 octane gasoline for 13.6 cents a gallon with a 6.4 percent rate of return.[47] In a subsequent assessment, Parsons actually lowered that estimate to 12.8 cents a gallon. Even then, OCR officials felt that Parsons was overly cautious. Their estimate was 11.0 cents a gallon in 1965. "If the coal people can produce it for 11 cents," noted a skeptical oil company official, "they would have ample profit of 2 cents a gallon right now."[48] Even though this figure was less than half any previous estimate other than the Bureau of Mines' in 1950, the OCR stuck to it

[45] GTAC Meeting Transcript, October 7, 1969, Box 3, GTAC/OCR/FRC, pp. 85–86.
[46] U.S. Congress, House, "Review of the Coal Research Program," vol. 5, OCR Budgetary Material, OCR/FRC.
[47] GTAC Meeting Minutes, October 8, 1962, Box 1, GTAC/OCR/FRC.
[48] GTAC Meeting Minutes, January 27, 1965, OCR Contract Files, Box 11, File No. 3, PG/OCR/FRC; also, Wall Street Journal, October 20, 1965.

tenaciously as late as 1968, by which time the project was already in deep trouble.

Despite construction delays and cost overruns, OCR officials and project managers remained optimistic about the technical promise of the Cresap plant. Until 1967, design changes and substitution of a newly discovered catalytic process using zinc chloride had accounted for most of the problems. But after six months of shake-down operations plagued by technical problems, this shared optimism gave way to frustration and a growing tension between OCR staff and the project's management. While maintaining a mien of confidence before the Advisory Committee, Neil Cochran, the OCR's Director of Utilization, complained formally to the project manager that continuing problems had to be solved quickly to avoid embarrassment of the OCR.[49] By November, he was recommending that Consolidation be declared in default of its contract if problems were not solved in 90 days.

Mechanical, design, and maintenance problems seemed to get worse rather than better as shake-down operations continued. Filters, compressors, rotating equipment, and other critical parts kept breaking down, even with continuous modification and frequent replacement. It seemed that the pulverized coal mixed with solvents continually clogged and damaged all sorts of valves, pumps, and pipes designed for more conventional liquids. Periodic problems with the critical carbonization and hydrogenation vessels that operated under high temperatures and pressure caused sustained shutdowns over the entire operating period from November 1966 through April 1970. Worst of all, when one section was up and operating, two or three others were invariably shut down for equipment repairs or replacement. Thus, the coal liquefaction system never did operate as an integrated whole.[50]

Contradictory perceptions of Project Gasoline's purpose seemed to have complicated its management as the operating problems worsened. Eric Reichl, the project manager for Consolidation Coal, coped with the problems as normal difficulties for a research endeavor.[51] The management of Continental Oil, drawn in by complaints from the Secretary of Interior, seemed to share Reichl's perspective and fully supported his efforts. But OCR officials grew increasingly alarmed and impatient, as if they had sold themselves on the belief that coal liquefaction was a proven technology, except for its commercial feasibility. When they did not get a fully operational plant for the costs they had estimated, they were quick to place blame on the contractor, initiate outside evaluations, and bring the Interior Department into deliberations with the contractor and its parent, Continental Oil.[52] Although the Interior Department did what it could

[49] GTAC Meeting Transcript, May 27, 1967, Box 2, GTAC/OCR/FRC, p. 22; N. Cochran to E. Reichl, May 11, 1967, OCR Contract Files, Box 11, File No. 3, PG/OCR/FRC.
[50] "Brief History of Cresap, West Virginia Pilot Plant Operations," November 9, 1971, in OCR Contract Files, Box 11, File No. 5, PG/OCR/FRC; also, "Monthly Operations Log," in DOI, Office of the Secretary, Equipment and Property Files, OCR Pt. 5, OCR/DOI.
[51] E. Reichl, interview.
[52] Memorandum, Chief, Division of Contracts and Administration to C. Moore, November 27, 1967, and G. Fumich to Secretary of the Interior, December 11, 1967, in DOI, Office of the

to pressure Continental Oil to take a more active financial and managerial role in Project Gasoline, it was not willing to make a public fight over the project's imminent failure. To allay congressional criticism and prevent a generalized attack on the OCR's budget, all parties involved quietly accepted Project Gasoline's termination in April 1970.[53]

Stewart Udall's oil shale initiative

While the coal industry's advocates pursued the nostrum of synfuels research, oil shale had been all but forgotten. The Bureau of Mines' experimental facility at Rifle, Colorado, had laid dormant since 1956 after the National Petroleum Council recommended its closure. Quite unexpectedly in November 1963, Interior Secretary Stewart Udall solicited public suggestions for "the orderly conservation and development of the federally owned oil-shale deposits in Colorado, Utah, and Wyoming."[54]

Several impulses seemed to lay behind this initiative. A number of western congressmen had an abiding interest in the timely development of oil shale by the private sector. Foremost among them was Wayne Aspinall, who did not think that government-funded synfuels research should exclusively benefit Appalachia.[55] A ruling by the Bureau of Land Management, cancelling 257 old placer-mining claims, had recently stirred up old issues regarding the government's responsibility for developing oil shale properties in the public domain. And the Interior Department had just begun negotiations to lease the plant at Rifle for private research. Since Mobil and Humble Oil (a subsidiary of Jersey Standard), two of the Seven Sisters, were the prospective tenants, news of this deal evoked cries of impropriety – a "giveaway" to Big Oil.[56]

Perhaps most significant was Secretary Udall's own conservation ethic which valued efficient, planned utilization of resources as well as protection.[57] Con-

Secretary, Procurement Files, OCR, Pt. 10; also, Memorandum for the Record, April 21, 1969. Meeting between officials of DOI, Continental Oil and Consolidation Coal, Equipment and Property Files, OCR Pt. 1, OCR/DOI.

[53] In 1972, the OCR nearly entered another $7 million contract with Continental Oil to convert the Cresap plant to the H-Oil process. But with President Nixon's initiative to reorganize energy research, that idea was modified and delayed until 1974, when ERDA, Fluor Engineers, American Electric Power, and Allegheny Power Corporation entered a much larger contract to convert Cresap to a demonstration facility for producing synthetic, low-sulfur fuel oil for utility boilers.

[54] "Remarks by Assistant Secretary of the Interior John M. Kelly Before the First Annual Oil Shale Symposium, Colorado School of Mines, April 30, 1964, Golden, Colorado," O&G Files, Files 403.3, O&G/DOI, p. 1.

[55] Wayne Aspinall, "Address to the National Petroleum Council," in NPC, Meeting Transcript, May 25, 1965, NPC/DOI, pp. 32–47.

[56] The Anvil Points experimental facility, at Rifle, was technically leased in 1964 to the Colorado School of Mines Research Foundation, in order to avoid the appearance of a "giveaway" of public resources to the oil industry. By prior arrangement, the Foundation had sub-contracted the research work to Mobil and Humble, the two companies that would actually pay for the lease. Although their patentable research results would remain proprietary, they agreed to share the information with government and to grant licenses at reasonable fees. See, U.S. Department of the Interior, Press Release, May 1, 1964, O&G Files, 1964–65, File 403.3, O&G/DOI.

[57] See Stewart Udall, *The Quiet Crisis* (New York: Avon Books, 1963).

tinued non-action, when so many problems and uncertainties surrounded America's oil shale resource, was inconsistent with this ethic. "If the national interest is to be served," said Udall in 1964, "and this resource [oil shale] is to make an optimum long-term contribution to the economic well-being of the Nation, the major public policy questions needed to be identified and evaluated at the outset."[58] To help clarify these issues, Udall appointed six prominent and relatively disinterested citizens to an Oil Shale Advisory Board.[59]

The technical, economic, and political problems associated with any development of oil shale were legion. From the Interior Department's perspective in the mid-sixties, the most pressing of these was legal clarification of the government's title to oil shale properties, blocking up of sufficiently large tracts for commercial development, and adequate geologic survey data on oil shale reserves. Other problems involved availability of water, control of reserves, recovery methods, waste disposal, capital costs, and the likely demand for shale oil. However, as public discussion progressed during the 1960's, these problems, while far from being resolved, tended to be overshadowed by distributive issues, such as shale-oil prices, competition, and federal revenues.

The oil shale deposits of primary interest were those of the Green River Formation, covering approximately 16,500 square miles of Colorado, Utah, and Wyoming as indicated by the shaded areas in Chart 8–1. The federal government believed that it owned about 80 percent of these lands, or of the mineral rights under them. But its title to thousands of tracts was obscured by a long history of unpatented claims, withdrawals, and leases. The Interior Department had tried to revoke 36,000 claims in 1930, but the Supreme Court rejected the attempt. In 1964, the Solicitor's Office of the Interior Department prepared to contest the unpatented claims once again, this time on the grounds that they had lapsed from inattention.[60] To complicate matters, 16,000 additional claims had been filed since 1954 under a loophole allowing claims on separate deposits of metalliferous minerals, such as the aluminum dawsonite that is finely interspersed in the marlstone known as oil shale. Although the Interior Department challenged these claims too, it faced lengthy litigation before either problem was resolved.

The presence of these unvalidated claims severely hampered the Interior Department's prerogatives for managing the shale resource. As long as the titles were clouded, the Interior Department admitted that "private investment is improbable and leasing of Federal lands or 'blocking up' of land ownership to

[58] Quoted in *Interim Report of the Oil Shale Advisory Board*, February 1, 1965 (Washington, 1965), p. 1.
[59] Joseph Fisher, president of Resources for the Future, was appointed chairman of the Oil Shale Advisory Board. Its other members were John Galbraith, the Harvard economist, Orlo Childs, Dean of the Colorado School of Mines, H. Byron Mock, an attorney previously with the BLM, Benjamin Cohen, an attorney, and Milo Perkins, a financial consultant, both of whom had served the government during the New Deal.
[60] *Ickes v. Virginia-Colorado Development Co.*, 295 U.S. 639 (1935), and *Union Oil Company of California, et al.*, 71 I.D. 169 (1964); also, U.S. Department of the Interior, *Prospects for Oil Shale Development* (Washington: DOI, 1968), pp. 28–31.

Figure 8-1
Green River Oil Shale Formation

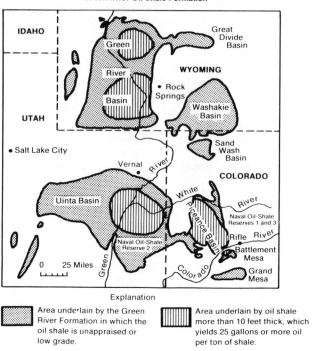

Explanation

Area underlain by the Green River Formation in which the oil shale is unappraised or low grade.

Area underlain by oil shale more than 10 feet thick, which yields 25 gallons or more oil per ton of shale.

Source: Geological Survey, Circular 523.

form economic production units is not possible."[61] Legal barriers to "blocking up" were particularly important. Except for the Naval Oil Shale Reserve, a patchwork pattern of land ownership with alternate units of public and private land prevailed throughout the oil shale regions. Exchanges would be necessary if developers of commercial-scale projects were to accumulate sufficient acreage of either private holdings or public leases. Since leases could not exceed 5,120 acres to any individual or corporation (under the Mineral Leasing Act), exchanges were all the more imperative.

The shale-oil content and value of federal properties was nearly as clouded as their title. Before any program of development could commence, the government needed to know how much shale it owned, how rich its deposits were, and how much was technically and economically recoverable on any given property. Chart 8–2 indicates only the roughest summary of this data. At a 60 percent recovery rate, it appeared that the richest deposits on federal properties might yield 288 billion barrels of shale oil, with private property contributing another

[61] Department of the Interior, *Prospects for Oil Shale Development*, p. 38.

Figure 8-2
Shale Oil Reserves by Land Ownership

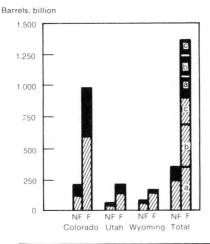

Barrels, billion

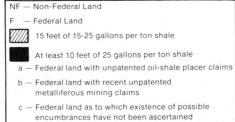

NF — Non-Federal Land

F — Federal Land

15 feet of 15-25 gallons per ton shale

At least 10 feet of 25 gallons per ton shale

a — Federal land with unpatented oil-shale placer claims

b — Federal land with recent unpatented
     metalliferous mining claims

c — Federal land as to which existence of possible
     encumbrances have not been ascertained

Source: U.S. Department of the Interior, Prospects for Oil Shale
Development (Washington: DOI, 1968), p. 15.

66 billion.[62] But to confirm these estimates on a property-by-property basis, it was obvious that the Geological Survey, Bureau of Land Management, and Bureau of Mines faced an immense job of measurement.

The government recognized various technical problems, including water availability, mining and refining methods, spent shale disposal, and resource conservation, but in the 1960's they seemed "subordinate" to issues of competition, economic policy, and the assurance of adequate government revenues. Early estimates of water requirements indicated that a one million barrel per day industry would need 145,000 acre-feet per year. Water availability in Wyoming and Utah appeared more than adequate. Although water supplies would be tighter in Colorado, because of U.S. treaty obligations to Mexico regarding the Colorado River, the Interior Department still felt there would be enough to support an industry of one million barrels per day.[63] Disposal of spent shale was

[62] Ibid., A–1, A–2.   [63] Ibid., 100–103.

also noted, but too easily dismissed. Since shale expands volumetrically by 30 percent when refined, a 60,000 ton per day plant would produce about 20 million cubic yards of powdery waste material each year. In an open pit mine, up to 1,000 feet of overburden would also require disposal, or at least storage. Where to put these materials, not to mention their final condition, was largely viewed as an engineering problem rather than a policy issue. Degradation of air and water quality was scarcely mentioned. For conservationists of Udall's generation, the potential for wasted shale resources seemed a more serious problem than environmental impact. Needless to say, those priorities would change shortly.

For the Interior Department to embrace even the most gradual utilization of oil shale, there had to be some degree of need and practicability. Although no one in 1964 foresaw any imminent shortage of liquid fuels, there was a growing conviction within the Interior Department and some elements of the oil industry that experimental and prototype work on oil shale should begin soon. "We have estimated," wrote an executive of Shell Oil to Udall, "that a minimum of ten years of serious effort would be required, and reliable forecasts indicate that within 10 to 15 years domestic crude oil production will be unable to meet the demand."[64]

It appeared to some energy analysts, including those at the Interior Department, that shale oil was again "coming into the competitive range." Various cost estimates that appeared during the 1960's indicated that shale oil could be produced at unit costs ranging from $1.46 to $2.68 per barrel, and be sold, with a reasonable return on investment, for $2.00 to $3.50 per barrel.[65] In 1964, the Interior Department estimated that a 50,000 barrel-per-day plant in Colorado, which would cost from $60 to $142 million, could produce shale oil at a price of $2.80 to $3.30 per barrel.[66] Another study done in 1967, using discounted cash-flow analysis, showed that a selling price of $4.34 per barrel would be necessary to yield a 20 percent rate of return on a first commercial plant. With a 12 percent rate of return, subsequent plants would only need to sell the shale oil for $2.98 a barrel, or 10 cents less than the price of crude oil at the time.[67]

Were these estimates realistic, it seemed certain that shale oil would be competitive if the real price of crude petroleum increased at all. Moreover, the

---

[64] W. A. Alexander to S. Udall, January 28, 1964, Office of the Secretary, Central Classified Files, Minerals and Fuels/Oil Shale, pt. 1, U.S. Department of the Interior, Washington, D.C.

[65] Edward W. Merrow, *Constraints on the Commercialization of Oil Shale*, prepared for the Department of Energy (R–2293–DOE), September 1978 (Santa Monica: Rand Corporation, 1978), Table B–1, p. 126; also, Henry Steele, "The Prospects for the Development of a Shale Oil Industry," in U.S. Congress, Senate, Judiciary Committee, Subcommittee on Antitrust and Monopoly, *Competitive Aspects of Oil Shale Development* (90th Cong., 1st Sess.), April–May 1967, pp. 542–558.

[66] U.S. Department of the Interior, "The Oil Shale Policy Problem," July 7, 1964, pt. 4, OS/DOI, p. 40.

[67] Department of the Interior, *Prospects for Oil Shale Development*, Appendix B, pp. 1–21. This study, prepared by Ezra Solomon, assumed no cost for the oil shale and a capital cost of $130 million.

actions of at least one private group appeared to confirm this. In 1964, The Oil Shale Corporation (TOSCO), Standard Oil of Ohio, and Cleveland-Cliffs Iron Co. undertook a joint venture (Colony Development Co.) to build and operate a 1,000 ton-per-day prototype plant. If that were successful, they planned to expand it into a commercial-scale plant costing $130 million and producing 58,000 barrels per day of shale oil by 1970.[68]

For once, it looked as if energy policy were to be planned rationally, with sensitivity to the market and commitment to long-term strategic interests. In a briefing paper for the Oil Shale Advisory Board, the Interior Department said that the question of oil-shale development "is not one to be answered from the standpoint of basic need but rather from that of competitive cost." Once the "world petroleum surplus" ended, shale oil would "have to compete with natural petroleum." The operative question was how to construct a resource policy that would neither hamper nor subsidize its development, but merely facilitate private initiative.[69]

This was certainly the approach that the oil industry wanted to see. In response to Udall's call for comments, most of the major companies urged the government to work out a careful and comprehensive set of leasing regulations before taking any affirmative action. A small portion of the shale lands should be set aside for purely experimental work by interested companies. Sometime after that, the Interior Department should begin a leasing program of commercial tracts "that assures orderly development." Although individual firms differed in their specific recommendations regarding lease size, royalties, development requirements, and the appropriateness of competitive bidding, nearly all of the major companies emphasized the need for orderly development.[70] During the same time that they were making these comments, however, at least four of the major oil companies submitted lease requests for more than 70,000 acres containing an estimated 200 billion barrels of shale oil.[71] Interior officials did not take those applications any more seriously than the suggestion by a number of small companies that President Hoover's withdrawal order be lifted.

There was less consensus among "citizens" than among oil companies regarding the appropriate course for a national policy on oil shale. In the spring of 1965, Secretary Udall's Oil Shale Advisory Board submitted a report distinguished only by its divisiveness. Board members could only agree in the most general terms that the objectives of federal policy should include the following: (1) encourage advancement of the technology, (2) encourage wide industry

---

[68] For a discussion of the original project, see U.S. Congress, Senate, *Competitive Aspects of Oil Shale Development*, pp. 308–331. Although the prototype plant was operated successfully, Colony repeatedly postponed its commercial development throughout the 1970's. By 1973, its estimated capital cost was $340 million, or $430 million in 1977 dollars (E. Merrow, *Constraints on the Commercialization of Oil Shale*, pp. 128–129).

[69] Department of the Interior, "The Oil Shale Policy Problem," p. 19.

[70] Correspondence from Shell Oil, Phillips Petroleum, Atlantic Refining, Union Oil, and TOSCO to Stewart Udall, Jan.–April, 1964, pts. 1–2, OS/DOI.

[71] E. W. Stanley to J. K. Galbraith, December 9, 1964, pt. 6, OS/DOI.

competition, (3) establish conservation goals and standards, (4) prevent land speculation, (5) assure reasonable revenues to the federal and state governments, and (6) set up the program so it could be administered effectively.[72]

Beyond this, there was no agreement. Ideological differences seemed to account for most of the discord among members of the Advisory Board. At one extreme, Milo Perkins and Byron Mock believed private enterprise should be turned loose on the shale lands, much as it had on the Outer Continental Shelf. They would lift the old withdrawal order, have competitive bids on large tracts, and provide minimal standards for performance and conservation.

Nearer the middle of the spectrum, Orlo Childs favored restricted commercial leasing, while Joseph Fisher would have government limit its leases to experimental tracts, contracting with industry for research.

At the other extreme, Benjamin Cohen and J. Kenneth Galbraith urged Secretary Udall to refrain from leasing the lands altogether and merely engage private firms to do specified contract research. They feared that the government would otherwise give away public properties worth trillions of dollars to a few large oil companies whose "current interest in leasing is related not to a desire for development but to a desire to control land." In this respect, they noted that there was an oil glut and that oil companies already controlled 168,000 acres of private shale lands. Finally, Cohen and Galbraith warned that with leases of any size, "the government would be offering a subsidy of unknown value for a development of unknown cost promising a return of unknown amount."[73]

Stewart Udall hardly needed this kind of advice. It was difficult enough to forge a consensus within the government, without an Advisory Board fueling the controversy. In Congress, Wayne Aspinall was pushing hard for rapid development of oil shale by industry. Toward that end, he was building support for revision of the depletion allowance. Aspinall's bill, promoted by Fred Hartley of Union Oil, would redefine the material to which the depletion allowance applied; that is, from oil shale (after mining) to shale oil (after retorting).[74] Within Interior, there seemed to be two camps. Cordell Moore, Assistant Secretary of Mineral Resources, favored large leases (5,000 acres), parcelled out slowly. "So as not to unduly upset the domestic petroleum industry," he cautioned, "it must be orderly and sufficiently programmed to phase in gradually over the entire development period."[75] The in-house agencies, however, preferred a large-scale program in which they would play the central role. Karl Landstrom, the Assistant Secretary of Public Lands, was sympathetic to this approach. He even suggested that "a federally sponsored private corpora-

[72] Oil Shale Advisory Board, *Interim Report to the Secretary of the Interior,* February 1965, in pt. 6, OS/DOI, pp. 6–7.

[73] Oil Shale Advisory Board, *Interim Report,* pp. 16–39.

[74] S. Udall to W. Aspinall, March 15, 1965, pt. 6, OS/DOI. The DOI's response to Aspinall's bill was lukewarm, for if the depletion allowance were changed for oil shale, the coal industry would certainly agitate for equal treatment.

[75] C. Moore to S. Udall, April 19, 1966, pt. 10, OS/DOI.

tion be considered for development of this resource." Another alternative "would be a government corporation."[76]

In January 1967, Stewart Udall announced a "Five Point Oil Shale Development Program" designed for minimal squawk. It offered something for everyone, but in limited amounts. Its objectives, with regard to competition, conservation, speculation, and government revenues, were similar to those recommended by the Advisory Board, with additional provision that national policy "encourage fullest use of all known mineral resources." The five points toward development were as follows:

1. Accelerated clearance of clouded titles;
2. Blocking-up of commercial tracts by exchanges of public and private lands;
3. Leasing of small, experimental tracts to develop various mining and processing methods, reserving larger commercial tracts, on which good conservation practices would be required, until the research and development work had been successfully performed.
4. *In situ* retorting by nuclear fission would be explored by the Atomic Energy Commission;
5. The Interior Department would also fund some research of mining and processing technologies, both by contract and by in-house agencies.[77]

Udall called for public comment on these guidelines and specific suggestions as to leasing regulations. His office was flooded with comments from irate citizens, congressmen, and all kinds of interest groups. The prospect of action sparked a raging controversy.

"Giveaway" was the cry that went up throughout the land. With the press commenting that as much as 5 trillion dollars were at stake, a lot of people concluded that the government was in cahoots with Big Oil to rape the public domain. People like J. R. Freeman, a newspaper editor in Colorado who had long been warning of a "Grabber Conspiracy," suddenly caught the attention of Congress and the national media. Freeman's series of 40 articles on "the oil shale scandal which dwarfs the Teapot Dome affair by a hundred times," even received the 1967 Herrick Editorial Award from the National Newspaper Association.[78] The pressure on Congress from concerned citizens was so great that Senator Philip Hart immediately convened his Subcommittee on Antitrust and Monopoly to hold hearings on the matter, while Senators Jackson and Proxmire urged Udall to delay issuance of leasing regulations until the Interior Committee could do likewise. Even the White House ordered Udall to undertake a

[76] C. Stoddard to Solicitor, May 25, 1966, and C. Moore to K. Landstrom, October 6, 1966, pt. 10, OS/DOI.

[77] Department of the Interior, Office of the Secretary, Press Release, January 27, 1967, File 403.3, Synthetic Liquid Fuels (1966–67), O&G/DOI.

[78] C. Moore to N. Peterson, January 12, 1967, and attached draft to J. R. Freeman, C. Moore Papers, Chronological File, Box 3, LBJPL; also, J. R. Freeman to R. F. Kennedy, January 25, 1968; J. R. Freeman to K. S. Landstrom, April 5, 1968; S. Udall to J. Inouye, April 17, 1968, pt. 15, OS/DOI.

more comprehensive study of oil shale development before moving ahead. So much for a rational energy policy.

Congressional deliberations at least translated the "Grabber Conspiracy" issue into a more sophisticated inquiry of the competitive aspects of oil shale development. Senator Hart's subcommittee was concerned that some points in Udall's five-point program "might contribute inadvertently to monopolization of that resource [oil shale] by the same corporations which presently sit astride our petroleum industry." Hart and like-minded congressmen felt that "the development of oil shale reserves should offer a unique opportunity for new sources of competition to penetrate the petroleum industry." Only government could guarantee that opportunity.[79]

The substance of the hearings revealed the contradictory nature of the issue. On the one hand, oil companies allegedly controlled ample shale properties already and had no intention of developing them for fear of undermining petroleum prices. On the other hand, it was feared that oil companies would monopolize oil shale development and reap huge profits at the public's expense. In a technical and economic sense, the hearings confirmed the concern for competition. Since the barriers to entry for commercial development of oil shale appeared more imposing than previously anticipated, major oil companies looked like the only private institutions with the resources necessary to do the job.

Another consideration was brought out in the 1967 hearings more clearly than before. This was the potential impact of oil shale development on the environment of the high plains. Spokesmen for half a dozen national conservation groups criticized Udall's plans in terms that were substantively different from the "good conservation practices" language used earlier in the decade. "The technology is a matter of considerable concern to us," commented the lobbyist for the Citizens Committee on Natural Resources, and "appears to us to create significant environmental problems."[80] Here was a quiet harbinger of a political force that would soon match the energy market in its impact on the development of oil shale. But for the time, distributive issues remained critical.

The upshot of this controversy was a set of leasing regulations that ignored most of the oil industry's suggestions and nullified what little enthusiasm there might have been for serious investment in oil shale. The most important change from the original five-point program was that an experimental tract could no longer be expanded into a commercial tract.[81] Among other important changes were limitation of the lease offering to three small tracts in Colorado, stiffer-than-expected requirements for environmental controls, "unduly high" royalty payments, bonus payments even in the event of project termination, and a limitation of only one tract per lessee.[82] Senators Paul Douglas and William

[79] U.S. Congress, Senate, *Competitive Aspects of Oil Shale Development*, pp. 2–3.

[80] *Ibid.*, 218.

[81] S. Udall to J. Dingell, January 18, 1968, pt. 15, and S. Udall to S. Hathaway, October 24, 1968, pt. 17, OS/DOI.

[82] M. Winston to S. Udall, December 19, 1968, and Sun Oil Co. to the Department of the Interior, December 18, 1968, pt. 18, OS/DOI.

Proxmire, protectors of the "public interest," wrote Udall to congratulate him for making changes that would thwart "the predators."[83]

On December 20, 1968, the Interior Department held a test lease sale at its Denver office that was the culmination of five years of planning. When the bids were opened, the disappointment was stunning. Only three bids were even submitted; two by TOSCO for $250,000 each, and a third for $625 by some anonymous entrepreneur. Secretary Udall hastily rejected the bids, attributing the program's failure to a combination of restrictive leasing terms and energy market conditions. With the issue of the depletion allowance unsettled, with import quotas under review by the incoming President, and with the economics of oil-shale technology still marginal, the government had simply not offered sufficient incentive for private firms to take a considerable risk. The Secretary sadly announced that he would take no further action on oil shale: "determination of what is in the best public interest will be left to the incoming Administration and Congress."[84]

The second synfuels program

The government's second synfuels program failed, in the first instance, because energy market conditions were not ripe. From at least 1959 until 1968, oil and natural gas were a glut on the market. Stabilization of declining prices and market share was the central problem that preoccupied public policy and private strategy. Above all else, the overhang of cheap foreign oil still dominated the domestic energy market as it had in 1953. Speaking in 1968, Assistant Secretary Cordell Moore observed that "our oil imports policy casts a long shadow over the prospects we have for bringing synthetic liquid fuels from coal and oil shale to market." Synthetic fuels were "much more vulnerable, much more sensitive to potential manipulation of oil import levels than is oil from conventional deposits. Depending on the decision made as to oil import levels over future years," said Moore, "the entry of synthetics to commercial markets could be delayed a decade or more."[85] These short-run circumstances overwhelmed the perceived longer-run need to develop a viable synthetic fuels industry rooted in abundant domestic energy resources. Lead-time of 10 to 20 years were simply beyond the planning horizons of major energy companies or the Congress. No matter how optimistic were the cost estimates for liquid coal or shale oil, the risks invariably appeared greater and the returns lower than for familiar, conventional fuels at stable real prices.

In a surplus oil market, neither politicians nor technocrats were able to frame the public policy issues of synthetic fuels in any cogent and practicable manner.

---

[83] P. Douglas to S. Udall, August 6, 1968, and W. Proxmire to S. Udall, August, 1968, pt. 16, OS/DOI.

[84] Department of the Interior, Office of the Secretary, Press Release, December 27, 1968, pt. 18, OS/DOI.

[85] J. Cordell Moore, "Remarks to the Oklahoma Independent Petroleum Association, Tulsa, Oklahoma, December 2, 1968," Box 1, "Oil Imports and National Security," Cordell Moore Papers, LBJPL.

The confused origins of both the coal-research and oil-shale programs attest to this problem. From 1958 until 1963, neither coal interests nor Congress could agree on whether coal research should be directed toward quick increases in coal sales or toward the larger but slower potential of a synfuels market. With oil shale, the Interior Department did not really know why it should have a program, other than the fact that the resources were there, existing policy was muddled, and Representative Aspinall wanted action. Although most parties agreed that oil shale and coal synthesis would sometime be necessary, the political process could not translate that certainty into concrete policy while excess capacity prevailed in conventional fuels.

Market conditions also shaped the political patterns of implementing policy in coal research and shale leasing. Creation of the Office of Coal Research and controversy over its sponsorship of synfuels pilot plants was the product of interfuel and intra-governmental politics. Coal-state congressmen viewed the OCR as a means of providing the coal industry with government subsidies to counterbalance some of the benefits received by the petroleum and nuclear industries. Western interests on the House Interior Committee were willing to tolerate something modest, given the coal industry's plight, but did not want to lose control of a potentially large-scale program that could gather momentum and sap government support for their own programs. Bureaucratic turf was also at issue. The Interior Department generally, and the Bureau of Mines in particular, did not wish to see their responsibility for resource policy diluted. The program for shale development was affected by similar frictions that involved the role of government-sponsored research, the appropriate extent of government planning, and the degree of public control. In 1968, the shale issue began shifting to the politics of business reform as part of a broader deterioration of business-government relations that presaged the end of glut and the emergence of scarcity.

Inept organization of business-government interaction stands out as another important reason that the second synfuels program failed. In both political and bureaucratic terms, the Office of Coal Research was unable to establish its autonomy, to build a network of intra-governmental support, or to effectively manage its contractors for the pilot-plant programs. With regard to oil shale, organization was virtually non-existent. Secretary Udall never did establish an organizational entity to promote and implement an oil shale program. Planning and development were handled with *ad hoc* staff support from the Solicitor's Office, the Bureau of Land Management, and the Assistant Secretary of Mineral Resources. The absence of well-organized, private clienteles exacerbated these bureaucratic deficiencies. For coal-research, the General Technical Advisory Committee was too fragmented, and perhaps too naive, to bring to bear the coal industry's potential political leverage. Oil shale had no clientele whatsoever, and Udall's Advisory Board obviously did nothing to crystalize external support for a substantive program.

Just as the second synfuels program appeared to reach a dead end, the very market conditions that had caused such political inertia began to shift. In 1969 and 1970, spare domestic oil capacity declined sharply, prices began to rise, and shortages of natural gas appeared imminent. Congress showed a quickening interest in all manner of synthetic fuels, and appropriations for the Office of Coal Research turned around suddenly to begin doubling on an annual basis. Eventually, even the OCR's bureaucratic problems were alleviated by government reorganization, and a prototype commercial leasing program for oil shale replaced Udall's experimental project.

Thus, despite its failure, the second synfuels program was to be the foundation of a major new initiative by the U.S. government during the 1970's, but only after the political economy of energy completed a fundamental shift from surplus to shortage.

Part III. The second energy transition: adjustment to depletion, 1969–1980

Our decision about energy will test the character of the American people and the ability of the President and the Congress to govern this Nation. This difficult effort will be the moral equivalent of war, except that we will be uniting our efforts to build and not to destroy.

Jimmy Carter, 1977

9. Energy crisis and structural change

America's energy crisis began symbolically in the third week of October 1973. Egypt and Israel had been at war for eleven days when President Richard Nixon announced his decision to resupply the Israeli Air Force. Two days later, King Faisal ordered a 25 percent cut in Saudi Arabia's oil output and an embargo against the United States. Other Arab members of the Organization of Petroleum Exporting Countries (OPEC) followed suit. The next week, OPEC unilaterally raised the price of oil from $3.00 to $5.11 a barrel. Two months later, OPEC raised it again to $11.65.

These events were the political and economic manifestations of secular trends and past policies; OPEC was merely the catalyst. Depletion of easily accessible oil and gas deposits in the United States, masked by the draw-down of reserve inventories, was the real cause. Public policies that maintained an artificial equilibrium between supply and demand had prevented gradual adjustment through the price mechanism. Thus, declining real prices had discouraged new supplies but had not dampened the growth of demand. As a result, the transition to shortage *appeared* abrupt, in the form of curtailments in the interstate gas market and a shift of control over oil prices from the Texas Railroad Commission to the government of Saudi Arabia.

Transition from abundance to shortage was accompanied by increased concentration in the energy industries. The surfeit of oil and gas during the 1960's inspired forward and backward vertical integration through a wave of mergers. Then, beginning in the mid-1960's, the realization of depletion and the prospect of shortage stimulated horizontal integration across competing fuel sectors. By 1980, most major oil companies, and some electric utilities and gas pipeline companies, owned substantial interests in coal production and reserves, oil shale and synthetic fuels technology, and various phases of the nuclear fuel cycle.

The effects of depletion, together with runaway demand, also contributed to an environmental movement that hit its stride in 1970. On the supply side, depletion pushed oil and gas exploration offshore to the continental shelf and into Alaska and other western wilderness areas. Coal mining also moved west to take advantage of strip-mineable reserves on the public domain in the environmentally fragile, high plains states. Meanwhile, the growing demand for elec-

193

tricity stimulated increased coal combustion and rapid commercial development of nuclear power. Pushed by the high economic growth of the 1960's, the
cumulative impact of these developments elicited political pressure for environmental regulation that peaked, not coincidentally, at the very time of the energy
crisis. During the 1970's, that regulation stimulated demand for low-sulfur oil
and natural gas by restricting expansion of coal and nuclear-powered electric
generation. At the same time, federal environmental policies reduced the availability of offshore leases and slowed the development of western coal and oil
shale. Thus, the environmental movement was both a product of depletion and
a factor in the perpetuation of energy crisis.

The conrescence of these three trends – depletion, concentration, and environmentalism – nearly overwhelmed a polity already shaken by a broader
crisis of confidence that stemmed from the Vietnam War. In January 1974, at
the height of the oil embargo, respondents to a Gallup poll blamed the energy
crisis primarily on oil companies (25%) and the Federal Government (23%).
Only a few (7%) blamed Arab states.[1] Neither industry nor government had
given the public advance warning of energy shortages. Even after they occurred,
there seemed to be no clear explanations or comprehensible data. The news
media only added to the confusion. Mistrust abounded, as to the reality of the
crisis and its causes. Past policies and prior relationships between business and
government were scrutinized and attacked. After 1968, the political process
shifted from intrafuel contention over market stabilization to intra-governmental politics and the punitive politics of business reform.

The energy crisis in the early 1970's was very real in the sense that physical
depletion of domestic oil and gas resources was behind it. However, short-
sighted public policies, consumerism, and business decision-making affected
the timing, severity, and economic impact that made transition from abundance
to scarcity a crisis. The purpose of this chapter is to explain the crisis in those
political economic terms, and to account for the mistrust and backlash that
accompanied it. The remaining chapters in Part III examine the process of
adjusting public policy to the longer-term realities of depletion and a world
energy market.

Domestic depletion and the OPEC shock

Depletion of America's oil and natural gas resources has been a long, gradual
process. The energy crisis, in which demand exceeded marketable supply at the
prevailing price, was far more abrupt. As late as 1971, there was no consensus
within industry or government, nor scarcely any warning, that a crisis was
imminent. By November 1973, it was a full-blown reality. Much of the subsequent debate and mistrust was a function of this abruptness, after years of
administered prices and inventory draw-down that had masked the transition
to scarcity. Still, the signs were there, had anyone been looking or had sufficient
perspective.

---

[1]   George Gallup, *The Gallup Poll, Public Opinion 1972–1977* (Wilmington: Scholarly Resources
Inc., 1978), vol. 2, p. 226.

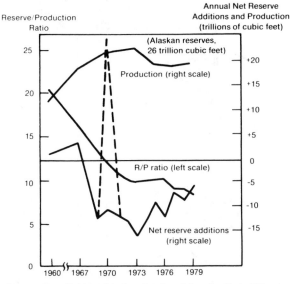

Chart 9-1
United States Annual Natural Gas
Production, Net Reserve Additions, and Reserve/Production Ratio
1960-1979

Source: Compiled from American Gas Association, <u>Gas Facts 1979</u>.

The course of depletion was similar for petroleum and natural gas since the two fuels are found either together or through a common exploratory process. The onset of crisis diverged somewhat because of different demand growth rates, price regulation of the interstate gas market, and the availability of imported oil. The first potential indicator that depletion might become a problem occurred in 1956 when the level of exploratory drilling peaked. Of course, that trend could have been no more than a response to declining return on investment or the fact that an immense glut of oil and gas had developed. But declining exploration, if continued, would inevitably lead to fewer gross additions to proved reserves.

The reserve-to-production ratio, for both oil and gas, peaked in 1960 and declined thereafter. (See Charts 9-1 and 9-2.) This was a key indicator, although perhaps mostly from hindsight. Were the ratio constant, it would have shown that new additions to proved reserves were keeping up with annual production. Expressed another way, the reserve-to-production ratio compares the growth of future supply to the growth of current demand. Between 1960 and 1973, the ratio for oil fell 36.7 percent (3.5 percent per year). The gas ratio declined 50.7 percent (5.3 percent per year). In effect, this was a draw-down of inventories that masked the economic effects of depletion and contributed to the suddenness of the shortages.[2]

---

[2]   Federal Power Commission, *1970 Annual Report*, p. 51.

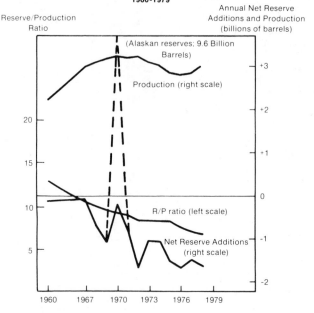

Chart 9-2
United States Annual Crude Oil Production,
Net Reserve Additions, and Reserve/Production Ratio
1960-1979

Source: Compiled from American Petroleum Institute, <u>Basic Petroleum Databook</u> (1976) and DeGolyer and MacNaughton, <u>Twentieth Century Petroleum Statistics</u> (1979).

With domestic exploration and production costs rising, and prices either stable or falling in real (uninflated) terms, the growth rate of new reserves fell below the growth of domestic demand (refer to Tables 9-1 and 9-2). The further these two growth rates diverged, the more rapid was the inventory draw-down for both oil and gas. In 1968, annual domestic production substantially exceeded new reserves and for the first time net new reserves turned negative. For both oil and gas, however, production continued to increase for a few years, until by 1972–73, net reserve shrinkage amounted to 30 percent of oil production and 75 percent of gas production. When production itself began falling due to the natural decline rates of existing oil and gas wells, the result was shortages, curtailments, and upward pressure on prices.

The depletion of oil and gas inventories with respect to demand growth occurred during the 1960's under the influence of the pricing and import policies described in Chapters 6 and 7. But it was the culmination of those trends in the exhaustion of unused productive capacity that actually destabilized prices and up-ended prior relationships between buyers and sellers (see Table 9-3). This was the most abrupt change, and the least anticipated, even though it

Table 9-1. *U.S. natural gas reserves and production, 1967–1979*

Year	Gross reserve additions	Production during year	Proved reserves at year-end	Net changes in reserves
1967	21.8	18.4	292.9	3.6
1968	13.7	19.4	287.3	−5.6
1969	8.4	20.7	275.1	−12.2
1970	11.2[a]	21.9	264.7	−10.4[a]
1971	9.8	22.1	252.8	−11.9
1972	9.6	22.5	240.1	−12.7
1973	6.8	22.6	223.9	−16.1
1974	8.7	21.3	211.1	−12.8
1975	10.5	19.7	202.2	−8.9
1976	7.6	19.5	190.0	−12.2
1977	11.9	19.4	182.9	−7.1
1978	10.6	19.3	174.3	−8.6
1979	14.3	19.9	168.8	−5.4

Note: Discrepancies due to rounding. Trillions of cubic feet.
[a]Excludes 26 trillion cubic feet discovered at Prudhoe Bay, Alaska.
Source: American Gas Association, *Gas Facts 1979* (Arlington, Va: AGA, 1980), p. 6.

Table 9-2. *U.S. crude oil reserves and production, 1967–1978*

Year	Gross reserve additions	Production during year	Proved reserves at year-end	Net changes in reserves
1967	2.96	3.04	31.38	−.07
1968	2.45	3.12	30.71	−.67
1969	2.12	3.19	29.63	−1.07
1970	3.09[a]	3.32	29.40	−.23[a]
1971	2.32	3.26	28.46	−.94
1972	1.56	3.28	26.74	−1.72
1973	2.15	3.18	25.70	−1.04
1974	1.99	3.04	24.65	−1.05
1975	1.32	2.89	23.08	−1.57
1976	1.08	2.82	21.34	−1.74
1977	1.40	2.86	19.89	−1.46
1978	1.35	3.03	18.20	−1.68

Note: Billions of barrels.
[a]Excludes 9.6 billion barrels discovered at Prudhoe Bay, Alaska.
Source: Compiled from American Petroleum Institute, *Basic Petroleum Databook* (1976) and DeGolyer and MacNaughton, *Twentieth Century Petroleum Statistics* (1979).

Table 9-3. *Landmarks in domestic oil and gas depletion*

	Crude oil	Natural gas
Exploration begins decline (peak year for number of exploratory wells)	1956	1956
Beginning of inventory draw-down (downturn of reserve/production ratio)	1960	1960
Maximum proved reserves	1966	1967
Annual production exceeds new reserves (net reserve additions turn substantially negative)	1968	1968
Production begins decline (peak year for annual production)	1970	1973
Demand exceeds marketable supply (estimated dissipation of spare production capacity)	1971	1970

was the critical measure of national security by which import quotas had been justified.

Productive capacity is an estimate of the maximum daily oil or gas output that could be obtained from all developed fields in the United States, with the pumping and gathering equipment already in place, without doing physical damage to the pools. Spare or "shut-in" capacity is the unused portion of this. Because there are so many thousands of wells and individual producers, all operating under different physical circumstances, it is nearly impossible to have a precise estimate of either figure.

With respect to natural gas, there were two indicators that full capacity utilization was reached in 1970. In that year, the unregulated price in the intrastate market of the southern Louisiana area surpassed the regulated price, suggesting that more gas was being demanded than was readily available. (Refer to Table 7-4.) In the regulated, interstate market, the first curtailments of deliveries to firm customers occurred at the same time. This too suggests that at the FPC's price, some customers could not buy enough natural gas. These developments marked the shift from a buyers' market to a sellers' market. Since the price mechanism was operative only in the relatively small intrastate market, the supply-demand disparity resulted in a quadrupling of new gas prices between 1971 and 1975 in that market. Producers naturally avoided committing what new reserves they had to the interstate market where the price had scarcely changed.

The demise of spare capacity in petroleum was even more dramatic, and of far greater consequence to the world political economy. Based on data provided by the National Petroleum Council and the American Petroleum Institute, the Department of the Interior estimated that total productive capacity as of January 1, 1968, amounted to 12.3 million barrels per day.[3] Since production in 1967 averaged 8.2 million barrels per day, spare capacity would have been 4

[3] Department of the Interior, *United States Petroleum Through 1980* (Wash.: DOI, 1968), pp. 30–31.

million, or approximately 25 percent. Twenty-six months later, in February 1970, the Texas Independent Producers and Royalty Owners Association asserted that the United States had no more unused productive capacity.[4] This conclusion was probably somewhat premature. But the latest date would be April 1972. It was in that month that the prorationing authorities of both Texas and Louisiana allowed production at 100 percent of market demand.[5] Industry analysts usually cite 1971 as the approximate date when full capacity utilization was achieved.[6]

Since domestic production in 1971 averaged 9.5 million barrels per day, one can only surmise that productive capacity had either declined sharply, or was grossly overestimated in 1968. The reality was probably a combination. If one assumed that no new productive capacity were being added between 1968 and 1971, the capacity loss of 2.8 million barrels would reflect a decline of 900,000 daily barrels each year, or about 10 percent of daily production which is close to the natural decline rate of oil wells. It would be more reasonable, however, to assume that productive capacity had been overestimated by something like 1 million barrels per day.[7] During the 1960's, it would have served the interests of domestic producers to exaggerate spare capacity to enhance their argument against increased oil imports. Were this the case, then it would appear that capacity only declined by 600,000 barrels per day per year. This would be feasible if additions to new capacity had substantially slowed.

Scarcely anyone recognized this decline in spare capacity until it had occurred. In 1968, the Department of the Interior accepted the National Petroleum Council's projection that domestic productive capacity would continue growing to about 14.5 million barrels per day by 1980. If, as the Interior Department estimated, daily production reached 11.5 million barrels by then, the United States would still have nearly 3 million barrels per day of spare capacity.[8] No projection could have been further from the mark. Still, it was not until early 1972 that oil companies and the federal government began to acknowledge the imminence of shortage. In a January 1972 hearing of the Louisiana Conservation Commission, Commissioner J. M. Menefee noted that production in his state was falling at about 15,000 barrels per day per month. "We're just about peaked out," Menefee told the state's oilmen, "and I think y'all realize it as well as we do."[9] On March 23, William Truppner, an assistant

4   U.S. Congress, Senate, Committee on Government Operations, Permanent Subcommittee on Investigations, *Staff Study of the Oversight and Efficiency of Executive Agencies with Respect to the Petroleum Industry, Especially as it Relates to Recent Fuel Shortages* (93rd Cong., 1st Sess.), Committee Print, November 8, 1973, p. 5.
5   Gulf Oil Corporation, Planning and Economics Department, "Monthly crude oil production and allowables for Texas and Louisiana," June 1973.
6   Interview with the author, Gulf Oil Corporation, Pittsburgh, PA., August 1980.
7   U.S. Congress Senate, *Staff Study of the Oversight and Efficiency of Executive Agencies with Respect to the Petroleum Industry*, p. 5.
8   Department of the Interior, *United States Petroleum Through 1980*, p. 32; also, National Petroleum Council, *Estimated Productive Capacities of Crude Oil, Natural Gas, and Natural Gas Liquids in the United States, 1965–1970* (Wash.: NPC, 1966).
9   U.S. Congress, *Staff Study of the Oversight and Efficiency of Executive Agencies with Respect to the Petroleum Industry*, p. 38.

director in the Office of Emergency Preparedness, wrote General George Lincoln, the Director, that the "nation has moved from a surplus crude oil situation . . . to one of deficiency." He urged that the import quota level on a percentage basis be abandoned, and that the program move to a demand footing.[10]

Nearly a year earlier, Sheik Ahmed Yamani, the oil minister of Saudi Arabia, had acknowledged that spare capacity outside of OPEC was virtually non-existent. In a discussion of Libya with George Piercy, an Exxon director, Yamani commented, "George, you know the supply situation better than I. You know you cannot take a shutdown."[11] And as Piercy explained, spare capacity was the key source of leverage in price negotiations between producers and consumers.[12] The United States no longer had that leverage, and OPEC did. If OPEC members controlled their own productive capacities, they could charge substantially higher prices, as long as U.S. demand remained relatively inelastic in the short run and U.S. pricing policies prevented domestic supply or demand from adjusting. All that remained was for OPEC to grasp the market power that the United States had abdicated.

The first step toward controlling productive capacity was taken by Muamer Qaddafi, shortly after he seized power in Libya in 1969. Qaddafi was the first Arab ruler since 1955 to seek an increase in price rather than output. He demanded an increase of 44 cents over the prevailing posted price for Libyan crude of $2.18 a barrel. The companies operating in Libya were shocked by this demand, although State Department officials thought it reasonable in geopolitical terms.[13] When Occidental Petroleum, the first company with which Qaddafi negotiated, balked at such an increase, the Libyan government cut the company's production by 50 percent in a few months. In September 1970, after the majors declined to backstop Occidental by providing crude oil at cost, Armand Hammer gave in to the Libyan demands. When the other companies were forced to follow, or lose their production too, a pattern of price leap-frogging between Libya and the Persian Gulf states was initiated. No sooner did the companies settle with Iran, Kuwait, and Saudi Arabia, than did Qaddafi demand another price and tax increase.[14]

In an effort to circumvent this pattern of destabilizing price negotiations, the major international oil companies decided to insist on unified negotiations between all the producing companies and all members of OPEC. To avoid antitrust prosecution and gain support for this joint-front strategy, the companies sought approval from the State and Justice Departments. In January

[10] *Ibid.*, 45.
[11] U.S. Congress, Senate, Committee on Foreign Relations, Subcommittee on Multinational Corporations, *Multinational Corporations and United States Foreign Policy* (93rd Cong., 2nd Sess.), August 1974, pt. 6, p. 70.
[12] *Ibid.*, pt. 5, p. 218.
[13] *Ibid.*, pt. 5, pp. 1–4.
[14] U.S. Congress, Senate, Committee on Foreign Relations, Subcommittee on Multinational Corporations, *Multinational Oil Corporations and U.S. Foreign Policy – Report* (93rd Cong., 2nd Sess.), Committee Print, January 2, 1975, pp. 122–126.

1971, just a week before negotiations opened in Tehran between the companies and the Persian Gulf countries, the State Department agreed to back the principle of unified negotiations and the Justice Department issued a Business Review Letter approving it. Thus, the Tehran meeting was to be a face-off between consuming and producing countries.

Later that same week, the United States government backed out. It remains unclear whether the reason was ineptitude, or some secret matter of state. But in a mission authorized by President Nixon, Assistant Secretary of State John Irwin visited Iran to discuss the oil supply situation with the Shah and his oil minister, Dr. Amouzegar. Those conversations apparently convinced Irwin that unified negotiations were unwise, for he promptly cabled Secretary of State William Rogers to recommend acceptance of separate negotiations with Persian Gulf and North African producers.[15] Rogers endorsed Irwin's recommendation, effectively withdrawing the government's political support at the very time that the oil companies were losing their market power as well. With this decision, almost 30 years of business-government cooperation in foreign oil policy came to an end.

In February 1971, the companies reached an agreement with the governments of the Persian Gulf states. It provided for a 30-cent-a-barrel increase in the governments' "take," and a promise of no leap-frogging for five years. Six months later, at Tripoli, the companies agreed to a 65-cent-a-barrel increase for Libya. These revenue gains, together with the obvious market power of the sellers, inspired a sense of economic nationalism that shortly translated into demands for greater participation. Midway through 1972, Colonel Qaddafi again set the precedent by nationalizing 51 percent of the producing operations in his country. Before the year's end, Saudi Arabia had negotiated an ownership position in Aramco, while Kuwait and Iran were well along with similar changes. Throughout 1972 and 1973, take-overs and buy-back arrangements escalated by a process similar to the price leap-frogging.

With oil markets extremely tight, the easy gains of economic nationalism inspired growing talk of an "oil weapon" throughout the Arab world. Restriction of supply was increasingly viewed as a political weapon that might be used to force changes in American foreign policy toward Israel. The outbreak of war in October provided the opportunity to test this weapon – an export embargo of the United States.

In the midst of this turmoil, representatives of the oil companies and OPEC met in Vienna to renegotiate the Tehran Agreement, two years ahead of schedule. The industry team offered to increase the posted price by 15 percent (from $3.00 to $3.45 per barrel). OPEC flatly refused, demanding instead a 70 percent price hike. Two months later, in Tehran, it raised the price another 130 percent, to $11.65 per barrel.

Besides disrupting the macroeconomies of most oil-importing nations, this price shock up-ended the traditional relationship between domestic and foreign oil, and competitive positions within and among the fossil fuel industries. With

[15] U.S. Congress, *Multinational Corporations and Foreign Policy (Hearings)*, pt. 5, pp. 145–173.

U.S. oil production declining and demand supported by price controls that Nixon had imposed in 1971, the new OPEC price was a short-run market-clearing adjustment to the long-run supply-demand disparity. It meant, more-over, that as long as OPEC restrained its own output, the entire superstructure of U.S. energy policy, and perhaps its ideological and political foundations, were irrelevant.

Mistrust and the data problem

Even before the OPEC shock, shortages of oil and natural gas elicited confu-sion and suspicion with regard to their origins. Abundance and stable prices had prevailed for more than two decades. Nothing as pedestrian as past policy, demand growth, and physical depletion could provide satisfactory explanation for so sudden a transition to scarcity and dependence. The news media em-braced drama rather than facts, and Congress was dismayed to discover that the federal government had no "independent" source of data as a check on the oil industry. Thus for many Americans – perhaps a majority – some degree of conspiracy among large oil and gas companies seemed a more compelling explanation of the crisis. Suspicion of conspiracy confused the issues, wasted an immense amount of congressional time, and gave weight to policy initiatives that were irrelevant to solving America's energy problems.

The producers of natural gas easily blamed federal regulation for their crisis. Through both supply and demand effects, inappropriate cost-based regulation had created, as Carl Bagge put it, "the worst of both worlds."[16] By the late 1960's, physical depletion and inflation were causing the long-run marginal costs of natural gas to rise sharply. However, the FPC's area rates were set on the basis of antiquated cost determinations. Even with two-tier pricing, which still restricted the producers' cash flow, these rates discouraged sufficient ex-ploration to replace reserves that were consumed. On the demand side, the cost-based rates that disregarded the commodity value of gas made it a bargain in comparison to substitute fuels. Other government policies, such as air pollu-tion controls and oil import quotas, had further stimulated demand for clean, cheap natural gas.[17]

Critics of the gas industry acknowledged the link between regulation and the crisis, but cast the causation in a different light. In their view, the gas industry had conspired to create the crisis as a means of circumventing regulation to attain higher prices. A coalition of groups that included the American Public Gas Association, the Consumer Federation of America, Energy Action, the U.S. Conference of Mayors, and various labor unions, farm organizations, and

[16] U.S. Congress, Senate, Committee on Commerce, *Natural Gas Regulation* (92nd Cong., 2nd Sess.), March 1972, p. 190.
[17] Federal Power Commission, Natural Gas Survey, Volume II, "Report of the Supply-Technical Advisory Task Force – Regulation and Legislation," December 15, 1972 (Wash., D.C., 1973), p. 563; for a list of economic experts that share this viewpoint, see U.S. Congress, House, Commerce Committee, Subcommittee on Energy and Power, *Natural Gas Shortages* (94th Cong., 1st Sess.), September 1975, p. 344.

state utility commissions claimed that "the producers are intentionally holding their gas off the market and thereby artificially creating a gas shortage in the hope that the contrived shortage can then be used as the basis for obtaining deregulation from congress or the setting of regulated interstate price by the FPC at the unregulated intrastate level."[18] Joseph Swidler, who had become chairman of the New York Public Service Commission after leaving the Federal Power Commission, was an influential, albeit cautious, proponent of this general proposition. Although Swidler acknowledged the impact of physical depletion, he still believed that "there is undoubtedly a great deal of short-term manipulation." The gas industry, said Swidler, "is in a position to fulfill its own prophecies, and if they prophesy a shortage, why, they can make pretty sure that there is not going to be a surplus when they have predicted to the contrary."[19]

This explanation of the gas crisis was rooted in several assumptions. Most consumer activists, and a great many other citizens, believed that the natural gas industry was uncompetitive – an oligopoly controlled by a few of the major oil companies. According to Lee White, a former FPC chairman and president of the Consumer Federation of America, no more than four companies "control between 70% and 99% of the total gas reserves" in each of the gas-producing areas. Such a concentrated structure, concluded White, "does not inspire any confidence."[20] Philip Hart, chairman of the Senate Subcommittee on Antitrust and Monopoly, shared this concern. Twice during the early 1970's, he induced the Federal Trade Commission to investigate allegations of anticompetitive behavior among gas producers.[21] This presumption of monopolistic behavior was significant in two ways. For the economist who accepted it (which few did), it justified the need for regulation that could transfer excess profits to the consumer and force the monopolist to increase output.[22] And for consumer activists, it provided the necessary rationale for believing that gas producers could act in concert.

A by-product of this monopoly interpretation was the conviction that the American Gas Association had intentionally under-reported gas reserve data beginning in 1968. It allegedly did this in reaction to the Court's affirmation of the Permian Area rates. According to a spokesman for small, municipal gas distributors, "there is a substantial body of evidence indicating that the producers, in order to force higher prices from the FPC and deregulation from Congress, have indeed manipulated reserve data in such a way to create the

[18] FPC, Docket No. RM75–14, "Application for Rehearing of the American Public Gas Association . . . [et al.]," September 1976, p. 31.
[19] U.S. Congress, House, *Natural Gas Act of 1971* (92nd Cong., 1st Sess.), September 1971, p. 271.
[20] U.S. Congress, House, Committee on Interstate and Foreign Commerce, Subcommittee on Energy and Power, *Long Term Natural Gas Legislation* (94th Cong., 2nd Sess.), Jan.–Feb. 1976, pp. 1710–11.
[21] U.S. Congress, Senate, Subcommittee on Antitrust and Monopoly, *The Natural Gas Industry* (93rd Cong., 1st Sess.), June 1973.
[22] For a theoretical explanation of how this effect would work, see James Griffin and Henry Steele, *Energy Economics and Policy* (New York: Academic Press, 1980), pp. 249–250.

impression that reserves have declined, when in fact they have not."[23] These reserve statistics, on which the FPC did indeed rely heavily, were compiled annually by the American Gas Association's Committee on Natural Gas Reserves. To preserve confidentiality, these data were not reported company-by-company. Instead, reservoir engineers from the producing companies met in subcommittees by producing areas and jointly computed estimates of reserves by area.

Controversy over reserve data was sparked by a Jack Anderson "revelation" in mid-1971 that alleged a disparity between AGA numbers and those aggregated from reports by pipeline companies to the FPC.[24] The Federal Trade Commission subsequently conducted a sample investigation of offshore Louisiana lease tracts, and in 1973, James Halverston, director of the Bureau of Competition, reported his conclusions to Senator Hart's subcommittee. According to Halverston, "serious underreporting by the natural gas producers to the Federal Power Commission of natural gas reserves has existed and continues to exist." He believed that the producers on the AGA's reserve committee "could provide the vehicle for a conspiracy among the companies involved to underreport gas reserves."[25]

While the FTC investigation continued, the issue of reserve data blended with related allegations that gas producers were shutting-in proved reserves. As evidence of this, critics pointed to a 1973 study by the Federal Power Commission which identified 168 offshore leases classified as "producible shut-in" by the Geological Survey. Yet another flap developed regarding problems that Gulf Oil was having with deliveries contracted to Texas Eastern Gas Transmission. Consumer activists accused Gulf of withholding 128 million cubic feet a day from delivery, presumably with the tacit approval of its buyer.[26]

Gas producers, usually backed by the pipeline companies, consistently refuted these allegations. Lease-by-lease, they explained the various reasons for shut-in reserves. Some were awaiting pipeline connections, field development, or work-over of the wells. Others were temporarily shut-in due to hurricane damage, or depleted, or simply contained inadequate reserves to be commercially feasible. And the Gulf-Texas Eastern problem turned out to be a legitimate mistake. Drilling logs had been badly misread (interpreting water as gas), leading to a 30 to 50 percent overestimation of reserves and a fixed-price contract that Gulf Oil could fulfill only by finding or buying more costly supplies. It was anything but intentional, given that Gulf Oil suffered a large financial impact from the contract for more than a decade.[27]

On the reserve data issue, the gas producers pointed to various other studies, conducted by the FPC, the U.S. Geological Survey, and the Federal Energy

23   U.S. Congress, *Long Term Natural Gas Legislation*, p. 1057.
24   Jack Anderson, "FPC Chief and Natural-Gas Rate Rise," *Washington Post*, June 14, 1971; also, "FPC Staff Disputed Industry Data," *Washington Post*, June 15, 1971.
25   U.S. Congress, Senate, *The Natural Gas Industry*, p. 223.
26   U.S. Congress, House, *Long Term Natural Gas Legislation*, p. 1301.
27   Interviews with the author, Gulf Exploration & Production Company, Houston, Texas, November 1980.

Office (created in 1973), none of which found gross inaccuracies in the AGA data nor evidence of collusive behavior for the purpose of under-reporting. Moreover, the Federal Trade Commission itself was unable to make a conclusive judgment. The Bureau of Competition eventually recommended that the Commission issue a complaint against the AGA for "concertedly maintaining a deficient natural gas reserve reporting program."[28] But the FTC's Bureau of Economics flatly disagreed. Its staff testified "that the AGA investigation has unearthed no information in support of allegations that the post-1967 downturn in reserves is a statistical contrivance of the AGA and its producer members." They felt that "the Bureau of Competition's complaint memos are based on incorrect interpretations of the testimonial evidence and invalid statistical comparisons."[29] The FTC eventually dropped its investigation.

In a broader sense, industry spokesmen challenged the logic of the conspiracy viewpoint. To withhold proved committed reserves would risk drainage from adjacent leases, would violate contracts, and would run afoul of state conservation regulations or federal lease requirements for offshore areas. As one industry executive acerbicly noted, "the producer is fully aware of the time value of money which deters withholding."[30] Even the gas distributors and pipeline companies most desperate for gas denied that producers were hiding or withholding any significant volumes of producible reserves. G. J. Tankersley, president of the East Ohio Gas Company and a past president of the AGA, pointed out that AGA members were not producers, but distributors and pipeline companies. There could be "no self-serving benefit" for them to manipulate reserve data, since it hurt their ability to raise capital and serve long-standing customers. "It absolutely defies logic," said Tankersley, "to conceive that the distributor would help create or publicize a false shortage."[31] Moreover, since state utility commissions regulated the distributors' rate of return, their profitability would not improve if gas prices rose, and they would likely lose ground in interfuel competition from coal-fired electricity and home heating oil.

As serious as it was, this dispute over the origins of the gas crisis and the possibility that it was contrived, paled in comparison to questions surrounding oil shortages and the OPEC price shock. The fact that it involved multinational oil companies – the "Seven Sisters" – over which the U.S. government had little control prior to 1974, made the oil crisis all the more suspect. And the government did not have a great deal of information on the complex movements of petroleum in international commerce. What little information there was came from the Church subcommittee hearings (1973–74), which reviewed the industry's cartel behavior prior to World War II and its oligopolistic conduct, with tacit government approval, during the postwar era. It is perhaps not surprising that in April 1973, people most frequently attributed energy shortages to

---

[28] Theodore Lytle, memorandum, Bureau of Competition to Federal Trade Commission, March 25, 1975, in U.S. Congress, House, Committee on Commerce, Subcommittee on Oversight and Investigations, *Natural Gas Supplies* (94th Cong., 1st Sess.), June 1975, vol. I, pt. 1, p. 15.
[29] U.S. Congress, House, *Natural Gas Supplies*, p. 606.
[30] U.S. Congress, House, *Long Term Natural Gas Legislation*, p. 630.
[31] U.S. Congress, Senate, *Natural Gas Regulation*, p. 296.

a conspiracy among utility and fuel companies. But in 1979, after six more years of intense public discussion, two-thirds of those polled still believed that oil companies had contrived the crisis and were continuing to withhold supplies to drive up prices.[32]

The conspiracy interpretation of the oil crisis stemmed from a historical conviction that the oil industry was an oligopoly which controlled government policy as well as world oil markets. Circumstantial evidence suggested that the oil industry was manipulating data, withholding supplies, squeezing independents, cooperating with OPEC, bribing the White House, and using the crisis as an excuse for eliminating environmental legislation. The industry's soaring profits in 1974, and its continuing diversification into alternate energy sources, provided plausible motives.

Although there were grains of truth in each of these allegations, the whole was smaller than the sum of its parts. But by reiterating every allegation indiscriminately and making large inferences from fragmentary non sequiturs, the news media gave credence to the public's suspicion of conspiracy. Among hundreds of examples, a *Newsweek* article in 1973, entitled "Is the Big Shortage Just Gas," was typical. "With the gasoline shortage becoming worse each day, growing numbers of Federal and state officials are asking: Is the shortage legitimate? Or is it due to a conspiracy by oil-industry giants to drive competitors out of business, boost their own profits and win major concessions." The article did not answer its rhetorical question. *Time* noted that independent marketers "suspect the major oil companies have contrived the shortage to force them out of business." The *New Republic* posited that "today the American public is caught in a pincer movement between a domestic cartel and a foreign cartel, essentially two arms of the same body." Jack Anderson cited secret documents in the *Washington Post* "proving" that Aramco executives urged the Saudi government to raise prices.[33]

In a thorough content analysis of how the major news periodicals reported the energy crisis and conspiracy thesis, Barbara Hobbie has presented some disconcerting findings. First, there was an immense gap between what those magazines reported and what most academic economists (who studied energy industries) believed. Second, she found that the periodicals largely ignored available evidence relevant to evaluating oil monopoly charges. Third, her content analysis revealed how heavily the news media relied on industry critics as

[32] *The Harris Survey Yearbook of Public Opinion, 1973* (N.Y.: Louis Harris & Associates, 1976), p. 235; also, ABC News/Harris Survey, May 28–29, 1979 (N.Y.: Chicago Tribune-N.Y. News Syndicate, Inc., 1979). In this 1979 poll, 1,200 adults nationwide were asked, "All in all, do you think the oil shortage is real, or do you think the oil companies are deliberately holding back on supplies in order to increase the price of gasoline?" Sixty-four percent felt that oil companies were holding back, while only 19 percent believed the shortage to be real.

[33] "Is the Big Shortage Just Gas?" *Newsweek*, July 2, 1973, p. 59; "Energy: A Federal Oil Firm," *Time*, February 24, 1975, p. 27; Melville Ulmer, "How to Treat Parasites: Thwarting the Cartel," *The New Republic*, February 15, 1975, p. 10; *Washington Post*, January 10, 11, and 28, 1974, cited in U.S. Congress, Senate, Committee on Government Operations, *Current Energy Shortages Oversight Series: Conflicting Information on Fuel Shortages* (93rd Cong., 1st Sess.), January 1974, pt. 4, pp. 547–550.

sources, giving their charges overwhelming weight and coverage in comparison to explanations by industry or academic spokesmen.[34]

Considering this general atmosphere of misinformation and mistrust, it is little wonder that Congress was drawn deeply into the search for answers and the allotment of blame. Between 1973 and 1975, at least 25 of the 39 permanent congressional committees investigated one aspect or another of the energy crisis. In the course of these hearings, the motives and practices of business executives were scrutinized and castigated more harshly than at any time since World War II. As Rawleigh Warner, the chairman of Mobil complained, "For God's sake, we're being treated like criminals."[35] And of course, they were, since the general charge was conspiracy.

No sooner had the embargo begun than Senator Henry "Scoop" Jackson and Representative John Dingell of Michigan moved to assert their leadership in matters of energy policy; Jackson through his chairmanships of the Interior Committee and the Subcommittee on Investigations, and Dingell by trading his chairmanship of the Subcommittee on Regulatory Activities for a new Subcommittee on Energy and Power. Both Jackson and Dingell took advantage of the news media's rarefied interest by conducting highly visible hearings in December 1973 and January 1974 to get to the bottom of the energy crisis. Those hearings were to set the tone for dozens that followed.

From the start, congressional investigation of possible conspiracy involved an impossible search for "objectivity," defined as energy industry data that could be verified by independent government sources and which would provide a straightforward explanation of the crisis. But as Wildavsky and Tenenbaum have noted in their superb study of the data problem, "as long as government did not own the industry, industry would remain the ultimate supplier of data."[36] Moreover, oil executives might cooperate as fully as possible, but since the suspicion of conspiracy was largely rooted in ideological conviction, there was little likelihood that their data would help.

The great data search had several underlying themes to which Representative Dingell alluded when he opened his committee's hearings: "In terms of getting the facts in the energy area, the federal government has completely delegated their responsibility to the oil industry. This deplorable situation has to end," said Dingell. "Whether or not there is an energy crisis, there most certainly is a crisis of confidence. The latter must be resolved before action on the former is possible."[37] This comment says a great deal about the change in business-government relations that had occurred. It suggests that prior relationships for transmitting information and advice were illegitimate, and that

[34] Barbara Hobbie, *Oil Company Divestiture and the Press: Economic vs. Journalistic Perceptions* (N.Y.: Praeger Publishers, 1977).
[35] Quoted in "The New Shape of the U.S. Oil Industry," *Business Week*, February 2, 1974, p. 55.
[36] Aaron Wildavsky and Ellen Tenenbaum, *The Politics of Mistrust* (Beverly Hills: Sage Publications, 1981), p. 301.
[37] U.S. Congress, House, Permanent Select Committee on Small Business, Subcommittee on Activities of Regulatory Agencies, *Energy Data Requirements of the Federal Government* (93rd Cong., 2nd Sess.), January–May 1974, pt. 1, pp. 3–4.

some alternative was feasible. It suggests that detailed economic intelligence, in addition to policy-making, is a governmental responsibility. By implying that the government was misled, it insinuates that the crisis was contrived. And most significantly, it presupposes that sound remedial policies were contingent on a sufficient, objective data base. This, as Wildavsky and Tenenbaum point out, was a great irony of the entire quest. It substituted data acquisition for real policy analysis regarding what needed to be done about price, supply, and demand, and how those goals could best be implemented.[38]

Spokesmen for the Federal Energy Office, the Office of Management and Budget, the Federal Power Commission, the Bureau of Mines, and the Department of the Interior testified at great length before the Dingell Committee as to the adequacy of the energy data they received from industry. An Exxon official representing the American Petroleum Institute further documented the extensive data submissions and analyses that the oil industry and its trade associations routinely made to the government. Still, several of the committee members remained dissatisfied. None of this information was truly "independent," in the sense that government employees (unsullied by employment experience in the oil industry) had not gathered it through observation and measurement in the field. As Representative Fernand St. Germain of Rhode Island concluded, "It is all well and good for Exxon and the other firms to say, 'Well, we have been providing the statistics and the figures.' The trouble is there have been no independent statistics."[39]

A frequently cited example of the government's data dependence was a multi-volume study entitled *U.S. Energy Outlook*, released by the National Petroleum Council in December 1972. When the study was undertaken in 1970, John McLean, the chairman of Continental Oil who directed it, told his counterparts that the National Petroleum Council was "the best qualified group if not the only qualified group in the U.S. today capable of doing the job."[40] Interior Secretary Rogers Morton confirmed that the study would be "of critical importance to the development of a sound and sensible policy on energy."[41] Although its scenarios and parametric projections were impressive, it completely failed to anticipate the OPEC price shock. Although it foretold of rising dependence on oil imports, it rejected any demand-dampening policies as ineffective. Its worst error was a price projection which suggested that a 1980 oil price of $4.90 a barrel (in 1970 dollars) would be enough to stimulate the most optimistic domestic supply scenario. For natural gas, a price of 38 cents per thousand cubic feet would have the same effect.[42] Oil and gas producers

[38] Wildavsky and Tenenbaum, *The Politics of Mistrust*, pp. 299–303.
[39] U.S. Congress, *Energy Data Requirements*, p. 123.
[40] National Petroleum Council, Meeting Transcript, January 16, 1970, NPC/DOI, pp. 19–20.
[41] National Petroleum Council, Meeting Transcript, March 4, 1971, NPC/DOI, 1971, pp. 15.
[42] National Petroleum Council, *U.S. Energy Outlook: A Summary Report of the National Petroleum Council*. (Wash.: NPC, 1972), pp. 3–4, 18–19, 39–41. In 1980 dollars, these estimates would have been $9.60/bbl. for oil and $.74/Mcf for natural gas. The NPC numbers were average wellhead costs, including a 15 percent return on net fixed assets. The report mentioned that if prices for existing production were kept low by government regulation, then the marginal cost of new production would be substantially higher.

were to rue these figures after 1974 when they tried to justify price decontrol to levels of $12 a barrel and $1.42 per thousand cubic feet.

Critics of the oil industry were adamant about the need for autonomous data. Martin Lobel, a Washington lawyer and industry gadfly, complained to the Dingell Committee that "there simply is no adequate, credible, objective base of real information." According to Lobel, "the only accurate data base is closely held in the hands of a few international integrated oil companies."[43] Christopher Rand, Lee White and others voiced similar frustrations. Ralph Nader, of whom the Dingell Committee was especially solicitous, explained that the data dependency of government was merely symptomatic "of the incestuous relationship between the Federal Government energy policy officials and the oil industry itself." Like Lobel, Nader criticized the Office of Oil & Gas for employing people with industry experience and for relying on the American Petroleum Institute and the National Petroleum Council as sources of data. Ralph Nader suggested that Congress establish a federal energy information agency capable of gathering "first-hand" information with its own geologists and economists. To facilitate this, he urged that "phony arguments about trade secrets, proprietary data, and national security" be jettisoned, in order that "all information relating to this energy problem should be disclosed." Finally, he proposed the establishment of a Federal Oil and Gas Corporation as a TVA-like yardstick against which the performance of private oil companies could be measured.[44]

While the Dingell hearings, and those in subsequent months, may have provided an interesting and detailed review of business-government data flows, neither the hearings nor the suggestions for improved data-gathering bore any relationship to the substantive policy issues of the energy crisis. They did, however, severely undermine the existing institutional mechanisms for cooperation between business and government. The discredited National Petroleum Council was effectively defunct for the remainder of the 1970's, the very time when it was most needed. The Federal Energy Administration was discouraged from employing personnel with any experience in the energy industries, and its formal data requirements of oil and gas companies evolved into an immense and costly burden of paperwork and red tape.

Senator Jackson was more interested in explaining the conspiracy than in reviewing the government's data base. Upstaging Dingell, he empaneled senior executives from the seven largest American oil companies and demanded they answer the public's questions:

The American people want to know if there is an oil shortage.
The American people want to know whether oil tankers are anchored offshore waiting for a price increase or available storage before they unload.
The American people want to know whether major oil companies are sitting on shut-in wells and hoarding production in hidden tanks and at abandoned service stations.
The American people want to know why oil companies are making soaring profits.
The American people want to know if this so-called energy crisis is only a pretext, a

---

[43] U.S. Congress, *Energy Data Requirements*, pp. 9–10.
[44] *Ibid.*, 136–137, 222–225.

cover to eliminate the major source of price competition – the independents, to raise prices, to repeal environmental laws, and to force adoption of new tax subsidies.[45]

If the oil companies failed to cooperate in answering these questions, Senator Jackson promised to "get the answers one way or another." His attitude was neither extreme nor partisan. "You are reaping the whirlwind of 30 years of arrogance," Senator Abraham Ribicoff told the oilmen, for engaging in conspiracy when there was no real shortage. Senator Charles Percy seconded Ribicoff's sentiments and Senator Jacob Javits spoke of the public's deep cynicism, "induced by problems we have in Washington respecting Watergate" and "by the suspicion that it is your companies who have brought on this crisis."[46]

For several days, the seven oil executives answered the committee's hostile questions and provided supplemental documentation demanded with a few hours' notice. Senator Jackson repeatedly reminded the panel they were testifying under oath, and was angered by the few negative responses to questions involving proprietary information. None of the extensive testimony had any apparent effect on the views of the committee, nor for that matter, on public opinion. As *Time* magazine aptly commented later that week, "the nation will probably remain split into two equally hopeful and equally helpless factions, the believers and the doubters. And as every American has come to know, a house divided against itself will be a little colder this year."[47]

Concentration and the antitrust backlash

Suspicion that the energy crisis was contrived by American companies rested logically on the conviction that the oil and gas industries were sufficiently concentrated and uncompetitive to carry out conspiracy. In order to withhold production, suppress alternate energy sources, squeeze independents, and cooperate with OPEC, major oil companies would need extraordinary control of the market, high entry barriers, and a large measure of ill will. Pre-1945 cartels, postwar trends toward vertical and horizontal integration, and the U.S. government's stabilization policies convinced many policy-makers and would-be reformers that industry structure accounted for the energy crisis. These perceived links between structure, collusion, and crisis were attended by less defined but more compelling apprehension of the oil industry's political power and influence on societal well-being. Thus, the natural and emotionally satisfying response to these presumptions was to attack the oil industry's structure by promoting legislation or litigation to dismember it.

With the exception of petroleum refining, the oil, natural gas, and coal industries had all grown more concentrated between 1955 and 1975. (See

[45] U.S. Congress, Senate, Committee on Government Operations, Permanent Subcommittee on Investigations, *Current Energy Shortages Oversight Series: The Major Oil Companies* (93rd Cong., 2nd Sess.), January 1974, pt. 2, pp. 113–114.

[46] *Ibid.*, pp. 114–119.

[47] "Policy: No Shortage of Skepticism," *Time*, January 28, 1974, p. 31.

Table 9-4. *U.S. energy industry concentration ratios, 1955–1975*

		4 Firm	8 Firm	20 Firm
A.	U.S. crude oil production			
	1955	21.2%	35.9%	55.7%
	1965	27.9	44.6	63.0
	1970	31.0	49.1	69.0
B.	U.S. petroleum refining			
	1951	33.5	56.4	80.7
	1970	32.5	57.5	84.3
	1975	29.1	51.1	80.3
C.	U.S. natural gas production			
	1955	18.6	30.4	48.1
	1965	19.9	32.6	50.1
	1970	24.4	39.1	57.5
D.	U.S. bituminous coal production			
	1955	17.8	25.4	39.5
	1970	30.2	40.7	56.5
	1975	26.4	36.2	50.6
E.	Production of U_3O_8 concentrates			
	1955	77.9	99.1	100.0
	1970	55.3	80.0	100.0
	1975	54.9	78.4	100.0

Source: Compiled from U.S. Federal Trade Commission, Staff Report, *Concentration Levels and Trends in the Energy Sector of the U.S. Economy* (Wash., D.C., 1974), and U.S. Treasury Department, *Implications of Divestiture: A Treasury Department Staff Study* (Wash., D.C., 1976).

Table 9-5. *Twenty largest U.S. oil companies concentration summary*

	Top 4	Top 8	Top 20
Production (1974)	26.0%	41.0%	59.8%
Reserves (1970)	37.2	63.9	93.6
Refining (1975)	29.1	51.1	80.3
Pipelines (1972)	33.7	55.6	86.6
Tanker capacity (1972)	14.4	20.5	25.3
Gasoline sales (1975)	29.1	49.9	71.5

Source: U.S. Department of the Treasury, *Implications of Divestiture: A Treasury Department Staff Study* (Wash., D.C., 1976), p. 48.

Tables 9-4 and 9-5.) But compared to most other basic industries, the primary fuel sectors remained relatively unconcentrated. In the international oil sector, where oligopoly had prevailed since the early 1950's, dominance by large firms had not grown at all (Table 9-6). Critics of the oil industry tended to dismiss

Table 9-6. *Relative distributive shares of U.S. companies in the free world oil production, 1962, 1972*

	1962	1972
Total free world crude oil and natural gas liquid production (000 b/d)	(20,172)	(41,933)
of which:	100%	100%
1. Exxon	13.2	11.9
2. Texaco	7.4	9.0
3. Gulf	8.4	7.7
4. Standard of California	5.5	7.5
5. Mobil	4.0	4.6
Subtotal for top five	38.5	40.7
Subtotal for other 20 U.S. companies	15.7	14.2
Total for 25 largest U.S. companies	54.2	54.9

Note: Based on barrels per day.
Source: U.S. Department of the Treasury, *Implications of Divestiture: A Treasury Department Staff Study* (Wash., D.C., 1976), p. 89.

these points as irrelevant in light of the alleged effects of vertical and horizontal integration and joint ventures.

The oil industry had indeed become more vertically integrated in the two decades prior to 1973. During years of surplus, producers had integrated forward into refining and marketing as a means of ensuring outlets for their crude oil. A number of independent refiners likewise integrated backward into foreign crude oil production in order to remain competitive with those cheaper sources of supply. While some of this integration involved start-up investments, most of it was accomplished by merger. Table 9-7 shows changes in rank among the largest companies over two decades. As of 1974, the top 20 firms included three new entrants (Occidental, Tenneco, and Amerada-Hess).

Economists have generally not felt that vertical integration is presumptively anti-competitive.[48] Rather, under certain circumstances, vertically integrated firms can use their economies of scale and transfer pricing to control bottlenecks (such as pipelines) and squeeze non-integrated competitors between costs and prices. These anti-competitive effects could be amplified, as Kahn and DeChazeau suggested in their 1959 study, by such public policies as the oil depletion allowance and the foreign tax credit.[49] Had this been the case over an extended period of time, one would expect to have seen an increase in crude oil

[48] For a valuable analysis of vertical integration in the petroleum industry, see the prepared statement of Edward J. Mitchell in U.S. Congress, Senate Committee on the Judiciary, Subcommittee on Antitrust and Monopoly, *The Petroleum Industry* (94th Cong., 1st Sess.), Jan.–Feb., 1976, Pt. 3, pp. 1852–1880.

[49] Alfred Kahn and M. DeChazeau, *Integration and Concentration in the Petroleum Industry* (New Haven: Yale University Press, 1959).

Table 9-7. *Major U.S. oil companies ranked by sales, 1954–1974*

1954	1974
1. Standard Oil-New Jersey	Exxon
2. Gulf	Texaco
3. Socony-Vacuum	Mobil Oil
4. Standard Oil-Indiana	Standard Oil-California
5. Texas Co.	Gulf
6. Shell	Standard Oil-Indiana
7. Standard Oil-California	Shell
8. Sinclair	Continental
9. Cities Service	Atlantic Richfield
10. Phillips	Occidental
11. Sun Oil	Tenneco
12. Atlantic Refining	Phillips
13. Continental	Union Oil (California)
14. Tidewater	Sun Oil
15. Pure Oil	Amerada-Hess
16. Union Oil (California)	Ashland
17. Standard Oil-Ohio	Marathon
18. Ohio Oil	Cities Service
19. Ashland	Getty
20. Richfield	Standard Oil-Ohio

Note: Segmented lines denote major mergers and acquisitions.
Solid lines indicate movement in relative position.
Source: U.S. Congress, Senate, Committee on Interior and Insular
Affairs, Subcommittee on Integrated Oil Operations, *The Structure
of the U.S. Petroleum Industry: A Summary of Survey Data* (94th
Cong., 2nd Sess.), Committee Print, 1976, p. 8.

self-sufficiency among the integrated majors, a decline in the number of non-integrated producers and refiners, collusive practices, and a higher profit level among the majors.

According to the work of other analysts, none of these measures has yielded any convincing evidence of monopolistic accomplishment.[50] In the domestic industry, entry barriers to production and even refining remained low enough

---

[50] Besides E. Mitchell as cited in note 48, see William A. Johnson et al., *Competition in the Oil Industry* (Wash., D.C.: Energy Policy Research Project, George Washington University, 1976); also, prepared testimonies of Richard Mancke, Edward Erickson, and Neil Jacoby, in U.S. Congress, Senate, *The Petroleum Industry*, Pt. 3, pp. 1891–1916, 2109–2129, and 2227–2238 respectively. With regard to natural gas, see testimonies of John Nassikas and Paul MacAvoy in U.S. Congress, Senate, Committee on Interior and Insular Affairs, Special Subcommittee on Integrated Oil Operations, *Market Performance and Competition in the Petroleum Industry* (93rd Cong., 1st Sess.), December 1973, Pt. 3, pp. 829–869 and 1032–1053 respectively.

Table 9-8. *Crude oil production and refining self-sufficiency, by area, of the 20 largest U.S. integrated oil companies, 1962, 1972*

Company	World crude oil production 1972	World refining % self-sufficiency[a]		U.S. crude oil production 1972	U.S. refining % self-sufficiency[a]	
		1972	1962		1972	1962
1. Exxon	5,009	97.3	81.1	970	94.3	65.2
2. Texaco	3,777	127.9	100.5	792	78.3	77.8
3. Gulf	3,214	165.2	175.5	561	73.1	70.7
4. Standard-California	3,159	154.3	121.2	462	56.7	73.3
5. Mobil	1,911	85.5	67.9	394	46.0	36.8
6. Standard-Indiana	815	78.6	54.9	487	50.9	45.8
7. Atlantic Richfield	652	86.6	89.8	401	56.2	63.7
8. Shell	638	63.7	65.0	638	63.7	65.0
9. Continental	588	115.5	113.7	220	64.9	85.5
10. Sun	469	85.4	74.2	285	69.0	51.7
11. Occidental	432	407.5	—	8	—	—
12. Marathon	424	135.0	107.5	181	78.4	86.5
13. Union	365	86.5	56.5	301	72.4	49.6
14. Phillips	363	59.6	73.6	268	49.2	58.2
15. Getty (except Skelly)	306	280.7	83.7	189	258.9	56.7
16. Amerada Hess	231	52.0	160.3	95	131.9	120.6
17. Cities Services	227	87.6	50.0	216	83.4	49.0
18. Tenneco	99	110.0	151.7	86	95.6	117.2
19. Skelly	89	111.3	124.6	88	110.0	122.8
20. Standard-Ohio	50	12.4	28.2	30	7.5	19.1

Note: In millions of barrels per day.
[a]Self-sufficiency is ratio of production to refinery runs.
Source: U.S. Department of the Treasury, *Implications of Divestiture: A Treasury Department Staff Study* (Washington, 1976), pp. 85–86.

so that some 10,000 independent producers and 130 refiners were operating in the early 1970's. Crude oil self-sufficiency among the integrated majors should have become very high if, as alleged, earnings on production was the profit center that allowed those firms to squeeze non-integrated competitors. Table 9-8 indicates that 14 of the 20 largest American companies became more self-sufficient worldwide, but not in their domestic operations. As of 1972, only 3 relatively small firms were self-sufficient in the United States, while all the larger firms continued to rely heavily on independent producers to supply their crude oil feedstock. And on the question of profitability, there has been no correlation between crude oil self-sufficiency and earnings. Moreover, between 1953 and 1972, the five largest international oil companies had lower rates of return (10.2%) than either domestic refiners (10.8%) or the 500 largest industrial firms that constitute Standard and Poor's index (12.4%).[51]

In the lexicon of anti-competitive relationships, joint ventures, exchange agreements, and interlocking directorates occupy a nether world between vertical and horizontal integration. The oil industry used joint ventures extensively, particularly for pipelines and bidding on offshore minerals leases. Crude oil and product exchanges among competing companies were also a common practice for reducing transportation costs, smoothing regional inventories, and assuring that refineries received oil with the required physical properties. As to interlocking directorates, the oil industry has had few if any primary links (where executives of competing firms sit on each other's boards) in the past 30 years, but quite a few secondary links (the same third party sitting on boards of two or more companies).[52] Once again, the issue was whether such relationships were presumptively anti-competitive, or in fact yielded anti-competitive effects.

Critics of these relationships linked them to the oil industry's integrated structure in the allegation of presumptive anti-competitiveness. Senator Robert Packwood of Oregon, co-sponsor of a divestiture bill, claimed that "the net effect" of these ties was "a lack of arm's length transactions and open buying and selling that underscore free market competition." Another congressman added that with such a structure, formal collusion was unnecessary (and thus the absence of evidence). Rather, industry leaders could individually "attune their policies to further cooperation rather than competition, among themselves."[53] Even the Federal Trade Commission, when it leveled charges of shared monopoly against the eight largest U.S. oil companies in 1973, could cite only "common course of action" and "interdependent behavior" as the basis for its argument that exchange agreements and joint venture pipelines should be illegal under Section 5 of the Federal Trade Commission Act.[54]

Most analytical studies have either contradicted the presumptive ill effects of these cooperative relationships, or at least shown them to be open to serious interpretative disagreement. Joint ventures on offshore lease bidding among independents have generally exceeded those among majors. Moreover, even joint bidding among majors has tended to increase the number of bids and to increase the government's royalty revenue.[55] The competitive effects of joint

[51] Edward Mitchell's testimony in U.S. Congress, Senate, *The Petroleum Industry*, Pt. 3, pp. 1873–1876; also, Standard Oil Company (Ohio), "Oil Profits: How Much? Where Do They Go?" Pt. 1, pp. 1137–1167.

[52] U.S. Congress, Senate, Committee on Interior and Insular Affairs, Special Subcommittee on Integrated Oil Operations, *The Structure of the U.S. Petroleum Industry: A Summary of Survey Data* (94th Cong., 2nd Sess.), Committee Print, 1976.

[53] U.S. Congress, Senate, *The Petroleum Industry*, Pt. 1, pp. 48, 210.

[54] U.S. Federal Trade Commission, Docket No. 8934, *In the Matter of Exxon Corporation, et al.*, "Complaint Counsel's First Statement of Issues, Factual Contentions and Proof," October 31, 1980, pp. 69–76, 102–104, 179–302.

[55] See, for example, Jesse Markham, "The Competitive Effect of Joint Bidding by Oil Companies for Offshore Lease Sales," in J. Markham and G. Papanek, eds., *Industrial Organization and Economic Development* (Boston: Houghton Mifflin, 1970); Edward Erickson and Robert Spann, "An

Table 9-9. *Coal production and reserve ownership by wholly or partially owned subsidiaries of 10 major U.S. oil companies, 1975*

Parent company	Coal company	Production (millions of tons)	Reserves (billions of tons)
Continental Oil	Consolidation Coal	54.2	10.8
Socal	Amax Coal (20%)	21.4	5.1
Occidental	Island Creek Coal	19.2	4.4
Ashland-Hunt	Arch Mineral Corp.	13.5	.2
Sohio	Old Ben Coal	8.3	.8
Gulf Oil	Pittsburg & Midway	7.3	2.6
Exxon	Monterey Coal	3.0	7.0
Atlantic Richfield	—	—	2.2
Sun Oil	—	—	2.2
Texaco	—	—	1.7
Total of 10 oil companies		126.9	35.3
Percentage of total U.S.		19.6	19.3

Source: Compiled from U.S. Department of the Treasury, *Implications of Divestiture* (Wash., D.C., 1976), pp. 56–57.

venture pipelines are somewhat less certain. While the Department of Justice has maintained that undersizing of oil pipelines and restricted access to non-owners has injured competition, studies by others have provided evidence to the contrary.[56] The record on exchange agreements suggests negative impacts on competition primarily when abused under individual circumstances. As a general rule, however, their contribution to efficiency and cost savings seems clearly to have outweighed their impact on competition.[57]

Unlike the issues of vertical integration and cooperative ventures, horizontal integration by the oil industry into coal, uranium, and other energy sources was a relatively new and visible trend. In the minds of its many critics, this horizontal merger movement in energy threatened the remaining bulwarks of interfuel competition and raised the specter of an energy industry dominated by multifuel leviathans. Once again, the operative political issue was whether the emergent energy companies were inherently undesirable, or explicitly anticompetitive through their manipulation of reserves, technology, and the mar-

Analysis of the Competitive Effects of Joint Ventures in the Bidding for Tracts on OCS Offshore Lease Sales," February, 1974, in U.S. Congress, Senate, *Market Performance and Competition in the Petroleum Industry*, Pt. 5, pp. 1691–1755; U.S. Congress, Senate, Committee on Interior and Insular Affairs, *Report to the Federal Trade Commission on Federal Energy Land Policy: Efficiency, Revenue, and Competition*, prepared by the Bureaus of Competition and Economics (94th Cong., 2nd Sess.), Committee Print, 1976, especially pp. 385–396.

[56] For careful recent analyses of oil pipelines, see Edward J. Mitchell, ed., *Oil Pipelines and Public Policy* (Wash., D.C.: American Enterprise Institute, 1979).

[57] W. A. Johnson et al., *Competition in the Oil Industry*, pp. 78–84.

kets for interfuel substitution. Although integration by petroleum companies into uranium mining and milling, geothermal steam, and advanced solar technologies is certainly significant, it is the involvement in coal, oil shale, and synthetic fuels that is of primary relevance to this study.

Gulf Oil's acquisition in 1963 of Spencer Chemical and its coal subsidiary, Pittsburg & Midway, marked the beginning of the petroleum industry's diversification into coal. This trend was part of a more general dispersion of the coal industry's ownership to other industrial sectors (such as, steel/smelting, electric utilities, railroads, and diversified manufacturing companies) that continued unabated through the 1970's. By the mid-1970's, petroleum and natural gas interests owned or controlled 12 of the 40 largest coal companies and about 23 percent of total coal output. Altogether, more than fifty oil or gas companies had acquired at least 38 percent (43 billion tons) of total proved coal reserves.[58] Table 9-9 lists the 10 major oil companies most involved in coal production and reserve ownership as of 1975. Despite these large numbers, it should be noted that except for Continental Oil, the coal operations of these firms contributed a very small share of their gross revenue.

With a few exceptions, the acquisition of coal properties by oil and natural gas companies was motivated by long-range forecasts of domestic oil depletion, increasing interest in utility markets, and the expectation that coal liquefaction and gasification would eventually be commercially feasible.[59] Continental Oil's rationale was typical. "We are convinced," said Chairman L. F. McCollum in 1965, "that the coal industry has attractive long-term prospects, particularly in supplying increasing requirements for generation of electric power." And besides power generation, there was an obvious fit between the research and development experiences of both Continental Oil and Consolidation Coal in synthetic fuels technologies.[60]

Involvement of oil companies in oil-shale properties and synfuels research was still more of a long-run hedge on depletion. As previously discussed, most of the major integrated firms had research and patent interests in the technology of coal hydrogenation dating back to the late 1920's. Their acquisition of oil-shale properties and mining rights began at about the same time, but accelerated during the 1950's and early 1960's. By 1974, sixteen of the major oil

---

[58] Richard Vietor, *Environmental Politics and the Coal Coalition* (College Station: Texas A&M University Press, 1980), pp. 17–34, 256–260; also, Federal Trade Commission, Staff Report, *Concentration Levels and Trends in the Energy Sector of the U.S. Economy* (Wash., D.C., 1974), pp. 67–95).

[59] In Gulf's case, it was actually Spencer Chemical's agricultural operations that inspired the acquisition. The Pittsburg & Midway subsidiary, with its considerable coal reserves and advanced liquefaction technology ("Solvent Refined Coal"), was a "tag-end Charlie" in the deal. Ironically, few of those involved even knew what they would do with the coal company. Gulf Oil Corporation, interview with the author, Pittsburgh, PA, August 1980.

[60] L. F. McCollum, quoted in *Time* magazine, October 22, 1965, p. 106; also, Continental Oil Company, "Statement by Continental Oil Company on the Consolidation Coal Company Acquisition," September 15, 1972, pp. 2–6, 35–41; also, "Memorandum for the Antitrust Division of the Department of Justice: Proposed Acquisition by Continental Oil Company of the Coal Properties and Related Operations of Consolidation Coal Company," February 7, 1966, pp. 27–28.

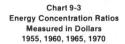

Chart 9-3
Energy Concentration Ratios
Measured in Dollars
1955, 1960, 1965, 1970

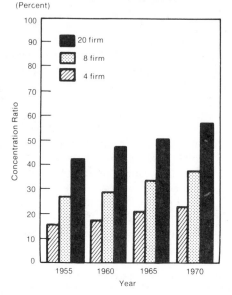

Source: U.S. Federal Trade Commission, Concentration Levels
and Trends in the Energy Sector of the U.S. Economy — Staff
Report (Wash., D.C., 1974), p. 142.

companies held 239 thousand acres of private oil-shale lands containing estimated reserves of 67 billion barrels. Still, the federal domain contained 80
percent of all oil shale deposits, including the highest grade ores, and oil
companies would be the most interested bidders in the 1974 prototype lease
sale (discussed at greater length in Chapter 13).[61] With the exceptions of Union
Oil and TOSCO, none of these companies had significant experimental operations prior to the OPEC shock.

Concentration in energy resulting from horizontal integration is a concept of
limited analytical value. Opportunities for substitution among various fuels are
so limited in the short-run that the notion of interfuel competition in a structural sense is extremely nebulous. As Continental's Howard Hardesty commented, "While the energy concept is useful in studying public policy, I don't
believe it is the relevant market for antitrust consideration."[62] However, to the
extent that concentration in energy production can be aggregated, Chart 9-3

[61] U.S. Congress, Senate, *Report to the Federal Trade Commission on Federal Energy Land Policy:
Efficiency, Revenue, and Competition,* Chapter 8, pp. 469–540.
[62] U.S. Congress, Senate, Committee on the Judiciary, Subcommittee on Antitrust and Monopoly, *Interfuel Competition* (94th Cong., 1st Sess.), June–October, 1975, p. 193.

does so, indicating a gradual trend toward greater concentration at one percent per year. More to the point was the fact that critics of the oil industry, including a substantial number of congressmen, believed that horizontal concentration in energy, together with vertical integration and joint ventures, posed a serious threat to the national interest.

For the first time since the divestiture of Standard Oil in 1911, the energy crisis of 1973–74 sparked a significant antitrust backlash that challenged the structural legitimacy of integrated oil and energy companies. In addition to media and political rhetoric (which itself was of no small consequence to public policy), the backlash expressed itself in three concrete initiatives: (1) a shared monopoly suit by the Federal Trade Commission seeking vertical divestiture of the eight largest oil companies, (2) legislation for vertical divestiture, and (3) legislation for horizontal divestiture or prohibition of further horizontal mergers. Henry Jackson appears to have been the catalyst for that reaction.

The Federal Trade Commission actually began investigating the oil industry in December 1971. But during the next 17 months, it did not request or examine any of the companies' documents nor interview any of their employees. However, on May 31, 1973, Senator Jackson wrote FTC Chairman Lewis Engman, requesting "a report within thirty days regarding the relationship between the structure of the petroleum industry and related industries and the current and prospective shortages of petroleum products."[63] On July 6, Engman sent Jackson a report captioned "Preliminary Federal Trade Commission Staff Report on Its Investigation of the Petroleum Industry." Even though the Commission had not evaluated the report, Jackson chose to publish it a week later as a committee print. Five days thereafter, the FTC issued a complaint against the eight largest oil companies, requesting vertical divestiture as the remedy for their "interdependent behavior." The Commission still had not reviewed company records, and took seven more years to issue formal charges (October 31, 1980).[64] To the defendants, at least, this sequence of events suggested that FTC action was politically motivated – the sort of "fishing expedition" prohibited by the "reason-to-believe" requirement of the FTC Act.[65]

The Commission charged that the eight large integrated oil companies had individually, jointly, and through "common course of action," maintained a "noncompetitive market structure at every level of the petroleum industry," especially crude-oil refining. Price leadership, competitive forbearance, exchange of pricing and production data, and self-imposed restrictions had all contributed. Most of all, they had taken a "common course of vertical integra-

---

[63] H. Jackson to L. Engman, May 31, 1973, quoted in *Federal Trade Commission vs. Standard Oil Company of California*, U.S. Court of Appeals, Ninth Circuit, "Brief for the Respondents," October 1979, p. 4.

[64] *In the Matter of Exxon Corporation, et al.*, FTC Docket No. 8934, "Complaint Counsel's First Statement of Issues, Factual Contentions and Proof," October 31, 1980.

[65] In *Hunt Foods and Industries, Inc. v. F.T.C.*, 286 F.2d 803, 806 (1961), the court had said that "[t]he Commission cannot have 'reason to believe' unless it is in possession of facts warranting such a belief."

tion" that suggested "interdependent conduct, accomplished with full knowledge that the other respondents were following the same common course of action for identical reasons."[66] The Commission candidly noted its frustration over the past 50 years during the course of 300 specific antitrust actions directed at the integrated oil companies. "The practice-by-practice approach to antitrust attack," said the Commission, "did not adequately address the industry's vertically integrated structure or its multilevel behavior."[67]

The Commission was also frustrated by the contribution of federal policies to anti-competitive behavior in the oil industry. Nearly one-fourth of the 450 allegations in the FTC's prediscovery statement involved practices sanctioned by federal law. The most serious of these were (1) market-demand prorationing by the states under the authority of the Interstate Oil Company Commission, (2) oil import quotas, (3) the oil depletion allowance on corporate income tax, and (4) joint bidding on federal offshore leases. For example, allegation no. 199 charged that the oil companies "have jointly and separately supported state prorationing laws and have urged state governments to maintain them." Allegation no. 201 added that the companies "have used the oil depletion allowance and state prorationing systems as vehicles for maintaining and strengthening their monopoly power." In allegation no. 117, the FTC complained that the companies "opposed the creation of exemptions to the oil import quota system," and noted in no. 264 that they had "urged the retention of an oil import quota and devoted considerable resources to convincing the Executive Branch of the Government to retain the quota."[68]

Of course, the Commission's perception of the anti-competitive effects of those government policies was perfectly accurate. But the eight defendants, recognizing the irony of one government agency attacking the statutory authority of others, were unwilling to dismiss it. They argued that the FTC could not blame them for the effects of government regulations that had been held constitutional. And with even greater irony, the oil companies admitted the ill effects of government policy on competition as part of their defense. Since "government regulation has so pervasive an impact upon both the structure of the industry and the specific acts and practices," argued the companies, "it cannot be contended that such structure, acts and practices constitute 'unfair' methods of competition."[69]

While the antitrust case dragged on through endless preliminary motions, impatient congressmen introduced bills proposing various forms of vertical and horizontal divestiture. Most prominent among these were the Petroleum Industry Competition Act of 1975 and the Interfuel Competition Act of 1975. The

---

[66] Exxon Corporation et al., "Complaint Counsel's First Statement of Issues," pp. 35–36.

[67] "Preliminary Federal Trade Commission Staff Report on its Investigation of the Petroleum Industry," in U.S. Congress, House, Permanent Select Committee on Small Business, Energy Crisis and Small Business (93rd Cong., 1st Sess.), July 1973, Committee Print, pp. 7–8.

[68] FTC Docket No. 8934, "Complaint Counsel's Prediscovery Statement," cited in In the Matter of Exxon Corporation, et al., "Joint Brief of All Respondents on Issues Relating to Government Action and Primary Jurisdiction," June 24, 1974, appendices A and B.

[69] Ibid., 4.

first one, co-sponsored by Senators Birch Bayh of Indiana and Phillip Hart of Michigan, would have required the eighteen largest companies to separate through divestiture their production, pipeline, refining, and marketing operations within five years. In a floor vote, this bill failed by a narrow margin of 54 to 45. The Interfuel Competition Act, which did not reach a floor vote, would prohibit anyone engaged in production or refining of petroleum or natural gas to acquire interests in coal, oil shale, uranium, geothermal, or solar fuels. It would also have required oil and gas companies to dispose of currently owned properties within three years.[70] Senator Edward Kennedy and Representative Morris Udall of Arizona were the principal sponsors of this horizontal divestiture.

The economic rationale for vertical divestiture was restoration of competition in the domestic oil industry. As Senator Bayh reasoned, "intense concentration and vertical integration" in concert let a small number of companies have "extensive control over an essential commodity." The fact that other industries were much more concentrated was irrelevant. "The undermining of th[e] free market economy by *any* industry is unfortunate," declared Bayh. But "in the case of the *oil industry* it is a danger of such magnitude and seriousness that it cries out for a firm solution."[71] For Bayh and the other supporters of vertical divestiture, it was "axiomatic" that more and smaller firms would result in lower prices for consumers. They ascribed no validity or legitimacy to the concept of economies of scale.

The economic brief for horizontal divestiture was similar. Acquisition of coal and uranium interests by oil companies threatened to destroy interfuel competition and, by implication, delay commercial development of alternate fuels that would undermine the profitability of oil. The very fact that coal and uranium prices had jumped in unison with the OPEC shock suggested a Btu-equivalent pricing conspiracy by the oil oligopolists. "It doesn't take much brilliance," declared Senator James Abourezk of South Dakota, "to figure that if an oil company can make high profits on oil during a shortage period, its managers will not be enthusiastic about developing a lower cost competitor."[72] This fear seemed confirmed by a widely quoted remark of Howard Hardesty, Continental Oil's president. When Abourezk had asked him, "Would you tell your coal subsidiary – or would you permit your coal subsidiary to undersell your oil subsidiary," Hardesty had responded, "No sir, under no circumstances." But elaboration of his answer in the very next sentence suggests that Hardesty was responding to the first part of Abourezk's question rather than the second. "We would not direct a coal subsidiary, a nuclear subsidiary, to have its price changed," added Hardesty, "so as to either compete readily against, or not compete against, another form of energy." Elaboration, of course, did not make good press.[73]

---

[70] U.S. Department of the Treasury, Staff Report, *Implications of Divestiture*, June 1976, summary version, p. 11.

[71] U.S. Congress, Senate, *The Petroleum Industry*, Pt. 1, p. 3.

[72] U.S. Congress, Senate, *Interfuel Competition*, p. 5.

[73] *Ibid.*, 194.

Political values, more than economic logic, compelled and sustained the drive for divestiture. Especially between 1975 and 1977, distrust of big business and democratic commitment to fragmented power read between every line of the divestiture argument. "[W]hen 5, or 8, or 20 huge companies dominate," said Abourezk, "the public interest is no longer represented." Or in Federalist terms, "the public has no concerted strength to counterbalance the strength of the companies."[74] Senator Kennedy made the political rationale explicit: "There are social and political consequences of coal and uranium acquisition by the oil companies." Kennedy argued that it would be undesirable were the oil industry to extend its "formidable level of political activity" into the coal and uranium sectors. The same kind of market control achieved through oil import quotas and other public policies would soon affect these traditionally competitive sectors. Illegal campaign contributions and foreign bribes might similarly be extended horizontally.[75] And departing from the relative cogency of this point, Senator John Durkin of New Hampshire cast the issue in the same metaphor and moralistic fervor of a Progressive muckraker: "We must act before this petroleum octopus violates and subverts any more of what is good, decent and fair in our political system."[76]

The Senate's near enactment of a divestiture bill in 1975 awakened the oil industry to the imminence of its political risk. At the American Petroleum Institute's annual meeting, Charles Spahr, the chairman of Sohio and president of API, warned that the threat of divestiture was the most important policy issue facing the industry. "If divestiture takes place," said Spahr, "the industry will have chaos for all time." Frank Ikard, the API's executive director, emphasized that divestiture was part and parcel of a broader sentiment for nationalizing the oil industry. Spahr and Ikard called for a concerted lobbying effort to avert the crisis, making the oil industry's views "visible and credible."[77]

The call for unity was scarcely superfluous. Earlier in the year, the Independent Gasoline Marketers' Council and the National Congress of Petroleum Retailers had given their support to vertical divestiture. The Independent Refiners Association of America had hedged on the issue, affirming its support for competitive crude oil markets and suggesting amendments to the antitrust laws and a federally chartered auction market for crude oil.[78] Not until a week before the API meeting did the Independent Petroleum Association of America issue a statement of moderate opposition to vertical divestiture.[79]

The integrated sector of the oil industry marshalled its human, informational, and political resources with unusual effectiveness. Between 1975 and 1978, senior executives challenged the rationale for divestiture in every possible

[74] Ibid., 4.
[75] Edward Kennedy, "Big Oil's Ominous Energy Monopoly," Business and Society Review, Summer 1978, pp. 16–20.
[76] U.S. Congress, Senate, The Petroleum Industry, Pt. 3, p. 2172.
[77] Oil & Gas Journal, November 17, 1975, pp. 22, 24.
[78] U.S. Congress, Senate, The Petroleum Industry, Pt. 1, pp. 175–77, 185–87, 240–42.
[79] Oil & Gas Journal, November 3, 1975, p. 27.

forum, while their public relations staffs labored to change media and public opinion. They had three basic arguments against divestiture. First, the oil industry was competitive. In support of this, industry defenders provided evidence of its relative lack of structural concentration, low barriers to entry at the production and retail levels, savings to consumers from the economies of scale that vertical integration allowed, and historically stable price and modest level of profitability.[80] A second argument focused on the economic damage that would be done by vertical divestiture. Scale economies would be lost, capital could not be accumulated or borrowed in quantities large enough to support high-risk exploration, and non-integrated American companies would lack the resources and leverage necessary to compete with national oil companies in the world economy. Finally, with regard to horizontal divestiture, the companies argued that their entry into coal and uranium increased competition, accelerated development by the infusion of capital, and would result in a needed transfer of technological and managerial know-how. The National Coal Association and the American Mining Congress reiterated these arguments. Confirmation by some academic experts and a number of government studies contributed vital credibility.[81]

By 1977, the divestiture movement was plainly losing momentum. Vertical divestiture had failed, and political interest in horizontal divestiture was waning. Advocates of divestiture modified their proposals so as to prohibit only future acquisitions. But even then, Congress had little interest.

There were several reasons for this. As already noted, the oil industry's campaign was unusually vigorous and effective. Then too, President Jimmy Carter and his Energy Secretary, James Schlesinger, opposed divestiture. The President wanted to preserve the institutional strength of major oil companies so they could function effectively in the global market, while making tougher use of antitrust laws and federal energy policy to control their behavior at home. There was also a conviction among many congressmen that divestiture would disrupt enactment and implementation of President Carter's National Energy

---

[80] See for example, American Petroleum Institute, *Witnesses for Oil: The Case Against Dismemberment* (Wash., D.C.: API, 1976), and testimony of Randall Meyer, B. R. Dorsey, and H. Hardesty, in U.S. Congress, Senate, *Market Performance and Competition in the Petroleum Industry*, Pt. 2, pp. 680–697, 697–702, and 783–795.

[81] For studies by academic experts, see Edward J. Mitchell, ed., *Vertical Integration in the Oil Industry* (Wash., D.C.: American Enterprise Institute, 1976); *Capitalism and Competition: Oil Industry Divestiture and the Public Interest*, Proceedings of the Johns Hopkins University Conference on Divestiture, Wash., D.C., May 27, 1976 (Baltimore: Center for Metropolitan Planning and Research, 1976); Edward J. Mitchell, ed., *Horizontal Divestiture in the Oil Industry* (Wash., D.C.: American Enterprise Institute, 1978); Frank N. Trager, ed., *Oil, Divestiture and National Security* (N.Y.: Crane, Russak & Co., 1977). For government studies, see U.S. Department of the Treasury, Staff Report, *Implications of Divestiture*, 1976; General Accounting Office, Report to the Congress, *The State of Competition in the Coal Industry* (Wash., D.C.: GAO, 1977); Tennessee Valley Authority, *The Structure of the Energy Markets: A Report of TVA's Antitrust Investigation of the Coal and Uranium Industries*, (TVA, 1977), in 3 volumes; and Department of Energy, Energy Information Agency, *An Analysis of Petroleum Company Investments in Non-Petroleum Energy Sources (DOE/EIA/8556-1)*, October 1979, Books 1 and 2.

Plan. With the Congress engaged in debate over conservation and price controls for oil and natural gas, divestiture increasingly came to be viewed as a punitive distraction from substantive issues.

Finally, and certainly most important, was the passing of crisis, easing of shortages, and stabilization of price. Divestiture was an extreme manifestation of the politics of business reform, evoked by energy shortage and rising price. As the market moved toward equilibrium, so did the focus of public policy. Although the second oil shock in 1979 engaged a brief recrudescence of the divestiture issue, it too faded as quickly as the shortage. Finally, in 1981, the FTC succumbed to overwhelming procedural problems, presidential opposition, and the reality of a post-OPEC world. It dropped its case against the eight largest oil companies.

Terminating the depletion allowance

Although the structure of the energy industries and its gradual trend toward concentration survived the energy crisis, the three government policies that had historically stifled competition did not. Market demand prorationing had become moot in 1972, once no spare productive capacity remained in the United States. President Nixon formally abandoned oil import quotas in 1973 since foreign oil no longer threatened domestic producers. The percentage depletion allowance survived the initial erosion of business-government relations, but not the political backlash to shortage. After 40 years of criticism and legislative attack, the first crack occurred in 1969, when Congress reduced it from 27.5 percent to 22 percent. Then in 1975, Congress terminated it altogether for large firms, only retaining the allowance for small producers at a lower rate.

The percentage depletion allowance, as discussed in Chapter 2, was a tax deduction that served as an incentive for oil exploration and as a dubious method for depreciating a capital asset (discovered crude oil in the ground). No matter what its substantive merits might have been, the depletion allowance was, as Senator Proxmire put it, "a symbol of privilege and inequity in our tax laws" since Senator Robert LaFollette's first attack on it in 1918.[82] As a symbol, it has repeatedly evoked intense political conflict between representatives of oil producers and would-be reformers.

The first postwar dispute occurred in 1950, as President Truman tried unsuccessfully to reduce the depletion allowance. At that time, Senators Paul Douglas of Illinois and Hubert Humphrey of Minnesota were the leading proponents of reform, while John Connally, Robert Kerr, and Lyndon Johnson were the chief defenders.[83] In 1958, Senator William Proxmire (D–WI) joined the reformers in another concerted effort, this time to have a graduated deple-

[82] *Congressional Record*, December 1, 1969, p. S15223.
[83] See U.S. Congress, House, Committee on Ways and Means, *Revenue Revision Hearings* (81st Cong., 2nd Sess.), 1950; U.S. Congress, House, Committee on Ways and Means, *Hearings, Revenue Revision* (82nd Cong., 1st Sess.), 1951; *Congressional Record*, 1951, pp. 1546–1549, 12309–12322; also, Ronnie Dugger, "Oil and Politics," *Atlantic Monthly*, 224, September 1969, no. 3, p. 71.

tion allowance. This battle was harder fought, and opened up some friction between domestic independents and the international majors. Senator Russell Long told Proxmire he should really concentrate on the multinationals, arguing that if oil imports were not curbed, "we shall not have any domestic industry to tax."[84] This time the vote was closer, with 30 Senators supporting a reduction of the depletion allowance. The battle was renewed again in 1963 at the initiative of President Kennedy. Kennedy proposed some modest limits to both the depletion allowance and the foreign tax credit. Senator Douglas tried to drive a wedge between independents and majors by raising the prospect of a compromise that would cut the allowance only for large companies. But neither this ploy nor public clamor was sufficient, and the depletion allowance remained intact on the illogical grounds that the domestic industry was already weakened by excess capacity.[85]

Resurgence of the depletion allowance as a legislative issue in 1969 was part of a broader initiative besides tax reform. True, as Russell Long noted, the Tax Reform Act of 1969 "emphasize[d] equity – that is what the whole affair is about."[86] Without a rate reduction in the depletion allowance, the "bill would be considered a mockery," said Proxmire, "a hypocritical, meaningless mockery by most Americans."[87] But criticism of the depletion allowance as one of the government's "three basic handouts" to the oil industry also emanated from Senator Hart's investigation of federal oil policies and the Cabinet Task Force review of oil import quotas.[88] As part of the existing relationship between business and government, the depletion allowance was called to question on substantive grounds that it was facilitating anti-competitive practices and thereby contributing to the emergence of shortage.

Critics of the depletion allowance argued in 1969 that: (1) it caused higher average production costs by subsidizing marginal producers; (2) it did more to subsidize the production wells of major companies than the wildcat exploratory wells of independents; and (3) it focused profitability in the crude oil production stage so that integrated firms could afford to run refining and marketing activities at cost, thereby squeezing independent refiners out of business.[89] In defense of the 27.5 percent rate, spokesmen for the oil industry claimed that any reduction in the depletion allowance would reduce domestic exploration

---

[84] *Congressional Record*, 1958, pp. 16895–16903.

[85] U.S. Congress, Senate, Committee on Finance, *Revenue Act of 1963* (88th Cong., 1st Sess.), 1963; U.S. Congress, House, Committee on Ways and Means, *President's Tax Message* (88th Cong., 1st Sess.), 1963; Peter Steiner, "The Non-Neutrality of Corporate Taxation – With and Without Depletion," *National Tax Journal*, XVI, No. 3, September 1963, pp. 238–251; and Paul Davidson, "Public Policy Problems of the Domestic Crude Oil Industry," *The American Economic Review*, LIII, No. 1, March 1963, pp. 85–108.

[86] *Congressional Record*, November 24, 1969, pp. S14944–45.

[87] *Congressional Record*, December 1, 1969, p. S15223.

[88] *Congressional Record*, December 1, 1969, p. S15236.

[89] See, for example, testimonies of Walter Mead, Alfred Kahn, and Walter Adams, in U.S. Congress, Senate, Committee on the Judiciary, Subcommittee on Antitrust and Monopoly, *Government Intervention in the Market Mechanism* (91st Cong., 1st Sess.), March, April 1969, Pt. 1, "The Petroleum Industry, Economists' Views," pp. 77–85, 132–154, and 304–317 respectively.

and that in view of growing import dependence, 1969 was precisely the wrong time to reduce or eliminate the depletion allowance.[90]

Opposition to the oil depletion allowance was emanating from too many sources in 1969 to be completely suppressed. There were those who traditionally believed it to be unfair and inequitable; those who felt it was economically inefficient; and those who balked at the government's deep involvement in stabilizing the market conditions of the domestic oil industry. Energy market conditions, and thus the political process, were just beginning to shift in 1969 from surplus to shortage. As a policy issue, the depletion allowance had not yet attracted widespread public interest nor stimulated deep-seated conflict between business and government, and the outcome reflected this transitory state.

As managers of the Tax Reform Act of 1969, Russell Long and Wilbur Mills engineered a compromise. The rate of the depletion allowance was reduced to 22 percent, and a minimum tax requirement of 10 percent on tax preferences was established. The industry estimated its revenue loss at $500 million per year.[91] The key vote, on an amendment to restore the rate to 27.5 percent, was 62 to 30 against, reflecting the relative division between oil-consuming and oil-producing states.[92] At the same time, amendments to enlarge the reduction or attack the foreign tax credit repeatedly failed by votes of approximately 55 to 35, with Southern Democrats and moderate Republicans from non-oil-producing states unwilling to further upset the status quo.[93] This equilibrium, however, like that of the oil market, was about to shift.

The politics of the Tax Reduction Act and the issue of the depletion allowance were entirely different in 1974–75, by which time shortage and rising price prevailed. The Watergate episode, and its revelations of illegal campaign contributions by oil companies, had further altered the political environment. Freshman congressmen, the so-called "Watergate Class," were determined to reaffirm congressional authority and legitimacy by reforming the committee system and, symbolically, by punishing "Big Oil." These objectives converged on the House Ways and Means Committee, whose once powerful chairman, Wilbur Mills, had been discredited by an embarrassing presidential bid, a long illness, and scandal.

The depletion allowance was no longer the only target of reform. The provision for expensing intangible drilling costs was also attacked. Critics estimated that by 1972, this deduction ($650 million), together with the depletion allowance ($1.7 billion), amounted to a tax subsidy of $2.35 billion.[94] Then too, there was the foreign tax credit which since 1951 had allowed oil companies to

---

[90] See, for example, U.S. Congress, *Government Intervention*, Pt. 2, "Industry Views," pp. 612–672.
[91] Petroleum Industry Research Foundation, Inc., *The Tax Burden on the Domestic Oil and Gas Industry, 1967–1970* (N.Y.: PIRF, 1971), pp. 20–23.
[92] *Congressional Record*, December 1, 1969, p. S15243.
[93] See Roll Call No. 12 (*CR* November 24, 1969, S15270) and Roll Call No. 168 (*CR* November 25, 1969, S15576).
[94] John M. Blair, *The Control of Oil* (N.Y.: Pantheon, 1976), p. 193.

credit their foreign income taxes against their U.S. income tax liability. Critics objected to the low effective tax rate that resulted from this, as well as the fact that foreign taxes to OPEC governments were indistinguishable from royalties since they were levied on the posted price.[95] The Internal Revenue Service estimated that if those taxes were deducted (as an expense) rather than credited, the difference would increase the tax liability for American oil companies by $1.1 billion in 1973 and $2.7 billion in 1974.[96] With OPEC in control of oil supply, critics questioned whether the incentive value of the tax credit was still appropriate.

Phased elimination of the depletion allowance and restrictions on the other two preferences were proposed in a bill entitled, "The Oil and Gas Energy Tax Act of 1974." While the old issues of incentive value, economic efficiency, competition, and fairness were still germane, some new ones took the limelight in political debate. Foremost was the question of oil industry profitability. If, as many believed, the industry's profits were "obscene," it seemed completely unreasonable that they should also benefit from extraordinary tax preferences. In this context, the proposed elimination of percentage depletion was commingled with legislative debate of President Nixon's windfall profits tax initiative. Closely linked to this point was the matter of the oil industry's overall tax burden. Critics both in and out of Congress alleged that the industry was paying an average of only 6 percent of its net income, while a few major companies paid almost no tax in 1973.[97]

The relationship between tax subsidies and price was an interesting issue. Consumer advocates who favored elimination of the depletion allowance tried to downplay the likely impact of such a reform on retail prices. The oil industry tried to maximize it. Their conflicting estimates ranged respectively from 3 tenths of a cent to 3 cents per gallon of refined product.[98] Similarly, proponents of tax reform argued that the OPEC-inspired price increases were a far stronger incentive for development of reserves than any tax preference. Oil industry spokesmen countered with the point that domestic oil prices were controlled by government, and that even were they decontrolled, it would be irrational to reduce exploration incentives in any way, under the circumstances of shortage.[99]

On this point, inconsistent ideological rhetoric seemed to obscure rational discourse. Critics of the depletion allowance, such as Hubert Humphrey, avowed their faith in capitalism and urged their opponents to "let the market forces work." In the same breath, however, Senator Humphrey rejected any thought of decontrolling domestic oil prices in exchange for abolition of the

[95] U.S. Congress, *Multinational Corporations and Foreign Policy (Hearings)*, pt. 4, pp. 13–162.

[96] Jerome Kurtz, Commissioner, Internal Revenue Service, in U.S. Congress, House, Committee on Government Operations, *Foreign Tax Credits Claimed by U.S. Petroleum Companies* (95th Cong., 1st Sess.), 1977, p. 374, 378.

[97] *Congressional Record*, June 20, 1974, p. S11163; also U.S. Congress, House, Committee on Ways and Means, *Hearings on Windfall Profits Tax* (93rd Cong., 2nd Sess.), 1974; also, American Petroleum Institute, *Petroleum Taxation and Energy Independence* (Wash., D.C.: API, 1974), pp. 6–10.

[98] API, *Petroleum Taxation and Energy Independence*, pp. 37–40.

[99] *Ibid.*, 27–33.

depletion allowance.[100] Similarly, oil industry managers, while urging price decontrol in the name of "free enterprise," continued to press for retention of all their tax preferences as well. Thus, the potential for a sensible policy that would substitute replacement-cost pricing for a distorting tax subsidy, was lost.

Ironically, a pragmatic reaction to this absurdity by one industry executive may have been the catalyst for destroying the industry's political unity. At the height of the OPEC embargo, Thornton Bradshaw of Atlantic Richfield (ARCO) broke ranks and announced his support for elimination of the depletion allowance. It had, he felt, become an "albatross" around the industry's neck, providing a target for the industry's critics that stood in the way of price deregulation.[101] Not only did this embarrass the other majors, but it alarmed the independent producers who suspected abandonment. Subsequently, they abandoned the majors. In a deal with Russell Long, the independents agreed to support a compromise to eliminate the allowance for major integrated companies, while retaining it at a rate of 15 percent for small producers.

The Energy Tax Act of 1974 provided for phasing-out of the depletion allowance, phasing-in a windfall profits tax, and reducing benefits for intangible drilling costs and foreign tax credits. If the package were enacted, according to an oil industry briefing paper, "domestic oil and gas activities will be drastically curtailed [and] the U.S. will cease to be a potent factor in international petroleum operations."[102]

Months of complicated parliamentary maneuvers between the Ways and Means Committee and the Democratic Caucus eventually resulted in the tabling of the bill by the House Rules Committee.[103] But in 1975, the Democratic Caucus succeeded in overturning the closed rule to get abolition of the depletion allowance passed as a floor amendment to the Tax Reduction Act of 1975. After Russell Long obtained the exemption for small producers in conference committee, the Act passed, and with it, an element of federal energy policy that had prevailed for nearly half a century.[104]

It is perhaps ironic that after condoning the depletion allowance during decades of domestic over-supply, Congress finally abolished it in a domestic supply crisis when it might actually have served the national interest for the very first time. The motive for eliminating it was primarily punitive, accompanied by a confused commitment to "fairness." That is not to say that the depletion allowance should have been retained, but merely that the decision was not tied to any rational concept of energy policy. Like the antitrust backlash, it resulted from extreme market disequilibrium and the effects of that imbalance on the

[100] Quoted in *Ibid.*, 28.

[101] *Washington Post*, December 25, 1973, A44.

[102] American Petroleum Institute, "Briefing Paper, Oil and Gas Energy Tax Act of 1974" (API, Washington, D.C., 1974), p. 1.

[103] For an excellent analysis of this legislative episode, see Edward F. Morrison, "Energy Tax Legislation: The Failure of the 93rd Congress," *Harvard Journal on Legislation*, Vol. 12, 1975, pp. 369–414.

[104] For analysis of the specific provisions and effects of the Tax Reduction Act, see Stephen L. McDonald, "Taxation System and Market Distortion," in R. J. Kalter and W. A. Vogely, eds., *Energy Supply and Government Policy* (Ithaca: Cornell University Press, 1976), pp. 26–50.

political process. By 1975, the prospect for constructive relations between government and the energy industries appeared to be reaching a nadir. But to fully appreciate what had happened to those relations, it is necessary also to look at the role of environmental regulation in the alienation of business and in the energy crisis itself.

The impact of environmentalism

On January 28, 1969, an offshore well operated by Union Oil in the Santa Barbara Channel sprang a leak. The resulting oil spill, and its damage to the California coast, sparked widespread concern that galvanized existing threads of conservationism into a national movement for environmental reform. The very presence of the rig in offshore waters was a result of rapidly increasing energy demand and depleted onshore reserves. The spill, or one like it, was inevitable in the course of producing more fuel from less accessible resources. Unfair coverage by the news media and inept public relations by Union Oil further undermined the oil industry's public image. As a consequence of this accident, the rate of offshore leasing was temporarily slowed, Congress enacted the National Environmental Policy Act, which had an immense impact on energy developments, and "public interest" lobbies turned to the courts to obstruct a wide range of energy projects.[105]

It was scarcely coincidental that the environmental movement and energy crisis occurred together when they did. They had common origins in rapidly increasing energy demand and even more rapid depletion of cheap domestic reserves of oil and natural gas. As domestic energy consumption grew 4.1 percent annually from 1960 to 173, the burden of effluents from fossil-fuel combustion began to exceed the environment's carrying capacity. On the production side, depletion of oil and gas reserves necessitated renewed reliance on coal, as well as oil and gas exploration in offshore and wilderness areas. To combat rising production costs, technologies of scale were increasingly applied; strip mining, larger power plants, remote pipelines, super tankers, and nuclear reactors. The immense scale of these energy systems, their drain on resources, and the cumulative effects of their effluents evoked widespread academic debate over the possible limits to economic growth.[106]

While the environmental movement came to encompass a wide range of ecological impacts, production and combustion of energy fuels remained preeminent problems. Three areas of environmental policy – air pollution control, environmental impact statements, and strip mining regulation – are good exam-

---

[105] See Carol Steinhart and John Steinhart, *Blowout: A Case Study of the Santa Barbara Oil Spill* (Belmont Calif.: Duxbury, 1972); John C. Whitaker, *Striking a Balance* (Wash., D.C.: AEI, 1976), pp. 264–272; U.S. Congress, Senate, Public Works Committee, Subcommittee on Air and Water Pollution, *Amendments to the Federal Water Pollution Control Act – Hearings* (91st Cong., 1st Sess.), February 1969.

[106] The limits-to-growth debate was sparked by a Club of Rome study published in 1972; Dennis Meadows et al., *The Limits to Growth* (N.Y.: Signet Books, 1972). The debate was recast in energy terms principally by Amory Lovins, *Soft Energy Paths: Toward a Durable Peace* (Cambridge: Ballinger, 1977), and Barry Commoner, *The Poverty of Power* (N.Y.: Alfred Knopf, 1976).

ples of how environmental reform related to the energy crisis, to the energy-policy process, and to the relationship between business and government.

Although the health effects of stationary-source air pollution emerged as a national concern in the early 1960's, the coal industry's leadership paid it little attention until 1965, when Mayor John Lindsay announced his intention to ban coal from New York City. By the time coal and the other energy-intensive industries formulated a public posture of supporting state and local regulation as opposed to federal intervention, the issue had been adopted by Senator Edmund Muskie of Maine and moved to the congressional arena. Muskie's efforts yielded the Air Quality Act of 1967, a law that environmentalists perceived as a victory for industry.[107] At best, the Act appeared to be a compromise since it ordered no emission standards and left to the States the responsibility for establishing and implementing standards for ambient air quality. The federal government, however, was charged with promulgating scientific health criteria for each of the major pollutants (e.g., particulates, sulfur oxides, and nitrogen oxides). The fact that these criteria were premised on health effects, rather than cost or technological feasibility, was a critical and overlooked provision that would evolve directly into the growth-limiting requirements of the Clean Air Act of 1970.

Because its ambient and emission standards were premised on scientifically determined health criteria (specific numerical effluent levels for each pollutant), the 1970 Act has been viewed as a radical departure in public policy.[108] Energy-intensive industries unanimously opposed its provision for federal air quality standards based on health. By arguing that cost effectiveness and technology should be relevant considerations, they cast themselves in a role of insensitive, faceless corporations that cared little for the elderly or those afflicted with lung disease. To observers of the political process, and certainly to members of the "public interest" lobbies, this unified opposition, and subsequent meddling with the implementation process, seemed part and parcel of the concentrated structure, anti-competitiveness, and self-interested conduct of the energy industries.[109]

Implementation of the Clean Air Act, between 1970 and 1975, affected energy supplies in several ways. To achieve the ambient air quality standards in polluted cities, powerplants had to switch from coal to low-sulfur fuels or retrofit with expensive clean-up equipment. Emission standards for new coal-burning plants required very clean Western coal and/or the installation of expensive and inefficient flue-gas scrubbing systems. Synthetic fuel plants appeared less feasible than ever. Although oil refineries and gas treatment plants had to reduce fugitive emissions in every way possible, they were far less affected than coal. It was no wonder that the National Coal Association bewailed the effects of these requirements on coal demand and delivered costs.

[107] For a more detailed history of these developments see Richard Vietor, *Environmental Politics and the Coal Coalition* (College Station: Texas A&M University Press, 1980), particularly Chapter 5.
[108] For this view of the political process, see Charles O. Jones, *Clean Air* (Pittsburgh: University of Pittsburgh Press, 1975).
[109] R. Vietor, *Environmental Politics and the Coal Coalition*, Chapter 6, pp. 155–193.

They came just when OPEC, the anti-nuclear movement, and domestic gas shortages had begun to restore the coal industry's interfuel competitiveness.

Two other provisions of the Clean Air Act had a significant impact on the energy supply-demand balance: vehicular emission standards and "prevention of significant deterioration." As subsequently implemented by the Environmental Protection Agency, the emission standards for automobiles (and trucks) necessitated catalytic converters and engine modifications which, according to automobile manufacturers, would cause losses in fuel efficiency of 15 to 20 percent. Since other analysts and the government disputed this, the industry's critics viewed this posture as another attempt by big business to use the energy crisis as an excuse for avoiding environmental responsibility.[110]

Prevention of Significant Deterioration (PSD) derived from the Court's interpretation of an objective, stated in both the 1967 and 1970 acts, of "protecting" as well as enhancing air quality. As implemented between 1974 and 1977, PSD became a set of restrictive ambient standards for clean-air regions of the United States. In effect, the PSD rules meant that few if any energy-intensive projects could be developed in a Class I (most restricted) region, and only a limited number in Class II areas. At the very least, PSD made siting of new facilities very difficult, and required use of the best available control technologies, regardless of expense. To energy industrialists, whose future plans for the western states included mine-mouth power plants, oil shale projects, and synthetic fuels plants, PSD seemed to be a radical manifestation of the limits-to-growth philosophy – the environmental movement at its worst.[111]

The National Environmental Policy Act of 1969 had similar effects on the supply of energy fuels. Richard Nixon signed the Act on January 1, 1970, originally intending to accomplish three relatively modest objectives: (1) a lofty declaration that environmental quality was a national goal, (2) creation of a Council on Environmental Quality to advise the President, and (3) a requirement that government agencies prepare a statement of environmental impact for any action they were contemplating that might "significantly" affect the environment.[112] The President certainly did not appreciate the ramifications of that provision.

Section 102 of the Act required that government agencies prepare environmental impact statements to evaluate the environmental impact of their proposed actions, any adverse consequences which could not be avoided, alternatives to their proposed action, any irreversible commitments of resources, and the relationship between short-term uses of the environment and its long-term productivity. Environmental interest groups skillfully transformed this

---

[110] U.S. Congress, Senate, Committee on Environmental and Public Works, *Report No. 95–127*, "Clean Air Act Amendments of 1977" (95th Cong., 1st Sess.), May 10, 1977, pp. 71–73; also, Richard Vietor, "Policy by a Single Criterion: A Decade's Experience with Emissions Control," in *Summary and Proceedings: Seminar on Issues Affecting the Future of the Motor Vehicle* (McLean, VA: The MITRE Corp., 1979), pp. 75–88.

[111] Richard Vietor, "The Evolution of Public Environmental Policy: The Case of 'No Significant Deterioration,'" *Environmental Review*, vol. III, No. 2 (Winter 1979), pp. 2–18.

[112] *Public Law 91–190* (January 1, 1970) 83 Stat. 852, 856.

requirement into a powerful tool for their activism. By successfully litigating for the widest jurisdiction and application of environmental impact statements, they succeeded in making Section 102 a major stumbling block to the development of energy resources and power-generating facilities.[113]

Like the Clean Air Act, the environmental accomplishments of the National Environmental Policy Act were of immense value to the public interest. By requiring agencies to develop in-house expertise and to articulate their decisions on an ecological cost-benefit basis, the Act dramatically changed the administrative procedures of agency decision-making. More than that, it reordered national priorities such that environmental impact became a new baseline in the regulation and allocation of public goods.[114] At the same time, however, it imposed a burden of red tape on those agencies most responsible for energy development. Consequently, lease sales, pipelines, new powerplants, and other energy projects were often delayed for months, or even years, while the environmental impact statement was prepared, circulated for public comment, challenged in court, and revised.

Two court decisions involving the National Environmental Policy Act especially affected the course of federal energy policy. In *Calvert Cliffs' Coordinating Committee v. AEC*, the court rejected the Atomic Energy Commission's procedures for developing environmental impact statements. It broadened the scope and meaningfulness of the Act's requirements, and transformed AEC licensing procedures into an imposing barrier to commercial expansion of nuclear power.[115] The AEC was thereafter required to make an independent assessment of all environmental impacts of any powerplant it licensed. Furthermore, the decision obliged the Commission (or any other agency) to perform an independent "balancing" of *all* factors involved, and to relate that analysis to its substantive decision. This meant that each agency, on each specific action, would have to act as an independent policy center rather than as a rational part of the larger system of environmental laws and enforcement agencies developing in state and federal government. And this was only half the problem. In the case of *NRDC v. Morton*, which involved a proposed offshore lease sale by the Interior Department, the court ruled that Interior's environmental impact statement should have contained an analysis of alternatives, including other energy projects for which other government agencies were responsible.[116] This meant that agency decision-making on energy development as well as environmental impact would be further atomized. Since this problem was already a barrier to

[113] For a thorough analysis of NEPA's judicial evolution, see Frederick R. Anderson, *NEPA in the Courts* (Baltimore: Johns Hopkins University Press, 1973).
[114] Testimony of Russell Train, in U.S. Congress, Senate, Committees on Public Works and Interior and Insular Affairs, *Joint Hearings: National Environmental Policy Act* (92nd Cong., 2nd Sess.), March 1972, pp. 11–16; also, Richard N. L. Andrews, *Environmental Policy and Administrative Change* (Lexington: D.C. Heath Company, 1976).
[115] *Calvert Cliffs' Coordinating Committee, Inc. v. U.S. Atomic Energy Commission*, 449 F.2d 1109 (D.C. Cir. 1971); also, testimony of James Schlesinger, Chairman of the Atomic Energy Commission, in U.S. Congress, Senate, *National Environmental Policy Act*, pp. 86–106.
[116] *Natural Resources Defense Council v. Morton*, 3 ERC 1558, 2 ELR 20029 (D.C. Cir. 1/13/72).

constructive relations between the public and private sectors, these broad interpretations left federal energy policy less coherent than ever.

Federal regulation of coal surface mining was another major objective of environmental activism that occupied the Congress fairly continuously from 1973 to 1977. For many environmentalists, surface mining epitomized the wantonness of industrial growth with its destruction of agricultural and timber resources, water courses and acquifers, and the aesthetic appeal of rural and wilderness environments. Conversely, the coal industry viewed federal regulation of strip mining as a serious threat. Western surface mining had been coal's only real growth sector since the mid-1950's, and would be crucial to future prospects for synthetic fuels. Coal-industry leaders felt that harsh federal controls would be the last straw in a succession of federal policies that had all but destroyed their competitive vitality. For government bureaucrats and many congressmen, regulation of strip mining posed a dilemma. Strip-mined coal was the most readily available alternative to greater dependence on imported oil, yet the demand for regulatory reform came at the height of the energy crisis. Thus, in December 1974, when he vetoed the bill for the first time, President Gerald Ford justified his decision as follows: "I find that the adverse impact of this bill on our domestic coal production is unacceptable at a time when the nation can ill afford significant losses from this critical energy resource."[117]

Environmental issues in the strip mining conflict revolved around (1) limits to expansion, (2) the effects of regulation on production costs, (3) the effects of regulation on relative competitiveness between eastern and western operators, and (4) division of authority between state and federal government. The first two of these were most germane to energy supply and energy policy.

Some of the environmental interest groups, and a fair number of congressmen, sought to limit as much as possible the kinds of areas in which strip mining could occur. At the extreme, Congressman Kenneth Hechler (D-WV) and eighty-eight co-sponsors sought to abolish strip mining altogether. Moreover, that was the avowed goal of CASM, the Coalition Against Strip Mining that coordinated the lobbying efforts of fifteen national and regional environmental groups. Short of this, environmentalists would prohibit strip mining where the federal government owned the coal but not the surface property (most of the Great Plains), in alluvial basins, on prime agricultural lands and steep slopes (over twenty degrees), and in national forests or grasslands. Energy interests largely succeeded in keeping these containment provisions out of the final Act.[118]

The regulatory issues that involved strip mining operations and reclamation standards were contested detail-by-detail. Environmental groups wanted to minimize the impact of mining operations and maximize the thoroughness of reclamation, irrespective of cost. Coal operators, especially in the East where the unit costs of mining and reclamation were relatively high, did all they could

---

[117] President Gerald Ford, quoted in Southern Coals Conference, *Commentary and Research Service* 36 (January 9, 1975), 2.

[118] R. Vietor, *Environmental Politics and the Coal Coalition*, chapter 4, pp. 85–126.

to minimize these provisions in order to remain as cost-competitive as possible with natural gas and nuclear electric generation. In this area, they were less successful. The Surface Mining Control and Reclamation Act of 1977 did contain effective control provisions, including restoration of land to approximate original contour, avoidance of water pollution and soil erosion, and lasting revegetation to a condition as good or better than the original. But, the licensing and enforcement of these requirements by an unwieldy federal bureaucracy posed significant administrative costs and far longer lead times for project development. When President Carter finally signed the bill into law, just two months after proposing his National Energy Plan, it represented a reasonable, yet very real compromise between the objectives of energy sufficiency and environmental quality.

Notwithstanding the obvious merits of these and the other policy accomplishments of environmental reform, the price was slower energy development and less coherent energy policy. Environmental regulations altered the supply and demand relationships among fuels by changing relative costs, and thus prices, between them. On the demand side, air pollution controls sharply curtailed coal use on the east coast, resulting in increased demand for low-sulfur residual oil and natural gas. The anti-nuclear movement, which effectively forestalled the only alternative to fossil-fueled, electric power generation, further focused demand on oil and natural gas.

On the supply side, policies to prevent water and land degradation helped delay mineral leasing and the construction of powerplants. By increasing the costs and risks of large-scale power projects at a time when oil and gas prices were controlled, those policies depressed new supply and intensified reliance on proved reserves of easily accessible oil and natural gas. This accelerated the draw-down of inventories and increased dependence on OPEC through 1979. Ironically, the higher costs of environmental protection probably helped the price mechanism to enforce conservation and eventually restore equilibrium to energy markets.

The most permanent and valuable impact of the environmental movement was the new baseline of environmental sensitivity and constraint that it created. Short of any real national emergency, fossil-fuel production by private firms, as well as government energy policy, would have to be responsive to environmental considerations. Although the two energy crises weakened public support of that baseline slightly, it has nonetheless shown an impressive resilience. Public opinion polls taken over the course of the 1970's reveal that environmental quality was not as high a priority in 1980 as it was in 1973. However, the polls also show that when asked about a trade-off between energy production and environmental protection, the polity has remained as committed to the latter as to the former.[119]

Environmental consciousness, and responsibility of the federal government for assuring a certain degree of environmental protection, appear to constitute a

[119] Council on Environmental Quality, *Public Opinion on Environmental Issues: Results of a National Public Opinion Survey* (Wash., D.C.: CEQ, 1980), pp. 6–8, 18–23.

secular change in the American political context that affected the relations between business and government. Because energy industries are inherently prone to adverse environmental impacts, they bore the brunt of this change, in terms of (1) constraints on their policy options, (2) deeper penetration by governmental command-and-control regulation into their day-to-day operations, (3) heightened animosity and conflict between energy corporations and government agencies, and (4) new institutional barriers to cooperative management of energy resources. During the 1970's, these effects made the adjustment to energy shortage no less difficult.

Ambivalence at risk

In Chapter 2, the postwar relationship between business and government, which prevailed during two decades of energy abundance, was characterized as ambivalent. The balance between market and administrative allocation of resources remained relatively stable. The policy issues revolved around problems of market stabilization, maintenance of market share, and price support. Those issues were usually resolved through intrafuel politics, or occasionally interfuel and intra-governmental contests. Broad clashes of the business-reform variety were rare, and government was more often a partner to the energy industries than a hardened, meddling foe.

In this chapter, I have tried to show that the energy crisis stemmed from the convergence in the early 1970's of three long-term developments. Depletion of domestic oil and gas reserves, structural concentration and integration of the energy industries, and the movement for environmental reform were interrelated historical developments. All three resulted from two decades of rapid economic growth in the face of static federal policies and a limited endowment of fossil-fuel minerals. The political backlash to this crisis threatened the ambivalence that had previously characterized relations between business and government.

During the last energy crisis, world war had sufficiently focused the national interest so that business-government relations shifted from ambivalence toward close and constructive cooperation. But in the 1970's, the national interest was so thoroughly ill-defined and lacking consensus that the lapse of ambivalence led instead to open conflict between business management and government authority, and to a breakdown of institutional channels for constructive interaction. In both cases, the traditional balance between market and administrative allocation of energy resources shifted sharply, albeit temporarily, toward government.

Adjustment of public policy to the onset of scarcity and the reality of higher-cost fuels is the subject of the next four chapters. The process of adjustment proved to be agonizingly difficult. In fact, during the entire decade of the 1970's, restoration of equilibrium in energy markets, and of ambivalence in business-government relations, remained at doubt.

10. Equity versus efficiency: oil price controls

Federal regulation of petroleum prices was partly coincidence, partly an extension of previous policies, and mostly a frustrating adjustment to domestic depletion and the power of OPEC. Direct federal control of crude oil prices lasted just short of a decade, from August 1971 until January 1981. The price of petroleum products was also regulated for most of that time, and quantities were allocated right down to the level of retail distribution. Congress, the Executive Branch, and the courts devoted a ridiculous amount of time and political energy to the issue of price controls. The oil industry was deeply affected, from strategic planning to daily operations. American consumers benefited, in the short-run, from lower prices. But, over the long-run, they paid dearly through distorted markets, a less efficient industry, and still greater dependence on imported oil. Relations between business and government reached their nadir on the price control issue, and the policy process left the public with an abiding distrust of the industry and its regulators.

This chapter does not attempt to document the literally hundreds of oil price regulations and their implementation by the Federal Energy Administration (FEA). Nor does it provide economic analysis of their costs and benefits to the whole economy, or their microeconomic impact on the oil industry.[1] The chapter largely disregards the immense structure of downstream price and product controls (such as refining, wholesale and retail distribution), except where it affected issues of crude-oil pricing. Even limited to crude-oil pricing, the story is complicated. As a guide, Chart 10-1 outlines the principal statutory rules over the course of the decade. Moreover, the reader should bear in mind that

---

[1] For more detailed history and economic analysis of oil price controls, see Charles R. Owens, "History of Petroleum Price Controls," in Office of Economic Stabilization, U.S. Department of the Treasury, *Historical Working Papers on the Economic Stabilization Program, August 15, 1971 to April 30, 1974* (Wash.: GPO, 1975), pp. 1223–1340; Anthony Copp, *Regulating Competition in Oil* (College Station: Texas A&M University Press, 1976); U.S. Congress, Senate, Committee on Energy and Natural Resources, *Regulation of Domestic Crude Oil Prices* (95th Cong., 1st Sess.), March 1977 (Committee Print); Paul W. MacAvoy, ed., *Federal Energy Administration Regulation; Report of the Presidential Task Force* (Wash.: American Enterprise Institute, 1977); Kenneth J. Arrow and Joseph P. Kalt, *Petroleum Price Regulation – Should We Decontrol?* (Wash.: American Enterprise Institute, 1979); Joseph P. Kalt, *The Economics and Politics of Price Regulation* (Cambridge: MIT Press, 1981).

236

Chart 10-1
Crude Oil Price Controls, 1971–1980

Program	Period	Price Regulations
Economic Stabilization		
Phase I (Cost of Living Council)	8/71 to 11/71	Economy-wide price freeze
Phase II	11/71 to 1/73	Controlled price increases to reflect cost increases with profit limitations
Phase III	1/73 to 8/73	Voluntary increases up to 1.5% annual for cost increases
Special Rule No. 1	3/73 to 8/73	Mandatory controls for 23 largest oil companies
Phase IV	8/73 to 11/73	Two-tier pricing; old oil at level of 5/15/73 plus $.35, new oil, stripper oil, and "released" oil uncontrolled
Reaction to Shortage		
EPAA (Emergency Petroleum Allocation Act)	11/73 to 12/75	Same as Phase IV plus mandatory product allocation, Buy-Sell Program (1/74)
(Federal Energy Administration)		Entitlements Program (11/74)
EPCA (Energy Policy and Conservation Act)	12/75 to 9/81	Lower tier (old) oil at $5.25 Upper tier (new) oil at $11.28 Stripper oil decontrolled (9/76) Composite price at $7.66 Provision for incentive and inflation increases
Compromising Decontrol		
COET Proposed (Crude Oil Equalization Tax) (Department of Energy)	4/77	Phased decontrol over three years with a graduated tax on the difference between old and new oil
Administrative Decontrol	6/79 to 9/81	Under EPCA authority, phased decontrol of lower and upper tier oil
Windfall Profits Tax	3/80 to present	Taxes on difference between controlled prices and market price; Tier One (lower tier and upper tier) at 70% Tier Two (stripper) at 60% Tier Three (newly discovered and tertiary) at 30%

oil price controls were intertwined with the other policy issues discussed in the previous chapter, as well as those developed in the chapters following this one.

What this chapter does do is to look at how market conditions precipitated change in policy and in the relationship between business and government. Even before the embargo in October 1973, the U.S. oil market had shifted from surplus to scarcity. During that transition, and through the immediate crisis period of the embargo, intrafuel politics dominated the policy process. When reaction to the crisis began taking hold in the spring of 1974, the political process escalated rapidly to a mix of intrafuel friction, intragovernmental strife, and the increasingly strident politics of business reform. This combination resulted in the Energy Policy and Conservation Act of 1975. By 1977, when Jimmy Carter announced his National Energy Plan, the politics of business reform had come to dominate energy policy and what was left of business-government relations.

Throughout these years, federal regulators struggled to implement faulty statutes on the basis of inadequate information, insufficient expertise, and ballooning constraints of bureaucratic procedure. For the oil industry, the *Federal Register* became more important than the geologist's report. As one executive put it, "The oil industry is placed in an uncomfortable and understandable posture of fighting for a position of preference within these government-imposed regulations, rather than competing with each other to provide additional supplies to the consumer."[2]

Fighting inflation with oil price controls

On August 15, 1971, President Nixon announced an extraordinary package of economic measures that included a 10 percent surcharge on imported goods, suspension of the dollar's convertibility to gold, and a freeze on all wages and prices. These actions were unprecedented during peacetime. They were "bold measures," designed to simultaneously curb inflation, unemployment, and balance-of-payments deficits. The price freeze eventually gave way to a series of price controls that finally expired in 1974 – except for the oil industry. The Cost of Living Council, which administered Nixon's Economic Stabilization Program, had singled out the petroleum industry for special treatment as early as March of 1973.

Although explicit government control of oil prices was new and seemingly discriminatory, it was scarcely a departure from a free market. Government had implicitly supported domestic oil prices for more than a decade by the combination of prorationing and import quotas. Until 1971, those controls maintained domestic oil prices at a level nearly 30 percent above the world market price. But just as Nixon imposed Phase I of his price controls, long-term trends were

---

[2] A. D. Bonner to Henry Jackson, July 31, 1974, in U.S. Congress, Senate, Committee on Interior and Insular Affairs, *Emergency Petroleum Allocation Extension Act of 1974* (93rd Cong., 2nd Sess.), July 1974, p. 314.

converging to close the gap of approximately $1.25 per barrel. With U.S. oil production approaching capacity, prices and then costs began to rise. Since domestic demand was inelastic in the short run, imported oil from the Middle East became the incremental unit of supply. Thus, foreign crude prices began to rise. With the price increase negotiated in Tehran in 1971, together with a 100 percent increase in tanker rates (due to Libyan export cuts and the closing of Tapline to Europe), the delivered cost of imported oil caught up with the domestic wellhead price early in 1973. This equalization was reflected in the fact that the value of an import ticket fell to zero.[3]

Imposition of economy-wide price controls thus coincided with the collapse of a 10-year-old system for petroleum-market stabilization. That system had entrenched distribution patterns, market share, and import allocation, as well as price. Prorationing had protected less efficient domestic producers from import competition, and quota allocations had equalized acquisition costs for refiners geographically and between integrated and non-integrated firms. Because federal price controls intervened at this juncture, gradual structural adjustment to the new market conditions was foreshortened. As a result, re-stabilization of market structure would necessarily become an adjunct to government price control.

During Phases I and II of wage-price controls, the Nixon administration did not view petroleum prices as a special problem. But the controls certainly created one. The Phase I price freeze occurred in mid-summer at a time when gasoline prices were relatively high due to seasonal demand. But the freeze also applied to home heating oil, the price of which had been soft the previous winter due to abundant inventories and was even lower in mid-summer when prices were frozen. With heating-oil margins fixed at a seasonal low, refiners sought to maximize gasoline production and lagged in their normal fall build-up of heating oil stocks.[4]

Distortion of the refining cycle was repeated and amplified during 1972 because Phase II controls maintained the disparity in margins between gasoline and heating oil. To simplify administration of Phase II, the Price Commission (predecessor to the Cost of Living Council) had authorized term limited pricing agreements for specific products. Although these were intended to provide the flexibility that refining seasonality required, they were not applicable to certain "sensitive" products, such as gasoline and heating oil. Price Commission staff informed the oil companies that, to increase the price of heating oil, elaborate

[3]   C. Owens, "History of Petroleum Price Controls," p. 1233; also, Martin Taschdjian, Office of Economic Analysis, Energy Information Administration, U.S. Department of Energy, *The Effects of Legislative and Regulatory Actions on Competition in Petroleum Markets* (Energy Policy Study, Volume 2), October 1979, p. 28.
[4]   William A. Johnson, "The Impact of Price Controls on the Oil Industry: How to Worsen an Energy Crisis," in Gary Eppen, ed., *Energy: The Policy Issues* (Chicago: University of Chicago Press, 1975), pp. 100–103; also, Robert Deacon et al., *Price Controls and International Petroleum Product Prices*, prepared for the Energy Information Administration, U.S. Department of Energy (DOE/EIA-6039-01), February 1980, pp. 2–3.

and lengthy public hearings would be necessary.[5] The New England congressional delegation had extracted a promise to this effect from the Administration.[6]

To avoid further damage to its public relations, the oil industry quietly took its price increases on other products that were covered by term limited pricing. Together with unseasonably cold weather, this resulted in heating oil shortages during the winter of 1972–73. Then in 1973, as refiners sought to rebuild heating oil stocks, gasoline inventories suffered. By June, there were lines at gas stations throughout the East. Both shortages hurt the oil industry politically and raised public suspicion that the industry was intentionally causing a crisis, either to crush competition from independents or to get high prices for crude oil and larger profits from its products.[7] This interpretation helped inspire the FTC's shared monopoly case, and contributed to a solicitude for independents that Congress made explicit in the Emergency Petroleum Allocation Act of 1973.

Phase III of Nixon's stabilization program began at the very height of the winter heating oil shortage in 1973. Phase III was designed to phase-out price controls through a program of voluntary guidelines with a target inflation rate of less than 2.5 percent. The Cost of Living Council's only lever for enforcement was the threat that it might selectively reimpose mandatory controls. Apparently, this did not daunt the oil industry. In an effort to recover costs that had accumulated for 17 months, heating oil prices jumped by 8 to 10 percent. Coming as it did on top of the shortage, this price hike was politically unacceptable. Senator Henry Jackson convened hearings on the shortages, and Treasury Secretary George Shultz, who was Chairman of the Cost of Living Council, called for hearings on oil prices.

At the various hearings, spokesmen for major companies cited extraordinary growth of demand spurred by unseasonably cold weather and curtailments of natural gas. They also tried to explain how Phase I and Phase II price controls had disturbed the refining cycle and had prevented pass-through of rising costs. An Exxon executive testified that, with gasoline prices relatively stable, the average price of all Exxon products could absorb the heating oil increase and still remain within "the letter and the spirit" of Phase III guidelines.[8] Other segments of the industry, notably independent refiners and wholesale jobbers, placed the blame on import quotas which had restricted heating-oil supplies along the East Coast.[9]

None of these explanations, however, was particularly compelling to con-

---

5   Warren B. Davis, Chief Economist, Gulf Oil Corporation, "Responsibilities of Business, Government and the Public for Solving U.S. Energy Problems," a paper presented at the conference on Businesses' Role and Responsibility in Modern Society, Washington, August 1974, p. 8.
6   C. Owens, "History of Petroleum Price Controls," pp. 1236–37.
7   For a different interpretation of these events which attributes conscious malice and cooperative behavior to the major oil companies, see Fred C. Allvine and James M. Patterson, *Highway Robbery: An Analysis of the Gasoline Crisis* (Bloomington: Indiana University Press, 1974); also, John D. Blair, *The Control of Oil*, Chapter 10.
8   U.S. Congress, Senate, Committee on Interior and Insular Affairs, *Fuel Shortages* (93rd Cong., 1st Sess.), February 1973, Pt. 2, pp. 552–561, 637–651.
9   *Ibid.*, Pt. 1. pp. 92–104, 187–199.

gressmen whose constituents were being told to pay more for fuel already being rationed. Oil companies and the Nixon administration had to share the blame. As Senator Edward Kennedy put it, "We already see the major oil companies seeking to take advantage of a situation they were substantially responsible for creating." Kennedy's solutions, which had wide-spread support, were that import quotas on heating oil be abandoned and that the Cost of Living Council rescind the price rise.[10]

After hearings and the publicity that attended them, the Council tried to figure out what to do. It's staff posited a peculiar, but evidently convincing, rationale. It recognized that prices were rising because domestic crude production and refinery capacity were insufficient. This insufficiency was apparently caused by uncertainty over price, which in turn was caused by Phase III: "There currently is no way for a company to determine with any degree of certainty whether a proposed price increase is compatible with the goals of the program." Given this line of logic, the conclusion was obvious: the way to remove the uncertainty generated by Phase III "is to be specific about what pricing flexibility oil companies can exercise."[11] In other words, reimpose mandatory controls – Catch 22.

On March 6, the Council issued Special Rule No. 1, by which it reimposed mandatory control over crude oil and product prices – but only for the 24 largest oil companies. These few firms, which the Council claimed were responsible for 95 percent of gross industry sales, would be allowed price increases of one percent, plus an additional half a percent if justified by increased costs. Presumably, by limiting the controls to so few firms, enforcement might be more feasible. Needless to say, this selective control pleased the independent refiners and distributors, and appealed to the antibig business sentiment of many congressmen.

What seemed like a good, or at least expedient, idea turned out to be a total failure: Its key premise was so flawed. The 24 largest oil companies did not control oil prices, least of all during a period of shortage. Independent refiners and distributors had other domestic and foreign sources of crude oil and product besides the major companies. And even when they bought from the majors at controlled prices, the voluntary guidelines scarcely inhibited them from raising the price for resale. Thus, not only did this two-tier application of controls result in a 30 percent increase in gasoline prices, but it did so at the expense of the major companies' profitability and market share. This made the majors even more reluctant to share their crude oil and refined products with independents. For the White House and the Cost of Living Council, the lesson was clear; mandatory controls should again be extended to the entire oil industry.

With inflation, particularly for energy and commodities, getting out of control, President Nixon announced a two-month freeze on consumer prices during the summer of 1973. Moreover, he specifically directed the Council to

[10] *Ibid.*, 212–216.
[11] Staff memorandum to CLC Deputy Director James McLane, cited in C. Owens, "History of Petroleum Price Controls," pp. 1240–1241.

formulate Phase IV measures that would control gasoline prices and stimulate domestic oil production. This was a difficult assignment since worldwide oil production was near capacity and nothing but a price increase could restore equilibrium between supply and demand.

There was another problem to be considered as well. Product shortages and price controls had begun to squeeze independent retailers in certain areas. Independent refiners were also suffering because import tickets, which had kept them competitive for more than a decade, no longer had value. The integrated majors, with ensured crude oil supplies, could balance lower refining and retail gasoline margins with profits from other operations. Thus, the Cost of Living Council had, as "a subsidiary but important goal, the maintenance of rigorous competition."[12] In other words, Phase IV controls would have to protect the independents from potential depredation.

Charles Owens headed the Council's Energy Policy Committee. Through discussions with more than 1,500 oil industry personnel, Owens and his staff tried to figure out control mechanisms that would achieve these diverse goals without introducing undesirable, unanticipated effects. But because the new round of controls would regulate prices for producers, refiners, resellers, and retailers, they would pose innumerable opportunities for market distortion, discrimination, and non-compliance. As the source of shortage and the beginning of the inflationary chain, crude oil was the crux of the problem. Even the major producers, who preferred no controls whatever, could think of no device other than multi-tiered pricing, that would stimulate domestic production and still prevent substantial price increases.[13]

Phase IV regulations, issued in August 1973, divided domestic crude oil production into two categories – "new" oil and "old" oil. To simplify enforcement, the pricing rules were set in dollar values rather than percentage increases over a base period. Old oil, initially priced at the May 1973 level of $4.25 per barrel, applied to the amount of oil from each oil property being produced in May 1972. New oil, which was free of controls, applied to production from new fields plus any production from old oil properties above 1972 levels. As a special incentive to increase production from existing properties, provision was made for "released" oil. This was an amount of old oil, equal to the amount of new production from an old property, that the Council released from price controls. By deregulating approximately 40 percent of all domestic oil, the Council hoped to stimulate exploration and new production, while still controlling inflation on most old production where development capital was already sunk. However, the creation of a two-tier price structure meant that, for refiners, there would also be a two-tier cost structure.[14]

---

[12] *Ibid.*, 1252.

[13] Interview with the author, Gulf Oil Exploration and Production Co., Houston, Texas, November 1980.

[14] The downstream price regulations of Phase IV were as follows: (1) refiners' prices were set at the May 1973 level, adjusted for the pass-through of increased import prices thereafter; (2) wholesale prices for oil products (other than gasoline and heating oil) were set at acquisition cost (the refiner's price) plus the absolute dollar markup that had prevailed in January; (3) retail sales of

Phase IV price controls were in effect for only three months before the oil embargo created a brief supply crisis in the United States. Still, that was enough time to reveal serious distortions of the market, to fragment the industry politically, and to trigger intense intrafuel lobbying for congressional relief. As Owens recalled, the communication lines to the Council were jammed: "calls, letters, and telegrams came from producers, refiners, retailers, trade associations, Congressmen, attorneys and state government."[15] The American Petroleum Institute could do nothing because its membership was at odds. Among crude oil producers alone, there was little agreement and no cooperation. The regulations affected each firm differently, according to past investment strategy, marketing arrangements, and crude position. Moreover, because the regulations related directly to price, there could be no inter-firm cooperation without running a serious risk of violating antitrust laws. Thus, the oil industry's political response was "rifle-like," rather than "shotgun," each company seeking to minimize its damage or maximize its opportunity.[16]

Although decontrol of new oil stimulated domestic drilling activity enough to reverse a 15-year decline, the two-tier pricing nonetheless dissatisfied producers, refiners, independent retailers, and congressmen from the Northeast. Independent producers wanted all oil decontrolled, while the major refiners preferred that it all be controlled. Since most refiners were net crude purchasers, they anticipated difficulty in passing through new oil price increases to their customers. Independent refiners were even more apprehensive, lest the integrated majors reserve their cheap old oil for themsleves, and offer only high-priced new and imported oil to the independents. Small producers were especially adamant about their stripper wells (producing less than 10 barrels per day). Even before the Council announced its Phase IV controls, the stripper lobby had swung into action. By October, an amendment to exempt stripper wells from price control had been tacked on to the Alaskan Pipeline Bill. Although the Council strenuously opposed it, the bill passed in November, and by January, the price of stripper oil had more than doubled.

The Cost of Living Council never intended for its price controls to become permanent. Phase IV was scheduled to expire at the end of April 1974. Once the market price stabilized under the supply impetus of decontrolled new oil, the Council planned to allow old oil prices to catch up. In fact, late in November 1973, the Council exercised its statutory discretion by raising the old oil price one dollar, to $5.25. Although OPEC had just raised its price from $3.00 to $5.11 (f.o.b. Persian Gulf), the congressional and news media's outcry at the price increase foretold intense political opposition to eventual decontrol.

Short-lived as they were, Phase IV controls had already established a regulatory baseline. Any semblance of industry political unity was shattered, at least until 1977, and a course of multi-tier crude oil pricing was set until 1981.

Throughout 1973, various legislative schemes had been proposed in Con-

gasoline and heating oil were set at the sales price to retailers as of August 1973 plus the absolute dollar markup as of January 1973.
[15] C. Owens, "History of Petroleum Price Controls," pp. 1282–1283.
[16] Interview, Gulf E&P Company.

gress to establish mandatory allocation of petroleum products. But it took an embargo on oil exports by the Arab members of OPEC to stifle dissent and galvanize sufficient congressional support for such a measure. In an address to the Nation on November 7, Richard Nixon warned that oil supplies would fall 10 percent short of demand. To cope with the expected emergency, the President called for voluntary conservation, relaxation of environmental standards, and accelerated production from the Naval Petroleum Reserves. He proposed a Project Independence to develop synthetic fuels, and urged Congress to grant him authority to allocate crude oil and petroleum products.[17] In a rare display of bipartisanship, Congress managed to enact the Emergency Petroleum Allocation Act (EPAA) in less than three weeks.

The illusiveness of decontrol

Even without the embargo, transition from energy surplus to scarcity, compounded by the effects of federal price controls, would likely have led to allocation by government. Enterprise was failing to deliver cheap energy, and the embargo provided a timely impetus. The Allocation Act tentatively substituted government for the market, to restore stability and assure distributive equity.

The Act gave the President 15 days to organize a Federal Energy Agency that would allocate all petroleum products to all end-users, in all regions of the country, as equitably and efficiently as possible. To avoid windfall profits and price gouging, it extended Phase IV price controls for another year. Market share within each sector of the oil industry was to be restored to 1972 conditions, with careful and early oversight by the Federal Trade Commission.[18] "Preservation of an economically sound and competitive petroleum industry" was among the Allocation Act's most pressing objectives, with special attention to "the competitive viability of independent refiners, small refiners, non-branded independent marketers, and branded independent marketers."[19] The Federal Energy Agency's statutory charter was, to say the least, ambitious.

During the months of actual emergency caused by the embargo, federal regulators were largely preoccupied with availability of crude oil and delivery of products to end-users. Market distortion, competition, and pricing issues were secondary, but not unrelated. OPEC had again raised the price of oil, effective January 1974, from $5.11 to $11.65 per barrel. As the price of new domestic oil rose to this market-clearing level, the disparity between it and old oil (fixed at $5.25) worsened the disruption of normal supplier-purchaser relationships. Trying to meet their own needs first, especially with regard to cheap old oil, the major integrated oil companies failed to renew many of the one-year supply contracts with independents as they were due to expire December 31. In the

[17] "Address to the Nation About Policies to Deal with the Energy Shortages, November 7, 1973," in *Public Papers of the Presidents: Richard Nixon, 1973*, pp. 916–922.
[18] Federal Trade Commission, Staff Report, "Evaluation of the Emergency Petroleum Allocation Program; Summary of Findings, Conclusions, and Issues," March 15, 1974.
[19] *Public Law 93–159* (November 27, 1973) Sec. 4 (b) (1).

absence of regulation, the entire market structure of independents, so long protected by surpluses and import quotas, threatened to collapse.

The new Federal Energy Agency (FEA) moved swiftly, ordering a complete freeze of supplier-purchaser relationships, from wellhead to gas pump. With the notable exception of oil from stripper wells, this freeze effectively established property rights to old oil for refiners purchasing that oil on December 1, 1973.[20] But by itself, this freeze did not insure "equitable" distribution of available crude oil among refiners, nor did it alleviate the cost disadvantage suddenly imposed on those refiners who had traditionally relied on imported oil. The first step toward solving these problems was a "buy/sell" program, under which each refiner with a smaller crude supply than the national average could purchase from refiners whose supplies exceeded the average. The program's initial purpose was merely to equalize capacity utilization among refiners during the immediate crisis, making no distinction between small, independent, and major refiners.

After the embargo ended and the supply situation eased, the FEA revamped this allocative scheme, so as to better serve the ostensible structural goals of the Act. On June 1, the Buy/Sell List Program took effect. The 15 largest integrated oil companies (excluding several that were classified as independent refiners) were required to sell crude oil to approximately 100 small and independent refiners, designated as "refiner-buyers."[21] The sales obligation of each "refiner-seller" was based on the ratio of its refinery capacity to the total capacity of all 15 firms on the Sell List.[22] Although designed for allocation, the Buy/Sell List Program affected refiner acquisition costs, once crude oil supplies were more readily available. Refiner-sellers could only change the weighted average price of their own feedstock (plus a 30-cent-a-barrel handling charge). Since the majors produced much of the controlled old oil, this selling price was considerably below the prices that refiner-buyers would otherwise have to pay for new or imported oil. And since even the refiner-sellers were net crude oil purchasers, they were forced to absorb the difference between their weighted average selling price and their replacement cost for new oil.

Although the Buy/Sell List Program solved the allocation problem, it did not sufficiently relieve disparities in refiner acquisition costs. The price gap of 100 percent between old and new oil left companies without access to old oil at a real competitive disadvantage. With the Executive Office in turmoil during the months surrounding President Nixon's resignation, the FEA Administrator, John Sawhill, did his best to cope with the situation. Members of his staff had

---

[20] Robert Deacon et al., *Price Controls and International Petroleum Product Prices*, p. 7. The exemption of stripper wells, which Congress had written into the EPAA, was unexpectedly damaging to small refiners, because they had relied disproportionately on stripper oil as a source of supply.

[21] Small refiners were defined as those whose refining capacity did not exceed 175,000 barrels per day. Independent refiners, regardless of their size, were those which had to purchase 70 percent or more of their crude oil feedstock.

[22] Statement of Frank G. Zarb, Administrator of the Federal Energy Administration, May 19, 1975, in U.S. Congress, Senate, Committee on Interior and Insular Affairs, *Oversight – Federal Energy Administration Programs* (94th Cong., 1st Sess) April, May 1975, pp. 522–524.

suggested a system of tickets for distributing rights to cheap old oil; very similar, but the reverse, of the Mandatory Oil Import Program. The independent refiner lobby was enthusiastic about such a program, the New England congressional delegation demanded it, and a group of 21 liberal senators supported it as a means of preserving competition.[23]

In November, the FEA adopted the Old Oil Entitlements Program. Its objective was to equalize the average cost of crude oil to all refiners. Entitlements, equal to the number of barrels of old oil produced monthly, were issued to all refiners in proportion to their refining capacities. Refiners with fewer entitlements than the amount of old oil they wished to process had to buy them from refiners with a surplus. The value of an entitlement was a large fraction of the price difference between old and new oil. In this convoluted manner, companies with cheap domestic oil were to subsidize their crude-short competitors, all in the interest of preserving "competition."

After the oil supply crisis had ended, in the summer of 1974, the American public, the news media, and the federal government began looking for explanations, placing blame, and considering national priorities and policy options. Throughout the oil industry, managers reassessed their circumstances in a drastically altered market and a new framework of government regulation. Uncertainty and mistrust abounded. With a handful of Arab governments apparently controlling both the supply and price of oil, two issues shared the public limelight with the Watergate hearings: the security of energy supply and the appropriate price of oil. The first of these was a long-term problem that would require long-term solutions. The second, however, was an immediate concern, to consumers, to the Ford administration, to Congress, and to the oil industry. A national debate ensued over what to do about oil prices and, more specifically, what to do about the Emergency Petroleum Allocation Act when it expired in February 1975. At no time during the next 18 months were the terms of the debate ever clear, nor were the positions of the major participants ever coherent or consistent.

Had the oil industry itself a clear policy agenda, the debate might at least have been polarized along ideological lines, between those with faith in the market and others with a preference for government. But after seven months of government allocation and price control, winners and losers were forming lines, and the industry was thoroughly divided. Some of the major integrated firms sought immediate decontrol, while others accepted the need for a gradual phasing-out. Independent producers opposed any thought of a windfall profits tax, although some of the larger firms thought it reasonable with sensible plowback provisions. Large independent refiners wanted controls continued temporarily, but the smaller ones preferred indefinite extension. Retail marketers, terminal operators, and wholesale jobbers all feared a margin squeeze and demanded some form of protection, although the jobbers eventually changed their minds.

---

[23] For a well-documented discussion of the origins of the Entitlements Program, see Neil De Marchi, "Energy Policy under Nixon: Mainly Putting Out Fires," in Craufurd D. Goodwin, ed., *Energy Policy in Perspective* (Wash.: Brookings Institution, 1981), pp. 466–473.

The firms that benefited and suffered most under the Buy/Sell List Program, and then Entitlements, argued and lobbied most intensely. The rift between Standard Oil of Ohio and Marathon, both medium-sized, partially integrated oil companies, epitomized this intrafuel conflict.

Sohio, with crude oil production of only 29,294 barrels per day, and a refining capacity of 427,000 barrels, qualified as an independent refiner by the Petroleum Allocation Act's definition. Before the energy crisis, explained Chairman Charles Spahr, "Sohio's investment of large sums of capital in the marketing and refining business provided a stable market for those companies who had production and had success in their efforts to find oil." Spahr added that, before the oil market had become inverted, import quotas had prevented Sohio from out-competing producers whose high-priced domestic oil was protected by government. As the market shifted in 1972–73, Sohio lost long-term supply contracts amounting to 120,000 barrels a day and remained competitive only thanks to the Allocation Act. As a refiner-buyer, Sohio was eligible to buy 152,000 barrels a day from its competitors at their weighted average cost. This alone, said Spahr, had prevented "any large market share distortion." Not surprisingly, Spahr urged that the Allocation Act be extended, even though he preferred a free market condition "in the long-run."[24]

Harold Hoopman, the president of Marathon, saw the issue in a completely different light. His company was relatively self-sufficient in crude oil, having pursued a strategy of intense exploration and development at a cost of lower returns to shareholders' equity. But now, as a result of the FEA's program, Marathon was on the Sell List, and thus deprived of "the well earned competitive advantage of lower refinery feedstock costs in comparison with those of its competitors who opted to pursue a different investment strategy." According to Hoopman, the Buy/Sell List Program was, at best, inefficient because it neither stimulated supply nor discouraged consumption. But worse than that, it was a "business welfare" scheme that had little bearing on the antitrust objectives of the Act. "It cripples competition in order to assure the preservation and economic viability of all individual competitors. It accomplishes this not by means of direct Government subsidies, but rather by compelling one competitor to subsidize another in utter disregard of the rights guaranteed by the fifth amendment."[25] Suffice it to say, Hoopman thought oil prices should be decontrolled and flatly opposed extension of the Act.

Congressmen who were unimpressed by Hoopman's eloquent brief at least took pause at some of the worst distortions created by the allocation program. It seems that six big companies – Sohio, Amerada Hess, American Petrofina, Ashland Oil, Commonwealth Refining, and Tenneco – received 40 percent of all transfers under the Buy/Sell List Program. In Ohio, for example, where Sohio's market share was 25 percent and Union Oil's only 4 percent, FEA rules had the effect of requiring Union to sell Sohio nearly a million barrels of crude oil, at $4 to $5 less per barrel than Union's replacement cost. In effect, Union

[24] Charles Spahr to John Sawhill, July 22, 1974, in U.S. Congress, Senate Interior Committee, *Emergency Petroleum Allocation Extension Act of 1974*, pp. 88–91.
[25] *Ibid.*, 94–96.

had "been directed to give one of its principal midwestern competitors a subsidy of more than $3.5 million."[26]

Still, ideological convictions ran deep. Expressing dismay at this sort of thing, Senator Howard Metzenbaum of Ohio could only conclude that "abuse of implementation by the bureaucracy" was responsible, rather than congressional intent or a flaw in the concept of price regulation.[27] Otherwise, how could it be that so many small businessmen in the oil industry wanted the price controls to continue, while the giants wanted them ended?

Indeed, the pro-regulation forces were politically impressive. At the head of the list was the Independent Refiners Association of America. As long as price controls were in effect, this group demanded an allocation system to match, preferably one "with an effective price equalization program." It was not as though the refiners supported price controls *per se*, but they wanted allocation continued, accompanied by entitlements.[28] Although noted for heavy campaign contributions, some of the refiners' political clout can be attributed to the support they received from their customers. The National Congress of Petroleum Retailers, which represented 47 associations of 70,000 gas station operators, also favored extension of controls. So did the New England Fuel Institute, whose membership numbered 1,300 independent distributors of home heating oil, and the Society of Independent Gasoline Marketers of America. In a letter to Senator Jackson, the Marketers claimed that "the only reason that the independent private brand segment of the industry exists today is because of the presence of the Mandatory Allocation Program."[29]

Against this coalition, the contrary advice of Exxon, Texaco. and the other international majors had little impact.[30] Even the independent domestic producers seemed to have lost some of their political clout. When John Miller, president of the Independent Producers Association, warned that continued controls would only destroy initiative, members of Congress retorted by asking how he justified an $11 price for oil that cost only $3.[31]

On the issue of oil price controls, the federal government itself was no less disjointed than the oil industry. During 1974, before the issues had been extensively aired, many congressmen remained unsure of their positions, frustrated by the industry's conflicting arguments and a lack of hard facts. Price controls were also a source of confusion within both the Nixon and Ford administrations. The Treasury Department and the Office of Management and Budget seemed to prefer decontrol, but could not decide how to implement it.

---

[26] *Ibid.*, 276.

[27] *Ibid.* In his study, economist Joseph Kalt concluded that ideology was the single most important factor in congressional policy on oil price controls throughout the 1970's. See Kalt, *The Economics and Politics of Price Regulation*, Chapter 6, pp. 237–283.

[28] U.S. Congress, Senate, *Emergency Petroleum Allocation Act of 1974*, pp. 127–135, 142–146.

[29] *Ibid.*, 328.

[30] *Ibid.*, 304, 314–315.

[31] U.S. Congress, House, Committee on Interstate and Foreign Commerce, Subcommittee on Energy and Power, *Hearings on the Presidential Energy Program* (94th Cong., 1st Sess.), February 1975, pp. 578–582.

The Council of Economic Advisers was torn between its preference for market prices and concern for inflation. The FEA was preoccupied with too many conflicting interests, and the White House was concentrating on a presidential transition. It took Gerald Ford until January 1975 to organize his administration's energy policy. By then, the Democratic Congress and its two key committee chairmen – Henry Jackson and John Dingell – had decided against decontrol. The result was a year-long intragovernmental conflict which produced a law that satisfied no one.

In his State of the Union Message for 1975, President Ford announced the Energy Independence Act of 1975.[32] His plan called for a strategic petroleum reserve, decontrol of new natural gas, delayed implementation of the Clean Air Act, and sundry measures to promote coal utilization and conservation. A critical part of this package was administrative decontrol of old crude oil (when the Allocation Act expired), together with congressional enactment of a windfall profits tax. The President felt that decontrol was the only means of stimulating the domestic oil supply. To stanch demand and encourage congressional cooperation in the meantime, Ford imposed a fee of up to $3 per barrel on imported oil, to be replaced by an excise tax when Congress passed his bill.[33]

Nearly all parties rejected the President's initial proposal for one reason or another. Immediate decontrol was deemed too abrupt and too unfair. Spokesmen for the Administration admitted the harshness of decontrol and its impact on inflation, but felt that quick action was necessary to reduce dependence on OPEC. Democratic congressmen disagreed. As the U.S. economy was slipping into deep recession, decontrol plus the proposed excise tax would cost consumers an estimated $24 billion.[34] Representative Dingell, who chaired the Subcommittee on Energy and Power, thought this trade-off too much: "Sudden decontrol of domestic old oil prices would be nothing short of disastrous for the U.S. economy."[35] Of equal concern was the President's apparent callousness to the impact of decontrol. "The program is cruel and unfair," complained Richard Ottinger (D-NY), "designed to sock the poor, the working man and the middle-income people by leaving allocation of the hardship entirely to the marketplace."[36] From this perspective, the price mechanism was simply illegitimate as a tool of energy policy.

Then too, there was the issue of monopoly profits, which really had two distinct aspects. First, with OPEC setting the price of oil, there was no "market price," only a market-clearing price. Neither the public nor most congressmen were willing to appreciate that distinction. What justification could there be for

---

[32] "Address before a Joint Session of Congress Reporting on the State of the Union, January 15, 1975," *Public Papers of the Presidents: Gerald Ford, 1975* (Wash.: GPO, 1977), p. 42.
[33] Testimony of Frank G. Zarb, in U.S. Congress, House, *Hearings on the Presidential Energy Program*, pp. 8–12.
[34] *Ibid.*, 20–21.
[35] U.S. Congress, House, Committee on Interstate and Foreign Commerce, Subcommittee on Energy and Power, *President's Decontrol Proposals* (94th Cong., 1st Sess.), July, September 1975, p. 2.
[36] U.S. Congress, House, *Hearings on the Presidential Energy Program*, pp. 175–176.

allowing old domestic oil to receive anything like a cartel, (i.e., OPEC), price? Congress had even passed a bill to roll back the Cost of Living Council's price from $5.25 to $4.25, and Nixon's veto barely sustained an attempted override. A spokesman for the Washington-based Public Interest Research Group said that Ford's proposal was "not really decontrol of prices so that they will be set by a free, competitive marketplace, but it is decontrol of prices so that they will now be set according to the OPEC price for oil."[37] John Sawhill, Henry Jackson, and a great many others opposed decontrol for this very reason. As Ralph Nader put it, "Gerald Ford is a sales agent for Exxon and the OPEC cartel."[38]

Excess profits for U.S. oil companies was the other aspect of the monopoly issue, and it carried over to the question of new oil prices. Although producers paid most of the price increase to OPEC governments in the form of taxes, their gross profits had gotten larger in relative terms. They also benefited from the appreciation of their domestic reserves which, if it were new oil, could be priced at the OPEC level. Quarterly profit gains realized by most of the major companies during 1974 caused widespread public anger. "The profits are incredible," complained Senator Jackson. "They are so embarrassing that one company has decided to take over Montgomery Ward." And yet, "the argument for the price increases is that you need the money to provide an incentive for new drilling."[39] Because it had no bearing whatsoever on energy, Mobil's acquisition of Montgomery Ward became a symbol of excess profits that discredited the industry's appeal for incentives.

There were several reasons why Ford's proposal for a windfall profits tax did not help. Even with such a tax, consumers would still be paying prices far in excess of apparent oil-production costs. It made no difference that the President promised to recycle the receipts through a reduction in income taxes. The public paid taxes only once a year, but paid at the gas pump almost daily. Moreover, the congressional energy committees distrusted the legislative agenda and doubted its outcome. While they were asked to approve immediate decontrol, the Administration spoke vaguely of discussions with the tax committees. As late as August 1975, neither Frank Zarb nor his deputy could provide firm answers on the progress of the tax. "We have yet to see any tangible evidence," complained Representative Timothy Wirth of Colorado, that the Administration "is serious about a wind-fall profits tax. Increasingly, there are a number of us who are beginning to believe that in fact this is something of a chimera."[40]

Wirth's concern was probably not unfounded. Political expedience, not principle, was the Administration's only commitment to the tax. And there was certainly no reason to think that Russell Long, the Senate Finance Committee chairman, would support such a tax, at least without gutting it. His people, the Independent Petroleum Association of America, adamantly opposed it. So did

[37] Ibid., 778.
[38] U.S. Congress, House, President's Decontrol Proposals, p. 6.
[39] U.S. Congress, Senate, Emergency Petroleum Allocation Extension Act of 1974, p. 41.
[40] U.S. Congress, House, President's Decontrol Proposals, p. 557.

the American Petroleum Institute, as long as it offered no relief for the plowback of profits into exploration.[41] The oil industry's failure to support the President's position probably provided the finishing blow. Regardless of their own motives, congressional opponents could not only point to the little guy and the independent refiners, but now to the independent and integrated producers as well. Until too late, the industry's leadership seemed to believe that the only likely alternative to Ford's pricing compromise was simply the expiration of existing controls. Nor was this the last time oil people made this particular tactical mistake.

Although accused of playing a "game of economic brinksmanship," President Ford was unwilling to concede a standoff. In mid-July, he made a major concession, offering a program of phased decontrol over a period of 30 months. New oil would be capped at $13.50 a barrel (including $2 of excise tax), while old oil caught up at 3.3 percent per month. To assuage producer opposition and win support from Senator Long, the windfall profits tax was modified to provide deductions for plowback.

But it was too late. In the wake of Watergate, a congressional revolt against Executive power had taken hold. Within weeks of overturning the oil depletion allowance, the House rejected the 30-month plan and voted to extend the Petroleum Allocation Act. The atmosphere was one of reprisal and reprobation. Every compromise was cast as a plum for "Big Oil." To make matters worse, a series of alleged exposés by NBC, Ralph Nader, and a host of newspapers had convinced the public that the energy crisis was a hoax concocted by the oil companies.[42]

The President offered yet another compromise: A 39-month phased decontrol would start slowly, so that its impact would be delayed until late 1976, after the next election. As Frank Zarb candidly noted, this schedule "would ease the concerns in the minds of some Members of Congress."[43] But with this plan, Ford had begun losing what little support he had previously enjoyed from conservative Republicans and oil-state Democrats. The initiative shifted to Congress, wherein the energy committees began to mark-up their own legislation – the Energy Policy and Conservation Act.

Late in the fall of 1975, the Energy Policy and Conservation Act (EPCA) emerged from a conference committee containing many of the provisions President Ford had wanted. However, its policy for crude-oil pricing was radically different. The congressional Democrats who managed the bills had decided to roll back the price of domestic oil and extend controls for at least 40 months. EPCA set three different prices for crude oil, not to exceed a composite price

---

[41] U.S. Congress, House, *Hearings on the Presidential Energy Program*, pp. 578–582, 594–595. Independent producers were especially chary of a windfall profits tax which they felt would affect them "most critically" in the event it were applied to new or stripper oil. The API seemed to appreciate the political necessity for some form of tax, but just could not accept one without reasonable plowback deductions.
[42] Richard Corrigan, "A Decision at the Polls May Not Hinge on the Price at the Pump," *National Journal Reports*, April 3, 1976, pp. 440–445; also, William Tucker, "The Wreck of the Auto Industry," *Harpers*, November 1980, pp. 45–60.
[43] U.S. Congress, House, *President's Decontrol Proposals*, p. 556.

initially set at $7.66 per barrel. "Lower tier" oil was old oil, held at the price of $5.25. "Upper tier" oil established an initial ceiling of $11.28 for what previously had been new oil, released oil, and stripper-well production. The highest tier applied to imported oil that the government could not control, and to stripper oil once it was exempted again in September 1976. The FEA could increase the composite to compensate for inflation and provide a 3 percent growth incentive, as long as the total did not exceed 10 percent each year. Larger increases had to be submitted to Congress. If the President wished to end controls at the end of 40 months, he would have to take positive action, subject to congressional review.[44] As long as OPEC and the U.S. price differed, the entitlements program would have to continue "to preserve competition."[45]

Gerald Ford disliked the pricing provisions of EPCA, almost as much as did oil producers. But EPCA was an omnibus bill that still contained much of his energy plan. After 16 months of effort, a veto would leave the President with an empty bowl when he faced the voters in New Hampshire's primary, just two months away. Although he resented being manhandled by Congress, Ford probably felt little remorse for the oil industry. Its support had been of little help. On December 22, the President signed EPCA into law, which probably cost him the Texas vote. His campaign strategy, like the EPCA, was a mistake.

Regulatory nightmare

The regulatory experience of price controls under the Energy Policy and Conservation Act bore a slight resemblance to that of import quotas under the Mandatory Oil Import Program. Once again, interaction of business and government was plagued by technical, bureaucratic, and political problems. Only with the FEA and price controls, all of those problems seemed infinitely worse. This was due, in part, to the inherent complexity of price controls, the breadth of the FEA's mandate, and the specificity of Congress' statutory instructions. Import quotas, involving physical units, were easier to estimate, implement, and enforce. Prices, on the other hand, are ephemeral measures of value, constantly affected by, and interacting with, subtle variations in the market. When government set price, even on a single type and source of crude oil, its unanticipated effects cascaded down through distribution channels and permeated the process of capital budgeting, from exploration investments to maintenance charges on stripper wells.

The FEA's task included setting multiple prices for crude oil and for a dozen refined products at each level of distribution; for allocating supplies of crude oil and products throughout the distribution chain; for balancing cost differentials among different categories of producers and refiners: and for doing all this

---

[44] *Public Law 94–163* (December 22, 1975).
[45] U.S. Congress, *Senate Report No. 94–516,* "Energy Policy and Conservation Act, Conference Report" (94th Cong., 1st Sess.), December 8, 1975, p. 203.

according to starting points and escalation schedules explicitly fixed in the EPCA. Moreover, the FEA's mandate included statutory objectives that were wholly contradictory. While protecting inefficient producers and refiners, it was to promote competition and maximize economic efficiency. While preventing inflation and enforcing rent control, it was to stimulate exploration and domestic supply.

Without disparaging the importance of these factors, it was the change in the market, and thus the political environment, that contributed most to the problems of implementing oil price controls. From 1972 on, shortage and upward pressure on prices prevailed in the U.S. domestic oil market. Moreover, the perception of shortage was worse than the reality. The fact that world oil markets had returned to temporary surplus by 1975 only complicated the policy issues and the regulatory problems. Until 1977, competition for market share within the industry was only one of several political interactions affecting the regulatory process. Oil companies were also caught in a political crossfire between activist congressional committees and the FEA, and between one administrative agency and another. Both the oil industry and the FEA labored in a hostile environment of public distrust, partisan rhetoric, and increasingly frequent attacks by the news media and so-called public interest lobbies. It is of little wonder that the record of oil price control during this period was among the most discouraging in the history of government regulation.

When the Federal Energy Administration set out to implement EPCA's provisions for crude oil pricing in 1976, it did so from a base of pre-existing regulations and the dependencies they had fostered. Thus, its starting point was the definition of old and new oil. (At the refining level, the FEA also began adjusting the Buy/Sell List and the Entitlements programs.) The FEA planned a three-stage process of formulating its major pricing rules. At each stage, it proposed alternatives, solicited and evaluated the industry's comments, issued its rule-making, and moved on to the next problem. Stage I restructured the price tiers. Stage II dealt with the process of escalation, and Stage III with incentives and adjustments. Industry participation was extensive and the regulators seemed willing to listen. But the complexity of the task, the diversity of advice, and the incremental process itself resulted in serious errors and inequities.

In the first round, there was widespread agreement that the number of price tiers should be limited to two for the sake of administrative simplicity. But as one FEA official had previously noted, "for every problem you solve, it seems you create two more."[46] For example, if the old category of "released oil" were to be eliminated, a new mechanism had to be devised to stimulate continued production of lower tier (old) oil. Natural decline rates had already pushed production from most old properties below the "Base Period Control Level" established by the Cost of Living Council in 1972.[47] Thus, there was a worsen-

---

[46] *National Journal Report*, May 25, 1974, p. 778.
[47] Federal Energy Administration, Energy Action No. 11, March 15, 1977, Enclosure B, p. 7.

ing disincentive to spend money on enhanced recovery, merely to maintain production of lower tier oil ($5.25), when failure to do so would allow an old well's production to decline still further into the stripper category ($11.28).

To alleviate this distortion, the FEA proposed shifting the base period from 1972 to 1975 and applying a decline rate to it. Assuming an accurate choice of the new base period and a realistic decline rate, this system would allow a gradual reduction of the amount of lower tier oil and leave enhanced recovery from old wells eligible to receive new oil prices. But this was easier said than done. Several firms, anticipating problems in the choice of a base period that did not mask previous efforts at enhanced recovery, offered contrary advice for determining decline rates.[48] As it turned out, the FEA overestimated the initial share of lower tier production, underestimated the decline rate, and did mask the fruits of earlier enhanced recovery efforts.[49] This, in turn, resulted in a sharper-than-expected decline of lower tier production that fouled up the statutory escalation of composite price.

In its Stage II ruling, the FEA decided that the composite price should be increased by 10 percent, the maximum allowed by law. At issue was how the increase should be divided between lower and upper tier oil. Firms with a larger portion of old oil obviously felt that the lower tier should receive the lion's share of the increase. In support of this view, Gulf noted that, since 1972, the unit cost of slowing production decline had increased by 21 percent annually. To minimize premature well-abandonment, the price increase should be as large as possible.[50] Firms with more upper tier oil took the opposite view. To stimulate exploration, the price of new oil should at least keep pace with inflation, and preferably close the gap that EPCA created between new oil and the world market price.[51] With conventional bureaucratic wisdom, the FEA chose to divide the increase equally between the two tiers. This too proved mistaken because it hastened the decline of lower tier production.

By the time Stage III of the implementation process was under way in May 1976, there was general agreement within the oil industry that after a few months' experience with the EPCA, the costs "of finding, developing and producing crude in the United States are outrunning the escalators applied to crude prices."[52] Not only was the lower tier price fostering well abandonment, or deterioration to stripper status, but the upper tier price was allegedly too low to justify the costs of new wildcat exploration, deep offshore drilling, or enhanced tertiary recovery.[53] Moreover, the system of crude-oil price controls

---

[48] Continental Oil Company, "Comments Regarding the Notice of Proposed Rulemaking (10 CFR Parts 210 and 212)," January 22, 1976, pp. 5–6; also, Gulf Oil Corporation, "Comments on Proposed Rule Making for Domestic Crude Oil Prices," January 23, 1967, p. 2.

[49] Interview, Gulf E&P Company.

[50] Gulf Oil Corporation, "Comments on Proposed Rulemaking for Domestic Crude Oil Prices – Phase II," March 17, 1976, pp. 2–3.

[51] FEA, *Energy Action No. 11*, Enclosure B, pp. 24–25.

[52] "Statement of Gulf Oil Corporation, Third Stage Implementation of EPCA," June 2, 1976, p. 2.

[53] Continental Oil Company, "Pricing Amendments – Third Stage Additional Incentives, Company Positions, Written Testimony," June 14, 1976.

was creating more problems than the FEA could handle within the framework of EPCA. As one executive noted, the third stage proceedings were "evidence that regulation requires an ever increasing maze of rules, amendments to rules and clarification of rules."[54] Although the FEA solicited comments on market-level pricing for stripper wells and various categories of high-cost production, it ultimately deferred to Congress where the only authority to amend EPCA lay.

Congress passed the Energy Conservation and Production Act in August of 1976. This law amended the pricing provisions of EPCA in three respects: (1) it expanded the definition of stripper-well properties; (2) it exempted stripper-well production from price controls altogether; and (3) it modified the requirements for escalating the composite price of crude oil.[55] The first two changes, although rationalized by pleas for optimal recovery, were the fruit of intense lobbying by independent producers and royalty owners. The third change was a more interesting halfway measure designed to cope with an emerging regulatory crisis.

Because lower tier oil production had declined unexpectedly, the FEA discovered in June that the actual composite price (based on four-month-old data) exceeded the statutory level by 14 cents a barrel. This meant that between February and the end of June, oil company receipts were $422 million more than Congress had allowed. This situation left the FEA with no choice but to freeze the price of upper tier oil on July 1st. In its amendments, Congress made a veiled effort to relieve this problem by decoupling the escalator from the rate of inflation. Henceforth, the FEA could increase the composite price (for 1977) by the maximum 10 percent, even if the inflation rate declined. But the conference committee was unwilling to admit that the composite-price ceiling was conceptually flawed. Instead, it attributed the problem to economic recovery and the fact that "EPCA has been more successful than expected."[56] Indeed, it was so successful that the price freeze had to extend for a year, thoroughly discouraging domestic exploration and stimulating even greater reliance on OPEC.

The regulatory problems of crude-oil pricing paled in comparison to the bureaucratic difficulties and political machinations of the Entitlements Program. But because the Entitlements Program was a mirror image of the Mandatory Oil Import Program, as developed in Chapter 6, only a cursory summary is warranted here. In a controlled market, lower tier domestic oil had all the same characteristics as cheap imported oil prior to 1970. And, like import tickets, entitlements were initially devised for a single purpose – to neutralize the impact of price controls on competition by equalizing refiners' acquisition costs. With the enactment of EPCA, fractional entitlements became necessary so that both upper and lower tier oil could henceforth be included in the system of "equitable" distribution.

---

[54] Continental Oil Company, "Statement by F. E. Ellis on Third Stage of Implementation of the EPCA: Additional Incentives for Domestic Crude Oil Production," June 1976, p. 1.
[55] *Public Law 94–385* (August 14, 1976).
[56] U.S. Congress, House, "Conference Report on H. R. 12169," in *Congressional Record*, August 4, 1976, p. H9359.

The program grew less and less simple. By 1978, the process of intrafuel politics had transformed entitlements into a system of illogical and inefficient subsidies. Independent refiners received immense cash transfers from the integrated companies, based on the rationale of preventing a "margin squeeze."[57] The distribution of entitlements was inversely graduated – a so-called small refiners' bias – allegedly to mitigate advantages that resulted from economies of scale.[58] This became an incentive, as one critic noted, "to bring out of mothballs every piece of refining junk that could be mustered, regardless of its inefficiency."[59] California refiners again had their own special arrangements, and another program of appeals and exceptions piled subsidy upon subsidy with no consistent logic other than political intimidation. The New England Congressional Caucus attained the crowning achievement by winning an entitlements allocation for importers of residual oil. But this incentive to import was so explicit that it highlighted the absurdity of the entire program and helped, finally to bring it under serious scrutiny.

During its brief existence, the Federal Energy Administration was subject to intense criticism from Congress, the oil industry, the news media, and consumer groups. This is hardly surprising in view of its political environment and a market characterized by shortage and rising price. Unfortunately, these conditions also prevented the development of an effective working relationship between oil-industry managers and FEA regulators. For the people involved, this was the most frustrating and painful aspect of the entire price-control episode.

Technical incompetence on the part of FEA staff was a major source of friction that hampered regulatory relationships. The distrustful political climate of Washington forbade the FEA from hiring more than a minimal number of experienced oil-industry personnel. Fewer than one out of twenty FEA employees had any industry background, let alone relevant experience, and those few were continually investigated and badgered by congressional committees.[60] Lawyers, accountants, and bureaucrats transferred from other agencies took

---

[57] Concern for a margin squeeze of independent refiners derives from the idea that crude oil profits are like subsidies to integrated oil companies that allow them to intentionally forego profits at the refinery level (which independent refiners can obviously not afford). This thesis was originally formulated in M. DeChazeau and A. Kahn, *Integration and Competition in the Petroleum Industry* (New Haven: Yale University Press, 1959). For an excellent analysis of the small refiner bias and refutation of the margin squeeze thesis, see Edward J. Mitchell, "The Small Refiner Subsidy," in U.S. Congress, House, Committee on Interstate and Foreign Commerce, Subcommittee on Energy and Power, *DOE Entitlements Program – Hearings* (95th Cong., 2nd Sess.), June 1978, pp. 524–534.

[58] See U.S. Congress, Senate, Committee on Interior and Insular Affairs, *Energy Action No. 2 – Small Refiners Entitlements* (94th Cong., 2nd Sess.), May 1976. In his article, Mitchell also points out that the economies of scale rationale is patently fallacious, because most of the refineries operated by large refiners (in terms of aggregate capacity) are as small as those operated by independent companies that qualified for the bias.

[59] J. L. Schweizer, "Consequences of Two-Tiered Crude Pricing," *Proceedings of the Symposium on Rate Design Problems of Regulated Industries* (1975), p. 173.

[60] William A. Johnson, "Why U.S. Energy Policy Has Failed," in R. J. Kalter and W. A. Vogley, *Energy Supply and Government Policy* (Ithaca: Cornell University Press, 1976), pp. 280–305.

several years, if at all, to acquire sufficient technical knowledge to formulate detailed pricing regulations that made any sense. And for much the same reasons, there was little or no cooperation between the FEA and the oil companies, either through informal or institutional relations. With FEA staff discouraged from lunching with industry officials and required to log each meeting and telephone conversation, any transfer of knowledge or mutual resolution of problems through personal interaction was unlikely. The National Petroleum Council, which during the 1970's was more or less defunct, had no relations with the FEA, and no other advisory councils filled the void. Although the API and some of the major companies tried to be responsive to requests for technical data, communications were tenuous, at best.[61]

Bureaucratic ineptitude went hand-in-hand with the FEA's technical difficulties. The Cost of Living Council had been a relatively small and reportedly energetic group, committed to inflation-fighting and trying hard to make its regulations work. But more than one industry official sensed changes in attitude and procedure when the FEA took over. Distrust of the oil companies accounted for part of this change, but so did organizational uncertainty and more rigid requirements of administrative procedure. Between 1974 and 1977, the FEA underwent three major reorganizations and had four administrators, while its personnel continued to increase rapidly.[62] All this time, the FEA's rule making required pre-notification, commentary, hearings, and formal promulgation, compounded by amendments, clarifications, exceptions and appeals.

In its first 24 months, the FEA published 5,000 pages of rules in the *Federal Register,* supplemented by multiple volumes of guidelines and explanations. The law required the FEA to gather extensive data from the industry, conduct continuous audits and frequent enforcement actions, and report everything in a formal and standardized manner.[63] The net effect of these requirements was that government intervention penetrated even the normal conduct of the oil industry's day-to-day business. Routine transactions required application and approval, or at least notification. Changes in supplier relationships, for example, generated two to three thousand applications monthly in 1976. The procedure for selling a refinery was nearly overwhelming.[64] While procedural inertia prevented progress, constant change fostered uncertainty. Productivity was lost in the shuffle.

Persistent political interference with the regulatory process further debilitated administrative effectiveness. Managers and regulators alike attested to the severity and disruptiveness of this pressure which left the FEA "between a rock

---

61 Interviews with the author, Continental Oil Company, Houston, Texas, November 1980.
62 The Federal Energy Office, originally in the Executive Office of the President, took over from the CLC. In April 1974, it became the Federal Energy Administration, a quasi-autonomous agency that was, theoretically, responsible to Rogers Morton, chairman of the President's Energy Resources Council. In 1977, the FEA was absorbed in a reorganization that created the Department of Energy. William Simon, John Sawhill, Frank Zarb, and John O'Leary were its successive administrators.
63 W. A. Johnson, "Why U.S. Energy Policy Has Failed," pp. 296–299.
64 P. W. MacAvoy, *Federal Energy Administration Regulation,* pp. 48–50.

and a hard place."[65] Political interference generally took two forms. First, there were daily complaints from individual congressmen in response to local pressures from dealers, jobbers, refiners, producers, and consumers. Invariably, the complaints were directed to senior officals who would then have to interfere with lower-level operations to get answers or make adjustments. Needless to say, this fostered an atmosphere of political intimidation among agency staff and professionals. Thus, an oil company might lay out a good technical solution to some regulatory problem, but the bureaucrat would often respond, "Yes, that makes sense, but it's politically infeasible."[66]

Narrowly focused oversight by congressional committees created other problems. Subcommittee chairmen, responsible for energy, economics, small business, and antitrust matters, took to conducting investigative hearings on extremely technical matters, either to mollify constituents or gain political recognition. John Dingell was especially skilled at getting industry spokesmen to criticize the FEA, an easy accomplishment which obviously damaged working relationships. "The next day when you showed up at the FEA," said one oilman, "you'd pay for it."[67]

Indeed, the industry did pay for it, as did consumers and taxpayers. Even aside from foregone production, distributional effects, and losses to economic efficiency, government regulation of crude oil prices was costly. Just the FEA's standard reporting requirements involved more than 200,000 industry respondents in a commitment of 5 million man-hours annually. One estimate suggests that refiners alone might have spent over $500 million a year on regulatory matters, and fuel-oil marketers something like $200 million.[68] Many of these costs were passed through to consumers, who also paid more for products because of allocative bottlenecks and the higher operating costs of small refineries under the Entitlements Program. For the taxpayer, the yearly tab was somewhere between $40 million (the budget for FEA regulatory programs) and $130 million (FEA's total administrative budget).[69] The benefits of price regulation were somewhat less.

Window of opportunity

Jimmy Carter became president three years after the Arab oil embargo. During that time, America's dependence on foreign oil increased from 36 to 46 percent of total consumption. Domestic production of crude oil declined meanwhile, by 10 percent. Whatever else they might have accomplished, oil price controls had certainly not helped restore equilibrium between supply and demand. With the Entitlements Program becoming a national embarrassment and the regulatory burden obviously mounting, Carter felt that change was in order, as part of his larger National Energy Plan.

[65] Interview, Continental Oil Company.
[66] Interview, Gulf E&P Company.
[67] *Ibid.*
[68] P. S. MacAvoy, *Federal Energy Administration Regulation*, pp. 47–48.
[69] *Ibid.*, 54–58.

During his campaign, Carter made relatively few promises regarding energy. He decried proliferation of nuclear power, spoke enthusiastically of conservation, proposed a cabinet-level energy department, and called for decontrol of new natural gas prices. This last suggestion, together with vague comments on the need for replacement-cost prices for oil, helped him win the votes of Texas and Oklahoma, deemed crucial to his victory. But not until after his election did Carter begin seriously to consider a policy for oil pricing.

James Schlesinger, a former secretary of defense and chairman of the Atomic Energy Commission, was the President's closest energy advisor. He shared the President's view that physical depletion of petroleum and natural gas posed an immense threat to American economic and political hegemony. Both Schlesinger and Carter were determined to redress the incoherence of U.S. energy policy, but they disdained the political process of coalition-building through piecemeal compromise. Schlesinger's own management philosophy seemed an admixture of his economics Ph.D. from Harvard and his experience in strategic planning. While sensitive to the realities of the market, he nonetheless believed that business and government should cooperate to develop resources in the common national interest. Toward this end, Schlesinger was determined that U.S. oil be priced at the world-market level and that EPCA's system of entitlements should be abolished. However, he also considered OPEC a cartel, and was loath to concede all the rents it created to domestic oil producers. For Schlesinger, at least, this reservation was more a philosophical commitment to political balance than a concern for distributional equity.[70]

After the inauguration, Schlesinger and a team of 15 advisors worked furiously for eight weeks to prepare a comprehensive National Energy Plan. In a dramatic televised address on April 18, 1977, Jimmy Carter announced the Plan which he characterized as "the moral equivalent of war." Its proposals would probably be unpopular, admitted the President, causing "inconvenience and sacrifice." But the alternative would likely be a "national catastrophe." Carter warned that "all the special interest groups in the country will attack the part of this plan that affects them directly," but he insisted that "there should be only one test for this program – whether it will help our country."[71]

The goals of the Plan were to reduce the growth rate of energy demand below 2 percent and to cut oil imports to 6 million barrels daily from a potential level of 16 million. To do so, the Plan comprised of more than one hundred legislative proposals, clustered in five basic categories: (1) conservation; (2) incentives to convert power plants to coal; (3) incentives for non-conventional energy sources; (4) natural gas pricing; and (5) the Crude Oil Equalization Tax.[72] This entire framework of policy was to be administered by a new Department of Energy, proposed in a separate reorganization bill. James Schlesinger would be its first Secretary.

During the next 18 months, Congress engaged in one of the most compli-

---

[70] James Schlesinger, interview with the author, March 1982.
[71] "Presidential Energy Address, April 18, 1977," Commerce Clearing House, Inc., *Energy Management*, 1977, pp. 739–743.
[72] Executive Office of the President, *The National Energy Plan* (Wash.: GPO, 1977).

cated and intense legislative battles of its history. Nearly a dozen committees were involved with the various pieces of the National Energy Act. Literally hundreds of industry groups, consumer and environmental organizations, and labor unions testified at the hearings and established semi-permanent command posts near the Capitol. Under extremely tight control by Majority Leader Tip O'Neill, the House passed Carter's package intact, in only five months. But in the Senate, the National Energy Plan came unhinged. It started when Southern Democrats, from the oil and gas producing states, took issue with the centerpiece of the Plan – the Crude Oil Equalization Tax.

The tax was designed as a compromise for the Democratic Party. Its aim was to impose world market prices on consumers, provide some incentive for producers, and to capture for the government the economic rents created by OPEC. Still, it was not decontrol. President Carter held to his view that "price controls on oil should be retained as long as world oil prices remain subject to arbitrary control."[73] The price of both lower and upper tier oil (discovered before April 1977) would be controlled indefinitely, increasing no faster than the general rate of inflation. New oil, discovered after April, 1977, would rise over a three-year period to the 1977 world price. Thereafter, it too would track the inflation rate. Oil from enhanced recovery and from stripper wells would be free of price controls. In conjunction with these pricing schedules, a tax would be levied on all domestic oil, equal to the difference between its price and that of OPEC. This "equalization tax," applied in stages over three years, would presumably force consumers to pay a price that reflected the replacement cost of petroleum products; that is, if refiners, on whom the tax would be levied, could pass it through to their customers.

The Carter administration estimated that its pricing proposal would have desirable economic effects from most any perspective. By 1980, the average price of oil would be only 16 percent higher in constant dollars than otherwise under the existing formula ($14.69 instead of $12.67 per barrel). Of course, this assumed that OPEC prices did not increase faster than inflation. With the equalization tax, this price would reduce demand for oil by 800,000 barrels daily in 1980, and by 3.9 million in 1985.[74] Meanwhile, domestic production of crude oil would be increased by 200,000 barrels a day.[75] Better yet, this increased production could be achieved without allowing producers to capture a windfall. The tax would reduce producer's revenues by $11 billion between 1978 and 1985.[76] Finally, and of no small consideration given the deficit in the budget, the equalization tax would generate substantial receipts by a popular means. Treasury Secretary Michael Blumenthal estimated that the equalization tax would

[73] *Ibid.*, 50.
[74] Congressional Budget Office, Staff Working Paper, *President Carter's Energy Proposals: A Perspective* (Wash.: GPO, 1977). p. 16.
[75] Executive Office of the President, *The National Energy Plan*, p. 96.
[76] Alvin Alm (Executive Office of the President, Energy Policy and Planning) to Henry Jackson, May 27, 1977, in U.S. Congress, Senate, Committee on Energy and Natural Resources, *Economic Impact of President Carter's Energy Program* (95th Cong., 1st Sess.) May 1977, p. 90.

gross $38 billion over five years which, after assorted refunds and reduced income tax liability, would leave $27 billion for the federal government.[77]

Not everyone agreed that the Crude Oil Equalization Tax was the best solution to the dilemma of oil pricing; least of all, the oil producers. James Schlesinger expected independent refiners to oppose it, if only because it would mean the end of Entitlements. But he did assume that producers would either support or acquiesce to a compromise that would decontrol new oil and effectively raise their revenues (compared to the EPCA program). His optimism was not entirely unfounded. Charles DiBona, president of the API, may have given Schlesinger the mistaken impression that the industry would accept such a tax, levied on refiners.[78] Then too, several of the largest companies, the "enlightened" ones as Schlesinger called them, had privately acceded to the plan, but refused to support it publicly. In part, they wished to avoid creating dissension within the industry, and they also thought they might "get it all" (i.e., decontrol without a tax).[79]

In public, the American Petroleum Institute opposed the Equalization Tax almost as pointedly as did independent producers. The API prepared its testimony carefully, so as to "serve as a benchmark throughout the legislative process." After going through several drafts in a subcommittee of industry tax experts, the statement was approved by the API's Public Issues Committee, then chaired by Jerry McAfee, chairman of Gulf Oil.[80] Harold Hoopman, of Marathon, made the presentation. Besides opposing the tax in principle, the API objected that it was too large and that refiners would have to absorb as much as one-third of it. Since this would reduce the industry's profits by an estimated $2.5 billion annually, it could scarcely be called an "excess" profits tax. However, "if concerns over 'excess profits' persist," allowed Hoopman, then a better approach would be an "excise tax applied at the wellhead," based on "the actual increase in revenue to each producer."[81] Subsequent testimony before the Senate revealed extensive qualifications to this apparent offer, including exemption of all new and high-cost oil, application to a declining production base of old oil, and allowance for state and local taxes and the impact of inflation.[82]

The Independent Petroleum Association of America did not mince words or show interest in compromise. It greeted the equalization tax much as it had President Ford's plan for a windfall profits tax: it "embodies the worst of all

[77] U.S. Congress, Senate, Committee on Finance, *Energy Tax Act of 1977* (95th Cong., 1st Sess.), August 1977, Pt. 1, p. 140.

[78] Interview with the author, Gulf Oil Corporation, Pittsburgh, PA., August 1980.

[79] Interview, James Schlesinger.

[80] Interview with the author, American Petroleum Institute, Tax Department, Washington, October 1980.

[81] U.S. Congress, House, Committee on Ways and Means, *Tax Aspects of President Carter's Energy Program* (95th Cong., 1st Sess.), May–June 1977, Pt. 2, pp. 124–125.

[82] U.S. Congress, Senate, Committee on Energy and Natural Resources, Subcommittee on Energy Conservation and Regulation, *Crude Oil Pricing Amendments of 1977* (95th Cong., 1st Sess.), September 1977, pp. 114–122.

possible options." It would hurt consumers and do nothing to increase supply.[83] Worse still, it would "become Government's new balancing mechanism for regulating the economics of the petroleum industry," a function that domestic producers no longer supported.[84] And if they no longer supported it, neither would Senator Russell Long.

Ironically, consumer advocates opposed Carter's pricing plan just as obdurately, because of its intended effect of transferring income from consumers to the government. Although pleased that it would prevent oil companies from getting windfall profits, the Consumers' Federation nonetheless urged Congress to abandon the idea because of its premise – "that domestic petroleum prices must be raised to the OPEC-determined 'world market price.'"[85] This source of opposition had a regional component as well. Senators who represented the industrial states of the Northeast thought that the tax would shift income away from their oil-consuming states by redistributing the tax receipts nationally.

While Senator Long killed the equalization tax in his Finance Committee, opponents of decontrol succeeded in blocking alternatives. Thus, when Jimmy Carter finally signed the National Energy Act in October 1978, it contained no provisions for oil pricing. Controls would simply continue as constituted under the 1975 Act. Oil producers had failed to "get it all," but were nonetheless satisfied at having defeated the tax. Many were convinced that price controls under Carter's plan might have been as costly and difficult to implement as existing regulations.[86] Consumerists viewed its defeat as a victory, even though existing policies would do nothing to reduce their dependence on OPEC. Political analysts blamed the Carter administration for springing the National Energy Plan on Congress and the public, and for failing to build a coalition of support through effective congressional relations.

With the benefit of hindsight, James Schlesinger concluded that political and economic circumstances had simply not been right. With real prices declining and supplies temporarily abundant, there had been no sense of urgency to break Washington's political inertia. Even with a windfall profits tax, oil price decontrol would be politically feasible only given a "window of opportunity": a supply crisis prior to a major price hike by OPEC.[87]

The Iranian revolution and sudden rise to power of Ayatollah Ruholla Khomeini came as a surprise to the U.S. government. So did the abrupt stoppage of Iranian oil production. As late as September 1978, the National Iranian Oil Company was producing 6 million barrels a day, very near its capacity. Revolutionary disorder, together with the departure of foreign technicians, resulted in a precipitous decline in output. By January 1979, Iranian oil production was virtually zero. Although it recovered somewhat by March, there was scarcely

[83] *Ibid.*, 41.
[84] U.S. Congress, House, *Tax Aspects of President Carter's Energy Program*, p. 225.
[85] U.S. Congress, Senate, *Energy Tax Act of 1977*, p. 717.
[86] Interview, Gulf E&P Company.
[87] Interview, James Schlesinger.

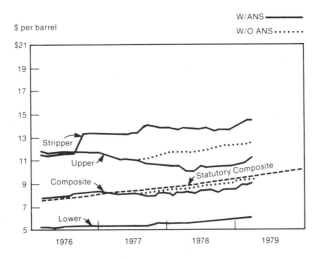

Chart 10-2
DOE Regulations — Crude Oil Prices
With and Without Alaska North Slope

Source: Gulf Oil Exploration and Production Co., Houston, Texas.

enough for domestic consumption. Moreover, without skilled technicians, Iran's production capacity had already begun to deteriorate. Continuing turmoil inside Iran, together with the intense xenophobia of its revolutionary government, offered little hope that oil exports would recover quickly.[88]

Prior to the curtailment of Iranian oil production, world oil prices had remained remarkably stable. Since 1974, crude oil prices had risen less than the average rate of inflation in industrialized countries. As of September 1978, the marker price of Saudi Arabian light crude stood at $12.70 per barrel (a U.S. landed cost of $14.03), scarcely a dollar above OPEC's posted price of January 1974. In the United States, the composite price of domestic oil was still about $4.00 a barrel below that of Saudi Arabia, and stripper oil, which reflected the market price, was about $14.00 (see Chart 10-2). Although the level of crude oil imports remained as high as in April 1977 (6.8 million barrels a day), domestic production, excluding Alaska, had declined by another 6 percent.[89]

For several years, OPEC members did not significantly expand their oil production capacity because the first price shock had created a surplus. Neither did U.S. producers, because of the uncertainty caused by price controls. As

[88] Parts of this section were previously published as a Harvard Business School case entitled, "Carter, OPEC, and 'Big Oil': 1979," No. 0-382–116 (Boston: HBS Case Services, 1982).
[89] U.S. Department of Energy, International Affairs Office of Market Analysis, International Energy Indicators, Feb. - Mar., 1982 (DOE/EIA0010/18), pp. 16–18.

Schlesinger explained, the Iranian crisis late in 1978 "stretched taut the world's productive capacity, led to sharp increases in spot prices, and provided a basis for higher than anticipated OPEC price increases."[90] In December, OPEC announced a 60-cent-a-barrel price increase, but on the Rotterdam spot market, prices skyrocketed from about $10.50 to $22.00 per barrel in less than three months. Schlesinger, who had been predicting another doubling of OPEC prices in the early 1980's, now realized that "developments in Iran [had] brought together the long-term and the short."[91] Quite possibly, the window of opportunity for oil price decontrol had opened; but it could be expected to close before long.

President Carter had not expected energy policy to be a significant political issue in 1979. He scarcely mentioned energy in his State of the Union Address. His "major domestic priority [was] to reduce inflation" since that was "the major domestic concern of the American people."[92] Obviously, this would be no less difficult if oil prices rose sharply. But the political risk of another shortage was an even worse prospect.

At least temporarily, the Iranian crisis complicated the Administration's oil pricing options and further polarized Congress. Under the provisions of EPCA, non-discretionary price controls would lapse at the end of May 1979. Before then, the President would have to choose a course of action from among four alternatives: (1) allow immediate decontrol; (2) implement a phased decontrol; (3) continue controls through August 1981; or (4) ask Congress to enact a new program.

Within the Administration, there was a range of views. Schlesinger and Blumenthal wanted decontrol. Hamilton Jordan objected to decontrol because of its political consequences, and Stuart Eisenstadt and Vice-President Mondale worried about the distributional effects and the apparent unfairness of allowing cartel prices to prevail.[93] Alfred Kahn, chairman of the Council on Wage and Price Stability, objected to price controls in principle, but nonetheless favored them under the current inflationary situation. The President himself had difficulty deciding. At the summit meeting in Bonn the previous July, Carter had pledged "that the prices paid for oil in the United States shall be raised to the world level by the end of 1980."[94] But he remained unwilling to concede windfall profits to domestic oil producers.

---

[90] U.S. Congress, Joint Economic Committee, *Hearings on the 1979 Economic Report of the President* (96th Cong., 1st Sess.), January 1979, Pt. 1, p. 6.

[91] U.S. Congress, Senate, Committee on Energy and Natural Resources, *Iran and World Oil Supply* (96th Cong., 1st Sess.), March 1979, Pt. 3, p. 6. Prior to the Iranian crisis, the expectation that OPEC would again double prices was not widely shared. Many observers agreed with Representative David Stockman, who wrote in the Fall of 1978 that "the global economic conditions necessary for another major unilateral price action by OPEC are not likely to re-emerge for more than a decade – if ever." See, David Stockman, "The Case Against a National Energy Policy," *The Public Interest*, No. 53, Fall 1978, pp. 20–21.

[92] "State of the Union Message, January 25, 1979," *Public Papers of the Presidents: Jimmy Carter 1979* (Wash.: GPO, 1980), p. 122.

[93] Interview, James Schlesinger.

[94] Quoted in *Wall Street Journal*, February 2, 1979.

Congressmen of all stripes were alarmed by oil price developments, and the potential for a supply crisis caused genuine panic. Symbolic of this concern, the chairman of the Joint Economic Committee chose Schlesinger as the first witness for the 1979 hearings on the President's Economic Report. The Energy Secretary warned that "unless we constrain demand, we will face either rapidly rising prices for oil or a reduction worldwide in income, output, and unemployment." Conservation was working, he conceded, but far too slowly, and rationing was no solution in the absence of "patriotic fervor." In response to criticism of the Administration's past policies, Schlesinger bluntly reminded the Committee that Congress had itself failed to resolve the issue of oil pricing.[95]

Despite the perilous supply situation, most Democrats still appeared to oppose decontrol. Many did not believe that either demand or supply of oil was at all price elastic. This was certainly the view of Charles Vanik of Ohio when he complained that "decontrol would result in horrendous profits to the oil industry which are not likely to be invested in developing new sources of oil."[96] Senator Dale Bumpers of Arkansas felt that decontrol would "be an outrageous breach of trust with the American people because the American people are not going to get anything in exchange for all this deregulation."[97]

As Schlesinger's efforts to promote decontrol became more and more apparent, this congressional rhetoric took on substance in the form of personal attacks. Speaking for the New England delegation, Senator John Durkin of New Hampshire suggested that Schlesinger resign, because he tolerated "profiteering at public expense" and shared "the oil industry's self-serving allusion that all will be well if we only pay higher prices."[98] Senators Deconcini (Arizona) and Metzenbaum (Ohio) carried these complaints one step further with a formal request for Schlesinger's resignation.[99] This strategy for blocking administrative decontrol would suggest that its congressional opponents realized they no longer had a majority of support in their own house nor the benefit of statutory inertia.

The Schlesinger-Blumenthal view eventually prevailed, and this time markets, timing, and political momentum favored presidential initiative. On April 5, in a nationally televised speech, President Carter announced that he intended to decontrol the price of oil gradually over the next 30 months. To prevent oil companies from reaping "huge and undeserved windfall profits," he also proposed a special tax designed to capture half of the expected increase in oil revenues. An Energy Trust Fund would be established, from which the windfall taxes would be recycled as energy credits for the poor, subsidies for mass transit, and the development of alternate energy sources.[100]

As originally proposed, the decontrol schedule was relatively simple. Upper-

[95] U.S. Congress, *Hearings on the 1979 Economic Report*, pp. 2–8.
[96] *Congressional Record*, March 21, 1979, p. H1535.
[97] *Congressional Record*, February 26, 1979, p. S1754.
[98] U.S. Congress, Senate, *Iran and World Oil Supply*, Pt. 2. pp. 5, 64.
[99] *Congressional Record*, March 14, 1979, pp. S2669–2671.
[100] "Energy Address to the Nation, April 5, 1979," *Public Papers of the Presidents: Jimmy Carter, 1979*, Vol. I, pp. 609–614.

tier oil would be allowed to rise to world prices in monthly increments. Volumes of lower-tier oil would be released into the upper tier at the imputed rate of production decline (1.5 percent). Oil from marginal properties and tertiary recovery could rise to the world price in two stages, and newly discovered oil would be exempt from controls immediately.[101] Assuming OPEC prices remained constant in real terms, pre-tax producer revenues would be $59 billion larger than without decontrol by 1985.[102]

Carter's Windfall Profits Tax was also simple, at first. A severance tax of 50 percent, adjusted for inflation, would be applied to producer revenues from the upper-tier price increases and from lower-tier production released to the upper-tier category. In the likely event that OPEC raised prices faster than inflation, an excise tax of 50 percent would apply to additional producer revenue resulting from the excess of OPEC prices over inflation. With no OPEC price hike, this schedule would impose a windfall tax liability of $25 billion on domestic producers, leaving about $30 billion in windfall revenue to be taxed at the conventional rate for corporate income.[103]

By adopting a strategy of administrative decontrol followed by congressional enactment of a windfall profits tax, Jimmy Carter had "bitten the bullet" – accepting the political consequences. Congress could blame him for decontrol, and then take credit for passing a punitive, if not confiscatory, tax. Henry Jackson and others believed it was a "terrible mistake" not to make decontrol contingent on enactment of the tax.[104] But Schlesinger was determined that decontrol begin immediately, before OPEC decided on a serious price hike; otherwise, the window of opportunity might close.[105] Because Carter had considerable administrative discretion, his strategy was to hold out the threat of continued regulation to gain Russell Long's acquiescence and to control excessive opposition by the oil industry. As it turned out, the more difficult task would be to keep congressional liberals from expanding the tax so much that it would leave no incentives for domestic oil production.

Chief executives of the major companies conceded, in private, that oil price decontrol was politically infeasible without a windfall profits tax. Moreover, this proposal was certainly a better deal for the industry than was the 1977 proposal, especially with the prospect of large increases in world prices. Once again, however, independent producers felt a windfall profits tax was "disastrous energy policy," and opposed it as adamantly as ever. Speaking for the Independent Petroleum Association, Jack Allen claimed that independents were responsible for most exploration and development of new oil, and would be injured most by the tax. Just because the major firms used their worldwide

---

[101] U.S. Congress, House, Committee on Interstate and Foreign Commerce, Subcommittee on Energy and Power, *Analysis of the President's April 5, 1979 Crude Oil Pricing Plan* (96th Cong., 1st Sess.), Committee Print, April 1979, pp. 4–6.

[102] Congressional Budget Office, *The Decontrol of Domestic Oil Prices: An Overview* (Wash.: CBO, 1979), p. 28.

[103] *Ibid.*, 38–39.

[104] Quoted in *Wall Street Journal*, April 24, 1979.

[105] Interview, James Schlesinger.

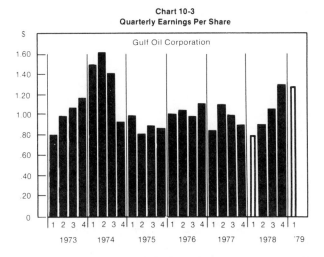

Chart 10-3
Quarterly Earnings Per Share

Source: Testimony of Jerry McAfee in U.S. Congress, Finance Committee,
Crude Oil Tax (96th Cong., 1st sess.), July 1979, p. 455.

profits to make non-oil acquisitions (Exxon was then trying to buy Reliance Electric), "it does not make sense," Allen argued, "to penalize the domestic petroleum producing industry because of public or political perceptions" of multinational companies.[106] Sensitive to the risk of an intrafuel rift, the major companies, represented by the API, decided to oppose the tax publicly in the hope of quashing disunity and minimizing the size and duration of the tax.[107]

Besides its intrafuel distributive aspects, the controversy over a windfall profits tax appeared to involve a trade-off between two substantive values: equity and efficiency. The Congressional Budget Office made a balanced effort to define this trade-off. The equity question related to the expectations of producers and the market power of OPEC. If producers made investments in exploration and development without expecting high OPEC prices, then the incremental revenue of decontrol could be considered a windfall. Also, if OPEC prices were the result of cartel behavior, rather than supply and demand, then the increment would also be a real windfall to domestic producers. Even if there was a windfall, that still left an issue of efficiency. That is, would the tax impair the ability of domestic producers to find and produce oil? Some econo-

---

[106] U.S. Congress, Senate, Finance Committee, *Hearings: Crude Oil Tax* (96th Cong., 1st Sess.), July 1979, pp. 210–217.
[107] Interview, Gulf Oil Corporation. One exception to this strategy was William Tavoulareas, president of Mobil. He annoyed his counterparts by proposing a compromise without informing the API Issues Committee. At a timely annual shareholders meeting, Tavoulareas offered to accept continued control of old oil prices (adjusted for inflation), in exchange for market pricing of all new oil, without a windfall profits tax. See W. E. Tavoulareas, "U.S. Crude Oil Pricing – A Proposal," delivered at Mobil Corporation's Annual Meeting, May 3, 1979.

Table 10-1. *Net income as a percentage of net worth, 10 years, 1969–1978*

Year	Petroleum	Total manufacturing
1969	11.9%	12.4%
1970	10.9	10.1
1971	11.2	10.8
1972	10.8	12.1
1973	15.6	14.9
1974	19.6	15.2
1975	13.9	12.6
1976	14.8	15.0
1977	14.0	14.9
1978	14.3	15.9

Source: Citibank, "Monthly Economic Letter," cited in Testimony of Jerry McAfee in U.S. Congress, Finance Committee, *Crude Oil Tax* (96th Cong., 1st sess.), July 1979, p. 456.

mists thought not, as long as it did not apply to new oil. Others argued for replacement-cost pricing of a depleting resource or claimed that risk made external financing so costly that oil companies needed a maximum cash flow.[108]

Both of these issues hinged on the oil industry's profitability, and in the spring of 1979, the most salient and politicized datum was the increase of 58 percent in the industry's first quarter profits over the year before. API spokesmen did their utmost to put the industry's profits in perspective.[109] Jerry McAfee tried to explain that the sharp first quarter increase was a fluke, and that longer-term measures of return on equity were far less impressive (see Chart 10-3 and Table 10-1). Moreover, the industry needed every bit of net income it received for capital expenditures in new exploration and production (Table 10-2). To many observers, however, these data merely showed that the oil industry was surviving under price controls. Opponents of decontrol remained unconvinced that future profits would look so modest.

For a few months, at least, congressional action on the Windfall Tax was reminiscent of the equalization tax. In June, the House passed a bill that would generate somewhat larger tax revenues than Carter requested. An amendment to increase the rate to 60 percent was not quite balanced by others to limit its duration beyond 1990 and to exempt certain marginal producers. In the Senate, the tax again ran into trouble, but this time it was temporary. The major companies apparently indicated they could live with a tax that made substantial

---

[108] Congressional Budget Office, *Decontrol of Domestic Oil Prices*, pp. 32–33.
[109] U.S. Congress, Senate, *Hearings: Crude Oil Tax*, pp. 253–257, 410–462, 515–546.

Table 10-2. *Net income, debt, and capital expenditures for a group of 27 petroleum companies*[a]

Term year	Return on equity (%)	Net income ($ bil.)	Capital expenditures ($ bil.)	Ratio of capital expenditures to net income	Long-term debt ($ bil.)
1972	9.4	6.9	13.2	1.9	21.9
1973	14.0	11.7	14.6	1.3	22.7
1974	17.3	16.4	22.9	1.4	25.6
1975	12.0	11.5	25.0	2.2	30.6
1976	12.9	13.1	26.8	2.1	36.2
1977	13.0	14.4	28.0	1.9	39.9

[a] The Chase Manhattan Bank.
Source: Testimony of Jerry McAfee in U.S. Congress, Finance Committee, *Crude Oil Tax* (96th Cong., 1st Sess.), July 1979, p. 462.

provision for plowback. President Carter greeted this idea with the first in a series of sharp rhetorical attacks on the oil industry. He called the plowback proposal a "charade" intended to "hoodwink the American people" and "plow under" the poor. He accused the industry of "selfishness."[110] Responding in kind, Russell Long asserted that the Windfall Tax threatened "the survival of freedom in this nation and on this planet."[111]

When OPEC prices began to rise in June, opposition to decontrol and support for a tax redoubled, much as Schlesinger had foreseen. A National Citizens' Coalition for the Windfall Profits Tax was formed, and Senator Kennedy denounced the Carter bill as a "fig leaf." Sensing this political momentum, Russell Long promptly shifted gears and admitted "that if we don't pass a windfall tax, the President is simply going to withdraw the [decontrol] plan and leave us in the mess we are in already."[112] With that, the Senate Finance Committee took up the bill, and the political debate snowballed into a classic distributional fight over the sources and uses of windfall tax revenues. Meanwhile, OPEC prices jumped from $14.55 to $18.00 to $26.00 per barrel over the next six months. As they did, the prospective windfall pie grew from $30 billion to nearly $300 billion.

In the ensuing paroxysm of political greed, cooperation within the oil industry broke down (as it did among proponents of the tax that were potential recipients of its revenues).[113] The conflict between independents and integrated majors became open and explicit when Senator Lloyd Bentsen of Texas

[110] Quoted in *Wall Street Journal*, April 24, 1979.
[111] Quoted in *Wall Street Journal*, May 8, 1979.
[112] Quoted in *Wall Street Journal*, June 18, 1979.
[113] Richard Corrigan, "Who'll Get the Largest Slices of the $1 Trillion 'Windfall Profits' Pie?" *National Journal*, November 10, 1979, pp. 1885–1888.

offered an amendment that would exempt the first 1,000 barrels of an independent producer's daily output. In return, the independents were willing to support an increase in the windfall tax rate to 75 percent. The Senate approved both amendments late in November, saving independents an estimated $10 billion and costing the majors about $22 billion.[114] By the time the conference committee met in December, every sub-group and individual firm had "started shooting for their own deals and particular needs."[115] Everyone lobbied for some kind of an exemption: Alaskan oil, offshore oil, deep wells, stripper wells, old oil, upper-tier oil, enhanced recovery, and so forth. The net effect of this intrafuel brokerage weakened the industry's ability to hold down the aggregate impact of the tax.

The conference committee finished its work on the Crude Oil Windfall Profits Tax Act in March 1980. Senate and House members agreed on a formula that would raise an estimated $227 billion in tax revenues by 1988. Independents lost their exemption, but did get a reduced rate. The major companies would have to pay variable rates of 50 to 70 percent on different vintages of crude oil. Basically, the Act divided oil production into three categories. Tier one, with a 70 percent tax rate, applied to old oil from fields in production prior to 1979. Tier two, at the 60 percent rate, included stripper oil and oil produced from National Petroleum Reserves. Tier three, liable to a 50 percent tax, included newly discovered oil (developed after 1978), production by tertiary recovery, heavy oil, and oil released from lower tiers as the program was phased-out over the next decade.[116]

Two weeks later, on the day Congress approved the Act, the *Wall Street Journal* published its lead editorial with a black border and entitled it, "Death of Reason." The tax, wrote the editors, "will sacrifice the nation's future security to its own unslakable thirst for revenues." It was "beyond belief that Congress would set out to destroy *this* industry in *this* decade." Many in the oil industry shared this view. Looking at the structure of three new tiers with their differential tax rates, it was difficult to see this as decontrol. At any rate, it would be hard to argue with the *Journal's* conclusion that "the evolution of this latest self-inflicted blow is bound up in the broader history of U.S. economic policy through the 1970's."[117] A week later, Jimmy Carter signed the bill into law.

The painful adjustment

There is no way to quantify precisely the economic costs and benefits of oil price regulation during the 1970's. However, most analysts have agreed that the benefit to American consumers was far outweighed by the costs. Crude oil price

[114] *Wall Street Journal*, November 28 and 29, 1979.
[115] Interview, Gulf Oil Corporation.
[116] U.S. Congress, House, *Report No. 96–817* (96th Cong., 2nd Sess.), "Conference Report: Crude Oil Windfall Profits Tax Act of 1980," March 7, 1980, pp. 92–115.
[117] *Wall Street Journal*, March 27, 1980.

regulation reduced domestic supply and stimulated imports.[118] Entitlements transferred up to $19 billion per year away from producers. Half or more of that revenue went to refiners rather than consumers.[119] Economic waste resulting from controls and entitlements is estimated to have cost between $1 and $6 billion annually.[120] Worse still, by providing a stimulus to domestic energy demand, price controls helped bolster the OPEC cartel, hurting other oil-consuming nations as well as ourselves.[121]

On the matter of preserving competition, there is little evidence that crude oil price controls or entitlements were of any benefit after the OPEC embargo. The FEA itself agreed that controls "denie[d] consumers the full benefits of competition" by fixing supplier-purchaser relationships and creating barriers to entry.[122] As early as 1975, the Federal Trade Commission concluded that decontrol would have no debilitating effects on small and non-integrated firms. "[W]e must again be careful," cautioned the FTC, "to distinguish between injury to specific competitors and generalized injury to the vigor of competition."[123]

Finally, the experience of oil price controls entailed considerable political costs. Public distrust of oil companies and animosity between the oil industry and government were heightened and reinforced for so long that any prospect for cooperation on substantive problems of energy policy in the 1980's became remote.

It seems reasonable to generalize on two conclusions that James Schlesinger drew from his experience. First, administrative allocation of energy resources cannot indefinitely run counter to the market. And second, it is doubtful whether economic efficiency and energy policy could be made compatible in the political environment of Washington that prevailed during the 1970's.[124]

---

[118] C. E. Phelps and R. T. Smith, *Petroleum Regulation: The False Dilemma of Decontrol* (Santa Monica: Rand Corporation, 1977); also, Stephen W. Chapel, *The Oil Entitlements Program and Its Effects on the Domestic Refining Industry* (Santa Monica: Rand Corporation, 1976); also, Calvin T. Roush, Jr., *Effects of Federal Price and Allocation Regulations on the Petroleum Industry*, Staff Report to the Federal Trade Commission (Wash.: GPO, 1976).

[119] K. Arrow and J. Kalt, *Petroleum Price Regulation*, p. 32.

[120] J. Kalt, *The Economics and Politics of Oil Price Regulation*, pp. 288–289.

[121] Robert Stobaugh and Daniel Yergin, *Energy Future* (New York: Random House, 1979), pp. 222–223.

[122] U.S. Congress, Senate, *Oversight – FEA Programs*, pp. 549–551.

[123] Federal Trade Commission, "Staff Report on the Effects of Decontrol on Competition in the Petroleum Industry," September 5, 1975, in U.S. Congress, Senate, Committee on Interior and Insular Affairs, *Oil Price Decontrol* (94th Cong., 1st Sess.), September 1975, p. 378.

[124] Interview, James Schlesinger.

11. Natural gas: the dilemma of regulatory transition

Under the effects of cost-based regulation, it took just 20 years of rapid growth and low prices to transform natural gas from a near-effluent to a scarce commodity. The 1968 downturn in net additions to reserves marked the beginning of a difficult transition in natural-gas regulation. By 1974, service to industrial customers in interstate gas markets had been widely curtailed – reaching 16 percent nationally, and worse in some areas.[1]

This chapter tells two interrelated stories. One is about regulatory process, and how adversary proceedings thwarted the Federal Power Commission's best efforts to change its regulatory standards. The other is about regulatory concepts, and how cost-based multi-tier rate regulation failed in a market of shortages and rising costs.

The adversary environment

When John Nassikas took over the chairmanship of the Federal Power Commission in August 1969, he announced that "What we need is a Nassikas round of gas rate increases."[2] That proved more easily said than done. In general terms, the political issues of gas pricing were similar to those for oil: mistrust and distributive equity. Much of the public and Congress believed that "Big Oil" had perpetrated the gas shortage intentionally. Thus, every decision by the Nassikas Commission was subjected to the closest congressional and media scrutiny for charges of ineptitude, impropriety, and unfairness.

But Nassikas faced an even greater challenge – surmounting barriers to change that the adjudicatory process and the weight of precedent imposed. The Federal Power Commission had neither the discretion of the Executive nor the authority of Congress to alter its own administrative criteria. The problems associated with natural gas were bound up with its historical treatment as a

[1] U.S. Congress, House, Committee on Interstate and Foreign Commerce, Subcommittee on Energy and Power, *Long Term Natural Gas Legislation* (94th Cong., 2nd Sess.), Jan.–Feb. 1976, pt. 2, pp. 1788–1789.
[2] *The New York Times*, September 21, 1969, p. 67.

public utility, and all that implied. Even in a crisis, "just and reasonable" was defined by three decades of regulatory precedent and judicial interpretation. Technical problems and bureaucratic behavior placed additional constraints on the Commission's flexibility. But worst of all was the host of interested groups and firms, from independent gas producers to residential consumers, that could use the panoply of adversary procedures – intervention, rebuttal, and appeal – to confound the process of regulatory transition.

After 1968, all three sectors of the natural gas industry loosely agreed that higher wellhead prices were needed to stimulate exploratory drilling and induce greater supply. But this did not mean that the principal participants in the FPC's rate proceedings were all pulling in the same direction. Far from it. The industry's consensus was a fragile alliance of necessity that left ample latitude for disagreement. Gas producers still wanted the wellhead price deregulated. The pipeline companies did not, but did favor somewhat higher prices or different rules that might block the flow of new gas reserves into the unregulated, intrastate markets. It was the distribution sector (not including municipally owned utilities) that had actually changed its stripes. By opposing higher field prices in the past, the large investor-owned distributors had provided the political support necessary for the Swidler and White commissions to hold the line on gas prices in the 1960's. Although they rarely went as far as the producers, these big urban utilities, with their quasi-consumerist briefs, now lent vital credibility to the advocates of higher prices.

Participation by the gas industry in regulatory proceedings was organized somewhat differently than by the trade groups that represented industry viewpoints to Congress. Under FPC procedures, the producers involved in any case could form *ad hoc* groups to formulate and present collective viewpoints. In the larger area rate cases, such a group might represent as many as twenty of the major oil and gas companies. The members of such a group chose a lead company with the resources necessary to prepare the elaborate briefs and technical support data. Occasionally, due to unique circumstances, one or two companies might file separate or dissenting views.[3] The Natural Gas Supply Committee, a trade group of the major producers formed in 1972, provided additional technical support. Transmission companies usually presented their briefs separately, except in the national rate cases of 1973–1976, when the Interstate Natural Gas Association of America presented the view of all. This organization represented all of the major interstate pipeline companies and included, until 1974, some 30 producers as associate members. Distributors were generally organized less coherently. In the national rate cases, one group of 30 to 50 firms was organized as the Associated Gas Distributors. Smaller groups of 10 to 15 firms each were jointly represented by law firms that specialized in regulatory adjudication. The primary trade group of large distributors, the American Gas Association, did not participate directly in regulatory proceedings.

[3] Interviews by the author, Gulf Exploration & Production Co., Houston, Texas, November 1980.

Groups outside the gas industry became more active in rate regulation as the gas crisis worsened. By 1974, these groups had coalesced in a loose consumerist coalition that struck a new adversary balance with the relatively unified industry.

The American Public Gas Association was the most active member of this coalition. Since 1961, it had represented more than 100 small, municipally owned gas distributors located primarily in the east-central states. Charles Wheatley, the Association's colorful spokesman, managed to intervene in the major rate cases, as well as lobby Congress persistently, with a professional staff of three. Since Wheatley believed that oil companies had fabricated the gas crisis, his position was invariably to oppose any rate increases. Other similar groups, such as the American Public Power Association and the National Rural Electric Cooperative Association, often supported the Public Gas Association in area and national rate cases. So did the Consumer Federation of America, once Lee White became its president. And in 1975, a small but well-funded group called the Energy Action Committee was organized in California by James Flug, actor Paul Newman, and Leo Wyler, chairman of TRE Corporation. With little concern for technical precision, the Energy Action Committee worked closely with these other groups on issues of gas price regulation. Its arguments usually centered on the monopolistic structure of the gas industry and the Commission's alleged responsiveness to producers' wishes. These groups, in turn, enlisted name-support from various organizations not ordinarily involved in gas regulation. Among these were the National Farmers Organization, the U.S. Conference of Mayors, and several labor unions.

Finally, there were three or four "consumer-oriented" state utility commissions that usually provided the most effective opposition to rate increases. Of these, the New York Public Service Commission was preeminent. Particularly under the chairmanship of Joseph Swidler, from 1969 to 1974, the New York Commission refuted cost and productivity data from gas companies and resolutely opposed the inclusion of non-cost criteria in the FPC's rate-setting methodology.

Each of these groups, and numerous individual firms, sought to manipulate the regulatory process in pursuit of its own objectives. The Federal Power Commission had a decided disadvantage when it finally tried to make changes. Any initiative beyond mere incrementalism ran counter to some existing procedure, criterion, or assumption affirmed somewhere in the mass of data, case opinion, and judicial ruling developed over the preceding decade. No matter how constructive and practical a change, opponents could cite a dozen precedents to controvert it. From the Natural Gas Act itself, to the Supreme Court's affirmation of the *Permian* decision, there were just too many ambiguities in the definition of "just and reasonable." Chairman Nassikas painfully acknowledged these limits to the Commission's discretion: "We are not regulating if we are compelled to accept a price offered by a producer in competition with the intrastate market – which cannot be sustained by evidence of costs." And if the Commission were "unable to prescribe prices under the Natural Gas Act to serve the interstate market," then "congressional change in the act is necessary, not Commission actions beyond delegated powers."[4]

Not only did costs remain the starting point, but the burden of proof for showing that a rate increase was "just and reasonable" rested with the industry. Even during the years of abundance, gas producers had difficulty validating costs. But in the 1970's, with a worsening gas shortage, accelerating inflation, rising interest rates, and a foreign cartel allegedly determining marginal energy prices, that cost-based burden became impossible to prove.

In terms of precedent, established data base, and bureaucratic inertia, two previous rate cases posed the most serious roadblocks to innovation by the Commission. After being in the works for nine years, the Permian and southern Louisiana area rate cases were upheld by the Supreme Court in 1968 and 1969. They were masterpieces of coherent administrative regulation that held the prospect of simultaneously providing price stability, consumer protection and producer incentive.[5] Precisely because of their coherence and completeness, these decisions constituted a new regulatory norm, just at the onset of the gas crisis. So as the Nassikas Commission grasped for emergency measures and sought solutions to the price competition of the intrastate market, its every action was tested against the evidentiary rationale and procedural legitimacy of the existing rate system.

Coping with crisis

Prior to 1969, warnings from gas producers of impending shortages were usually dismissed, since they were inevitably accompanied by requests for higher rates. Then, in September 1969, the FPC published a staff report that underscored the implications of the worsening trend in reserves.[6] Two months later, John Nassikas broke the news to the Senate Interior Committee that all was not well in the gas industry. Actual curtailments of committed gas supplied to industrial customers began in 1970. Although small at first, these curtailments by the pipeline companies grew rapidly, reaching 3.7 trillion cubic feet by 1977 (see Chart 11-1). Curtailments meant higher fuel costs, plant closings and layoffs of workers, and eventual disruption of public services in the areas most affected.

The earliest curtailments fell exclusively on "interruptible" customers – those industrial users whose contracts specified that their service could be temporarily interrupted during periods of peak demand. These customers were generally electric utilities or large industrial plants that maintained alternate power facilities in order to benefit from the bargain rates for interruptible

---

[4]   U.S. Congress, Senate, Committee on Commerce, *Federal Power Commission Oversight: Wellhead Pricing* (93rd Cong., 2nd Sess.), February 1974, p. 57.
[5]   See, for example, *Public Utility Fortnightly*, "Supreme Court Decisions on Gas Rate Cases," and "Impact of Area Pricing on Production and Demand," December 10, 1968, pp. 29–32, 76–78.
[6]   Federal Power Commission, *A Staff Report on National Gas Supply and Demand* (Washington: FPC, Bureau of National Gas, September 1969).

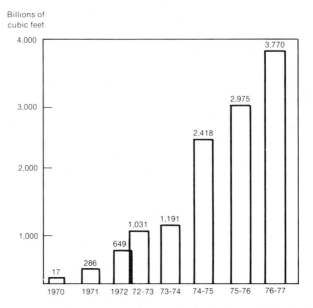

Chart 11-1
Firm Curtailments
by Interstate Pipelines, 1970-77
(Intercompany Sales Eliminated)

Source: 1970-72 data from FPC, Natural Gas Survey (Wash., D.C., 1975), Vol.
1, P. 105; 1972-77 data, reported on Sept. — Aug. basis, from FPC, 1976 Annual
Report, p. 16.

service. This arrangement served the interest of pipeline companies too, allowing them to manage seasonal load variations more efficiently. But when the gas
shortage came, and curtailments were no longer temporary nor limited to interruptible customers, the FPC was forced to devise some criteria for rationing.

As usual, the Commission approached the problem on a case-by-case basis,
examining particular circumstances and then moving gradually towards a generalized policy.[7] From the start, its deliberations focused on the need for a
manageable system that would have the least direct impact on the fewest end-
users. Human need, consumer protection, and safety were real concerns. The
problem of relighting pilot flames on 50 million gas burners easily identified the
top priority user. Any curtailment schedule must "meet the basic objectives of

[7]   The principal cases in this evolution included, United Gas Pipe Line Co., *Opinion No. 606,* 46
FPC 786 (1971); *International Paper Co. v. FPC,* 476 F. 2d 121 (5th Cir. 1973); El Paso Natural Gas
Co., *Opinion No. 634,* 48 FPC 931 (1972); and Arkansas Louisiana Gas Co., *Opinion No. 643,* 49
FPC, 53 (1973).

protecting deliveries for residential and small volume commercial consumers who cannot be safely curtailed on a daily basis."[8]

Setting forth priorities involved adjudicatory skirmishes and litigation among the various types of intermediate users. The Commission eventually settled on eight priority-of-service categories, which it issued in January 1973. Top priorities after residential consumers went to small commercial concerns and industrial uses for which gas was a vital process ingredient. The middle range of priorities went to dependent industrial customers ranked by size, with larger firms getting lower priorities. Interruptible customers were similarly ranked in the bottom three categories.[9]

Each pipeline company had to apply this schedule *pro rata* to its customers in each category, starting with the largest interruptible customers. Not until curtailments reached 100 percent in any category were they to impinge upon the next highest priority. This system was relatively nondiscriminatory among similar customers within the service area of each pipeline company. Of course, some pipeline companies were worse off than others, and their curtailments penetrated more deeply into the high-priority categories. This did result in some sharp regional disparities. On the other hand, a salutary effect of this system was that it stimulated conservation by users in the middle-priority categories and a permanent reduction of demand by customers in the lowest-priority categories. After several years of regular, semi-annual curtailments, many of the largest industrial users converted to more reliable (and expensive) fuels, such as coal or residual oil. In this manner, the rationing system operated effectively through 1979, until curtailments generally subsided below the threshold of non-interruptible requirements.

If the allocation of scarce resources had been the Commission's only responsibility, then its regulatory record might have earned some plaudits. But even as it carried out rationing, the Federal Power Commission started to promulgate a series of innovative, primarily short-term measures, intended to stimulate the flow of new gas supplies into the interstate market. Since these departed from established patterns of cost-based rate making, they proved most controversial. And in order to avoid lengthy adjudicatory disputes that could defeat the timeliness of these actions, the Commission chose to exert its seldom used rulemaking authority. Although this too met with resistance, the Commission was at least able to implement these initiatives while disputes were being settled in the courts. Five new measures, in conjunction with increases in area rates, contributed some short-term relief to the supply crisis in the interstate natural gas market.

The first change made by the Nassikas Commission redressed an inequity that dated back fifteen years. In the mid-1950's, pipeline companies that produced some of their own gas had petitioned to receive a rate of return on their

8   Arkansas Louisiana Gas Co., *Opinion No. 643*, 49 FPC, 64 (1973).
9   Utilization and Conservation of Natural Resources – Natural Gas Act, Docket No. R-469, *Order No. 467*, 49 FPC 87 (1973).

exploration and production investments that was comparable to that earned by independent oil and gas producers. Although the Commission approved this in 1959, it was overturned by the courts in 1960.[10] Upon remand, the new Swidler Commission decided, in 1962, to allow only the standard six percent return that pipelines received on their overall investment.[11] After that, the transmission companies had little incentive to expand their exploration and production activities; some cut back dramatically.[12]

In October 1969, the FPC finally rejected cost-of-service valuation of gas produced by transmission companies. It ruled that they could receive (that is, charge themselves) the applicable area rate for gas from newly acquired leases. This decision, although promptly challenged by user groups, was eventually affirmed.[13] It was especially important since the intrastate market was attracting the new reserves of independent producers at prices above the regulated ceilings. At least with the prevailing area rates, the interstate pipelines could try to help supply themselves.

In a related effort to lock new reserves into the interstate system, the Commission introduced a program in 1970 whereby pipeline companies could advance venture capital to producers to expand exploration and development. Advanced payments for this could be charged to the pipeline company's rate base.[14] During the next two years, pipeline companies advanced about $1.25 billion for this purpose, reportedly eliciting an additional 9.5 trillion cubic feet of gas reserves.[15] Pleased with this progress, the Commission extended the program for two more years, and expanded it to include payments for the acquisition by pipeline companies of a working-interest in wells they financed.[16] But with this, the Commission apparently overreached its grasp. The New York Public Service Commission challenged the order. In January 1975, a circuit court overturned the Commission, reasoning that as long as Congress "prescribed a system of regulation by an agency subject to court review the courts may not abandon their responsibility to acquiescing in a charade or rubber stamping of nonregulation in agency trappings."[17]

In yet another attempt at structural innovation, the FPC proposed in 1970 to exempt small producers from regulation. The exemption would apply to com-

---

[10] FPC, El Paso Natural Gas Co., Docket No. G–4769, *Opinion No. 326,* 22 FPC 260 (1959); *El Paso Natural Gas v. FPC,* 281 F 2d 567 (1960).

[11] El Paso Natural Gas Co., *Opinion No. 366,* 28 FPC 688 (1962).

[12] Howard Boyd, retired chairman, The El Paso Company, interview with the author, November 1980; also, compilation of research and development expenditures, reported in Federal Power Commission, *Statistics of Natural Gas Companies,* 1956–1968 (Washington, 1969).

[13] Pipeline Production Area Rate Proceeding (Phase I), *Opinion No. 568,* 42 FPC 738 (1969), aff'd *City of Chicago v. FPC,* 458 F. 2d 731 (D.C. Cir. 1971), cert. denied, 405 U.S. 1074 (1972).

[14] *Order No. 410,* 44 FPC 1142.

[15] John Nassikas, "The National Energy Crisis – Revisited," Speech, National Press Club Luncheon, Washington, D.C., April 10, 1973.

[16] *Order No. 499,* 50 FPC 2111.

[17] *P.S.C. of New York v. FPC,* 511 F. 2d 338 (D.C. Cir. 1975). This same court had previously upheld the Commission's earlier version of this rule. See, *P.S.C. of New York v. FPC,* 467 F. 2d 361 (D.C. Cir. 1972).

panies that produced less than 10 billion cubic feet of gas annually.[18] By this definition, all but about 70 of the 4,700 producers were "small," and together accounted for about 15 percent of total gas output. Small producers were responsible for the lion's share of exploratory drilling. Even their dry holes contributed to the industry's general knowledge of gas reserves and helped guide the major producers to productive deposits. The sharp decline in exploratory drilling over the past decade was thought to reflect the increasing risk and shrinking margins for these small operators. What gas they did have they tended to sell locally, to avoid the administrative and legal overhead of regulatory compliance. As the price gap widened between intrastate and interstate markets, small producers disproportionately abandoned the interstate pipeline companies. Thus, the FPC figured that the starting point for reversing the gas shortage lay with the small producers. It hoped "not to increase contract prices, but to facilitate the entry of the small producer into the interstate market and to stimulate competition among producers to sell gas in interstate commerce."[19]

Chairman Nassikas also had some other motives for trying to decontrol small producers. By eliminating the need to certificate 99.8 percent of all producers, the Commission could relieve its own regulatory burden in order to concentrate on larger matters. In political terms, a regulatory exemption for small producers would alleviate the criticism and pressure from that powerful, independent constituency, and still leave to Congress the issue of substantive deregulation.

All logic aside, the Commission's proposal met with fierce resistance. More than seventy interested parties filed comments and participated in an unusual rule-making conference. Only the small producers themselves endorsed the idea. Consumer advocates and the activist state commissions opposed it, accusing the FPC of subverting the Natural Gas Act by *de facto* deregulation. They argued that the Commission had no authority to allow any rates not justified on a cost-basis, and that the rule would lead to significantly higher consumer prices. The transmission and distribution sectors split on the issue, with a number of companies suggesting extensive modifications to the FPC's proposal.

Large producers flatly opposed the exemption, ostensibly because they might not be able to pass through to the pipelines their own costs of purchasing from small producers at prices higher than area rates.[20] But the real reason was politically motivated. Deregulation was already a subject of congressional discussion, with legislation pending to deregulate small contracts (as opposed to small producers). Integrated oil companies were sensitive to the implications of being decoupled politically from the small independent producers with whom the real grassroots political power of the industry lay. If the FPC succeeded in exempting all small producers, their support for deregulation would be dissipated and the big companies would stand alone.

In 1971, the Commission went ahead and promulgated its small-producer

---

[18] Notice of Proposed Rulemaking, Docket No. R-393, Exemption of Small Producers from Regulation (35 *Fed. Reg.* 12220, July 30, 1970).
[19] Exemption of Small Producers from Regulation, *Order No. 428*, 45 FPC 455 (1971).
[20] *Ibid.*, 454, 458.

exemption, qualified by the provision that if their prices did not meet the Commission's specified criteria, then pipeline purchasers would have to absorb the price differential in their rate of return. In a strange alliance with state utility commissions, the major producers pressed an appeal, and in 1974, the Supreme Court overturned the FPC. Even if the change "would make a small dent in the consumer's pocket," said the Court, "the Act makes unlawful all rates which are not just and reasonable, and does not say a little unlawfulness is permitted."[21]

Besides structural changes, the Commission undertook several emergency measures designed to snatch new supplies from the intrastate market long enough to alleviate the worst seasonal peaks of curtailments. For example, in the fall of 1973, when the Commission realized that a severe fuel shortage would likely occur in the forthcoming winter heating season, it issued an order allowing 180-day emergency sales at unregulated prices. Typically, a coalition of user-groups quickly got a restraining order. Ten days later, after some hasty revisions by the Commission, the Supreme Court vacated the stay, allowing an extra 200 billion cubic feet of emergency gas to meet the minimum requirements of the winter heating demand.[22] Eventually, however, the same group prevailed and convinced the court to strike down the 180-day rule. A judge concluded that the FPC had "attempted to remedy the shortfall of supply in the interstate market by authorizing a supplemental injection of large quantities of gas through sales freed from the constraints of meaningful regulation."[23]

The most controversial of the Commission's discrete responses to the shortage was an optional certification policy, adopted in August 1972. This was an alternative procedure for producers willing to forego certain benefits of the area-rate system. It allowed them to enter firm contracts with consenting pipeline purchasers at prices above the area rates. But to acquire such a certificate, the producer had to offer gas from entirely new wells and waive any claims to possible increases in the area rates for flowing gas. Under this option, the Commission would weigh a proposed contract against intrastate prices, gas from nonconventional sources, and substitute fuels – the "economic and market factors in an intercompetitive fuel economy."[24] If it survived court scrutiny, this new process promised a significant departure from traditional, cost-based regulation.

As always, consumer groups reacted vehemently to this optional rule. In an unusual development, 21 congressmen, primarily liberal Democrats, challenged the rule in court, with the Consumers Union and the New York Commission intervening on their behalf. In their brief, the congressmen chastened the Commission for trying "to change the substantive standard for regulating interstate sales by producers of natural gas from cost-plus-reasonable-return to market price. Such a drastic change is, in effect, a change from regulation to

21 *FPC v. Texaco, Inc.*, 417 U.S. 380 (1974).
22 *FPC v. Consumer Federation of America et al.*, Sup. Ct. No. A-608 (December 20, 1973).
23 *Consumer Federation of America v. FPC*, 515 F. 2d 347 (D.C. Cir. 1975).
24 John Nassikas, "The National Energy Crisis," 1973, p. 21.

Table 11-1. *Area rate increases by the Federal Power Commission, 1970–1973*

Area	Opinion	Date	Previous ceiling price[a]	New ceiling price
Appalachia	411 (44 FPC 1112)	10/70	28.0	24.0–34.0
Hugoton-Anadarko	566 (44 FPC 761)	9/70	17.0	19.9–20.0
Texas Gulf Coast	595 (45 FPC 674)	5/71	17.0	23.1
Southern Louisiana	598 (46 FPC 86)	7/71	20.0	26.0
Other southwest	607 (46 FPC 900)	10/71	20.5	21.9–23.5
Permian Basin	622 (50 FPC 390)	8/73	16.5	32.4

[a]Prices shown here are the highest of various vintages and among various subregions in an area. Cents per thousand cubic feet.
Source: The respective opinions cited above.

*non*regulation," and that was the prerogative of Congress alone. And worse yet, the "Commission's assumption that higher prices will bring forth some gas is unjustified."[25] Senators too put the Commission on notice that its action was "a blatant and arrogant usurpation of the legislative function," and was "manifestly anticonsumer and proindustry."[26]

The commissioners themselves sometimes found it difficult to agree on the optional certificate rule. In January 1974, for example, the FPC approved a contract of the Southern Natural Gas Company for a block of gas being developed in Escambia County, Alabama. The Commission split 3–2 on the decision. There was no internal consistency regarding the appropriate price. The staff had recommended 35 cents, the dissenting commissioners 41 cents, the administrative law judge 50 cents, and the majority of commissioners 55 cents. To make matters worse, on the night before the decision, all five commissioners received telegrams from Southern Natural, warning that the project would be scrubbed if a certificate for 55 cents were not issued within 24 hours. Nassikas himself felt that this decision carried the optional rule too far. In his dissent, he characterized the majority's approval as a "travesty of regulatory justice."[27] Any departure from the convention of cost-based pricing was evidently a wrenching experience.[28]

While working at these structural and procedural changes, the Federal Power

[25] U.S. Court of Appeals (D.C. Circuit), *John E. Moss*, et al., "Brief for Petitioners," in U.S. Congress, Senate, *Federal Power Commission Oversight* (1974), p. 393.
[26] U.S. Congress, Joint Economic Committee to Kenneth Plumb, Secretary, Federal Power Commission, May 12, 1972, *Ibid.*, p. 387.
[27] Southern Natural Gas Company, Docket No. CP73-154, *Opinion No. 686*, 51 FPC 423 (1974).
[28] The Commission eventually approved a dozen or so contracts under the optional certificate rule, all of which were contested by consumer organizations. Although a circuit court sustained the new policy in principle, it rejected the first specific certificate on the grounds that the Commission had assigned too much weight to non-cost factors. *John E. Moss, et al. v. FPC*, 502 F. 2d 461 (D.C. Cir. 1974), and *Consumers Union of the U.S., Inc. v. FPC*, 510 F. 2d 656 (D.C. Cir., 1974).

Commission issued a string of area-rate decisions between 1970 and 1973. Each was intensely contested, but five were eventually upheld. As Table 11-1 indicates, these decisions increased rates from 17 to 35 percent, except for the Second Permian opinion, which sought to cover a five-year lag with a whopping 96 percent increase. The Second Southern Louisiana proceeding set two important precedents. It was a reconsideration of the 1968 decision, upon petition by producers, to which the Commission had agreed. And it was settled by a consent agreement among 77 distributors, all of the interstate pipelines, and 46 producers.[29] Since the producers voluntarily accepted a 26-cent rate, consumer groups would subsequently cite this case as evidence that 26 cents provided adequate incentive to produce and sell gas in the interstate market. Producers, on the other hand, viewed it as a breakthrough in the FPC's recognition that prevailing rates were too low.

Nationwide rate-making

While struggling with the mixed results of these short-term measures, the Federal Power Commission initiated another course of action that Chairman Nassikas viewed as the long-term restructuring of natural gas regulation. It began in 1970 with a study of the current *nationwide* cost of producing gas. Its purpose was to reconsider rate of return and evaluate "whether the market mechanism will adequately protect the consumer interest."[30]

This proceeding led to the issuance of the FPC's landmark Opinion No. 699 in June 1974, establishing a uniform price of 42 cents per thousand cubic feet for new natural gas. This price applied to all gas in the lower-48 states, both onshore and offshore, from wells newly begun or reserves newly committed to the interstate market, after December 31, 1972.[31] Upon rehearing, the Commission revised the price to 52 cents and extended its application to flowing gas upon expiration of existing contracts. It also provided for biennial review, to "determine if that rate was sufficient to bring forth the supply of gas."[32] New gas would henceforth be priced at the new rates established by each review, so as not to create multiple vintages.

Accordingly, the FPC reiterated this entire process during the next two years, culminating in the issuance of Opinion No. 770 in July 1976. That decision did reconstitute vintages, but established prices of $1.42 for new gas in the period 1975–76, $1.01 for the period 1973–74, and 52 cents for old gas under new contracts.[33]

---

[29] Area Rate Proceeding (Southern Louisiana Area), Docket No. AR61-2, *Opinion No. 598*, 44 FPC 86 (1971); aff'd, *Placid Oil Co., et al. v. FPC*, 483 F. 2d 880 (5th Cir. 1978).

[30] Initial Rates for Future Sales of Natural Gas for All Areas, Docket No. R-389-A; 35 *Fed. Reg.* 11638 (1970); and FPC, *1971 Annual Report*, p. 42.

[31] Just and Reasonable National Rates for Sales of Natural Gas, Docket No. R-389-B, *Opinion No. 699*, 51 FPC 2112 (1974).

[32] *Opinion No. 699-H*, FPC 1604 (1974), and FPC, *1974 Annual Report*, p. 42.

[33] National Rates for Jurisdictional Sales of Natural Gas, Docket No. RM75-14, *Opinion No. 770* (Washington: FPC, 1976).

Together, these two national rate cases spanned most of the period of America's gas crisis and involved virtually every firm in the industry as well as all other conceivably interested parties. The proceedings laid bare many of the economic and ideological conundrums of rate regulation, as well as the political limitations of administrative adjudication.

1. *Adversary process*

Even before taking up the substantive issues, the FPC had to contend with two serious controversies regarding procedural matters. The first was resistance by consumer activists to the very idea of increasing rates and reviewing them every two years. "The most fundamental element underlying the current and projected natural gas shortages," complained Consumers Union, "is the regulatory uncertainty surrounding the prices."[34] Similar in its logic to the idea of "inflationary expectations," this argument complemented the view that crisis had been contrived by concerted industry action. In its most generous light, if gas producers believed that economic rates on their properties would increase more rapidly than the carrying costs, where was the incentive to hasten development? Of course, the consumer coalition actually put it far less generously, implicating the Commission in the shortage conspiracy: "The gas 'shortage' is therefore nothing but a self-fulfilling prophecy caused by a Commission pricing policy which permits higher and higher rates because of greater and greater supply shortfall and not on the basis of costs."[35]

The other procedural issue related to the FPC's decision to use rule-making, rather than formal adjudicatory procedures, because of the scope of these national cases and the urgency of the gas crisis. This meant doing without the trial-like hearings, complete with oral testimony and cross-examination under oath. Instead, the Commission would rely on an evidentiary record that consisted of the rule-making notices, staff studies, written briefs and supplemental studies from all parties, a public conference, and two rounds of written replies.[36] These opportunities for participation and redress notwithstanding, consumerist intervenors claimed to "have suffered a complete denial of their procedural rights guaranteed by both the Natural Gas Act and the due process clause of the Fifth Amendment." To the extent that it was serious, this complaint stemmed from distrust of the industry's reserve data on which the FPC relied for computing productivity – a major element of the cost determination. "Without an adversary hearing," said one group, "the setting of nationwide rates for gas producers is nothing more than a ritualistic exercise of computing industry rates based on industry data."[37]

Objections to rule-making evinced an ideological commitment to the adver-

[34] Docket No. R-389-B, "Response of Consumers Union of United States, Inc. To Commission's Notice of Proposed Rulemaking," May 1973, pp. 1–2.

[35] Docket No. RM75-14, "Motion of American Public Gas Association, et al., for a Stay of Opinion No. 770," 1976, p. 51.

[36] *Opinion No. 699*, 51 FPC 2220–2224.

[37] Docket No. RM75-14, "Motion of American Public Gas Association," pp. 4–5.

Table 11-2. *Determination of productivities (excluding Alaska) from FPC Opinion No. 770*

	Non-associated (trillions of cubic feet)	Drilling footage (millions)	Productivity (Mcf/ft) (thousand cubic feet per foot drilled)	
1966	16.1	24.4	662	
1967	17.3	21.5	803	
1968	12.3	20.7	597	
1969	6.9	24.1	286	
1970	9.4	22.9	409	
1971	8.6	22.6	379	
1972	7.6	26.7	284	
1973	3.7	35.6	104	
1974	6.7	38.9	172	
1975	9.9	41.9	237	
1966–1974	88.5	237.4	373	
1966–1975	98.5	279.3	353	
1967–1975	82.4	254.9	323	FPC's chosen "range of
1968–1975	65.1	233.4	279	reasonableness" for Opinion
1969–1975	52.7	212.7	248	No. 770

Source: Federal Power Commission, Docket No. RM75–14, *Opinion No. 770* (Wash., D.C.: FPC, 1976), p. 35.

sary process itself. Senator James Abourezk of South Dakota urged the Commission to behave like the "quasi-judicial agency" that Congress had intended it be. For the new rates to be legitimate, said Abourezk, they must be "tested in the crucible of adversary hearings."[38] This faith in the efficacy of adversary process was a facet of American ideology that rejected technocratic efficiency and with it, any possible cooperation between business and government. But in view of the technical and economic complexities posed by natural gas regulation in the 1970's, it would seem that some issues of national economic policy exceeded the capacity of the adversary process to deliver any solutions whatever. At least the FPC, under Nassikas' chairmanship, had evidently begun to think so.

2. Costs

Although the FPC claimed to have "considered" non-cost factors in both of its national rate proceedings, computed costs remained more than "the point of departure in arriving at a just and reasonable rate." The Commission maintained that the $1.42 rate for new gas was "fully cost-based and justified."[39] It

[38] Docket No. R-389-B, "Statement of Senator James G. Abourezk," May 29, 1974.
[39] *Opinion No. 770*, p. 1.

was composed exclusively of 13 components of cost, and included no arbitrary increments ascribed to non-cost factors.[40] Although each and every cost component was contested, three aspects of the Commission's methodology were critical and involved significant departures from the area-rate cases: productivity, taxes, and rate of return.

"Productivity," said the Commission, "is the cornerstone of the analysis used to determine the cost of 'new' gas."[41] Each component of the unit costs for gas actually produced was determined by dividing the industry's overall costs for that component by the chosen productivity rate. The Commission defined productivity as annual additions of non-associated gas reserves divided by successful drilling footage. Table 11-2 shows this data for the period 1966–1975, together with averages for several different base periods.

Disagreement between producer and consumer groups centered on two aspects of productivity. As the table shows, the calculations relied entirely on reserve data from the American Gas Association – data that consumer activists believed were "manipulated." Furthermore, the base period used to determine average productivity was crucial since the trend over time had been downward. Because lower productivity meant higher costs, consumer groups wanted the longest base period to reflect the oldest productivity data; producers urged the Commission to rely on the few most recent years. By way of compromise, the FPC averaged two productivity figures that represented a "range of reasonableness." In Opinion 770, for example, it chose a high of 323 and a low of 279, yielding an average productivity of 300 thousand cubic feet of gas per foot drilled. This was the basis for unit-cost computations. Compared with the 522 figure used by the Commission in 1974, this represented a 57 percent decline in productivity in two years – a change that nearly satisfied the producers but which the consumer groups found incredible.

Prior to Opinion 770, the FPC had excluded federal income taxes from its determination of costs for natural gas producers. In the first national rate proceeding, producers had urged the Commission to include income taxes in the cost computation. The Commission rejected that proposal, but reversed itself in 1976 over the objections of its own staff. "Tax treatment," explained the Commission, "has been altered to reflect the tax liability resulting from the repeal of the percentage depletion allowance." (Congress had done away with it in the Tax Reduction Act of 1975.) Thus, in 1976, the FPC included a large new cost component representing the 58 percent marginal tax on corporate income, adjusted to compensate for cost savings from expensing intangible drilling costs. Consumer groups shouted foul.[42]

Rate of return was another important part of the Commission's national rate decisions. In the area cases, the Commission had adopted a 12 percent rate of

<hr />

[40] The factors of cost in the FPC's methodology for national rates were as follows: (1) successful wells, (2) recompletion and deeper drilling, (3) lease acquisition, (4) other production facilities, (5) dry holes, (6) other exploration, (7) exploration overhead, (8) operating expenses, (9) return, (10) return on working capital, (11) net gas liquids credit, (12) regulatory expense, and (13) royalty. Income taxes were added in Opinion No. 770.

[41] *Opinion No. 770*, p. 33.

[42] *Ibid.*, 4, 81–86.

return. But recognizing the need for additional exploration incentives and the upward trend in interest rates, the FPC raised it to 15 percent in Opinion 699 (1974). Although less than the rate of 18 percent that producers requested, any increase was too much for consumerists.[43] Undaunted, the Commission contended that the rate was compatible to that of other industries, and stuck to it in 1976 as well.

Putting together these components of cost – 37 cents for exploration and production, 3 cents for operating costs, 22 cents for royalties, 38 cents for taxes, and 42 cents for return on investment – the Commission arrived at $1.42 per thousand cubic feet of gas in 1976.[44] This exercise probably came closer to a realistic determination of costs than had any previous decision. But the question remained, was it enough?

3. *Vintages*

Gas producers (and economists) might have thought so had it not been for the Commission's return to "vintaging" in the 770 Opinion. Multi-tier pricing of old and new gas, as discussed in Chapter 7, dated from the beginning of the Permian Area rate proceedings in 1961. Alfred Kahn, its leading proponent at that time, had thought that it would provide incentive for exploration and still protect consumers from paying economic rents to producers for gas already developed. This system, however, masked the marginal cost of new gas to consumers because it was "rolled-in" with the larger cushion of cheaper, "old gas." Thus, it stimulated demand without helping supply. As Professor Stephen Breyer aptly described it, this amounted to a system of rent control. Its effect on natural gas was no different than on urban rental housing – shortages.[45]

Given the effects of inflation on costs and interest rates in the early 1970's, vintaging posed a serious problem for the Nassikas Commission. If separate vintages continued to proliferate, the result would be an ever-widening gap between revenues and replacement costs and disincentives to commit new reserves to purchase contracts (for fear of getting locked into an "old" price). Following this logic in Opinion 699, the Federal Power Commission decided on a rate system that would phase out separate vintages as existing contracts expired. Old gas would then be eligible for new-gas rates. To continue this gradual standardization, the price of all gas eligible for the national rate would increase with each biennial review.[46]

Although producers were delighted by this idea, the distributors could find "no rational or legal basis for abandoning the two price system." Doing so, they felt, would "not provide any incentive for the commitment of new gas reserves to the interstate market."[47] Worse still, the New York Public Service Commis-

---

[43] Docket No. 389-B, "Reply Comments of the New York Public Service Commission," May 29, 1974, pp. 4–6.

[44] *Opinion No. 770*, Exhibit 30, p. 125.

[45] Stephen Breyer, *Regulation and Its Reform* (Cambridge: Harvard University Press, 1982), pp. 240–260.

[46] *Opinion No. 699*, pp. 2215, 2274, 2278.

[47] Docket No. R-389-B, "Reply Comments of the Associated Gas Distributors," June 1, 1973, pp. 7–8.

sion viewed it as a disincentive: "A producer will have no inducement to spend money in additional exploration or development to secure higher rates for its gas when it can get the identical price without lifting a finger." This was "the opposite of using price as a regulatory tool."[48] As with crude oil, it seemed patently unfair that consumers should be made to pay 42 cents or more for natural gas that cost less than a dime to develop, just because of the OPEC cartel.

The elimination of vintaging in the 1974 case was a giant step in the transition away from cost-based rate making. But it was evidently too large a step to repeat in the second national rate decision. In 1976, the Commission had enough difficulty justifying the drastic cost and tax revisions that hiked the new gas price from 52 cents to $1.42 in the space of two years. To have applied this to old gas as well would have exceeded the tolerance of political realism. So as a compromise, which producers failed to appreciate and consumers failed to acknowledge, the Commission reestablished a three-tier price system that Congress would eventually extend into the 1980's.[49]

4. Market mechanism

When the FPC first announced its national rate inquiry, it called for comments on the appropriateness of considering the "market mechanism," as well as costs, in its rate deliberations. Gas producers and pipeline companies responded to the Commission's call by explaining and documenting the relevance of rising interest rates, intrastate-market prices, interfuel competition, and the commodity value of natural gas. They also pointed to the prevailing prices of non-traditional gas sources (liquefied natural gas for $1.50 per thousand cubic feet and Alaskan gas estimated to cost $1.55) as indicators of the level at which national rates should be set.[50] The distributors were more circumspect in this regard. They suggested a 6.5 cent exploration incentive, qualified by a plowback requirement, as the only non-cost factor that the FPC should consider.[51] Consumer groups opposed consideration of any non-cost factors since they believed that monopoly, not the market mechanism, was determining intrastate and interfuel prices.

Although the Commissioners no doubt gave some thought to these factors, they chose to disregard them in their first national rate decision. Opinion 699 made no mention of market-related considerations.

But the new rate of 42 cents was still not enough to match prices being offered for gas in the intrastate market. The gap that had opened in 1968 between intrastate and interstate prices had just kept widening. By 1974, average price in the unregulated markets of Texas and Louisiana was nearly twice the regulated price, and contracts for new gas went for nearly four times as

---

[48] Docket No. R-389-B, "Reply Comments of the New York Public Service Commission," May 29, 1974, p. 4.

[49] *Opinion No. 770*, pp. 12–13.

[50] Docket No. 389-B, "Comments by the Interstate Natural Gas Association of America," May 7, 1974, pp. 3–4.

[51] Docket No. 389-B, "Reply Comments by the Associated Gas Distributors," June 1, 1973, pp. 7–8.

Table 11-3. *Comparison of interstate and intrastate wellhead prices for natural gas, 1971–1976*[a]

Year	Interstate (1)		Intrastate (2)		Texas intrastate (3) average six highest new contracts
	Long-term contracts	Total average contracts	Permian	So. Louisiana	
1971	23.9	27.0	24.1	26.2	34.0
1972	24.5	29.5	30.0	29.5	44.0
1973	24.6	36.7	n.a.		66.0
1974	26.2	45.8	91.0(3)		160.0
1975	26.3	57.0	127.5		212.0
1976	142.0		154.9(4)		n.a.

Note: Cents per thousand cubic feet.
[a]Weighted average of new contract prices. Interstate figures averaged nationally by long-term contracts and the total average of long-term contracts plus optional certificates, small producer exempt contracts, and limited-term contracts. Intrastate figures by area for 1971–72, then averaged nationally from 1974 through first half of 1976.
Sources: (1) U.S. Congress, House, Commerce Committee, Subcommittee on Energy and Power, *Long-Term Natural Gas Legislation* (94th Cong., 2nd Sess.), pt. 1, p. 470; (2) K.E. Wedemeyer, *Interstate Natural Gas Supply and Intrastate Market Behavior* (New York: Arno Press, 1979), pp. 143–44, 152; (3) FPC, Docket No. RM75-14, "Joint Supplemental Comments of Indicated Producer Respondents," July 24, 1975, p. 4 and Appendix B; (4) FPC, Docket No. RM75-14, *Opinion No. 770* (Wash., D.C.: FPC, 1976), p. 114.

much (Table 11-3). The unregulated price appears to have followed that of crude oil, its nearest interfuel substitute.

Whether or not competition accounted for this price run-up was disputed intensely by producers and consumer groups. Spokesmen for producer interests claimed that this data showed the "classic" market response, wherein competition among buyers stimulated new drilling and new reserves at costs that exceeded the FPC's ceilings. Only when gas prices approached the Btu-equivalent price of crude oil did demand slacken, restoring relative stability.[52] But if, as consumer groups believed, crude oil prices were monopolistic, then they merely created an umbrella that allowed oil companies to raise unregulated natural gas prices well above costs. The New York Public Service Commission reasoned that "the intrastate market cannot be workably competitive because prices in that market tend to approach the price of competitive fuels which must be purchased by the consumer, which are in turn determined in large part by the price that the OPEC nations require to be paid for their crude oil." And since "the OPEC crude oil price is determined by a cartel, the entire energy market in the United States is 'noncompetitive.' "[53] From this perspective, the intrastate gas market was scarcely a model for deregulation.

[52] Docket No. RM75-14, "Joint Supplemental Comments of Indicated Producer Respondents," July 24, 1975, p. 4.
[53] *Ibid.*, 8.

Table 11-4. *Total reserve additions: interstate versus intrastate, associated and non-associated gas (excludes Alaska)*

Year	AGA reserve additions excluding revisions	Interstate new supply[a]	Percentage	Inferred intrastate new supply[b]	Percentage
1966	14.8	10.0	68	4.8	32
1967	14.8	9.9	67	4.9	33
1968	9.8	6.4	65	3.4	35
1969	9.6	6.2	64	3.4	36
1970	11.3	3.5	31	7.8	69
1971	11.1	2.2	20	8.9	80
1972	10.7	5.0	47	5.7	53
1973	10.1	1.7	17	8.4	83
1974	9.7	2.4	25	7.3	75
1975	10.0	1.3[c]	13	8.7	87

Note: Trillions of cubic feet.
[a]Form 15, FPC, excluding revisions.
[b]Derived by assuming that intrastate reserve additions are equal to the difference between total AGA reserve additions and the reserve additions committed to the interstate market.
[c]Preliminary.
Source: FPC, Docket No. RM 75-14, *Opinion No. 770-A* (Wash., D.C.: FPC, 1976), p. 116.

Regardless of why, the expansion of intrastate markets was certainly aggravating the supply crisis in the interstate markets. Given a choice, gas producers sold as much of their new supply as possible to intrastate customers paying far higher prices. Table 11-4 shows that the proportion of new reserves committed annually to the interstate market shrunk from 68 to 13 percent in 10 years. In effect, the intrastate market had become a sluice that diverted more and more new gas from the interstate markets, around which the FPC had erected a barrier of price ceilings.[54]

In their briefs for the second national case, producers relied more heavily on market-related arguments and evidence. For the first time, they claimed that gas prices should rise to the level of marginal energy costs. At the very least, this meant parity with intrastate gas prices. With curtailments rising, distributors grudgingly acceded to this demand, as long as it did not apply to offshore gas, produced on the federal domain. The pipeline companies were more desperate still. Curtailments were forcing them to give up industrial customers to competing fuels, and were even raising the unit costs of transmission, as the flow of gas fell below the capacity of their pipelines. Although they too urged the FPC to set national rates at the intrastate level, they were willing to entertain any solution – including the notion of extending regulation to the intrastate market.

[54] U.S. Congress, House, Committee on Interstate Commerce, Subcommittee on Communications and Power, *Natural Gas Act of 1971* (92nd Cong., 1st Sess.), September 1971, p. 229.

While they did not openly advocate that, the very thought was a source of friction between them and the producers.[55]

Consumer groups would not accept regulated prices raised to the intrastate level. The only feasible solution, given their philosophical premises, was that the FPC should begin regulating the intrastate price as well:

Congress could not have meant for the FPC to throw up its hands when discrimination by the intrastate market is severely crippling the interstate market and conclude that it is powerless to do anything to stop the discrimination, but may only surrender to the discrimination by unlawfully deregulating the interstate market through the setting of the interstate rate at the unregulated intrastate level.[56]

Although the Federal Power Commission again set a rate that was fully cost-justified in 1976, it did rely on non-cost criteria for some of its supporting rationale. Since the intrastate price of $1.55 was not much higher than the new rate of $1.42, the Commission thought its rate appropriate. If "workable competition" was lacking in the intrastate markets, then the 13-cent differential was justified. If intrastate markets were in fact competitive, then the $1.55 probably reflected a short-run imbalance between demand and supply, and the Commission's new price would hopefully approximate the long-run equilibrium level.

As to interfuel parity, the regulators were equally confident. "Regardless of the origin of today's energy pricing structure" (e.g., OPEC cartel vs. competition), the new rate was "near" the commodity value of energy and would, over time, "lead to a gradual reduction in excess demand." Prices for No. 6 residual oil, the fuel that competed with natural gas for marginal industrial demand, ranged from $1.28 to $1.43 per thousand cubic feet of Btu-equivalent gas in 1975.[57]

The regulatory transition

The national rates promulgated in Opinion 770 marked the Federal Power Commission's final attempt to correct the problems of regulation, by regulation. Its decision – based on recent cost data and the reaffirmation of vintaging – took regulatory adjustment about as far as possible without legislative intervention. The process of regulatory transition severely tested the authority and resources of an independent commission charged with the responsibility for managing natural gas in the public interest.

Adjudication proved unsuited to a market of rising costs and severe shortage. Just the problems of case precedent and established procedure were enough to stifle innovation. But as sources of inertia, their effects were magnified by ideological conflict that politicized the process. Rebuttal, intervention, and the

---

[55] In 1974, this incipient split caused the pipeline companies to force producers to give up their membership in the Interstate Natural Gas Association of America. The Association would then be free to take whatever position its remaining members deemed necessary.

[56] Docket No. RM75-14, "Motion of American Public Gas Association, et al., for Stay of Opinion No. 770," p. 60.

[57] *Opinion No. 770*, pp. 109–124.

rules of evidence were meant for judicious deliberation – not battle. In the years of the gas crisis, the adversary process and its pursuit as a matter of principle contributed little to the national interest at a time when change was obviously needed.

This is not to say that the FPC, under the leadership of John Nassikas, did not make some heroic efforts and accomplish some imaginative reforms. But in the end, the Commission failed because of its inability to abandon the time-honored concept of cost-based rate regulation and the artificial distinction between old and new gas. Reliance on historic costs and treatment of gas production as a utility function was deeply rooted, not only in precedent, but in the minds and careers of the Commission's professional staff. The idea of marginal-cost pricing for a depleting resource was difficult to accept. And in an inflationary economy, duplicating the market mechanism with regulation was harder than ever.

Opinion 770, regardless of its considerable merits, merely set the agenda for executive and legislative decisions soon to be made by the incoming Administration of Jimmy Carter.

12. Natural gas: the consequences of scarcity

The political and economic consequences of natural gas shortages went far beyond the purview of conventional rate regulation. While the Federal Power Commission struggled to adopt procedural reforms, Congress haltingly reassessed and eventually amended the Natural Gas Act of 1938. Its nine-year effort to do so was more complicated and intensely fought, even than the issue of oil pricing. Meanwhile, market pressures and the cost-basis of regulation encouraged the industry to pursue high-cost sources of gas to supplement depleting domestic reserves. Development of these sources – synthetic gas, liquefied natural gas, Alaskan gas, and imported gas – raised complicated issues of public policy that required administrative supervision by the Executive branch of government.

For the first time since the 1950's managers of the gas industry got involved in political activities beyond adjudication. They did not fare well. Intrafuel conflict compromised the industry's political effectiveness while politicization of pricing and the rhetoric of equity undercut its legitimacy. Over the course of the 1970's, the means of business-government interaction in managing natural gas policy seemed to get less, rather than more, effective.

The high-cost supplements

Shortly before leaving the Federal Power Commission in 1970, Carl Bagge drew an interesting parallel between the intrastate gas market and commercial development of high-cost, supplemental sources of gas. Both represented "breaches" by market forces in the "dike" of cost-based rate regulation. "When this occurs," said Bagge, "regulatory policy cannot continue to operate as it has in the past, with or without more rational alternatives to cost based pricing."[1] A significant gap between the price of regulated domestic gas and that of supplemental sources made no economic sense. But it was financially and politically feasible in the context of regulation.

When demand for new gas outstripped additions to domestic reserves in the

[1] Carl Bagge, "Broadening the Supply Base of the Gas Industry," *Public Utilities Fortnightly*, October 26, 1970, pp. 26–27.

292

late 1960's, American pipeline companies started to develop supplemental sources. The principal domestic opportunities were coal gasification and Alaskan natural gas. Foreign sources included pipeline imports from Canada and Mexico, and liquefied natural gas (LNG) imported from North Africa, Indonesia, or the Persian Gulf. These sources were relatively costly, entailed greater risk, and if imported, involved decisions by foreign governments.

Regulation not only created demand for these supplements, but also justified their high costs prematurely. In cost-based rate regulation, the rate of return allowed each company was set as a percentage of its rate base. The rate base consists of a company's productive assets. Thus, one way to increase overall return is to increase the rate base by investing in additional plant such as an LNG terminal or a coal gasification facility. Moreover, regulation did little to discourage high-priced supplies even where no investment was involved. Since rates were also based on cost-of-service, a pipeline company or distributor could pass higher sourcing costs through to its customers if no cheaper sources were readily available. This was the incentive behind gas imports from Canada and Mexico. Pipeline companies could subsidize the high cost of supplemental sources to end-users by averaging those costs with their much larger volume of cheaper domestic gas. This is called "rolled-in pricing." Since market share and security of supply were the strategic objectives of most regulated pipeline companies, development of high-cost sources was a logical step.

Synthetic gas

As of 1970, prospects for producing synthetic gas from coal were moving along two separate tracks: commercialization of the relatively proven Lurgi technology, and continued experimental development of potentially more efficient, second-generation technologies. The Lurgi process looked to several large transmission and distribution companies like a quick and secure means of fulfilling existing commitments. For coal producers, it was a huge new market, potentially. No financial involvement by the government was thought to be necessary.

In 1968, El Paso Natural Gas formed a joint venture with Consolidation Coal, a subsidiary of Continental Oil. ConPaso, as it was called, leased 40,000 acres of coal reserves from the Navajo tribe in New Mexico and applied to the FPC in 1972 for certification of a project to produce 288 million cubic feet a day of synthetic gas. The capital cost was estimated at $605 million (for both plant and mine), resulting in a unit cost of $3.00 per thousand cubic feet. Since that was 10 times as much as the prevailing area rates, the project would not be competitive without benefit of rolled-in pricing.[2]

While the ConPaso project was pending revisions, a similar project named Wesco was proposed by Texas Eastern Transmission, Pacific Lighting, and Utah International. Pacific Lighting, a large west coast utility, would take all of

---

[2]   Inform, Inc., *Energy Futures: Industry and the New Technologies* (Cambridge: Ballinger Publishing, 1977), pp. 436–438.

the gas produced at cost plus 15 percent return on its investment. Wesco was the first gasification project to receive full consideration by the FPC. The Commission claimed authority over the pricing of the synthetic gas and certification of the project. In 1975, it approved an initial price of $1.38 per thousand cubic feet, but admitted that inflation would probably result in a rate closer to $1.70 by the time construction was completed. The key issue in this case was Texas Eastern's need for a cost-of-service rate that guaranteed the highly uncertain costs of this first commercial project. This posed a regulatory dilemma. The Commission hesitated to guarantee an "all-events tariff" for fear of promoting unsound projects. But because of the risks involved, Texas Eastern could not readily attract investors without some assurance that it could charge any rate necessary to recover costs. In the Wesco case, the FPC approved only an initial rate for the first six months, promising to watch developments closely and review the rate situation upon start-up.[3]

Together with this chicken-and-egg dilemma, rising costs during the 1970's overran the commercial feasibility of coal gasification. Even the tripling of marginal energy prices by OPEC failed to restore the competitiveness of synthetic gas. In fact, by pushing up the price of coal feedstock, it actually contributed to the cost escalation of gasification projects. A study by the Rand Corporation estimated inflation in the general price level accounted for about 12 percent of the cost run-up. Increases in the cost of capital (interest rates) and the compliance costs of environmental regulation were other major factors. The largest factor, according to the Rand study, was improving knowledge of design and scale-up costs that were grossly underestimated in the early planning stages.[4] These elements of escalating cost eventually led to abandonment of the ConPaso and Wesco projects, and indefinite delay of other less advanced plans.

Of the various gasification projects conceived in the early 1970's only one – the Great Plains Gasification Project – made progress towards construction. A consortium of transmission and distribution companies, eventually headed by American Natural Resources, organized this project for gasifying North Dakota lignite. The group filed its first application with the FPC in 1975, proposing two-phased construction of a plant that would produce 250 million cubic feet a day of gas. As costs escalated, new firms joined the consortium while others dropped out, and the FPC application was revised repeatedly. In 1979, the Federal Energy Regulatory Commission (successor to the FPC) rejected the consortium's application; capital costs were then estimated to be $900 million.[5] The project needed a rate that covered more anticipated cost increases as well as some kind of direct financial backing from the federal government. When the

---

3   *Opinion No. 728*, 53 FPC 1278 (1975).
4   Edward W. Merrow et al., *A Review of Cost Estimation in New Technologies: Implications for Energy Process Plants* (Santa Monica: Rand Corporation, 1979), R-2481-DOE; also, Edward W. Merrow, *Constraints on the Commercialization of Oil Shale*, prepared for the Department of Energy (R-2293-DOE), September 1978.
5   Cameron Engineers, Inc., "Status of Synfuels Projects, August 1979," in U.S. Congress, Senate, Committee on the Budget, Subcommittee on Synthetic Fuels, *Synthetic Fuels* (96th Cong., 1st Sess.), Committee Print, September 29, 1979, p. 232.

Carter administration took up the problem in 1980, it did so as part of its larger plan for a federal synfuels corporation.

Liquefied natural gas

Liquefied natural gas is another technical system with potential for supplementing the natural gas supply of the United States. An American named Godfrey Cabot first developed the technology for commercial application in 1914. Liquefaction involves freezing natural gas to -260 degrees to reduce its volume by a factor of more than 600, thus providing convenience in transportation and storage. The early commercial attraction of LNG was for peak-shaving by utilities. In periods of low use, natural gas would be liquefied and stored in cryogenic tanks. During peak demand periods, the LNG was regasified and fed directly into the distribution pipeline, gas turbine, or boiler. This minimized a supplier's base-load capacity. Although the technology is not complex, the volatile gas is so highly compressed that safety of LNG systems requires great care. In 1944, an LNG plant in Cleveland, Ohio, failed, causing a fire that took 131 lives and destroyed several blocks of buildings. There have been no other major accidents since then, but safety remains a political issue in the siting of LNG plants.

Interest in LNG for ocean transport developed in the early 1960's when energy planners in Europe and Japan tried to find a way to utilize the immense, worldwide reserves of natural gas that were being flared incidental to oil production. Although transoceanic LNG delivery required large capital outlays, the delivered cost would be commercially feasible if the gas could be purchased at a nominal price. By 1973, seven baseload LNG systems were in operation, moving natural gas from Brunei, Libya, southern Alaska, and Algeria, to Japan, continental Europe, and the United Kingdom. Total international LNG commerce amounted to 1.8 billion cubic feet a day.[6]

The Federal Power Commission approved the first long-term project for the continental U.S. in 1972. Distrigas Corporation began delivering 40 million cubic feet a day from Sonatrach, the Algerian national oil company, to Boston, Massachusetts, for peak-shaving in 1973. The delivered price, before regasification at Boston Harbor, was $1.37, and the FPC allowed rolled-in pricing by the receiving utility company. While several baseload LNG import projects were in planning stages, only one – El Paso Algeria – would be operational by 1980.

El Paso Natural Gas got involved in LNG development in the early 1960's because the company's founder, Paul Kayser, believed that gas shortages in the United States were inevitable. El Paso exploration crews discovered several huge gas fields in the Algerian Sahara and subsequently developed them for Sonatrach.[7] In 1968, the year U.S. gas production exceeded new discoveries,

---

[6] Edward Faridany, *LNG: 1974-1990, Marine Operations and Market Prospects for Liquefied Natural Gas* (London: Economist Intelligence Unit, Ltd., 1974), p. 20.
[7] Howard Boyd, retired chairman of the El Paso Company, interview with the author, November 1980.

El Paso began discussing LNG with Sonatrach. The following year it signed a contract for 1 billion cubic feet a day at a base price of 30 cents per thousand cubic feet. The capital cost of the project was estimated at about $1.7 billion, of which El Paso would bear 40 percent and Sonatrach 37 percent. The rest would be shared by three utilities that would distribute the gas on the U.S. east coast.[8] Although the FPC approved the project in 1972, it ordered that the LNG be priced incrementally so that consumers would recognize the real costs of using it for baseload supplies.[9]

As other large-scale projects for importing LNG were submitted to the FPC by Tenneco, Trunkline, and Pacific Lighting, the prospect of growing dependence on foreign sources of gas started to draw attention in both Congress and the White House. After the oil embargo, policy-makers were loath to see new dependencies spring up with the *ad hoc* proliferation of LNG systems. In 1975, President Ford suggested that LNG imports be limited to 1 trillion cubic feet a year from any one country and no more than 2 trillion in all. To implement this guideline, the Federal Energy Administration asserted discretionary authority over FPC decision-making on imports. Its criteria would include "such issues as pricing, government financial assistance, regional import dependence, [and] source of supply."[10]

By the time President Carter was preparing his National Energy Plan in the spring of 1977, pending applications to import LNG already exceeded the previous administration's guidelines. James Schlesinger, the President's energy advisor, felt that imported LNG was not a long-term secure substitute for domestic natural gas, but at best, a transitional option. In the National Energy Plan, he abolished Ford's fixed ceiling and substituted a more flexible policy of case-by-case review. The evaluative criteria were much the same.[11] In a government reorganization that created the Department of Energy in 1977, responsibility for gas imports was transferred from the independent FPC to the new Energy Regulatory Administration. This gave the Executive, through the new Secretary of Energy, direct statutory control that President Ford had lacked.[12]

The Federal Power Commission, however, had already approved an application by Trunkline for another large Algerian project and had allowed a revision of the El Paso project to provide rolled-in pricing. Participants claimed it was necessary because of cost overruns that had increased delivered cost to about $1.25 per thousand cubic feet.[13] For Schlesinger, this was more than enough

---

8   John A. Brickhill, "Statement with Respect to Supplemental Gas Supplies and Prices," in U.S. Federal Power Commission, Docket No. R-389-B, May 16, 1973, pp. 20–32.
9   U.S. Federal Power Commission, *Opinion No. 622*, June 28, 1972.
10   Gerald Ford, "Presidential Energy Message to Congress," February 26, 1976, and "Fact Sheet," in Commerce Clearing House, Inc., *Energy Management*, 1976, pp. 688, 698.
11   Executive Office of the President, *The National Energy Plan* (Washington: GPO, 1977), p. 57.
12   Department of Energy Organization Act, 42 USC 7101, Title III, Sec. 301 (b).
13   U.S. Federal Power Commission, *Opinion No. 786*, January 21, 1977, and *Opinion No. 796*, April 29, 1977.

dependence on Algeria – a country viewed in Washington as politically radical and not very stable. Late in 1978, the Economic Regulatory Administration rejected two other LNG projects involving Algeria, but approved one to import from Indonesia.[14]

The policy framework that evolved under Schlesinger's direction was broader and more complex than merely choosing among LNG projects. Schlesinger was concerned with the strategic and foreign-policy implications of the multi-billion-dollar LNG projects that tied domestic consumers to foreign supplies for 20 years or more. And since imported LNG required the benefit of rolled-in pricing, it not only affected domestic gas prices, but also the terms and feasibility of other supplemental sources.

Schlesinger priorities for supplemental gas were as follows: (1) new domestic gas stimulated by higher prices, (2) Alaskan gas, (3) synthetic gas from domestic coal, (4) existing Canadian imports, (5) Mexican imports at "reasonable prices," and (6) imported LNG.[15] These priorities were based on Schlesinger's analysis of strategic considerations, Carter's domestic political objectives, and the Department of Energy's estimates of comparative national economic benefits. By these criteria, an Alaskan gas transportation system appeared to be a higher priority for the nation.

Alaskan gas

Alaskan gas became a potential supplemental source in 1968, upon discovery of an immense hydrocarbon field at Prudhoe Bay, on the North Slope of Alaska. The field's proved gas reserves amounted to 26 trillion cubic feet, and geologists suspected that adjacent areas held additional reserves. The problem was getting it to U.S. markets at anywhere near competitive prices. The consortium that built the Alaskan oil pipeline had serious technological difficulties, regulatory delays, and very substantial cost overruns. To avoid repeating that experience, Congress enacted the Alaskan Natural Gas Transportation Act in 1976. It specified the terms, timetable, and procedure by which the President would select one of three competing proposals to deliver Alaskan gas. It also prohibited exportation of North Slope gas to Japan.[16]

Two consortia of gas pipeline companies submitted proposals to the Federal Power Commission in 1974. One group, named Arctic Gas, proposed to build a 48-inch-diameter pipeline east from Prudhoe Bay along the coast of the Beaufort Sea into Canada. From there, it would run south down the Mackenzie Delta, carrying both Alaskan and Canadian frontier gas into Alberta, and then on to markets in eastern Canada and the American Midwest. Its capital cost, estimated at $8.1 billion (1975 dollars), would yield a delivered price of $1.72

[14] Economic Regulatory Administration, *ERA/DOE Opinion No. 3*, December 18, 1978, and *ERA/DOE Opinion No. 4*, December 21, 1978.
[15] James Schlesinger, "Gas Prospects and Policy," remarks before the National Association of Petroleum Investment Analysts, New York, January 9, 1979.
[16] Alaskan Natural Gas Transportation Act of 1976, 15 USC 719.

per thousand cubic feet.[17] The other proposal, from the El Paso Natural Gas Company, entailed an "All American" route that its management believed was more consistent with President Ford's goals for energy independence. El Paso would build a gasline, parallel to the existing oil pipeline, from Prudhoe Bay to the south coast of Alaska. There, the gas would be liquefied and moved via a fleet of 11 LNG tankers to California to serve west coast markets. By displacing gas previously piped west to California, it would indirectly increase supplies elsewhere in the United States. Although its estimated capital cost was only $6.6 billion, the delivered price was somewhat higher, at $2.09 per thousand cubic feet, because of its higher operating costs. Either project would need an all-events tariff, and possibly government financial assistance, to attract investors.[18]

Northwest Energy Company, at one time a member of the Arctic group and before that, a subsidiary of El Paso, submitted its own proposal in July 1976. Northwest formed a consortium of American and Canadian firms with a plan to build a 1,600 mile pipeline, down the oil pipeline corridor to Fairbanks, and then southeast across Canada following the Alcan Highway to Alberta. There it would branch with delivery systems to eastern Canada and Chicago. Its estimated cost was $6.7 billion, with a delivered price of $1.79. Northwest claimed it could finance the project entirely from private sources, although it too would require an all-events tariff. Proponents of the Alcan project, as it was called, touted its minimal impact on the environment (using previously developed right-of-ways) and characterized it as a truly cooperative venture between the U.S. and Canada. This claim was especially pregnant after the Berger Commission in Canada ruled out the Arctic Gas project because of its negative impact on Canadian arctic wilderness areas and on the life-styles of the native (Eskimo) population.

To facilitate prospects for a trans-Canadian pipeline, the U.S. State Department had already negotiated a "Transit Pipeline Agreement" with the government of Canada. It covered existing and future pipelines and provided guarantees of throughput and non-discriminatory treatment of hydrocarbon flows with regard to taxes or other monetary charges.[19] Shortly after this agreement was concluded, the Federal Power Commission announced its decision, based on a record-breaking 235 volumes of evidence. The Commissioners split 2–2 between the Arctic and Alcan systems, agreeing that an overland route was "preferable because of its greater reliability, easier expansibility, greater efficiency in terms of gas consumed in route, and lesser environmental impact."[20]

[17] The Companies Comprising the Arctic Gas Project, *More for Less: A Summary Statement of the Advantages to the United States of the Arctic Gas Project* (Washington, 1977); also, U.S. Congress, Senate, Committee on Energy and Natural Resources, *Decision and Report to Congress on the Alaskan Natural Gas Transportation System* (95th Cong., 1st Sess.), Committee Print, No. 95-56, 1977, p. 117.
[18] U.S. Congress, Senate, Committees on Commerce and Interior, Joint Hearings, *The Transportation of Alaskan Natural Gas* (94th Cong., 2nd Sess.), March 1976, pp. 1559–1571.
[19] U.S. Congress, Senate, *Decision and Report on ANGTS*, pp. 151–153.
[20] U.S. Federal Power Commission, *FPC News Release No. 23113*, May 2, 1977.

Together, the treaty and the FPC's recommendation pretty much eliminated El Paso's project from the running. That company had organized most of its political support within the State of Alaska. Although it did win some early support from environmental groups that opposed the Arctic Gas project, most of them transferred their support to Alcan after FPC studies indicated problems with seismic stability at the liquefaction-plant site. As to Washington, El Paso had relied on President Ford's stated concern for keeping energy sources as independent as possible.[21]

President Carter announced his selection of Alcan in September. Secretary Schlesinger emphasized its benefits to the U.S. economy, its environmental soundness, and its symbolic significance for future cooperation and interdependence between Canada and the United States.[22] He also noted the fact that Alcan required no direct government aid other than the allowance of rolled-in pricing.[23]

Imports from good neighbors

One reason for the Carter administration's commitment to energy cooperation with Canada was the fact that Canada was already the oldest and largest supplemental source of natural gas for the United States. Since 1965, imports from the province of Alberta had grown 12 percent annually until 1973 when they peaked at just over 1 trillion cubic feet.[24] But Canada's National Energy Board had decided that domestic gas reserves were inadequate for Canada's own future demand. Accordingly, it rejected all pending applications for new gas exports, imposing a freeze that lasted until 1981. Gas exports continued under existing long-term contracts to northern-tier cities in the United States.

By agreement between the Canadian federal government and Alberta, gas export prices were linked to the Btu-equivalent price of imported oil or alternate fuels available in U.S. markets. Prices had thus been relatively stable until 1974.[25] In November of that year, the price for exports was increased to $1.00 per thousand cubic feet, marking the first in a series of substantial, unilateral price hikes.[26] Although considerably higher than regulated rates in the United States, Canadian prices maintained an approximate parity with the Btu-equivalent price of No. 6 residual oil. Since residual was the usual substitute fuel for

[21] Interview, Howard Boyd. See speech by Gerald Ford in the House of Representatives, *Congressional Record*, August 3, 1973, pp. H7297-H7309, in which he argued vigorously against a trans-Canadian oil pipeline on national security grounds.

[22] U.S. Congress, House, Committee on Interstate and Foreign Commerce, Subcommittee on Energy and Power, *Natural Gas Pipeline from Alaska* (95th Cong., 1st Sess.), September 1977, pp. 163–184.

[23] For a careful analysis of Alcan's commitments, see Arlon Tussing and Connie Barlow, "The Alaska Highway Gas Pipeline – A Look at the Current Impasse," A Report to the Alaska State Legislature (Juneau: Legislative Affairs Agency, 1979), pp. 20–27.

[24] American Gas Association, *Gas Facts 1979* (Washington: AGA, 1980), p. 31.

[25] G. C. Watkins, "Canadian Oil and Gas Pricing," in the Fraser Institute, *Oil in the Seventies* (Canada: The Fraser Institute, 1977), pp. 89–124.

[26] Economic Regulatory Administration, *ERA/DOE Opinion and Order No. 14*, February 16, 1980, p. 6.

natural gas to interruptible customers that constituted marginal demand, the Canadian price was tolerable, although not appreciated, by the FPC and by Schlesinger when he assumed authority for international gas commerce. And since it supplied dependent customers, the U.S. government couldn't do much about it anyway.

In 1977, the prospect for natural gas imports from Mexico presented radically different circumstances and questions of policy for the U.S. government. The administration of President Lopez Portillo had begun a concerted effort to expand exploration and development of Mexico's hydrocarbon resources. These efforts proved immensely and immediately successful. Mexico's estimated reserves of oil and natural gas (reported jointly) jumped from 11 to 46 billion barrels of oil-equivalent. The natural gas portion of this amounted to 70 trillion cubic feet.[27]

These were timely discoveries. Mexico had just experienced an economic crisis that resulted in the restructuring of its foreign debt and a 50 percent devaluation of the peso; the energy discoveries seemed like "divine intervention." To Jorges Diaz Serrano, the Director General of Mexico's national oil company, Pemex, it seemed obvious that to overcome the crisis, "it was necessary to use that source of wealth likely to produce immediate returns."[28] That source was surplus natural gas from the new southern oilfields which Pemex was flaring at a rate of more than 500 million cubic feet a day.

Early in 1977, Pemex commenced negotiations with several American pipeline companies that were eager to tap into the huge Mexican gas supply. The Mexican government planned to build a 42-inch-diameter pipeline that would deliver natural gas 600 miles from southern Mexico to the city of Reynosa near the American border. In April, and again in June, Diaz Serrano visited Washington to discuss with James Schlesinger the prospects for exporting as much as 2 billion cubic feet a day to the United States. Schlesinger explained that under existing regulations, the U.S. government would have to approve the pricing aspects of the project. He also made clear that a price above that recently set by Canada ($2.16) would be unreasonable, and that a pricing formula linked to a crude-oil escalator was also unsuitable. The Mexicans, however, felt that natural gas was a premium fuel and should be priced at parity with other high-quality fuels such as No. 2 Distillate (home-heating oil).[29]

In August, Pemex called six American pipeline companies to Mexico City to sign a letter of intent. It called for deliveries of gas rising gradually over three years. The price was stipulated as the monthly average, Btu-equivalent price of No.2 distillate oil at New York Harbor.[30] At the time, that meant an initial price

[27] U.S. Congress, Senate, Committee on Foreign Relations, *Mexico's Oil and Gas Policy: An Analysis*, prepared by the Congressional Research Service (95th Cong., 2nd Sess.), Committee Print, December 1978, p. 17.

[28] Diaz Serrano, "Report of the Director General of Petroleos Mexicanos," Mexico City, March 18, 1978 (mimeo).

[29] James Schlesinger, interview with the author, December 1979; also, Jorges Diaz Serrano, interview with the author, November 1979.

[30] Economic Regulatory Administration, Docket No. 77-003-NG, Tenneco Inter-America, Inc.

of $2.60 per thousand cubic feet. The six firms formed a consortium called Border Gas and filed preliminary application for the FPC's approval.[31] Bilateral negotiations continued sporadically for the remainder of the year, but finally collapsed four days before Christmas when Schlesinger declined to approve the terms of the deal.[32]

While the timing of the gas pipeline project had seemed ideal for Mexico, it came at a politically difficult juncture for the Carter administration. Congress was heatedly debating the President's National Energy Plan and was bogged down with the natural gas amendments. The President's bill proposed a fragile compromise to price new domestic gas at $1.75 with escalation linked to the Btu-equivalent price of regulated, domestic crude oil. The initial price in the Mexican gas deal was 50 percent higher. To approve it during the congressional debate would anger both consumer and producer interests and undermine the Administration's legislative rationale.[33]

Approval of the Mexican gas sale would also have conflicted with Schlesinger's priorities for supplemental gas sources. A higher price for Mexican gas would put irresistible political pressure on the Canadian government to seek parity. This condition risked the start of a leap-frogging dynamic between Canada and Mexico that Schlesinger, recalling the pricing actions of Libya and Iran in the early 1970's, wished to avoid.

Worse still from the Carter administration's viewpoint was a complex link between the price and volume of Mexico's gas and the Alaskan gas pipeline. Schlesinger believed that Alaskan gas offered the greatest long-run benefits for the United States, once the problem of upfront capital costs was solved. The existing supply of cheap domestic gas (with an average price of 69 cents in 1977) could be viewed as a cushion of subsidy, available to any particular source of high-cost gas via rolled-in pricing. Schlesinger preferred to apply the cushion to Alaskan gas, and as a second choice, domestic coal gasification. Since Mexican gas would be rolled-in under existing statutes, its importation in such a large quantity and at such a high price would raise average gas prices and erode the cushion otherwise available for Alaskan natural gas.[34]

Price stability was another consideration. Secretary Schlesinger objected to

et al., August 11, 1977. Members of the Border Gas group were to receive the following portions of gas: Tenneco, 37.5 percent; Texas Eastern, 27.5 percent; El Paso, 15 percent; Transco, 10 percent; Southern Natural and Florida Gas, 10 percent jointly.

[31] *Platt's Oilgram* and *Oil Price Handbook*, 1977. Platt's quotation for No. 2 Distillate (at New York Harbor) was 35 cents a gallon for August 1977. At 42 gallons per barrel, with a Btu-conversion factor of 1 to 5.71, this figures out to a price of $2.60 per thousand cubic feet. The same calculation based on the September 1979 quotation of 68.5 cents a gallon comes to $5.04 per thousand cubic feet.

[32] U.S. Department of Energy, "Chronology of U.S.-Mexican Gas Discussions," January 30, 1979 (mimeo).

[33] For the reaction of domestic producer interests, see *Oil and Gas Journal*, September 12, 1977, p. 58; also, *Chemical Week*, September 14, 1977, p. 14.

[34] For an analysis and explanation of this effect, see Arlon Tussing and Connie Barlow, "Marketing and Financing Supplemental Gas: The Outlook for, and Federal Policy Regarding, Synthetic Gas, LNG, and Alaska Natural Gas" (Anchorage: Institute of Social and Economic Research, 1978), Chapter 5.

direct, contractual linkage of the natural gas price to world oil prices, much less imported No.2 Distillate. He believed that the relevant substitute was residual oil, and even then, there was no good reason for the United States to endorse the establishment of a worldwide commodity price for energy.[35] If OPEC raised its prices again soon, the contractual price of Mexican gas would increase proportionately. As things turned out, the second oil shock had just that effect. Had the 1977 deal been approved, the price of Mexican gas would have reached $5.04 by September 1979, even before deliveries had begun.[36]

At their summit meeting in February 1979, Presidents Carter and Lopez Portillo agreed to renew bilateral consideration of Mexican gas imports. In September, after months of arduous negotiations, the two governments finally compromised on a price of $3.62, but for only 300 million cubic feet a day, less than a sixth of the original amount. The initial price, about the same as residual oil, would escalate with the international price of crude oil.[37] Although Schlesinger was no longer Secretary of Energy, he nonetheless felt the deal was consistent with the interests of the United States. The price was in line with that of Canada, the escalator was appropriate, and the volume was small enough so as not to undermine the pricing of Alaskan gas.[38]

At the beginning of the 1970's, supplemental sources of gas were economic anomalies, made feasible by the failures of regulation. By the end of the 1970's, they were political anomalies, feasible only if the federal government supported them. The Alaskan gas pipeline was stalled. With its cost estimated at $40 billion, sponsors were making quiet inquiries about the possibilities for getting financial support from the government. Commercial coal gasification had still not gotten started due to regulatory and financial difficulties. The Great Plains Gasification Project was delayed by rate litigation, even though the Energy Department had guaranteed its debt up to $1.5 billion. Imported LNG had proven unreliable. In 1980, a new Algerian government demanded a 400 per-cent price increase in order to obtain Btu-parity with OPEC oil. When the U.S. government balked, Algeria terminated deliveries. After seven rounds of bilateral negotiations, the two governments remained more than a dollar apart. The El Paso Company could only look on as a bystander and report an immense loss on the project. The Mexican government had announced its intention to hold gas exports at the existing low level for the foreseeable future. And finally, there was Canadian gas, no longer any cheaper than gas from Mexico. In February

[35] Interview, James Schlesinger. In Schlesinger's view, the United States was a monopsonistic buyer (of Mexican gas) in a buyer's market, since gas and oil were not fungible in the short run. Diaz Serrano acknowledged this point when he described the United States as "the only feasible market" for Mexican gas; see J. Diaz Seranno, "National Trunk Line for Distribution of Natural Gas," before the Chamber of Deputies, Mexico City, October 26, 1977, English translation in U.S. Congress, Senate, Committee on Energy and Natural Resources, *Mexico: The Promise and Problems of Petroleum* (96th Cong., 1st Sess.), Committee Print No. 96–2, March 1979, Appendix B.
[36] See footnote 32.
[37] Economic Regulatory Administration, Docket No. 79-31-NG, "Application of Border Gas, Inc. for Authority Pursuant to Section 3 of the Natural Gas Act to Import Natural Gas from Mexico," November 6, 1979; also, *ERA/DOE Opinion and Order No. 12*, December 29, 1979.
[38] Interview, James Schlesinger.

1980, Canada announced an immediate price increase to $4.47 per thousand cubic feet. The leapfrogging impulse that Schlesinger had sought to avoid with Mexico was initiated by Canada. Although the Carter administration had to accept those terms for flowing gas, it refused to approve any new contracts at that price until a deal was worked out to reinstate Btu-parity with residual oil.[39]

In both Canada and the United States, there was a growing surplus of natural gas that would delay development of supplemental sources for as much as another decade.

Congressional quagmire

While Nassikas struggled with regulatory reform and Schlesinger set priorities for supplemental gas, Congress slowly and grudgingly addressed the underlying problem – the Natural Gas Act. Finding a politically acceptable formula for amending the Act proved no less difficult in the 1970's than it had two decades earlier. Each time Congress ignored or defeated another proposal, the gas shortage worsened, public and industry pressure intensified, and the issue loomed larger on the next year's legislative calendar. Congress passed the Natural Gas Policy Act in 1978, only after severe winter curtailments had caused considerable hardship and economic loss.

Political debate evolved through three recognizable stages. From 1969–1973, Congress considered partial deregulation and structural reform of FPC procedure. From 1974–1977, a momentum toward complete deregulation developed, but did not succeed. Finally, as a part of President Carter's National Energy Plan, a compromise program emerged for commodity price regulation accompanied by gradual decontrol of new gas. Throughout, the same issues predominated: distributive equity between producers and consumers, economic regionalism, the competitive versus monopolistic nature of energy markets, and the tensions between cost-based and commodity-based rate regulation.

The Murphy Bill, first introduced in 1969 by Representative William Murphy of New York, did not receive serious attention from Congress until 1971. By then, curtailments had begun and all three sectors of the gas industry were generally united on behalf of higher prices and the need for remedial legislation. The bill was an assortment of partial measures aimed at making regulation more palatable to producers without seriously alienating consumer groups. On this second count, it failed completely. Murphy's bill contained three important provisions. First, it would guarantee producers "sanctity of contract," meaning that once the FPC approved a sales contract at a particular price, it could not order refunds when it later determined that the "just and reasonable" rate should be lower. Second, the bill would remove small contracts (under 10 million cubic feet a day) from normal FPC regulatory requirements. This would affect 93 percent of all transactions, but only a quarter of all gas sold.

[39] Economic Regulatory Administration, *ERA/DOE Opinion and Order No. 14A,* April 23, 1980, Appendix II.

Third, the bill would make explicit the FPC's authority to consider non-cost factors in its rate determinations.[40]

Although spokesmen for the gas industry unanimously supported the proposed legislation, neither producers nor pipeline companies felt it went far enough. Nor were they confident that it would provide the incentives necessary to alleviate projected curtailments. On behalf of the Natural Gas Supply Committee, Kenneth Vaughan acknowledged that the bill was "a realistic attempt to make regulation consistent with the industry being regulated." Still, he complained that it did not provide adequate discretionary authority for the FPC to use price to stimulate supply.[41] But it was the endorsement of distributors that most impressed congressmen. Witnesses for the American Gas Association and several companies carefully explained how circumstances had changed, compelling them to join with the producers in seeking higher prices and legislative reform.

One other industry voice joined with the gas people in endorsing the Murphy Bill. Carl Bagge, who had left the FPC to become president of the National Coal Association, complained that it was less than deregulation, but "an important step in the right direction."[42]

There was no doubt in the minds of consumer advocates that this legislation was just that – a step in the direction of deregulation. Viewing it as a Trojan horse, they mobilized strong opposition to the proposal. Charles Wheatley, Joseph Swidler, and David Calfee (of Ralph Nader's organization) were the principal spokesmen for this opposition. They raised all the arguments regarding data manipulation, reserve withholding, supply inelasticity and monopoly that were already being aired in the regulatory forum. Swidler accounted for the distributors' support of the bill by arguing that producers had them and the pipeline companies over a barrel. "It is not hard in a period like this," concluded Swidler, "for the producers to mass a great deal of support."[43]

The Federal Power Commission's position in this controversy was an important balancing factor. Even though Chairman Nassikas supported some of the concepts in the Murphy bill, he opposed its specifics in 1971 and continued to hedge on the 1972 version. The sanctity of contract provisions appeared to pose difficulties for the Commission's rate-making procedure. The small contract exemption seemed superfluous since the Commission had already deregulated small producers. And Nassikas viewed the injection of non-cost criteria as excessive, possibly prohibiting the FPC from applying any cost-based criteria.[44] This faint-heartedness by the Commission hurt the perceived legitimacy of the bill. It never made it out of committee.

Beginning in 1973, the energy crisis seemed to polarize the gas question

[40] U.S. Congress, House, Committee on Interstate Commerce, Subcommittee on Communications and Power, *Natural Gas Act of 1971* (92nd Cong., 1st Sess.), September 1971, pp. 20–27.
[41] *Ibid.*, 162.
[42] U.S. Congress, Senate, Committee on Commerce, *Natural Gas Regulation* (92nd Cong., 2nd Sess.), March 1972, p. 191.
[43] *Ibid.*, 141.
[44] *Ibid.*, 46–49.

between two fundamental choices; Congress could deregulate the wellhead price of gas (or at least new gas), or else extend regulation to the intrastate markets as well. The growing gap and resulting depletion of interstate reserves militated for one or the other. Of course, this made the prospect of continued and expanded regulation even less acceptable to producers and to politicians ideologically predisposed against regulation. As a result, most bills introduced between 1974 and 1977 were either deregulation measures or counter-proposals for expanding the FPC's jurisdiction. A Republican-Dixicrat coalition supported deregulation, as it had during the Truman and Eisenhower years. Democratic consumerists from the urban Northeast favored broader federal regulation.

The historical parallel was incomplete, however, even though consumer spokesmen like Lee White drew on it for rhetorical effect. Both the energy economy and the political environment had changed. Consumer groups that opposed deregulation were now better organized for political action. Moreover, their political premise was reversed. When the *Phillips* decision had forced the regulation of wellhead prices for interstate commerce, consumer activists had welcomed it as a desirable departure from the *status quo*. But by 1976, the groups opposing deregulation saw regulation as the norm. So much so, in fact, that the unregulated, intrastate market seemed quite illegitimate. The Commission, said Charles Wheatley, "is powerless to deal with the efforts of the natural gas companies subject to its regulation to pursue what they believe is a major loophole in the Natural Gas Act." Thus, it could not "prevent discrimination against the interstate market by natural gas companies [selling] gas in the intrastate market at unregulated prices."[45] No less an authority than Joseph Swidler also adopted this extraordinary logic. "If regulation were extended to the intrastate market," said Swidler, "it would become feasible to exempt the smaller producers because *closing the intrastate loophole* [emphasis added] would release large volumes for the interstate market."[46] This was the Tar Baby, run amuck.

Price inelasticity of supply was the argument used most effectively by consumer advocates to oppose deregulation. By January 1976, the FPC's efforts to stimulate supply by raising prices had been underway for five years. As anti-deregulation people inevitably pointed out, the regulated price for new natural gas had already risen from 16 to 52 cents, and the Commission was on the verge of increasing it again to $1.42. And yet, curtailments were still climbing while reserve commitments to the interstate market kept shrinking. Where was the new supply that price hikes had stimulated?

Industry spokesmen had two answers which, no matter how true, seemed to carry little weight in political dialogue. First, they said, the price increases still lagged inflation of costs. Second, they noted that the decline in new drilling had in fact reversed. As evidence that the market mechanism was truly working,

---

[45] U.S. Congress, House, Committee on Interstate Commerce, Subcommittee on Energy and Power, *Long-term Natural Gas Legislation* (94th Cong., 2nd Sess.), January-February, 1976, p. 1710.
[46] *Ibid.*, 977–978.

producers pointed to recent data from intrastate markets. In Texas, price was finally levelling off, signaling that demand and supply had nearly reached equilibrium.

The polarized venue of legislative options also revealed a divergence of interests within the gas industry. Those differences, while subdued in 1976, augured a more serious breach in the future.

At one extreme, the smaller, independent producers desperately sought nothing short of deregulation, even if just for themselves, leaving the major integrated oil companies under the FPC's thumb. Independents were especially opposed to any thought of regulating the intrastate markets in which they did a disproportionate share of their business. They also felt unjustly saddled with the monopoly-conspiracy critique that slopped over from attacks on the majors. As in the oil issue, they characterized themselves – "4,000 small producers" – as vigorous, if not cutthroat competitors.[47] Although preferring general deregulation, the Independent Petroleum Association was not unsympathetic to other bills that would deregulate only the independents. Obviously, this was not even a partial solution from the perspective of the majors. They would support nothing short of total decontrol.

The transmission sector was beginning to waiver. Although it supported decontrol, it did so partly to avoid incremental pricing. But the preeminent concern of pipeline companies was the interstate-intrastate price imbalance. Although left unstated, it was evident that legislation to extend regulation to the intrastate market would also solve that problem.

The American Gas Association did not take a position on the legislative options in 1976. Its membership was divided between deregulation and expanded regulation. Either way, distributors would receive more gas, but the latter approach might be cheaper.

In the final days of the Ford administration, two bills languished in conference committee. By a narrow margin, the Senate had voted to deregulate new natural gas. The House had only passed a substitute amendment that exempted small producers from FPC jurisdiction. With a presidential election pending and consensus obviously lacking, the conference could not reconcile the differences. With that, the initiative passed to Jimmy Carter.

The Carter promise

In the heat of their campaigns, presidential candidates make many promises that no one in Washington takes very seriously. But in October 1976, Jimmy Carter wrote a letter to the governors of the gas-producing states in which he clearly endorsed deregulation of new natural gas.[48] Like other new presidents after a couple of months in Washington, Carter apparently discovered that political issues such as gas deregulation were a good deal more complex than anticipated. By February 1977, it appeared that his Administration had mixed

[47] U.S. Congress, House, *Long-term Natural Gas Legislation*, pp. 579–591.
[48] *Wall Street Journal*, February 24, 1977.

feelings on the subject. Both John O'Leary, the Federal Energy Administrator, and Cecil Andrus, the Interior Secretary, declined to endorse deregulation. James Schlesinger hedged on the issue, hinting that the President might have changed his mind.

More than likely, the Administration was buckling under public anger at the severe gas shortages during January and February. The President had supported an Emergency Natural Gas Act that Congress rushed through in the last week of January. It authorized President Carter to order pipeline companies to transfer gas from surplus to shortage areas. It also empowered him to waive controls on the price that interstate pipelines could pay producers, at least until July. Sales under those emergency orders brought prices in the range of $2.25, or 58 percent above the new gas price most recently approved by the FPC.[49] As a precursor of the market price, this experience foretold of large political costs to deregulation, possibly shaking the Carter administration's prior resolve.

The National Energy Plan included a proposal to amend the Natural Gas Act. It turned out to be the single most controversial legislative problem in the entire package. As a Senate report later noted, "few bills in national history ran such a legislative gauntlet as did the Natural Gas Policy Act of 1978."[50] Schlesinger and his staff had devised a compromise between producers and consumers and between the Sun Belt and the Northeast. Although President Carter felt it was a fair and practical approach, it was not the promised deregulation. "By helping bring natural gas supply and demand back into balance," read the Plan, "this pricing proposal would be a first step toward deregulation." If so, then "by the mid-1980's, it might be possible and desirable to move further toward establishing full market pricing."[51]

The Carter team proposed to continue FPC regulation, but to substitute commodity-pricing for cost-based rate making. New gas would be priced at the Btu-equivalent price of domestic crude oil. At the beginning of 1978, that would be approximately $1.75 per thousand cubic feet, and would escalate according to a formula based on inflation. Old interstate gas, upon contract expiration, could be rolled-over at a price determined by the FPC, up to $1.42. To the amazement of gas producers, that was the part of the compromise in their favor. On the other side, the Carter proposal extended federal regulation to the intrastate market, allowing it the same price of $1.75 as for new gas. The only difference would be that roll-over contracts in the intrastate markets could move to the prevailing new gas price. Pipeline companies too were asked to sacrifice. High-cost, supplemental gas sources (except for Alaska) would be incrementally priced and allocated to industrial, rather than residential, users. The net effect of these proposals, according to the National Energy Plan,

[49] Federal Power Commission, "Summary of the General Orders Issued Under the Emergency Natural Gas Act of 1977," in U.S. Congress, House, Commerce Committee, Subcommittee on Energy and Power, *National Energy Act*, (95th Cong., 1st Sess.), May 1977, Pt. 2, pp. 780–819.
[50] U.S. Congress, Senate, Committee on Energy and Natural Resources, *Energy Initiatives of the 95th Congress* (96th Cong., 1st Sess.), 1979, p. 43.
[51] Executive Office of the President, *The National Energy Plan* (Washington: GPO, 1977), p. 53.

"would be about as much gas" as under total deregulation; "but in addition, windfall profits would be prevented."[52]

When Schlesinger's group devised the National Energy Plan, it largely avoided consultations and the usual process of running ideas "up the flagpole" with the various interested groups and key congressmen. Instead, it had opted for the dramatic announcement after developing the program internally. This unfortunate decision reflected the technocratic character of Carter's key policy advisors and the political naivete of his White House staff. This element of surprise may have elicited even more negative responses by industry groups than otherwise. And, since the Administration had laid no groundwork of committee support in the Congress, with the possible exception of Speaker Tip O'Neill, congressmen were free to disassociate themselves from any unpopular provision. In other words, the process, as well as the content of the Plan, contributed to an extraordinary legislative battle that ensued almost immediately.

Because of O'Neill's support, the House moved more quickly to take up the substantive issues of the legislative proposals. A special Energy Committee was formed, and O'Neill appointed the members with great care. Before making his selections, O'Neill reviewed a 1975 test vote on gas deregulation. He made sure that 18 of the 32 committee members he appointed had voted against deregulation and were therefore likely to support the President's proposal.[53] In the hearings, Schlesinger argued that cost-based regulation, rather than regulation *per se*, had caused the gas shortage. By switching to commodity-based price regulation, the Administration's bill would bring about a rational price relationship among substitute fuels.[54]

As might be expected, neither industry nor consumer groups could discern elements of compromise in the President's gas bill. Energy Action, the Consumers Federation, and the American Public Gas Association all came out swinging against every aspect of the bill except for its incremental pricing and regulation of intrastate gas. They called it *de facto* deregulation, a cave-in to the monopoly power of OPEC and the major oil companies, and a gross windfall for producers. Behind this rhetorical posturing were ideological convictions that Lee White expressed in the clearest, simplest terms. "The whole concept of cost-based regulation is far and away the most equitable system to use," said White. "We believe price to be one of the most regressive techniques for rations and allocation that there is."[55] This view flatly rejected the market mechanism as an effective means of distributing resources. The invisible hand, or even a slightly visible one, did not assure equity, which is what these groups evidently cared most about. The immensity of the ideological gap, between consumerists and most energy-industry managers, helps explain why Congress had such difficulty legislating a satisfactory compromise.

Gas industry spokesmen lambasted the Carter proposal and endorsed instead the deregulation bills that were reintroduced in Congress. The indepen-

52 *Ibid.*, 53–55.
53 *Wall Street Journal*, April 22, 1977.
54 U.S. Congress, House, *National Energy Act*, pp. 68–70.
55 *Ibid.*, 1173–1174.

dent producers were most upset. "Contrary to what candidate Carter promised," said A. V. Jones on behalf of the Independent Petroleum Association, "President Carter's proposal would perpetuate controls indefinitely with no hope of achieving competitive market prices." It was not just the gas bill to which they objected, but the entire Energy Plan: "We find the Carter energy proposal to be poorly conceived, poorly drafted and internally inconsistent," said Jones. It "contains all the elements for economic chaos at home and political nightmares on the international front." To these businessmen, the Carter administration exhibited an attitude of unwarranted fatalism about future prospects for domestic energy production and the elasticity of domestic supply.[56]

Were it not for the incremental pricing provisions, Carter's gas bill might have satisfied the distribution and transmission sectors. They could live with the proposed price levels, if applied equally to the intrastate and interstate markets. But the provisions for incremental pricing appeared to impede commercial development of high-cost, supplemental gas sources. If industrial users had to bear the full cost of synthetic gas, or expensive imports from Mexico and Canada, without benefit of rolled-in pricing, then those projects would be far less competitive with alternate fuels. Since the interstate pipelines and large distribution companies were the principal sponsors of most such projects, they were the ones threatened by the prospect of incremental pricing.[57]

As early as June, in the Senate hearings, one could detect the beginnings of fragmentation among the various industry groups. The White House eventually recognized this tendency and manipulated it with some effect toward getting its gas bill enacted. On the surface, the entire industry still supported deregulation, but when pressed, were willing to indicate their minimum needs. For example, a spokesman for the Independent Gas Producers Committee testified that regulation of multi-national energy companies and regulation of independents were actually separate issues. The multi-nationals were involved in foreign projects and offshore operations, "necessarily intertwined with extensive governmental regulations" and "economic controls." But not so with independents. Exempting independents "while imposing realistic ceiling prices" on the integrated majors "will rapidly increase competition within the industry."[58] This, of course, was bad news for the major companies that had no congressional allies of their own.

The pipeline companies also identified their minimal needs. Richard O'Shields, of the Interstate Natural Gas Association, preferred "to achieve parity with the intrastate market by asking the Congress to deregulate the price of 'new' natural gas." But if a "ceiling price is to continue in the interstate market," it "should be applied to all gas."[59] This left the major producers

[56] *Ibid.*, 254–257, 329.
[57] *Ibid.*, 1225.
[58] U.S. Congress, Senate, Committee on Energy and Natural Resources, *Natural Gas Pricing Proposals of President Carter's Energy Program (Part D of S. 1469)* (95th Cong., 1st Sess.), June 1977, pp. 235–245.
[59] *Ibid.*, 592.

focusing on complete deregulation and distributors primarily opposing incremental pricing. With the opposition so dispersed, the President's legislative managers could take hope.

Meanwhile, the House Subcommittee on Energy and Power attached an amendment to the Carter bill, providing for deregulation of new natural gas. This move elicited an unusually harsh public statement by the President who called it a "ripoff" by the big oil companies. Perhaps that helped, for the full Commerce Committee reinstated the President's original proposal by a 22 to 21 vote. President Carter declared "a major victory for the American consumer."[60] With the Speaker riding close herd over the bill, it moved intact from the Commerce Committee to the Ad Hoc Energy Committee and then on to the House floor. In August, the deregulation forces narrowly failed in a final attempt to amend the legislation in floor debate. Two days later, the House passed its version of the President's Natural Gas Policy Act.

Resistance to the entire National Energy Plan was more intense in the Senate. There, the Majority Leader had less control and northeast consuming states had less proportionate representation. In September, the Senate Energy Committee deadlocked 9–9 on a vote to substitute a gas-deregulation bill for the President's. As a result, the bill went to the floor without the committee's endorsement. An intense debate ensued in which Senator Henry Jackson tried to defend the Administration's bill against an onslaught of criticism from the Republican-Dixiecrat coalition. A test vote, which showed the strength of deregulation sentiment, triggered a four-day filibuster by Senators Metzenbaum and Abourezk. After a vote of cloture, the filibuster continued in a thinly disguised form. The two senators insisted on debate and roll-call votes for each of 508 amendments that had been introduced previously.[61] After several more days, the President withdrew his support for the filibuster and Vice-President Mondale ruled each amendment out of order as Senator Byrd brought them up in rapid succession. The Senate then adopted an amendment that provided for deregulation of wellhead prices on new natural gas after two years of gradual increases following the Btu-equivalent price of No.2 home heating oil.[62]

When the conference committee convened in December, it faced what seemed to be an insurmountable negotiating task. The House and Senate gas bills were completely different in principle and particulars. After three months of deliberation, Senator Jackson got the President's support for a fragile compromise in which new gas would be regulated according to the Administration's price schedule until 1985 when deregulation would take hold. Thrown in was a liberalized definition of "new gas," moderation of the incremental pricing provision, and sanctity for existing gas contracts. By this point, President Carter desperately wanted some kind of legislation so that the entire energy package would not fail. That would be a defeat of major proportions for his Administra-

---

[60] *Wall Street Journal*, June 30, 1977.
[61] *Congressional Record*, September 22, 1977, pp. S15322–S15365, and September 26, 1977, pp. S15595–S15604.
[62] U.S. Congress, Senate, *Energy Initiatives of the 95th Congress*, pp. 45–46.

tion. The White House pulled out all the stops in pressuring the industry to accept the compromise. The pipelines and distributors were willing, and finally, the major oil companies grudgingly withdrew their opposition.

Still, the congressional negotiations dragged on for months to iron out the details and obtain final approval of each house.[63] Not until the early hours of Sunday, October 15, did the Senate vote cloture on another filibuster by Senator Abourezk, and then vote passage of the Natural Gas Policy Act of 1978. With relief, but little enthusiasm, Jimmy Carter signed it on November 9th.

After 40 years, the nation had a new policy for regulating natural gas – a complicated, 60-page act that would be difficult, if not impossible, to administer. The Act established nine price categories, each containing several subcategories that identified different gas sources, well depths, commencement dates, etc. New gas was allowed a price of $1.75 with an inflation-plus escalator until 1985 when it would be deregulated. This applied to both the interstate and intrastate markets. Old interstate gas was priced in three vintages ranging from 29 cents to $1.45 plus inflation, but would remain regulated indefinitely. Expiring contracts for flowing interstate gas were allowed 54 cents plus inflation; for intrastate gas, $1.00 or the old contract price. Deep gas, from below 15,000 feet, got the new gas price until early decontrol. Gas from stripper wells earned the highest price ($2.09 plus inflation), but remained regulated. Alaskan gas from Prudhoe Bay would remain regulated at a price to be set by the Federal Energy Regulatory Commission, but would be allowed rolled-in pricing as its one subsidy.[64] Other high-cost supplemental sources were to be priced incrementally for industrial users until the point at which that price reached the Btu-equivalent price of crude oil. Thereafter, their price would again be rolled-in.

Consequences of scarcity

The shift from surplus to shortage in the domestic market for natural gas posed new managerial problems for the industry and new regulatory problems for the government. After 1968, natural gas was clearly a rising-cost industry, increasingly dependent on marginal deposits, deeper drilling, offshore and foreign sources, and exotic technologies. What had been a relatively simple business became a high-risk, capital intensive enterprise in a politically volatile sector of the economy. Existing mechanisms of governmental decision-making staggered under the weight of these changes.

Shortages and public criticism forced the various sectors of the gas industry to close ranks. New policies to revalue natural gas and stimulate supply were in the interest of producers, pipeline companies, and distributors (not to mention consumers). This general consensus made possible the FPC's upward revision

[63] U.S. Congress, Senate, *Conference Report No. 95–1126*, "The Natural Gas Policy Act of 1978" (95th Cong., 2nd Sess.), August 18, 1978.
[64] Federal Energy Regulatory Commission, "Fact Sheet – Natural Gas Policy Act of 1978" (Washington: FERC, 1980).

of prices and the Carter administration's legislative compromise. But it was a fragile consensus that easily broke down at the point of hard bargaining and fine tuning. This, together with consumerist opposition to market-pricing, made reform more difficult and the outcome more complicated.

Over the course of the 1970's, the character of business-government relations in the gas sector changed dramatically. The balance, however, between administrative and market allocation of gas resources, changed little. On the one hand, the executive branch of government assumed greater authority over supplemental gas sources. By 1980, it appeared that enterprise could not develop large-scale projects for gas importation, LNG, or coal gasification without the cooperation, and perhaps financial support, of government. Price regulation, on the other hand, had evolved from a cost-of-service basis to administered commodity pricing – a closer approximation of the market. If the complexity of the Natural Gas Policy Act did not become overwhelming, then this seemed to be a tolerable outcome.

What stands out is the inefficiency of the policy process; it could not have been more inept. The adjustment to high-cost energy, and the issues of equity that entailed, was certainly a difficult challenge. But the legislative and administrative problems described in this chapter can only be attributed to institutional failure – the exclusive reliance on adversary process to make microeconomic policy.

13. National energy management

Energy crises in the decade of the 1970's strained the balance between market and administrative allocation of energy resources. Shortages, dependence on insecure foreign sources, and startling increases in price convinced the majority of Americans that government should intervene in a *comprehensive* manner to redirect the behavior of energy producers and consumers. With few exceptions after 1970, politicians, consumers, and business leaders shared a consensus that the United States needed a coherent national energy policy. But there was no agreement on the substance of such a policy. It derived from political choices between supply-stimulus and demand-reduction, direct and indirect allocative mechanisms, and centralized and decentralized organization. Unfortunately, the political process rarely made these choices explicit, nor considered their relationship to market price.

For all the effort spent in formulating a national energy policy, its effects, in the absence of sensible pricing policies, were bound to be marginal. At the time of the first OPEC shock, petroleum and natural gas together accounted for 77 percent of total energy consumption in the United States. Domestic supply of these two fuels, at prevailing administered prices, was the problem. Direct combustion of coal, which accounted for 18 percent of consumption, had some potential as a substitute, but was constrained by its impact on the environment. Nuclear power, with only 1.2 percent of the market, had already begun to stagnate in the face of virulent opposition. Hydro-power, which contributed 4 percent of energy consumption, had nearly reached its physical potential, while solar power held great promise, but in the long-term at best. Clean-burning synthetics from coal and oil shale, together with some enhanced recovery of conventional liquids, appeared to have the greatest potential on the supply-side of the energy balance.

Opportunities on the demand-side, although more abundant, were recognized belatedly, were difficult to implement politically, and were relatively ineffective if not linked to price. Demand-reduction ran counter to the values of a people accustomed to abundance, and served few of the organized constituencies that traditionally influenced public policy. Thus, serious attempts to mandate conservation and coal-substitution only began with the Ford administra-

313

tion; taxation as a means of demand-management was rejected politically for reasons similar to those that hampered price-adjustment.

This chapter examines the four areas of public policy, other than oil and gas pricing, that were at the heart of national energy management: (1) policy planning based on forecasts of supply-demand balances, (2) government reorganization, (3) sponsorship of synthetic fuels, and (4) conservation and demand management. While needed improvements were achieved in all four areas, the net result was far from comprehensive, and it is doubtful whether the ends justified the means.

Energy planning: the elusive equilibrium

As early as 1970, the prospect of domestic energy shortages had evoked an interest in forecasting and policy planning not seen since World War II. Government officials and energy managers alike were highly uncertain about the future course of energy supply, demand, and imports. Moreover, so many policy issues were coming to a head, including import quotas, gas pricing, taxation, R&D and leasing, that their inter-connectedness was increasingly apparent to those responsible for decisions.[1] Senior managers in the energy industries were frustrated in their own planning efforts by the internal contradictions and inconstancy of Washington's energy and environmental policies. "Piecemeal handling of energy problems," warned a spokesman for Skelly Oil in 1971, "is getting us deeper and deeper in trouble." In a similar, representative vein, a SoCal executive urged that "a more coordinated, consistent approach to energy matters at all government levels is essential."[2] But achieving coherence in public policy was easier said than done. To do so would require a convincing plan, a legislative package well enough designed and managed to survive the pressures of fragmentation in Congress, and organizational changes necessary to implement the resulting program.

Most major efforts at national energy planning during the 1970's had three components: (1) a set of economic and political assumptions, (2) alternative models of future energy supply and demand balance based on those assumptions, and (3) recommendations for changes in government policy. The purpose of planning was to disseminate information and provide a rational, rather than *ad hoc*, framework for public policy. Of the half-dozen major planning projects undertaken during the decade, three stand out as the most comprehensive and politically influential.[3] In December 1972, the National Petroleum Council

---

[1] H. M. Dole to J. H. Abernathy, January 20, 1970, and NPC, Agenda Committee, Meeting Transcript, January 20, 1970, NPC Files (1970), NPC/DOI.

[2] G. W. Selinger to N. G. Dumbros, June 17, 1971, and C. J. Carlton to N. G. Dumbros, June 21, 1971, in National Petroleum Council, Energy Outlook Files, Gulf Oil Corporation, Pittsburgh, PA.

[3] Another planning project that had a widespread intellectual, if not political, impact was the Ford Foundation's Energy Policy Project. The Project, begun in 1971 under the direction of F. David Freeman, involved more than 20 book-length studies, prepared largely by academic experts. The final, integrating report probably succeeded in shifting the orientation of public policy somewhat closer to a conservationist ethic. See, Ford Foundation, *A Time to Choose – America's Energy Future* (Cambridge: Ballinger, 1974).

Table 13-1. *Supply-demand balances for 1985 from* U.S. Energy Outlook

	1970 actual	Case I[a]	Case II[a]	Case III[a]	Case IV[a]
Total domestic supply	59.4	111.5	100.4	90.0	77.6
Total imported supply	8.4	13.4	24.5	34.9	47.3
Total domestic demand[b]	67.8	124.9	124.9	124.9	124.9

Note: Quadrillions of BTU's.
[a]Case I assumes recommended changes in government policy resulting in high levels of exploration and discovery, healthy coal, nuclear and synfuels industries, and minimal environmental delays. Case IV assumes no constructive changes in policy. Cases II and III are intermediate scenarios.
[b]Intermediate demand case in which energy demand grows 4.3 percent annually.
Source: National Petroleum Council, *U.S. Energy Outlook* (Washington: NPC, 1972), pp. 15, 29–32.

released *U.S. Energy Outlook*, a multi-volume report based on two years of work by more than a thousand industry personnel. Two years later, the Federal Energy Administration published *Project Independence Report*, "the most comprehensive energy analysis ever undertaken" in the FEA's own view.[4] And in April 1977, James Schlesinger's Energy Policy and Planning group in the Executive Office of the President released *The National Energy Plan;* the most explicit of the three in terms of proposals, but the least carefully documented by econometric modeling.[5]

In aggregate terms, Tables 13-1, 13-2, and 13-3 summarize the supply-demand balances forecast for 1985 by each of the plans. Although these numbers do a gross injustice to the depth of analysis behind all three plans, they do show the broadest differences in orientation and purpose. The NPC study, done by industry prior to the first OPEC shock, was clearly oriented toward the supply-side of the energy balance. Its recommendations were the most general, since they originated outside of government. Project Independence, just after the shock, looked at both supply and demand. The reality of significantly higher oil prices, the flexibility of the Project's econometric model, and the relative impartiality of its technocratic authors, account for this balance. Since it originated within government, but not the Executive Office, it posed options for public policy, but not recommendations. Finally, the National Energy Plan was oriented more toward demand-reduction and conservation. In part, this reflected the philosophical preference of its principal authors and of the President for whom it was prepared. Moreover, by 1977, its authors were preoccupied with steadily increasing dependence on imported oil, together with a continuing decline in domestic oil and gas production.

[4] Both of these planning projects yielded multiple volumes of supporting documentation and analysis. The summary volumes were entitled, National Petroleum Council, *U.S. Energy Outlook: A Summary Report*, December 1972 (Wash.: NPC, 1972); and, Federal Energy Administration, Project Independence, *Project Independence Report*, November 1974 (Wash.: GPO, 1974).
[5] Executive Office of the President, *The National Energy Plan* (Wash.: GPO, 1977).

Table 13-2. *Supply-demand balances for 1985 from* Project Independence Report

	1972 actual	Base case	Accelerated supply	Conservation	Accelerated supply & conservation
$7/bbl. oil price					
Total domestic supply	60.4	84.2	92.6	79.6	88.5
Total imported supply	11.7	24.9	17.0	19.6	11.2
Total domestic demand	72.1	109.1	109.6	99.2	99.7
$11/bbl. oil price					
Total domestic supply	60.4	96.3	104.2	91.8	96.3
Total imported supply	11.7	26.6	0	2.4	0
Total domestic demand	72.1	102.9	104.2	94.2	96.3

Note: Quadrillions of BTUs.
Source: Federal Energy Administration, *Project Independence Report* (Washington: GPO, 1974), p. 34.

Table 13-3. *Supply-demand balances for 1985 from* The National Energy Plan

	1976 actual		1985 without plan		1985 with plan	
	(MMB/D)	(Quads)	(MMB/D)	(Quads)	(MMB/D)	(Quads)
Total domestic supply	30.0	60.0	37.1[a]	74.2	40.0	80.0
Crude oil	9.7		10.4		10.6	
Natural gas	9.5		8.2		8.8	
Coal	7.9		12.2		14.5	
Nuclear	1.0		3.7		3.8	
Other	1.5		1.7		1.7	
Refinery gain	.4		.9		.6	
Total imported supply	7.0	14.0	11.5	23.0	6.4	12.8
Total domestic demand	37.0	74.0	48.3	96.6	46.4	92.8

Note: In Millions of Barrels per Day and Quadrillions of Btu's.
[a]Details do not add up due to rounding.
Source: Executive Office of the President, *The National Energy Plan* (Wash.: GPO, 1977), pp. 165–166.

When the National Petroleum Council agreed to prepare a long-range energy forecast and policy recommendations in 1970, its members expected it to "influence energy policies here in the United States and in the Western Hemisphere for a very long time to come."[6] As it turned out, the report did not have a

[6] National Petroleum Council, Committee on U.S. Energy Outlook, Meeting Transcript, November 16, 1970, NPC/DOI, pp. 8, 20.

lasting impact, in large measure because it failed to use good price assumptions as the basis for forecasting supply and demand.

One reason for this was the Council's long-standing sensitivity to the anti-trust laws. Warren Davis, a Gulf economist who chaired the coordinating committee for the study, chafed at this constraint from the outset. Normally in indicative planning, said Davis, the allocation of demand "should be determined by the relative prices of the various fuels." But "this method of operation is not feasible for committees of the NPC, because it would involve economists from competing companies getting together and discussing their forecasts of price trends."[7] Because of this limitation, and also because of the prevailing conviction among energy economists that demand was relatively insensitive to price, the Council estimated demand by extrapolating from the present growth rate of 4.2 percent per year. Thus, as Table 13-1 indicates, the Council suggested that without constructive changes in public policy (Case IV), 38 percent of U.S. energy demand would have to be supplied from foreign sources by 1985. And putting the cart before the horse, it estimated prices based on the average unit revenues required to support assumed levels of energy production.[8]

With this strained methodology, the National Petroleum Council justified policy recommendations that suited the preconceptions of most council-members. The major recommendations, in approximate order of importance, were as follows: (1) a coordinated and consistent national energy policy, (2) realistic environmental standards with minimal delays, (3) decontrol of natural gas field prices, (4) accelerated leasing of mineral rights in Alaska, the Outer Continental Shelf, and the lower-48 states, (5) maintenance of oil import quotas, (6) more favorable tax incentives (including restoration of the depletion allowance to 27.5 percent), and (7) expanded research and development of synfuels, efficient energy use, and control of effluents.[9] *U.S. Energy Outlook* made it clear that industry felt government had a crucial role, but only as a facilitator of supply.

For the participants in Project Independence, government's role was not so clear-cut. The Project evolved out of efforts by senior officials in the Office of Management and Budget and the Federal Energy Office to get a grip on energy-market conditions and to make some sense out of President Nixon's more-or-less random energy initiatives. William Simon, the FEA administrator, got the project started as an interagency review, coordinated by Eric Zausner at the head of a team of economic modelers. For six months during 1974, several hundred staff from 25 government agencies prepared detailed background studies on each fuel sector (production and consumption) and each area of significant resource constraint. Meanwhile, the Zausner group created a

7 W. B. Davis, "A Proposed General Method of Operation for the Working Subcommittees and Task Groups of the National Petroleum Council's Committee on U.S. Energy Outlook," December 17, 1980, in Energy Outlook Files, Gulf Oil, Pittsburgh, PA.
8 *U.S. Energy Outlook*, pp. 3, 7, 15.
9 Correspondence to N. G. Dumbros, Chairman, NPC Government Policies Subcommittee, January 1971, Energy Outlook Files, Pittsburgh, Pa.; also, NPC, *U.S. Energy Outlook*, pp. 9–14.

complicated econometric model, which integrated hundreds of macroeconomic and energy-sector variables, as a means for evaluating any specific policy initiative. John Sawhill, Simon's replacement as FEA Administrator, wanted the model (Project Independence Evaluation System, or PIES) and the *Report* completed by November, to be used for input to the 1975 State of the Union Message.[10]

The *Project Independence Report* did not recommend a package of energy policies. However, the policy assumptions associated with forecasts of various levels of supply and demand did "provide a framework for developing a national energy policy."[11] Although most of the Project's architects, and certainly the Nixon and Ford administrations, were relatively committed to market-oriented solutions to energy shortages, the *Report* indicated a significant role for government if oil imports were to be reduced. Even for the base case, government would have to facilitate nuclear powerplant licensing, phased implementation of the Clean Air Act, moderate leasing of coal and OCS properties, Alaskan gas, and phased deregulation of new natural gas. Much more would be necessary for accelerated development of supply. Commercial development of synthetic fuels from coal and oil shale would require new financial incentives; all leasing programs would have to be accelerated; siting and licensing for nuclear plants would require streamlining; and Congress would have to deregulate new natural gas promptly, and modify the Clean Air Act.[12]

If the nation were to achieve demand reductions indicated in the Conservation Case, still more direct action by the federal government would be necessary. Among the options for the transportation sector were a gasoline excise tax, mandatory fuel-efficiency standards, and subsidies for mass transit. But all of these together would accomplish less than half the projected savings. Tax credits for investments in energy-reduction, as well as mandatory standards for lighting, appliances, and thermal efficiency, could be used to further reduce demand in the residential, commercial, and industrial sectors.[13]

The National Energy Plan was put together under the direction of James Schlesinger during the first eight weeks of the Carter administration. The team that produced it included Alvin Alm from the EPA, S. David Freeman from the Office of Science and Technology, Robert Nordhouse from the staff of the House Commerce Committee, and several of Schlesinger's staff from his days at the AEC and Department of Defense. None of the group had any experience in the energy industries.[14]

The Plan focused on the reduction of oil imports by 5 million barrels per day by 1985. Table 13-3 indicates that conservation would account for two-fifths of

[10] Neil De Marchi, "Energy Policy Under Nixon: Mainly Putting Out Fires," Chapter 6 in Craufurd D. Goodwin, ed., *Energy Policy in Perspective* (Wash.: Brookings Institution, 1981), pp. 458–466.

[11] FEA, *Project Independence Report*, i.

[12] *Ibid., 64–65.*

[13] *Ibid.,* 160.

[14] James L. Cochrane, "Carter Energy Policy and the Ninety-fifth Congress," Craufurd Goodwin, ed., *Energy Policy in Perspective*, pp. 551–556.

this savings, while increased domestic supply, primarily in the form of coal, would account for the other three-fifths. The oil and gas pricing policies discussed previously would accomplish some improvement in supply, some reduction in use, and significant substitution of coal for industrial uses. These conservation effects would be reinforced by a host of tax incentives, the centerpiece of which was a gas-guzzler tax penalty on fuel-inefficient automobiles. Price incentives for the substitution of domestic coal would be reinforced by a statutory prohibition on fueling new powerplants with gas or oil. Thus, as an integrated whole, the Plan would combine more accurate price signals with administrative guidance to push supply and demand together in a more stable, less dependent, equilibrium.

National energy planning was difficult enough on paper. But to convert such comprehensive blueprints into effective statutes was all but impossible in the absence of a grave national emergency. Despite Jimmy Carter's assertion that energy crisis was indeed the "moral equivalent of war," none of these plans survived the legislative process intact.

In April 1973, Richard Nixon outlined a "comprehensive, integrated national energy policy" that contained all but one of the National Petroleum Council's recommendations (continuation of oil import quotas). Wherever possible, Nixon used his executive authority to accelerate leasing, to promote energy conservation in government operations, and to extend compliance deadlines in the Clean Air Act. Still, most of his recommendations required congressional action, and there he met with little success. The Administration introduced bills to provide tax credits for oil and gas exploration, deregulation of new natural gas, changes in siting and licensing requirements for nuclear power plants, reorganization of the government's energy and resource agencies, and a larger R&D budget.[15] Only on the last item did Congress cooperate, and even Nixon's executive actions, with the exception of abandoning import quotas, were delayed or reversed by litigation.

Gerald Ford devoted most of his first year in office to national energy planning. In his 1975 State of the Union Message, Ford announced "a plan to make us invulnerable to cut-offs of foreign oil." The President asked Congress "to act within 90 days on a comprehensive energy tax program," decontrol of oil and gas prices, and "a massive program" to increase supply by funding development of a synfuels industry, encouraging nuclear power, and moderating the excesses of environmental regulation. Admitting that "it will require sacrifices," the Republican President called up the memory of Franklin Roosevelt in the mobilization crisis of 1942.[16] However, the Energy Independence Act, the omnibus bill discussed in Chapter 10, met with stubborn resistance from the Democratic 94th Congress. Executive leadership was not in vogue, least of all

---

[15] Richard Nixon, "Presidential Energy Message to Congress, April 18, 1973," Commerce Clearing House, Inc., *Basic Energy Documents* (Wash.: CCH, 1973), pp. 504–517.
[16] Gerald Ford, "The President's 1975 State of the Union Message Including Economy and Energy," January 15, 1975, in U.S. Congress, Senate, Committee on Interior and Insular Affairs, *Economic Impact of President Ford's Energy Program* (94th Cong., 1st Sess.), January–February 1975, pp. 699–712, and accompanying White House Fact Sheet, pp. 713–760.

for oil and gas price deregulation on which the Ford plan hinged. Once Congress rejected those key provisions, and the tax policies that accompanied them, the comprehensive program fell apart, with only bits and pieces surviving as disjointed titles in Congress' own Energy Policy and Conservation Act.

As a Democrat, Jimmy Carter at least had a partisan advantage over his predecessors. Still, it took nearly 18 months for Congress to finally pass his 400-page National Energy Act. By most estimates, its 200 sections represented about 60 percent of the substantive content originally proposed by the Administration. Looking back on the political process and its mixed results, Schlesinger took a philosophical view. If holism was the only measure of success, then the National Energy Plan had failed. But if the Act moved the nation 60 percent closer to a sound national energy policy, then that was indeed an accomplishment.[17] Of course, this view was not necessarily shared in Houston, and it remained to be seen how well the institutions of government were structured to administer this national energy strategy.

Energy organization: the elusive coherence

Prior to the OPEC shock, the U.S. federal government was not organized to deal with the concept of energy. As previous chapters have shown, institutional problems within the Interior Department, between its agencies and Congress, and the statutory and judicial limits on the Federal Power Commission, contributed in no small measure to the ineffectiveness of federal energy policy. Only the Atomic Energy Commission seemed to function efficiently, and that in itself became an object of intense criticism by environmentalists after 1971. With the advent of the Environmental Protection Agency, the Occupational Health and Safety Administration, and the Price Commission in the early 1970's, this disparate structure for managing the energy industries became less coherent than ever. "The present dispersion of effort among some 61 different government agencies," complained John McLean, the chairman of Continental Oil, "creates delays and confusion and will inevitably tend to accentuate whatever energy shortages may lie ahead."[18] Enactment of the Federal Advisory Council Act in 1972, albeit a needed reform, disarmed the only remaining institutional channel for coordinating relations between business and government.

Under these circumstances, it is little wonder that proposals for reorganizing the government's energy functions attracted growing support within Congress, the executive branch, and the private sector. But the purpose of reorganization, and how best to do it, was subject to diverse interpretation. In general, proposals that emanated from the executive branch sought to centralize and increase administrative authority. Proposals from Congress were more likely to emphasize administrative autonomy, budgetary authority, and oversight. And those from the business community envisioned a reduction of regulatory inter-

---

[17] James Schlesinger, interview with the author, March 1982.
[18] John G. McLean, "Action on the Energy Front," a speech before the API Division of Production, March 7, 1972, Houston, Texas, p. 13.

vention through consolidation. Although several major oil companies supported a Department of Energy or Natural Resources, their objective was limited to achieving "greater consistency and promptness of action with respect to the existing areas of government involvement."[19]

In 1973, President Nixon proposed a Department of Energy and Natural Resources, to "provide leadership across the entire range of national energy." But as with planning, such a massive reorganization looked better on paper than in reality. All kinds of interests within the bureaucracy had reason to fear and obstruct such a change. Outside of government, too, there were organized groups with a vested interest in maintaining the separation between resource management, price regulation, energy development, and environmental protection. That rationale accounted for pressure from the anti-nuclear movement to divide the Atomic Energy Commission into two agencies: one for R&D and the other for environmental and safety regulation.

Anticipating a long fight over full-scale reorganization, both the President and Senator Henry Jackson introduced legislation to reorganize energy research and development right away. Jackson's bill, the Federal Non-Nuclear Energy Research and Development Act, would create five independent, government-owned energy development corporations; one for each new energy source (oil shale, gasified coal, liquefied coal, solar, and geothermal).[20] Nixon's bill would split the AEC in two, creating a Nuclear Regulatory Commission and the Energy Research and Development Administration (ERDA). ERDA would be a fairly straightforward merger of the research functions of the Atomic Energy Commission, the Office of Coal Research, and the Bureau of Mines. The Administration claimed that ERDA, headed by a single administrator, could provide better coordination and more flexibility in energy development, and would be more consistent organizationally with a Department of Energy and Natural Resources, if and when Congress approved that proposal.[21]

The 93rd Congress passed modified versions of both bills late in 1974, and ignored the cabinet-level reorganization. The Energy Reorganization Act of 1974 established ERDA as an independent administrative entity with a single administrator. ERDA's internal structure had been a point of substantive contention, since advocates of soft-energy technologies feared that the massive nuclear R&D transferred from the AEC would overwhelm other ERDA activities. Thus the law designated six assistant administrators, one each for nuclear, national security, fossil fuels, solar, geothermal, and advanced power systems.[22] This measure insured that ERDA was organizationally suited to

[19] *Ibid.;* also, Gulf Oil Corporation, "Gulf Energy Statement," February 1973, Pittsburgh, Pa., p. 2.

[20] U.S. Congress, Senate, Committee on Interior and Insular Affairs, *Energy Research and Development Policy Act* (93rd Cong., 1st Sess.) June–July 1973, pp. 2–60.

[21] U.S. Congress, Senate, Committee on Interior and Insular Affairs, *Background and Goals of the Federal Nonnuclear Research and Development Effort* (94th Cong., 2nd Sess.), Committee Print, July 1976.

[22] *Public Law 93-438*, October 11, 1974, in U.S. Congress, House, Committee on Science and Technology, *Principal Energy Research and Development Legislation* (95th Cong., 2nd Sess.), Committee Print, December 1978, pp. 51–79.

implement the programmatic aspects that were left in the Federal Non-Nuclear Energy Research and Development Act.[23]

Although creation of ERDA did succeed in consolidating the government's energy-research activities, it by no means solved the broader organizational problem of formulating and implementing coherent national energy policy. Under President Ford, authority for federal energy policy was divided between four large bureaucracies: ERDA, the Interior Department, the FPC, and the Federal Energy Administration. Frank Zarb, as President Ford's FEA Administrator, had tacit responsibility for coordinating overall energy policy. But with a restive Congress unwilling to accept the Administration's leadership, and with separate oversight committees challenging the decisions of every energy bureaucrat, the argument for a cabinet-level reorganization looked better with each passing month.

Jimmy Carter proposed a Department of Energy two months before his election, before his staff conceived the National Energy Plan. The need for a single Department of Energy seemed obvious from the technocratic perspective shared by Carter, Schlesinger, and O'Leary. As outsiders, after eight years of Republican leadership, they felt no bureaucratic threat from reorganization. For Congress too, the disarray of the Nixon-Ford years had been sufficiently frustrating to make the prospect of cabinet-level coherence amenable, at least to the Democratic majority. With relatively little controversy, Congress passed the Department of Energy Organization Act in August 1977.

The Department of Energy combined most of the Interior Department's energy-development responsibilities with those of ERDA, the Federal Energy Administration, and the Federal Power Commission. To satisfy Carter's environmental constituents, the Interior Department was left relatively intact with control of federal leasing and administration of public lands; the EPA remained untouched. The new department was to be managed by eight assistant secretaries responsible for R&D, energy-resource applications, national security, nuclear waste management, competition/consumer affairs, international programs, intragovernmental affairs, and environmental impact. It would also encompass two quasi-independent agencies: the Energy Information Administration and the Economic Regulatory Administration. The Information Administration would provide energy data from "independent sources," so that government would no longer need to rely so exclusively on industry. The Economic Regulatory Administration would control gas imports and enforce oil price regulations. Finally, the new Department would include a nearly-autonomous Federal Energy Regulatory Commission, to replace the FPC.[24]

Although it did centralize the government's energy functions, the Department of Energy scarcely fulfilled its promise of coherence, coordination, and efficiency. By 1980, it had become a real disappointment for many congressmen who voted for it, and a campaign issue that symbolized Ronald Reagan's attack on Big Government. As a conglomerate from the outset, the De-

---

[23] *Public Law 93-577*, December 31, 1974, *ibid.*, 80–118.
[24] *Public Law 95-91*, August 4, 1977, *ibid.*, 1–50.

partment of Energy was very large (10,000 employees and a budget of $20 billion) before its management had time to develop an organization. During its first year of operation, its senior management was preoccupied with the difficulties of marshalling the National Energy Plan through Congress. When Schlesinger, O'Leary, and other top officials were not working on that, they were busy defending the Department's actions before increasingly hostile oversight committees. Less than a month after Congress enacted the Plan, the Iranian crisis and then the second oil shock brought new chaos to U.S. energy markets that evoked attacks on the Department of Energy from all sides. Secretary Schlesinger, whose strengths did not include organizational behavior and public relations, was unable to alleviate the Department's worsening image. The Department of Energy was indeed a huge, centralized bureaucracy with all the inflexibility, unresponsiveness, and procedural inefficiency inherent in such organizations.

It was in part due to these organizational problems that the Carter administration reversed course in 1979 and proposed to decentralize administration of energy policy. For a crash program to commercialize synthetic fuels, the Department of Energy would be neither an effective instrument nor a good symbol. Accordingly, President Carter proposed that Congress establish two new agencies: an Energy Security Corporation to subsidize commercial synfuels projects, and an Energy Mobilization Board with authority to short-circuit regulatory barriers for "fast track" energy projects.

To justify yet another energy agency, the Carter administration cited historical examples of government-owned corporations like the Tennessee Valley Authority and the Reconstruction Finance Corporation, created "to meet other urgent national needs." The Energy Security Corporation would have four attributes that the Department of Energy was lacking: (1) a clear focus, (2) independence from political and procedural constraints, (3) flexibility in the use of market-oriented incentives, and (4) a business perspective. Together, these atributes would hopefully allow the Corporation "to choose the most economic and expeditious approach," without being "needlessly hampered by other policymaking and policy implementing demands."[25]

Even with such autonomy, the Energy Security Corporation could make little progress if regulatory and environmental roadblocks were not removed. Thus, the need for an Energy Mobilization Board to cut through red tape. The three-member Board would have the authority to set binding deadlines for federal, state, and local agencies to reach decisions and grant licenses, and to accept a single environmental impact statement for each project. Under certain circumstances, it could suspend federal laws for projects that Congress had designated as "fast track." Litigation involving priority projects would be resolved quickly by a Temporary Emergency Court of Appeals.

At the height of the second energy crisis, both sides of Congress approved the Energy Security Corporation (renamed the Synthetic Fuels Corporation)

25 The White House, "The President's Program for United States Energy Security: The Energy Security Corporation," August 1979, pp. 9–12.

and the Mobilization Board, but with significant differences in their bills. By the time the conference committees got down to serious negotiations in the spring of 1980, the threat from OPEC had already subsided, and opponents were fully mobilized. Late in June, the House voted down the conference version of the Mobilization Board by a margin of 101 votes. Ninety-eight Republicans reversed themselves, and liberal Democrats remained steadfastly opposed. "The left and the right ganged up on this," complained John Dingell in reference to the odd coalition of environmentalists and states' rights advocates.[26] Congress did approve the Synthetic Fuels Corporation, relatively intact.

For faithful advocates of synfuels like Representative Moorehead of Pennsylvania, the Synthetic Fuels Corporation was "a message to OPEC," long overdue. For its critics, including many conservative Republicans, the Corporation looked like just another boondoggle. "Will this be any better than the Department of Energy?" was the common concern.[27] The answer to that would depend more on the market than on organization, but judging from the government's record on synfuels during the past decade, it could scarcely be worse.

Synfuels revitalized

Even before the OPEC price shocks of 1973–74, domestic shortages of natural gas and demand for clean fuels lent new credence to the government's previous programs for encouraging development of synthetic fuels. In 1971, when President Nixon first addressed incipient energy problems, he called for "greater focus and urgency" with the synfuels projects in progress. He announced a "cooperative program with industry to expand the number of pilot plants" and "the orderly formulation of a shale oil policy – not by any head-long rush toward development but rather by a well considered program in which both environmental protection and the recovery of a fair return to the Government are cardinal principles."[28]

With the energy supply-demand balance tilting toward shortage, these measured initiatives at least revived the faltering synfuels program. In the next two years, congressional appropriations outstripped the capacity of the Office of Coal Research to commit funds to contract research. In fiscal year 1974, the OCR was able to use only $62 million of its $128 million authorization.[29] It managed to get construction under way for three liquefaction pilot plants, five high-Btu gasification pilot plants, and new process-development work on a wide range of synthetic fuels technologies. Even the ill-fated Project Gasoline at Cresap, West Virginia, was rejuvenated as a $45 million liquefaction "test

[26] *Wall Street Journal*, June 30, 1980.
[27] *Wall Street Journal*, June 27, 1980.
[28] Richard Nixon, "Presidential Energy Message to Congress," June 4, 1971, in Commerce Clearing House, Inc., *Energy Management* (Washington: CCH, 1973), pp. 401–411.
[29] U.S. Congress, Senate, Interior Committee, Subcommittee on Energy Research and Water Resources, *Nonnuclear Energy Research and Development Fiscal Year 1976 Authorization* (94th Cong., 1st Sess.), March 1975, p. 410.

facility." For pilot plants alone, the government committed $280 million, with industry contributing an additional $50 million. In fact, private sector financial involvement and participation in policy were vital new elements of the synfuels program that increased its prospects for success.

Two developments in the early 1970's were responsible for transforming the synfuels program into more of a joint, public-private venture. Congressional criticism of Project Gasoline and other slow-moving projects placed much of the blame on the fact that contracting firms had no risk in the projects. Had they more at stake, it was thought, they would be more inclined to provide their best talent and impose greater efficiency on design and implementation of the projects. In response to these complaints, the Office of Management and Budget issued special guidelines for the Office of Coal Research, suggesting that industry contribute one-third of the cost of any new pilot plants.[30] Coal executives serving on the General Technical Advisory Committee reacted with indignation to this policy, since it made no sense to them to commit retained earnings to research for which the government would control patent rights.[31]

The natural gas industry, however, not only approved of the joint-venture guidelines, but helped create them. For gas companies under cost-based rate regulation, expenditures on R&D did not reduce return on equity. The American Gas Association had already participated on a 50-50 basis with the Office of Coal Research to develop one small pilot plant. By 1971, given the dismal state of domestic gas reserves and the costs of other supplemental sources, natural gas companies were taking coal gasification even more seriously. In January, the AGA submitted a formal proposal to the Interior Department for an eight-year, jointly funded program to test seven processes at pilot-plant scale, select the best, and construct a commercial demonstration plant by 1978.[32] An agreement was signed in August. Somewhat scaled down, the $30 million program would run four years, to construct, operate, and test six pilot plants. Government would contribute $20 million, while the AGA put in $10 million. A second phase, involving a commercial demonstration plant, was to be negotiated at a later date. The program would be jointly managed by the Director of Research for the AGA and the Director of the Office of Coal Research. To resolve any intractable differences, the agreement designated a three-member steering committee, composed of the Assistant Secretary for Mineral Resources, president of the National Academy of Engineering, and president of the AGA.[33]

Judging from subsequent evaluations, this model organization for program

---

[30] Office of Management and Budget, "Circular A–100," December 18, 1970, Equipment and Property Files, OCR Pt.3, OCR/DOI.
[31] GTAC Meeting Transcript, January 12, 1971, Box 4, GTAC/OCR/FRC, pp. 30–33.
[32] Statement of Herbert D. Clay, chairman of the AGA Government Relations Committee, reprinted in U.S. Congress, Senate, Interior Committee, *Energy Research and Development Policy Act* (93rd Cong., 1st Sess.), June 1973, pp. 686–688.
[33] "Agreement between the United States Department of the Interior and the American Gas Association for the Cooperative Coal Gasification Research Program," August 3, 1971, in *ibid.*, pp. 652–658.

management was far more effective than the OCR's politicized contract management during the 1960's. Projects, plant sites, and funding levels were determined according to technical and economic merit. By 1976, most of the pilot plants had operated successfully, yielding the data necessary to design commercial demonstration plants.[34] Although this formal arrangement for joint management was not reproduced, it did set a precedent for cost-sharing and closer public-private cooperation in most other synfuels projects.

The Nixon administration's pre-embargo planning for oil-shale development proceeded similarly along a measured, albeit more controversial, course. Congress contributed by shifting the 15 percent depletion allowance from oil shale to shale oil in the Tax Reform Act of 1969. Walter Hickel, Nixon's new Interior Secretary, followed up by designating an Oil Shale Task Force within the Department. Taken together, these two developments seemed to rekindle public controversy over a "giveaway." Regional commercial boosters, western congressmen, and the governors of Colorado, Wyoming, and Utah urged Hickel to avoid Udall's mistakes and conceive a program more palatable to business in order to stave off imminent energy crisis. Just the opposite course was urged by concerned citizens, newspaper editors, and several eastern congressmen who feared a massive giveaway of public wealth to Big Oil. Organized environmentalists and state conservation officials warned that oil shale development posed a significant threat to the ecology of the high plains.[35] Recommendations from the oil industry were noticeably absent.

Temporarily at least, environmental pressures prevailed. In May 1970, just two weeks after Earth Day, Hickel remanded a draft leasing plan, scheduled for release, on the grounds that it did not provide adequate analysis of the costs of land restoration after mining. With environmental advocacy so intense, the Nixon administration wisely decided to move cautiously with oil shale.[36]

In 1971, Interior Secretary Rogers Morton took up his predecessors' burden of formulating oil-shale policy in a new political context of institutionalized environmentalism. Morton seemed to have a reasonable grasp on the terms of the policy problem. "The need to have large amounts of shale oil available in the future is now quite evident," said Morton. "The heart of the current issue is if this development can proceed in harmony with the existing environment."[37] Government needed to establish "stable economic and regulatory policies," but then it would be up to private enterprise to develop the resource and produce its energy.[38] On the basis of these principles, Morton set out to implement a proto-type oil shale leasing program.

[34] AGA, *Coal Gasification Pilot Plant Research Program, Third Quarter Fiscal Year 1973*, in *Ibid.*, 659-666; also, Energy Research and Development Administration, *Coal Gasification, Quarterly Report*, September 1976 (ERDA 76-93/3), pp. 47–50.
[35] Correspondence files, Office of the Secretary, Central Classified Files, Minerals and Fuels/Commodities and Products, Oil Shale, Pts. 1 and 2 (January 1969 to July 1970), OS/DOI.
[36] U.S. Congress, Senate, Interior Committee, Subcommittee on Minerals, Materials, and Fuels, *Oil Shale Development* (91st Cong., 2nd Sess.), May 21, 1970, pp. 6–8, 23–27.
[37] R. Morton to D. Evans, April 19, 1971, Oil Shale, Pt.5, OS/DOI.
[38] R. Morton to H. R. Sharbaugh, president, Sun Oil Co., January 10, 1972, Oil Shale, Pt.7, OS/DOI.

The Nixon administration encouraged "private sector participation in the design of the program."[39] The Interior Department's Oil Shale Coordinator, Reid Stone, directed the program's development while serving as co-chairman of the NPC's Oil Shale Task Group for *U.S. Energy Outlook*. The program presumably benefited from Stone's close cooperation with task-force members from Union Oil, Standard Oil of Ohio, and Cleveland-Cliffs Iron, the three companies most experienced in oil-shale development.[40] The Interior Department also reviewed criticisms of the 1968 leasing program, conducted field studies and held 15 public meetings with environmental and citizens groups in the shale regions, and analyzed environmental and socioeconomic impact studies prepared by the state governments of Colorado, Wyoming, and Utah.[41] Secretary Morton released the Program Statement and Preliminary Environmental Impact Statement in July 1971.

The leasing program envisioned by Morton was to proceed expeditiously through six stages over an 18-month period. Core drillings by interested firms would begin immediately, leading to nominations by industry of prospective development sites. For industry, these two steps alone were major improvements over the centralized and allegedly misguided site selection implemented by Udall. Following nominations, the Interior Department would select six lease tracts, two each in Colorado, Wyoming, and Utah, of 5,120 acres each. It would then prepare a site-specific, Final Environmental Impact Statement, reflecting public comments on the Draft Statement. Finally, the Secretary would decide whether or not to proceed with a competitive lease sale scheduled for December 1972.[42]

The lease form itself was of utmost interest to prospective shale developers. The new leasing terms contained several major changes from the 1968 lease that were responsive to industry's complaints. First of all, the 5,120 acre tracts, if carefully chosen, appeared large enough to sustain commercial-scale operations for 20–30 years each. And if problems developed, the lessee would suffer less under the 1971 lease. If the project appeared infeasible after a couple of years, the lessee could surrender the lease and the Interior Department would waive the last two installments on his bonus bid. Moreover, the new lease contained no production requirements, an important change for uncertain bidders. Under the Udall program, a lessee would lose the lease if commercial production had not begun by the twelfth year. The 1971 lease imposed a progressive schedule of royalty payments in lieu of production which, at $8.5

[39] "Decision Statement of the Secretary of Interior on the Prototype Oil Shale Leasing Program," November 28, 1973, in U.S. Congress, Senate, Interior Committee, Subcommittee on Minerals, Materials, and Fuels, *Prototype Oil Shale Leasing Program* (93rd Cong., 1st Sess.), December 1973, p. 8.
[40] National Petroleum Council, Other Energy Resources Subcommittee of the Committee on U.S. Energy Outlook, *An Initial Appraisal by the Oil Shale Task Group, 1971–1985* (Washington: NPC, 1972).
[41] U.S. Congress, Senate, Interior Committee, Subcommittee on Minerals, Materials, and Fuels, *Hearings: Oil Shale* (92nd Cong., 1st Sess.), November 15, 1971, pp. 29–30.
[42] U.S. Department of the Interior, *Program Statement for the Proposed Prototype Oil Shale Leasing Program, June 1971* (Washington: DOI, 1971).

million over 20 years, was neither an incentive nor disincentive to production. Since the new lease form was not designed to promote experimental work, it did not contain the requirement of the 1968 lease that any patents derived from work on the tract be licensed at reasonable rates. In 1971, it was thought that the absence of this requirement would give firms more of an incentive to take the risks of being first in commercial shale development.

Unique terms for environmental control were probably the most important aspect of the 1971 lease form. Although environmental provisions of the old lease were strict, they had involved "open ended requirements with many unknowns." The 1971 program involved stricter controls (a mine restoration plan and compliance with the Clean Air Act of 1970 and the Water Pollution Control Act of 1972), but they would be spelled out in the actual lease. Furthermore, the new lease form authorized an offset of unforeseen environmental costs against royalties, at the discretion of the Secretary. This provision was explicitly designed "to achieve the maximum possible environmental integrity while allowing an oil shale industry to achieve commercial stature."[43]

Nine major oil companies and several other interested firms drilled core samples, nominated 23 tracts for development, and participated jointly with the Interior Department in baseline environmental studies.[44] But the program was delayed by environmental opposition and by compliance with the requirements of the National Environmental Policy Act. As the courts were just then interpreting it, the Act required an environmental impact statement that evolved through three drafts, two rounds of public hearings, extensive interagency review, and full consideration of policy options other than developing shale. Despite intense and sincere efforts by virtually every branch of the Interior Department to make its Draft Environmental Impact Statement a model of the genre, environmental organizations were totally dissatisfied.[45] The Natural Resources Defense Council, for example, found the Draft Statement "inadequate in its discussion of both environmental impact and alternatives."[46] In the face of threatened litigation, the Impact Statement went back to the drawing boards for another year so that the final statement, released in September 1973, might be beyond reproach.

When environmentalists deemed the final Statement completely inadequate, the future pace of oil-shale development began to look less certain.[47] Still,

[43] "Comparison of the Department of the Interior 1968 and 1971 Oil Shale Leasing Programs and Lease Forms," in U.S. Congress, Senate, *Hearings: Oil Shale*, pp. 97–138.

[44] List of lease-site nominators (including American Petrofina, Ashland Oil, Atlantic Richfield, Gulf Oil, Marathon, TOSCO, Shell, Sohio, Superior, and Sun Oil), in Oil Shale, Pt.7, OS/DOI; also, Office of the Oil Shale Coordinator, "Program Decision Option Document: The Proposed Prototype Oil Shale Leasing Program," October 1973, in U.S. Congress, Senate, *Prototype Oil Shale Leasing Program*, pp. 216–220.

[45] Department of the Interior, internal memoranda reviewing the Draft Environmental Impact Statement, June–August 1972, Oil Shale, Pt.8, OS/DOI.

[46] Natural Resources Defense Council, "Comments on Prototype Oil Shale Leasing Program, Draft Environmental Impact Statement," February 29, 1972, in Oil Shale Pt.7, OS/DOI, p. 25.

[47] The Institute of Ecology, Environmental Impact Assessment Project, *A Scientific and Policy Review of the Prototype Oil Shale Leasing Program Final Environmental Impact Statement*, October 29,

Secretary Morton gave the go-ahead. Two choice tracts in Colorado (tracts C-a and C-b) would be sold, by sealed bid, on January 8, 1974. The Secretary declared that every reasonable precaution had been taken to protect the environment. The leases were designed to encourage orderly commercial development, with royalties and rents that insured adequate revenues for government.

Seven days before the sale, OPEC raised the price of crude oil to $11.65 a barrel.

Synfuels for energy independence

The Arab oil embargo, followed closely by OPEC's fourfold price increase, had a profound impact on both the political and economic rationales for synthetic fuels. Finally, after three decades of anticipation, the national security justification for synfuels was consummated. Both government and business grudgingly acknowledged domestic depletion and agreed that synthetic fuels were, in Frank Zarb's words, "the most promising near-term developments in alternate sources." Speaking for the oil industry, W. T. Slick of Exxon likewise cast synfuels as "obvious supplements for the transition from today's energy systems to those of the next century."[48] Synfuels had appeared commercially infeasible as long as foreign oil was available for $1.75 a barrel. But with Saudi light crude priced at $11.65, and new natural gas bringing $1.60 per thousand cubic feet in Texas, shale oil and even coal synthesis were certainly competitive. At least, it seemed so for a time.

After November 1973, the policy at issue was not whether government should subsidize development of synfuels, but rather, how fast and in what manner. Although public debate of this issue was tied to proposals for government reorganization, three possible approaches could be discerned: (1) a business-as-usual approach that emphasized the socioeconomic and environmental impacts of synfuels, (2) an accelerated program of shale leasing and coal synthesis with federal funding for an array of pilot and demonstration plants, and (3) a crash program for commercialization, financed by grants, loans, and price guarantees from the federal government.

Environmental activists and advocates of limited, decentralized growth generally preferred the first approach. A majority of Congress, federal bureaucrats, and managers of the energy industries supported or accepted the need for an accelerated program, in principle. For the third option, two conditions would be

1973 (Washington: EIAP, 1973). More than a dozen scientists contributed to this 200-page critique which found almost nothing praiseworthy in the DOI's Final EIS. The assessment recommended that Secretary Morton cancel the lease sale and give more serious consideration to alternatives that emphasized greater research, a slower pace, and more participation and control by the government.
[48] Frank Zarb, FEA Administrator, "Energy Policy and Technology's Role," *Energy Technology II: Proceedings of the 2nd Energy Technology Conference,* May 1975 (Washington: Government Institutes, Inc., 1975), p. 11; W. T. Slick, Senior Vice President, Exxon, "Commercialization of New Energy Technology," *Energy Technology III: Proceedings of the 3rd Energy Technology Conference,* March 1976 (Washington: Government Institutes, Inc., 1976), p. 10.

necessary: a perception of severe energy shortages and the personal commitment from a politically effective President.

In the aftermath of the first OPEC shock, it was increasingly apparent that only large oil and natural gas companies had the research, capital, and managerial resources needed to put together commercial-scale synfuels plants. Major companies like Exxon, Texaco, and Gulf, which had accumulated substantial coal and shale reserves and built up their R&D departments since the mid-1960's, were well-positioned to take advantage of whatever synfuels policies the government might develop. But even for those companies, the government first needed to alleviate certain "institutional barriers and uncertainties" that still threatened private investment in synfuels technology: "potential price controls on synthetic fuels; changing requirements for protection of the environment; [and] delays in regulatory and leasing policy." It would be useless for one agency to throw money at synfuels while six others erected road-blocks.[49] Even then, energy prices would have to keep rising, at least as fast as inflation.

Before Congress or the Ford administration could act, the Office of Coal Research initiated a project to involve government directly in commercial demonstration of synthetic fuels. In May of 1974, it published a request for proposals to design and build a plant for demonstrating conversion of high-sulfur coal to clean, liquid fuel for use in electric powerplants. Since technologies for coal liquefaction were the least advanced, this request appears to have been politically or bureaucratically motivated. Perhaps the Office of Coal Research needed to commit more of its excess appropriations, and to establish itself with a major project before it was absorbed into the Energy Research and Development Administration.[50]

Although several contractors were expected to participate in the preliminary design phase, only one submitted a complete proposal and was awarded the contract. The winner was Coalcon, a joint venture between Union Carbide and Chemical Construction Corporation (Chemico) that was organized just a month prior to the issuance of the request. Coalcon would head a consortium of 15 large companies which had signed letters of intent to share the non-government portion of the $237 million project. The technology would be Union Carbide's hydrocarbonization process, on which the company had reportedly spent $100 million over 30 years of research to develop. After an elaborate site-selection process in which six states competed vigorously, ERDA chose New Athens, Illinois as the location for the 2,600 ton-per-day plant (one-fifth com-

[49] W. T. Slick, "Commercialization of New Energy Technology," p. 13.
[50] Mel Horwitch, "Liquecoal" (Boston: Harvard Business School, Case Services Inc., 1978). The contract was subsequently signed just two days before ERDA absorbed the OCR. The request required bidders to submit detailed information in 90 days on environmental compliance, management organization, costs, and financing. It pointedly suggested that implementation of the contract be divided into four phases with a total estimated cost of about $150 million: (1) preliminary design, (2) demonstration-plant design, (3) construction, and (4) test operation. The OCR would fund the first two phases and split the cost of the second two 50-50 with the contractor.

mercial size) that would produce 3,900 barrels a day of liquid fuel and 22 million cubic feet of high-Btu gas.

After less than a year, the project was in serious trouble. Chemico had dropped out of the venture in December, and Phase I was already months behind schedule.[51] By 1976, cost estimates for the project had increased to $440 million before Phase I was even completed, and Union Carbide concluded that it might be prudent to operate a pilot plant before proceeding on a demonstration-scale. In August 1977, ERDA quietly terminated the project on grounds that it was no longer economically viable.[52] In a report to Congress, the General Accounting Office was sharply critical of the haste with which the Office of Coal Research had awarded the contract, the original cost estimates, and poor planning and bad management by ERDA.[53] Not an auspicious start.

Even with relatively generous appropriations from Congress, ERDA's efforts to demonstrate the commercial feasibility of synthetic fuels progressed slowly. Although several of the gasification and liquefaction pilot plants held great promise, high interest rates and the inflation of construction costs made it apparent that extraordinary funding would be necessary to accelerate the program. The Ford administration regrouped around a plan which the White House announced in February 1976. The "Synthetic Fuels Commercial Demonstration Program" would provide $11 billion to help industry finance construction and operation of at least 12 demonstration plants. Its purpose was to provide information on the commercial and environmental feasibility of various technologies for high- and low-Btu gasification, direct coal liquefaction, oil shale, and biomass conversion. The projects would have to be modules of commercial-scale plants, for which loan guarantees and price guarantees would be the primary incentives. In most cases, industry would be expected to contribute 50 percent of the project costs. ERDA would administer the program.[54]

Despite the balanced and measured appearance of this program from a national-planning perspective, the Ford administration was still unable to muster adequate support from Congress. Modified versions of the program, pruned to $6 billion and then $4 billion, were introduced and debated by the 94th Congress, but to no avail. By 1976, crude-oil inventories had fully recovered, and inflation-adjusted oil prices were actually declining. Under these circumstances, support even for ERDA's regular research began to wane, and many congressmen found it politically unpopular to vote for big-ticket loan and price guarantees which would likely be awarded to highly profitable, major oil companies. "Is this truly to get knowledge," asked Representative Richard Ottinger somewhat cynically, "or is it to finance the major energy companies in commer-

[51] Energy Research and Development Administration, Office of Fossil Energy, *Coal Demonstration Plants, Quarterly Report*, September 1976 (Washington: ERDA, 1976), pp. 7–14.
[52] *The Wall Street Journal*, August 22, 1977.
[53] General Accounting Office, *First Federal Attempt to Demonstrate a Synthetic Fossil Energy Technology – A Failure* (EMD-77-59), August 17, 1977 (Washington: GAO, 1977).
[54] Energy Research and Development Administration, *Fact Book: Proposed Synthetic Fuels Commercial Demonstration Program* (Washington: ERDA, March 1976).

cial production of these fuels?" Others were concerned with federal deficits or the possibility that credit for synfuels would crowd out investment in intermediate technologies, such as enhanced recovery, heavy oil, and deep natural gas.[55]

Spokesmen for the energy industries remained ambivalent to the idea of large subsidies for demonstration plants. Natural gas pipeline companies were generally enthusiastic, although some preferred that the program be directed at full-scale, commercial plants. Within the oil industry, divergent strategies, shaded by the ideologies of individual executives, effected contradictory views on the incentive policies of government. Exxon, for example, with its tremendous capital resources, felt that demonstration was an unnecessary stage of development. Once technology and commercial feasibility were reasonably established at the pilot-plant stage, Exxon was prepared to move directly to a commercial plant.[56] A company like Atlantic Richfield, with far fewer resources, but with an advanced position in oil shale, vigorously supported subsidies for demonstration. Gulf Oil took a position of tepid endorsement. Demonstration subsidies were attractive, but with oil prices and government pricing policy in a highly uncertain state, Gulf was unwilling to make any firm commitment of its own capital to such a joint program. As an API spokesman acknowledged, "there is no consensus among our member companies on the need for this program."[57]

A similar lack of consensus extended to the incoming Carter administration. In his campaign, Jimmy Carter had pledged to protect the environment, in part through federal regulation of strip mining and amendment of the Clean Air Act. Hasty commercial development of synfuels conflicted with these legislative goals, and the President personally agreed with the environmentalists who voted for him – that synfuels were, at best, a necessary transitional evil like light-water nuclear reactors. Conservation, not high-technology supply stimulus, would be the focus of the first National Energy Plan. Several of Carter's key energy advisors were less willing, however, to rely so heavily on demand-dampening incentives. John O'Leary, head of the FEA and then Deputy Secretary of Energy, had long chafed at government's short-sightedness in regard to synfuels. Likewise, F. David Freeman, a key architect of the NEP and leading advocate of conservation, had urged prompt development of oil shale as early as 1970 when he directed the energy staff of the Office of Science and Technology.[58] And Secretary Schlesinger, although more concerned with issues of energy pricing, also felt that government and business should cooperate in getting some proto-type synfuels plants under way.

Without any clear consensus in the energy industries, Congress, or the Administration, special funding for commercial demonstration was not forthcom-

[55] U.S. Congress, House, Commerce Committee, Subcommittee on Energy and Power, *Synthetic Fuel Loan Guarantees* (94th Cong., 2nd Sess.), March–August 1976, vol.I, pp. 77–82.
[56] W. T. Slick, "Commercialization of New Energy Technology," pp. 13–15.
[57] U.S. Congress, House, *Synthetic Fuel Loan Guarantees*, vol.II, pp. 14–26, 353–371.
[58] S. D. Freeman, "Strategic Oil Supply and the Naval Petroleum Reserves," November 1970, Gulf Oil Co., National Petroleum Council files (Pittsburgh, Pa.).

ing. Still, with shortages of natural gas causing widespread plant closures during the winter of 1976–77, there was pressure on ERDA to show that government was doing something. If ERDA could stretch its regular budget, and if reasonable cost-sharing by industry could be encouraged, then at least a couple of projects might be started. During the first few months of the Carter administration, the government did sign five contracts that could lead to commercial demonstration of coal gasification. Three projects involved consortia of gas utilities that grew out of the previous joint ventures between government and the American Gas Association. A fourth involved Continental Oil in a $370 million project to demonstrate the British Gas/Lurgi slagging gasifier. The fifth project somewhat resembled Coalcon. W. R. Grace, the prime contractor, was new to the field, and planned to demonstrate low-Btu gasification with no particular technology in mind. In all five instances, the Department of Energy would fund the preliminary design phases, while the private participants shared construction and operating costs on a 50-50 basis.[59] The program was designed to progress on a competitive basis, with only the two most successful plants actually getting funded for construction.

Demonstration of coal liquefaction took a different course. Of the four most advanced technologies (Ashland Oil's H-Coal, Exxon's Donor Solvent Process, SRC-I and SRC-II), only Solvent Refined Coal had been fully tested in pilot plants. SRC-II was Gulf Oil's process for producing heavy oil. SRC-I was a derivative that had been tested at a power plant in Alabama by Southern Services. In the case of SRC-II, renewed initiative for commercial demonstration came from both the firm and the government. At Gulf, those involved with SRC had made tentative arrangements through foreign subsidiaries to interest Mitsui & Co. and Ruhrkohle AG in the project. In turn, those firms had gotten their respective governments interested as well. Then, in the spring of 1977, James Schlesinger personally suggested to Jerry McAfee, Gulf's chairman, that Gulf commit itself to a major synfuels project.[60] The idea appealed to McAfee, although he hesitated to commit Gulf to significant financial participation.

After more than a year of negotiations, Gulf and the Department of Energy signed a contract to design an SRC-II demonstration plant. Gulf would put in an additional $50 million, bringing its total contribution to $100 million. Mitsui and Ruhrkohle would make similar contributions, and the governments of Japan and West Germany each agreed to commit about 25 percent of the estimated $1.6 billion cost. The Department of Energy's share, with help from Senator Byrd on appropriations, would be $600 million. The 6,000 ton-per-day plant would be built near Morgantown, West Virginia, with construction scheduled to begin in 1980. The Department of Energy made similar arrangements to demonstrate SRC-I in a joint venture with Southern Services, Wheelabrator-Frye, Air Products and Chemicals, and the Commonwealth of Ken-

[59] U.S. Department of Energy, *Fossil Energy Program Report*, August 1978 (DOE/ET-0060-78), pp. 57–89.
[60] Gulf Research & Development Company, interviews with the author, Pittsburgh, Pa., December 1982.

tucky. The two projects would compete through the design phases, with the most advanced getting final authorization.[61]

While the government's energy agencies were trying to organize a program to demonstrate coal synthesis, the Interior Department was overseeing efforts to demonstrate shale-oil production. Initial results of its Prototype Lease Sale had been deceptively encouraging. In the spring of 1974, four consortia of oil companies made acceptable bids on the lease tracts in Colorado and Utah. Rio Blanco Oil Shale Project, a joint venture between Gulf Oil and Standard Oil of Indiana, bid $210 million for tract C-a, the choicest lease containing an expected yield of 4.07 billion barrels of oil. Fifty miles away, tract C-b went for $117 million to Atlantic Richfield, Ashland Oil, Shell Oil, and TOSCO. As partners in Colony Development Co., these four firms were already involved in planning a commercial plant. The two lease offerings in Utah, U-a and U-b, went for $75 and $45 million respectively, to the White River Shale Oil Corporation. The parent firms, Phillips Petroleum, Sun Oil, and Sohio, planned to develop the two tracts as a single project since their total expected yield was only 510 million barrels.[62]

In compliance with the terms of their leases, all three groups spent the next two years gathering baseline environmental data, doing geotechnical and engineering research, and preparing their Detailed Development Plans. The leases stipulated that developers put together a thorough scientific profile of the environment's condition prior to disruption. This research would create a "baseline" against which pollution controls and reclamation standards could be monitored. These Plans were necessary not only for the operator, but for the more than 30 federal, state, and local government agencies that would participate in regulating the environmental and socioeconomic impacts of the shale operations. Approval by the Interior Department of the Development Plans and the baseline studies would be necessary before the operators could proceed to actual development.

The thoroughness of these studies had a number of interesting effects on the projects. First, the baseline environmental studies revealed to the operators just how expensive and difficult it would be to protect a relatively fragile ecosystem from massive industrial development. Incident to these studies, the two lessees in Colorado discovered that for certain categories of emissions, air pollution from natural sources intermittently exceeded the ambient air quality standards of the Clean Air Act. For other categories, however, the air quality in shale country was pristine – so much so, in fact, that mining and refining operations would inevitably result in emissions that exceeded the EPA's standards for Prevention of Significant Deterioration. In other words, prior to any development whatsoever, it appeared that the air quality was at once too dirty and too clean to proceed.[63]

[61] U.S. Department of Energy, *Fossil Energy Program Summary Document*, March 1979 (DOE/ET-0087), pp. 101–104.

[62] U.S. Congress, Senate, Interior Committee, Subcommittee on Minerals, Materials, and Fuels, *Hearings – Oil Shale Leasing* (94th Cong., 2nd Sess.), March 1976, pp. 32–34.

[63] Richard Vietor, "The Evolution of Public Environmental Policy: The Case of 'No Significant Deterioration,'" *Environmental Review*, III, No.2 (Winter 1979), pp. 2–19.

The Detailed Development Plans were even more revealing. The White River group not only had air-pollution problems, but discovered that the shale on their tracts fractured in a manner that made underground mining difficult or impossible. They also found that title to their leases was unclear and would be contested in the courts. In developing its plan for open-pit mining on tract C-a, the Rio Blanco group realized that to maximize recovery of shale, off-site storage of overburden and disposal of spent shale would be necessary. However, federal law prohibited leasing the adjacent properties for such a purpose. In planning a residential community for their workers at the nearby town of Rangely, the C-a developers could not find enough private land to buy, and federal lands were not available for sale.[64]

These problems, albeit very real, were modest compared to larger uncertainties regarding cost and competitiveness. During the two years of environmental and development planning, inflation, energy market conditions, and most of all, national energy policy, were completely unpredictable. For all three operating groups, preparation of the Plans revealed that the capital and operating costs to develop oil shale had been grossly underestimated. Inflation in construction costs, unanticipated costs of environmental protection, and better knowledge resulting from complete mine and plant designs resulted in revised estimates two or three times higher than the original ones.[65] The White River group, for example, reported that in two years, the estimated cost to construct a 100,000 barrel-per-day plant had increased from $600 million to more than $1.5 billion, while still in the design stage. Thus, for a 15 percent return on a 100-percent equity basis, the price of shale oil would have to exceed $20 a barrel (in 1975 dollars).[66] With estimates of crude oil prices for 1980 ranging from $11 to $20, and some analysts even suggesting that OPEC might collapse, it was nearly impossible for any responsible management to justify the risk of $1 billion in a first-time-ever venture.

Worse even than the market, however, was the uncertainty associated with national energy policy. To prospective shale developers, attitudes in Washington were more volatile than the energy market itself. "In February 1974," recalled an Ashland Oil executive, "there was a sense of urgency in the air as a result of the oil embargo and a certain momentum had started to build for a national energy policy that would support development of synthetic fuels." But by November 1976, "this feeling has since disappeared," and with it, "the incentive for industry."[67] President Ford's comprehensive energy policy had failed in Congress, and the Energy Policy and Conservation Act had reimposed oil-price regulation. Thus, "the situation where product prices could be subject to some form of control while ever-increasing expenses are not" was "one area of greatest concern."

[64] U.S. Congress, House, Interior Committee, Subcommittee on Minerals, Materials, and Fuels, *Oversight – Prototype Oil Shale Leasing* (94th Cong., 2nd Sess.), November 30, 1976, pp. 33–50.
[65] Edward W. Merrow, *Constraints on the Commercialization of Oil Shale*, (R-2293-DOE), September 1978 (Santa Monica: Rand Corp., 1978).
[66] White River Shale Project, "A Position on Oil-Shale Development," *Shale Country*, II, No.8 (August 1976), p. 16.
[67] U.S. Congress, Senate, *Oversight – Prototype Oil Shale Leasing*, p. 48.

The government's policies on incentives for synfuels was another. With proposals for demonstration programs, tax credits, and loan guarantees repeatedly being introduced and rejected, there was "no assurance that the political actions needed to make oil-shale development commercially attractive will occur."[68] One group might go ahead with a plant on its own, only to find its competitors subsidized by government at some point in the future. Or, a company might start a commercial shale-oil plant, and then lose it in a horizontal divestiture mandated by Congress. "It is time to stop haggling about the form government synfuel participation should take," urged a TOSCO executive. "There has to be a way for government and industry to wed resources on equitable terms; and each should go to the last mile to find the way before lead time runs out."[69]

Without a crisis in the market, such a wedding was apparently not possible. By December 1976, the Prototype Leasing Program was a shambles. TOSCO, Atlantic Richfield, and Shell dropped out of their C-b group, and all three groups applied for lease suspensions. The Interior Secretary granted them on the grounds that problems with air pollution, rock fracturing, and off-site land requirements were beyond their control. But Congress viewed the situation in a different light. Lee Metcalf, chairman of the Senate Subcommittee on Minerals and Fuels, only wanted to know "how long is the Department prepared to reserve this important public resource for the exclusive use of lessees who have so thoroughly documented their inability to develop the leases."[70]

But there did not seem to be many interested replacements. Occidental Petroleum picked up the abandoned leases to the C-b tract, but it had a long way to go in its experiments with in-situ (underground) retorting. No one was any longer interested in the Utah leases (except the governor of Utah), and if open-pit mining was environmentally infeasible, then even the rich C-a tract looked a lot less attractive. Among private developers, only Union Oil continued serious planning, but its management would not proceed until Congress created a satisfactory investment and regulatory climate.

It was the Ayatollah, not Congress, that made the difference. The Iranian Revolution and second oil-price shock provided as much a window of opportunity for government-sponsored synfuels as for oil-price decontrol. The anticipated shortage of crude imports in 1979 and the implications of continuing political instability in the Middle East reinvigorated the national security argument for domestic synthetic fuels. Optimists had convinced themselves that the supply disruption in 1973 was a unique event. Its repetition in 1979 evoked the chagrin of "fool me once, shame on you; fool me twice, shame on me." The price shock, and the Carter administration's decision to decontrol domestic oil prices in conjunction with a windfall profits tax, created the necessary economic opportunities. With OPEC oil selling for $28 a barrel by Christmas 1979, $20 shale oil again looked attractive to private developers. Moreover, if Congress

---

[68] White River Shale Project, "A Position on Oil-Shale Development," p. 16.
[69] Charles H. Brown, quoted in *Shale Country*, II, No.12 (December 1976), p. 6.
[70] U.S. Congress, Senate, *Oversight – Prototype Oil Shale Leasing*, Appendix I, p. 57.

did enact a windfall profits tax, substantial revenues would be available for government sponsorship of synfuels.

By mid-1979, President Carter's energy advisors found him much more receptive to the need for stimulating domestic fuel supplies. In the National Energy Plan, the goal of conservation was to reduce, not eliminate, reliance on imported oil, "obviating the need for immediate massive development of all energy sources simultaneously."[71] But Congress had watered down its provisions for conservation and eliminated its toughest two measures for reducing demand: the excise tax on gas-guzzler automobiles and the Crude Oil Equalization Tax. Because of this, said the President in April, "we have now lost precious time." Oil imports were still 43 percent of domestic demand, and domestic production continued to decline. A month earlier, the accident at the Three Mile Island nuclear powerplant had "demonstrated dramatically that we have other energy problems." For all of these reasons, the President had concluded that "now we must join together in a great national effort to use American technology to give us energy security in the years ahead."[72]

Oil price decontrol, together with a windfall profits tax, would generate an estimated $140 billion in federal revenues over the next 12 years. President Carter proposed an energy trust fund to dispense the lion's share of these funds ($88 billion) to the Energy Security Corporation to subsidize development of 2.5 million barrels per day of synthetic fuels production. The rest of the Trust Fund would be used to finance a Solar Bank, energy assistance for the poor, various projects to improve mass transit, and as incentives to encourage conversion by utilities from oil to coal, development of unconventional natural gas, and residential conservation.[73] Taken together, these proposals were designed to reduce oil imports by 4.5 million barrels per day by 1990. The centerpiece of this second national energy plan was a crash program for commercialization of synthetic fuels.

This initiative sparked a rush of other legislative proposals and widespread debate over the necessity and feasibility of developing synfuels on a crash basis. For the first time during the decade, the debate focused explicitly on the costs, benefits, and appropriateness of government's role in energy development at each of three levels: mere R&D (with limited demonstration), like the Department of Energy's current program; accelerated demonstration of 10 to 12 prototype plants, as proposed by the Committee for Economic Development; and the crash commercialization embodied in the Administration's proposal. Carter's goal was to stimulate 2.5 million barrels per day of synfuels production by 1990. Toward this end, the Energy Security Corporation would be given a range of financial tools: indirect subsidies, such as loan and price guarantees, as well as direct involvement through loans, product purchases, and government-

---

[71] Executive Office of the President, *The National Energy Plan* (Washington: GPO, 1977), p. 60.
[72] "Energy Address to the Nation, April 5, 1979," *Public Papers of the Presidents: Jimmy Carter, 1979*, (Wash.: GPO, 1980), Vol.I, pp. 609–614.
[73] Office of the White House Press Secretary, "Fact Sheet on the President's Import Reduction Program," July 16, 1979.

owned, company-operated plants. The 96th Congress considered at least six other bills with similar provisions, although none was as comprehensive nor contained production targets as ambitious as the President's.[74]

Four considerations seemed to predominate opposition to the President's proposal. Environmental interest groups objected on several grounds. Commercialization of synthetic fossil fuels was obviously a shift in emphasis away from the conservation and solar objectives so prominent in the first National Energy Plan. On a commercial scale, synfuels plants would have many of the same characteristics that elicited ideological opposition to nuclear power: capital intensive, centralized, environmentally destructive, and energy-inefficient. What was new, however, was that a crash program guided by an Energy Mobilization Board might run roughshod over the body of regulatory, adjudicatory, and participatory controls that the environmental movement had cultivated for a decade. Thus, the program threatened not only the environment, but environmentalism.[75] Although the political influence of environmental groups was at a low ebb in the midst of perceived energy emergency, they had some powerful backing for conservative Republicans who viewed it as an immense expansion of government's intervention in the economy.

Academic economists and management consultants objected to the new synfuels plan on grounds of effectiveness and feasibility. For the economists, misallocation of resources by administrative fiat was a fatal flaw. Robert Pindyck, for example, argued convincingly that massive subsidies would crowd out private investment, select and lock-in technologies that might not be competitive, encourage waste and cost overruns, and artificially stimulate energy demand by disguising real price signals as tax purchases. "By any rational economic criteria," warned Pindyck, "subsidy programs such as that proposed by the Administration are wasteful to the utmost, detrimental to the economic health of the country," and "unlikely to contribute significantly to solving our energy problems."[76] Management experts, including several consulting firms commissioned by Congress, objected less to synfuels subsidies than to the magnitude of the program. They pointed to organizational difficulties, bottlenecks with specialized equipment, infrastructure, and manpower, and the opportunities for mistakes so evident from past experience.[77]

The implications of a crash program for the relationship between government and business was among the most contentious issues, politically. If enacted, President Carter's proposal would substantially shift the means of allocating

[74] U.S. Congress, Senate, *Synthetic Fuels Report*, pp. 5, 9–13.

[75] See, for example, David Masselli, Energy Policy Director, Friends of the Earth, in U.S. Congress, Senate, Committee on Banking, Housing, and Urban Affairs, *Energy Financing Legislation* (96th Cong., 1st Sess.), July 1979, pp. 697–702.

[76] Testimony of Robert Pindyck, in *Ibid.*, pp. 151–160; also, Paul J. Joskow and Robert Pindyck, "Synthetic Fuels," *Regulation*, October 1979, pp. 18–24, 43.

[77] U.S. Congress, Senate, Committee on the Budget, Subcommittee on Synthetic Fuels, *Costs and Economic Consequences of Synthetic Fuels Proposals* (96th Cong., 1st Sess.), September 1979, and *Synthetic Fuels Report* (Committee Print), appendices I-III, pp. 55–392; also, Panel Discussion by the authors of *Energy Future: Report of the Energy Project at Harvard Business School*, in U.S. Congress, Senate, *Energy Financing Legislation*, pp. 604–656.

capital in the energy sector from market mechanisms to centralized, administrative authority. The business community itself was uncertain whether or not economic conditions warranted such a shift, and if so, how managerial authority and responsibility for outcomes would be divided. Prospective developers of synfuels had certainly been urging government incentives and, indeed, the sort of coherence in national energy policy that Carter's second energy plan represented. And yet, any enthusiasm for the synfuels program was tempered by the record of energy policy, by the President's anti-business rhetoric, and by the fact that it would be funded by a tax that the energy sector thought patently unfair.

This ambivalence was reflected in a report on synthetic fuels issued by the Committee on Economic Development (CED) in the same month President Carter made his proposal. The business executives that wrote the report saw an "immediate need" to develop about ten commercial-size plants, "sufficient to demonstrate the technology, environmental effects, and economic viability." To do so, they estimated a cost of $15 billion, only $2 billion of which need come from government: "This effort should place primary reliance on the technical and financial resources of the private sector and on the incentives provided by market forces." But because of the unusual risks involved, "some added governmental action will also be needed."[78]

Although this approach appealed to the ideologies of many managers, those experienced with synfuels knew that $2 billion would not go very far towards the development of an industry. A single plant, like the Great Plains Gasification Project, might need more than $1 billion from government, on top of rate-structure subsidies from the FERC. What the CED was suggesting was equivalent to a first phase of the President's plan: synfuels capacity of 500,000 barrels a day by 1987, at a cost of about $20 billion. The idea of a two-part program for commercializing synfuels received widespread support from analysts, businessmen, and congressmen who acknowledged the need for government action, but feared the consequences of undue haste.[79]

The year-long legislative battle over President Carter's synfuels program nearly matched the intensity of the windfall profits debate. The bill that President Carter finally signed in June of 1980 gave him most of what he had proposed, but in a two-phased approach that slowed the pace, reduced some of the risks, and sought to limit government's role to that of a banker. The Energy Security Act authorized the Synthetic Fuels Corporation to commit $17 billion of budgetary authority, through a wide range of financial mechanisms, to commercial synfuels projects. Three billion dollars was provided for "fast track" projects, even before the Corporation was operational. At the end of four years,

---

[78] Committee on Economic Development, *Helping Insure our Energy Future: A Program for Developing Synthetic Fuel Plants Now* (New York: CED, 1979), pp. 2–6. A number of committee members took exception to the report's consensus, mostly on two issues: (1) that the report grossly understated the likely cost of synfuels plants, and (2) that it understated the government's necessary role.
[79] U.S. Congress, Committee on Science and Technology, Subcommittee on Energy Development and Applications, *The Pros and Cons of a Crash Program to Commercialize Synfuels: A Report* (96th Cong., 2nd Sess.), February 1980, Committee Print.

it would have to get approval from Congress for a "comprehensive strategy" to attain the production goals identified in the Act. Only then would the additional $68 billion be forthcoming.[80]

Carter's program appeared to convince executives in the energy companies that the federal government was finally serious about synthetic fuels. That, together with an OPEC price of $34 a barrel, seemed to change the market-outlook for synthetic fuels. Oil shale, if not coal synthesis, appeared competitive at last. This rare confluence of high oil prices and favorable public policy posed strategic opportunities for firms whose production and reserves of domestic crude oil had declined the most during the 1970's, and whose competitive position in refining flexibility was the weakest. Three firms whose downstream assets were most vulnerable by both these measures were Gulf, Union, and Exxon. Union announced it would build its commercial plant with a price guarantee from the Department of Energy. Gulf and Standard of Indiana resolved some of their problems on the C-a tract and accelerated work on their engineering design for a huge commercial plant. Exxon, which had lacked a significant position in shale, bought out Atlantic Richfield's stake in Colony for $400 million, and subsequently announced its intention to build a $3 billion plant as the first wave of a $500 billion shale-oil industry.[81]

By the time Jimmy Carter left office, he could take some satisfaction from the supply-side accomplishments of his National Energy Plan. Although far from certain, the prospects for synthetic fuels looked better than at any time since World War II. Six demonstration projects for advanced liquefaction and gas-ification were making steady progress. Three commercial shale-oil ventures seemed on solid footing, and the Great Plains Gasification Project had begun construction with loan guarantees under the Defense Production Act. But even with commercial development of synthetic fuels, the gap between domestic supply and demand would remain unacceptably large unless the growth of demand slowed considerably. Yet, throughout the decade of energy crises, the same political problems that hampered rational energy pricing had likewise undermined implementation of an effective strategy for demand management.

Energy demand management and conservation

Prior to the onset of oil and gas shortages, few Americans had given much thought to energy conservation. In a nation where extraordinary abundance of all sorts had prevailed for a generation, conservation equated to inconvenience or reduced standard of living, neither of which had much popular appeal. For planners in government and in the energy industries, stabilization of surplus had been the object of energy policy for two decades. Even when demand was addressed for the purpose of planning supply, it was assumed to be relatively price inelastic, much like any essential commodity.

[80] Public Law 96-294; also, U.S. Congress, House, Report No. 96-1104 (96th Cong., 2nd Sess.), "Conference Report on Energy Security Act," May 1980.
[81] The Wall Street Journal, June 18, 1980; also, "Synthetic Fuels: The Processes, Problems and Potential," The Lamp, Summer 1980, pp. 3–11.

Thus, it is perhaps understandable that this myopia cleared only gradually over the course of the 1970's. But even as it did, organized political support for effective conservation was lacking. By their nature, energy producers had no vested interest in demand reduction, while individual consumers had no wish to pay for it. For their part, politicians were generally unable or unwilling to link their conservation programs explicitly to the forces of the price mechanism. Thus, much of what Congress eventually did enact by way of conservation policy ran counter to the market instead of guiding it toward the desired ends.

Three types of policy can be distinguished among the melange of conservation measures proposed or implemented during the Administrations of Nixon, Ford, and Carter: (1) mandated fuel-efficiency standards, (2) interfuel substitution (from oil and gas to coal or nuclear), and (3) tax penalties or incentives designed to dampen demand. The first two of these proved to be the most feasible politically, but the least practical in the absence of complementary price signals to the consumer. Similarly, Congress embraced tax incentives to encourage thermal efficiency because they were relatively non-controversial, but repeatedly rejected tax penalties on gas and oil usage although they held the greatest potential for savings.

The Nixon administration was too disorganized by Watergate and too preoccupied with supply to promote or implement conservation policies after the first oil shock. A mandatory 55 mph speed limit and some energy-saving rules for federal office buildings were about its only accomplishments. On its own initiative, however, Congress enacted the Energy Supply and Environmental Coordination Act in June 1974. This law set an important precedent as well as a new standard for regulatory ineptitude. It required the Federal Energy Administration to issue orders, on a case-by-case basis, prohibiting large powerplants from burning natural gas or oil if they had a capability for coal. The FEA could require new plants to use coal, and order some existing plants to switch to coal.

To justify a conversion order, the Act required the FEA to make a series of statutory findings in each case regarding coal supply and transportation, financial practicability, and impact on service. Furthermore, both FEA and the Environmental Protection Agency had to insure full compliance with all environmental requirements. After a lengthy process of public comment and hearings, an order could be issued that triggered an environmental impact statement and another round of comment and hearings. Since the combined costs of conversion and environmental compliance were large, and the savings from fuel substitution remained small as long as government controlled prices of residual oil and natural gas, electric utilities and large industrial firms had little incentive to comply without a fight. Moreover, local consumer and environmental groups with which they had to coexist were invariably opposed. This program failed to obtain a single conversion in three years of operation, which left fuel substitution as an unsolved problem for Carter's National Energy Plan.[82]

[82] For a review of this program, see U.S. Congress, Senate, Committee on Energy and Natural Resources, Subcommittee on Energy Production and Supply, *Coal Conversion Legislation* (95th Cong., 1st Sess.), March 1977.

The Ford administration could at least benefit from the perspective on supply and demand balance provided by the *Project Independence Report*. With their general orientation toward market mechanisms, President Ford and his advisors chose a package of conservation measures that relied primarily on taxation to amplify the effects of their proposed decontrol of oil and gas prices. Gerald Ford explicitly linked conservation to market-clearing prices for oil and natural gas. He imposed a $2.00-a-barrel tariff on imported oil, until after decontrol, when domestic oil would carry a $2.00 excise tax in addition to the windfall profits tax. To accompany the decontrol of natural gas, Ford proposed an excise tax of 37 cents per thousand cubic feet, equivalent to the excise tax on oil. The entire package was designed to reduce demand immediately by 900 thousand barrels (equivalent) per day, as well as raise $16 billion in revenues to finance a proposed cut in personal income taxes. Ford generally tried to avoid mandatory conservation measures. Instead of proposing mandatory fuel-efficiency standards for automobiles, he extracted agreements in writing from domestic automobile manufacturers to improve fleet-average fuel efficiency by 40 percent in five years. That pledge, however, was contingent on the President's commitment to relax the auto emission standards of the Clean Air Act.[83]

Linked as it was to price decontrol, this conservation program got a hostile reception from the 94th Congress. The windfall profits tax notwithstanding, the program appeared to put nearly all of the burden on consumers, especially the poor, and none directly on industry. For many in Congress who believed that industry was largely responsible for the problem, this seemed patently unfair. Accordingly, Congress not only rejected price decontrol and the excise taxes, but it tried to make automobile manufacturers and utilities themselves pay the conservation premium. The Energy Policy and Conservation Act established mandatory fuel economy standards for automobiles and light trucks. If manufacturers or importers failed to attain these standards, they would be liable for a substantial civil penalty. Similarly, the FEA's authority to order coal conversions was expanded, and the House even tried (unsuccessfully) for a statutory ban on the use of natural gas in powerplants.[84] It made politicians feel better to obscure the end-costs of conservation from the consumers who would inevitably pay them anyway.

By the time Jimmy Carter took office, the government's energy policies seemed almost designed to discourage conservation and stimulate demand, especially for imported oil. At regulated prices, low sulfur oil and natural gas were the preferred boiler fuels in comparison to coal, with costly flue-gas scrubbers, or nuclear, with skyrocketing capital costs and intense environmentalist opposition. In the transportation sector, the clash between price signals and mandated fuel economy was even worse. Motorists had just begun adjusting their consumption patterns to the first price shock before the government helped stabilize the real (inflation-adjusted) price of gasoline. Between 1977

[83] "The President's 1975 State of the Union Message including Economy and Energy," in U.S. Congress, Senate, *Economic Impact of President Ford's Energy Program*, pp. 699–760.
[84] U.S. Congress, Senate, *Report No. 94-516*, "Conference Report on the Energy Policy and Conservation Act" (94th Cong., 1st Sess.), December 8, 1975, pp. 119–122.

and 1979, there was a resurgence of demand for big cars at the very time domestic automobile manufacturers were hastily down-sizing their products. In the residential sector, households were turning their thermostats back up and postponing improvements in insulation, regardless of a modest tax credit. Only in the industrial sector, where large savings in wasted heat and electricity were readily available, had conservation begun making significant progress. But there too, prevailing utility rate structures remained a disincentive.

The time seemed ripe for a National Energy Plan, the object of which, as Schlesinger put it, "is first to achieve a much higher level of conservation and fuel efficiency than we have achieved in the past." Substitution of coal for oil and gas was secondary, while "a rational pricing system" came third.[85] The Plan contained at least 35 separate non-price proposals designed to force or induce energy conservation. No sector was overlooked, and nearly every administrative device conceivable was proposed. If anything, it was too much for Congress to cope with.

For the single most serious problem of gasoline consumption, the National Energy Plan proposed harsh remedies. A graduated, "gas-guzzler" excise tax of up to $2,488 would be imposed on automobiles that exceeded fleet-average standards for fuel economy. Moreover, if savings in gasoline consumption did not attain the Plan's targets, a standby gasoline excise tax (that could be as much as 50 cents a gallon) would take effect anytime after 1978. Both of these tax penalties would operate on top of market-clearing oil prices to be obtained through the Crude Oil Equalization Tax.

For existing residential and commercial buildings, the Plan proposed sizeable new tax credits to induce weatherization and solar heating. For the poor, the government would provide $130 million in subsidies for such improvements. For industry, the Plan offered a 10 percent investment tax credit for energy-saving equipment. Investments in cogeneration (of electricity and process steam) were encouraged by regulatory exemptions as well as the tax credit. For electric utilities, an entire section of the Plan was devoted to rate reforms designed to discourage peak-load demand and more generally link prices to marginal costs. Finally, the National Energy Plan not only proposed to strengthen the mandatory coal-conversion program, but would tie it to significant tax penalties and incentives. Beginning in 1983, utilities would pay a graduated tax of 90 cents, rising to $3.00 per barrel, to burn residual oil. The tax penalty for using natural gas would be the Btu-equivalent. But the Plan also provided either a 10 percent investment tax credit or rebate of penalties to cover the cost of converting to coal.[86]

Eighteen months later, Congress accepted a few of the Plan's mandatory conservation measures, but rejected the more effective tax penalties. Even

[85] U.S. Congress, Senate, Committee on Energy and Natural Resources, *Economic Impact of President Carter's Energy Program* (95th Cong., 1st Sess.), May 3, 1977, p. 7.
[86] "The President's Address to a Joint Session of Congress, April 20, 1977," in U.S. Congress, Senate, Committee on Energy and Natural Resources, *The President's Energy Program* (95th Cong., 1st Sess.), Committee Print, May 1977, pp. 17–21; also, Executive Office of the President, *The National Energy Plan*, pp. 35–47.

modest tax proposals, according to one analyst, were too "regressive or un-popular or too complicated."[87] The National Energy Act contained no standby gasoline tax, and its gas-guzzler penalty was innocuous. Instead, the Act dou-bled the penalty for automobile manufacturers whose products exceeded the fleet-average mileage standards. On coal conversion, Congress rejected the tax penalties and credits. It did, however, prohibit use of oil and gas in new electric generating facilities and strengthen the government's authority to order conver-sion of existing facilities. Tax incentives for energy-saving investments in build-ings did survive, but at modest levels compared to what Carter had proposed. Utility rate reform also survived, but more on a "recommended" than obliga-tory basis.

The net effect of the National Energy Act's conservation program would be measured in thousands rather than millions of barrels per day of demand reduction. But however disappointing to its proponents, it was more than an incremental step. Together with the Carter administration's programs on the supply-side, even these limited policies for curbing demand had carried na-tional energy management about as far as the boundaries of the American political economy would tolerate in peacetime.

Administrative versus market allocation

The contentious drift toward national energy management was a political con-sequence of declining domestic fuel reserves and an overdue adjustment to the realities of the international energy market. Although there was an energy crisis, it was never severe enough to warrant the degree of national management that attended energy shortages during World War II. And yet by 1980, in com-parison to a decade earlier, it could reasonably be said that the United States finally had something like a national energy policy. Centralized government institutions had been created and authorized to stimulate supply and discourage demand.

Even so, this national policy remained an adjunct, not a substitute, for the market. Producers and consumers of energy fuels would still respond primarily to market prices, shaded at the margins, either effectively or ineffectively, by national policy. There is no inherent reason for the outcome to have been ineffective. Its failures must only be attributed to inadequacies of the political process, institutional barriers between business and government, and misper-ceptions of economic reality. These are central among the conclusions consid-ered in the next and final chapter.

[87] Robert Bamberger, "Energy Conservation in the Transportation Sector," in U.S. Congress, Senate, Committee on Energy and Natural Resources, *Energy Initiatives of the 95th Congress* (96th Cong., 1st Sess.), Committee Print, May 1979, p. 167.

14. Business, government, and public policy

The foregoing chapters tell the story of government intervention in energy markets for nearly 40 years. It is a saga, not of heroes and villains, but of ineffective institutions and administrative process. For readers convinced that big business contrived the energy crisis, the story must be disappointing. For those committed to theories of regulatory capture or public-interest reform, the story should be frustrating. And for managers, bureaucrats or others who would like to see a more effective industrial policy, the story should put the relationship of business to government in a critical perspective.

In this chapter, I offer my own conclusions regarding the government's record in energy policy, a few prominent views by others of the political economy, and some implications of this history for public economic policy.

Past policy – the record

There are any number of angles from which we can exercise the prerogatives of hindsight. All of them involve some degree of normative judgment. For example, we could contrast the government's energy policies to hypothetical alternatives that might have brought more desirable long-term results. We might compare inept implementation to the potential achievements of wiser legislators and bureaucrats. Or we could speculate how policy might have been were private interests not so self-interested. What I have settled for, however, is to consider how effectively government interacted with business in dealing with problems of market failure or public goods.

On the basis of these criteria, the government's domestic policies for fossil fuels generally failed. They reduced economic efficiency in return for marginal gains in equity, temporary and misleading stabilization of markets, and little or no benefit to national security. For evidence of this, we need only look to a few key areas of energy policy: synthetic fuels, oil imports, natural gas, and oil price controls.

Involvement of government in synthetic fuels has been argued on grounds of national security, depletion of domestic liquid fuels, excessive financial and technical risk, and aid to a sick coal industry. If we assume, as I do, that these reasons justify some role for government, then why have efforts over 35 years

345

failed to demonstrate the feasibility of a commercial-scale plant? Two plants, one each for shale and coal synthesis, would have provided baseline data and real experience with the economic, engineering, and environmental problems involved. And yet the taxpayer's cost would have been modest compared to the depletion allowance or the Atomic Energy Commission's budget for reactor research.

The obvious answer is that market conditions undermined both public and private commitment to such a venture. This is true, but only indirectly. Otherwise, governments would never undertake long-term capital projects such as dams or highways. In the case of synfuels, surpluses of conventional fuels and the absence of sustained crises relieved both business and government from any pressure to resolve the political problems of dividing authority and sharing risk. Executives in the private sector, even desperate coal operators, were preoccupied by a fear that government would do too much. Despite the fact that synfuels never seemed competitive, they would not concede responsibility to a government agency or public corporation. Conversely, Congress was unwilling to provide adequate, unfettered incentives to get industry to do it. In fact, to avoid political opposition from the oil industry, or criticisms of a giveaway to Big Oil, government initiatives were explicitly restricted so as not to impinge on the domain of "private enterprise." It was this failure of institutional relations that left administrative agencies without the financial or technical resources, and especially the political autonomy, necessary to get any kind of a job done.

Oil import quotas, which I previously characterized as the balance wheel of U.S. energy policy, were the worst possible means for controlling dependence on foreign energy sources. Although protection for uncompetitive domestic oil producers provided the political impetus for quotas, we could stretch our imaginations to justify quotas as providing a public good (national security) or as a remedy to a market imperfection (instability). Even so, the quota program was still inefficient economically and politically. As told in Chapters 5 and 6, the program for allocating physical quantities reduced wholesale and retail competition, favored the least efficient refiners, produced absurd distortions in distribution channels, penalized consumers, depleted domestic reserves, and helped alienate OPEC-member governments.

There were more efficient alternatives. If national security had been a serious objective, then direct subsidies to shut-in productive capacity could certainly have insured military preparedness at a smaller cost to consumers. A strategic petroleum reserve, stocked with output from marginal wells, could have served the same objective, satisfied influential small operators, and maximized recovery of marginal oil. This might have achieved public objectives with only a minimal disturbance to the market (i.e., average costs in the domestic oil industry). Finally, if market stabilization was the objective, and were it more readily admitted, then a tariff would have worked, without the administrative overhead incurred by quotas.

Although mentioned at the time, none of these options was considered seriously. Once again, failure of institutional relations was a major reason. To intervene formally, the Eisenhower administration needed national security for an excuse. Price stabilization was not acknowledged as an acceptable role for the government. And since domestic oil producers had to suppress the ideological implications of seeking federal protection, they too dismissed more explicit options. The fact that both industry and the government were internally divided on the broad issue of import protection complicated matters. Rather than focusing on the most rational options, the quota program merely evolved out of prior efforts to keep peace in the industry by voluntary arrangements. Once President Eisenhower agreed to quotas, complicated rules were needed to accommodate each sector of the industry and the conflicting interests of the Departments of State, Interior, and Justice.

The record in natural gas price regulation is easy to criticize, and not too difficult to explain. But suggesting an alternative, short of non-regulation, is more of a challenge. The Federal Power Commission's administered pricing of natural gas caused all sorts of allocative distortions; price differentials between interstate and intrastate markets, and between conventional domestic sources and foreign sources, were the worst. But the most obvious failure was the creation of shortage. With the benefit of hindsight, there are few economists who have not flatly blamed those shortages on the regulatory practices of the FPC. Tiered, cost-of-service rate making stimulated demand and discouraged supply, inevitably creating a gap between the two. It worked temporarily by drawing down inventories (proved reserves).

How could this have happened? Well, in the broadest sense of ideas, I already suggested an absence of economics. In the legislative debates of the 1940's and 1950's, the gas issue was cast either as an administrative problem involving physical resources or a moral struggle of the "people" versus the "interests." These themes were reiterated in the 1970's, although moderated by acknowledgment that the price mechanism did serve a purpose.

In the earlier period, the huge surplus of natural gas reserves relieved the pressure on business and government to find a rational solution, consciously and explicitly. Gas producers stonily denied even reasonable concerns about uncompetitive pricing, and savored the political execution of Leland Olds. Spokesmen for gas consumers in the Congress were just as unbending, allowing their own political rhetoric to drown out reason. The Eisenhower administration merely sat on the sidelines until casting an indignant but irresolute veto. Responsibility for policy returned by default to the adjudicatory arena of commission regulation.

Formal rate proceedings with constant judicial review, whether on a case-by-case or area basis, was about the least efficient and least flexible method one can think of to administer a commodity market. It was the last refuge from common sense in which process overwhelmed substance – again a failure of institutional relations. Formulas, precedent, and evidentiary briefs replaced administration. Broad standing for intervenors cast the decision-making process in an adversary mode that lent itself to decision-by-compromise. To quiet competing claimants, new gas was priced too low, while cheap old gas was misallocated. In the process, participants and the Commission alike lost sight of the ball.

If the natural gas industry were sufficiently uncompetitive to create unwarranted economic rents, the federal government could have done something besides cost-of-service rate making. A windfall profits tax, as Stephen Breyer has suggested, would have been better suited to the problem. But as we saw in oil, such a tax imposes its own variety of distortions and inefficiencies. Another less equitable possibility would have been to regulate just the largest producers, those that might have controlled wellhead prices. A better option would have been to raise prices annually to an estimated, market-clearing level. But none of these alternatives was pursued prior to the onset of crisis.

In fact, the record of gas regulation exemplifies a more general failure of public policy to adjust to changing market conditions *soon enough*. Although the availability of huge inventories contributed to this unresponsiveness, institutional factors were even more responsible. Too few regulators and congressmen recognized or understood the tension between supply, demand, and price. Even for those that did, bureaucratic inertia was usually overwhelming. Either administrative procedure, regulatory lag, or legislative process delayed rational change until too late. The same was true, to a lesser extent, in the private sector. Most large firms that had painstakingly adjusted their operations to a regulatory regime were hesitant to seek radical change until operating conditions became all but intolerable. And finally, when a need for change was at last recognized, institutional mechanisms for achieving consensus, within or between business and government, were inadequate.

Regulation of crude oil prices during the 1970's was as inefficient and counter-productive as these other policies, but better justified in a political sense. The first oil crisis was a serious shock to the American economy. Not only did it precipitate shortages (possibly caused by existing regulations), but it contributed to inflation in a manner that affected low-income households disproportionately. OPEC's control of prices did create huge, short-term rents for domestic oil producers. To have ignored these effects, and let the market clear by itself, would have been impossible and inappropriate in a liberal democratic state.

But the cure was worse than the disease. The story of oil price controls in Chapter 10 attests to an institutional failure of relations among Congress, the oil industry, and the bureaucracy. In Congress, rhetoric and solicitude for conspiracy ran rampant. Political entrepreneurs in both houses seized on the energy crisis as an opportunity to pillory corporate executives and build committee fiefdoms. The industry showed little leadership or collective initiative. While the international firms defended their motives, domestic producers jostled for favorable positions in the emerging web of regulation. Trade groups were powerless in the face of internal dissent, as were advisory committees, which Congress was in the process of reforming out of existence. Bureaucrats, meanwhile, spun out allocative rules and procedures that no one could understand, much less enforce. They did not know the energy business, and could scarcely talk to people that did. Their organizations – FEA, ERDA, and DOE – were hobbled by administrative procedure and nitpicking congressional oversight.

Rational remedies were available, however. A simple wellhead tax, with exemptions for the plowback of rents into exploration, could have been coupled to a rapid phase-out of price controls. Three successive administrations proposed some form of price decontrol with a tax on windfall profits. None succeeded until 1980 because congressmen could not agree on the details, major oil companies would not admit their willingness to compromise, and the press could not get the story straight. The result was a default to the fine print of the *Federal Register*. For six years, rent controls were allowed to stimulate demand, depress supply, and give OPEC the chance to do it again.

All of these energy policies had something else in common besides their inefficiencies. At least by intent, they were oriented to supply. Almost no thought was given to demand management in energy, prior to 1973. But hindsight is a real problem here. Except for the very long run, no one in or out of government had reason to think about curbing consumption. Surpluses had prevailed too long. Depletion of fossil fuels was invisible, unlike that of timber, water, or wilderness, and elicited no outcry by concerned citizens. For producers, the problem was finding markets for products. For consumers, there were no problems.

It might be argued that someone in government ought to have recognized the effects of oil import quotas and static gas prices on domestic energy demand, at least by 1967. Perhaps, but there was no agency, including the Interior Department, with any real responsibility for long-term planning. And few policy makers, as I already noted, were sufficiently sensitive to the market to anticipate the inevitable squeeze.

After 1973, scapegoating and issues of distributive equity got in the way of sensible demand management. Preoccupied with rents, Congress could not use the price mechanism to discipline consumers. Since energy problems were blamed on industry or the Arabs, any use of tax penalties on energy-users was just as unpalatable. A few incentives for residential conservation, or fuel-efficiency standards that appeared to penalize business, were all that Congress could muster. Even the National Energy Act coddled consumers, despite Carter's plea for sacrifice.

Although Carter's successor embraced market prices, he pointedly rejected any administrative measures for constraining energy demand in the eighties. It remains to be seen if price alone will induce a healthy energy equilibrium.

Theories and propositions

Most theories of public policy suffer from at least one of three problems. Some describe only a piece of the regulatory process – either policy formation, implementation, or outcome. Some are static. They depend on a snapshot of public issues and the political process at a point in time, and then generalize for situations that change over time. There are some dynamic models, but they tend to invoke a linear evolution in which private power or government control of business simply grows and grows indefinitely. In most of these, elegance and simplicity is too much a premium.

As noted in Chapter 1, regulatory capture, public-interest reform, and bureaucratic ineptitude are concepts that historians and political scientists use to explain the government's policies toward business. We have certainly seen elements of all three sporadically through the history of energy policy. The Oil Import Administration might be considered a candidate for the capture model, while the Federal Power Commission presumably exemplifies public-interest regulation. Promotion of synfuels, by a succession of agencies, evinced most of the problems of public bureaucracy. But even these examples, which are the best I can think of, reveal shortcomings in all three models.

An obvious problem is that each model only applies under particular circumstances. Natural gas producers never captured the FPC. Concern for the public interest was not a serious force behind oil import quotas. One might conclude that each model does accurately describe regulation under certain circumstances, were it not for the facts. In the 1930's, independent oil producers opposed market-demand prorationing. In 1959, and for several years thereafter, oil importers opposed mandatory quotas. Yet according to private interest theories, it is the regulated industry that acquires regulation and controls it. Well, perhaps the Oil Import Administration was captured later in its "life cycle?" But no, we saw how its support from the oil industry deteriorated as exemptions and extensions proliferated. In natural gas regulation, there was a similar deterioration of relations between the regulated and regulators. And then, even consumers ("the public interest") became disenchanted, once FPC pricing policies precipitated shortages.

Another model we should consider briefly is the idea that big business controls government in some general manner. Stated flatly, this appears simplistic, but it is a major theme in the literature of public policy. The work of Charles Lindblom, most recently in *Politics and Markets*, epitomizes this view. Unless the definition of control is restricted to so "grand" a matter as the maintenance of a private enterprise system, the history of energy policy refutes this notion – especially if the emphasis is on *big* business. At least in domestic affairs, there were a score of situations where small business interests or so-called consumerists exercised political power at the expense of the largest companies.

This hardly suggests that big business is without political power, or that under certain circumstances, that power is not excessive or abused. Those circumstances are defined by market conditions and constrained by the structural diversity of industry and government. Lindblom and others overlook these constraints by assuming a linear accretion of power and the ability of corporate managers to exert it effectively. If that were true, then certainly by 1977, a handful of major oil companies, with over half-a-trillion dollars in assets, would easily have dominated public policy and public opinion. But they did not.[1]

The models I find useful, that do help explain a complex history, are

[1]   Charles Lindblom, *Politics and Markets* (New York: Basic Books, 1977). For critical commentaries on Lindblom, see Robert Hessen, ed., *Does Big Business Rule America?* (Washington, D.C.: Ethics and Public Policy Center, 1981).

qualified by institutional or economic circumstances; if things were this way, then the political process worked that way. As James Q. Wilson has noted, correction of overly simple theories need not preclude useful generalizations. For example, Wilson's model, which identifies four types of political process tied to various circumstances of distributive costs and benefits, explains important aspects of the energy-policy history even though his political types don't always match my own.

Were the idea of distributive costs and benefits linked to changes in an industry's price structure – the importance of which Wilson himself has observed – it would be even more useful a concept.[2] As markets change over time, the perceived size of costs and benefits change, even to the point where benefits become costs, and vice versa. For example, natural gas distributors were content with the FPC's control of wellhead prices as long as they could expand their market share by drawing down underpriced inventories. But in 1969, once the long-term costs of this policy became apparent (or began to rise), they changed their stance on cost-of-service pricing, and thus changed the political process, even before consumers entered the fray. The same could be said for the oil import program, oil price controls, and the ebb and flow of support for synfuels.

In other words, it is the market, with its frictions, imperfections, and externalities, that determines distributive circumstances. It follows that changes in supply relative to demand, or costs relative to price, precipitate movement from one distributive circumstance to another.

Like Wilson, Breyer acknowledged different structural situations in his book, *Regulation and Its Reform*. "Mismatch" between the economic structure of an industry and the purpose or tools of regulatory policy applied to it is Breyer's basic explanatory framework. He too is willing to sacrifice "theoretical comprehensiveness" for "generalizations that are broad enough to cover more than one regulatory situation but specific enough to impart useful knowledge."[3] On this basis, Breyer's analysis of natural gas price controls, as a mismatch of rent control and cost-of-service ratemaking, explains that part of the history brilliantly, without the risk of misapplying to energy policy his analysis of natural monopoly or excess competition.

Valuable as it is, Breyer's concept of structural mismatch does not go far enough to explain how the politics of regulation change. One wonders what facilitates the kind of public-interest reform that Breyer himself espouses. The rise of political entrepreneurs, or the advent of majoritarian politics, would be Wilson's answer, and presumably Breyer's.

But it is the change in market equilibrium, and thus the price structure of industry, that provides the impetus for significant changes of economic policy, by whichever political process those circumstances evoke. This point is the key to a useful and durable concept of business-government relations. And it is the

---

2   James Q. Wilson, ed., *The Politics of Regulation* (New York: Basic Books, 1980), pp. 357–394.
3   Stephen Breyer, *Regulation and Its Reform* (Cambridge: Harvard University Press, 1982), pp. 1–7, 240–260.

point of departure for the propositions I made in Chapter 1, which are summarized below:

1. Market disequilibria precipitate policy issues and subsequent government initiatives;
2. Political processes differ according to prevailing conditions of supply and price (surplus induces political conflict within and among industries, and shortage leads to political conflict within government or between business and government);
3. Despite its superior resources, business exercises limited influence on public policy, in part because of its structural diversity, and that of the federal government;
4. Administrative management of markets is likely to suffer from inherent problems that include faulty statutory design, incomplete data, bureaucratic constraints, and imposition of contradictory criteria;
5. Over time, the breadth of government intervention in business fluctuates within limits set by ideology, institutions, and the market's own tendency to clear.

I think these generalizations provide an explanatory framework that is sufficiently flexible and dynamic to relate the economic and structural conditions of business to the political process and institutions of government, as they change over time. It accommodates theories of private-interest capture as well as public-interest reform, and it helps explain the breakdown of regulatory mismatches and the shifts in costs and benefits that precipitate changes in public policy.

Business and government

Taken together, these propositions have several implications for the objectives of government intervention in business, for the tools of intervention, and for the institutional channels through which policy is made and carried out.

Markets, we have seen, are a force regardless of the extent of administrative intervention. They cannot be ignored or bottled up indefinitely without repercussions, usually negative. Proponents of price controls, import quotas, synfuels, or conservation too often disregarded the pressure of supply on price, or eventually, of price on demand. As Carl Bagge put it, the market is like a balloon; squeeze it in one place and it bulges out in another. Allocative distortions or failed projects were results of ignoring the market, not of intervention *per se.*

But however resilient, markets are rarely perfect, as too few businessmen will admit. They are rife with imperfect competition and social externalities, and they cannot deliver public goods such as equity, security, or long-term planning. Moreover, a system of private enterprise precludes by definition the sorts of voluntarism and cooperation necessary to provide for such goods. Denying these limitations has too often left businessmen on the defensive and without a legitimate voice in public policy.

These observations return us to the broad definition of business-government relations as the balance between market means and administrative means for allocating economic goods. Had the limitations of each means been better recognized by the people involved, then the balance struck could only have been more effective. During periods of surplus, businessmen might have thought twice before engaging government to distort competition through intrafuel and interfuel politics. They might at least have anticipated the likely consequences: divisiveness within the industry, loss of political credibility, and increasingly distorted markets. In periods of shortage, businessmen might have exercised some leadership had they admitted the unfairness of monopoly profits or the need for publicly sponsored research. Politicians swept up in the politics of business reform might have thought more clearly about the causes of shortage. If so, then the impulse to fix prices and profits could have been linked to supply and demand.

Another way to put this, as Chalmers Johnson has, is the need to perfect "market-conforming methods of state intervention in the economy." Intervention can guide the market, alter its course, and repair its imperfections, but should preserve competition and relationships between supply, demand, and price as much as possible. This is necessary, as Johnson notes, "to avoid the deadening hand of state control and the inevitable inefficiency, loss of incentives, corruption, and bureaucratism that it generates."[4]

What would constitute more effective microeconomic policy than the energy programs of the recent past? There would be several prerequisites: (1) understanding of industry's organization and market structure, (2) clear and simple statute, (3) policy tools that minimize repercussions, and (4) institutional reforms to facilitate these principles.

Consider again my favorite problem – oil imports in the early 1950's. A world petroleum market was evolving rapidly, shifting supply to a long-term surplus. With foreign oil so abundant and inexpensive, the market would not support high enough prices for marginal producers in the United States to survive. And without foreign sources of oil, domestic refiners could not compete with importers. High domestic prices, moreover, could only stimulate demand, which in the absence of policy, would be satisfied by imports. Had the Eisenhower administration understood this in 1954, its decisions could only have been more effective.

When the functions of making policy and carrying it out are blurred, any potential for administrative effectiveness is reduced, if not lost altogether. Traditionally, the purpose of statutes was to state broad objectives, delegate administrative responsibility, and make provision for funding – little else. These are things that Congress could do well. But in the postwar era, as we have seen, Congress became increasingly involved in designing the procedural details of policy. These they invariably botched.

Take the Natural Gas Policy Act of 1978 as an example. What good was accomplished by Congress spending 18 months writing page after page of legislation specifying trivial categories of production, definitions, field conditions, and percentages? Its members had no experience, no technical skills, and could not anticipate peculiar circumstances or the future course of energy markets. Despite concern about bureaucratic discretion and the proliferation of

4   Chalmers Johnson, *MITI and the Japanese Miracle* (Stanford: Stanford University Press, 1982), pp. 317–318.

administrative law, Congress should have stuck to its business; just stated the objectives of gradual decontrol and better allocation of incremental costs, qualified by a need to protect residential consumers. Then provide for oversight by the General Accounting Office and give competent bureaucrats the authority and resources necessary to implement the law.

Even the clearest policy, however, can suffer from inept choice of policy tools. In most instances of energy policy, intervention failed in proportion to its degree of detailed involvement in the day-to-day affairs of business. At the risk of overstating my case, I would suggest this principle: passive tools of intervention are better than active ones. A tariff is better than a quota. A windfall tax is better than price controls. National rate-making is less harmful than area rate-making, and a case-by-case approach is futile. If a synfuels plant is desirable, get industry to build it with the minimal subsidy and assumption of risk that is needed to succeed.

Market-conforming methods of intervention are not easily devised, but they do *not* require collegial relations between managers and civil servants. In fact, conflict is probably the only means for developing methods of intervention that are effective. But to resolve conflict, to share technical expertise, and to work out practical details of compliance, there needed to be institutional mechanisms for rational deliberation. The problems of economic policy had become too complex to manage by formal adjudication or congressional oversight.

Advisory councils, despite their past problems, are the only institutional means I know for carrying on relations between business and government sensibly. The National Petroleum Council was one model, but certainly not the best nor only one. With dedication to the process, and with appropriate organization and safeguards, deliberative councils composed jointly of business and government officials could have made policy work better. So might have technical councils and smaller, less unwieldy business councils. The objectives of any such council need only have been to reduce heavy-handed bureaucratism and to channel, not enhance, the influence of business along more constructive lines.

Relations between business and government in energy could have been worse. The balance between competitive markets and administrative direction might have failed altogether, giving way to monopoly power or statism. But that never happened, even through the politics of scarcity and the politics of glut. Still, inefficiency need not be prerequisite to a healthy ambivalence, nor a necessary price for equity. If the utility of markets were more widely recognized, and their limitations more readily admitted, then the interaction of business and government in America would surely contribute more to the national good in the future than it has in the turbulent, postwar past.

Index